DRAVIDIAN THEORIES

DRAVIDIAN THEORIES

R. SWAMINATHA AIYAR

MOTILAL BANARSIDASS
Delhi Varanasi Patna
Bangalore Madras

First Published: Madras, 1975
Reissued: Delhi, 1987

MOTILAL BANARSIDASS
Bungalow Road, Jawahar Nagar, Delhi 110 007

Branches
Chowk, Varanasi 221 001
Ashok Rajpath, Patna 800 004
24, Race Course Road, Bangalore 560 001
120 Royapettah High Road, Mylapore, Madras 600 004

ISBN : 81-208-0331-0

PRINTED IN INDIA
BY JAINENDRA PRAKASH JAIN AT SHRI JAINENDRA PRESS, A-45 NARAINA INDUSTRIAL AREA, PHASE I, NEW DELHI 110 028 AND PUBLISHED BY NARENDRA PRAKASH JAIN FOR MOTILAL BANARSIDASS, DELHI 110 007.

A NOTE ON THE BOOK

This book has a long and chequered history. It began as a trickle of talks by the author to a small audience, under the auspices of the South Indian Teachers' Union, over fifty years ago. Only Tamil scholars, and those with a background of English education and general knowledge, such as teachers, could be expected to be interested in those days. No more than a few dozen people attended the talks. An abridged report was published in the Madras Tamil daily " Swadesamitran "

The Tamilian Education Society, Madras, (founded in 1917 by a few enthusiasts under distinguished guidance, which had for its main object " the propagation of modern scientific knowledge among the Tamil masses through the medium of Tamil ") felt that a wider publicity for the lectures among the teachers and the educated public would provide useful results. At its request, Mr. R. Swaminatha Aiyar wrote down his thesis a little more fully, after careful consideration of possible criticisms. This was published serially in 1922-23 as supplements to THE TAMILIANS' FRIEND (*Tamilar Nēśaṉ*), the Tamil Journal of the Society, and attracted rather more attention.

Since Mr. R. Swaminatha Aiyar's theories covered not merely the Tamil language, but also the other languages of the Dravidian group, he followed up his thesis, which was published by him in Tamil first, by writing a number of articles in English to some journals, particularly in the Andhra area, and he read too a number of learned papers at several conferences of scholars in Madras, Poona (1919), and elsewhere. He delivered a series of lectures on the Philology of the Dravidian languages in the capacity of a Special Reader of the Calcutta University. These lectures are referred to by the author in Appendix II-A (p. 552). They attracted the attention of a few scholars in those areas and elsewhere. Linguistics had not yet become an object of wide study. It was true that Dr. Caldwell and a few others had put forward their views. Some accepted them wholesale, while others were too little inclined to investigate such an abstruse matter. Mohenjo-Daro had not been discovered, and nothing was known of the Indus Valley civilization and of the language and script of the seals discovered there.

During all this period, Mr. R. Swaminatha Aiyar was gathering more and more material, much of which confirmed him in his theories, and some of which suggested that certain ideas, which had been put forward by him, perhaps needed revision. So he decided to write them out more fully and elaborately, and to publish them in the form of a book. His attitude was one of detachment in his conclusions, but one of close attachment to truth in his selection and presentation of data. He had his manuscript material typed with diacritical marks, explanations, quotations, and indications of the authorities which he had referred to, either to agree with or to differ from. He gave it to the Madras Law Journal Press for printing. But the author died before the printing was completed.

The problem was what to do next. The material had been examined by some scholars like Professor S. Kuppuswami Sastri and others, who decided that the book should be completed. Dr. Chintamani, one of the Professor's pupils, was assigned the work of going through the manuscript and the proofs. Dr. Chintamani too did not live to complete the work ; Professor Kuppuswami Sastri had died earlier. For a long time, the printed material lay almost neglected in the premises of the Madras Law Journal Press, and in course of time the paper perished and could no longer be bound and issued as a book.

Ultimately some eminent personages were willing to sponsor the publication. The Madras Law Journal Press was willing to do the laborious and extremely difficult work of printing the work over again, though almost all those who had something to do with the work in the previous attempt were no longer there, owing to death or superannuation; and the Press wrote to the present writer in 1968 asking him to help with the proofs. But the difficulties connected with printing—proof-reading, correcting, and checking—were almost insurmountable. There were hardly any with a scholarship approaching that of the learned author in its range or depth in so many languages and dialects of the country. It extended from Vedic Sanskrit to Classical Sanskrit, and to the various Sanskrit-based dialects of North India, and also to the early classical, later classical, and dialectal forms of the various Dravidian languages of the South. However, the sponsors were so convinced of the utility, at least as a jumping-off ground or basic point, of the pioneering work of Mr. Swaminatha Aiyar (pioneering because he disagreed with Dr. Caldwell and propounded other theories) that they persisted with the work. The Press had printed twenty-one formes, when again the work got bogged down and had to be re-started after a time. It has now been completed, though some material is missing.

On behalf of those who corrected the proofs, the writer of the present note submits that they did their best, but that their best fell far short of legitimate expectations. There are a number of mistakes in proof-reading, numbering etc. They hope that the scholars who go through this work will help to correct at least some of the mistakes and inaccuracies that may have been unwittingly allowed to creep in, and be good enough to intimate them to the publishers.

Apart from such inaccuracies, the major conclusions of the author may not find ready acceptance at the hands of those who are convinced of the truth of the influential theories that he assails. This is natural, and there would be nothing wrong if his views were criticised, provided the criticism was done dispassionately in the interests of truth. With regard to the deciphering of the Mohenjo-Daro seals, for example, there has been a long and lively controversy in our time, and there seems little prospect of its terminating decisively in favour of any particular solution. Nevertheless, no one regrets the controversy, as it is bound to further the truth in the long run.

Mr. Swaminatha Aiyar's work is placed before the public as a pioneering contribution to a field of study in which there have been too few workers. Whatever be the absolute value of his work, all earnest workers will salute his memory as that of a painstaking scholar who laboured long over it with single-minded devotion, more than fifty years ago, in the cause of linguistic science. His labours should help promote national integration, by showing how, over two or three millenia ago, people living in different parts of India lived in linguistic amity taking freely from neighbouring languages and thereby enriching their own.

What Mr. R. Swaminatha Aiyar has so generously and warmly said of Dr. Caldwell's book, namely, "This book is a storehouse of information on everything Dravidian, and bears evidence, on every page of it, to the immense learning of the author, his indefatigable research, his genius for analysis, and his familiarity with the grammars of almost all the languages of the world", will apply equally well to his own book.

Maharajanagar *P. N. Appuswami*
Tirunelveli-11

A NOTE ON THE AUTHOR

Mr. R. Swaminatha Aiyar was one of the galaxy of brilliant men who were born and bred in the Tanjore District in the nineteenth century. He belonged to a generation which produced several giants of learning, who were as versatile as they were profound, and whose moral stature matched their intellectual greatness.

He was a contemporary of Sir P. S. Sivaswami Aiyar (and therefore of Sri V. Krishnaswami Aiyar as well), and continued as his close associate and friend, with mutual respect and admiration. Both were erudite, soft-spoken, and believed in an extraordinary degree in integrity, and hard and sustained work ; and they practised their beliefs throughout their lives, respecting themselves as much as they did others.

Like so many other great men of those days, Mr. R. Swaminatha Aiyar also commenced his life as a school master in the Districts, serving as such from 1880 to 1884. In 1885, he was appointed Assistant Professor of Mathematics in Presidency College, Madras, and served in that capacity, till 1888. In 1889, he entered the Revenue Department, and served as a Head Clerk, till 1892. In 1893, he became a Senior Assistant in the Board of Revenue, and held that post, till 1894. In 1895, he became Registrar of the Revenue Department in the Board of Revenue. In 1896, he returned to the profession of teaching, and was appointed Professor of Mathematics in Presidency College, a post which Mr. C. H. Stuart had held before him. In 1897 he was appointed as " Famine Assistant ", again in the Revenue

Department. He seems to have a so held the appointment of Tamil Translator to the Government of Madras.

In 1910 and later, he served as Treasury Deputy Collector, and as Administrative Deputy Collector in various districts of what was the Madras Presidency. He served in the Telugu areas, in Godavari, Kakinada, Jammalmadugu, and other places, and in the Tamil Districts of Coimbatore, and Tirunelveli.

His intellectual qualities and his cultural background made him interested in the physical and moral well-being of the community, looking upon himself, as he did, as its servant. He moved with the people closely, and ascertained at first hand their needs and requirements of everyday life. Because of his proficiency in their language and dialects, he was also interested in their cultural and linguistic activities. Because of this, he was also able to perceive and understand the nuances of language and dialect in an extraordinary degree. The knowledge he had cultivated of Vedic Sanskrit and of Classical Sanskrit, from his boyhood, at a time when such knowledge was more prevalent and valued, was of great help in preparing his mind for linguistic study. So too his knowledge of the Classic Tamil of the Sangham and later periods helped him in his study of the dialects of the Tamil country.

Thus, by birth, early training, bent of mind, and the opportunities provided by his occupation, he became eminently fitted for the work he dedicated himself to later on in life.

Mr. R. Swaminatha Aiyar was a linguist, administrator, mathematician, grammarian, educator, scholar, orientalist, and polymath, a versatile genius. The writer of this note used to marvel at his phenomenal knowledge, memory, powers of analysis, marshalling and synthesis, faculties which he was able to draw upon easily and almost spontaneously. It never occurred to this writer then to ask him how he had learnt so much and so well, what books he used, where he got them from, and what were the methods which he used to arrange, analyse and index them, in order to draw upon them and to use them.

R. Swaminatha Aiyar was profound, yet very likeable, widely and deeply learned, yet disciplined and modest; and with a scholar's sense of humour, yet mild and gentle.

31 3-75 *P. N. Appuswami*
Maharajanagar
Tirunelveli-11

DEDICATION

To

All lovers of the languages

of India

In the hope that through them

India

Will become integrated well and truly

As a great nation

CONTENTS

CHAPTER III

THE ALLEGED DRAVIDIAN CHARACTERISTICS IN INDO-ARYAN

CHAPTER IV
ARYAN LITERATURE AND INSCRIPTIONS

CHAPTER X

Pro-Dravidian Past Tense Forms

CHAPTER XI

CAUSAL FORMATIONS

CHAPTER XI-A

ARYAN GERUNDIAL SUFFIXES

CHAPTER XI-B

ARYAN PRESENT PARTICIPLE SUFFIXES

PAGE

CHAPTER XI-C

ARYAN ABSTRACT NOUN SUFFIXES

CHAPTER XI-D

THE ARYAN VERB-FORMS

Kri, *Kriṇu* and *Grihṇa*

CHAPTER XI-E

DIACRITICAL MARKS

The following is a list of the diacritical marks used in this book, following the style of the 'Tamil Lexicon' published by the University of Madras. They are arranged in the English alphabetical order to facilitate easy reference.

d = .. = द्	ñ = ஞ = ञ	th = .. = थ
ḍ = .. = ड	ṅ = ங = ङ	ṭh = .. = ठ
dh = .. = ध	r = ர = र	i = இ = इ
ḍh = .. = ढ	ṟ = ற = ..	ī = ஈ = ई
l = ல = ल	ṛ = .. = ऋ	ï = குற்றியல் இகரம் (half of இ)
l = ள = ळ	ś = ச = श	
ḻ = ழ = ..	ṣ = ஷ = ष	u = உ = उ
n = ந = न	s = ஸ = स	ū = ஊ = ऊ
ṉ = ன = ..	t = த = त	u̇ = குற்றியல் உகரம் (half of உ)
ṇ = ண = ण	ṭ = ட = ट	

CONTRACTIONS AND ABBREVIATIONS

Note : The numbers refer to pages

A.	.. Āraṇyaka
A.H.I.	.. Ancient and Hindu India *by* V. A. Smith
Aham	.. Akanāṉūṟu
A.G.	.. Avestan Grammar *by* Kanga
A.S.	.. Anglo-Saxon
B.	.. Bengali
B.A.G.	.. A Grammar of the Aryan Vernaculars of India *by* John Beames, 26, 27, 45, 197, 219, 498, 503, 511, 512, 517, 520, 534
Brug.	.. Brugmann, 106
C.D.G.	.. Comparative Grammar of Dravidian Languages *by* Caldwell
C.I.	.. Census of India
Col.	.. Śollatikāram
Coll.	.. Colloquial (Speech)
Cilap.	.. Śilappatikāram
Du.	.. Dutch
D.P.G.	.. 454
E.I.	.. Epigraphia India, 181, 257, 261, 315, 394, 509
Ep. Ind.	,, ,,
G.	.. Gauda
G.M.G.	.. Gundert's Malayalam Grammar, 379
Ger.	.. German
H.	.. Hindi
H.G.G.	.. Grammar of the Gaudīya Language (Hoernle) 29, 45, 251, 234, 448, 451, 455, 509 512, 517, 518, 523, 527, 534

I.A.	..	Indian Antiquary
Ind. Ant.	..	Indian Antiquary
I.S.	..	
Icel.	..	Icelandic
J.A.V.S.		233
J.R.A.S.		Journal of the Royal Asiatic Society, 81, 268
J.A.V.		172 452
K.	..	Kannada (Kanarese)
K.A.	..	Kanga's Avestan Grammar (Vocabulary) 233
K.A.G.	..	Kanga's Avestic Grammar, 73, 152, 173, 174, 175, 183, 485, 494, 533
KAG	..	Kanga's Avestan Grammar, 177, 183 452
K.K.G.	..	Kanada Grammar *by* Kittel, 152, 264 396, 397, 399, 425, 438
Kan.	..	,, ,,
Kali	..	Kalittokai
K.A.V.	..	,, ,,
Kural	..	Tiru-k-Kural
L.S.	..	Linguistic Survey of India
Lith.	..	Lithuanian
M.	..	Malayalam
Ma.	..	Malayālam
Mal.	..	,,
M.V.G.	..	Macdonnel's Vedic Grammar, 179, 180, 192, 481, 483, 494, 533
O.	..	Oriya
P.P.G.S.	..	Prākṛt Grammar, Pischel, 117, 149, 178
P.P.G.	..	Pāli Grammar, 155, 177, 183, 497, 514
Pr.	..	Prākṛt
Prak.	..	,,
Paisi. Lang.	..	Paisācī Language
Pattu.	..	Pattu-p-pāṭṭu

Puṟam	..	Puṟanāṉūṟu
S.	..	Sanskrit
S.I.I.	..	South Indian Inscriptions
Skt.	..	Sanskrit
Swed.	..	Swedish
T.	..	Tamil
Tam.	..	Tamil
T.A.S.	..	Travancore Archaeological Series, 28, 266, 272
T.A.		Taittirīya Āraṇyaka, 225
T.B.	..	Taittirīya Brāhmaṇa, 226, 227
Tel.	..	Telugu
Tol.	..	Tolkāppiyam
T.S.	..	Taittirīya Samhita, 87
T.S.I.	..	226
Var.	..	Vararuchi (Prākṛta Prākāśa)
V.F.J.	..	343
W.S.G.	..	Sanskrit Grammar *by* Whitney, 172, 192, 456, 459
W.S.G.	..	Whitney's Sanskrit Grammar, 180, 192. 452, 294, 533
W.G.G.	..	519

NAME INDEX

The Number refer to pages in the book

C

LANGUAGES REFERRED TO

A

ANGLO-SAXON
ANTARBEDI
APABHRAMŚA
ARDHAMĀGADHI
ĀRṢA PRĀKRIT
ARYAN (VERNACULARS)
ASSAMESE
AUSTRIC FAMILY
AUSTRO-ASIATIC GROUP
AVESTIC

B

BALTO-SLAVONIC
BAORI
BADAGA (OLD KANARESE), (KUINJU)
BENGALI
BĒRADI
BHILL—DHAR STATE, KANDESH, NAHIKANTHA, NIMAR, RAJ-I-A
BĪHĀRI
BRĀHŪI
BUNDELI
BURGANDI

C

CELTIC
CHATTĪSGARHI

CEN-TAMIḺ
CHENCHU
CHENTSU
CŪLIKAPAIŚACI

D

DĀRDIC
DĀSARI
DRĀVIDA BHĀṢA
DRAVIDIAN (GROUP)
DUTCH

F

FINNISH

G

GAUDA (NORTH), (SOUTH)
GAWAR BATI
GERMAN
GHISADI
GŌLARĪ
GŌṆḌĪ, GŌNDI, (MADRAS)
GOTHIC
GREEK
GUJARĀTI (GUZERATI)

H

HALABĪ
HEBREW
HINDI (EAST—WEST)
HŌLĪYA

I

ICELANDIC
INDO-ARYAN (GROUP), (VERNACULARS), (OLD), (LANGUAGES)
INDO-EUROPEAN (GROUP)
INDO-GERMANIC
IRANIAN

K

KAIKĀDI (DIALECT)
KĀLAMI
KALASA
KAMATHI
KĀNARESE (MODERN), (OLD)
KANNADA (KANARESE)
KAṆḌH
KOḌAGU
KŌLĀMI
KŌMTAU
KORA
KORAVA
KŌṬA
KUI
KUMAUNI
KURUKH
KURUMVĀRI

L

LAHNDA
LATIN
LITHUANIAN

M

MĀGADHI
MAHĀRASTRI
MAIPATI
MALAYĀLAM
MALTI
MALTO
MARĀTHI
MĀRWARI
MON-KHMER
MUṆḌĀ
MUSSALMĀNI

N

NAIKADI
NĒPĀLI (NAIPALI)
NEWĀRI
NORTH GAUDA
N.W. LANGUAGE

O

ORIYA

P

PR. (Prakrit)
PAHĀRI
PAHLAVI
PAIŚĀCI
PAIŚĀCHA (LANGUAGES)
PALI (LITERARY)
PĀNCĀLI
PANJABI
PASAI
PERSIAN (OLD), (NEW)

POGULI
PRAKṚITS (SECONDARY), (PRIMARY), (TERTIARY)
PRAKṚT
PRĀKṚT (ĀRSHA)
PRO-VEDIC

R

RĀJASTHĀNI
RAMBĀNI

S

SANSKRIT
SAURASENJ
SCYTHIAN (GROUP)
SCYTHIAN
SCYTHIC—TURANIAN
SEMITIC (GROUP)
SINDHI
SINGHALESE
SLAVONIC (OLD)
SWEDISH

T

TAMIL (DIALECTS), (MODERN), (MEDIAEVAL), (OLD)
TELUGU
TEUTONIC (LANGUAGES)
TIBETO—BURMAN
TIBETO—CHINESE GROUP
TODA
TOṬA
TUḶU
TURANIAN

V

W

Y

EDICTS, INSCRIPTIONS ETC.

CHAPTER I

DRAVIDIAN THEORIES

1. THE POSITION OF INDO-ARYAN AND DRAVIDIAN AMONG THE LANGUAGES OF INDIA

THE chief languages of India are grouped under four main heads, *viz.*,

1. the Indo-European, comprising the Iranian and the Indo-Aryan branches ;

2. the Dravidian, including Brāhūī spoken in the Khante of Kelat ;

3. the Austro-Asiatic, comprising the Mon-Khmer and the Muṇḍā sub-families and

4. the Tibeto-Chinese.

Of these the Tibeto-Chinese and the Mon-Khmer groups are spoken chiefly in the territories on the East and on the North-East, while the languages included in the Iranian branch are mostly confined to similar areas on the West. Excluding these and confining attention to India proper, that is, to the country known as India from the earliest times, the languages spoken therein may be grouped under three main heads, *viz.*, 1. the Indo-Aryan, 2. the Dravidian and 3. the Muṇḍā ; these have been in contact with one another from prehistoric times and may be expected to have greatly influenced one another. The speakers of the Muṇḍā group number about four millions roughly and are now to be found chiefly in the plateau of Chota-Nagpur and in the adjoining hills and jungles ; they are all aboriginal people of low culture and social status. The languages of this group are steadily being supplanted by Indo-Aryan forms of speech ; the habitat of this group was once very much more extensive extending perhaps over the greater part of Northern India. The Indo-Aryan languages are spoken by about 230 millions of people inhabiting Northern and Western India and Deccan ; these languages are traceable to the Vedic language through the Prākṛts and the Apabhraṁśas which arose out of the corruption and the breaking up of the Vedic dialects. The Dravidian family comprises all the principal languages of Southern India and the speakers thereof number about 64 millions, including the Brāhūīs and the small tribes speaking Dravidian dialects in the Central Provinces and Chota-Nagpur, and up the banks of the Ganges at Rājmahāl. The small Dravidian communities in the North and in Central India, scattered like islets in a sea of Aryan population are it is stated, being rapidly Hinduized and their language adopts an ever increasing Aryan element till it is quite superseded by Aryan speech. This process has been going on for centuries and is still going on. (Linguistic Survey of India, Vol. IV, p. 278.)

Kumārila Bhaṭṭa (7th Century A.D.) discusses in his *Tantravārtika* the meanings of certain Non-Aryan (*mleccha*) words which he says belongs to the Drāviḍa-bhāṣā. The phrase Drāviḍa-bhāṣā is taken by some Dravidian scholars to indicate a division of the Dravidian family of languages into two groups, Āndhra and Drāviḍa and following this supposed classification it has been usual to divide the family into two main groups Āndhra and Drāviḍa. Professor Sten Konow, in Volume IV of the Linguistic Survey of India undertaken in connection with the Indian Census of 1901, appears to have thought that Brāhūī should be regarded as an independent third group, but subsequent Census Reports recognise only two groups Āndhra and Drāvida, while Gōṇḍī etc., partaking of the characteristics of both the groups are shown as an intermediate group. The cultivated Dravidian languages are Tamil, Malayalam, Kanarese and Tulu belonging to the Drāviḍa group and Telugu belonging to the Āndhra group. Of these five, Tamil, Malayalam, Kanarese and Telugu possess inscriptions and extensive literatures ; the speakers of these four languages number 60.2 millions. The speakers of Tuḷu number about 6 millions ; while the speakers of all other Dravidian languages, *viz.*, Koḍagu, Toṭa, Kora, Kurukh, Malti and Brāhūī, belonging to the Drāviḍa group, Kalāmī and Kaṇḍh or Kuī belonging to the Āndhra group, Gōṇḍī etc., comprising the intermediate group, number only about 3.2 millions.

The following table exhibits the distribution of the population (Census of India, 1921) :

Family, Sub-family, Branch.		*No. of languages spoken.*	*No. of speakers in millions.*
Languages of India	..	220	314.389
(i) Austric Family	..	19	4.529
Muṇḍā branch	..	7	3.974
(ii) Tibeto-Chinese Family	..	162	12.885
(iii) Dravidian Family	..	14	64.128
Drāviḍa group	..	7	37.286
Intermediate group	..	5	3.057
Āndhra language	..	1	23.601
N. W. language	..	1	.184
(iv) Indo-European Family (Aryan Sub-family)	..	25	232.847
Iranian branch	..	2	1.982
Dardic branch	..	4	1.304
Indo-Aryan branch	..	19	229.561

2. THE SCOPE OF THE PRESENT WORK.

The cultivated Dravidian languages abound in Sanskrit words and words of Sanskritic origin to such an extent that learned scholars once entertained the opinion that these languages were descended from Sanskrit like the modern languages of Northern India and the Deccan. But a closer acquaintance with the Dravidian grammatical structure led to the abandonment of this extreme view, and Bishop Caldwell's "*Comparative Grammar of the Dravidian Languages*" contributed not a little to this result. The almost universal opinion held at present in regard to these languages is that they attained their development long anterior to the advent of the Sanskrit and Prākṛt-speaking immigrants into India and that, though the subsequent commingling of the Aryan and the Dravidian races has introduced a very large number of Aryan culture words into the Dravidian languages, they continue to be wholly Dravidian as well as the basic portion of their vocabularies ; and it is also claimed for these languages that the simplicity of their structure has exercised a profound influence on the grammatical structure of Sanskrit and of its descendants on Indian soil, and that a considerable proportion of Sanskrit roots is of Dravidian origin. The pendulum has thus swung back to the opposite extreme ; for if the theory of direct descent from Sanskrit erred on one side, the current theory which assigns a remote antiquity to the development of the Dravidian languages and regards their structure as unaffected by contact with Aryan idioms errs equally on the other side. The materials collected by the present writer in the course of a detailed examination of the subject would seem to lead to the inference that a very considerable majority, if not all, of the Dravidian grammatical forms have arisen from suffixed elements borrowed from Sanskrit and the Prākrts during the last twenty or twenty-five centuries, and that the basic portion of the Dravidian vocabulary not traceable directly or indirectly to Sanskrit or other Aryan sources is not very large. To deal fully with the various aspects of the question, it will be necessary to consider it under the heads (i) basic portion of the vocabulary, (ii) nominal declension and (iii) conjugation of verbs. It is proposed to deal in the following pages with the last and most important of these heads, *viz.*, conjugation of verbs, leaving the other two for a future occasion.

A finite verb in Dravidian languages consists in most cases of a verbal base, a pronominal termination, and certain intermediate particles or letters which indicate the tense and mood of the verb. It is these particles and letters which are referred to as *tense and mood signs* in the title of this book ; and an attempt will be made in the following pages to trace the etymology of all such signs in use in the cultivated Dravidian languages.

The pronominal terminations are either pronouns or modifications of pronouns and show the person and grammatical number of the verb, and in most cases the gender also in the forms of the third person. In colloquial Malayalam the finite verb contains no pronominal termination, but consists merely of the verbal base and a tense or mode sign and is common to all persons, numbers and genders. Thus Malayalam *koḍuttu* 'gave' [= *koḍu* (verbal base)+*tu* (past tense sign)] contains no personal termination like the Tamil *koṭuttēṉ* = *koṭu*+*tu*+*ēṉ*. The Malayalam form is like the English forms 'shouted,' 'created' etc., which are common to all persons, numbers, and genders. Similar forms occur, though to a limited extent, in other Dravidian languages also and it will be shown hereafter that, in the earliest stage of the development of these languages, that is to say, in the pro-Dravidian period, the verb consisted merely of the base and the tense or the mode sign. If these signs or the majority of them can be shown to be of Aryan origin, it follows that the Dravidian languages must have been under Aryan influence from earliest times.

The verbal bases and pronouns naturally come under the head vocabulary and are not dealt with directly in the following pages. But opportunity is taken from time to time to indicate incidentally that some of the commonest of them are of Aryan origin.

3. BISHOP CALDWELL'S DRAVIDIAN THEORY.

The originator of the current Dravidian theory was the late Bishop Caldwell who followed the Danish philologist Rask in classing Dravidian as a member of the so-called Scythic family. He probably began his "*Comparative Grammar of the Dravidian Languages*" (1856, 2nd edition 1875) with the object of combating the theory then held by some scholars that these languages were directly descended from Sanskrit, but he went much further than this. Having disposed of this theory in the Introduction (pages 45 to 56) to his Grammar he devoted the body of the work to comparing the Dravidian languages with one another and to determining theirs affinities with the other language-groups of the world—Indo-European, Semitic and Scythic—the last including the language of the Finns, the Magyars, the Tartars, the Turks, and the Chinese and all the other languages included in the term Turanian in the terminology of later years. In conclusion, while acknowledging the existence of a very large percentage of Sanskrit and Indo-Aryan words in the Dravidian vocabularies, he maintained that the Dravidian languages had no structural relationship with Sanskrit and attemped to prove that the grammatical affinities of these languages were mainly Scythic-Turanian in the nomenclature of later years, occasionally Semitic, and that, where the affinities were Indo-European, these did not come into existence on Indian soil, but belonged mostly to the pre-Aryan period of the pre-historic past when the Aryans and the Turanians were living as one undivided race. The book is a store-house of information on everything Dravidian, and bears evidence on every page of it to the immense learning of the author, his indefatigable research, his genius for analysis, and his familiarity with the grammars of almost all the languages of the world. Further the conclusions arrived at by the eminent author were expressed in no halting or faltering tones, many of the discussions on controvertible points being wound up with some such phrases as '*I have no doubt*' '*I have little doubt*' '*It cannot be doubted*' '*We can scarcely err in supposing*' etc. It is no wonder, therefore, that the work produced an immense sensation at the time, the views expressed therein being accepted by almost every scholar of note, and that the theories propounded therein have continued to dominate the Dravidian field for nearly seventy years. Among those who accepted these theories in their entirety special mention must be made of Dr. H. Gundert and Dr. F. Kittel, two missionary names, which Dravidian scholars should always hold in grateful remembrance for the Dictionaries and Grammars bearing these names.

The theory of direct descent from Sanskrit was based wholly on the extraordinary proportion of words of Sanskritic origin in the Dravidian vocabularies and took no note of the dissimilarity of the Dravidian grammatical forms to the Sanskrit forms. Bishop Caldwell had no difficulty in demolishing that theory, but he installed in its stead the equally untenable Scythic theory which it took many years of discussion to dislodge from its position. It is no disparagement to a pioneer worker, however eminent, to have it said that subsequent workers discovered serious errors in his work. The materials necessary for a historical treatment of the Dravidian question were not available in Bishop Caldwell's time and generalising on the imperfect and incomplete materials then to hand, he has sown the Dravidian field with a large number of questionable etymologies and equations which now impede progress at every step. Most of these etymologies, analogies, and equations will be fully dealt with in the following pages, but a few of them may be mentioned here to show how fundamental Bishop Caldwell's misconceptions were.

i. There is a class of Telugu forms ending in-*ṉ* which are called *drutaprakṛtika* ; the final -*n* of these words is often not pronounced except when the words are followed by vowels. Bishop Caldwell regarded the final -*n* of many of these words as put in for the purpose of preventing hiatus between two consecutive vowels in a certain class of cases just as -*y* is put in for the same purpose in the remaining class of cases called *kala* (C.D.G. pages 72-74). The *druta* of the copulative conjunction *un*, of the benedictive suffixes *edum* and -*tan* and of the third person aorist form *ceppunu* appears as-*m* in other languages : in these and in most other cases this *druta* or final -*n* is an essential part of Telugu suffixes and post-positions and enables us to trace the relationship of Telugu forms with the corresponding forms in other languages. To ignore this *druta*, as Bishop Caldwell does, as merely euphonic and adventitious, will have the same effect on these words as phonetic spelling will have on such words as *doubt*, *should*, *alms*, *receipt*, etc., in English.

ii. Bishop Caldwell also considered it probable that the -*n* of the Tamil-Telugu past tense forms in -*inta* and the -*d* of the past tense forms of some verbs in Kanarese were euphonic. Thus the past relative participles—Tamil *kāṭṭiṉa* ' that showed '; Telugu *koṭṭina* ' that beat '; Kanarese *māḍida* ' that made '—were according to him made up as follows :—

Kāṭṭiṉa=*Kāṭṭu*+*i*+(*n*)+*a*
Koṭṭina=*koṭṭu*+*i*+(*n*)+*a*
Māḍida=*māḍu*+*i*+(*d*)+*a*

the intervening-*n*- and -*d*- being put in to prevent hiatus. He also had an alternative theory that the -*n*- and -*d*- were perhaps the signs of the preterite and either way he arrived at the equation *d*=*n*, the former letter being the older (pages 390-394). The fact that modern Malayalam which separated very late from Tamil shows neither -*d*- nor -*n*- in the forms under consideration shows how untenable these theories are, especially the former.

iii. He also got together a number of Tamil forms—*irukkiṉṟaṉaṉ* 'he is'; *irundaṉaṉ* 'he was'; *poruḷaṉa* 'things that are real'; *varuṉa* 'things that will come'; *eṉmaṉār* 'they will say'—which he analysed as follows :—

1. *irukiṉṟaṉaṉ*=*irukkiṉṟa*+(*ṉ*)+*aṉ*
2. *irundaṉaṉ*=*irunda*+(*ṉ*)+*aṉ*
3. *poruḷaṉ a*=*poruḷa*+ *ṉ*)+*a*
4. *varuṉa*=*varu*+(*ṉ*)+*a*
5. *eṉmaṉār*=*eṉma*+(*ṉ*)+*ār*

the intervening -*n*- being put in, according to him, to prevent hiatus (C. D. G. pages 74-75). There are forms in Old Tamil like *irundaṉṟu* 'it was', *vandaṉṟu* 'it came' etc., in the third person neuter singular, which in accordance with the above analysis should be resolved into

6. *irundaṉṟu*=*irundu*+(*ṉ*)+*tu*
7. *vandaṉṟu*=*vandu*+(*ṉ*)+*tu* etc.,

where -*ṉ*- does not fill up any hiatus between vowels. This shows that Bishop Caldwell's analysis is wrong. The forms must be resolved thus :—

1. *irrukkiṉṟaṉaṉ*=*irukkiṉṟu*+*aṉ*+*aṉ*
2. *irundaṉaṉ*=*irundu*+*aṉ*+*aṉ*
3. *poruḷaṉa*=*poruḷ*+*aṉ*+*a*
4. *varukuṉa*=*varu*+*kuṉ*+*a*
5. *enmaṉār*=*eṉ*+*maṉ*+*ār*
6. *irundaṉṟu*=*irundu*+*aṉ*+*tu*
7. *vandaṉṟu*=*vandu*+*aṉ*+*tu*

It can be shown that, in each of these cases, the intermediate -ṉ- is an integral part of suffixes derived from Aryan.

It is on the basis of instances like these that he arrived at his conclusion that the Dravidian languages resembled Greek in using the letter -ṉ- to prevent hiatus between vowels. (C. D. G. Introduction page 76.)

iv. His equation that the Tamil formative suffix-*ku* was the same as the Telugu -*cu* and the Kanarese -*su* (pages 97-98) entirely overlooks the fact that there are Telugu forms in which the -*k*- of the original -*ku* suffix has not been palatalized. The Telugu suffix-*cu* was a late addition to Telugu roots and does not appear to have been adopted in the pro-Dravidian period when -*ku* was fully established in Tamil. The view taken in the following pages of the -*cu* suffix is that it has arisen from an older -*tyā* or -*tu* suffix, but Bishop Caldwell actually warns his readers against this view and against the illusory resemblance of the Tamil *veiccu* (*veittu*) to the Telugu *veici* 'having placed' (pages 396-397).

4. THE VIEWS OF GUNDERT, KITTEL AND POPE.

Dr. Kittel was a profound scholar of the Kanarese language and literature, and his Kannaḍa-English Dictionary published in 1894 is the best that has appeared of any Dravidian language ; his Grammar of the Kannaḍa language published in 1903 deals exhaustively with the grammatical forms of the ancient, the mediaeval, and the modern Kanarese and embodies the results of the labours of a life-time. Dr. H. Gundert, a profound scholar of the Malayalam language and literature belonged to an earlier generation, and his Malayalam-English Dictionary (1872) in which, in addition to his own life-work, he has utilised the materials collected in the sixteenth and seventeenth centuries by the Portuguese and Italian missionaries of Verapoli is a monument of research ; his Malayalam Grammar (2nd edition 1868) appears to have been the first grammar that has been published in that language. These scholars accepted Bishop Caldwell's theories in their entirety and supplemented his work by doing for the Dravidian vocabularies what Bishop Caldwell had done for the common grammatical framework of the languages. Dr. Gundert's Dictionary furnishes under each Malayalam word information as to whether the word is to be found in other cultivated Dravidian languages also and, if so, in what other languages, and in cases where the word is common to all the five cultivated languages, *viz.*, Tamil, Malayalam, Kanarese, Tuḷu and Telugu, the Roman numeral 5 is written after the word. In Dr. Kittel's Dictionary the information under this head is much fuller, the allied words and roots in all the five languages being given in great detail. The vast heap of materials brought together in the works of these authors is of great help to the Dravidian student in constructing a pro-Dravidian vocabulary, but the want of familiarity of these scholars with the Vedic dialects and with the Prākṛts (secondary and tertiary) arising out of these dialects detracts much from the value of the theories propounded in their works. This is specially the case with the long list of roots given in the Introduction to Dr. Kittel's Dictionary which Sanskrit is supposed to have borrowed from the Dravidian ; the list includes a selection from the lists previously published by Bishop Caldwell and Dr. Gundert.

Dr. G. U. Pope was a distinguished missionary, well versed in Tamil language and literature, but he did not accept Bishop Caldwell's theories ; and in a series of articles in the Indian Antiquary he suggested enquiry as to whether in these theories " certain things have not been taken for granted rather too suddenly in regard to the Dravidian dialects". He was the first to point out that the law of the harmonic sequence of vowels did not obtain in most of these dialects. He was further of opinion,

1. " that between the languages of Southern India and those of the Aryan family there are many deeply seated and radical affinities ;

2. that the differences between the Dravidian tongues and the Aryan are not so great as between the Celtic (for instance) and the Sanskrit ; and

3. that, by consequence, the doctrine that the place of the Dravidian dialects is rather with the Aryan than with the Turanian family of languages is still capable of defence". He illustrated these positions by means of copious illustrations and pointed out that " the resemblances (appeared) most frequently in the more uncultivated Dravidian dialects " and that " the identity (was) most striking in the names of instruments, places, and acts connected with a simple life". He also promised " to consider derivative words " in a future paper " and to show that the prefixes and affixes (were) Aryan " ; but no such paper appears to have been published.

5. DR. STEN KONOW'S VIEWS.

The next great landmark in the history of Dravidian philology was the publication in 1906 of Volume IV of the Linguistic Survey of India which gives specimens of the chief Dravidian languages and of their dialectic varieties. The preparation of this volume was entrusted to Dr. Sten Konow of Christiana and Sir G. A. Grierson, the editor of the series, is jointly responsible with him for the theories put forth in the volume. Unfortunately the area for which the Government of India ordered a linguistic survey in connection with the Census of 1901 did not include Southern India where the cultivated Dravidian languages are spoken and where the vast majority of the Dravidian speakers live.

The Editors have, however, thought it advisable to give a short sketch of the principal Dravidian languages without reference to habitat, in order to make it easier to compare and classify the North Indian members of the family included within the scope of the Survey. Hence only short accounts are given of Tamil, Malayalam, Kanarese and Telugu while theminor Dravidian dialects of the South, *viz.*, Kodagu, Tuḷu, Toḍa and Kōṭa are not described at all.

At pages 278 to 282 of the volume these scholars give a summary of the results of the fifty years discussion since the first publication of Bishop Caldwell's book. It is impossible to explain in detail here how most of the Turanian affinities elaborated by the latter have had to be given up, but the net result will be clear from the following extract (page 282).

"The denomination 'Scythian' is a very unhappy one. The Scythian words which have been handed down by Greek writers are distinctly Iranian, *i.e.*, they belong to the Indo-European family. But nevertheless the name has been used as a common designation of all those languages of Asia and Europe which do not belong to the Indo-European or Semitic families. Moreover, those languages cannot, by any means, be brought together into one linguistic family. The monosyllabic languages of China and neighbouring countries are just as different from the dialects spoken in Caucasus or from the speech of the Finns and Magyars, as is the Indo-European family. The points in which they agree are such features as recur in almost all languages, and they are by no means sufficient to outweigh the great and fundamental characteristics in which they differ from each other. In regard to the Dravidian languages the attempt to connect them with other linguistic families outside India is now generally recognized as a failure and we must still consider them as an isolated family."

It is but natural that such attempts should fail, for the Vedic Aryans probably entered India about 4,000 years ago, and if, as is held by many, the Dravidian languages were spoken not only in the South but also in the West and the North-West of India formerly, these languages must have been in contact with the Aryan dialects now for forty centuries. However this may be, confining attention to the Dravidian languages spoken now in the Deccan and Southern India and to the historic period in which large Hindu, Jain, and Buddhistic colonies are known to have been established in the South, we may confidently say that the Dravidian languages have been in close contact with the Aryan dialects certainly for the last 2,000 years, probably for 2,500 years; and we know that several aboriginal races have abandoned their mother tongues and are now speaking Aryan languages, while many indigenous dialects are now being rapidly Aryanised under our very eyes. In regard to the cultivated languages—Tamil, Malayalam, Kanarese and Telugu—which have a literature and a grammatical standard and which have remained practically unchanged for a considerable period, it must be remembered that the Brahmans, Jains and Buddhists who first cultivated these languages were full of northern learning and would have greatly Aryanised their structure. In these circumstances it was illogical, to say the least, to minimise, ignore, and reject as Bishop Caldwell did, Sanskritic and Aryan analogies, and to take a jump over the Himalayas and the Hindukush in search of analogies in distant Finland, Hungary, Lapland, Caucasus, Japan etc., on the basis of an unproved assumption that the Dravidians came from the West and must have been speaking a Turanian language originally.

In regard to the question whether or not the Dravidians are autochthonous to India, the Editors of the Survey remark :—" With regard to the Drāviḍas, some authorities believe that they arrived in India from the South, while others suppose them to have entered it from the North-West where a Dravidian language is still spoken by the Brāhūīs of Baluchistan. The Brāhūīs do not belong to the Dravidian race but are anthropologically Iranians, *i.e.*, they have merged into the race of their neighbours. It is possible that the same is the case with the Dravidian tribes of the South wherever they came from, but anthropology only tells us that the Dravidian race comprises Muṇḍas and Drāviḍas, and we have no information to show that the Drāviḍas are not the original inhabitants of the South " (L. S., Vol. IV, page 5).

The alleged relationship of the Dravidian languages with the Muṇḍā is examined at pages 2-5 of the volume and the conclusion arrived at is that the two families only agree in such points as are common to most agglutinative languages, that there is no philological reason for deriving them from the same original and that they form two quite independent families.

The Editors express an equally emphatic opinion that all " attempts to show a closer connection with the Indo-Germanic family have proved just as futile " (Vol. IV, page 282).

The aim of the present writer is to show that a closer relationship with the Indo-Aryan languages, than that allowed by Bishop Caldwell or by the Editors of the Linguistic Survey of India *does* exist, but not in the sense that the Dravidian is derived from the Indo-Aryan, like the modern Aryan languages of Northern India and of the Deccan.

6. THE ARYAN ELEMENT IN DRAVIDIAN VOCABULARIES

(A selection from Bishop Caldwell's Supposed Pure Dravidian words.)*

* The author's typescript does not contain this list of words.

The conclusion which the materials collected by the present writer lead to has been briefly stated in section 2 above ; it is to the effect that most of the Dravidian grammatical forms have arisen from suffixal elements borrowed from Indo-Aryan and that the non-Aryan element even in the basic portions of the Dravidian vocabularies is not considerable. This position is utterly at variance not only with the views of European scholars but also with those of Indian scholars generally ; for though there may be many Indians who hold the opinion that there is a much larger admixture of the Aryan element in the Dravidian vocabularies than that allowed by Bishop Caldwell and Prof. Sten Konow, there are perhaps few or none who think that the Dravidian grammatical elements are derived from Aryan sources. The reason for this appears to lie in the circumstance that the Aryan elements compared with the Dravidian languages have till now been taken mostly from classical Sanskrit. For instance, at page 48 of the Introduction of Bishop Caldwell's Comparative Grammar some sixty words of primary importance (not including pronouns and numerals) in Tamil are contrasted with their equivalents in Sanskrit and the conclusion arrived at is that the two languages have no common basis. The Sanskrit words chosen are from classical Sanskrit and not from the Vedic idioms or from the spoken Prākṛts.

Though classical Sanskrit had its roots in a dialect similar to the Vedic idioms, it latterly became, owing to various causes, an artificial, literary language confined almost wholly to books and ceased to be the home speech even of the learned. Similarly Māhārāṣṭrī, Pāli and other literary Prākṛts, though originally they were popular idioms, became highly artificial in course of time. Words relating to philosophy and the sciences are no doubt often borrowed from books, but wherever there is a large infusion of foreign words and idioms in the spoken language of a people, we have to look for their source in the spoken speech—the colloquial and vulgar idioms—not in literary works. These idioms and elements adopted at first in the popular speech ultimately find their way into literature and into books.

To ascertain to what extent Dravidian language and grammar have been affected by Aryan forms of speech we must compare the former with the popular Aryan idioms prevailing at the time when the Aryans and the Dravidians first came in contact, and not with an artificial language confined only to books. For a similar reason it will be seen that as much importance, if not more, is attached in this book to colloquial, vulgar and dialectic Dravidian idioms as to standard and grammatical forms.

We proceed to illustrate these observations by about a dozen examples under each head and begin with a selection from the words given at page 48 of the Introduction to Bishop Caldwell's Comparative Grammar. It must be borne in mind that the equivalences exhibited below hold good only in regard to the root-forms of the words instanced and not in regard to the terminations showing number, gender etc. Thus the Tamil word *Irāmaṉ* (a proper name) corresponds to the Sanskrit *Rāmaḥ*, both the words being in the masculine nominative singular ; but the equivalence is only in regard to the root-forms, the Tamil *irām* and the Sanskrit *rāma*. The final short vowels of Sanskrit words of two or more syllables are quiescent, and are at last elided in popular speech and as no Tamil word can begin with *r*- an on-glide *i* -is inserted ; thus we get the Tamil form *irām*-. The Sanskrit termination *ḥ* (for *s*) has no connection with the Tamil *aṉ* which is an entirely different formation derived from the Indo-Aryan *ant*. So also the S. *mṛgaḥ* and the T. *māṉ* both meaning a deer (item 10 below) are equivalent only in regard to their root-forms, (*i.e.*) S. *mṛga* and T. *mā*

(=Pr. *maga*). The -*ṉ* of *māṉ* was a masculine sign in its inception.

Again take the S. *uṣṭra* 'a camel.' Having regard to the limited number of consonants in Tamil the combination *ṣṭra* can exist only as *ṭṭa* in Tamil ; the initial *u*- of the word will become *o*- and the final short *a*- will become quiescent ; the form which *uṣṭra* should take in Tamil will thus be *oṭṭu*. But the actual forms are *oṭṭai*, *oṭṭakam*, *oṭṭakai* ; the first of these is equivalent to *uṣṭra* and the second and the third to *uṣṭrakaka*. The words *vēṅkai*, *erumai*, *kutirai* in the table below should be similarly derived from *vyāghraka*, *hērambaka*, *aśvataraka*, all containing a pleonastic-*ka*.

It is unnecessary to explain such niceties in detail at this stage.

	English	*Sanskrit*	*Tamil*	*Proposed word.*
1.	hair	*keśa*	*mayir*	S. *śmaśru*
2.	mouth	*mukha*	*vāy*	S. *vac*
2. (a)	nose	”	Tam. *mūkku* Tel. *mukku*	S. *mukha*
3.	ear	*karṇa*	*śevi*	S. *śrava* S. *śravika*
4. 4. (a)	hear	*śru*	*kēḷ* *kēṇ* (Tuḷu)	S. (*ā*) *karṇ*
5. 5. (a)	eat	*bhakṣ*	*tiṉ* *tu*	S. *tṛṇu* S. *tṛ*
6. 6. (a)	walk	*car*	*ēg-u* *śel*	S. *yā* or *i* S. *car*

	English	Sanskrit	Tamil	Proposed word.
7.	night	*nak*	*irā* *iravu*	S. *rā-tri*
8.	mother	*mātṛ*	*āyi*	*yāy* (Paiś)
9.	tiger	*vyāghra*	*puli*	*vēṅgai* (Tamil)
10. 10. (a)	deer beast	*mṛga*	*marai* *māṉ* *mā*	S. *mṛga* (*maraga*) Pr. *maga* Pr. *maga*
11.	fire	*agni*	*tī*	S. *tējas*, *tij*
12. 12. (a)	snake	*sarpa*	*pāmbu* *aravu* *arava* (m)	S. *prasarpa* (**pasap*) S. *sarpa* (**sarapa*) S. *sarpaka* (**sarapaka*).
13.	village	*grāma*	*ūr*	S. *pura*
14. 14. (a)	buffalo	*mahiṣa*	*erumai* *māḍu* 'cattle'	S. *hēramba* (ka) S. *māhiṣa*
15.	horse	*aśva*	*kutirai*	S. *asvatara* (ka)
16.	hill	*parvata*	*malai*	*poruppu* (Tam)

The first three columns are from Bishop Caldwell's book. The fourth column contains words now suggested for comparison. The lines 2 (a), 4 (a), 5 (a), 6 (a), 10 (a), 12 (a) and 14 (a) are also additions now suggested.

1. The Sanskrit word *śmaśāna* ' a cemetery, a burning ground ' has become *mayāṉam* in Tamil, by the loss of the first consonant *ś*-and the weakening of the second -*ś*-into-*y*-. The word *mayir* has arisen from a similar modification of *śmaśru* ' the beard, the hair on the body '.

2. In classical Sanskrit the word *vāc* means ' voice, sound, speech '; but in Vedic Sanskrit it also meant the ' mouth '[1] as the footnote quotations will show.

2. (a) It may also be pointed out here that the Dravidian word *mūkku* must be affiliated to the Sanskrit *mukha* which means not only ' mouth,' but is also applied to the ' beak ' of birds and the ' snout ' or ' muzzle ' of lower animals. Greek *uvk-tue* ' nose,' Latin *mucus* ' snivel ' may also be mentioned here (Curtius Greek Etymology, page 162).

3. The Sanskrit word **śravika* ' ear ' with a *ka* suffix is probably the original of the Tamil *cevi*.

---

1. ' *Svayam ēva mantram bruvāṇā patnī jalam siñcantī satī paśōr aṅgāni āpyāyati* " *vāk tē āpyāyatām* " *iti mantrēṇa vācam* ; " *prāṇas ta* " *iti nāsikē* ' (Srautapadārthanirvacanam, page 170).

The wife of the sacrificer sits by the side of the slaughtered victim and washes the various parts of its body pronouncing certain mantras. One of the parts washed is the mouth and she washes it (*vācam*) saying ' *vāk tē āpyāyatām* ' ' let your *vāk* be refreshed.' Another is the nostrils and she washes them saying ' let your *prāṇa* be refreshed. ' Compare also the following passage in the Taittirīya Upanisad :—' *kṣēma iti vāci* ; *yogakṣema iti prāṉapānaych* ; *karma iti hastayoḥ* ; *gatiriti pādayoḥ* ; *vimuktiriti pāyau* (T.A. 5-15).

6. The correct etymological syllabification of *ēku* is *ē-ku.* It is well known that an original *yā* often becomes *ē* in Dravidian languages.

7. The Tamil word *i-rā* is identical with the root form of *rā-tri.*

8. The Old Tamil form of *āyi* is *yāy*; allied forms occur in the Paiśāca languages of the North-West India and are connected with the Sanskrit verb *jāyate* 'he is born.' (*Vide* page 75 of Grierson's Paiśāca languages).

9. The Sanskrit *vyāghra* is obviously the original of the Tamil *vēṅkai.*

10. In Prākṛt the Sanskrit-*ṛ*-often changes into-*ā*- and *mṛga* 'deer, antelope' becomes *maga*; in Pāli it is *magō* (nominative singular). The Tamil words *mā* 'a beast, an animal' and *māṉ* 'a deer' are both derived from the Sanskrit *mṛga* through Prākṛt *maga*, the final -*ṉ* in *māṉ* being probably a masculine termination. Compare Tamil *marumakaṉ* 'nephew', *marumakaḷ*, *marumaka* 'niece,' which have become respectively *marumāṉ*, *marumāḷ*, *marumā.*

The vowel-*ṛ*-changes also into-*ar*-and with a glide vowel (*svarabhakti*) between-*r*-and-*g*-the word *mṛga* will become *maraga*, and this will give the form *marai.*

12. The Sanskrit *sarpa* 'a serpent' will become *sarapa* with a glide vowel between-*r*-and-*p*-also **sarapaka* with a pleonastic *ka.* These two altered forms will give *aravu* and *aravam.* While **prasarpa* 'which creeps along' or **apasarpa* 'which glides away' might have given rise to *pāp* through the intermediate **pasap.* For a large number of examples in which Tamil elides-*s*-in Sanskrit words, *see* Section 31 below.

13. In many well known instances of names of towns and villages, *pura* has become *ūr* in historical times.

(a) Daśapura, a place of pilgrimage mentioned in a grant of Daḍḍa IV of the first half of the 7th Century is the modern Man-Dasōr in Western Malwa (E.I. Vol. V, page 38).

(b) Rājyapura where an inscription of Mathanadeva (960 A.D.) has been found is now Rājōr or Rājōrgaḍh, a village on a lofty range of hills in the Rājgaḍh district of the Alwar State in Rājputāna (E.I. Vol. III, page 265).

(c) Sihapura which, according to Ceylon tradition was the original home of the earliest Aryan immigrants is now Sihōr.

(d) Āḍūr is Pāṇḍipura in a Western Cālukya inscription of the 8th Century A.D. and is Pāṇḍiyūr in the later inscriptions of the Western Cālukyas and the Kadambas (I.A. Vol. XI, page 69).

(e) Hatti-mattūr is Mattūra in a Bhairanmatti inscription of the 11th Century A.D. (E.I. Vol. III, page 231) and is Maḷtavūr in an inscription of the 8th Century (E.I. Vol. VI, page 161).

(f) Sirūr (Dhārwār) appears as Śrivūra in an inscription of the 9th Century A.D. (E.I. Vol. VII, page 202).

Such instances may be multiplied. They show that the initial-*p*-of the Sanskrit *pura* or *pūr* becomes *v*-intervocally and is ultimately lost in course of time, and that the Dravidian *ūr* ' a village ' is probably a *tadbhava* of *pūr* or *pura*.

Similar changes have taken place in the Telugu *prōlu* ' a town or village ' as the following names will show :—

Bhaṭṭiprōlu, Cēybrōlu, Nidadavōlu, Razōle, Kurnool (formerly Kandenavōlu).

14. (a) ' Buffalo ' is only a specialised meaning of *mahisa* as *mahā* and *māhēyī* mean ' a cow ' and *māhiṣaka* means a shepherd ' generally, as also ' a buffalo herdsman.' The

word *mahiṣa* or *māhiṣa* corrupted into *māṣa and with the last vowel quiescent appears to be the original of *māḍ* pronounced *māḍu*. Sanskrit *ṣ* changes into *ḍ* often in Tamil, as in the following words for instance :—

S. *varṣa* 'a year,' *śiṣya* 'disciple,' *mēṣa* 'a sheep,' *vēṣa* 'a disguise' etc., which exist as *varuḍam*, *śīḍaṉ*, *mēḍam* etc. in Tamil.

The word *māḻ* means 'a cow' in a Tamil dialect (I. S. Vol. IV, page 347).

15. The initial *a* of words is often lost when the accent is distant as in the Aryan vernacular forms *ham*, *hāmi*, *hake*, *hagge* for the Sanskrit *aham* 'I' (cf. below). The spirant-*ś*-is pronounced-*kh*-in some dialects in the north, *e.g.*, Skt. *dṛś* 'see'; *Īṣvara*, a proper name, *Vibhīṣaṉa* 'Rāvaṇa's brother' etc. ; which become *dēkh*, *ikhbal*, *bibikhan* etc., in the north. We thus get a possible *khvtaraka* which may be the original of *kutirai* in Tamil and *guṟṟamu* in Telugu by the *samprasāraṇa* of *va*. The Sanskrit *aśvatarī*, Prākṛt *assatarī*, *asatarī* etc., exist as *attiri*[1] in Tamil ; this last appears to have meant, not a mere mule, but a valuable riding animal used by noblemen in the Tamil country formerly.

The above notes and remarks do not certainly constitute the last word in regard to some of the words dealt with here, especially **prasarpa* and **aśvatarka* which look like artificial formations. But the notes bring out clearly that a comparison of Dravidian words with words of the same meaning given in the dictionaries of classical Sanskrit is not enough for the purpose of determining whether these words have any Indo-Aryan affinities and will often lead to fallacious results.

---

1. Kōvalan the hero of Cilappatikāram rode on an *attiri* in his palmy days. *vāṇa vaṇkaiya ṇattiri yēṟa* (Cilap. VI, l. 119) 'the man of high munificence riding an *attiri*'.

S. 7. THE ARYAN ELEMENT IN DRAVIDIAN VOCABULARIES—(*Contd.*)

(*a*) SPECIMENS OF SANSKRIT WORDS IN DRAVIDIAN CHANGED BEYOND ALL RECOGNITION

Criticising the theory (now abandoned) that the Dravidian languages were derived directly from Sanskrit, Bishop Caldwell said that :—

(1) " It overlooked the circumstance that the non-Sanskritic portion of the Dravidian languages was very greatly in excess of the Sanskrit.

(2) " It overlooked the still more material circumstance that the pronouns and numerals of the Dravidian languages, their verbal and nominal inflexions, and the syntactic arrangement of their words—everything, in short, which constitute the living spirit of a language—were originally and radically different from Sanskrit.

(3) " The orientalists who held the opinion of the derivation of the Dravidian languages from Sanskrit, relied mainly on the circumstance that all dictionaries of Dravidian languages contained a large number of Sanskrit words scarcely at all altered, and a still larger number which, though much altered, were evidently Sanskrit derivatives. They were not, however, aware that such words are never regarded by native scholars as of Dravidian origin, but are known and acknowledged to be derived from Sanskrit, and that they are arranged in classes, according to the degree in which they have been corrupted, or with reference to the medium through which they have been derived. They were also unaware that true Dravidian words, which form the great majority of the words in the southern vocabularies, are placed by native grammarians in a different class from the above-mentioned derivatives from Sanskrit and honoured with the epithets ' national words ' and ' pure words.'

(4) " The Orientalists who supposed the Dravidian languages to be derived from Sanskrit were not aware of the existence of uncultivated languages of the Dravidian family, in which Sanskrit words are not at all, or but very rarely, employed, and they were also not aware that some of the Dravidian languages which make use of Sanskrit derivatives, are able to dispense with those derivatives altogether, such derivatives being considered rather as luxuries or articles of finery than as necessaries. It is true it would now be difficult for Telugu to dispense with its Sanskrit : more so for Kanarese ; and most of all for Malayalam:—those languages having borrowed from Sanskrit so largely, and being so habituated to look up to it for help, that it would be scarcely possible for them now to assert their independence. Tamil, however, the most highly cultivated *ab intra* of all Dravidian idioms, can dispense with its Sanskrit altogether, if need be, and not only stand alone but flourish without its aid."

He also said :—

" In general no difficulty is felt in distinguishing Sanskrit derivatives from the ancient Dravidian roots."

These statements are due to a radical misapprehension as to the origin of the so-called " ancient Dravidian roots." The Tamil alphabet is entirely unable to represent or express Sanskrit words as it contains in each *varga* of consonants only two sounds—unaspirate tenues and nasals—as against the five sounds of the Sanskrit alphabet, and there is reason to believe that the alphabets of Telugu and Kanarese were equally deficient in former times. Sanskrit words which had already undergone great mutilation in the Prakṛts underwent further corruptions in the Dravidian languages, so that most of them have been transformed out of all recognition and it is impossible to identify many of them as Sanskrit *tadbhavas* without a familiar knowledge of the laws of sound obtaining in the Prākrts. This is the reason why Indian grammarians have regarded a very large class of such words as pure Dravidian unconnected with Sanskrit, but the majority of these supposed Dravidian words can be shown to be very corrupt *tadbhavas* of Sanskrit. The following selection will illustrate this point.

1. Tamil : *kāṇam* ' gold, a gold coin '

Sanskrit : *kārṣāpaṇa* ' a coin or weight.'

Prākṛt : *kāhāvaṇō* ; Hindī : *kahān* : Oriyā, *kāhāṇ* : Bengālī : *kāhaṇa* (B.A.G. Vol. 1, page 355.)

2. Tamil : *aṭi* ' a man's foot.'

Sanskrit: *aṅghri* ' a foot, foot-step '; Hindī and Gujarātī: *eḍi* ; Pānjābī : Marāṭhī : *eḍa,* Bengālī : *eḍi* ' heel '; Singhalese: *aḍiya* ' a foot, ' *eḍi* ' feet, ' (B.A.G. Vol. 1, page 134 ; I.A. Vol. XI, page 201).

3. Tamil : *mutunīr, munnīr* ' the sea '.

S. *samudra* ' the ocean.' Singh. Old : *hamuda* ; *muhuda* (with transposition of consonants), later *mūda* (I.A. Vol. XI, page 213), so that *mutunīr* is literally ' water of the ocean.'

4. Tamil : *vai* ' paddy stalks,' *vayal* ' a paddy field,' *Vide* S. 26 below where these are traced to a secondary derivative from the Indo-Iranian *vrīhi* ' rice, the rice plant.'

5. Tamil : *nel, nellu* ' paddy.'

Vide S. 27 below where these are traced to the Vedic *nīvāra* ' wild paddy.'

6. Tamil : *puṟavu, puṟā, prā* ' a dove.'

S. *pārāvatah,* ' a dove '; Pr. *pārāvo, pārāo* (Var : IV. 5).

7. Tamil : *pāvai,* ' a name of the goddess Pārvatī.'

S. *pārvatī*. Pr. *pavva*. (B. A. G. Vol. I, page 185).

The following three items (8), (9) and (10) exhibit some of the changes which the Indo-Aryan conjunct consonant *ṁs* undergoes.

8. Tamil *vīcam* 'one sixteenth part, containing twenty *muntiris*,' a *muntiri* being the smallest fraction in Tamil arithmetic.

S. *viṁśati* or *viṁśa* 'twenty.' H. *bīs* ; M. *vīs.* ; B. *bīc* ; G. *Vīs* (B.A.G. Vol. I, page 155). The Tamil form corresponds to **viṁśakam.*

9. Tamil *vaṅkiṣa* 'a race, family, lineage' ; *vāḻai* 'the plantain' ; *mūṅkil*, *vēy* 'the bamboo.' These words appear to be derived from the Sanskrit *vaṁśa* (1) 'a race, family, lineage.' (2) 'the bamboo.'

It is well known that *anusvāra* is pronounced in Oriyā and Bengālī as ṅg (B.A.G. Vol. I, page 275), thus *aṁśa* 'share' should be pronounced *aṅgṣa* and *siṁha* 'lion' should be pronounced *siṅgha.* A few words in Tamil appear to arise from a similar pronunciation of M in a nexus. One of these is the Tamil *ciṅkam* 'a lion' ; another is the semi-literary word *vaṅkiṣam* which is the equivalent of **vaṁṣaka.* The form equivalent to *vaṁśa* will be *vaṅgiṣ* which appears to be the original of the Tamil *mūṅkil.* *Vide* S. 8-b below.

If the *anusvāra* is elided and the vowel preceding it is lengthened as in the case of *viṁśa* (=vīc) in item No. 8, then *vaṁśaka* will become *vāṣaka* which is the original of the Tamil *vāḻai* 'the plantain'—the bamboo and the plantain being apparently called by the same word *Vaṁśa* as they grow in clusters. The Tamil *vēy* 'the bamboo' appears to be due to the form *vāś* (=vaṁsa) T. *vedir* 'the bamboo'= S. vētra.

10. Tamil : *tiṅkaḷ*, 'the moon', 'a month'.

S. *trīṁśa* 'thirty' takes the form *tīs* 'thirty' in the Aryan vernaculars of the North ; this change is analogous to that of *viṁsa* (=vīc) (Number 8 above).

In Tamil, Malayalam and Kanarese *triṁśa* appears to have taken the form **tiṅgṣ* or **liṅgaṣ* (with a glide vowel *a*) which is the original of *tiṅkaḻ* 'a month.' Just as *vīcam* literally 'twenty' stands for a quantity represented by twenty of the smallest fractions, so *tiṅkaḷ* literally 'thirty' stands for 'a period of thirty days,' *i.e.*, 'a month.'

11. Telugu : *āvā* (*lu*), Tamil : *aiyavi* 'mustard.'

S. *sarṣapa* 'mustard.' Pāli *sāsapa*.

When both the *s*'*s* are elided the word becomes *āava* which gives the forms *āvā*, *ayava*, with a junction consonant in the latter form.

12. Tamil : *eṟumbu*, *uḻuva* ; Malayalam : *eṟumbu*, *iṟumbu*, *uṟumbu* ; Kanarese : *iṟuve*, *iṟive*, *iṟumbe*, *iṟumbu*, *iṟuva*, *iṟuhe*, *iṟvu*, *iṟve* ; all meaning 'the ant.'

The Telugu word is *cīma* which was probably **cirma* originally. This **cirma* which has apparently given rise to the other Dravidian words mentioned above through the weakening and the ultimate loss of the initial *ś* appears itself to have arisen from the Sanskrit *krimi* 'an ant' (Lith: *kirmi*) through the palatalisation of *k*.

13. Bahvṛca 'the Ṛg-Veda' literally 'having many verses' ; bahvṛc 'the Ṛg-vedic Brāhmans.' These have been corrupted into the Tamil *paviḻiyam* 'the Ṛg-veda' which occurs in a Travancore inscription of the 9th Century (T.A.S. Vol. I, page 8). By the time of Nacciṉārkkiṉiyar it had become *pauṭiyam* and *pauṭikam*. (Commentaries on Kalittokai, Introduction, and Tolkāppiyam, Eluttu. Pāyiram).

14. Tamil *umpaḷam*, *umpaḷikkai* 'tax-free lands given for subsistence.' This appears to be derived from the same source as the Aśokan form *ōbalikē* 'tax-free' which occurs in the Paderia pillar inscription (E. I. Vol. V, page 5). Dr. Buhler derives *ōbalikē* from *apabalika* 'tax-free.'

Tamil *campaḷam* 'wages, salary,' is probably connected with *samabalika* 'half-tax-free.'

15. Tamil *kātam* 'a distance of about ten miles.' This appears as *kāvatam* in Old Tamil where it seems to denote a shorter distance and is traceable to the Sanskrit *gavyūti* 'a distance of two krōśaś' equal to about four miles.

These words illustrate what corruptions the original Sanskrit words have undergone and how it is impossible to recognize many of them as of Aryan origin without a detailed investigation in each case.

16. Tamil : *kālai* 'the morning, to-morrow morning.' *kiḻakku* 'the east'.

S. *kalyam* 'dawn.' Pr. *kallam.* Sindh. *kālha, kalha* ; G. M. *kāla* ; O. *kāli* ; B. *kāli, kāila.* These words mean 'to-morrow' also 'yesterday.' (B.A.G. Vol. I, page 350).

17. Tamil : *mālai* 'the evening' ; *mēṟku* 'the west.' S. *malam* 'impurity,' *malina* 'dark.' H. M. *maila,* G. *maḷa, mēla,* P. *maḷa, mala, mila* (Hemacandra II. 138 ; B.A.G. Vol. II, page 175).

18. Tamil : *teṉ* 'southern,' *teṟku* 'south.'

S. *dakṣiṇah,* 'south.' Pr. *dāhiṇō.* E.H. *dāhin* 'right.' *dachin* 'south.' K. *dachan* 'south.' (H.G.G. S. 116 note. B.A.G. Vol. 1, page 310).

Dāhin has apprently become the Tamil *teṉ.*

The termination *-ku* in *kiḻakku, mērku* and *teṟku* are obviously imitations of the terminations of the Sanskrit forms *prāk* 'eastern,' *avāk* 'southern,' *pratyak* 'western.' *udak* 'northern.' *viṣvak* 'in all directions,' *tiryak* 'horizontal' etc., *Kīḻ, mēl* are obviously connected with the Prākṛt words from which the Tamil *kālai* 'the morning' and *mālai* 'the evening' are derived ; *teṉ* is contracted from *dāhin.* These three words are not found in Kanarese and Telugu, and are obviously derived by Tamil from Sanskrit.

Bishop Caldwell thought that the termination *-ku* of these names was the sign of the fourth case. He also thought that *kilakku* ' the east ' and *mēṟku* ' the west ' were derived from the Tamil words *kīl* ' below ' and *mēl* ' above ' and that they were so called from the nature of the Tamil country which sloped down from west to east. This explanation is ingenious but the use of the same words in Malabar is fatal to it (C.D.G.).

(b) SPECIMENS OF SANSKRIT WORDS IN DRAVIDIAN DISGUISED PARTLY BY A CHANGE IN THE PRONUNCIATION OF VOWELS

The Dravidian languages have all the vowels of Sanskrit except the artificial ṛ and ḷ, but even here the Dravidian pronunciation differs from that in Sanskrit.

Sanskrit grammarians regard that *i*, *u* are natural elementary vowels and that *ē*, *ō*, the *guṇa* vowels and *ai au*, the *vṛddhi* vowels are produced from these by shifting the accent to them. On the other hand the Indo-Germanic philologists regard the *guṇa* vowels *ē*, *ō* as representing the normal stage from which the low grade vowels *i*, *u*, arise in un-accented syllables. From Comparative Grammar the latter seems to be the correct view and it also agrees with Vararuci's Prākṛt rules which generally substitute *ē*[1] and *ō*[2] for the first *ai* and *au* of Sanskrit words and also for first *i* and *u* in many cases. This is another reason why Dravidian words should be compared with the corresponding words of spoken Prākṛts, not with the words of the artificial classical Sanskrit The following table will illustrate this point :

---

1. *aita ēt* (Var. I-33) ' *e* is substituted for the first *ai* '.
2. *auta ōt* (Var. I-41) ' *o* is substituted for the first *au* '.

Sanskrit words containing the lowest grade vowels.	*Derivative Sanskrit words containing* vrddhi *or the highest grade vowels.*	*Allied words in Tamil.*
1. *śiśu* 'a child'	*śaiśavam* 'childhood'	*cēy*<*cēc* 'a child, youth'.
2. *piśā*-'a demon'	*paiśāca* 'pertaining to a demon'	*pēy*<*pēc* 'a demon'.
3. *Śibi* ('name of a king')	*śaībya* 'a descendant of Śibi'	*cempiya* (a title of Cōḷa kings supposed to be descended from *Śibi*).
4. *kumāra* '.a boy'	*kaumāram* 'childhood'	*kommai* 'youth' *komara* 'ayouth'
5. *kuṭila* 'crooked'	*kauṭilyam* 'crookedness'	*koṭum* 'crooked'
6. *krūra* 'cruel'	*krauryam* 'cruelty'	*koṭumai* 'cruelty'
7. *itara* 'the other' 'opposite of'		*etir* (v), 'oppose' *ētilar* 'neighbours'. K. *idaru, idiru, iduru, edaru* etc., 'the front, opposition'.
8. *puṣya* 'name of a constellation'	*pauṣī*, *pauṣa*, 'the full moon and the month connected with the constellation.'	*pōki* (*pōṣī*) *poṅgal* (*pōkki*) (feasts occurring in the month.)

Sanskrit words containing the lowest grade vowels.	*Derivative Sanskrit words containing* vṛddhi *or the highest grade vowels.*	*Allied words in Tamil.*
9. *cīra* 'a cloth'	*celam* 'a cloth'	*cēlai* 'a cloth'.
10. *cūḍā* 'a lock on the crown of head'	*cauḷam* 'the ceremony of tonsure'	*cōḻiya* '(a caste wearing front locks).'
11. *sīra* 'a plough'	*sairika* 'pertaining to a plough'.	*ēr* 'a plough'
12. *triliṅga*	*trailiṅgya*	*teluṅku* 'the Telugu language'.
13. ..	*maurya* 'a dynasty of northern kings'	*mōriyar* 'the Mauryas'.
14. ..	Pr. *kaila, kāli, kāla* from S. *kalyam* 'the morning'	*kīḻ, kiḻa-k-ku* 'the direction of morning or of light'.
15. ..	*maila, mēla, mala,* from S. *mala,* 'Dark'	*mēl, mēṟku* 'the direction of evening or of darkness'.
16. ..	*dāhin,* from S. *dakṣiṇā,* 'the South'	*teṉ, teṟku,* 'the direction of the south or the right side'.

For the explanation of the words in the second column of items 14, 15 and 16 see the notes under items 16, 17, 18 of (a) above.

S. 8. THE ARYAN ELEMENT IN DRAVIDIAN VOCABULARIES—(*Contd.*)

Specimens of Sanskrit words in Dravidian disguised by changes in the initial or final consonants

It often happens that the relationship of Dravidian words to Sanskrit forms is disguised by a change in the initial, or the final, consonants and escapes notice altogether.

(*a*) Initial *r* or *l* in Sanskrit or Aryan sometimes corresponds to *n* in Dravidian :

Sanskrit		Dravidian	
lāṅgalam	'a plough'	Tam : *nāñcil*	'a plough'.
lōkanam	'seeing, perceiving'	Tel : *nākali* Tam : *nōkku*	'sight'.
lalāma	'a sign, mark, or an ornament for the forehead'	Drav : *nāmam*	'a caste mark on the forehead'.
lalāṭam *niṭala* Pr: *nalāḍa*	'forehead'.	Tel : *netti* Tam : *neṟṟi* Kan: *netti*	'the head'. 'the forehead'. 'the forehead, the crown of the head'.
lāṅgūlam (Foreign) *langhōr*	'a tail' 'an anchor'	Pāli : *naṅguṭṭham* 'a tail' 'an anchor'. Tam : *naṅkūram*	

In the above instances the relationship is obvious. The following instances are suggested on the same analogy.

Sanskrit	*Dravidian*
rāṣṭram 'a kingdom, a country'	T. : *nāṭu* 'a country'.
roga 'a disease, an ailment' *rujati* 'it pains'.	T. : *nōy, nōvu* 'a disease'. *nōvu, nō* (v.i.) 'pain'.
rak, tak (v.t.) 'taste'.	Tam. : *nakku* (v.t.) 'lick'.
	Tel. *nāku* 'lick'.

The word *rāṣṭram* becomes *raṭṭham* in Pāli and *raṭṭa* may become *laṭa* through the loss of one of the *ṭ's* and the compensatory lengthening of *a*. *Vide* S. below. In '*lāṭa dēśa*' and in '*lārikē*'[1] of the Old Greek geographers which are the old names of the coast portion of Guzerat the word *lāṭ* is said to be a corruption of *rāṣṭra* apparently through *rāṭa*; the form *lāṭ* may have given rise to the Dravidian *nāṭu*.

(*b*) Often the initial *p*, *v*, or *b*, in Sanskrit is replaced by *m* in Dravidian. Such a change takes place even in the Dravidian languages themselves.

(1) Tam : *vāṉam, māṉam* 'the sky,' 'rain'; Tel : *vāna*; Kan : *bān*. These words arise from the Vedic *māna*. 'the aerial regions'.

(2) Tam : *viṇ* 'the sky'; Tel : *minnu*.

(3) Tam : *vāṭṭi* 'time' as in 'so many times'; Tel : *māṭi, māṟu*. All these words arise from the Sanskrit *āvṛtti* having the same meaning.

(4) Tam : *muḻi, viḻi, miḻi*, 'the eye-ball'.

(5) Tam : *viḻuṅku, miḻuṅku* (v.t.) 'swallow'.

(6) Tam : *veruḷ, miraḷ* 'be frightened, startled as a horse.

---

1. *Vide* Lassen's explanation of 'larika' quoted in I.A. Vol. XIII, page 345.

(7) Pr : *vakuḷa*, *bakuḷa*, *makuḷa* 'a kind of flower tree' ; Tam : *makiḻam*.

(8) Tam : *vaṇṇāṉ* 'a washerman' ; Mal : *vaṇṇāṉ*, *maṇṇāṉ*.

(9) Tam : *viṉai* 'an action, business' ; Mal : *viṉa*, *mina*. The form *miṉakkeṭu* 'idle away time' occurs also in Tamil.

(10) Tam : *vacūri* 'small-pox' ; S. *masūrikā*.

(11) Tam : *vaṇaṅku* ; Kan : *maṇagu* (v.i.) 'bend, be submissive'

(12) Tam : Mal : *mīḷ*, *vil* 'to return, to bring back' connected with the S. *āvṛt* 'to return'.

(13) S. *vandhyā*, 'a barren woman' ; Kan : *bañje* ; Tulu : *bajji* ; Mal : *macci* ; Tam : *vandi*.

There is no doubt about the identities in the above cases. The following identities are suggested on the same analogy.

Sanskrit	Dravidian
(i) *bṛndam* 'a collection' Pr : *vranda* 'a crowd' (Var : *vanda*, iv-27.)	Tam : and Kan : *Mandai* 'a flock, a herd, a crowd'.
(ii) *vārtā* 'a word, speech'	Tam : *maṟṟam* 'a word, speech (*vide* S. below)'.
(iii) *varṣa* 'rain', also *mṛṣ* 'sprinkle'	Tel : *māṭa*. Kan : *māṭu*. Tam : *maḻai* 'rain.'
(iv) *vaṁsa* i. 'the bamboo' ii. 'a family, line, a race'	Tam : *mūṅkil* 'the bamboo'

	Sanskrit	*Dravidian*

(v) Hindī ; *bōlī* 'a word, a language' ; Tam : *moḻi* 'a word, a language'.

(vi) *vyrddhi* (=*vi*+*ṛddhi*).

Tam : *miti* 'poverty' 'want'. This will become *viḍḍhi* in Prākṛt 'non-prosperity, ill-luck, misfortune'.

Telugu : *bottigā* 'completely, entirely'.

	Sanskrit	Dravidian
(vii)	*pūrta* 'completed' *pūrti* 'completion'	*muṟṟilum* 'entirely'. *muṟṟu* 'completion'.
(viii)	*vāraya* (v. t.) 'cover, hide'	*maṟai* (v. t.) 'hide, cover'
(ix)	*vāri* 'water' *vārida* 'a cloud' literally 'giver of water'	*māri* 'rain'

Note.—The words *moḻi* and *māṟṟam* stand isolated, there being no Dravidian roots from which they can be derived.

The word *bōlī* is said to arise from Sans : *brū* to 'speak, say' ; this becomes *mrū* in Persian.

(*c*) One of the peculiarities of Paiśācī noticed by Vararuci (x. 4.) is that one of its particles of comparison is *piva* instead of the Sanskrit *iva*, e.g., *kamalam piva mukham* instead of *kamalam iva mukham*, 'a lotus-like face'. The reason for this appears to be the habit of pronouncing the final *m* as *mp*. Thus in Telugu all words ending in *-mu* may now be pronounced as if they ended in *-mbu* ; a similar practice may have formerly obtained in Tamil to a more or less limited extent.

Sanskrit	*Tamil*
1. *vyōma* ' the sky '	*vicumpu* ' the atmosphere '.
2. *dāman* (*n*) ' a rope '	*tāmpu* ' a well-rope, a tether' *cāmaṇi* ' long rope for tying cattle'.
3. *upadāma* ' a short rope '	*tumpu* ' a short rope attached to the long rope'.
4. *cūrnam*[1] ' powder '	*cuṇṇāmpu* ' camphor powder ' formerly ; but now ' slaked lime'.[1]
5. *vīryam* ' bravery '	*vīmpu* ' rivalry, swaggering'.
6. *srama* ' military exercise, drill '	*cilamp* (am) ' fencing sword play ', also *cilamam*.
7. *kṛmi* ' an ant '	*eṟumpu* ' an ant'.
8. *ślēṣma* ' the phlegmatic humour '	*irumal*, also *iyumpal* ' coughing'.

(*d*) There is little or no change in some of the following *tadbhavas*, but they escape recognition owing to a difference in application and use.

Sanskrit	*Tamil*
1. *vaṭu* ' a young man '	*vaṭu* ' small tender mango berries'.
2. *pōta* ' the young of animals '	*pōttu* ' a sapling '.

1. Even now in the daily offerings to the deity the *tāmbūla* is described as *karpūracūrṇa-samyuktam* 'with camphor powder'.

Sanskrit	*Tamil*
3. S : *kiñcit* ' a little ' Pāli : *kiñci* ' a little', *kōci* any, some '	*koñcam* ' a little'.
4. *kula* ' a clan, race '	*kulai* Compare Kan : *gole*, *gone* ' a bunch'.
5. *mac* (v. t.) ' grind, pound '	*maci* (v. t.) 'mash, food etc.' ' reduce to a thin pulpy consistence'.
6. *vac* (v.t.) ' blame, censure ' *vācya* ' blamable, censurable ' Prākṛt : *vacca*	*vacai* (subs. ' reproach, censure'. *vacavu* (subs.) ' abuse'. *vai* (v.t.) ' abuse.'
7. *ucchṛ* (v. t.) ' raise, be erected ' *ucca* ' high, raised '	*uyar* (v. t.) ' rise, be erected'.
8. *kratu* (Vedic) ' intention' purpose, design '	*karuttu* ' intention, purpose, design'.
9. *vahitram* ' a boat, raft, **vōdhram*	*ōḷam* ' a boat, a raft'.
10. *drōṇī* ' a trough or tub ' Pāli: *dōṇi* 'a trough or boat'	*tōṇi* ' a boat, ' a raft '.
11. *bahu* (adj.) ' much, many ' *bahumānam* ' great respect, high esteem, a gift given by a superior to an inferior '	*veku* (adj.) ' many ' *vekumāṉam* ' regard, respect'. ' honour ' a gift as a mark of regard.
12. *mah*	'*miku*'

The illustrative words given in this article and in articles 6 and 7 are enough to demonstrate that the statement, that there is no difficulty in recognising Sanskrit derivatives from the ancient Dravidian roots, involves a fundamental misconception. The further statement that the Tamil language can stand alone and dispense with the aid of Sanskrit altogether is equally erroneous. This statement of Bishop Caldwell, based doubtless on the opinions of Indians who did not know Sanskrit, has been very often repeated by people who have made no independent investigation of the subject. As a matter of fact, however, a very large number of words which Tamil scholars cherish as Cen-Tamiḻ or pure Tamil have turned out on examination to be Aryan *tadbhavas*, very corrupt, vulgar *tadbhavas*. Things and men are judged by what they are,—not by what they were in the past and there is nothing degrading in a language beginning mainly with a stock of *tadbhava* words. The literary Prākṛts, Pāli, Ardhamāgadhī, Māhārāstrī, etc., have had humble beginnings and originally consisted of nothing but low, corrupt, vulgar Sanskrit *tadbhavas*. Malayalam, which has now got a body of literature cherished by the people and which is the vehicle used for conveying religious, philosophical and scientific truths to millions of inhabitants, has, as we know, arisen from corrupt Tamil.

No systematic investigation has been made as to what percentage of the words till now regarded as pure Tamil can thus be shown to have a Sanskritic or Aryan origin and any estimate that can be ventured on this point will be more or less a guess. But considering

(i) that a very large number of the commonest words and verbal bases, till now regarded as pure Dravidian, turn out to be Sanskrit *tadbhavas* ;

(ii) that the Demonstrative and Interrogative pronouns have been derived from Aryan sources ;

(iii) and that most of the tense and modal suffixes used in Dravidian are of Aryan origin,—it may be safely presumed that the non-Aryan element in the vocabulary of the Dravidian languages will not be considerable.

S. 9. ANALYSIS OF NON-PRONOMINALISED VERB-FORMS DRAVIDIAN : TAMIL, MALAYALAM, KANARESE AND TELUGU

The formation of Dravidian tense and moods is best illustrated by taking a number of verb-forms and analysing them into their component parts.

(1) Tamil present relative participle *paṭikkiṟa* 'that reads'=*paṭi*+(*k*)+*kiṟu*+*a*.

Here *paṭi* -is a Dravidian verbal base ; -*kiṟu* -is the Sanskrit root *kṛ* 'do' used as an auxiliary and is a present-tense sign ; and -*a* is the relative participle suffix with Aryan affinities, being in fact the remote demonstrative base -*av* with the final-*v* dropped.'[1]

(2) Tamil benedictive forms *vāḻi*, *vāḻiya*, *vāḻiyar* as in the sentence *vāḻi vēndaṉ*, *vāḻiya vēndaṉ*,*v* *āḻiyar vēndaṉ*, all meaning "long live the king". *Vāḻi*=*vāḻ*+*i* ; *rāḻiya*=*vāḻ*+*iya* ; *vāḻiyar*=*vāḻ*+*iyar*.

Here *vāḻ* "prosper, flourish" is a Dravidian verbal base ; *i*, *iya*, *iyar* arise from imitating the intermediate syllables in the Vedic optative third person (middle voice) :—

Singular	Dual	Plural
bhuñj-ī-ta, 'may he eat'	bhuñj-īyā-tām may these two eat'	bhuñj-ī(y) r-an 'may they eat'.

The long vowels in these syllables are shortened into *i*, *iya*, *iyar* and the forms *vāḻi*, *vāḻiya*, and *vāḻiyar* are used indiscriminately in all persons and numbers. It is very

1. *Vide* S. 16 (a) 'Aryan affinities of Dravidian Pronouns'.

probable that the final syllables of Vedic forms had already been lost in colloquial Aryan idioms from which the borrowing must have been made.

(3) Tamil conjunctive participle *aḻaittu* 'having invited' = *aḻai*+(*t*)+*tu*.

Here *aḻai* 'invite' is a Dravidian verbal base; the suffix *-tu* is of Aryan origin, being a corruption of *-tvā*.

(4) Malayalam future tense *aḻikkum* 'will destroy' *aḻi*+(*k*) *ku*+*m* (common to all persons and numbers).

Here *aḻi* 'destroy' is a Dravidian verbal base; *ku*<*kṛ* 'do' is an aorist sign of Aryan origin which has latterly lost its force and is now a meaningless addition to the base in some moods and tenses; *-m* the sign of the future, is also of Aryan origin.

(5) Malayalam present tense *kāṭṭunnu* 'shows' = *kāṇ*+ *tu*+*kunnu* (common to all persons and numbers).

Here *kāṇ* 'see' is a Dravidian verbal base; *-tu-* is a causative suffix of Aryan origin as also *kunnu* the sign of the present tense; the initial *k-* of *kunnu* is elided as *kāṭṭu* is an unaccented base.

(6) Malayalam infinitives *aḻiya* (ancient form) *aḻikka* (modern form) 'to be destroyed' = *aḻi*+*ku*+*a*.

Here *aḻi* 'be destroyed' is a Dravidian verbal base; *-ku* has the same origin as in example 4 and *-a* is an infinitive suffix also of Aryan origin, the ancient form occurring in books being apparently in imitation of Tamil which elides the initial consonant of *-ku*; but in the popular speech of Malabar this *-k* appears to be always retained in infinitive forms.

(7) Kanarese conjunctive participle *tinisi* 'having caused to eat' = *tin*+*i*+*su*+*i*. Here *tin* 'eat' is a Dravidian verbal base; *-i-* is a causative suffix of Aryan

origin, *-su-* is the remnant of an Aryan conjunctive participle suffix which has latterly become an integral part of Kanarese causal bases, and *-i* is a conjunctive participle suffix of Aryan origin.

(8) Kanarese impersonal imperatives *geyyaḻī*, *geyyaḻ* let (him, her, it, them, me or us) do'=*geyyu*+*alī*, *geyyui* +*aḻi*.

Here *geyyu* 'do' is a Dravidian verbal base, *alī* and *aḻi* appear to be derived from a Vedic gerundive suffix.

(9) Kanarese aorist (present-future) relative participles *ēṟisuva*, *ēṟipa* (Old Kanarese) 'which raises *i.e.*, causes to rise'=*ēṟu*+*i*+*sa*+*pu*+*a*, *ēṟu*+*i*+*pu*+*a*.

Here *ēṟu* 'rise' is a Dravidian verbal base; *-i-*is an Aryan causative suffix, *-su-*has the same origin as in example No. 7 above, *-pu-* is the present-future sign of Aryan and *-a* is the relative participle suffix. In *ēṟisuva* the present future sign *p* coming after an unaccented vowel has become softened to *v*.[1]

(10) Telugu imperative second person plural *koṭṭimpundu* 'cause to be struck'=*koṭṭu*+*i*+*pu*+*uṇḍu*.

Here *koṭṭu* 'strike' is a Dravidian verbal base; the causative suffix *i* the root extension suffix *pu* and the termination *uṇḍu* are all of Aryan origin.

(11) Telugu subjunctive *naḍacinam* 'if (I, we, you, he, she, it, they) walked'=*naḍa*+*cu*+*in*+*an*.

Here *naḍa* 'walk' is a Dravidian verbal base; *-cu-* is a formative syllable of Aryan origin; *-in-* the sign of the past tense and *-am* the subjunctive suffix are also of Aryan origin.

(12) Telugu verbal noun *cēyaḍamu* 'doing'=*cēyu*+*aḍamu*.

---

1. *Vide* 'Aryan Affinities of Dravidian Pronouns'.

Here *cēyu* 'do' is a Dravidian verbal base; and *aḍamu* is a verbal noun suffix of Aryan origin.

In the above examples attention is mainly directed to the suffixes, which are considered to be of Aryan origin. The bases are referred to as Dravidian, not because it is admitted that they are of non-Aryan origin, but solely for the purpose of indicating that they were in use in Dravidian dialects as verbal bases at the time when the Aryan suffixes were first imitated or borrowed. As a matter of fact *paṭi*, *vāḻ aḻai*, *aḻi*, *geyyu*, *ēṟu*, *koṭṭu*, *naḍa*, *cēyu*, *tiṉ* are mostly corrupt Sanskrit *tadbhavas*.

The grammatical forms instanced in this article and, by implication, the vast majority of Dravidian grammatical forms will then be formations obtained by suffixing Aryan words and particles to Dravidian bases most of which are obviously of Indo-Aryan origin.

S. 10. SPECIMENS OF HYBRID FORMATIONS IN UNCULTIVATED DRAVIDIAN

One obvious objection to the theory is that, although one language may borrow words from another language even on a very extensive scale, it never borrows its grammar in the wholesale manner indicated, and that this theory of hybrid formations is *prima facie* improbable. This objection does not take account of the circumstance that such borrowings are taking place at present before our eyes. The following instances of Dravidian borrowing may be cited from the pages of Volume IV of the 'Linguistic Survey' of India.

(*a*) Gōlarī or Hōliyā is a dialect of Kanarese spoken by Gōlars or Gōlkars,—a tribe of nomadic herdsmen in the Central Provinces, and by Hōliyās a low caste of leather workers in the same provinces (p. 385). The authors of the 'Linguistic Survey' are of opinion that in consequence of local corruptions resulting from intercourse with Aryan neighbours the dialect is not uniform everywhere (p. 385). The past tense is formed with the dental sign *-t* or *-d*, but the conjunctive participles in *-tu* or *-du* are very rare except in compound tense forms ; in fact the dialect seems to have almost forgotten their use. In their stead it has formed new participles with the help of the suffixes *ke* and *ko* :—

māḍke ' having made ' ;
hōgyā ' having gone ' ;
kaltkō ' having stolen ' ;
ōḍki ' having fun ' ;

tindkū ' having eaten '. This is stated by the authors of the ' Linguistic Survey ' to be due to the influence of the surrounding Aryan dialects (p. 387).

(*b*) Gōṇḍī is the principal Dravidian language of Northern India and is spoken by about one million people (L.S. IV p. 472). It has no well-defined linguistic boundaries, the speakers being almost everywhere scattered among people employing other languages. In the North it meets with Eastern and Western Hindī and Rājasthānī, to the West we find Marāṭhī, to the South Telugu, to the East Telugu, Oriyā, Halabī, and Chattīsgarhī (p. 473).

" All forms of Gōṇḍī abound in Aryan words ; Aryan speech is gradually supplanting the old Dravidian language of the Gōṇḍs and it is probably only a question of time when Gōṇḍī shall have ceased to exist as an independent form of speech " (p. 485). The regular Gōṇḍī past tense *kītān* ' I did,' is formed by adding the same suffix *-t-* which occurs in the form *-tt-* in Tamil and *-d-* in Kanarese. The conjunctive participles are formed by adding *cī* or *sī* to the root ; these suffixes are often strengthened by an additional *-kun* which the editors of the Linguistic Survey say is *probably* of Aryan origin (p. 384).

Example :—*kīsī-kun* 'having made';
huṛsī-kun 'having seen';
vāsī-kun 'having come';
iñjī-kun 'having said'.

(*c*) Most of the Aryan vernaculars of Northern India form their conjunctive participles by adding *-i-* to the root; this *-i-* is a reduction of the Prakritic *-ia-* which arose from the Vedic *-yā*. From the habitual neglect of the final short vowels the participles often assume the form of the bare stem and it has become customary to strengthen these participles by affixing to them *kari* the conjunctive participle of the verb *kṛ* 'to do' (B.A.G. Vol. III, page 231). This *kari* becomes often *kai, ke, kar*; the usual substitution of *ya* for *e* produces *kya*, and other forms of *kari* occurring in the Aryan vernaculars are *ki, ku, kō*. Example :—

dekh-kari, dekhi-kari, dekhi-kē 'having seen';

bharkai 'having filled';

jā-kō 'having gone'; *dōkki* 'having concealed'.

It is these *ki, kū, ke, kō*, that Gōlarī is stated to have adopted.

A few of the Aryan vernaculars of the North use *kan* or *kane* for strengthening the old conjunctive participles. Thus Nepālī has *garī-kan* 'having done,' *khāī-kan* 'having eaten'; *basī-kan* 'having sat'; Eastern Rājasthānī is said to reduplicate *kane* while Mārwārī is said to use *kar-ne* (H.G.G.S. 491). It is these suffixes that Gōṇḍī is stated to be imitating when it adds *kun* to its conjunctive participles.

(*d*) Burgaṇḍī is a dialect of Tamil and is spoken by a vagrant tribe in Nimar and in the Central India Agency. The editors of the Linguistic Survey say that the dialect is apparently dying out (L.S. IV p. 343). Certain past tense forms in the language contain a suffix *yō* which the

Editors surmise to be that of a past participle passive and that it is probably borrowed from Rājasthānī (p. 344). Example :—

ēleyōs ' he went ' ; *āgeyōs* ' it happened ' ;
ākyō ' done ' ;
vāngyōt ' I drove'.

It is usually stated that the Dravidian languages will be found in their greatest purity in localities far removed from civilized centres and that the Dravidian philologist in search of uncontaminated Dravidian forms should study the dialects of the aborigines living in the interior in jungles and in mountain fastnesses. This will be no doubt true if we were sure that the so-called aborigines have always inhabited the localities where we do find them. But this is not always the case.

(*e*) Kōṭa, the language of the Kōṭas, a small tribe of helot craftsmen inhabiting the Nilgiri hills and exceedingly filthy in their habits may be mentioned in point. Bishop Caldwell considered their language as a very old and very rude dialect of Kanarese which was carried thither by a persecuted low caste tribe at some very remote period. On examining the vocabulary of the language[1] however, we find that almost all their nouns end in *-e*. The personal and demonstrative pronouns[2] also exhibit this peculiarity:— *āne* ' *I* ' ; *nāme* ' we ' ; *nī* ' thou ' ; *nīve* ' you ' ; *avane* ' he ' ; *avare* ' they ' (epicene) the final *-e* of which corresponds to the *-e* of the Prākṛtic words *hake*, *hage* (=*ahake*) 'I', *amhe* 'we', *tuphe* 'you', *śe* 'he' etc. This characteristic reminds one of

1. *Vide* lists of Kōṭa and Chentsu words in B. H. Hodgson's Miscellaneous Essays relating to Indian subjects. Vol. II (1880).

2. Bishop Caldwell's Comparative Grammar of Dravidian Languages, page 512.

the Māgadhī Prākrt described by Prākṛt grammarians, one of the peculiarities of which was that the nominative singular of its *a* bases ends in *e* as opposed to the Śaurasēnī-*ō*. But this rule is not universally observed in any of the Prākṛts that have survived in literary works. The language of the Śvētāmbara canonical works in which this and other Māgadhī characteristics are only partially observed is therefore called Ardhamāgadhī. The final *e* in the Kōṭa words shows that the dialect should have been influenced possibly by the old Māgadhī speaking Jains who emigrated to the Karnāṭa country in the fourth century B.C. in consequence of a severe famine in Magadha.

(*f*) Chentsu. The Chentsus of the Nallamalai hills in the Kurnool district are another instance in point. Mr. Gopalakrishna Chetti, the author of the Kurnool District Manual, considers them to be indigenous, probably the descendants of aboriginal savages, and has noted that they speak the language of the surrounding Telugu population. But the Muhammedan historian Ferishta, whom he refers to, has recorded that the language of the Chentsus could not be understood by their neighbours. The Chentsu words, of which we have a list collected in the last century, are obviously Hindī words. These facts lead to the inference that the original language of the Chentsus has died out and been replaced by Telugu. If these facts be admitted, it follows necessarily that the ancestors of these so-called aborigines must have come from the North, in the wake probably of a conquering army and, having been stranded in the midst of Dravidians, must have taken refuge in the hills and jungles and gradually reverted to barbarism.

CHAPTER II

WAS THERE A PRE-ARYAN SOUTH-INDIAN CIVILIZATION?

S. 11. THE TESTIMONY OF THE PERIPLUS

We have to draw attention in this chapter to the speculaons of some eminent Orientalists and Dravidian scholars of the last century on the occurrence of some supposed South-Indian words in Hebrew and in Greek, and to the inferences drawn from these words in regard to the culture attained by the primitive Dravidians. A large amount of new linguistic and archaeological material has since come to light which tends to throw doubt on the conclusions arrived at by these Orientalists and Dravidian scholars. But writers who have made no independent investigation of the subject still continue to repeat these overdrawn estimates of pre-Aryan culture, often without the limitations and qualifications subject to which the estimates were originally made. Fanciful and grossly exaggerated accounts in regard to the nature and extent of this culture are now current not only among patriotic South-Indians but also among a class of English historians of South-India who take their cue from the late M. Kanakasabhai Pillai's book entitled *The Tamils, Eighteen Hundred Years Ago* (1904). The belief that the primitive Dravidians had attained a considerable degree of culture before the arrival of the Aryans in India and the notion that the Dravidian dialects have produced deep and organic changes in Sanskrit phonology, vocabulary and grammar are at the root of many a deep-seated misconception now current in regard to the Dravidian languages ; and it is impossible to determine the true affinities of these languages unless the misconceptions are removed at the outset.

The second of these questions, *viz.*, the changes alleged to have been brought about in Sanskrit phonology and grammatical structure by the influence of Dravidian dialects, have been examined in the last chapter. It is proposed to devote the whole of this chapter to an investigation of the first of these questions and to subject to a rigid test the evidences adduced in support of a *pre-Aryan* South-Indian civilization.

In forming an estimate of things pre-historical, we have in most cases necessarily to rely on the merest shadow of a probability ; nevertheless, we have to take into account all the available materials likely to influence that estimate.

The Periplus of the Erythraean Sea, an anonymous work in Greek supposed by some to have been written in the 1st century A.D., and by others to have been begun in the 1st century but added to by subsequent writers and finally completed in the 3rd century, contains " the best account of the commerce carried on from the Red Sea and the coast of Africa to the East Indies during the time that Egypt was a province of the Roman Empire "[1]. Mr. McCrindle, a translator of the work, says that there is internal evidence that the author was a merchant of Egypt and that the work was not a mere compilation from the narratives or journals of other merchants and navigators, but that probably the author had himself visited some of the seats of trade which he has described. This is also clearly the opinion of Mr. W. H. Schoff who, in the introduction to his translation of the Periplus of the Erythraean Sea, refers to it as " this plain and painstaking log of a Greek in Egypt, a Roman subject, who steered his vessel into the waters of the great ocean and brought back the first detailed record of the imports and exports of its markets and of the conditions and alliances of its peoples ". The work is frequently referred to as an authority in all discussions about the trade relations between the East and the West in ancient times.

---

1. McCrindle's Translation in the I.A. Vol. VIII, page 107 *et seq.*

One material fact of far reaching consequences which comes to light even on a cursory perusal of the work is that, in the pre-Christian centuries and up to about the time of Pliny (who died in 79 A.D.), the trade between Arabia and the Indian ports—*i.e.*, by implication the trade between the European countries and Indian ports, was performed in small vessels which kept close to shore, and followed its windings ; this will be evident from para. 57 of the Periplus[1] But a little before the time of Pliny, one Hippalos, by observing the bearing of the ports and the configuration of the sea, discovered the direct route across the Arabian sea by taking advantage of the South-West monsoon ; and at the time when the Periplus was written, this direct route was usually taken by vessels trading between Egypt and India. It is needless to remark here that, when the trade was carried on by coasting vessels, there would have sprung up *entrepots* in Arabia, in Persia and in Sindh; and that, when foreign names of merchandise got naturalized in European languages, it is the names current in the *entrepots*, and not necessarily the names at the places of production, that would have been so naturalized.

a. Pearls :—In para. 35 of the work reference is made to 'much diving for the pearl-mussel '[2] at the mouth of the Persian Gulf ; from para. 36 it appears that the pearls were inferior in quality to the Indian pearls but that great quantities of them were exported to Arabia and Borygaza (Broach)!!

b. Gold :—From para. 36 of the work it also appears that gold was exported from the ports of Apologos and Omana in Persia to Barygaza (Broach) ; para. 56 says that a great quantity of coin was imported into the Malabar ports, and it

1. *Vide* also Mc Crindle's Introduction (I.A. Vol. VIII, page 108).

2. ' very many pearl fisheries' according to Mc Crindle's translation.

appears from para. 49 that gold and silver coin was imported into Barygaza to be exchanged at a profit for the coin of the country. Para. 38 mentions a port Barbarikon in southern Sindh on one of the mouths of the Indus, but para. 39 mentions gold and silver plate among the imports of this place and not among its exports, though gold was found far up the Indus.

c. Rice, *Pippalī*—Pepper : It may also be noted here that according to the Periplus the only Indian port from which rice (*royza*) was exported was Barygaza (Broach); this was also the only port from which *pippalī* (piper longum) was exported. Pepper (piper nigrum) was exported only from the Malabar ports.

d. At page 227 of this translation of the Periplus Mr. W. H. Schoff at the end of his notes on the articles traded in by the author of the Periplus quotes the following extract from a letter by the Zamorin of Calicut to the King of Portugal carried by Vasco da Gama on his return from India fourteen centuries later : " In my Kingdom there is abundance of cinnamon, cloves, ginger, pepper and precious stones. What I seek from thy country is gold, silver, coral and scarlet."

Of the abovementioned Malabar products of the XVth century A.D. :—

1. Cloves—*lavaṅgam*—(Caryophyllon) were not indigenous to India and were probably not known in this country much before the 5th century A.D. (Watt,[1] page 627).

2. Ginger (*zingiber*) is not mentioned in the Periplus as an article of export though supposed to be indigenous to the Malabar coast. " It is not known in a truly wild state, but is doubtless a native of tropical south-east Asia " (Watt, page 1139).

3. Cinnamon. Only malabathron, the leaf Laurus Cassia, is mentioned in the Periplus.

---

1. Watt's Commercial Products of India, Birds.

4. Pepper. Mr. W. N. Schoff says (page 213) "The antiquity of the trade in pepper is not so easily shown as that in other spices. There is no certain mention of it in the Egyptian inscriptions. In the Hebrew scriptures it is unknown, nor has it a place among the *mint* and *anise* and *cummin* of the Gospels. Herodotus has no bit of folklore to attach to it. Theophrastus indeed in the 4th century B.C. knows it as a medicine and Dioscorides distinguishes between black, white and long pepper."

S. 12. PROFESSOR MAX MULLER ON SOME FOREIGN WORDS IN THE HEBREW TEXT OF THE BOOKS OF KINGS AND CHRONICLES

"And the navy also of Hiram, that brought gold from Ophir, brought in from Ophir great plenty of almug trees, and precious stones." I. Kings X-11.

"And the king made of almug trees pillars for the house of the Lords, and for the king's house harps also and psalteries, for singers : there came no such almug trees, nor were seen unto this day." I. Kings X-12.

"For the king had at sea a navy of Tharshish with the navy of Hiram : once in three years came the navy of Tharshish, bringing gold, and silver, ivory, and apes and peacocks." I. Kings X-22.

The above is repeated practically in the same words in II. Chronicles X-10, 11, 22 ; but what appears as Almug in the Kings appears as Algum in the Chronicles, the exact transliteration of the Hebrew forms being almuggion and algummim ; these words are interpreted as meaning 'sandal wood'. The word for 'pea-cock' in Hebrew Text is *tuki* or *tūki*. The Hebrew words for 'ivory' appear to be *karnoth shen* (the horn of tooth) and *shen habbim* (tooth of Habb), and that for apes is *kōf*. It is admitted on all hands that *almug* or *algum*, *tuki* or *tūki*, *habb*, and *kōf* are all foreign words in Hebrew.

In his Lectures on the Science of Language, Professor Max Muller drew attention to the occurrence of these foreign words in the Hebrew text, and discussed their significance. He thought that *Ophir* of the Bible was in Southern Sindh where Ptolemy placed a district called Abiria immediately above Patalene and where Hindu Geographers located a people called *Abhīra* or *Ābhīra*, his view being that the name *Abhīra* was corrupted into *Ophir* by Pheonician and Jewish merchants. He was also of opinion that *habb* was a corruption of the Sanskrit *ibha* ' elephant ', that *tuki* was ultimately traceable to the same as the Sanskrit *śikhī* (*śikhin*) ' peacock,' that *kōf* was the same as the Sanskrit *kapi* ' monkey ' and that *algum* was a corruption of the Sanskrit *valguka* ' sandal-wood'. " All these articles " he argued, " ivory, gold, apes, peacocks, are indigenous in India, though of course they might have been found in other countries likewise, not so the algum tree at least, if the interpreters are right in taking algum or almug for sandal-wood. Sandal-wood is found indigenous in the coast of Malabar only, and one of its numerous names there and in Sanskrit is *valguka*. This *valgu[ka]* is clearly the name which Jewish and Phoenician merchants corrupted into *algum* and which in Hebrew was still further corrupted into *almug*." And the conclusion which he drew from the occurrence of these supposed corrupt Sanskrit names in the Books of Kings was that so early as the time of Solomon (10th century B.C.) Sanskrit language had extended to Southern Sindh and even the Malabar coast.

As already remarked, the testimony of the Periplus that gold was not exported from Barbarikon or from any Indian port is a fatal objection to the location of *Ophir* in India, and it is now admitted by many scholars that this place must be located in Arabia; it is also generally agreed that *habb* and *kōf* are not derived from Sanskrit but from the Egyptian language. We have thus left only *tūki* and *algum* which, however, Bishop Caldwell claims as Dravidian.

S. 13. LIST OF WORDS ADDUCED BY BISHOP CALDWELL AND OTHERS AS EVIDENCES OF A PRE-ARYAN SOUTH INDIAN CULTURE

For the purpose of ascertaining the degree of civilization attained by the Tamils prior to the advent of the Aryans in South India, Bishop Caldwell made a detailed analysis of the accounts of India given by Ctesias, Megasthenes and Arrian, Ptolemy's Geography, Pliny's Natural History, the Periplus of the Erythraean Sea, the accounts of travellers and stray references to India and matters Indian, contained in the works of classical writers. The results of his examination are summarised in the Introduction to his *Comparative Grammar of the Dravidian Languages.* They may be arranged under the two heads :—

1. Dravidian names of articles of commerce adopted in foreign languages ; and

2. Dravidian names of South Indian towns and tribes occurring in the works of classical writers.

A. NAMES OF ARTICLES ADDUCED BY BISHOP CALDWELL

1. Hebrew *tuki* or *tūki :* Bishop Caldwell objected to Professor Max Muller's derivation of these words from the Sanskrit word *śikhin* 'peacock' on the ground that the latter was already represented in Tamil by the *tadbhava ciki* and contended that they were derived from the Tamil-Malayalam word *tōkai* which ordinarily meant 'a tail' in modern Tamil but was used for the peacock itself in the old Tamil poems. He also asserted that a dialectic pronunciation of *tōkai* was *tōgai* from which he derived Arabic *ṭawas*, Greek *taōs*, Latin *pavo* and English *pea-* (fowl), and contended that the word *tōkai* itself was derived from the verbal base *tok* or *tōk*, *tuk or tūk* 'hang' which, he said, was made up of the ultimate root √ *tō* or √ *to*+-*ko* or-*ku* a formative addition. Referring to this derivation Professor Max Muller remarked " if this etymology be right, it would be an important confirmation

of the antiquity of the Tamulic languages spoken in India before the advent of the Aryan tribes". Bishop Caldwell quotes this remark in the Introduction to his Comparative Grammar and observes in his usual manner " I have no doubt this etymology is right and that the inference deduced from it is well founded." (Introduction : C.D.G. page 92).

2. Hebrew *algum* or *almug* : Bishop Caldwell accepted Professor Max Muller's derivation of these words from the Sanskrit *valguka* ' sandal-wood ' another meaning of which is ' beautiful ' : and expressed the opinion that *valguka* itself ' seems to be identical with, or derived from, the Tamil-Malayalam *a̱laku* or *a̱laku* ' beauty ' (*Ibid.*, page 92).

3. Hebrew *ahalim* or *ahaloth* ' Aquilaria Agallocha ': Proverbs VII, 17 etc.; here the harlot is represented as saying to the brainless young man " I have perfumed my bed with myrrh, aloes, and cinnamon". The words in the Hebrew text for ' aloes ' appear as *ahalim* and *ahaloth.*

There are two Indian words with which *ahalim* could have been identified, *viz.*, the Sanskrit *agaru* (*a-guru* ' not heavy ') and the Tamil *akil* pronounced *ahil.* Bishop Caldwell prefers to derive it from the latter rather " than from the Sanskrit *agaru* though both are ultimately identical " the probable reason being that the Hebrew transliteration showed a *h* (*Ibid.* page 92).

4. Greek *oryza* 'rice' : " It cannot be doubted " Bishop Caldwell says " that we have here the Tamil *arici* ' rice, deprived of the husk,' this being the condition in which rice was then, as now, brought up in India for export " (*Ibid.* page 92).

Dr. Kittel goes further and derives the Sanskrit *vrīhi* itself from Dravidian (No. 126 in the Preface to his Dictionary). " This term (*vrīhi*) being without a perceivable root in Sanskrit is no doubt connected with the Dravidian *akki* (or *arki*, Tamil *arici* ; Malayalam *ari* ; Tuḷu *ari*, *akki*) and Telugu *vari*. The syllable *vri* is the same as Telugu *vari* and syllable *-hi* has been formed of Kanarese and Tuḷu *-ki* and Tamil *-ci*. In common Tamil the Sanskrit word *vrīhi* is written *viriki* ; Tamil *k* often stands in the place of *h*".

Here Dr. Kittel seems to construct a hypothetical pro-Dravidian **variki* or **varigi* from which, he says, the Sanskrit *vrīhi* is derived. If we ask why not assume *vrīhi* itself, an actual word, as the original instead of constructing a hypothetical form, the reply will probably be 'How could a Dravidian product have an Aryan name ?' Prof. P. T. Srinivasa Iyangar goes one step further than Dr. Kittel and asserts that *vrīh* is the Sanskritised form of *arici* itself.

5. Ctesias's *karpion* : Bishop Caldwell says :—" The earliest Dravidian word in Greek of which we know the date was *karpion*, Ctesias's word for cinnamon. Herodotus describes cinnamon as 'the *karpheas* (dry sticks) which we after the Phoenicians call *kinnamomon*'. Liddel and Scott say :— 'the word bears a curious likeness to its Arabic name *kerfat*, *kirfah*'. This resemblance must, I think, be accidental seeing that Herodotus considered 'cinnamon' alone as a foreign word...... The word mentioned by Ctesias seems, however, to have a ṛeal resemblance to the Arabic word and also to a Dravidian one."

This word, Bishop Caldwell adds, is " *karuppu* or *kārppu* e.g., Malayalam *karappa-(t)-tailam* 'oil of cinnamon' ", and that " other forms of this word are *karappu*, *karuva*, *karuvā* the last of which is the most common form in Tamil." These words he derives from the Tamil-Malayalam word *karu* 'black, pungent' remarking that the latter meaning " doubtless supplies us with the explanation of *karuppu* cinnamon ".

It must be mentioned here that the word *karpion* is not a word used by the Greeks at any time, but is a representation by Ctesias in Greek characters of the name which he pretends, and is supposed, to have heard from his Persian informants, as that of a resinous Indian tree. Also that 'cinnamon' was not one of the exports from the Malabar ports in the time of the Periplus and that the name *karpion* or anything resembling it does not occur at all in that work.

6. Greek *ziggiberis* 'ginger'.

This word is generally believed to come from the Sanskrit *śṛṅgabēra*, Pāli *siṅgivēra* through the Arabic *zanzabil* (Watt's Com. Products, page 1139). But Bishop Caldwell accepts Dr. Gundert's view that the Tamil-Malayalam word *iñji* or *iñci* must have originally begun with as *s*- as the Kanarese parallel word is *suṇṭi*. It is stated that "*iñci* 'ginger would naturally take the addition of *vēr* the Dravidian word for root" (C.D.G. page 465). Dr. Burnell accepted this view and said "*iñci* was probably in an earlier form of the language *siñci* as we find it still in Kanarese *suṇṭi*. Ginger is chiefly exported even now from Malabar and in earlier times the Greeks procured it almost exclusively from that province, so that there is every probability that the word is Dravidian, not Sanskrit. If we look at the form of the Sanskrit word, it is impossible to doubt that it is a foreign word altered by the Brahmins who by their pedantry disguise all they meddle with" (I.A. Volume I, page 352).

The final conclusion of these scholars was that the word *zingiber* came from the assumed Dravidian word *ciñcivēr* (ginger root) and that *śṛṅgabēra* was homophonous Sanskrit for the Dravidian word.

Here a hypothetical pro-Tamil *ciñcivēr* is constructed from which the Greek *ziggiberis* is stated to have been derived. If we ask why not adopt the actual word in Pāli *viz.*, *siṅgivēram*, as the original, the reply would probably be 'How could a Dravidian product have an Aryan name?'

B. NAMES OF TRIBES AND PLACES GIVEN BY BISHOP CALDWELL

In regard to the names of places and tribes Bishop Caldwell found that the word *Tamiḻ* itself was derived from the Sanskrit word *Draviḍa*, and remarked that " a similar peculiarity meets us with regard to almost all the names of South Indian peoples—Cōḻas, Kēraḷas, Āndhras, Kaliṅgas etc., which so far as is known at present, are Sanskrit, not Dravidian. The word Karnāṭaka alone appears to have a Dravidian origin." The word Karnāṭaka is claimed by Brahmin Paṇḍits to be Sanskrit, but Bishop Caldwell agrees with Dr. Gundert in deriving Karnāṭa from the Dravidian *kār-nāṭu* ' black country'.

In regard to the names of places he remarks that the names given by Ptolemy proved that the Brahmins had by that time established themselves at various points in the Karnatic and given names to some of the principal localities." The following words are admitted to be Sanskritic :—

Madoura, ' Madura ' ;
Pāndae, ' Pāṇḍyas' ;
Pāndion, ' Pāṇḍiyan ' ;
Komaria, (Cape) ' Comorin '; probably also
Kory, ' Kōṭi ' ; perhaps also
Khaberis, 'Kāvēri'.

As many as twenty-four of the places mentioned had names ending in *-our* or *-oura* the Dravidian word meaning ' town'. Bishop Caldwell also noted that the form Pāndion and still better the plural from Pāndiones faithfully represented the Tamil masculine termination *-an* as distinguished from the old Kanarese termination *-am* and the Telugu termination *-uḍu*.

It will be shown below that *-an*, *-am*, *-adu* arise from the Indo-Irainan *-ant*.

S. 14. NAMES ADDUCED BY OTHER DRAVIDIAN SCHOLARS

1. Sanskrit *pippalī* 'long pepper', *vide* No. 107 in the Preface to Dr. Kittel's Kanarese-English Dictionary.

Dr. Gundert appears to take this word to be *pippala* and to explain it as meaning 'great excellent fruit,' Dravidian *piri* (Kan. *hiri*) being 'great' But Dr. Kittel thinks that much dependence cannot be placed in this derivation; and suggests that if *tippalī* which is the Dravidian equivalent of *pippalī* could be the original form, then Dravidian *tin* 'irritation' may be thought of as furnishing the root syllable.

All scholars agree that *pippalī* is the original of the Greek *peperi* and we may therefore ignore the suggestion that *tippalī* may be the original form of the word. Dravidian scholars have not stopped to enquire why there is a 'r' in the Greek form instead of a 'l', why there were no exports of *pippalī* from the Malabar ports even so late as the time of the Periplus and why such exports were confined at that time to Barygaza (Broach).

2. Sanskrit *marīca, marica, vēllaja* 'black pepper'. In No. 113 in the Preface to Dr. Kittel's Dictionary it is stated:—

"Dr. Gundert says that *marīca,* is connected with Telugu *miriya*, Tamil *miḷaku* 'black pepper'. There cannot be the least doubt about it. See Dravidian *meḻasu* etc., *marīca* and *vēllaja* (not to be derived from a *vēlla*) are identical with *marīca.* The leading idea is unknown."

It will have been noted from the remarks made already the pepper was probably unknown to the Greeks before the 4th century B.C.

3. Sanskrit *muktā* 'a pearl'. In No. 73 in the Preface to Dr. Kittel's Dictionary it is stated:—

"Dr. Gundert, arguing that Tamil fishermen had not waited for the Aryan tradesmen to give a name to the most precious object caught by them in their profession, believes that the Aryans adopted the now so-called Dravidian *tadbhava* *muttu* (*mōti*) ' a pearl ' and attached an etymology to it that somehow suited their own ideas. He thinks *muttu* to mean " the first or best " (of gems) connecting it with the Dravidian *muttu* (*mutal* ' first '). Dravidian *mūḻku,* however, may be compared and the meaning be ' the immersed one,' but as the original idea cannot be fixed, one must be content with saying that *muktā* appears to have been borrowed from Dravidian."

But Dr. Gundert and Kittel seem to have been unaware of the existence of pearl-fisheries at the mouth of the Persian gulf which were much nearer the Punjab, the seat of the earliest Aryan settlements in India, than the Kolkhoi pearl-fisheries. Surely the Aryans, who had connections with Assyria even in the 14th century B.C., knew pearls produced so near their settlements and had a name for the article before they ever heard of the Kolkhoi fisheries. If the Sanskrit *muktā* and the Dravidian *muttu* are related, the probability is that the latter was derived from the former.

Para. 59 of the Periplus says :—

" From Komari towards the south this region extends to Kolkhoi where the pearl-fisheries are ; (they are worked by condemned criminals) ; and it belongs to the Pāṇḍiyan Kingdom." Though there were tribes of fishermen on the coast, there were apparently as yet no professional divers in the time of the Periplus and condemned criminals had to be employed for diving for pearl-oysters, a perilous occupation in waters infested by sharks. Mr. Schoff quotes Marco Polo who says that the sharks had to be charmed away and that the " fish-charmers are termed Abraiaman (Brahmans)." " There can be little doubt " says Mr. Schoff " that this kind of protection was sought by the divers at the time of the Periplus, and Yule observed it still in force, one of the Brahmans exercising this ancestral office being a Christian".

He infers from these circumstances that the Kolkhoi pearl-fishing industry " dates from a time after the Aryan invasion of Southern India " (Schoff's Periplus, pages 240, 241), Shark-charms are considered necessary even at the present day (Encycl. Britt).

It would seem therefore that the Kolkhoi fishermen did wait for the Aryans to come south and teach them the art of diving for pearl-oysters. If this is a justifiable inference, there will be nothing surprising in ' pearls' having a Sanskrit name.

It may be mentioned in passing that there was another art, that of training and teaching elephants, which the Dravidians did not know till the Indo-Aryans came and settled amongst them. For an old Tamil work says that the language in which the elephants were given directions was *vaṭamoḻi* " Northern language " (*i.e.*) Sanskrit.

S. 15. BISHOP CALDWELL'S PICTURE OF PRIMITIVE DRAVIDIANS. ARYAN CIVILIZATION OF THE SOUTH

1. The words given in the two preceding articles are the most important of those that have been adduced as evidences of a pre-Aryan Dravidian civilization in Southern India ; and the discussion under each word clearly brings out the mental attitude and prepossessions with which the question was approached by the great Dravidian scholars of the last century who originated the current theories about Dravidian languages.

These scholars appear to have been deeply impressed by the circumstance that *Tūki* and *Algum,* supposed to be corruptions of Tamil words, had found their way into Hebrew so early as the time of Solomon, and Bishop Caldwell seems to have thought Ophir was in South India or thereabouts ; for he says :—

"It seems probable that Aryan merchants from the mouth of the Indus must have accompanied the Phoenicians and Solomon's servants in their voyage down the Malabar coast towards Ophir (wherever Ophir may have been) or at least have taken part in the trade." (Intro. C.D.G. page 122). From this maritime trade with the West so early as the tenth century B.C. these scholars argued that the Tamils had attained a considerable degree of culture before the arrival of the Aryans in the South and they could not conceive how any special product of South India could have an Aryan name in its native home.

Thus in regard to 'ginger' and 'rice' for instance, the names current in the European languages and in the Dravidian languages of Southern India indicate that the original forms giving rise to the names must have been something like *śiñcivēr* and *variki* or *variji*. Instead of accepting the actual Pāli *siṅgivēram* and the Sanskrit *vrīhi* as the originals, these scholars construct the hypothetical words *śiñcivēr* and *variki* from which they derive ' not only the current Dravidian words but also the Pāli and the Sanskrit forms on the ground that these products of the South must have been familiar to the Dravidians before the arrival of the Aryans, and that the latter must have adopted the Dravidian words. So also in regard to words like *marīca* ' black pepper,' *muktā* ' pearl ' etc., these scholars are positive that Sanskrit must have borrowed and transformed Dravidian words. Here a pre-Aryan Dravidian culture is assumed and is brought forward to support the Dravidian origin of the words *arici*, *iñci*, *miḷaku*, *muttu* etc. ; the present-day writers, on the contrary, assume the Dravidian origin of the words and they adduce these as evidences of a pre-Aryan civilization.

2. Another noteworthy feature is that the Aryan civilization of the South is not conceived by these scholars to have been the result of any large movements of population

from the North to the South, but to have been brought about by a number of small colonies of Aryans, chiefly Brahmans, settled in the midst of the Dravidians. Bishop Caldwell speaks of the Brahmans having established themselves at various points in the Carnatic by the beginning of the Christian era According to him the earliest Dravidian civilization in the South was that of the Tamils of the Pāṇḍya kingdom; he says that " This civilization was probably indigenous in its origin but seems to have been indebted for its rapid development at so early a period to a succession of small colonies of Aryans chiefly Brahmans " ; and that " the leader of the first or the most influential Brahmanical colony was Agastya whose date is placed between the age of the Rāmāyaṇa and that of the Mahābhārata " (Intro. C.D.G. pages 119, 220).

" Though the primitive Dravidians were probably unacquainted with the higher arts of life, they do not appear to have been by any means a barbarous or degraded people. Whatever may have been the condition of the first tribes, it cannot be doubted that the Dravidians properly so called had acquired at least the elements of civilization prior to the arrival amongst them of Brahmans." (Ibid, page 117).

The assumption that the Aryan civilization of the South was effected by small colonies of Aryans, chiefly Brahmans who adopted the speech of the Dravidians, is irreconcilable with the theory put forward in the present book in regard to the cultivated Dravidian languages. If these languages were originally non-Aryan, the extensive changes that have taken place in them even in the popular dialects, could only have resulted from an influx of large bodies of Aryan speaking (not necessarily Aryan from an ethnical point of view) immigrants from the North.

(3) From the evidence of words in use among the early Tamils Bishop Caldwell[1] has drawn a picture of the Primitive

1. Bishop Caldwell does not give the Tamil words he relies on. These have been supplied within brackets wherever obvious

Dravidians in which he says among other things, "They had kings (Tam : *kō*) who dwelt in 'strong houses' and ruled over small districts of country (Tam : *nāṭu*). They had 'minstrels' (Tam ; *pāṇar*), who recited 'songs' (Tam : *pāṭṭu*) at 'festivals' (Tam : *cāṟu*) and they seem to have had alphabetical 'characters' (Tam : *eḻuttu*) written with a style on palmyra leaves. A bundle of these leaves was called 'a book' (Tam : *cuvaṭi*) ; they were without hereditary 'priests' and 'idols' and appear to have had no idea of 'heaven' or 'hell,' of 'soul' or 'sin' ; but they acknowledged the existence of God whom they called *kō* or king—a realistic title little known to orthodox Hinduism. They created to his honour a temple which they called *kō-y-il* (God's house). They had 'laws' and 'customs' (*vaḻakkam, marapu*) but no 'lawyers' or 'judges'. Marriage (*maṇam, maṉṟal, varaivu*) existed among them. They were acquainted with the ordinary metals, (*poṉ, veḷḷi, cempu, irumpu*) with the exception of tin, lead and zinc ; with planets which were ordinarily known to the ancients, (*nāyiṟu, tiṅkal, cevvāy, viyāḻaṉ, veḷḷi*) with the exception of Mercury and Saturn. They had medicines (*maruntu*), hamlets and towns (*ūr, pati, paṭṭaṇam*) but no cities ; canoes, boats and even ships, (*ōṭam, tōṇi, paṭaku, kappal*) but no foreign commerce ; no acquaintance with any people beyond sea except in Ceylon ; and no word expressive of the geographical idea of 'island' or 'continent' They were well acquainted with 'agriculture' (*vēḷāṇmai*) and delighted in 'war' (*pōr*). They were armed with 'bows' (*vil*), 'arrows' (*ampu, kaṇai*) and 'spears' (*vēl, īṭṭi*). All the necessary or ordinary arts of life including spinning (*nūṟṟal*), weaving (*neytal*) and dyeing (*cāyam*) existed among them. They excelled in pottery (*pāṉai, tāḻi*) but were unacquainted with higher arts. They had no acquaintance with 'sculpture' or 'architecture' ; with 'astronomy' or even 'astrology' ; and were ignorant not only of every branch of 'philosophy' but even of 'grammar' (*Ibid.* pages 117-118).

The above modest picture may be contrasted with the claim made at the present day by some persons who speak of the Dravidian contribution to the civilization of the world. Even this comparatively unpretentious account exhibits pre-Aryan Southern India as a country teeming with millions, living in organised communities under petty chiefs and engaged in agriculture, industry and trade, inland as well as coasting; but it is doubtful whether this is justified by the earliest accounts that we have of South-India in the Rāmāyaṇa and in the face of the evidence of Archaeology that, when the Aryans arrived in the South, the Dravidians were in the Stone Age of culture and were unacquainted with the use of metals. There might have been an agriculture of some sort, but the control over the forces of nature must have been very limited and the land could have supported only a sparse population. However this may be, it must be admitted that the evidence offered in regard to the social condition of primitive Dravidians and the method of proof adopted are unexceptionable; for if these Dravidians were well acquainted with agriculture and other ordinary industries, the products of these industries must now have Dravidian names and the products in which South India had a monopoly for long ages must also be known to the world by their Dravidian names. We shall presently put this evidence to the test.

S. 16. Mr. V. Kanakasabhai Pillai.

Numerous writers have written about South India and its Dravidian inhabitants since the time of Bishop Caldwell and it will be difficult to find even one of them who has not quoted that great orientalist as his authority for his statements. But it has happened nevertheless that the modest picture which Bishop Caldwell gave of the pre-Aryan Dravidian culture has gradually expanded till it has now become a highly developed civilization of considerable proportions. It will be needless to trace the various steps in this process of exaggeration, but we may give one or two typical instances.

Mr. V. Kanakasabhai Pillai, the author of 'The Tamils Eighteen Hundred Years Ago,' was a Tamil scholar of note and was the first to bring to the notice of the English-knowing public the contents of many of the classics of the Caṅkam Period. He was also the first to point out that there was no Cochin backwater at the beginning of the Christian era, that the eastern coast of the present backwater was then the sea coast and that Karūr, the old Kēraḷa capital, was not the modern Karūr on the banks of the Amarāvatī, but the ruined Tirukkarūr on the banks of the Periyār. He has also otherwise added to our knowledge of the conditions of Malabar in those early days, but his intense patriotism appears to have biassed his conclusions and his account of the various component elements of the population of South India and of Tamil civilization can only be described as a few facts diluted with a great deal of imagination.

Mr. Kanakasabhai Pillai says in his book :—

"The oldest of the tribes who dwelt in the Tamiḻ-akam were the *Villavar* and the *Mīṉavar* literally bow-men and fisher-men."

"These semi-barbarous tribes were conquered by the Nāgas, who were a very numerous and civilized race, and who at one time or other ruled a great portion of India, Ceylon and Burma. They are mentioned in the Rāmāyaṇa, and the Nāga Capital, which probably lay in the heart of Dakhan, is described in that epic." (page 39).

This description is accepted practically in full by Dr. L. D. Barnett in the Cambridge History of India, Vol. I, page 595, where it is stated :

" To the oldest stratum of pre-Dravidian blood belonged the savages termed by the ancient poets *Villavar* (bow-men) and *Mīṉavar* (fisher-men) of whom the former may be identical with the modern Bhīls, while the latter may have descendants in the Mīnas. Another group is that termed by the poets Nāgas, a word which in Hindu literature commonly denotes a class of semi-divine beings, half-men and half-snakes, but is often applied by Tamil writers to a warlike race with bows and nooses and famous as free-booters."

Mr. V. A. Smith, the historian, also accepts the statement that *Villavars* and *Mīṉavars* formed the most ancient elements in the South Indian population.

That the ancient poets termed any savages *Villavars* and *Mīṉavars* appears to be an addition of Dr. Barnett since it is not found in Mr. Kanakasabhai Pillai's book. The ancient poets did not know of, or refer to, any savages named *Villavar* or *Mīṉavar* nor did they make any distinction among the population of South India as old inhabitants and new immigrants. The account of the conquest of South India by the Nāgas and of the civilization of these conquerors is wholly a creation of Mr. Kanakasabhai Pillai's imagination, as also the interpretation bow-men and fisher-men.

Mr. Kanakasabhai Pillai was apparently of opinion that the higher caste Tamils were a superior people quite apart from the rest of the Tamil population and from the Telugu and Kanarese people. He therefore asserted that these higher caste Tamils were later immigrants and thought that the peculiar letter *ḻ* of the Tamil alphabet was doubtless brought in by these immigrants. He says in his book :—

"This letter, I understand, occurs only in some of the Tibetan languages. It indicates most clearly that the primitive home of the Tamil immigrants must have been in the Tibetan plateau. That they were not of Aryan descent is proved not only by the continued antagonism they displayed towards the Aryans, but also by the ancient Sanskrit works in which the Drāviḍas are spoken of as an alien people. That the Tamils had attained a high degree of civilization before the advent of the Aryans is established indisputably by the fact that the pure Tamil language is so copious and exact that it can do well without borrowing Sanskrit words. In fact, in the ancient Tamil classical works, the terms relating to music, grammar, astronomy and even abstract philosophy are of pure Tamil origin; and they indicate most clearly that those sciences were cultivated by the Tamils long before the arrival of the Brahmans or other Aryan immigrants. The Tamils obtained a knowledge of these sciences most probably from China, through Bengal or Burma, with both of which countries they had direct and constant intercourse." (pages 51, 52).

As the pure Tamil words relating to music, grammar, astronomy and even abstract philosophy, which Mr. Kanakasabhai Pillai relies on, are not mentioned by him, it is unnecessary to examine that question here. Such statements are freely indulged in by people who have no knowledge of Sanskrit. It must, however, be mentioned that the sound *ḻ* was however very common in old Kanarese, as common as in Tamil, and Telugu scholars have traced *l* in some Telugu inscriptions.

There are several other things of a similar nature in Mr. Kanakasabhai Pillai's book which may be mentioned here:—

(i) He locates the city—Bhōgavatī—of the Rāmayaṇa, the Nāga Capital (Kiṣkindhā Kānda, sarga 41) in

Dakhan. It is clear from the epic itself that it is near the southern end of the earth, across the Indian and Southern oceans, only one side on this stage of the abode of the departed souls presided over by Yama. Mr. Kanakasabhai Pillai is apparently thinking of the modern city of Nagpur.

(ii) " It was from the Nāgas that the Aryans first learnt the art of writing : and hence the Sanskrit characters came to be called Dēvanāgarī" (page 45).

(iii) " Tamil had, indeed, one advantage over Kanarese and Telugu, and this lay in the circumstance that its literary cultivation by the Aryan immigrants led by Agastya began a few centuries earlier."

But Mr. Kanakasabhai Pillai thinks that the tradition of Agastya leading the first colony of Aryans into the Podiya Hills does not deserve credence and Dr. Barnett agrees with him. Mr. Kanakasabhai Pillai's reason for discrediting the tradition is that, according to the Rāmāyaṇa, the hermitage of Agastya was only two yōjanas from Pañcavaṭī, on the banks of the Godāvarī. He, therefore, thinks that the story of the Agastya of the Podiyal Hills must have been of later growth—after the Brahmans had gained ascendancy in the South ; and Dr. Barnett agrees in this view.

This criticism of the Agastya legend is not conclusive. Sargas 40-43 of the Kiṣkindhā Kāṇḍa of Rāmāyaṇa in which Sugrīva gives instructions to the Vānara chiefs sent in search of Sitā are an interpolation which displays a knowledge of the geographical and other details, especially of Southern India, which were unknown to the original author of the poem. To him the peninsula south of the Gōdāvarī was a blank as no rivers or kingdoms south of the Gōdāvarī are mentioned in the original Rāmāyaṇa. If Rāma crossed the sea at Rāmeś-varam, he must have crossed the rivers Kṛṣṇā and Kāvērī on his way and must have passed though the Cōla and the Pāṇḍya kingdoms ; but these are not mentioned anywhere in the epic except in the Sarga in which Sugrīva gives instructions. But the original author knew that Agastya lived somewhere in the south, that a stranger could not reach his hermitage without a guide, and that he had to pass by, or in sight of, *pippalī* forests[1] on the way. The mention of *pippalī* forests is conclusive on the point and clearly shows that the original writer knew that Agastya's hermitage was somewhere in the south past the pepper forests of Malabar, but had no clear conception of the distance. Mr. Kanakasabhai Pillai's criticism thus falls to the ground. It will also be noted that the interpolated sarga 41 correctly locates Agastya on the top of Malaya near the Tāmraparṇi.

Mr. Kanakasabhai Pillai also imagined that the Limirikē, Dymirikē, Damirikē of the Greek writers was a transliteration of the Tamiḻakam.

Before accepting the identification we may ask why the Greeks used the medial *d* in the transliteration when they had a tenue *t*, why an *i* was used for *a*, and how the intervocal *k* in the Tamil word pronounced like a spirant came to be represented by *k*, not by *kh* or *h*.

Mr. Kanakasabhai Pillai's view is wholly untenable but some writers continue to repeat it. Greek writers mention not only Damirikē but also Āriake, Lārike. In these three words the termination *kē* or *ikē* is evidently the Greek termination signifying 'locality'. Limirikē, Dymirikē, Dimirikē

---

1. On the way to Agastya's hermitage Rāma says to Lakṣmaṇa,

"*Pippalīnām ca pakvānām vanādasmādupāgataḥ.*
Gandho'yam pavanotkṣiptaḥ sahasā kaṭukodayaḥ".
(Āraṇyakāṇḍa : Sarga 11, verse 51).

"The smell wafted by the winds from the *pippalī* forests bearing ripened fruits is very pungent".

2. Bhandarkar's Early History of the Dakhan, p. 3.

apparently mean the land of the Limirs, Dymirs, Damirs which may be different transliterations of the Prākṛt *damiḍa*. But we must note that the country so variously designated did not include the whole of the Tamil land as the region about Cape Comorin and the Coromandel coast are outside Damirikē, according to both the Periplus and Ptolemy's map. In any case we can confidently say that Damirikē is not a transliteration of the latter poetic word Tamiḻakam = *Tamiḻ+akam* " the home of the Tamils ".

It has been thought necessary to make large quotations from Mr. Kanakasabhai Pillai for criticising him, because his fancies have been taken to be facts by unsuspecting foreign writers and are finding their way into standard works. His ' patriotic ' book was never taken seriously in South India ; it is now presented to South Indians as genuine history by foreign historians of South India.

S. 17. Mr. V. A. Smith.

(*a*) The following extracts from Mr. V. A. Smith's " Early History of India ", 3rd Edition (1914), pages 438-443 may be quoted here :—

" The Greek geographer Ptolemy, who wrote his treatise about A.D. 140, was well acquainted with Southern India, which he called Damirikē, a good transliteration of Tamiḻakam, *r* and *ḻ* being interchangeable but unfortunately corrupted in the manuscripts into the unmeaning form Limyrikē owing to the frequent confusion between Λ and Δ[1]. In his time one languge only, the Tamil, was spoken over the whole area, Malayalam, now the speech of Malabar, not having been developed as a separate tongue till some centuries later. The population comprised various elements, of

1. Ptolemy bk. VII : Chap. 1, page 85; transl : Mc Crindle : Ind. Ant : XIII, page 367. The Peutingerian tables correctly give the names a Damirikē (Ind. Ant. III—144).

which the Villavar, or bow-men (Bhils) and Mīṉavar or fishermen (Mīnas) are supposed to have been the most ancient The Tamils seem to be later immigrants.

"The early Tamil poetical literature, dating according to competent expert opinion from the first three centuries of the Christian era gives a vivid picture of the state of society of that period. The Tamils had developed an advanced civilization of their own, wholly independent of Northern India. Immigrants from the North, who had settled at Madura and some other cities sought to introduce Hindu notions of caste and ceremonial, but met with much opposition and the caste system, which for many centuries past has been observed with special strictness in the South was then inchoate and imperfect[1]".

"Tamil land had the good fortune to possess three precious commodities not procurable elsewhere, namely, pepper, pearls and beryl. Pepper fetched an enormous price in the markets of Europe, and was so highly prized that when Alaric the Goth levied his war indemnity from Rome, in A.D. 409, his terms included the delivery of 3,000 lbs. of pepper. The pearl fishery of the Southern sea, which still is productive and valuable has been worked for untold ages, and always attracted a crowd of foreign merchants. The beryl or aqua-marine gem, which as Pliny truly observed, is closely related to the emerald was highly esteemed by both Indians and Romans, and often furnished material for the choicest achievement of the engraver's art. Its scarcity except in India tempted clever Indian forgers to fabricate imitations made from rock-crystal. Three Indian mines are recorded, namely (1) Punnata, where Ptolemy noted that beryl was found, close to Kittūr on the Kabbani river,

---

1. The Tamils Eighteen Hundred Years Ago, pages 3, 10, 39.

a tributary of the Kāvirī (Cauvery) in the south-west of Mysore ; (2) Padiyūr or Pattiāli, 40 miles E.S.E. from the town of Coimbatore where a mine was worked successfully as late as 1820 ; and (3) Vāniyambāḍi in the north-east corner of the Salem District, not far from the Kolar Gold Field. The large and numerous hoards of Roman gold coins found in the districts where the mines were situated, testify to the activity of ancient commerce in the gems of Southern India. The fact that the mineral corundum, a variety of the ruby and sapphire, found abundantly in Salem and Coimbatore bears a purely Tamil name (*kurandam*) affords another indication of the familiarity of ancient Europe with the products of the Indian gem mines."

Here Mr. Smith adopts several of Mr. Kanakasabhaī Pillai's specialities—aboriginal Villavar and Mīṉavar and the later Tamil immigrants. It is surprising that he should also have accepted Damarikē as a good transliteration of Tamiḻakam notwithstanding the *d, i, k* of the transliteration and that he should not have noted that the suffix of the transliteration is found also in Āryakē and Lāṛike. It may be remarked that Ptolemy transliterates the name of the town Tagara as using an initial tenue.

It is curious that, of the three precious commodities of which the Tamil land had the monopoly, not one should be known by its pure Tamil name in Europe. Vaiḍūrya of which *beryl* is a shortened form is obviously a Sanskrit formation. *Kurandam* the supposed pure Tamil name of *corundum* is a shortened form of the Sanskrit *Kuruvindam* and the word *muttu* is not known outside the Dravidian country. There were no professional pearl-divers at the time of the Periplus and from the fact of Brahman shark-charmers being found indispensable Mr. Schoff, transl ator of Periplus, suspects that the pearl-fishing industry perhaps dates from a time after the

Aryan occupation of South India. Mr. V. A. Smith's 'untold ages' must, therefore be accepted with considerable reserve.

In regard to the age of the early Tamil literature Mr. Vincent Smith accepts what he calls 'competent expert opinion' that the literature dates from the first three centuries of the Christian era ; but South Indian scholars are not at all agreed on the question, many of them inclining to the sixth or seventh century.

Mr. Smith apparently thinks that the South Indian civilization as described in the early Tamil literature was wholly independent of Northern India and that the immigrants from the North were confined at that time to Madura and some other cities. This view is entirely erroneous. Chapter V of Cilappatikāram which describes the first day of the annual Indra-festival lasting for one month mentions the following deities as possessiong temples within the city of Pukār *i.e.*, Kāvēripaṭṭiṇam :—

(1) Śiva, (2) Subrahmaṇya, (2) Balarāma, (4) Viṣṇu, (5) Indra,[1] the supreme deity of the Vedic pantheon (11 169-173) ; it is also stated that Indra's idol was bathed on the Viṣu (equinox) day which was the full-moon day of the month of Cittirai. (1. 168.)

Chapter VI of the poem enumerates eleven dances or dramatic representations enacted during the festival. These were :—

1. It appears from Chapter IX (ll. 9-15) that the under-mentioned deities also had temples in the city :—(6) the Kalpa tree (7) Indra's elephant Airāvata (8) Indra's weapon Vajra (9) Kailāsa (10) Subrahmaṇya's lance (11) Śātavāhana (12) Śāstā (13) Arhan (14) the Sun (15) the Moon.

1. Śiva's dance in front of the burning Tripura (11. 40-42),

2. Śiva's *pāṇḍaraṅgam* dance as Bhairavi (11. 44-45),

3. Kṛṣṇa vanquishing the elephant despatched by Kaṁsa against him (11 46-48),

4. Kṛṣṇa vanquishing Bāṇa (11 48-49),

5. Subrahmaṇya vanquishing Śūrapadma (11 49-51)

6. The umbrella dance of Subrahmaṇya in front of the Asura army (11 52-53),

7. The pot dance of Kṛṣṇa in the city of Bāṇa (11 54-55),

8. The dance of Kāma in the form of a hermaphrodite (11 56-57),

9. The dance of Durgā with wooden legs (11 56-57),

10. The dance of Śrī-devī in the form of a fascinating maiden (11 60-61),

11. The dance of Indrāṇī in the fields at the northern gate of Bāṇa's city (11 62-64).

Kāma festival was celebrated as now in the month of Phālguna (XIV-11 111-112).

i. Public Worship. The deities mentioned above are either Vedic or Purāṇic ; the dances represented striking and noteworthy incidents of Hindu mythology. It is obvious that the whole system of public worship had become Aryanized.

ii. The names of months. The system of naming the twelve months after the names of the full-moon constellations had been taken over from the Aryan together with the actual names of the months. It does not appear that the Tamils had at any time, any other names for the months.

iii. The names of planets. The Hindu planets (Grahas) were then called by their Sanskrit names :—*Cantiraṉ*, ' the

Moon', '*Kuru*' Jupiter', *Aṅkārakaṉ*, ' Mars' (Cilappatikāram XIV-1-195).

iv. The Brahmans. Chapter VI of Cilappatikāram refers to the Varunapputar (35), that is, the patron deities of the four castes, and to the *Nālvakai varunattaṭaṅkākkambalai*) (163-165) ' the ceaseless noise created by the four (assembled) castes'. The Brāhmaṇas were not confined to a few cities as supposed by Mr. Smith but had also settlements on the banks of the Cauvery (X-143-147) and in other country parts of which the following are mentioned incidentally in the epic :—Talaiccenkāṉam (XV-11), Taṅkāl (XXIII-75), Vayalūr (XXIII-119), Māṅkāṭu (XI-53). Kāppiya-t-tolkuṭi (XXX-83). It is also stated in the epic that the smoke of the offerings of Brāhmaṇas in their Yāgas becomes the nucleus (embryo) of rain clouds[1]. In Chapter XXIII the guardian deity of Madura states that the Pāṇḍya king always followed the counsel of Brāhmaṇas, never listening to the advice of sycophants (II 31-32) and relates how he made suitable amends when he once incurred divine displeasure in consequence of a Brāhmaṇa being put in chains by his agents. In Chapter XXI when Madura is burning, the God of fire is instructed not to injure Brāhmaṇas, ascetics, cows, chaste women and the old and the young (53-54). The kings of Kēraḷa were even then, as they are doing now, rewarding learned Brāhmaṇas versed in Vedic lore and on important occasions they used to distribute, as they do now, their own weights in gold (*tulābhāram*) as rewards to Brāhmaṇas (XXVI-174-176).

v. Pilgrimage to holy places. People went on pilgrimage to Tirupati, Śrīraṅgam and other holy places as they

1. That the rains are due to the Yāgas performed by the Brāhmaṇas is the teaching of the Smṛtis.

2. *Vide* the notes called Arumpada Urai.

are doing now. Rāmēśvaram had not apparently attained its present sanctity then ; Cape Comorin was then held specially sacred and the people of the Tamil country as well as those from Northern India went to Kanya-Kumārī to wash off their sins. This cape appears to have been regarded then as the site of Rāma's anikat[1]

The above are a few items throwing light on the social condition and civilization of Southern India culled from Cilappatikāram stated to have been written in the second century A.D. by a Buddhistic monk, brother to the Cēra king Ceṅkuṭṭuvaṉ. Other early Tamil works containing similar descriptions of early Tamil society are the Maṇimēkalai and the Paripāṭal. It appears from the former of these that the whole system of Indo-Aryan philosophy, orthodox and heterodox, had been bodily transplanted to the south. The latter work confines its description to Madura and its neighbourhood. A perusal of the poems included in the Paripāṭal will show clearly that the major portion of the Hindu mythology, especially the portion relating to the incarnations of Viṣṇu, the birth of Kumāra, his heroic exploits and his marriage with Indra's daughter and with Valli, has been adopted by the Tamil poets. It is the boast of one of these poets that the citizens of Madura are roused from their sleep in the morning not by the crowing of the cock as in the capital cities of the Cēra and the Cōla kings but by the sound of the Vedas recited by the Brāhmaṇas[2].

It will be seen from the above that the picture of South Indian society as given in the early Tamil poetical literature does not differ much from what it is now. Indo-Aryan philosophy, Indo-Aryan gods and system of worship, Indo-Aryan divisions of time and chronology and generally Indo-

1. Maṇimēkalai, V. 1-37.
2. Paripāṭal, page 175. V. Swaminatha Aiyar's edition.

Aryan ideals of life had been adopted in the South. There were no doubt fewer Brāhmaṇas than now ; there were also Buddhist and Jain ascetics who enjoyed perhaps as much honour as the Brāhmaṇas. But it will be wholly incorrect to say that the South Indian civilization of the period was indepéndent of Northern India.

(*b*) The following extracts from Mr. Smith's " Ancient and Hindu India " (1920) may also be given here :—

" *Dravidian culture.* The Brahmanical ideas and institutions, although universally diffused in every province, have not been wholly victorious. Pre-historic forms of worship and many utterly un-Aryan social practices survive, especially in the peninsula, among the peoples speaking Dravidian languages. We see there the strange spectacle of an exaggerated regard for caste co-existing with all sorts of weird notions and customs alien to Brahman tradition. While it is not improbable that the Dravidian civilization may be as old as or even older than the Indo-Aryan Brahmanical culture of the north, which was long regarded in the south as an unwelcome intruder to be resisted strenuously, the materials available for the study of early Dravidian institutions are too scanty and imperfectly explored to permit of history being based upon them ".

" *Distinct Dravidian civilization.* Where the Brahmans succeeded in making their way into the kingdoms of the peninsula, including the realms of the Āndhras, Cēras, Cōḷas and Pāṇḍyas, they found a civilized society, not merely a collection of rude barbarian tribes. The Dravidian religion and social customs differed widely from those of nothern India........Even now, when Hindusim, with its strict caste rules and its recognised system of law, has gained the mastery, the old and quite different Dravidian ideas may be traced in a thousand directions. The ancient Dravidian, alphabet called Vaṭṭeḻuttu, of Semitic origin, is wholly distinct from any of the nothern alphabets. Tradition as recorded in the ancient Tamil literature indicates that from very remote times wealthy cities existed in the south and that many of the refinements and luxuries of life were in common use. The good fortune of Tamil Land (Tamiḻakam) in possessing such eagerly desired commodities as gold, pearls, conch, shells, pepper, beryls, and choice cotton goods attracted foreign traders from the earliest ages. Commerce supplied the wealth required for life on civilized lines and the Dravidians were not afraid to cross the seas. Some day, perhaps, the history of Dravidian civilization may be written by a competent scholar skilled in all he lore and languages required for the study of the subject, but at present the literature concerned with it is too fragmentary, defective and controversial to permit of condensation."

The remark about Vaṭṭeḻuttu appears to reproduce Dr. Burnell's exploded view and does not apparently take into account the later researches of Dr. Buhler and Mr. T.A. Gopinatha Rao.

Nothing can be farther from the truth than the statement that the Brahmanical culture of he North was regarded as an intruder to be strenuously resisted ; it appears from the early Tamil literature that this culture had been adopted.

Cōḷa, Cēra and Pāṇḍya are dynastic names and Mr. Smith seems to be under the impression that these dynasties are of South Indian origin. But early Tamil literature says that they were of northern extraction.

In regard to the succession of ages in India culture, Mr. V. A. Smith says :—

" In Southern India stone-tools were superseded directly by iron, without any intermediate stop. The time when iron became the ordinary material of tools and weapons is called the Iron or Early Iron Age. In Northern India the case is different. There the metal first used for tools, harpoons, swords, and spear-heads was copper, practically pure. Copper implements and weapons, often of peculiar forms, but sometimes closely resembling those found in Ireland, have been discovered in large numbers in the Central Provinces, Chutia Nagpur, old beds of the Ganges near Cawnpore and elsewhere. Silver objects are associated with them, but no iron. Probably copper-tools were in use when the Rgveda hymns were composed, but commentators differ. Iron certainly was known to the authors of the Atharvaveda, a very ancient book, and was in common use in 500 B.C. We may safely assume that the metal was utilized in Northern India from at least 1000 B.C. It may have been introduced much earlier, and from Babylonia. The earliest of the copper-tools may well be as old as 2000 B.C. In Southern India, the discovery or introduction of iron, may have occurred much later and quite independently."

In regard to the Dravidian languages Mr. V.A. Smith says :—

" The family or group of tongues second in importance is the Dravidian in the peninsula, comprising Tamil, Telugu, Malayāḷam, Kanaresa and Tulu, besides some minor tongues. Both Tamil and Telugu have rich literatures. The Tamil is the principal and perhaps the oldest language of the group. The grammar and structure of the Dravidian speech differ wholly from the Aryan type. The most ancient Tamil literature, dating from the early centuries of the Christian era, or even earlier, was composed on Dravidian lines, and independent of Sanskrit models. The latter literature in all the languages has been largely influenced by Brahmanical ideas and diction. The linguistic family is called Dravidian because Drāvidian was the ancient name of the Tamil country in the far south. In fact, Tamil is really the same word as the adjective Drāviḍa."

S. 18. Professor J. Kennedy.

In an article entitled " Early Commerce of Babylon with India " published in J.R.A.S. 1898, Professor J. Kennedy examines in detail the evidences that have been adduced to prove the existence of such a commerce from the time of Solomon and comes to the conclusion that there was no intercourse prior to the 7th Century B.C.

In regard to Algum or Almug trees mentioned in the books of Kings and Chronicles he says that what has been adduced " is satisfacory proof of an Indian trade in the time of the author of Kings. But was it sandal wood that Solomon received or something else that was taken for sandal wood centuries after the destruction of the temple...... The wood was used for props and the inclined ascents to the temple and the palace. I know few material less fitted for such purposes than sandal wood."

In regard to *Tukīyīm* or pea-cocks he says :—

" Peacocks come with silver and gold, not from Ophir, but from Tarshish (I-Kings, X-22 ; 2 Chronicles, IX-21). ' *Thuki*, the Hebrew for pea-fowl, is certainly Dravidian' and derived from the Tamil *tōkei* or *tōgei* (Caldwell, page 66, 1st Edition). Now we happen to know, on independent evidence, that peacocks were exported from India at the time when the books of Kings and Chronicles were composed ; but here again there arises the question of identity. The exports of silver from Tarshish are decisive against any Indian locality, and the LXX says nothing about pea-fowl."

He also rejects the suggestion that Solomon received his apes from India and comes to the conclusion that Ophir must be sought for among the Semites and that he could see no archaeological or literary evidence for a maritime trade with India prior to the 7th Century B.C. He, however, holds the view that "rice, peacocks, sandal wood, every known article which we find imported into Babylon by sea before the 5th Century B.C. brought with it a Dravidian, not a Sanskrit designation" and that these articles are known by their Tamil names in Europe.

In an article entitled "The Gospels of Infancy" published in the J.R.A.S., 1917, he draws attention to the existence of an Indian firm of traders at Nippur[1] so early as the 5th Century B.C.

"Among the business tablets of the great banking house tablets of Murashu and Sons at Nippur which cover the latter half of the 5th Century B.C. we find records of their dealings with certain Indian merchants and if there were Indian merchants at Nippur there must have been Indians in other places in Babylonia. And they must have come from the west coast; for about the same time articles of Indian provenance, rice, peacocks and the like became known for the first time in Greece. Sophocles, Aristophanes and others mention them; and they were known under Dravidian names. This Indian colony carried on trade with Barygaza in the time of Periplus and it was still flourishing in the 7th Century A.D."

S. 19. THE CAMBRIDGE HISTORY OF INDIA. DR. BARNETT.

The latest contributions of British Scholars in regard to the ancient civilization of South India and of the Dravidians are contained in Chapters II, XXIV, XXV and XXXI of Volume I of the Cambridge History of India edited by E. J. Rapson, M.A., Professor of Sanskrit in the University of Cambridge. These contributions embody the considered

1. *See also* pages 51 and 52 of Professor P. T. Srinivasa Aiyangar's 'History of India' (1923).

views of Orientalists and other scholars in regard to these questions and are worth quoting *in extenso.*

L. D. Barnett, Litt.D., says :—(Vol. I, pages 593-594),

" The great peninsula of India from the Vindhya mountains southward to Comorin, is the home of the Dravidian peoples. And here at the outset we are faced by a difficulty of terms.

" The word Drāviḍa comes from an ethnic term Draviḍa or Dramiḍa, in Pāli Damiḷa which is apparently identical in origin with the adjective Tamil ; and thus a title which is apparently applicable to a single branch, the Tamils, is extended to a whole family. Again, not only is the term ' Dravidian ' used sometimes to denote all the members of the one ethnic family, but it is also employed to designate all the cognate languages spoken by that family—the Tamil, Malāyāḷm, Telugu, Kannaḍa (Kanarese), and various minor dialects—without regard to the possible differences of race among the groups speaking these tongues ; and further more by a deplorable looseness of terminology, it has been applied by anthropologists to a group of races characterised by common physical features,[1] who are chiefly inhabitants of the peninsula, and for the most part, but by no means entirely, use languages which are variants of Dravidan speech. Lastly we must note that an ancient Tamil tradition speaks of a *panca-Drāviḍam* or five Dravidian regions understanding thereby the Tamil, Āndhra, Telugu and Kanarese countries, the Mahārāṣṭra or Marāṭha provinces and Gujarāt. The conclusion which is suggested by a review of all the available data is as follows :—

" At some very early date several millennia before the Christian era, the greater part of India was inhabited by a

1. These features are very dark hue, long head, broad nose, abundant and sometimes curly hair, and dark eyes.

dark negroid race of low culture characterised more or less by the physical features now known as Dravidian. This early people, however, should more properly be termed pre-Dravidian. In course of time another race, higher in culture and speaking a language of 'Scythian' affinities, from which are derived the tongues now known as Dravidian, gradually made its way from the north or north-west—probably through Baluchistan—into the plain of the Indus, and thence ultimately passed down into the regions south of the Vindhya. This race may be called the proto-Dravidian. Wherever it came, it mixed its blood to a greater or less degree with that of the earlier inhabitants. From this combination have arisen the Dravidians of history who have preserved few traces of the physical characteristics of the proto-Dravidians, whatever these may have been.[1] Most of the pre-Dravidian tribes in the countries south of the Vindhya adopted the speech of the proto-Dravidians, while they absorbed their blood, notably in the centre and south of the peninsula, the Tamil, Kaṉṉaḍa and Telugu regions. In Gujarāt the waves of Aryan immigration gradually submerged Dravidian blood and speech ; in Mahārāṣṭra the same influences obliterated the language and the same has happened in Kaliṅga (now Orissa and part of the Circars) where a Dravidian language, the Telugu, survives only in the southern districts.

" Long before the beginning of the Christian era the Dravidian South had developed a considerable culture of its own, and its inhabitants had developed themselves into powerful kingdoms, some of which carried on a thriving trade with western Asia, Egypt, and later with the Greek and

1. It is possible that the 'Scythian' features that have been observed among the Marāṭha Brahmans, Kunbis, Coorgs and Telugus may be survivals of proto-Dravidian characteristics.

Roman Empires. The chief of these were three Tamil kingdoms, the Āndhras, Kaliṅga and Mahārāṣṭra."

This extract from Dr. Barnett's article requires a few explanatory and critical remarks.

a. Scythian and Dravidian.—The Scythian affinities referred to are the affinities asserted to exist in the Dravidian languages by Bishop Caldwell who, following the Danish philologist Rask, uses the term Scythian in the sense of what have later been generally called Turanian—non-Aryan and non-Semitic—languages. The existence of these affinities is, as we have seen, denied by the editors of the Linguistic Survey of India and by the generality of scholars.

The phrase ' Scythian features' in the foot-note is adopted from Sir Herbert Risley, who, in his classification of the populations of India, places the broad-headed peoples inhabiting the belt of country on the west of India between Gujarāt and Coorg in the Scytho-Dravidian group. This brachycephalism, Sir Herbert Risley thought, was possibly due to the absorption in the population of Western India of swarms of nomadic peoples who poured into India for a number of centuries about the beginning of the Christian era and " whose out-landish names were conveniently summed up in the generic term Scythian ". Sir Herbert defended the supposed brachycephalism of these Scythians on the ground that they came from the Central Asian steppes " a region occupied exclusively by broad-headed races ".[1] Dr. Barnett, differing from Sir Herbert Risley, appears to think that this brachycephalism is possibly due to the proto-Dravidians who settled in India before the arrival of the Aryans. A third theory, that of Professor E. J. Rapson, is that the disturbing influence was due to the invasion of a broad-headed Alpine race which

1. Census Report of India, 1901, Vol. I ; Imperial Gazetteer of India, New Edition, Vol. I, page 292.

inhabited the plateau of Western Asia (Anatolia, Armenia and Iran) and that these seem to have come into Western India, as the Dravidians also most probably came, through Baluchistan.[1]

There are other theories about the original home of the Dravidians. We have Sir W. Hunter's Central Asian theory which is rejected by Sir Herbert Risley. Mr. Kanakasabhai Pillai postulated a Central Asian Mongolian origin to the higher strata of Dravidian society. The editors of the Linguistic Survey think that " we have no information to show that they (Dravidians) are not the original inhabitants of the South (of India) ". Huxley treated them as Australioid ; Pischel classed them with Singhalese and Veddahs as people of uncertain origin. Then we have the theory of the submerged Lemurian Continent and some others.

b. Maritime Commerce.—The supposed thriving trade with Western Asia and Egypt and later with the Greek and Roman Empires rests on the assumption that *tōgai*, *pippali*, *arici*, *iñcivēr*, and *karuppu* or *kārppu* are indigenous Tamil words which have found entrance into foreign languages. It must again be noted, in passing, that there is no such word as in Greek.

c. Panca-Dravidam.—Reference is made in the extract to " an ancient Tamil tradition " which speaks of " a *pañca-Drāviḍam* or five Dravidian regions understanding thereby the Tamil, Āndhra or Telugu, and Kanarese countries, the Mahārāṣṭra or Marātha provinces, and Gujarāt ". If, by this, it is intended to convey the idea that there was such a tradition among the Dravidians as opposed to the immigrant Aryans a most emphatical denial should be given to the statement. Bishop Caldwell understood this so-called tradi-

1. Cambridge History of India, Vol. I, page 45.

tion to refer to five Dravidian languages and thought Marāṭhī and Gujarātī were erroneously included in it (Intro : C.D.G., page 117). The only tradition recorded in Tamil grammars about languages other than Tamil is that the Tamil land is surrounded by seventeen countries in which other languages are spoken, but the authors of these works appear to have had no idea that some of these were related to Tamil, *e.g.*, Telugu, Kanarese, Tuḷu, Koṭagu ; for these names occur mixed up indiscriminately with the names of non-Dravidian languages.[1]

The various sects of Brahmans in India do not all follow the same *ācāras* and the Smṛtis divide them into two main classes with reference to these *ācāras viz.*, the Northerners and the Southerners[2], who have usually been called the Gaudas and the Drāviḍas in later times, Gauḍa and Drāviḍa being the most prominent sects of the two classes. And as in the Vedic cosmogony, everything is regarded as five-fold[3]. The Skanda Purāṇa[4] refers to the people living north of the Vindhya mountains as the Pañca-Gauḍas *viz.*, Sārasvata, Kānyakubja, Gauḍa, Maithilika and Autkala ; and to the people living south of the Vindhyas as the Pañca-Drāviḍas *viz.*, Karnāṭa, Tailaṅga, Gujjara, Āndhra and Drāviḍa. Tailaṅga and Āndhra refer apparently to one and the same people ; so it is usual to omit one of these two and substitute

---

1. *Vide* page 161 Nannūl Edition (1918) by Mahāmahōpādhyāya V. Swaminatha Aiyar.

2. Smṛticandrikā, Vol. I, page 21.

3. Pañcabhirdhātā vidhāvidam yat tāsām svaśrīajanayat pañca pañca (T. S. IV. 3-11).

4. Sārasvatāh kānyakubjā gauḍamaithilikautkalāḥ.
Pañcagaudā iti khyātā vindhyasyōttaravāsinah.
Karnāṭāścaiva tailaṅgā gujjarā rāṣṭravāsinaḥ.
Āndhrāśca drāviḍāḥ pañca vindhyadakṣiṇavāsinah.

Mahārāstra instead. This is the origin of the so-called tradition about *pañca*-Drāvidas ; it refers neither to regions nor to languages but to peoples—Brahman sects[1], Drāviḍa and Gauḍa being convenient substitutes for Southern and Northern. This supposed tradition appears to be one of the grounds for Dr. Barnett's assumption that Gujarāt and the Marāṭha country were peopled by Dravidans when the Aryans arrived in India.

If there is one tradition regarding Tamil language and literature which is more ancient and more widely spread than others, it is that the sage Agastya of the Potiya hill wrote the first Tamil Grammar and was the author of various Tamil treatises. That a Sanskritist wrote the first Grammar is fully borne out by the arrangement of the alphabet which follows the Sanskrit order unscientifically relegating the special Tamil letters to the end and by the circumstance that the Tamil letter .·. corresponding to the Sanskrit *visarga* bears the name *āytam*, a *tadbhava* of the Sanskrit *āśrita* 'dependent'. Dr. Barnett is one of a small band of oriental scholars who have devoted their lives to the task of interpreting the East to the West and it is unfortunate that he should discredit this tradition (apparently following Mr. Kanakasabhai Pillai) and should speak of the undoubted Brahman tradition of *pañca*-Drāviḍas regarding the sects of southern Brahmans as 'an ancient Tamil tradition'.

S. 20. PROFESSOR RAPSON :—(*Vol. I, Cambridge History of India, pages* 41, 42 *and* 49).

" It would seem probable that the original speakers of the Dravidian languages were invaders and that the ethnographical Dravidians are a mixed race. In the more habitable regions the two elements have fused while representatives of

1. *Vide* the contribution of Mr. John Beames at page 160 of the Indian Antiquary, Vol. V.

the aborigines are still to be found in the fastnesses to which they retired before the encroachments of the new comers. If this view be correct, we must suppose that the aborigines have, in the course of long ages, lost their ancient language and adopted those of their conquerors. The process of linguistic transformation which may still be observed in other parts of India would seem to have been carried out more completely in the South than elsewhere.

" The theory that the Dravidian element is the most ancient that we can discover in the population of Northern India must also be modified by what we now know of the Muṇḍā languages, the Indian representatives of the Austric family of speech, and the mixed languages in which their influence has been traced. Here according to the evidence now available it would seem that the Austric element is the eldest and that it has been overlaid in different regions by successive waves of Dravidian and Indo-European on the one hand and by Tibeto-Chinese on the other. Most ethnologists hold that there is no difference in physical type between the present speakers of Muṇḍā and Dravidian languages. This statement has been called in question ; but if it be true it shows that racial conditions have become so complicated that it is no longer possible to analyse their constituents. Language alone has preserved a record which would otherwise have been lost.

" At the same time there can be little doubt that Dravidian languages were actually flourishing in the western regions of Northern India at the period when languages of the Indo-European type were introduced by Aryan invasions from the north-west. Dravidian characteristics have been traced alike in Vedic and Classical Sanskrit, in the Prākrts or early popular dialects, and in the modern Vernaculars derived from them. The linguistic data would thus appear to be arranged in the order Austric, Dravidian, Indo-European.

"There is good ground then for supposing that before the coming of the Indo-Aryans, speakers of the Dravidian languages predominated both in Northern and Southern India ; but as we have seen, older elements are discoverable in the population of both regions and therefore the assumption that the Dravidians are aboriginals is no longer tenable." (pages 41, 42).

"The Dravidian languages, with the exception of Brāhūī, are now confined to the peninsula south of the Vindhya and Ceylon ; but it is supposed that at the period of the Aryan invasions they prevailed also in the North. This inference is derived from the change which Indo-European underwent after its introduction into India, and which can only be explained as the result of some older disturbing element. The oldest form of Indo-Aryan, the language of the Rg-Veda is distinguished from the oldest form of Iranian, the language of the Avesta, chiefly by the presence of a second series of dental letters, the so-called cerebrals. These play an increasingly important part in the development of Indo-Aryan in its subsequent phases. They are foreign to Indo-European languages generally, and they are characteristic of Dravidian. We may conclude, therefore, that the earlier forms of speech by which Indo-European was modified in the various stages of its progress from the North-West were predominatingly Dravidian.

At the present time Dravidian languages are stable only in the countries of the South where they have developed great literatures like Tamil, Malayāḷam, Kanarese and Telugu. In the northern borders of the Dravidian sphere of influence, the spoken languages which have not been stereotyped by literatures are, as each succeeding Report of the Census of India shows, still continuing to retreat before the onward progress of Indo-Aryan." (page 49).

The Dravidian characteristics referred to in the above extract are discussed briefly in Volume IV of the Linguistic Survey of India. The chief of them are : 1. the adoption of the so-called cerebral letters in the Indo-Aryan forms of speech. 2. the irregular change of ṟ into ḻ and *vice versa.* 3. the increasing use of conjunctive participles instead of verb forms. 4. the formation of the active past participle and of the perephrastic future. These will be discussed in detail in the next chapter ; but it may be mentioned here in anticipation that most of these Dravidian characteristics in Aryan, when examined at close quarters, turn out to be Aryan characteristics in Dravidian.

22. ARCHAEOLOGICAL EVIDENCE.

i. Sir J. H. Marshall, K.C.I.E., Director-General of Archeology, India says :—(Cambridge History, Volume I, pages 612-615).

" With the palaeolithic peoples of India we are here scarcely concerned. Their rough-chipped implements have been found in large numbers in the southern half of the peninsula and in deposits, which indicate that countless centuries must have elapsed between their last appearance and the dawn of Vedic history, while the forms of the implements themselves, strikingly unlike those of the neolithic age, have suggested to some writers that their authors may not even have had an ethnical connection with the later inhabitants of the land. The neolithic races on the other hand are invested with a more immediate interest for the historian, not only because there are good reasons for supposing that some of the existing peoples of India—notably the Dravidians—are directly descended from them, but because this phase of civilization was preserved in some parts of the country until medieval and probably more recent times. The stone weapons and utensils which are specially characteristic of it are found scattered over a much wider area than the more rudimentary palæoliths, though mainly in regions where the trap-rock used specially in their manufacture abounds. They exhibit a remarkable variety, illustrated by at least a hundred distinct types, some of which belong to the polished, others to the unpolished class. With few exceptions, however, they are identical in form with similar objects from Western Asia and Europe, and this identity has led to the supposition that the Dravidian peoples, with whom the neolithic culture in India appears to have been peculiarly associated, once dwelt in the highlands of Western Asia and penetrated thence by way of Baluchistan into India ; and at first sight, the survival in Baluchistan of a Dravidian language, Brāhūī, would seem to support this view. Other linguistic considerations, on the other hand, have been thought to point to the conclusion that the Dravidians were indigenous in the Dakhan and spread thence over a part of Northern India.

" As the stone age passed gradually away in Northern India, it appears to have given place, not to an age of bronze, as it did in most parts of Europe, but to one of copper.

" At what date iron came to supplant copper in the north of India is uncertain, but literary evidence from Vedas seems to indicate that it was introduced in the second millennium B.C. It was about the same time too that it came into general use in Mesopotamia.

" In Southern India there was no copper age, and iron probably did not take the place of stone till about 500 B.C. Up to that time the Aryans of the north seem to have possessed no very distinct knowledge of the south of the Peninsula which was at once isolated and protected against invasion by the natural defences of the Vindhya hills and the trackless jungles of Central India, and when at last they penetrated through these barriers they found the Dravidian and other races in the south still in the neolithic stage of culture. The supposition that iron was first conveyed into Southern India by sea from Egypt has nothing to commend it."

ii. Professor Rapson says :—(Vol. I, page 56).

"The pre-historic archaeology of India has not attracted the attention which it deserves and many interesting problems connected with the earlier cultures and their relations to the culture of the Ṛg-Veda remains to be solved ; but there is a general agreement as to the succession of cultural strata in Northern and Southern India. The discoveries of ancient implements seem to prove that in the North, the Stone Age is separated from the Iron Age by a Copper Age ; while in the South no such transitional stage has been observed—implements of stone are followed without a break by implements of iron. Bronze, it appears, is not found anywhere in India before the Iron Age. If these facts may be held to be established, we must conclude that the chief metal of the Ṛg-Veda *ayas* (Latin *aes*) was copper ; and the absence of a Bronze Age in India would seem to indicate that the earlier inhabitants were still in the Stone Age at the time when the Aryans brought with them the use of copper. Iron was probably not known in the age of Ṛg-Veda ; but undoubtedly occurs in the period immediately following, when it is known to the Yajurveda and Atharvaveda as *śyāma-ayas* or 'black copper'. Its use was introduced by Indo-Aryan colonizers into Southern India where the Stone Age culture still prevailed.

"Described in its simplest terms, the earliest history of India is the story of the struggle between two widely different types of civilization, an unequal contest between metal and stone."

a. South Indian Rākṣasas mentioned in the Rāmāyaṇa.

Archaeological deposits and remains never mislead and are more reliable than theories based necessarily in great part on assumptions. We have had a plethora of theories about the original home and the ethnic relationships of the proto-Dravidians. But, wherever they came from, there seems to be now no doubt that the Dravidian inhabitants of Southern India were in the Neolithic stage of culture, most of them probably but little removed from the condition of barbarians, till about the latter half of the first millennium B.C. This is entirely in accordance with the accounts preserved in the Rāmāyaṇa of the peoples whom Agastya and Rāma encountered in Southern India. Agastya had a long struggle in the South with Ilvala and Vātāpi, chiefs of cannibal tribes. In the middle of the Dakhan, Rāma had frequently to war with Rākṣasas whose king Rāvaṇa lived in Ceylon. The following are some of the synonyms for Rākṣasa in the Sanskrit Dictionaries :—

1. *kauṇapa-* 'eater of corpses.'
2. *kravyād, kravyāda-* 'eater of raw flesh.'
3. *āsrapa-* 'drinker of blood.'
4. *yātudhāna, yātu-* 'cannibal.'

More than seven millions of the population of this Presidency still continue to be carrion-eaters.

b. The Telugu Māls.

Māli, Sumāli, and Mālyavān are the names of three brothers, Rākṣasa chiefs—mentioned in the Rāmāyaṇa—of whom the last was Rāvaṇa's maternal grandfather ; Dhānyamālā was one of Rāvaṇa's wives and Jambumālı was one of his sons ; Mēghamālī and Mahāmālī are the names of two of the lieutenants of Khara, half-brother of Rāvaṇa. Vasiṣṭha married a Caṇḍāla girl named Akṣamālā. So many names ending in or containing *māl* or *mālī* would seem to indicate that *māla* was a tribal name or a title of distinction among Rākṣasas which has survived to the present day in the name Mālas of the Telugu country. If this surmise is correct we might also infer that Janasthāna was in the delta of the Godāvarī or there abouts; it was on the banks of the Godāvarī that Rāma fought with Khara and his fourteen thousand.

23. AN EPIGRAPHIST'S VIEW OF PRIMITIVE DRAVIDIAN CULTURE.

MR. H. KRISHNA SASTRI.

Brāhmī inscriptions in the Pāṇḍya country.

The views entertained by epigraphists on the question of early Dravidian civilization, based, as they are, almost wholly on lithic records, must be assigned a prominent place in all discussions about this question.

Till recently the earliest indigenous records available in the Tamil country did not take us further back than the 7th or the 8th Century A.D. During the last fifteen years, however, certain cave inscriptions have been brought to light which are all in Brāhmī characters of the early Aśokan type. These inscriptions have till now been found in eleven different localities in the districts of Madura and Tinnevelly and the number of inscriptions copied is over forty. They have resisted all attempts at interpretation, but epigraphists appear to be of opinion that though written in Brāhmī they must contain a strong Dravidian element. In a paper[1] read at the Poona Conference of Orientalists, introducing these inscriptions to the public, Rao Bahadur H. Krishna Sastri, Government Epigraphist for India says :—

" Our present knowledge of the history of southernmost part of the Indian Peninsula, derived mostly from indigenous inscriptions does not extend farther back than the

1. Pages 327—348 of Volume containing Proceedings and Transactions of the Poona Oriental Conference.

7th Century A.D. The possibility, however, of the existence of a long-standing earlier civilization and dominion is suggested by references to the kingdoms of Cōḻa, Pāṇḍya, and Kērala-putta bordering on that of the great Mauryan emperor Aśoka and to the mutual commercial relations said to have existed between the countries of Pāṇḍu (*i.e.*, Pāṇḍay) and Rome, as gathered from the statements of early foreign travellers. Nearer home we have the further evidence of the epics Rāmāyaṇa and Mahābhārata and a host of literary references including those of Pāṇini, Kātyāyana, Kālidāsa and Varāhamihira which lead to the same conclusion. Still the data for the existence of a purely Dravidian civilization distinct from the now-existing super-imposed Aryan element of literary, political, religious and scientific thought, is but indefinitely postulated and the evidence in proof thereof, scantily put forth. We are asked to look for traces of the ancient Drāviḍas of Southern India in the Dasyus, Kirātas, Vyādhas and Śabaras of Sanskrit literature whose modern representatives are again assumed to be the hill tribes of the present day with their crude customs and manners. It is not possible to believe that the Dravidian civilization which, if it deserved that name at all, must have counted in it elements such as civil administration, military organization, commercial adventure, religious forecast, and scientific enquiry should have dwindled down into nothing but fetishism and ill-bred lawlessness of the aboriginal of Southern India. Much less would it be reasonable to work back from the rude elements of aboriginal institutions to arrive at the essentials of the Dravidian civilization. It appears therefore more scientific to suppose that the Dravidian elements of civilization that existed at the time when the Aryans came into Southern India were at once recognised by the conquerors and fast became assimilated with those of the superior and superimposed civilization of the latter the two races becoming entirely mixed up and the uncivilized element in society which must have existed even then, finding shelter only in mountains and forests as it does to this day. Consequently I understand that the elements of Dravidian civilization, if any, have to be worked out purely from literature and possibly also from a comparative study of civilized institutions both Nothern and Southern. Epigraphical research too, in my opinion, contributes a little in this direction as will be recognized in the present paper dealing with the natural caverns and Brāhmī inscriptions of Southern India. Before proceeding to give the preliminary readings of these Brāhmī records and discussing their importance as regards the Dravidio-Aryan elements that may be contained in them, I would try to acquaint the reader with a general description of these very interesting monuments—the natural caverns so called...

"Who were the authors of these beds and Brāhmī inscriptions? Firstly, it is useful to inquire whether, previous to their occupation by the authors of these beds and inscriptions, however they might be, there had been others who were using them. Secondly, whether the beds and the inscriptions were contemporaneous. The late Rai Bahadur V. Venkayya was of opinion that the inscriptions and beds were synchronous, and we may accept his view since stone beds have been noticed in the Buddhistic caves of Bhājā, Kudā, Jannār, Ajaṇṭa and Koṇḍivte and since Brāhmī inscriptions in question are sometimes found written on the beds themselves, as already observed. As regards the first question, I may refer to Mr. Parker who, in describing the ancient temples of Ceylon, makes elaborate references to thousands of natural caverns or rockshelters which formed once the abodes of the wild Vaeḍḍas, who, he believes, abandoned them in pre-Chiristian times, just when Buddhists entered Ceylon, and converted these into residences for their ascetics. The Vaeḍḍas themselves are traced by him to the Cōḻa and

Pāṇḍyan Tamils. It is not improbable that as in Ceylon the natural caverns in the Madura and Tinnevelly Districts may have been occupied in pre-Buddhistic times by indigenous aborigines who were perhaps the ancestors of the Vaeddas of Ceylon or similar wild hill tribes. One point of difference, however, between these caverns and those of Cyelon is in the provision made in the former for stone beds for the use of the Buddhist occupants. Another is that the language of the **Brāhmī** inscriptions on these caverns, far from being pure Buddihistic Pāli as in Ceylon, seems to be a mixed dialect in use among the then inhabitants of Southern India, perhaps the Vaeḍḍa ancestors spoken of above. Certain peculiarities of the alphabet too which are noticed below may also distinguish these records from the almost contemporaneous Pāli records of Ceylon."

The Dravidian element in the Brāhmī inscriptions.

The following are given in Mr. Krishna Sastri's paper as Dravidian words occurring in the inscriptions :—

1. *koṭu kuṭū*, *kuṭupitā*, *koṭupita*, *kotupitō*.—The last three of these are compared with the Tamil *koṭṭuvittān* ' caused to be cut', and also with Childer's Pāli verb *koṭṭiēti*.

2. *nāṭu* occurring in Ivañjenāṭu, Euminaḍu are stated to be ' apparently Tamil'. *Nāṭu* ' a district.'

3. *Ūra*, *ora* or *ura* occurring in Erukkoṭura, Koṭiora etc., are equated with the Tamil *ūr* ' a village."

4. *uṭaiyu*.—It is stated that this may correspond to *uṭaiyāṉ* ' a chief'.

5. *ēri*, *ēri* in Tamil means ' a tank '.

These identifications are suggested by Mr. Krishna Sastri with reserve.

24. The real question at issue is between North and South, not between Aryan and Dravidian.

It will thus be apparent that even in the earliest period of South Indian history there was a mixture of Aryan and Dravidian and as we go further and further back the assumed primitive Dravidian culture recedes further and further from us like a willo ' the wisp. Nevertheless, many writers assume such a culture partly on *a priori* grounds and partly on the evidence of words instanced by Bishop Caldwell and others. We, however, saw on what slender basis it has been assumed that India was trading with the Euphrates valley in the 14th century B.C. and even earlier. We may safely leave out of account such extravagant estimates of the antiquity of South Indian culture and confine our attention to sober views like those for instance of Professor J. Kennedy, who after a detailed examination of the data available, comes to the conclusion that there is no literary or archaeological evidence of any trade between India and the West prior to the 7th century B.C.

It will be seen that Prof. J. Kennedy while narrowly scrutinizing the evidence for early commercial intercourse accepts without question Bishop Caldwell's statement that *oryza, tuki, algum* etc., are Dravidian names. Hence he infers that the Indian merchants at Nippūr must have come from the west coast of India, which does not exclude the possibility of their having come from Dravidian ports ; for, how could the articles traded in have had Dravidian names, it they had not been brought from Dravidian ports ?

The ports of Barygaza and Suppāra with which Babylonia traded in the 5th and 6th centuries B.C. are unfortunately outside the limits of what is now regarded as Dravidian India and the theory of the articles having had Dravidian names cannot be supported unless it be shown that these ports were within such limits in those early times by interpreting the ' ancient Tamil Tradition about *Pañca Drāviḍiam* so as to include Mahārāṣṭra and Guzarat. We can now see the full significance and import of Dr. Barnett's Statement, (already quoted).

" Long before the beginning of the Christian Era, the Dravidian south had developed a considerable culture of its own, and its inhabitants had developed themselves into power ful Kingdoms, some of which carried on a thriving trade with western Asia, Egypt and later with the Greek and Roman Empires. The chief of these were the three Tamil Kingdoms, the Āndhras, Kaliṅga and the Mahārāṣṭra." He includes Mahārāṣṭra under Dravidian Kigndoms and appends the following foot-note—

The Tyrians apparenty imported thence ivory, apes and pea-cocks (*Tamil tōkai,* Gr: *Ταως.*) as we know from I, Kings, X-22 and II Chronicles, IX-21. Somewhat later we find India—to a large extten Southern India—exporting pepper (*πεπερι,* Tamil *pippalī*), rice (*ορυξα* Tamil *arici*) ginger (*ξιγγιβερις* Tamil *iïci-vēr*) and cinnamon (*καρπιου,* Tamil *Karrupu* or *Kārppu*) besides specious stones, coral, pearls, cloth, muslin, silk, tortoise-shell etc. See J. Kennedy J. R. A. S. 1898, pages 241 ff.

In this foot-note Dr. Barneet brings together all the Indian (supposed Dravidian) words on the strength of which a pre-historic Dravidian commerce is postulated. In regard to the Babylonian trade, the knows facts of the case are two :— 1. There was a maritime trade between Nippūr and India in the fifth and sixth centuries B.C. 2. About the same time articles of Indian provenance such as rice (*ορυξα*) and peacocks become known in Greece under (supposed) Dravidian names. On these the following superstructure is raised.

i. arici (*oryza*), tōkai (*toas*) etc. must have been some of the articles of trade between Nippūr and the Indian ports ;

ii. these ports were doubtless Barygaza and Suppāra, the former of which was trading with Nappūr in the time of the Periplus ;

iii. the articles with (supposed) Dravidian names were transmitted from Nippūr to Greece ;

iv. the country about the ports must then have been peopled by Dravidians, an exceedingly probable supposition; as,

v. the country now called Gujarat and Mahārāṣṭra formed part of the traditional *pañca drāviḍam* of the ancient Tamils ; and as,

vi. the Dravidians must once have been in occupation of the whole of the west cosat and of western India as for north as the Panjab, as is clear from the Dravidian influences observable even in the Vedic idioms.

None of the items i to vi is a 'hoistorical fact' as we understand the phrase but all are inferences from assumed premises. It has been pointed out already that there is no Tamil tradition in regard to *pañca-drāviḍam;* that this Indo-Aryan phrase refers to sects of Brahmans, not to regions ; and that the supposed Dravidian influences in Indo-Aryan are really Indo-Aryan influences in Dravidian.

a The meaning of the terms Dravidian.

We now proceed to consider whether the words relied on in support of the existence of such trade since the 7th century B.C. are really native South Indian words or have been borrowed by South-Indian Dravidians from the speech of the Aryan or Aryanised immigrants from the North. Here it is necessary at the outset to guard overselves against the ambiguty of language, for many Dravidian scholars seem to think that if an idea or word, common to the Indo-Aryans and the South Indian Dravidians has no counterpart in the Indo-European languages outside India, then the Indo-

Aryans must have borrowed it from the Dravidian language which it is assumed as in the extract from Dr. Barnett's articles above, were spoken in the North and North-west when the Aryans arrived in India. The words ' Dravidian languages, are now applied to a family of languages having certain common characteristics and the vast majority of the speakers of which are confined to South India. This family includes the four cultivated languages dealt with in this book besides a number of minor dialects. This is the sense in which Dr. Barnett used the words and the Dravidian characteristics referred to by Professor Rapson as having been traced in Indo-Aryan idioms are characteristics as found in the Dravidian languages spoken at the present day. We must be careful to use the words ' Dravidian ' in this sense and no t in the indefinite sense of ' Pre-Aryan Indian'.

b. The original home and wanderings of the Indo-Germanic race (Wiros).

It was till recently generally thought that the oldest probable domicile of the Indo-Germanic rac e was the steppe country of Southern Russia[1] and that at some distant date unknown to us the Aryan or Asiatic Branch of the race the ancestors of the Iranians and the Indo-Aryans wandered eastwards from the original home, and were settled for sometime on the banks of the Jaxartes and the Oxus, the oasis of Khiva being probably one of the most ancient seats of the Asiatic Branch. Thence, still a united people, they appear to have followed the courses of these rivers into the high-lying country round Khokand and Badakshan, where they separated, one portion marching south, over the Hindu Kush into the valley of the Kabul, and thence into the plains of India ; and the other, westwards toward what is now Merv and

1. Sir G. A. Grierson's article in Vol. I. Census of India 1901. Also Imperial Gazetteer, Vol. I.

Eastern and the other, westwards toward what is now Merv and Persia. After the separation, the once common Aryan speech developed on two different lines and became, on the one hand the parent of the Indo-Aryan, and on the other hand, that of the Iranian family of languages.

A new theory in regard to the original home and the wanderings of the Indo-Germanic race which is rapidly gaining ground is expounded by Dr. P. Giles in Chapter III entitled 'Aryans' in Volume I of the Cambridge History of India. In this theory the original home is located in the area comprising modern Hungary, Austria and Bohemia and the route taken by the Eastern Banch is assumed to be across the Bosphorus or Dardanelles and across the plateau of Asia-Minor or along its fertile slopes on the south side of the Black Sea. The recently discovered inscriptions at Boghas Koi in Cappodocia and the tablets of Tel-el-Amarna appear to lend strong suport to this theory which appears to be rapidly supplanting the previous one.

c. North versus South.

Whatever was the original home of the race it is not denied that after separation from the Indo-Europeans, and later from the Iranians, the ancestors of the Indo-Aryan branch of the race must have sojourned in many places and must have developed new ideas by contact with alien races and made additions to their vocabulary. Such new ideas and words may have been evolved *ab intra* or may have been borrowed, or evolved *ab intra* in part and borrowed from others in part ; if borrowed they need not necessarily have been borrowed from the Drvavidians, supposing that Dravidian languages prevailed in the North and North-west when the Aryans arrived in the country. The supposition that they so previled rest wholly on the assumption that Dravidian charactreistics have been traced in Indo-Aryan idioms. The reasons for this assumption are examined in detail in the next chapter and the conclusion arrived at there is that what are called Dravidian characteristics in Aryan are really Aryan charactreistics in Dradivian, that in most of these characteristics, the present Dravidian languages present a dim and distorted image of Indo-Aryan, that the above assumption is due to mistaking the image to be the original and the original to be the image, and that therefore it cannot be held to have been established that the Dravidian languages were spoken in the North and the North-west when the Aryans entered India.

However this may be, the question we are corsidering in this chapter is somewhat different. The question here is whether there was a pre-Aryan South Indian civilization, that is to say, whether the primitive South Indian Dravidians -speaking languages which have since become Tamil, Malayā-lam, Kanarese, and Telugu—were in possession of certain ideas and culture at the time when Aryan or Aryanised tribes came from the North and settled among them, or borrowed the ideas and culture from the nothern tribes. The question is not between Aryan and non-Aryan, nor between Aryan and Dravidian, but between the North and the South. No idea or word can be claimed as belonging to the primitive Dravidian stock of the South which is known, or can be shown to have travelled from the North to Southern India during the Aryan period of Indian history, *i.e.*, after the Aryans had occupied Hindustan or even the Punjab.

In the discussions that follow, the notes given under each word should be taken as in continuation of the notes given in sections 14 and 15 above.

25. GREEK *oryza* SANSKRIT *vrīhi-s* THROUGH IRANIAN, OR DIRECTLY FROM IRANIAN.

Bishop Caldwell's assertion that the Greek *oryza* was the same as the Tamil *arici* is still being repeated though philo-logists and eminent scholars have more than once pointed out that the Greek word cannot be so derived. The Periplus of the Erythraean Sea does not mention rice as exported from the Tamil country but only from Barygaza (Broach) and the rice exported from this port is described in the Periplus as produced is Orissa and Ariake. Why should Bishop Caldwell assume that rice was likely to become known in Europe by its Tamil name?

In the 5th Edition of his Greek Etymology published in 1879 four years after the publiation of Bishop Caldwell's Dravdian Grammar (2nd Edition, 1875,) George Curtius says of *oryza* (page 575) :

" It is clearly a borrowed word and, as is recognised by Pott and Benfey, seems not so much directly to resemble the Sanskrit *vrihi-s* (*m*) in sound as to be an attempt at reprsenting a related Persian form which has a sibilant instead of *h*............................... Pictet gives the Afghan *urishi* which also has a vowel in the place of *v*. The Greek by-form *oryda* coms nearer to Armenian *birinz* and the modern Persian *biring* "

Skeat quoting Raverty gives (*vide* Etymological Dictionary of the English Language) the following Old Persian forms preserved in the Pushtu (Afghan) :—*wrijzey*, *wrijey* 'rice' ; *wrijza'h* ' a grain of rice'.

There is a discussion on the point in Watt's Commercial Products of India (page 825) :—

In spite of the temptation to derive the Arabic *alruzz*, *aruzz*, *uruzz*, *wiz*, etc., from the Tamil *arici* modern philogogists are agreed that they cannot be so derived, but come from the Old Persian word *virinzi* or *virinza*, the modern equivalent of which is *biring*. Sir C.J. Lyall states that *virinza* is exactly the equivalent we should expect of the Sanskrit word for 'rice' *vrīhi*, and the names point to the time when the two branches of the Aryan race dwelt together and developed the respective pecularities of their language from a common or original tongue. The Persians did not borrow the cultivation of rice from the Indians ; the plant existed in the region where the two races dwelt together before their respective migrations."

Indo-Germanic philologists tell us that the original Indo-Germanic palatal medial aspirate *-gh-* had become *zh-* in the primitive Aryan period and that this latter sound became *-h-* in Sanskrit through an intermediate stage *-jh-* while it became *-z-* in Iranian and was further changed into *-d-* in Old Persian (Brug : I Ss. 396-402). They also tell us that the original Indo-Germanic velar medial aspirate *-gh-* became *-jh-* in the primitive Aryan stage and that both these latter sounds became de-aspirated in Iranian thus becoming *-g-* and *-j-* while in Sanskrit *-gh-* remained unaffected and *-jh* became partly *-h-* and partly *-j-* (Brug: I. S. 462).

Thus the Greek by-form *orynda* referred to by Curtius must have arisen from an Old Persian form **virinda* (Iranian * *virinza* or **virinzi*).

The followng table gives a number of Aryan words having *-h-* or *-j-* Sanskrit, *-z-* in Iranian and *-d-* in Old Persian. The words *vrihi, wrizey, *virinzi, birnj, virinda,* which are on all fours with the words in the table must also have been derived from primitive Aryan.

Sanskrit.	Iranian	Old Persian.	Remarks.
1. *aham*	*arem*	*adamt*	The 1st pers : pron : sing: Brug: III. S. 439).
2. *hasta*	*zazta*	*dasta*	'The hand' (Brug: III. S. 263).

Sanskrit.	Iranian		Old Persian.		Remarks.
3. *jrayah* (extent)	*zrayas*		*drayah* 'the *draya* sea'		(Brug : I. S. 402.
4 *josa* '*favour*'	*zaosa* 'favour'		*dauster* 'friend'	do	do
5. *dehī*	*uz-daeza*		*dīda*		(Brug. I : S 405).
6 *gūhati* 'hides'	*gaozaiti* 'hides'		*gaudaya* 'hide'	(Imper- ative)	do do
7. *vrīhi*	*wrijzey* *wrijey*	Pushtu	*biring* * *virinda*		'*rice*'
	oryza	Greek	*orynda* *birinz*		*Greek.* Armenian

The net result of the discussion is :—

i. that rice was not exported from the Tamil country even so late as the beginning of the Christian era, when there was direct trade between the Malabar coast and Egypt. If rice were exported to Babylonia or European countries from the Malabar ports in earlier times coast-wise, an improbable supposition, it is not necessarily the Tamil name of the article that would have found entrance into the European languages, but the name current in the entre-pots ;

ii. that there is, therefore, nor reason to suppose that the European and Arabic names for rice ' were derived from its Tamil name, and

iii. that the Sanskrit, Iranian, Pushtu and Old Persian names for ' rice ' appear to be derived from a primitive Aryan name *vrizhi* or *vrizhi* in complete accordance with established sound-laws.

---

*Note.—The change of *-z-* to *-d-* is also very common in Singhalese and occurs occasionally in Telugu and Marāṭhī.

Professor P. T. Srinivasa Aiyangar's assumption that *vrīhi* is the Sanskritized form of Tamil *arici* and Dr. Kittel's surmise that it is derived from Dravidin *variki* must now be abandoned.

26. TAMIL *arici* < SANSKRIT *vrīhya* OR ARYAN *vrijhya*.

1. It appears to have been assumed by every body that has taken part in the discussion of the relation between *arici* and *oryza* that the former is an original South Indian word ; but this is altogether improbable.

2. The other South Indian words for 'rice' *i.e.*, the husked grain, are :—Tamil *ari ;* Mal. *: ari ;* Kan. ; *akke* Tuḷu *aoi, akki ;* Koḍagu *ikki ;* Tel. *biyyamu.*

3. The names for unhusked paddy are—Tamil, Malayāḷam, Kanarese, *nel* or *nellu;* Tel.; *vari* (sing). *vaḍlu* (plural); Singh ; *wī*. The form *vari* occurs in Tamil poetry and in Malayālam, but in the latter it means wild uncultivated paddy. *Navara* in Malayāḷam means variety of quick-growing paddy.

4. Of these *ṉel, ṉellu, ṉavara, navira* containing an initial *ṉ* appear to have a different etymology from the rest and will be considered in the next para. Singh : *wi* and the Tam-Mal. and Tel. *vari* obviously arise from an apocopated *vrihi, vrī* becoming *wī* and *varī* ; at least this is the derivation which Dr. E. Euller gives of the Singh : *wī* (I.A. Vol. XI, page 213). The word *varī* appears to have also existed in Old Persian in the sense of 'paddy'; for *sapīd vari* (Sanskrit '*śvēta vrīhi*) 'white rice' is the name of' husked rice' in Modern Persian.

5. Of the names for the husked grain in Kanarese, *akki* arises from the usual Kan. substitution of *-k-* for the palatal in *arici,* while the Mal. and Tuḷu *ari* arises from the weakening of *-c-* into *-y-*, and the ultimate loss of the last syllabel in *arici.* Koḍagu *ikki* must have arisen from an original *irici.*

6. The Tamil *arici* and *irici* and the Telugu *biyyamu* though entirely dissimilar in appearance are, it is suggested, derived from the same word *vrīhya or Vrījhya*, secondary formatives meaning 'arising or produced from *vrīhi* or *vrījhi*', the unhusked grain.

7. The conjunct consonant *vri*—being unfamiliar to Dravidian, *vri*-will be simplified into *vī*- or *ri*- by the elision of one of the consonants, or converted into *vari*- or *viri*- by the insertion of a glide vowel between.

8. It is a rule in Tamil that final *-ya* may be replaced by *-i*. Thus *vrījya* will have given rise to *rici*, and *varici* as all palatal sounds are represented by only one character in Tamil, *viz.*, *-c-* pronounced *-s-* when single. The former of these forms with a prothetic vowel will become *arici* and *irici* (=*akki* and *ikki*), and the latter is apparently the original of the literary Tamil word *valci* 'food'. The existence of two different prothetics *-a-* and *-i-* cleary shows that the original form was *rīci* and that it has been differently treated by the two dialects Tamil and Koḍagu. The Telugu *biyyamu* is obviously derived from *vrīhya* or *vrijhya* (> *viyya*, *biyya*)."

9. Another secondary derivative mentioned in the Nighaṇṭus is *vraiheya* in the sense of 'place for *vrīhi*' or 'connected with *vrīhi*' which may ultimately become shortened into *bayya* and *baiy*. The name of paddy straw which is *bai* in Tuḷu and *vai* in Tamil-Malayāḷam as in *vai-k-kōl* (paddy stalks) appears to be derived from *baiyya* or *baiy ;* these names may also be derived from *vari*. In any case the initial labial of *bai* and *vai* shows their unmistakable cousinship with the Singhalese *wi*.

Has the Tam-Mal, *vaya-l* 'a paddy field' any connexion with *baiyya*<the Taddhita *vraiheya ?* Dr. Gundert's Malayāḷam Dictionary connects this *vayal* with the Kan. and Tel. *bayal*, *bayilu*, *bayalu* which are entirely different

words meaning 'outside, publicity, open space etc.' and corresponding to Tam-Mal. '*veḻi*' and Sanskrit '*bahir.*'

27. DRAVIDIAN *nel* OR *nellu*<SANSKRIT *nīvāra.*

1. It will be noted that Tamil, Malayāḷam and Kanarese which used *nel* or *nellu* as the name of the unhusked grain (paddy) are employing *arici, ari, akki* to indicate the husked grain (rice). The words *nel, nellu, navara* and *navira* irresistibly remind one of the Vedic *nīvāra* whatever may be the origin of this word. It probably signified at first paddy growing wild without cultivation in swamps.

2. A fifth form *neṟu* is suggested by the Tuḷu *neji* 'paddy'; for in a certain class of words final *-ji* or *-ji* in Tuḷu corresponds to *-ṟu* in Tamil and Kanarese.

Thus Tuḷu[1]		appears as
	1. *āji* 'six'	*āṟu*
	2. *kañji* 'calf'	*kaṉṟu, karu*
	3. *toj* 'appear'	*tōṉṟu, tōru*
	4. *baji* 'empty'	*vaṟu, bāri,*
	5. *mūji* 'three'	*mīṉṟu, mīṟu*

This justifies the inference that corresponding to Tuḷu *neji* there must have been a form **neru* 'paddy' in Tamil and Kanarese which must have been the original of the modern *nel* and *nellu.* We thus have the following sequence of successive forms *nīvāra, navara, naviṟa,* **neṟu, nellu, nel.*

28. GREEK *πεπερι*—SANSKRIT *pippalī* THROUGH IRANIAN.

According to Watt's Commercial Products of India "this is a perennial shrub, native of the hotter parts of India from Nepal eastwards to Assam, the Khasia hills and Bengal, westwards to Bombay, and southwards to Travancore, Ceylon and Malacca. As manifesting antiquity of knowledge

1. *Vide* foot-note at page XVI of the Preface to Dr. Kittel's Kanarese English Dictionary.

it may be mentioned that the Sanskrit name *pippalī* was originally given to this plant and only within comparatively recent times it has been transferred to blackpepper. Long-pepper is mentioned by Pliny and is referred to in the Periplus."

Long-pepper is mentioned in the Periplus under the name *peperi makron* as one of the exports from Barygaza (Broach) while the pepper exported from the Malabar ports is referred to simply as *pēperi* (Ind : Ant : VIII pages 143 and 147). Long-pepper is also called *māgadhī* (native of Magadha) in Sanskrit which name is reproduced in an old Tamil Nighaṇṭu, Cūḷāmaṇi. The name *pippalī* occurs in the vocabularies of Tamil, Malayāḷam, Kanarese and Telugu ; it exists also in the form ' *tippali* in the popular dialects of the first three, *t*-being substituted for the initial *p*- in popular speech as the result of dissimilation, just as the Sanskrit *pipīlikā* ' an ant ' becomes *kupullika* in Pāli.

Brugmann says " Old Iranian had only *-r-* as opposed to the Armenian-European *-r-* and *-l-* and Sanskrit *-r-* and *-l-*. Old Persian had *-l-* only in loan words "[1] (Vol I, page 209).

In the Linguistic Survey of India we find—" Most European languages possess an *-l-* as well as an *-r-*........

In Sanskrit *-l-* is used in many words where other languages have *-r-* and *vice versa*. The Old Iranian dialects did not possess and *-l-* and its irregular use in Indo-Aryan makes it probable that we are face to face with an alien

---

1. Dr. P. Giles says (Cambridge History of India Vol. I, page 741) "In India *-r-* is often found in words where the languages of the same stock in Europe show *-l-* ; *-l-* also, though not as frequently, found for *-r-* ; in the Old Persian of the achaemenid inscription *-l-* is found only in two foreign words and has otherwise been entirely replaced by *-r-*."

influence. Now it seems almost certain that such an influence can only have been Dravidian. The change of *-r-* to *-l-* is, as has long ago been pointed out by Bishop Caldwell, quite common in Dravidian Languages (Vol. I page 279)".

Bishop Caldwell says " In the Dravidian family this interchange of *-r-* and *-l-* is one of very common occurrence. Sometimes *-l-* is corrupted into *-r-* ; but in large number of cases *-r-* appears to be the original and *-l-* the corruption.... This change of *-r-* to *-l-* though not uniform is an exceedingly common one, and one which may be regarded as characteristic of colloquial Tamil. It is common in Malayāḷam also. Seeing that a tendency to change *-r-* to *-l-* exists and operates in Dravidian languages, especially in Tamil, it may be concluded that in those ancient roots which are the common property of several families of languages and in which an interchange appears to exist between *-r-* and *-l-*, *-r-* was the original and *-l-* the altered sound that is, that the form with *-l-* is less ancient than the form with *-r-*." C.D.G. page 56.

The change of the *-l-* of *pippalī* into *-r-* of *πεπερi* shows that the Greeks must have first become acquainted with the article through the Iranians at a time when there was no *-l-* in the Iranian alphabet (*c. f.* Weber I.A. Vol. II, pages 146, 147) ; that is before the Achaemenian (500 B.C.) or Old Persian period when they had learnt to tolerate *-l-* in loan words. As there do not appear to have been any exports of ' longer-pepper ' from the Malabar ports even so late as the time of the Periplus it would seem that *pippalī* was not a southern word but a North Indian word which travelled south along with the *pippalī* industry, *i.e.*, the cultivation of *pippalī* and the collection of *pippalī* fruits as forest produce. The Greeks had become acquainted with the article long, long before South Indian began to export it.

29. TAMIL *miḷaku* < SANSKRIT *marīca*—PRAKRIT *mirc*.

But what about *piper nigrum* which was for long ages the special product of Malabar and to secure the trade in which the Greeks and the Moors vied with each other? Long-pepper used chiefly in medicine is not much in evidence before the public, while 'black-pepper' enters into the daily food of the people. What is the Tamil-Malayāḷam name for the latter? And was this name imposed upon the world and adopted in other languages as one would expect would have been the case under the circumstances? The Sanskrit name for it is *marīca* and various *tadbhavas* from it are in use in Northern India, such as, *gul-mise*, *miri*, *miri-cung*, etc. Telugu, as usual, adheres closely to the Sanskrit form, and has *miriyamu*, *miremu* (singular); *miriyālu* (plural). Kanarese has *menasu*, *meḷasu* and *melasu*; Tuḷu *munaci*; and Tamil-Malayāḷam *miḷaku*, thus showing the difficulty experienced in the Dravidian country in pronouncing a North Indian *-n-*. Having regard to Bishop Caldwell's rule in regard to the interchange of *-r-* and *-l-* the Tamil form is obviously drived from, and is later than, the Sanskrit form.

In old Tamil black-pepper was also called *kari*, a word not in popular use at present except in the sense of 'pungent condiments' in which 'black-pepper' or 'capsicum' is a chief ingredient; this word appears to be derived from the Sanskrit *khara* 'sharp, pungent' which is Indo-Germanic in origin.

There is also a Vedic root marc **mṛc*[1] which means 'hurt, injure' and the participle '*marcayat*' means 'keen

---

1. *yat kṣureṇa marcayatā supeśasā vaptrā vapasi keśān* 'When you remove the hair with a sharp burnished 'razor' (Ekāgnikāṇḍa II-1).

sharp' ; the word *marīca* appears to be connected with this root. The Avesta has a root *mark* (*mərəñch*) 'kill.'

It is claimed by Dravidian scholars that *pippalī* is a Dravidian word on the *a priori* ground apparently that a Dravidian product should have a Dravidian name. But the Greek form *πέπερι* is not synchronous with the pre-Aryan period of Indian history, for if the Iranians had then spread over Iran as far as the Persian Gulf it is natural to presume that the Indo-Aryans also had spread over a considerable portion of Hindustan. Further when the word came to South India the true Dravidians here were unable to pronounce it correctly and substituted *ti* for *pi-*.

Throughout India at all times *pippalī* meant only 'long-pepper', and this, which gave rise to the Greek name *πεπερι* appears to have been the only pepper known to the Greeks at first. Black-pepper '*piper nigrum*' was obviously unknown outside Malabar at first. When subsequently this article became known to the Greeks the name *πέπερι* appears to have been transferred to it, *pippalī* becoming the Greek *peperi makron* thereafter. The names *miḷaku, marīca* or *mirach* never got adopted in Europe.

It would seem from the facts stated above that *pippalī* and *mirch* are North Indian words that have been adopted in South India in the Aryan period of Indian history. The first Greek writer to mention pepper belonged to the 4th century B.C. There is no evidence that the primitive South Indians knew of its properties or cared to cultivate it prior to the arrival of the Aryans in Malabar.

30. TAMIL *karappa, karuvā*<ARABIC *qarfah*<GREEK *Karphea*.

Ctesias's Carpion.—Ctesias had exceptional opportunities for acquiring knowledge about India since he resided for seventeen years at the Persian court as physician to the king

Artaxerxes Mnemon. He has, however, been condemned as a deliberate liar not only by the consentient voice of antiquity but also by the generality of the learned in modern times. The following is taken from an article (Chapter XVI) by Mr. E. R. Bevan, M.A., in the Cambridge History of India (Vol. I, page 397) :

"Ctesias apparently was a deliberate liar. Modern writers urge that some of his monstrosities—his dog-faced men, his pygmies and so on—can be paralleled by the statements in old Indian books. This shows that Ctesias was not above saving himself the trouble of fresh invention when statements sufficiently sensational were furnished him by other.......... One of his most monstrous animals, the creature as large as a lion, with a human face, which shoots stings out of the end of his tail, called in the Indian language, says Ctesias, *martikhora*—as a matter of fact the word is Persian—Ctesias affirms that he had himself seen, as one was sent as a present to the Persian King. This gives the measure of the man. No doubt his wildest statements about the fauna and flora of India can, if sufficiently trimmed, be made to fear a sort of resemblance to something real, but it seems ingenuity wasted to attempt to establish these connexions."

Bishop Caldwell, has, however, exercised his ingenuity to establish such a connexion between *karpion* and the Tamil-Malayāḷam *karappa* (*-t-tailam*) 'cinnamon oil' and *karuvā-* (*p-paṭṭai*) 'cinnamon bark.' It will be noted that Ctesias's *karpion* is on all fours with his *martikhora*, an imaginary thing, having an imaginary Indian name stated to have been presented to the Persian King and to have been seen personally by Ctesias.

Ctesias was a physician, and a physician to a king and a man of talent. He would certainly have known cinnamon —Greek *karphea* (dry twigs)—which the Greeks called *kinnomomon* after the Phoenicians. He does not use either of these words in connexion with the Indian tree exuding the fragrant oil, but distinctly says that the Greeks called it *myroroda* (unguent roses) and his description of the oil refers only to its extra-ordinary smell and fragrance and seems to show that it was prized only as an unguent. There is nothing in it to suggest pungent taste. Bishop Caldwell's assumption that Ctesias referred to cinnamon oil and that his glowing description applied to the coarse, inferior Malabar trees which are very poor in oil is hardly justifiable. *Khara* 'rough, hot, pungent' is an Indo-Aryan word of Indo-Germanic origin ; there is a Vedic word *kṣāra* ' acid, caustic, pungent ' of which the Prākṛt *khāra* and the Dravidian *kāram* ' pungency ' are *tadbhavas*. It has already been suggested that the Tamil *kari* ' black pepper, pungent condiments' appears to be derived from *Khara*. It is possible to form derivatives *karuppu, kārppu* ' pungency from *khara* and *kāru*,' but such derivatives are not now in use either in Tamil or in Malayāḷam. It will be shown in a latter part of this work that *-pu* the Dravidian suffix forming verbal nouns and abstract nouns is of Aryan origin. It will thus be seen that if, as is held by Bishop Caldwell, the words *karappa* and *karuvā* are of Indian origin, then their bases and terminations are both Aryan.

But they do not appear to be of Indian origin. Their most probable derivation is that given in Dr. Gundert's Malayalam-English Dictionary, *viz.*, that they are traceable to the Greek *karphea* through the Arabic *qarfah*. The most decisive argument against Bishop Caldwell's assumption is that cinnamon is not mentioned as an Indian export in the Periplus. China then supplied fine cinnamon and the trade in the coarse, inferior Malabar stuff had probably not yet begun. It is hardly likely as supposed by Mr. Schoff that the Malabar stuff was kept from the knowledge of the Greek traders and secretly sold to the Arabs.

31. TAMIL *iñci* < SANSKRIT *śṛṅgi* OR *Śṛṅgabera*.

The names given to this article in the Indian languages, especially Dravidian, are most instructive. Ginger was originally a special product of Malabar and is an indispensable requisite in every household either green or in a dry state. Green ginger is called *ārdrakam* 'moist, wet, liquefying' in Sanskrit and dry ginger *śuṣkārdrakam* or merely *śuṣkam* which is an Indo-German word meaning 'dry' (Brug : I sections 332, 413). There is also a Sanskrit root *śuṇṭh* 'purify, dry up, from which two derivatives are formed *śuṇṭhi* and *śuṇṭhyam* both of which are also used names of dried ginger.

In addition to these, there is the word *śṛṅgaveram*, Pāli *singivāram*, which is applied both to the green and the dry articles ; Skeat in his Etymological Dictionary of the English Language explains this word as "hornshaped from the horns on it."

It is well known that the Sanskrit *ārdra* has become *alla*[1] in some of the Prākṛts (P.P.G.S. 294) ; and *ārdraka* in the forms *alla*, *allamu* is in use in Telugu, Kanarese and literary Tamil in the sense of 'green ginger' ; the word appears to exist also in the northern vernaculars in the forms of *ādrak*, *āda*, *ālē*, *allam*, as the name of the plant.

Śuṇṭhī exists as *soṇṭī* in Telugu, *suṇṭ* in Kanarese and *cuṇḍi* in Malayāḷam and all these words mean 'dry ginger *cukku* is the form which *śuṣka* assumes in Tamil-Malayāḷam and also means 'dry ginger.' *Śauṇṭhi* appears also to exist in the northern vernaculars as *sōṇṭh*, *suṇḍh*, *suṇḍhi*, *suṇth*, *suṇṭh*.

1. C. F. Pāli *allaīvaro* 'having a wet *cīvara*'.

The above were the usual etymologies given of the various Indian names for 'green ginger' and 'dry ginger' till Drs. Gundert and Kittel appeared on the scene. Dr. Gundert derived *śuṇṭhī* from Dravidian *curuḷ* 'contract, shrivel up, shrink." Dr. Kittel pointed out that 'dry ginger' was called *cukku, cucca, cuccu, cuṇṭi, coṇṭi, coṉṟi* in Tamil and compared these words with the Dravidian root (*curka* Tamil *curuṅku*) 'contract, shrivel up, shrink'; the last six names are obviously derived from two different bases *śuṣka* and *śuṇṭhya*, but Dr. Kittle does not apparently note this and derives them all from one root. It is in view of these forms with an initial *ś*- or *c*- that Bishop Caldwell and Drs. Burnell and Gundert considered that the Tamil *iñci* must have had an initial *ś*- formerly, that the Sanskrit *śṛṅgabera* was an imitation of the (supposititious) Tamil *ciñcivēr* and that the European *zingiber* was derived from the Tamil name.

There is absolutely no reason to suppose, as Dr. Burnell did, that the Sanskrit Pandits converted *ciñcivēr* into *śṛṅgabera* with the object of disguising the Tamil origin of the word. There are several other plant and vegetable names in Sanskrit containing *śṛṅga* :

1. *karkaṭaśṛṅgī* name of a tree ;
2. *ajaśṛṅgī*, a plant having fruits like goats' horns ;
3, 4. *śṛṅgī, śṛṅgikā* which denote (a) a kind of medicinal plant (b) a kind of poison ;
5. *śṛṅgakāṇḍaḥ* ;
6. *śṛṅgakaḥ* ;
7. *śṛṅgajam* ;

Śṛṅgabera means 'horn shaped' or 'antler shaped' and aptly describes the root of the ginger plant ; in Singhalese *śṛṅgabera* has become *hingur*, later *ingur* ; and it is likely that the Tamil *iñci* is only a corrupt appocopated form of this word or of *Śṛṅgikā* or *Śṛṅgī*.

Tamil reduces the initial conjunct consonant *śṛ-* of Sanskrit words to *ś-* and ultimately elides it. Before adopting the words as its own, it also elides *s-* and *ś-* in most Sanskrit words as can be seen from the following table :—

Sanskrit	*Meaning*	*Tamil form.*
śramana	Buddhist mendicant	camana amaṇa
śrāvaṇa	Name of month	āvani
śroṇā	Name of a constellation.	ōnam
śraviṣṭhā	-do-	aviṭṭam
śreṣṭhī Pāli : sēṭṭhī	Foreman of a guild, a wealthy merchant	ceṭṭi ; eṭṭi, (title given by king).
śreṇi	A line, a row	
Pāli : niṣseṇi Telugu niccena	A ladder	ēṇi (a ladder)
śrotra	Revealed scriptures	ōttu
āśrita	Dependent (adj.)	āytam (a dependent letter)
mārgaśira	Name of a month	mārkali
sarṣapa Pāli : sāsapa	mustard.	Tam : aiyavi Tel : āvālu
sīsa	lead	īyam
śmaśru	hair	mayir
śmaśāna	a cemetery	mayāṉam
simhala Pāli : sihala	Ceylon	Īḻam
sahasra	one thousand	āyiram.

Sanskrit	*Meaning*	*Tamil form*
sneha	oil	ney
sūcī	a needle	ūci
sabhā	an assembly	avai
suparna	having beautiful features.	Uvana
samaya	fit time, opportunity	amaya
śulka	toll	ulku
sarpa (*sarap)	a snake	aravam
sandhyā	evening	anti
śāṭaka	cloth	āṭai

ālāpasallāpa intimate and familiar conversation : alavalāvu.

These instances might be multiplied indefinitely. Dr. Burnell's remarks extracted previously deserve consideration, but unfortunaretly the Periplus does not mention any exports of ginger from the Tamil country or from India. The cultivation of the plant, at any rate for export purposes, seems to have been of late growth and there is no valid reasons to postulate a suppositious *ćiñcivēr* especially as *allam*, *ćukku*, *suṇṭi* and *soṇṭi* are of Aryan origin. Probably the cultivation of the plant began only after the establishment of Aryan colonies in South India and taking all circumstances into consideration it looks as if the Tamil *iñci* is a corruption of the Sanskrit *śṛṅgī*, as the Singhalese *ingur* and *hingur.* are of *Śṛṅgabera.* Further the assumed loss of an initial *c*- or *ś*- is itself an admission that the word is foreign. Why should there be any loss in indigenous word to which people have long been accustomed? It is only in strange foreign words that such changes occur.

32. SANSKRIT *mayūra*, *nīvāra*, *agaru* NORTH INDIAN *jōwār*.

We are now in a position to decide definitely as to the claim for priority between (1) *mayūra* and *mayil* ' peafowl ',

(2) *nīvāra* and *nel* ' unhusked rice ' ; *agaru* and *akil* ' Aquilaria Agallocbum ' ; (4) *jowar* and *cōlam* ' Sorghum Vulgare.' The Sanskrit forms containing the liquid *ṛ* are clearly the earlier ones and the Tamil form containing *ḷ* are derived therefrom. In regard to *akil* however the contention of Bishop Cadwell must be conceded, *viz*, that it was the original of the Hebrew word *ahalim* or *ahaloth*, not the Sanskrit word *agaru* (C.D.G. Intro : Page 92), for it is well known that in Tamil an intervocal single *k* is not pronounced like the English *k* but nearly like the English *h* ; its exact sound is that of a deep guttaral spirant. Thus *pakaḻ* ' day-time,' *tōkai* ' a tail,' *vēkam* ' smell, ' *pākam* ' share ' etc. are pronounced nearly like *pahal*, *tōhai*, *vēham*, *pāham* etc., and the Tamil *aki* pronounced *ahil* is more likely to have given rise to the Hebrew *ahalim* than the Sanskrit *agaru* (which is *aguru*) pronounced as it is written though it may have been the original of the Tamil *akil*.

(*b*) Sanskrit *candana* ' sandalwood.'

The following is an extract from para 39 of McCrindle's introduction to his translation of the Periplus (I. A. Vol. VIII, page 15).

" 39. *Σανδαρακη* and *σασὰμιναξὺλ* Logos of Sandalwood and Sasama (*santatum album*) exported from Barygaza to the ports of Omana and Apologos (36).

Σαντάλινα is a correction of the Ms. reading *σαγάλινα* proposed by Salmasius. Kosmos Indikopleustes calls sandalwood *τξαδὰνα*. For *σασὰμινα* of the Ms., Mr. Stuckius proposed *σησὰμινα*—a futile emendation, since seasme is known only as a leguminous plant from which an oil is expressed, and not as a tree. But possibly red-saunders wood (*Pterocarpus santalinus*) may be meant."

There is no doubt that sandalwood is a special product of South India, about seven-eighths[1] of the world's supply being produced in Mysore ; in old times it must have been a monopoly of South India. Red-saunders too is confined to South India[2]. There is no mention of it either in the Periplus among the exports from South Indian ports ; but certain logs of wood are mentioned among the exports from Barygaza (Broach) which Salmasius by an emendation of the text takes to be *σανὰλῖνα* sandalwood. The real sandalwood is first mentioned centuries later by Kosmos Indikopleustes as *τξαδανα*. It is doubtful whether the Periplus really means sandalwood or red-saunders, by *Σανδαρακη* and *σασαμινn* mentioned among the exports from Barygaza ; having regard to the localities in which they are now produced there is no warrant for such an assumption.

Unless fresh evidence is forthcoming we must conclude that there were no exports of sandalwood logs from South India even so late as the beginning of the Christian era, when the country had become partly Aryanized.

Lastly *candana* cannot be a pure Tamil name ; for according to *Tolkāppiyam* I—62, no Tamil word can begin with *ca*.

(*c*) Hebrew *Almug*, *Algum*.

These words need not detain us long. *Almuggim* and *algummim* were brought to Solomon from Ophir as hewn timber in immense quantities and used for props ; the girth of sandal wood is not sufficiently large for such a purpose ; and as pointed out by Professor J. Kennedy few materials are less fitted than sandalwood for such a purpose. This appears to be also the opinion of other scholars. The identification of algum with sandalwood must therefore be given up.

---

1. Watt's Commercial Products, page 978.
2. *Ibid*, page 909.

It may be mentioned in passing that the Sanskrit *valguka* means also 'woop' generally.

It is unnecessary to stop here to consider Bishop Caldwell's suggestion that Sanskrit *valgu(ka)* is derived from the Tamil *aḻa-ku* or *aḷa-ku* 'beauty; these words seem to be related to the Sanskrit *alam-kṛ*, 'adorn'.

33. HEBREW *tuki*— GREEK *τ α ῶ ς* : OLD TAMIL *tōkai*.

(*a*) The identification of the Hebrew *tuk* (with the old Tamil *tōkai* 'a peacock was one of Bishop Caldwell's earliest, and by assuming a dialectic variety *togei* for the latter word he has connected the Arabic *ṭawas* Greek *τ α ῶ ς*, Latin *pavo*, English *peacock*) with the Tamil word. These relationships having been accepted by Professor Max Muller, all subsequent writers have assumed these equations as a matter of course and regard them as unassailable as propositions in pure mathematics. There are, however, insuperable objections to the identification. The meanings of *tōkai* and the connected words in the Dravidian languages are as follows :—

1. *Tamil, tōkai* : 'plumage, a tail, a peacok's tail, skirt or order of a cloth, a peacock.'
2. *Malayalam. tōka* : 'what hangs down, a tail.'
   toṅgal : 'frapery, plumage, pendulous ornament.'
3. *Kanarese. tōke* — 'anything that hangs down, a tail.'

sōge, sōgu : (1) 'the peculiar leaf of palms, sugarcane and the screw pine ;
(2) a peacock's feather or tail ;
(3) a ship's rudder ;
(4) a peacok.'

4. *Telugu. toka* : 'a tail.'

In Marāṭhī *sōgā* means 'the skirt of a garment, crailing on the ground.'

It will be seen from the above that *tōkai* usually means 'a tail' in Dravidian languages and that Tamil is the only language in which the word means 'a peacock,' *i.e.*, 'the bird with the tail,' and even here it is only in Old Tamil that has come down to us in poetical works of the early Christian centuries that the word means 'a male peacock' by a figure of speech. The corresponding word in Kanarese is *sōge* which means 'a tail' and 'a peacock.' In this language *sōge navil* 'a *navil* with a tail' means 'a peacock' as opposed to 'a pea-hen'; here also it is by a figure of speech that *sōge* has come to mean the male of the species.

Instances are given later on, of initial *s-* having become *-t-* in Tamil and one possible explanation is that the Dravidian *tōka* 'a tail' and the Kanarese *sōge* 'a peacock' have fallen together in the Tamil *tōkai.*

(*b*) It may be doubted, indeed, whether *tōkai* in the secondary sense of 'a peacock' ever got into ordinary speech. Another serious objection to Bishop Caldwell's identification is that the rendering *tōkai* should be *tūhi* in Hebrew characters, not *tūki.* For intervocal single *-k-* is, as explained by Bishop Caldwell himself, pronounced like *-h-* in Tamil (C.D.G. pages 23-24)[1] An exactly parallel case is that of the Tamil *akiḻ* (S. *agaru*) Aquilaria Agallocha which appears as *ahalim*, *ahaloth* in the Hebrew Text in the Proverbs, which Bishop Caldwell says should be derived from the Tamil *akil* and not the Sanskrit *agaru.*

(*c*) Pea-fowls are now plentiful in all the drier parts of India and abound in Gujarāt, Kach and Rajputāna. On would expect that it is the name current in Barygaza

1. Manimēkalai XIX-62 where *tōkai* means 'the male of the species.

or thereabouts that would travel with the bird to Babylonia. How does it happen that the Tamil name of the bird goes to the court of Solomon ? When it was believed that Ophir was in South India or thereabours and that Phoenicians and Solomon's servants voyaged down the Malabar coast once in three years it might have been accepted without question that Solomon's peacocks were procured from the Tamil country. It is now believed by most scholars that Opir was not in India. Mr. Schoff thinks that " the location of Ophir in India is impossible."[1] It is also certain that pea-fowls were procurable in Northern India. It is, therefore, *a priori* imporbable that the Hebrew *tūki* is derived from the Tamil name for ' peacock.'

For these reasons it is impossible to accept Bishop Caldwell's identification.

(*d*) In Chapter XVI of Volume I of the Cambridge History of India Mr. E. R. Bevan says :—

" The peacock which was introduced into Greece during the second half of the fifth century B.C. retained in his designations evidences both of his Indian origin and of the route—*via* the Persian empire—by which he had been conveyed (*Mysikos Oevis*) " (page 396). It is not merely the Indian origin that is involved here ; Bishop Caldwell's explanation of τ α ῶ ς is based on the assumption that the bird was procured from the Tamil country, the southernmost portion of the peninsula. Of course it does not occur to Mr. Bevan to call into question the usually accepted explanation of the Greek τ α ῶ ς and he reconciles the two explanations. It is, however, clear that the Greeks thought that the peacock was a native of Media, not of India. We have seen that *oryza* and *peperi* were derived by the Greeks from words current in Persia. Similarly Arabic *ṭawas*

1. Translation of the Periplus—p. 170.

and Greek might ταῶς have been derived from a name current in Media or thereabouts. The objections to Bishop Caldwell's derivation of these words from Tamil *tōkai* are :

1. There is no dialectic variety *togei* ; Bishop Caldwell transliterates intervocal single *-k-* by the character *-g-* but he admits that both in Tamil and in Malayāḷam intervocal single *-k-* is pronounced like *-h-* (C.D. G. p. 23).

2. He does not account for the initial cerebral of the Arabic word. It is hardly likely that the Arabic name is derived from the Greek word. It is thus clear that the original of the Hebrew *tūki* and the Greek ταῶς must be sought for outside the Tamil country.

(*e*) It may finally be pointed out that the root *to-* or *tu-* and the suffix *-ku-* of the base *tonu* have Aryan affinities, the suffx being a modification of the Aryan root *kṛ* ' to do.'

34. Conclusion.

What is known as Dravidian civilization is really the civilization of Aryan and Aryanized immigrants from the North.

We have now discussed most of the evidence relied upon in support of the assumed existence of a pre-Aryan material civilization in Southern India. This evidence consists merely of a number of European and Hebrew words claimed to be Dravidian and non-Aryan : *viz.*, *Oryza*, *gingiber*, *karpion*, *algum*, *tūki*.

The earliest reliable account of Soth Indian trade is furnished by the Periplus of the Erythrean sea, which may be taken to describe this trade as it existed in the first three centuries of the Christain era, South India, especially, the Tamil land, then appears as carrying on a direct maritime trade with Egypt, the chief exports from South India being black pepper and pearls of superior quality in great quantity, ivory, fine siks, spikenard from the Ganges, malabathrum transparent precious stores, diamonds, jacinths, tortoise shall etc. But this was in a period subsequent to the establishment of very many Aryan colonies in the south if not also to the Aryanization of the south and subsequent also to the establishment of a direct intercourse with Africa and the Red Sea coast by the discovery by Hippalus in the first century A. D. of the annual monsoons. In earlier times the trade of Southern India with foreign countries was carried on entirely by coasting vessels. The clay tablets unearthed in Babylonia disclose that in the 5th and 6th centuries B.C. there was a maritime trade between the west coast of India and that country, but this trade appears to have been carried on with the ports of Barygaza and Suppara and not with any ports in Dravidian India. Barygaza and Suppara were apparently entreports for the South Indian trade at the time.

1. *Oryza.*—From the Periplus we find that the only Indian port that exported rice in the first three centuries of the Christian era was Barygaza and that the Malabar ports did not export this commodity even after the establishment of direct trade with the Greeks. If we also remember that Malabar has now to import part of the rice required for her consumption, it will be seen how improbable it is that the South Indian name for rice should ever get known to the Greeks or get adopted in the Greek language. As a matter of fact philologists including Pott, Benfey, Curtius, Pictet and Skeat are agreed that the word *oryza,* which it may be noted in passing was in use in Greece even in the 5th century B.C., is from a lost Iranian word which is equivalent to the Sanskrit *vrīhi* according to the laws of letter change obtaining between the Indo-Aryan and Iranian languages. Thus the Sanskrit *vrīhi* is not a word coined on Indian soil but belongs to the stock of the words inherited by Sanskrit from the Indo-Iranian parent tongue.

The names for rice in use in the South Indian languages look like the *debris* of the Sanskrit *vrīhi* or vrijhi.

Telugu	.. *vari*	
Malayāḷam	.. *ari*	
Tamil	.. *arici*	
Kanarese	.. *akki*	(ariki—ariśi)
Kodagu	.. *ikki*	(iriki—irisi)

Dr. Kittel constructed out of these debris a supposititious '*varigi*' and asserted that the Sanskrit *vrīhi* was derived from this. This theory must now be given up in view of the fact that *vrīhi* must have had its origin in Central or Western Asia where the Indo-Aryans and the Iranians were living together. But was there a non-Aryan South Indian form *varigi*? If so, it is indeed surprising that the Indo-Iranians in Central or Western Asia and the Dravidians in South India should have independently hit upon two names for rice so nearly alike.

Further, Dr. Kittle's word does not account for the Telugu *biyyamu* which obviously is the Sanskrit secondary formation *vrīhyam*, nor for the *wī* of Singhalese, the *vai*, *bai* of Tamil and Tulu. There seems to be little doubt that the European names for 'rice' are derived from the lost Iranian *wrizey*, while the South Indian names are derived from the Sanskrit *vrīhya* or *vrījhya*.

The hypothetic form *varigi* of Dr. Kittel reminds one of the Telugu grains *variga* and *varaga* and the Tamil grains *varaku*, *kēḻvaraku* (*rāgi*). If these also are to be traced to the Sanskrit *vrīhi* (previously *vrītjhi* and *vrīghi*), as apparently they should, then South India must be poor indeed in indigenous grain names. Naturally so : for, as pointed out by Sir J. H. Marshall, when the North Indian Aryans at last broke through the barriers of hill and jungle that separated them from the Dekkan and penetrated in the South in the first millennium B.C., they found the South Indians in the neo-lithic stage of culture.

(*b*) *zingiber*:—The Periplus does not mention any exports of ginger from any Indian port at all. There is no mention of any Greek name for this commodity dating from the pre-Christian era. The trade in this commodity thus appears to have come into existence late. Drs. Gundert and Kittel mix up the various South Indian names of this article derived from three different roots of which *inci*, *cukku*, *cuṇṭi* are types and construct therefrom a hypothetical *Śīncivēr*, asserting that the Greek word '*ziggiberis*' is derived from this form and that the Sanskrit *Śṛṅgabera* was a pedantic modification of the same form. As pointed out above, there are undoubted Sanskrit names containing the conjunct *śṛ*- which Tamil has dropped when adopting the names and *Śṛṅgī* would have become *iñci* in the usual course in Tamil. The Greek name is apparently of late origin, dating long after the establishment of Aryan colonies in the South.

(*c*) *nīvāra* is another word of importance in this connection, of which *navira*, *navara*, *nel* and *nellu* are obvious corruptions and the three words *vrīhi*, *nīvāra* and *Śṛṅgabera* have an important bearing on certin aspects of South Indian cilivization. *Vrīhi* and *nīvāra* occur in the Vedas and *Śṛṅgabera* is also very old being found in Pāli in the form *Siṅgivèra*.

The representatives of *nīvāra* are found in four languages of Southern India, Tamil, Malayāḷam, Kanarese and Tuḷu; the representatives of *śṛṅgabera* are found in Tamil, Malayāḷam and Singhalese, while those of *Śuṣka* (dried ginger) an Indo-Iranian word, are found only in Tamil and Malayāḷam. The representatives of *vrīhi* exist only in Telugu, Kanarese, Tuḷu, Malayāḷam, Tamil and Singhalese. The popular names of these articles in other parts of India are generally derived from words admitted into Sanskrit in later times.[1] This fact seems to show that the people who

1. *Vide* names in Watts' Dictionary of Economic Products of India.

brought the above words to South India must have been in contact with the Nothern Aryans during Vedic times and must have separated from them before the latter had adopted other and later names for the articles.

(*d*) *karpion* :—The Cinnamon trees of Malabar appear to be of a very inferior kind and the main use to which their bark is now put appears to be to adulterate the Chinese bark[1]. The Periplus mentions no exports of Cinnamon from India. The Cassia leaf exported in the time of the Periplus, if any Malabar leaf was exported, must have been grouped under *Malabathrum*. This *Malabathrum* though exported from Malabar ports appears to have been a product of the interior[2] or to have come from outside India (Paras. 56, 63 and 65 of the Periplus). It is unlikely that Ctesias's glowing description has any reference to these inferior trees. The names *kaṟappu* and *karuvā* are not mentioned in the Periplus and appear to be very late reflexes of the Arabic names *kerfat* and *qartah* traceable to the Greek *kerphea* which is at least as old as the time of Herodotus and older than that of Ctesius. If the names *kaṟappu* and *karuvā* are Indian words, then they are of Aryan origin, for both the base *kaṟ*- 'sharp' and the suffix *-pu* are Aryan.

(*e*) *algum*.—There were no exports of sandalwood from any South Indian port at the time of the Periplus. There were exports of some wood from Barygaza which by an emendation of the text of the Periplus, have been understood to be sandalwood. Considering the distance of Barygaza from Mysore and the Western Ghats, the places of production of sandal, it is unlikely that the wood exported from Barygaza was sandalwood. As pointed out by Professor J. Kennedy

1. P. 315 *Ibid*.

2. "All brought from countries further east" according to McCrindle.

sandalwood is not of sufficient girth for use as pillars and props etc., and it is unlikely that the *algum* and *almug* of the Hebrew texts meant sandalwood. Bishop Caldwell's identification of *algum* with the Tamil *a̱laku* 'beauty' is fantastic, to say the least of it, the suffix *-ku* of the *a̱laku* is probably from the Sanskrit root *kṛ* 'do' and the word is obviously related to the S. *alaṁkṛ* (v.—t.) 'adorn'

(*f*) *tūki*.—In regard to peacocks it is unnecessary to repeat the objections detailed above to the identification of the Hebrew *tūki* with the Tamil *tōkai*, and of the Arabic *ṭawas* and Greek *ταῶς* with a hypothetical Tamil *tōgei*. But the identifications, even if admitted, do not materially strengthen the theory of a Dravidian civilization. If peacocks were once confined to Southern India, an improbable supposition, then they must have borne a South Indian name wherever they were transported, and there would be nothing surprising in the Hebrew name for its being derived from a Tamil word. This fact will only show that the bird was a native of South India and gives no indication as to the state of civilization of South Indians at the time. The real implication lies in the picture, which Bishop Caldwell tacked to his identification, of the Phoenician merchants and Solomon's servants making voyages once in three years down the Malabar coast towards Ophir for bringing 'gold, silver, ivory, apes and peacocks'. This still continues to fascinate a few Dravidian scholars.

In conclusion *algum* appears to be some unknown foreign word which Professor Max Muller and Bishop Caldwell thought to be Indian. Karpion which rests solely on the authority of Ctesias had perhaps no South Indian connection. *Arici* and *iñci* are obviously corruptions of North Indian words.

The theory of a pre-Aryan, South Indian civilizatio therefore fails to the extent to which it is thought to be supported by the testimony of these words. *Nellu*, *tippali* or *pippali* and *miḷaku* also have come from the north. That black-pepper, the practical monopoly of the Malabar coast in the past and so eagerly sought after by the Europeans, is not known by its South Indian names *kaṟi* or *miḷaku* in Europe indicates that these names came late in the field. So far as an inference can be formed from the testimony of the words mentioned above, we can safely say that what is known as the Dravidian civilization of the South is really the civilization of Aryan and Aryanised immigrants from the North.

The discussion in this chapter and the extracts from various authors who have written about South India bring out how little is known in Europe about the real South India of the past and how apt scholars are to repeat the statements of previous writers without much scrutiny. Such statements frequently repeated acquire a progressively increasing fictitious authority as years roll on. It has thus come about that people think that *karpion* is a Greek word, that *Damirike* is a good transliteration of Tamiḷakam and that *vrīhi* and *Drāvida* are Sanskritised forms of *arici* and *Tamil*.

It is also surprising that historians should implicitly accept certain details of ancient South Indian history which the late Mr. Kanakasabhai Pillai evolved out of his inner consciousness, namely that the ancient inhabitants of South India were *villavars* and *mīṉavars*, literally 'hunters and fishermen', that these were conquered by a civilized race called *Nāgas* who were in their turn displaced by Mongolians from Central Asia who reached India through Tibet and the Himalayan passes. The first two items find a place in Mr. V. A. Smith's *Early History of India* and in the *Cambridge History of India*. The last item is not noticed in these books as the theory of a Mongolian irruption through middle Himalayan passes is opposed to the current theory, that the Dravidians came from the highlands of Western Asia and entered India by the North-West.

Even a writer like Professor J. Kennedy who has re-examined the evidence usually accepted without question in proof of the ancient maritime trade between India and Babylonia and has rejected part of it, has expressed the opinion that ' rice, peacock ', etc., were known in Greece in the 5th Century B.C. by their Dravidian, *i.e.* Tamil names. This was, however, unavoidable as the greatest authority on South Indian languages had declared that *oryza*, *tawas*, *algum*, etc., were derived from Tamil words. Bishop Caldwell was indeed a great magician. He pronounced a spell and there sprung up a vision of Phoenician seamen voyaging with Solomon's servants down the West coast of India to Ophir once in three years to bring gold, silver, algum, peacocks and apes. This vision still fascinates some Dravidian scholars, though it has been pointed that the Hebrew *algum* was not wanted for its scent, but to be used as props and pillars for which sandalwood was wholly unfitted, that peacocks could be had in plenty in Guzerat and that there was no gold or silver for export from India. The whole vision rests on Bishop Caldwell's opinion that *oryza*, *algum*, and *tawas* are derived from Tamil words. It is time that the spell is broken.

CHAPTER III.

THE ALLEGED DRAVIDIAN CHARACTERISTICS IN INDO-ARYAN.

35. THE NON-ARYAN ELEMENT IN SANSKRIT VOCABULARY.

The changes stated to have been introduced into the Aryan dialects of India by the influence of the Dravidian languages are arranged by the Editors of the Linguistic Survey under three heads :

1. Vocabulary,
2. Phonology and
3. Inflexional system.

In regard to the first head, some scholars appear to hold the extreme view that all words common to Dravidian and Sanskrit which are not traceable in any of the other Indo-Germanic languages, must have been borrowed by Sanskrit from the Dravidian languages.

Professor Sten Konow gives a fair summary of the controversy on this point in the Linguistic Survey of India. (Vol. iv, pp. 278—9).

" There are in all Indo-Aryan languages a considerable number of words which cannot apparently be identified in other Indo-European languages. This is specially the case in modern vernaculars and the old opinion was that such words had, generally speaking, been borrowed from the language of the tribes which inhabited India before the Aryan invasion. The steady progress of philological studies in later years has enabled us to retrace an ever-increasing portion of such words to Sanskrit, and many scholars now hold that there have hardly been any loans at all. It has, however, been overlooked that it is not sufficient to show that a word is found in Sanskrit or even in the Vedic dialects, in order to prove that it belonged to the original language of the Aryans. If Bishop Caldwell is right in the opinion just quoted, the foreign element must reach back into the oldest times, and it is necessary to trace the dubious words not only in Sanskrit but also in other languages of the Indo-European family. This is exactly what modern philology has in many cases failed to do. There are, for example, a number of verbal roots in Sanskrit which do not appear to occur in other Indo-European forms of speech. The same is the case with a considerable portion of the vocabulary. We cannot here go into details, the less so, because we do not as yet possess a complete etymological dictionary of Sanskrit. There is, however, every probability for the supposition that at least a considerable portion of such words and bases has been borrowed from the Drāviḍas. Lists of such words will be found in most of the works dealing with Dravidian philology, *e.g.*—in Bishop Caldwell's Grammar and in the Rev. F. Kittel's Kanarese Dictionary. I shall only mention one instance. The word Śiva is already in the Vedas used as an epithet of the God Rudra and it is known that Śiva has become one of the principal deities of the Hindu pantheon. It has been asserted that this use of the word *Śiva* must be explained from a Dravidian *Śiva* 'red'. Now the word *Rudra* in the Ṛg Veda often seems to mean 'red', and it seems probable that the conception of the God Rudra-Śiva has a tinge of Dravidian ideas. I have mentioned this word because it shows how fundamental the Dravidian influence on the Aryans can have been, not only philologically, but also on the whole method of thought."

According to an analysis made many years ago by Professor Edgern, 530 of the Sanskrit roots given in the Dhātupātha have representatives in Greek or in the Iranian, the Italic, the Teutonic, the Slavonic and the Celtic languages.[1]

1. *Vide* Dr. Buhler's article entitled Roots of the Dhātupāṭha in The Indian Antiquary, Vol. xxiii, p. 144.

From Curtius's Greek Etymology we find that 671 of Greek roots have representatives in the other languages of the Indo-European family.[1] The smaller number found in Sanskrit is perhaps due to the earlier migration of the Asiatic Branch from the original habitat of the Indo-Europeans, but it is obvious that both the Greeks and the Indo-Aryans have made very large additions to the stock of words inherited by them from the parent language.

It cannot, therefore, be denied that the old Indo-Aryan which the Aryan immigrants into India developed while they were still in the North-West—the Panjab and Afghanistan—contained a large number of roots and words which did not belong to the Indo-Germanic stock. Much of the new addition was no doubt borrowed from the non-Aryan languages outside India and it is possible that a portion thereof has been derived from pre-Aryan languages spoken in the North-West. But in whatever manner it has been derived and whatever elements it is composed of, this old Indo-Aryan is undoubtedly the original to which the Vedic dialects, the classical Sanskrit, the Prākṛt languages including the Apabhraṃśas and the Modern-Aryan vernaculars are traceable. If there is no reason other than the similarity between Dravidian and Indo-Aryan sound-forms and words to suppose that the Dravidians once occupied the North-West of India, then the natural presumption will be that these words have really travelled from the north to the south and have been derived by the Dravidian languages of the south from immigrants speaking dialects arising from the old Indo-Aryan.

Professor Sten Konow's opinion that, in the case of the Indo-Aryans, a considerable portion of the new roots and words should have been borrowed from the Drāviḍas is based

1. Curtius's Greek Etymology, 5th Edition (English Translation), p. 407.

on the theory that the Drāviḍas were in occupation of the West and the North-West of India when the Aryans arrived in the country; and this theory again is based on the assumption that Dravidian characteristics have been traced in the Vedic and classical Sanskrit.

As Professor Sten Konow points out, it is impossible to enter into details here and we must content ourselves with examining some typical instance of alleged borrowings from the Dravidian languages. We have an amusing instance in the case of the Vedic *karmāra* 'a smith' which is alleged by some writers to have been borrowed from the Dravidian *Karumā* 'a smelter',—a neolithic people unacquainted with the use of metals possessing a word for 'smelter'.

A long list of Sanskrit words—the names of indegenous South Indian products—like *vrīhi* (rice, rice plant), *śṛṅgabera* (ginger), *muktā* (pearl), *marīca* (black pepper), *pippalī*, (long pepper), *candana* (sandalwood), *mayūra* (peacock), etc., have been instanced by Dravidian scholars as having been adopted by Sanskrit from Dravidian languages with some modifications, but it can be proved in most of these cases that the Dravidian name of the product has travelled South from the North during the Aryan period of Indian History. But it may not always be possible to disprove assertions made solely on the basis of the theory that the Dravidians once occupied the North-West of India, otherwise than by showing the theory to be improbable. It is, therefore, necessary to subject to a critical examination the Dravidian characteristics alleged to have been found in the Indo-Aryan languages, which form the basis of this theory.

36. Śiva, Śivaratri.

(*a*) *Siva* :—In regard to the typical instance of *Śiva* mentioned by Professor Sten Konow, it is no doubt true that the deity Rudra is regarded as *red* or tawny in colour[1] and that the word *Śiva* is used in the Vedas as an epithet of this deity[2]. For *tāmra*, 'coppery' red and *aruṇa* 'red, ruddy, of the colour of the morning sky' *babhru* 'deep brown, tawny,' *sumaṅgala*, 'yellow coloured very auspicious' are some of his epithets, as also *Śiva* and *Śivatara*. These last two words, however, do not mean 'red' but 'propitious' and 'highly propitious this will be apparent from the other epithets along with which these two words occur, *viz.*, *śambhu, śaṅkara*, 'causing happiness', *mayobhu, mayaskara* 'causing pleasure, satisfaction'.

Rudra as depicted in the Taittirīya Saṁhitā is a fierce destroying deity, and the hymns addressed to Him are intended to propitiate Him by calling Him and His weapons good, beneficent, propitious. The word *Śiva* occurs seven times in the first Anuvāka of 'Rudram'—a hymn addressed to Rudra.

(T. S. iv—5) In the Taittirīya Saṁhitā :—

(*a*) yā ta iṣuś śivatamā śivam babhūva te dhanuḥ
śivā śaravyā yā tava tayā nō rudra mṛḍaya
yā te rudra śivā tanūraghorāpāpakāśinī
tayā nas tanuvā śantamayā giriśantā bhickāśīhi
yāmiṣum giriśanta haste bibharṣyastave
śivām giritra tām kuru mā hiṁsīḥ purusam jagat
śivena vacasā tvā giriśācchā vadāmasi.

1. Asau yastāmro aruṇa uta babhrus sumaṅgalaḥ. (T. S. iv. 5-8.)

2. Namas somāya ca rudrāya ca namas tāmrāya cārunāya ca namaś śaṅgāya ca paśupataye ca nama ugrāya ca bhīmāya ca
Namaś śambhave ca mayobhave ca namaś saṅkarāya ca mayaskarāya ca namas śivāya ca śivatarāya ca. (T. S. iv. 5-8.)

(*b*) niśīrya śalyānām mukhā śivo nas sumanā bhava.

Here we have

(1) *ta iṣuśśivatamā* 'Your most beneficient arrow'

(2) *śivam te dhanuḥ* 'Your beneficent bow'

(3) *śivā śaravyā tava* 'Your auspicious aim'

(4) *te śivā tanus śantamā* 'Your auspicious form (body), most beneficent'

(5) *iṣum haste śivām kuru* 'please render the arrow in Your hand beneficent to us'

(6) *śivena vacasā tvā vadāmasi* 'we address You with propitiating words'

(7) *śivo nas sumanā bhava* 'be propitious and well disposed towards us.'

It is with the same object that Rudra himself is called *śiva, śivatara, śambhu, śaṅkara, mayobhu, mayaskara.* Of these *śiva, śambhu* and *śaṅkara* have now become Rudra's names. It is the merest accident that the Sanskrit *śiva* 'beneficent' has the same sound as the Dravidian *śiva* (= *civa*) 'red'. Have those that assert an etymological connexion between the two words been able to quote a single passage from the Vedas in which *Śiva* the epithet of Rudra means 'red'?

(*b*) *Śivarātri* : Another instance can be quoted from the Vedas of a similar propitiation by the epithet *śiva.* The fourteenth night of the dark half of the month (lunar) of Māgha is called *śivarātri.* At the time of the Kauṣītakī Brāhmaṇa this must have been the winter solstice night, *i.e.*, the night immediately preceding the sun's turning to begin his northward course. For it is stated in the Brāhmaṇa (XIX—3).

Sa vai māghasyāmāvāsyāyāmupavasati udaṅṅavartsyan
upeme vasanti prāyaṇīyena atirātreṇa
yakṣyamāṇāḥ tadenam prathamamāpnuvanti ||

"He (the sun), indeed, rests on the new moon day Māgha, being about to turn towards the north. Thus they rest, who are about to perform the rites of the Prāyaṇīya Atirātra. Thus they reach him for the first time".[1] The Brāhmaṇa here refers to the Gavām Ayana sacrifice which begins with a Prāyṇīya Atirātra ; the sacrifice lasts for a year and in the middle of it, the sun reaches the highest point (the Summer Solstice) of his annual course.

Śivarātri thus coincided with the winter solstice at one time, and was then the longest and probably the coldest night of the year ; in high latitudes, the sun would have appeared only for a few hours above the horizon and may not have been visible at all in consequence of mists and fogs. The following passage occurs in the Pariśiṣṭa of the Ṛgveda."

prapanno'ham śivām rātrim bhadre
pāram aśīmahi bhadre pāram aśīmahi.
(Maṇḍala X, Anuvāka 10—16)

"I seek the protection of the beneficent night, Oh ! Propitious One ! may we (safely) reach the other side ? Oh ! Beneficent One ! may we (safely) pass the night ?"

The same idea occurs in the Taittirīya Saṁhitā :—

Citrāvaso svasti te pāram aśīya ityāha
rātrir vai Citrāvasuḥ, avyuṣṭyai vā
etasyai purā brāhmaṇa abhaiṣuḥ.[2] (T. S. 1, 5—7.)

"It is stated 'Hail Citrāvasu ! May I reach your other side !' Citrāvasu is night ; in former days the Brāhmaṇas were afraid that it may not dawn."

Putting these passages together and Sāyaṇa's commentary on the last it may be inferred that the propitiatory

1. As per G. Thibaut I.A. Vol. xxiv, p. 87.

2. Hemantartau rātrerdīrghatvena prabhātam na bhaviṣyatyeveti kadācid brāhmaṇā bhītāḥ (Sāyaṇa bhāṣya.)

"As the nights are long in the *hemanta* (dewy) season the Brāhmanas were at one time afraid that it may not dawn at all."

prayer was addressed to the longest night of the year which got its epithet *Śiva* at the same time perhaps as Rudra got His. The fourteenth night of the dark half of Māgha ceased to be the winter solstice night more than three thousand years ago ; at a later period, Rathasaptamī—the seventh day of the bright half of the month (lunar) of Māgha was considered to be the first day after winter solstice. Later still the first day of the the solar month of Makara was considered to be the day after the winter solstice ; and now the winter solstice coccurs on the 22nd December. But Māgha Bahula Caturdaśī still continues to be called *Śivarātri*, the current traditional explanation being that it is a night sacred to Śiva.

(*c*) The above examination shows that the statement that the use of Śiva as an epithet of Rudra must be explained from a Dravidian *civa* ' red ' is merely an assertion. We must now proceed to examine the alleged Dravidian characteristics in Indo-Aryan phonology and inflexional system.

S. 37. Alleged Dravidian Influence on Sanskrit Phonology.

The cerebral sounds in Sanskrit :—The most important item under the second head ' Phonology ' is the evolution of the cerebral sounds on the Sanskrit alphabet, but scholars are not agreed on this point, some of them holding that these sounds might have been developed *ab intra* by Sanskrit itself, while others hold that the sounds must have been borrowed from Dravidian. Pages 32 to 48 in Bishop Caldwell's Dravidian Grammar contain a detailed discussion on the point from which it will be seen that the names Caldwell, Benefey, Norris and Trumpp appear among those of scholars who held the latter view, while the names Wilson, Buhler and Beames are ranged on the opposite side. The former argued that the cerebral sounds which are a special feature of the Dravidian languages are of Tartar origin and are not found in any of the Indo-Germanic alphabets west of the river Indus, while they exist side by side with the dentals in all the Indo-Aryan alphabets east of the Indus, and that their presence in Sanskrit and other Indo-Aryan dialects must be due to Dravidian influence. The late Mr. John Beames, I.C.S., argued on the other hand that the Indo-Germanic languages possessed only linguals and that these had become partly dentals on Indian soil. He said :—

" The sounds of this series as expressed by the Teutonic branch of the family, are among the harsher, though not absolutely the harshest, notes of the series. In expressing *-t-* and *-d-* we, the Teutons, touch with our tongues the gum or fleshy part of the palate just above the teeth. The Southern European races form the contact lower down, just where the osseous substance of the teeth issues from the gums, thus producing a softer sound than the Teutons. The Persians and Indians form it low down on the teeth almost at their edge thus producing the softest sound of all. This Indian sound, being the result of impact on the teeth is a true dental. We, Teutons have no dental sounds at all while the Italians have semi-dentals. The Indians have, however, in addition to their true dentals another series produced by contact at a point, very little if at all higher than the Teutonic contact, so that they possess, so to speak, the highest and lowest notes of the scale, but not the intermediate ones."

The following remarks of Professor Sten Konow extracted from the Linguistic Survey of India (Vol. IV, page 279) contain a very fair presentment of the controversy :—

" It seems to be a general rule that a people which invades a foreign country, to some degree adopted the pronunciation of its new home, partly as a result of the influence of climate, and partly also on account of the intermixture with the old inhabitants. This has also generally been supposed to have been the case in India. Thus there has been a long discussion as to whether the Aryans have adopted the cerebral letters from the Drāvidas or have developed them independently. Good reasons have been adduced for both suppositions, and the question has not as yet been decided. The Indo-European languages do not seem to have possessed those letters. They had a series of dentals which were not, however, pronounced as pure dentals by putting the tongue between the teeth, but probably as alveolars, the tongue being pressed against the root of the upper teeth. It is a well known fact that these sounds have in India partly become dentals and partly cerebrals. The cerebrals are in most cases derived, irom compound letters where the old dentals were preceded by an *-l-* Similar changes also occur in other Indo-European languages, and it is therefore quite possible that the Indo-Aryan cerebrals have been developed quite independently. The cerebral letters, however, form an essential feature of the Dravidian phonology, and it therefore seems probable that Dravidian influence has been at work and at least given strength to a tendency which can, it is true, have taken its origin among the Aryans themselves."

This seems a more careful and more accurate statement of the question at issue than that contained in S. 21 above in which Professor Rapson does not seem to recognize the possibility of an independent development of the cerebral letters and appears to think that their adoption in Sanskrit can only be explained as the result of an older disturbing element.

38. Alveolar Sounds in Dravidian

It is well known that the English *-t-* and *-d-* are not pure dentals nor cerebrals but alveolar sounds produced by pressing the tip of the tongue against the root of the teeth. It has been surmised that the original Indo-European languages possessed only these alveolar sounds and that these have become partly dentals and partly cerebrals on Indian soil. In the language of the Avesta they have become whole dentals.

This change of alveolars into dentals in some cases and in some languages and into cerebrals in others can be exemplified by what has taken place in the Dravidian languages themselves. Sanskrit has five classes—*vargas*—of consonants, *viz.*, gutturals, palatals, cerebrals, dentals and labials. Tamil-Malayāḷam has in addition a sixth varga : gutturals *k*, *ṅ*, palatals *c*, *ñ* ; cerebrals *ṭ*, *ṇ* ; dentals *t*, *n* ; labials *p*, *m* ; the sixth varga *ṟ*, *ṉ*. This sixth class is placed at the end of the alphabet, after the liquids and semi-vowels, but the rules given in Tolkāppiyam for the pronunciation of the Tamil *ṟ* and *ṉ* show that their place of articulation is above that of the dentals and below that of the cerebrals. A single intervocal *r* is pronounced like a harsh *ṟ* but the sound of the doubled *ṟṟ* is entirely different.

Dr. Gundert

In the scheme of transliteration prefixed to Dr. Gundert's Malayāḷam dictionary it is stated :—

"*ṟa* (the sixth varga) has three different pronunciations.

1. *ra* doubled (*rra*) is marked *tta* (resembling *t t* in utter).
2. *ra* combined with *n* (*nra*) is marked *nda* (resembling *nd* in binder).
3. Initial and medial *r* is marked *r*."

In a foot-note it is added *rr* has semi-dental, *nr* dento-gingival pronunciation.

Dr. Gundert thus identified the sounds of *rr* and *n r* with those of the English alveolar *t* and *tt* and *nd*.

BISHOP CALDWELL.

In Tamil, their pronunciation now is somewhat different. Bishop Caldwell says in his Grammar (page 20):—

"*r* when doubled is pronounced *ttr* though written *rr*. The *t* of this compound differs both from the soft dental *t̠* of the fourth varga and from the cerebral *ṭ*, and corresponds very nearly to the emphatic final *t* of our English interrogative what. This sound of *t* is not expressed in writing, but in pronunciation it is never omitted ; and it is one of those peculiar Dravidian sounds which are not derived from Sanskrit and are not found in it......."

Again, in another place, "The hard rough *r* of the Dravidian languages is not found in Sanskrit and is not employed in pronouncing Sanskrit derivatives. It is found in Telugu poetry and elegant prose, and the grammarians insist upon using it ; but in the modern dialect of the Telugu it is seldom used. In Kanarese the use of this letter is confined to the poets and the ancient dialect. It is evident that it was originally contained in all the dialects ; though, possibly through the influence of the Sanskrit, it is now seldom used except in Tamil and Malayāḷam in which it holds as firm footing as ever" (page 29).

"The letter *ṉ* (not the dental *n* but the final *n* of Tamil), a letter which is not found in Telugu, is often prefixed in Tamil to the rough *r* for the sake of euphony, when the compound *ṉṟ* acquires the sound of *ndr*........In another class of words the *n* which prefixed to *r* is radical, and should be followed by *d* according to rule (*e.g.*, in the preterites of verbs whose root ends in *n*) ; but *r* is suffixed to *n* instead of *d* in consequence of which the sound of *ndr* is substituted for that of *nd*" (page 30).

He considered the *r* radical and *n* euphonically prefixed in the words *mūṉṟu* ' three ' (Kanarese *mūru*) and *oṉṟu* 'one' (for *oru*) ; but radical and *r* euphonically substituted for *d* in the words :— *eṉṟu* (*endru*) ' having spoken ' instead of *endu* and *ceṉṟu* (*cendru*) ' having gone ' for *cendu* (which is used instead of the less euphonic celdu) (page 30).

He does not distinguish the final -*ṉ* of Tamil by any diacritical remark and it is clear that he did not recognise that its place of articulation was alveolar, higher than that of the dental *n*.

Mr. C. P. Venkatarama Aiyar.

In a paper read at the First Oriental Conference at Poona (1919) Mr. C. P. Venkatarama Aiyar, M.A., (now Headmaster, Training School, Tanjore), discusses the exact pronunciation and place of articulation of the hard Dravidian *r* and after a detailed examination of the available facts bearing on the question arrives at the conclusion " that the hard *r* is an alveolar plosive and that the hard *r* and its corresponding nasal with which the enumeration of the Tamil consonantal system ends, are characteristics Dravidian consonants which are still preserved in Tamil."[1]

INCONSISTENT VIEWS OF DRAVIDIAN SCHOLARS.

Every one can easily satisfy himself by making the attempt that it requires an effort to pronounce a purely dental *n* except when in combination with a dental consonant *t* or *d* as in Sanskrit *anta* ' end,' *manda* ' slow.' In all other cases generally the *n* which is formed without any effort is the alveolar *n* : e.g.

English : now, when, then, in.

1. Proceedings of the First Oriental Conference, Poona, Volume I, Summaries of Papers, pages lxxxi to lxxxiv.

Sanskrit : *ananta* 'endless,' *nāga* 'a snake,' *bhavān* 'your honour,' *gacchan* 'going.'

Tamil : *tiṉ* 'eat', *eṉ* 'say'.

When the preterites of the roots *tiṉ* and *eṉ* are formed, by suffixing *du*, the combinations *tindu*, *endu* require a change of articulation in pronouncing the conjunct *-nd-* and this is avoided by converting the dental *d* into an alveolar mute, when the combination will come to have the same sound as in the English *and, binder, sand.* We may regard the character of this alveolar mute as the Tamil-Malayāḷam *ṟ*. This is in effect what Dr. Gundert says, but the pronunciation of *ṟ* and *ṟṟ* being somewhat different in Tamil, Bishop Caldwell did not recognize their true nature.

Most of what we know of the phonology of the old Dravidian languages is derived from Tamil-Malayāḷam, Kanarese and Telugu ; of these Tamil is considered to have developed in full the most charactersistic of Dravidian features. If Indo-Germanic languages originally possessed only alveolars and if these sounds became cerebrals in many cases on Indian soil through Dravidian influence, how came the most important of the Dravidian languages to possess these alveolar sounds long after Sanskrit had converted its alveolars into dentals and cerebrals, and how comes it that Tamil—the most typical of the Dravidian languages—still possesses them ? Bishop Caldwell and Mr. C. P. Venkatarama Aiyar consider them to be characteristic Dravidian consonants not found in Sanskrit, and Bishop Caldwell goes to the length of saying that their disappearance in modern Kanarese and Telugu is probably due to the influence of Sanskrit. We thus have two sets of Dravidian scholars, one set ascribing the cerebralization of Sanskrit alveolars to Dravidian influence, the other set ascribing the disappearance of Dravidian alveolars to Sanskrit influence It is obvious that there is considerable misapprehension in the matter and the question requires detailed examination.

39. CEREBRALIZATION OF LIQUID-DENTAL IN SANSKRIT AND OF SIMILAR COMBINATIONS IN DRAVIDIAN.

(*a*) *The rule of Fortunatov* (Uhlenbeck, Sanskrit Phonetics S. 44).

As pointed out by Professor Sten Konow (S. 37 above) " cerebrals are in most cases derived from compound letters where the old dentals were preceded by *l*." This has been established by Fortunatov, who after a detailed examination arrived at the following results :—" Idg. *r* dental remained unchanged but in combination of *l* and a following dental the *l* disappeared and the dental was lingualized." Thus in Sanskrit :—

paṭa-s ' woven stuff, cloth, garment ' (cf. O. Slav. *platino*, Russ. *polotno* ' linen '.

paṭala-m ' cover, veil, mass ' (Ice. *feldr.* ' cover ').

paṭu-s ' sharp ' (Gr. πλατυς ' saltish brack ').

vaṭa-s (*vaṭa-m, vaṭī*) ' snare ' (Lith. *valtis* ' thread, net,' Russ. *voloti* ' thread ').

hāṭaka-m ' gold ' (O. Slav. *zlato*. Russ. *zoloto*).

kuṭhara ' axe ' (Lat. *culter*).

pāṇi-s ' hand ' (Lat. *palma*).

paṇa-s ' wager, stake, prize, wages, a coin ' (Lith. *pelnas.* ' wages ').

bhāṣate ' speaks ' bhashati ' barks ' (Lith. *balsas* ' voice tone ').

pāṣāṇa-s Vedic *pāṣya* ' stone ' (O. H. G. (felis).

The combinations *lt, lth, ln̲, ls* &c., are now rare in Sanskrit all such having been converted into the corresponding cerebrals as shown above or into *rt, rth, rn, rs*, etc., by the change of Idg. *l* into *r*. These latter combinations have also been cerebralized in a few instances, the original and the modified words now existing side by side in Sanskrit :—

bhaṭa 'soldier' *bhṛta-s* 'hired' (Gr. φερω)
kaṭa-s 'mat' *kartana-m* 'weaving' (Gr. κύρτος)
kaṭu-s 'sharp' **kartu-s* (Lith. *kartus*).
naṭa-s 'dancer' *nartaka-s* 'dancer'.

Some Indo-Germanic philologists appear to be of opinion that cerebralizations of the latter kind are due to external Prākṛtic influences, while the cerebralizations of the combinations *l* and dental, have developed *ab intra* owing to the operation of causes within the Indo-Germanic languages themselves. Other scholars prefer to believe that all those cerebrals which go back on a combination of a liquid (*r* or *l*) dental are due to Prākṛtic influence. There appears also to be a third school of philologists who appear to be of opinion that there was a cerebralizing tendency in the Indo-Germanic languages themselves and that the Prākṛt influence referred to above has merely strengthened this tendency.

In the Prākṛt languages the combinations *rt*, *rth*, *rd*, *rdh*, have, as a rule, and subject to exceptions, been converted into *ṭṭ*, *ṭṭh*, *ḍḍ* and *ḍḍh*. Examples of this change and of the exceptions to the rule will be found collected in P.P.G. Ss. 289-291. Another set of combinations which were occasionally cerebralized were *tr dr* (*vide* Ss. 292-4 *Ibid*).

(*b*) *The Dravidian treatment of the combinations* lt, rt, nt *in verb-forms.*

Dravidian scholars take up the question at this stage and assert that the Dravidian languages were being spoken in the North and the North-west of India when the Aryans entered the country and that the Prākṛt influence referred to above is merely the influence of Dravidian languages.

This assertion can be shown to be untrue in the case at least of Tamil (including Malayāḷam) and Kanarese. There are a number of verbal bases in Tamil ending in *-l*, *-ṉ* and in some of the verbal forms of these bases the final consonants *-l* and *-ṉ* come in intimate contact with the initial *t-* of the suffixes. This intimate contact sometimes converts both the consonants into alveolars but never into cerebrals. When the base ends in *-r* no change takes place in the initial *t-* or the final *-r*.

Base.		Verbal noun with suffix-*tal*.	Conjunctive participles with suffix-*tu*.
vil	'sell'	*viṟṟal*	*viṟṟu*
kal	'learn'	*kaṟṟal*	*kaṟṟu*
kol	'kill'	*koltal* or *kōṟal*	*koṉṟu*
cel	'go'	*celtal* or *cēṟal*	*ceṉṟu*
tiṉ	'eat'	*tiṉṟal*	*tiṉṟu*
pār	'see'	*pārttal*	*pārttu*
tīr	'settle'	*tīrttal*	*tīrttu*

In Kanarese such verbal forms do not contain even alveolars and the initial dentals of suffixes do not undergo any change. Thus :—

nil 'stand' has the conjunctive participle *niltu*, *nindu* ;
kal 'learn' ,, ,, *kaltu* ;
nūl 'spin' ,, ,, *nultu* ;
kur 'love' ,, ,, *kurtu* ;
kuḻir 'bend, stoop' ,, ,, *kulitu* ;
nār 'smell' ,, ,, *natu* ;
an 'lean, recline' ,, ,, *antu* ;
kun 'bend, stoop' ,, ,, *kuntu*.

In Telugu there do not appear to be standard grammatical forms in which the initial *t-* of the suffixes comes in intimate contact with *-l-* or *-r-* of the bases ; but in the case of the roots *anu* 'say', *kanu* 'see or bring forth,' *konu* 'buy, take,' *vinu* 'hear,' *tinu* 'eat,' *-n-* comes in intimate contact with the initial *t-* of the present participle suffix *-tun* and the past tense suffix *-ti*, and the resulting combination *-nt-* is cerebralized into *-ṇṭ-* as in *aṇṭunu* 'saying,' *koṇṭunu* 'buying,' *aṇṭānu* 'I say', *koṇṭānu* 'I buy' etc.

(*c*) The Dravidian treatment of the combinations *-lt-*, *-rt-*, *-nt-* in nominal declension.

In Telugu the initial *t-* of the oblique case suffix *-ti-* comes into intimate contact with the final *-l* or *-r* of the nouns declined and then the combinations *-lt-* and *-rt-* are replaced by a single cerebral *-ṭ-* except in a few cases where *-t-* appears in the place of the combination. Caldwell's grammar enumerates about 50 words as belonging to this class. In some cases, where the nouns contain *-ll-* or *-nn-* the combinations *-llt-* and *-nnt-* are replaced by *-ṇṭ-*.

Nouns.	Oblique form.
nōru 'the mouth'	*nō-ṭi*
ēru 'a river'	*ē-ṭi*
nudur 'the forehead'	*nudu-ti*
aṅgili 'the palate or throat'	*aṅgi-ti*
guppili 'the fist'	*guppi-ti*
kundēlu 'a hare'	*kundē-ti*
nāgali 'a plough'	*nāga-tt*
rōkali 'a large pestle'	*rōkati*
illu 'a house'	*iṇṭi*
pallu 'a tooth'	*paṇṭi*
villu 'a bow'	*viṇṭi*
kannu 'the eye'	*kaṇṭi*

In pronominal declension cerebrals appear in the oblique plural forms *vāṭi*, *vīṭi* of the pronouns of the third *avi*, *ivi*;

these oblique forms correspond to the oblique forms *avaṟṟu*, *ivaṟṟu* of Tamil and to the Kanarese declensional form containing the augment *-ar-* (K. K. G. Ss. 124, 125, 136). In non-pronominal declension there is an oblique case suffix in Tamil and Kanarese beginning with a dental, but it remains a dental as in Tamil : *marattu*, Kanarese : *marada* 'pertaining or belonging to a tree' and undergoes no change of class. Thus, as in the case of *verb forms*, only alveolars or dentals appear in nominal declension in Tamil and Kanarese and no cerebrals.

(*d*) No tendency in Tamil and Kanarese to cerebralize.

The illustrations given in (*b*) and (*c*) above bring out a marked difference in the phonetic peculiarities of Tamil and Kanarese on the one hand and Telugu on the other. The combinations *-lt-*, *-rt-*, *-nt-* occurring in grammatical forms are cerebralized in Telugu while they are converted into *alveolars* in literary Tamil and remain unchanged in Kanarese. There is thus no tendency in Tamil or Kanarese to cerebralize the combinations *lt*, *rt*, *nt* occurring in inflexions ; such a tendency does exist in Telugu, but only in regard to these combinations. It will be seen from the examples given in (*a*) above that *-ls-* became *-ṣ-* and *-ln-* became *-ṇ-* in the pro-Sanskrit period; and no doubt through the continued operation of causes producing these changes, Idg. *-rs-* and *-rn-* have become *-rṣ-* and *-rṇ-* in Sanskrit : as in *dharṣāmi* 'I dare,' *varṣ* 'rain,' *karṇa* 'the ear,' *varṇa* 'colour' (Uhlenbeek S. 44). This change cannot possibly be attributed to Telugu for in *tadbhava* words as opposed to *tatsama* words Telugu avoids *ṣ* and *ṇ*; thus, Sanskrit: *harṣa* 'joy,' *karṣaṇa* 'cultivation' *śirṣa* 'head,' *paruṣa* 'harsh,' *bhāṣā* 'language.' Prākṛt: *vanna* (*varṇa*) 'colour, sound, letter' exist as *arasa*, *karisanamu*, *sēsa*, *parusa*, *bāsa*, *vanne* in *accau* (pure) Telugu.

In these circumstances it is difficult to assent to the view put forth by some Dravidian scholars that the Prākṛt influence, referred to by the Indo-Germanic philologists, which cerebralized dentals in Sanskrit was exercised by the Dravidian languages.

40.—(*a*) ALVEOLAR PRONUNCIATION IN DRAVIDIAN OF THE FINAL DENTALS OF SANSKRIT DERIVATIVES.

In Malayāḷam the symbol ൽ besides expressing final *-l* serves also for the Sanskrit consonants *-t* and *-d* which in that language are pronounced *l*, e.g., *ut*, *tat*, *mat* etc., *adbhuta* 'wonderful,' *utsāha* 'energy,' *tātparyam* 'real meaning,' *camatkāram* 'cleverness,' and in the 5th case singular of nouns *tasmāt*, *Rāmāt* etc., in all of which the final consonants *-t*, *-d* of words or syllables are pronounced as *-l* which has about the same place of articulation as the alveolar *-t*.

In Tamil, the Sanskrit words (1) *adbhuta* 'wonderful,' (2) *Padmanābha* 'a proper name,' (3) *tatkāla* 'that time,' (4) *mudga* 'a kind of pulse,' etc. in which class, (5) *pataṅga* 'a bird' may perhaps be also included, are converted into (1) *aṟpudam*, (2) *Paṟpanāpaṉ*, (3) *taṟkālam*, (4) *muṟkam* and (5) *paṟavai*.

The final *-ṉ* of Tamil words denoting masculine singular is derived from Sanskrit *-nt* as is pointed out below. Later on it is shown that Tamil replaces the final consonants *-t* and *-d* of Sanskrit *tadbhavas* by *-l* and *-n*.

(*b*) ALVEOLARS AND CEREBRALS FROM THE INDO-ARYAN CONJUNCT *-tr-*.

Another surprise is in store for us when we proceed to examine in what classes of words these alveolar sounds are found in literary Tamil. The Sanskrit word *Sūtra* 'a thead, a string, a coil' gives rise to the Sanskrit denominative root sutra[1], 'coil round' from which the Tamil *cuṟṟu* 'envelope, coil round' is derived. The Sanskrit root *mā* 'measure' gives rise to the word *mātrā* 'a measure, a little quantity, a small measure'; it is from this *mātrā* that the Tamil word *māṟṟu* in *poṉmāṟṟu* 'fineness of alloyed gold' (measure of pure gold) appears to have been derived.

The above instances in which the double *-ṟṟ-* arises from the Sanskrit *-tr-* furnish the reason why the Tamil pronunciation of *-ṟṟ-* resembles, as pointed out by Bishop Caldwell, that of *-ttr-*. But in some cases the alveolar *-ṟṟ-* derived from *-tr-* has been replaced by the cerebral *-ṭṭ-*. Thus *mātrā* and *mātram* exist also in the form *maṭṭa* as in *maṭṭa vilai* 'low price,' *accu maṭṭam* 'an Acin (pony) of small stature,' *maṭṭa-p-palakai* 'carpenter's square' *atu maṭṭum* 'that only (and nothing more).' The Sanskrit *chātra* 'a pupil, a student' has come *caṭṭaṉ* in Tamil.

A number of Sanskrit words will be given later on below in which *-tr-* is replaced by *-ṟṟ-* or *-ṟ-* in Tamil.

(c) ALVEOLARS AND CEREBRALS FROM THE INDO-ARYAN CONJUNCT *-rt-*.

Another Sanskrit conjunct which becomes *-ṟṟ-* in Tamil is *-rt-*. Thus the Sanskrit *vṛtha* 'in vain, useless', *vārttā* 'unsubstantial,' *varttam* 'chaff' appear to be connected etymologically with the Tamil *veṟṟu*, *veṟu* 'empty,' *vaṟumai* 'poverty.' The Sanskrit *vārttā*, 'a word, speech,' which has become *vātta* in Prākṛt and exists as *bat* in Hindi and as *vat* in Guzerati, Panjabi, Mahārāṣṭrī etc., appears as *māṟṟam* in literary Tamil.

A number of Sanskrit words will be given later on where the combination *-rt-* is replaced by *-ṟṟ-* or *-ṟ-* in Tamil.

---

1. *Sūtra veṣṭane.* The root sūtra is used in the sense of 'surrounding, twisting, coiling round.' Dhātupāṭha, 1908.

In most cases however, the Sanskrit *-rt-* is represented by *-tt-* in Tamil and other Dravidian languages.

For instance :—

arthavarṇa ' a synopsis ' ; *aṭṭavaṇai* ;
tīrtha ' a fording place ' ; *tiṭṭu* ;
nandyāvarta ' a flower plant ' ; *nantyāvaṭṭai* ;
pratimā ' a picture, statue ' ; *paṭimam* ;
vṛtta ' round ' ; *vaṭṭam*, *vaṭṭu* ;
ālavarta ' a fan made of cloth ' ; *ālavaṭṭam* etc.

These have probably been adopted from the Prākṛts.

(*d*) TAMIL *-ṟ-*, *-ṟṟ-* AND *-ṉ-* ARE IMITATIONS OF THE PRO-SANSKRIT DENTAL SOUNDS.

There seems to be now no doubt that the Tamil *-ṟ-* had originally the sound of an alveolar plosive and if Sanskrit dentals were originally sounded as alveolars then the Tamil *-ṟ-* substituted for the Sanskrit letters in the examples given in (*a*) above truly represent the pro-Sanskrit sounds of *-t-* and *-d-*; *-l-* and *-n-* which are also substituted in certain connections have nearly the same place of articulation as the pro-Sanskrit *-t-* and *-d-*.

The combination *-tr-* became cerebralized in Prākṛt only in a few instances ; in the vast majority of cases *-r-* was assimilated with *-t-* and the combination was replaced by *-tt-* or *-tth-*; the combinations *-rt-*etc., were no doubt cerebralized in a very large number of instances in Prākṛt but *-r-* also became assimilated to *-t-* and the combination replaced by *-tt-* in a considerable number of cases. (P.P. P. G. Ss. 281-294). In these cases of assimilation *-ṟṟ-* of Tamil will truly convey the pro-Sanskrit sound of *-tt-*. But *-ṟṟ-* must have been substituted for *-tr-* and *-rt-*, at least for *-tr-* even in cases where there was no assimilation and this is apparently the reason why a liquid *-ṟ-* intrudes itself in the Tamil pronunciation of *-ṟṟ-* which is sounded as *-ttr-* and not like a pure alveolar as in Malayāḷam. The list which will be given later on will leave little room for doubt that there is now in literary Tamil a considerable number of words containing *-ṟṟ-* or *-ṟ-* which are merely adaptations of Sanskrit words containing *-tr-* or *-rt-*. The conjunct *-ṟṟ-* which was originally substituted for *-tr-* and *-rt-* has since lost one *-ṟ-* in some of the words in the list.

It is thus clear that the alveolars *-ṟ-*, *-ṟṟ-* *-n-* which are supposed to be peculiar to Tamil occur very frequently in Tamil adaptations of Sanskrit words in the place of *-t-*, *-tt-*, *-tr-*, *-rt-*, *-nt-*, and this circumstance goes to confirm the view held by some philologists that the Idg. dentals were pronounced like alveolars.

(*e*) CHANGE OF ALVEOLARS INTO DENTAL AND CEREBRALS IN DRAVIDIAN.

As is now generally admitted, the alveolars *-ṟṟ-* and *-ṉṟ-* existed also formerly in other cultivated Dravidian languages. But in colloquial and vulgar Tamil *-ṟṟ-* and *-ṉṟ-* become respectively *-tt-* and *ṉṉ* ; Sometimes *-ṉṟ-* is also pronounced and written *-nt-*. In Telugu they generally become *-ṭ-* or *-ṭṭ-* and *-ṇṭ-* or *-ṇḍ-* respectively ; in Kanarese *-ṟṟ-* becomes *-tt-* or *-ṭṭ-* and *nr* becomes *nd*, so that it is only in literary Tamil that the alveolar sounds are preserved. The subjoined table illustrate the changes.

Literary Tamil.	Colloquial and vulgar Tamil.	Kanarese.	Telugu.
cuṟṟu 'envelope, coil round'	*cuttu*	*suttu*	*cuṭṭu*
puṟṟu 'ant hill'	*puttu*	*huṭṭu* } *puttu* }	*puṭṭa*
māṟṟam 'a word'		*matu*	*māṭa*

Literary Tamil.	Colloquial and vulgar Tamil.	Kanarese.	Telugu.
vēṟṟu 'empty, profitless'	*vĕttu*	*bari*	*veṭṭi* *utta*
uṟṟu 'a spring of water'	*ūttu*	*ūṭe*	*ūṭa*
eṉṟēṉ 'I said'	*eṉṉu* 'having said'	*endenu*	*aṇṭini*
tiṉṟēṉ 'I ate'	*tiṉṉu* 'having eaten'	*tindenu*	*tiṇṭini*
eṉṟu 'sunshine'			*eṇḍa*
ñāṉṟu 'a day'			*nāḍu*
kuṉṟu 'a hill'	*kuṉṉu*		*koṇḍa*
oṉṟu 'one'	*oṉṉu*	*ondu*	*oṇḍu*
avaṟṟiliṟundu 'from then'		*avaṟin* (Old Kanarese)	*vāṭinuñci*
ivaṟṟil 'in these'		*ivaṟalli* (Old Kanarese)	*vīṭilō*.

To sum up :

(i) Scholars tell us that the original Indo-Germanic language possessed no true dentals but only alveolars; this view receives remarkable confirmation from the circumstance that in the Old Tamil adaptations of a class of Sanskrit words, Tamil alveolars *-ṟ-*, *-ṟṟ-* and *-ṉṟ-* take the place of the Sanskrit dentals.

(i) Scholars also tell us that these alveolars have become dentals in some cases and cerebrals in others in Sanskrit. Old specimens that have come down to us of Tamil, Kanarese and Telugu contain alveolars side by side with dentals and cerebrals; the alveolars have now become dentals in some cases and cerebrals in others. In this change the Dravidian languages resemble the Indo-Germanic and Sanskrit. This change is certainly not due, as supposed by Bishop Caldwell, to the influence of Sanskrit.

(iii) The view of a number of Dravidian scholars that the external influence which cerebralized the pro-Sanskrit combinations of a liquid (*ṛ* or *ḷ*) dental was exercised by the Dravidian languages is altogether *improbable.* In Old Tamil the combinations *-lt-* and *-nt-* are converted into alveolars, not cerebrals ; the combination *-rt-* undergoes no change. None of these combinations undergo any change in Kanarese. They do become cerebralized in Telugu but this may be due to the fact that that language being nearest to the idioms of the North has been more under the Prākṛt influence which cerebralized the Sanskrit liquid dental. Telugu does not tolerate the cerebrals *ṣ* and *ṇ*.

The known facts of the case are best explained on the supposition that there emigrated into South India a body of Indo-Aryans in the pro-Sanskrit period when the Sanskrit dental letters still retained the Indo-Germanic alveolar sounds. These sounds thus brought to the South persisted longer here than in the North, where they were soon lost under what the Indo-Germanic philologists describe as Prākṛt influence. We know there has been a continuous stream of immigration from the Prākṛtic North to the South throughout the historic period and the alveolar sounds of the South have also disappeared, but more slowly, from the spoken languages through the same Prākṛt influence. We see here, not Dravidian influence on Sanskrit, but some influence acting on Dravidian and Sanskrit alike.

The theory that the cerebral letters of Sanskrit are due to the influence of Dravidian languages as known to us must be definitely rejected.

41. CHANGES IN THE INFLEXIONAL SYSTEM OF SANSKRIT.

Materials and Method.

In regard to the inflexional system some writers attribute to the influence of the Dravidian dialects every change that has taken place on Indian soil in the grammar of Aryan languages. The most comprehensive statement to this effect is probably contained in 'The Age of the Mantras' already quoted from, in the last chapter. At page 6 of this book it is stated :—" In the course of its growth in India, on account of the constant influence of the Dravidian tongues, this (Vedic) language lost the subjunctive mood, many infinitive forms and several noun declensions, forgot its richly varied system of real tenses and adopted turns of expression peculiar to the Dravidian idiom. Compare :

Sanskrit *kṛtavān*, Tamil *ceytavaṉ* ;
Sanskrit *iti cet* after an assertion to indicate a condition,
Telugu *ante* ;
Sanskrit *kiñca* ;
Telugu *maṟiyunnu* ;
Sanskrit *tasya kṛte dattam* instead of *tasmai dattam* ;
Telugu *vani koraku iccinadi* "[1].

In considering whether, and if so, to what extent, Dravidian influences have affected Aryan inflexion, we must broadly distinguish between borrowing of materials and mere imitation of method. If it is shown that Indo-Aryan has borrowed any suffixes, auxiliaries or particles from the Dravidian, then we have tangible evidence of Dravidian influence. Where, however, the evidence consists of similarity of methods, no definite conclusion can be drawn. For, the Vedic language which was originally highly inflexional had been undergoing a process of disintegration for over three thousand years till there is nothing left of it now as a spoken language except the neo-Aryan vernaculars of northern India and the Dekhan which are not synthetic but analytical. Parallel instances are the

---

1. In the work referred to the words are not given with proper transliteration.

evolution of the highly analytical modern English from the inflexional Anglo-Saxon and that of New Persian from Old Persian through Pahlavi. When a language loses its inflexional character, it must express grammatical cases by separate particles prefixed or post-fixed to nouns, must form sentences by means of auxiliaries affixed to uninflected participles and must change the order of words in the sentence so as to avoid the ambiguity which the loss of inflexions would produce if the old order were still retained. These and other changes of a similar nature may be wholly illusory and misleading as evidence of imitation of method, and cannot obviously be relied upon. The point may be amply illustrated by taking the first verse in the Saṅksepa Rāmāyaṇa :—

" Tapassvādhyāyaniratam[1] tapasvī[2] vāgvidām[3] varam :

Nāradam[4] paripapraccha[5] Vālmīkir[6] munipuṅgavam[7]."

'Constantly engaged[1] in tapas and svādhyāya, practising[2] tapas, the best of those[3] skilled in speech, Nārada[4] asked[5] Vālmīki[6] the best[7] of munis.'

In the English rendering one cannot say which is the subject, which the object, which of the adjuncts qualify the subject and which the object. But in the Sanskrit original No. 6 is in the nominative case as also its adjunct No. 2, while No. 4 and its adjuncts 1, 3 and 7 are in the accusative case and the sense is easily made out. In uninflected analytical languages we must therefore enter into some convention in regard to the position of the subject and of the object, and of the adjuncts with reference to the nouns they qualify, and must strictly adhere to the convention. The oft-repeated oracular statement " The Greeks the Romans shall conquer " is wholly ambiguous for want of a convention of this sort.

Granting that some such conventions are necessary, it has been argued that the conventions adopted by the Indo-Aryan vernaculars appear to be imitated from Dravidian. A few points which have been prominently mentioned under this head may be considered here :—

" With regard to the inflexion of nouns we may mention the use of postpositions as case-suffixes, the postpositions being usually the same in the singular and the plural. This peculiarity, the Indo-Aryan vernaculars share with Dravidian, but also with the other non-Aryan languages of India, and it would not therefore be safe to base any conclusion upon this fact. Still it is remarkable that the postpositions are often added not to the base but to an oblique form, just as is the case in Dravidian, where the oblique form is commonly used as a genitive. The use of a separate oblique form is, moreover, most extensive in languages such as Marathi and Bihari, where the Dravidian influence must presumably have been strongest. Note also that the genitive is, in both families, an adjective "[1].

" The order of words in modern Indo-Aryan vernaculars, with the governed before the governing word and the verb invariably at the end of the sentence, is also in agreement with Dravidian principles. It is, however, here also possible to think of an influence exercised by other non-Aryan languages, and I only mention the fact that both families agree also in this respect." [2]

The use of separate words as case-suffixes is of the very essence of an analytical language. The use of different suffixes for the different numbers which are already expressed by the number signs attached to the nouns is a needless complexity rightly dispensed with by Aryan vernaculars as

---

1. Linguistic Survey of India, p. 280.
2. Linguistic Survey of India, p. 281.

by other analytical languages. In these two respects modern English about six thousand miles away follows the same methods which the Indo-Aryan vernaculars follow. But it may be asked why these vernaculars have postpositions instead of prepositions. In this respect they follow the Vedic idioms in which case-signs are post-fixed to nouns. The placing of the governed word before the governing word and of the verb at the end of the sentence is a necessary consequence of using post-positions instead of prepositions. The case-suffix is related not only to the noun to which it is attached, but also to the verb-form governing the noun. Example :—

	1	2
Tamil :	Rāmaṉ-ai	kēṭṭāṉ
Translation :	Rāma of	enquired he.
		He enquired of Rāma.

The case-prefixes are called appropriate prepositions in English in their relation to the verbs and come between the verb and the noun it governs. In Sanskrit they are called *upasarga* and are prefixed to the verb ; in this language also they come between the verb and the governed word.

	1	2	3
Tamil :	pacu-v-ai	cuṟṟi	varukiṟāṉ
	1	2	3
Sanskrit :	gām	pari	kramati
(literal translation)	cow	round	comes he
English :	he	comes round (the) cow.	

Thus it is seen that a mere change from post-positions to prepositions produces the entire reversal of the order of words in sentence.

The post-positions are added not to the base but to an oblique form even in the case of English pronouns which have a base, an oblique form and a genitive case as :—

Nominal	Oblique	Possessive.
I	me	my
thou	thee	thy
he	him	his
she	her	her
they	them	their.

In the case of all these pronouns the case-signs are attached to an oblique from and the genitive is an adjective.

It may be argued that the change from the inflexional to the analytical type was itself due to Dravidian influence. How is this established ? Is there any evidence that any of the Dravidian languages were spoken in anything like their present form in the Brāhmaṇa or the Sūtra period ? We have no specimens of these languages which can be ascribed to a period earlier than the end of the 1st century A.D. and the grammatical changes that have taken place since clearly indicate that the languages must then have been in a state of flux.

In the case of Anglo-Saxon and Old Persian the influence appears to have come *ab intra* ; and the facts adduced below would seem to show that in the case of the Vedic language also the changes arose probably *ab intra* and are not necessarily the result of imitation of Dravidian methods. There are certain points in which all agglutinative and all analytical languages must necessarily agree, and no valid inference can be drawn in regard to their origin or influence from such points of agreement.

These discussions become of minor importance in view of the main argument in this book—that in its essential characteristics, what is called Dravidian is made up of elements to be found in Old Indo-Aryan and is merely a phase of Indo-Aryan

42. Pro-ethnic Dravidian Verb.

a. It is also desirable at the outset to settle what was the pro-ethnic form of the Dravidian finite verb. Modern Malayāḷam uses as finite verbs indeclinable verbal forms which are the same for all persons, numbers and genders, and have no personal endings. Thus *paḍi-k-kuṉṉu, paḍi-t-tu, paḍi-k-kum* from the verbal base *paḍi* 'read' are used as finite verbs in the present, the past and the future tenses respectively in all persons, numbers and genders. In Old Kanarese, verbal forms produced by affixing *-ku, -gu, -kum, -gum* to the base were common to all numbers and genders of the third person. In Old Tamil, finite verbs of the form *ceyyum, naṭakkum, varum* etc., from the bases *cey,* 'do' *naṭa* 'walk' *vā* 'come' etc., were common to all the three singulars and the neuter plural of the third person. There were also other verbal forms in Old Tamil in which the personal terminations were of the most rudimentary kind ; this is often the case even now in some Tamil dialects like Burgaṇḍi. In Telugu verbal forms like the past *koṭṭedu, koṭṭe*; the aorist *koṭṭunu*; the futures *koṭṭedunu, koṭṭendeni, koṭṭeni, koṭṭini*; from the verbal base *koṭṭu* 'strike' are common to the three singulars and the neuter plural of the third person, and the analogy of Kanarese and Malayāḷam suggests the inference that some of these forms were probably used in other numbers and persons also in former times. In a specimen of the Beradi dialect of Telugu given in the Linguistic Survey of India (Vol. IV, p. 604), the following past tense forms are used in the singular without any personal endings :—

aḍigiti	'he asked',	*agati*	'I became'
osti	'I came'	*agati*	'you became.'

Can we infer from all these that the Dravidian verb was originally uninflected, that is to say, had no personal endings?

b. Bishop Caldwell says "When the Dravidian entered India the verb must, I think, have been without personal terminations and therefore without gender", (C.D.G. Introduction, page 75). In another place he says "It would appear, therefore, that the Dravidian verb was originally uninflected; and this may partly account for the circumstance that Malayāḷam so readily lost the inflexions which, in common with Tamil, it had acquired. The period when the Dravidian verb was uninflected must have been long prior to the separation of the parent tongue into dialects, in all which, even in the rudest, a system of inflexions has been developed" (C. D. G. page, 377).

The Editors of the Linguistic Survey say:—"the pronominal suffixes are not necessary for the conjugation of the Dravidian verbs, and they are very often dropped in common speech. In Malayāḷam they are never used, but the tenses are replaced by participles without any distinction of person and number. Such participles are also in other dialects used as conjunctive participles. In Gōṇḍi we occasionally also find them employed in the same way as in Malayāḷam. In High Tamil we find a similar state of affairs. Such participles probably represent the oldest stage of the development of the Dravidian verb and they have long been recognized as the bases of the so-called tenses *i.e.*, the compound nouns or nouns of agency used as such (L.S. Vol. IV-page 295)." Following these authorities it has been assumed throught the following pages that the Dravidians were originally using as finite verbs indeclinable verbal forms which have since come to be called participles and verbal nouns.

c. A parallel instance outside India is furnished by the evolution of the past tense in New Persian. "The third person singular of the past tense is the perfect participle ending in *-t* or *-d* alone. The other persons of the tense are formed by attaching to this participle the persons of the auxiliary *ah* 'be'. Thus from *kuṣ* 'killed' are formed the tense forms :—

Sing.	*kuṣṭ-am*	*kuṣṭ-i*	*kuṣṭ*
Plur.	*kuṣṭ-im*	*kuṣṭ-id*	*kuṣṭ-and.*

The past tense as thus formed is a creation of the New Persian. In Pahlavi the participle alone served to express all persons. Example :

kart I did, thou didst, he did and so on"[1].

"In the pre-classical period the past tense of transitive verbs was not constructed as shown above ; but a passive construction was employed (after the example of Old Persian, the Pehlavi, as also the Sanskrit and the Hindi) the agent of the act was put in the oblique case (originally the genitive) the object of the action became the subject and the shorter form of the two participles was employed in the passive."[2].

It may be remarked in passing that even the oldest Dravidian specimens available, do not furnish any instance of such passive constructions or use of the oblique case for the agent. It would seem, therefore, that, so far as we can judge from the available materials, the Dravidian past tense has been evolved from the conjunctive participle, not from the past participle passive.

---

1. J.T. Platts's Grammar of the Persian Language (Vol. I, pages, 173-174, S. 96).

2. J.T. Platts's Grammar of the Persian Language (Vol. I, page 175, S. 96).

d. We see from the above history of the New Persian past tense how the third person singular in a tense paradigm often comes to be left without any personal ending. Certain indeclinable forms like the Pehlavi *kàrt* or the English *did* are originally common to all persons and numbers; gradually the first and the second person singular and plural and the third person plural come to be differentiated by suitable personal endings, thus leaving the original form exclusively for the third person singular. In Dravidian which appears originally not to have recognised neuter plural the form for the third person singular was, as it is even now in some cases, used also for this plural.

We may also note here in anticipation that of the non-pronominalised Telugu forms in (*a*) above *koṭṭe* and *koṭṭenu* are corruptions of forms which have given rise to two of the four Telugu past tense paradigms; while *koṭṭiti* perhaps the latest of Telugu past forms—has been unable to retain its place in the third person. The forms *koṭṭunu*, *koṭṭedunu*, *koṭṭedini* have been superseded by *koṭṭuta* and *koṭṭeda* in other persons and numbers.

43. THE INCREASING USE OF PARTICIPLES IN LATER SANSKRIT.

We are now in a position to examine the various items in which Aryan dialects are said to have imitated Dravidian methods on Indian soil. The Editors of the Linguistic Survey say (L. S. IV, p. 280-281):—

"If we compare the Dravidian, and the Indo-European verb we are at once struck by a considerable difference. The Indo-European languages have developed a richly varied system of real verbal tenses, while the Dravidians do not use ordinary tenses but employ forms which can best be described as participles or nouns of agency derived from such participles. The Dravidian verb in this respect also differs from the Tibeto-Burman one, which can most properly be described as a verbal noun.

The Dravidian participles are commonly used without any addition, as conjunctive participles in subordinate sentences. In other cases they are used in the same way in some dialects, but usually prononominal suffixes are added in order to indicate the person of the subject. The same is, to a great extent, the case with ordinary nouns of agency, when they are used as verbs.

It is easy to see how a corresponding tendency has gradually pervaded the Indo-Aryan language and changed their whole appearance.

In the Vedas we still find the Indo-European principle of using a varied system of verbal tenses. But already in the old Epics all this has changed. According to Professor Whitney, the number of verbal forms in the Nala-carita and the Bhagavadgītā is only one-tenth of that found in the Ṛg-Veda In classical Sanskrit almost every verbal tense was replaced by a participle, and in the modern vernaculars there are only traces of the old tenses, and new ones have been formed from the old participles, just as in the case with the Dravidian forms of speech. The use of personal terminations in many Indo-Aryan vernaculars and the substitution of the nominative for the agent in some of them point in the same direction.

Side by side with this development we find that the conjunctive participle is used more and more in secondary sentences, another point of analogy with the Dravidian languages. In the Epics this form is used thrice as often as in the Vedas and in later literature its use is steadily increasing."

Every particular in the above enumeration, especially the replacement of tenses by indeclinable verbal forms is a step in the transition from the synthetic to the analytic stage and these steps may have been taken in the natural course of evolution without being suggested by Dravidian forms. What Dravidian or Turanian example did English followed when it discarded almost all inflexions and came to tolerate such a sentence as "*I got up* early in the morning, *had* a bath before taking coffee, *got on* horseback and *rode* twenty miles." The verbal forms *got up, had, got* and *rode* have no endings to indicate person, number or gender and are exactly the same as the Malayāḷam forms *eḻunnu, snānam, ceydu, kudara ēṟi, savāri ceydu.* In Telugu, the forms will be *lēci, snānamu cēśi, gurramu yekki, savāri cēśinānu* the last only having a personal ending. Again there is absolutely no inflexion in the forms of the tense. "I, you, he, she, it, we, you, they had done." English has succeeded in doing what they did only on a very limited scale in classical Sanskrit. This use of uninflected participles is a revolt of the progressive human mind against the tyranny of unnecessary and bewildering inflexions. English which has thrown off this tyranny is easy to learn and to speak and has acquired a power of expression hardly inferior to that of any language ancient or modern. Sanskrit had within itself forms and modes by the free use of which the Epic writers attempted to throw off the yoke of inflexions, but the process did not proceed very far in classical Sanskrit which soon ceased to be a spoken dialect and became stereotyped nearly two thousand years ago. The simplification was, however, continued by the speakers of the Prākṛts and the Apabhraṁśas so thoroughly that the present Aryan vernaculars of India are almost wholly analytical with occasional exceptions.

The substitution of the nominative case for the agent has its analogue in the evolution of the past tense in modern

Persian and appears to be another instance of unnecessary detail dispensed with in the course of simplification.

Let us look at the reverse side af the picture. If the Dravidian finite verb was at first an unchanging participle and had no personal ending, might it not be argued that the Aryan speakers of Dravidian began to attach these endings to the final verb in a sentence in imitation of Sanskrit. In Old Tamil personal endings are also added to verbal forms in subordinate clauses[1]: is it not reasonable to suppose that this was due to the earliest Aryan cultivators of Dravidian-Brahmans, Jains, and Buddhists imitating Old Aryan idioms which preceded classical Sanskrit?

Again taking the Dravidian conjunctive participles and verb forms instanced above *eḻunnu*, *ēṟi*, *ceydu*, *lēci*, *cēśi*, *yekki*, *cēśinānu*, it will be seen from the explanations given above that the aim of this book is to show that the tense signs —*nnu*, -*i*, -*du*, -*ci*, *śi* -*inu* in the above examples are corruptions of Aryan particles. If this is a fact, Dravidian must have borrowed Aryan particles wholesale, and there is no point in saying that Indo-Aryan has imitated Dravidian. If the roots and the tense and mode signs of Dravidian are taken from Indo-Aryan, then Dravidian is not a separate entity.

44. Loss of many infinite forms in Sanskrit.

The loss of many infinitive forms in Sanskrit has been attributed to Dravidian influence by some writers, but without any justification whatever. The infinitive had a

1. *a. uṇarndanar koḷalē—uṇarndu koḷalē* (Tol. II, 19) "it must be understood."

b. paliccinir kaḻimin (Pattu. X-360) 'pass (the spot) after offering up a prayer'.

c. uḷḷinir cērir āyin. (Pattu. X-65) 'if you go (there) thinking of..'.

variety of forms in the Vedas, but all these were merely cases of verbal nouns ; and the case-form most commonly used as infinitive was the dative though objective infinitives were also frequent ; the genitive, ablative and locative infinitives were rare. The dative infinitives like *kartave* *kṛ* 'do'), *śrotave* (*śru* 'hear') are not known to later Sanskrit in which only the objective infinitives in *-tum* like *kartum*, *śrotum* now survive.

In the Dravidian languages there are two ways of forming infinitives. One form is the dative case of verbal nouns, as Telugu *cēyuṭaku*, *cēyadāniki*, Kanarese *geyyalige*, Tamil *ceyarku*, 'for doing' ; and this dative form is mentioned in Tolkāppiyam which is supposed to be the oldest Tamil work extant ; the objective case form is unknown to the Dravidian languages. If Sanskrit has discontinued the dative form and adopted the objective form universally, it cannot certainly be through Dravidian influence.

The other mode of forming infinitives in Dravidian is by adding *-a* to the root, as, Telugu *cēya*, Kanarese *geyya*, Tamil *ceyya*. The older form of this *-a* is *-an* in Telugu which appears to have become *-al* in Tamil and Knnarese ; this suffix *-an* is probably derived from Prākṛtic forms.

45. Loss of the Vedic subjunctive mood.

The remark that the Vedic language lost its subjunctive mood through the influence of the Dravidian appears to be equally unjustifiable and shows a misapprehension of the functions of this mood in that language and of the circumstances under which the mood became latterly a superfluity. The Vedic subjunctive had a value similar to that of the optative and its fundamental meaning was one of requisition, less peremptory than the imperative, but more so than the optative. In principal sentences the difference in the values of these moods was only one of degree ; in fact when the subjunctive mood gradually fell into desuetude its forms for the first person—as in *bhavāni*, *bhavāva*, *bhavāma*—were taken over by the imperative which originally had no forms in the Vedas for the first person (W.S.G. SS. 533-a ; 574-a 578).

The subjunctive mood was also used in the Vedas in subordinate clauses in such connections as would be expressed in English by the conditional clauses 'if it should be etc.,' 'lest it should be etc.', 'in order that it may be etc.' ; but here also its functions were shared by the optative which even in the earliest Vedic period had come to be used in dependant clauses with relative pronouns and conjunctions, as a regular means of expressing the conditional and contingent. (W.S.G.S. 576-b). A part of its functions being fulfilled by the imperative and the rest having been taken over by the optative the subjunctive became a superfluity in the language and fell into disuse. It is not easy to see how this disuse can be attributed to the influence of Dravidian.

In the Avestic language also the imperative had originally no forms for the first person; the subjunctive forms of this person were subsequently taken over by the imperative (J. A. V. S 447 note).

46. THE ARYAN INDECLINABLE PRESENT PARTICIPLE.

The present participle was always declined in Vedic and classical Sanskrit and in literary Prākṛts so as to agree with the subject in number and gender. But some of the modern Aryan vernaculars use an indeclinable form of the participle, and whenever this is the case the Editors of the Linguistic Survey remark that such usage is due to the example of the adjoining Dravidian languages. On examining the question, however, it is seen that the indeclinable present participle occurs often in the Aśoka inscriptions of the 4th Century B.C.; and the neo-Aryan vernaculars have doubtless inherited it from the Māgadhī Apabhraṁśā. The suffixes of one of the Telugu present participles and possibly also of the Kanarese present participle appear to be derived from the termination of the Aśokic participle.

47. The sanskrit periphrastic future.

The Editors of the Linguistic Survey say that " the periphrastic future is used very sparingly in the Brāhmaṇas and only becomes more frequent in the later literature. It is, as is well known, formed from the noun of agency by adding the verb substantive in the first and second persons. Now the noun of agency is a present or indefinite form, not a future. In the Dravidian languages, on the other hand, the indefinite present is commonly also a future. The analogy becomes still more striking when we remember that the verb substantive is only added to the first two persons, just as nouns of agency in the Dravidian languages are used without any additions as verbs in third person singular, while pronominal suffixes are added in the first and second persons. Forms such as *kartāsmi* ' I shall do,' *kartāsi* ' thou shalt to,' *kartārah* ' they will do ', thus directly correspond to the Gōṇḍ *kiatona.* 'I do,' that is, ' I am a doer ' ; *kiatoni* ' thou doest '; *kihtor* ' they do ". (L.S. IV-page, 281).

The above remarks overlook the circumstance that there is a periphrastic future in the Avesta in which the forms of the third person are as in Sanskrit the *nomen agentis* inflected for the three numbers :

netā *netārau* *netāraḥ*

In the first and second persons the singular *netā* is compounded with the corresponding forms of the Avestic verb *ah* ' to be ' in all numbers (K. A. G. S. 471). Brugmann when dealing with periphrastic formations in the Indo-

Germanic languages mentions similar forms in which infinitival words are used with the verb substantive to express the future (Brug. IV S. 899). It will be noted that on the analogy of *netāsmaḥ* instead of *netāsmi*, the first person plural is *netāsmaḥ* and not *netāraḥ smaḥ*; similarly we have in the Avesta *patmahi* 'we will protect' *patasto* 'you will protect' (K. A. G. S. 471).

These forms are a certain token that the component words had become fused into one word even in the Indo-Iranian period (C. F. Brug. IV, 896).

This instance shows the danger of assuming that, if a form not found in the Vedas is found in later Sanskrit, it must have been borrowed from a foreign source. The existence of such a form in the Avesta has demonstrated in this case that classical Sanskrit has inherited materials from some unknown Aryan dialects of India which are not represented in the existing Vedas.

48. The Sanskrit Active Past Participle.

The Editors of the Linguistic Survey say that "forms such as the Sanskrit *kṛtavān* 'one who has done are also peculiar to the later Sanskrit. The suffix -*vat* is of course Aryan, but it is not easliy understood how an active form can be arrived at by adding the suffix to a passive participle. In the Dravidian languages on the other hand a participle is active as well as passive[1] and a noun of agency is formed from it in all dialects. Thus from Tamil *ceytu* 'having done' we form *ceytavaṉ* 'one who has done.' The close agreement between *kṛtavān* and *ceytavaṉ* is of course partly accidental. There cannot, however, be any reasonable doubt about the former having been influenced by the latter. In Sanskrit *kṛtavān* is an anomalous form without analogy in connected

1. The corresponding Telugu form will be *cēśinavā-ḍu*.

languages, while Tamil *ceytavaṉ* is quite regular " (L.S. IV, page 281).

Here also the Editors of the Linguistic Survey have overlooked the existence in the Avesta of forms identical with those in Sanskrit. The following are some of the examples given in Kanga's Avestan Grammar, of past participles active, formed from past participles passive by suffixing the termination *-vat* (K.A.G. S. 563).

Root : *vərəz.* ' to work ' p.p.p. *varsta.* p.p.a. *varstavat.*

Root : ṣā ' to become propitious ' p.p.p. ṣāna. p.p.a *ṣānavat.*

49. The Dravidian Terminations of the Nominative Masculine Traceable to the Indo-Germanic *-nt-* through Indo-Aryan.

The Indo-Iranians had inherited two present participles one active and the other passive, *viz.*, *bharat*, *bhriyamāṇa*; two future participles, active and passive, viz., *bhariṣyat*, *bhariṣyamāṇa*; but only past participle, passive, viz., *bhṛta*. In coining an active participle for the past they followed the model of the present and future participles active, and chose the suffix *-vat* so that all the three active participles may have practically identical declensions. In the nominative masculine singular *-ts* disappears leaving only *-n*, as *bhavan*, *bhariṣyan*, *bhṛtavān*. In the masculine nominative dual and plural and accusative singular and dual, the full conjuct *-nt* appears and thereafter only *-t*.

		Present.	Future.	Past.
Nominative	Sing.	*bharan*	*bhariṣvan*	*bhṛtavān*
,,	Dual.	*bharantau*	*bhariṣvantau*	*bhṛtavantau*
,,	Plur.	*bharantaḥ*	*bhariṣvantaḥ*	*bhṛtavantaḥ*

		Present.	Future.	Past.
Accusative	Sing.	*bharantam*	*bhariṣyantam*	*bhṛtavantam*
,,	Dual.	*bharantau*	*bhariṣyantau*	*bhṛtavantau*
,,	Plur.	*bharataḥ*	*bhariṣyataḥ*	*bhṛtavataḥ*
Instr.	Sing.	*bharatā*	*bhariṣyatā*	*bhṛtavatā*
		etc.,	etc.,	etc.

If the object was merely to imitate Tamil, this could have been secured better by using the suffix *-van* which contains no *-t* and would show *-n* all case forms like Tamil, as :—

**bhṛtavān*, **bhṛtavānau*, **bhṛtavānaḥ*,
**bhṛtavānam*, **bhṛtavānau*, **bhṛtavānaḥ* etc.

The contention that the Sanskrit participle was based on the Tamil model is clearly untenable.

On the other hand it will be abundantly clear from an examination of the Dravidian forms Tamil *ceytavaṉ*, Old Kanarese *geydavam*, Modern Kanarese *geydavanu* etc., that the masculine singular nominative of the demonstrative pronoun has in every case imitated Aryan forms. This demonstrative is *avaṉ* in Tamil and Malayāḷam, *avam* in Old Kanarese, *avanu* in Modern Kanarese, but the Old Kanarese form is still retained by the Badagas on the Nilgiris; it is *vāḍu* or *vāṇḍdu* in Telugu, *ondu* in Madras Gōṇḍi, and *eañju oañju* in Kūi. The Tulu demonstrative singular masculine remote and proximate are *aye* and *imbe*. In the table below, these demonstratives are compared with the masculine nominative singulars of the Aryan present participles which they imitate ; the *-nt* of these participles is, as is well-known Indo-Germanic in origin.

Dravidian.	Dravidian forms.	Aryan forms.	Aryan dialects.
Tamil. Malayāḷam.	*avaṉ*	*bharān*	Vedic

Dravidian	Dravidian forms.	Aryan forms.	Aryan dialects.
Old Kanarese, Badaga	*avam*	*bhavam*	Ardhamāgadhī
Telugu	*vāḍu, vaṇḍu*	*bharanto*	Pāli
Madras Gōṇḍi	*ondu*	*bharantu*	Apabhraṁśa (P.P.G. 327).
Kūi.	*eañju*	*baras* (from *barns*)	Avestic (K.A.G. Ss. 132 & 133.) (P.P.G.S. 397).
Tulu	*aye*	*drvae* (from '*dru* run')	Avestic (K.A.G. S. 134).

The correspondences in this table gives us a clue as to the kind of Aryan influence to which the various parts of Southern India were subject in the earliest times. The Old Kanarese *avam* imitating *bhavam* one of the forms assumed by the nominative masculine of the present participle *bharat* in Māgadhi and Ardhamāgadhī betrays Jain or Buddhistic influence, while the Tamil *avaṉ*, which corresponds to the Vedic *bhavān* arising from the loss of *-ts* in the *bhavants* probably indicates that the earliest Aryan influence in the Tamil country was Brāhmanic. Telugu and Madras Gōṇḍ forms indicate Pāli influence. The Kūi termination *-ñju* may be taken to arise from the palatalization of Telugu *-ṇḍu*; perhaps so, but there is also the possibility of there having been an Aryan dialect in India possessing the Avestic form *baras* but not represented in Sanskrit or the Prākṛts, and the Kūi language might have received the termination *-ñju* from the lost dialect. There is nothing very special in the form *baras*, the termination of which arises from ans. C. F. Sanskrit *vidvāṁsa*. In the case of the *aye* we have to postulate the existence of a similar dialect not represented in Sanskrit or the Prākṛts. Or we may expl .in the final *-e* in *aye* as due to the Māgadhī influence, and regard the initial *a-* as equivalent to *av-* the vowel being lengthened in compensation for the loss of *-v-*; this Māgadhī influence appears also in *imbe* the Tulu proximate demonstrative and the long- *ā* also appears in *-aḷ* 'she,' *-ār* 'they (epicene),'

50. THE TELUGU *-ṇḍu* HAS ARISEN FROM THE INDO-ARYAN *-ntu*.

In the table given in the previous paragraph the Telugu cerebrals *-ṇḍ-* or *-ḍ-* corresponds to the Sanskrit *-nt*. As will have been seen from the examples given in S. 39 above Telugu appears to have a predilection for the cerebral *-ṭ-* and *-ḍ-*, for what is dental or alveolar in Kanarese and Tamil is very often converted into a cerebral sound in Telugu.

(i) *aṇḍu, uṇḍu* : There is a Telugu form of respectful accosting, viz., *ēmaṇḍi*, and the respectful form request is *ceppaṇḍi, dayacēvaṇḍi* etc. These correspond to the Sanskrit idiom in which the persons addressed are put in the third person, as in *āgacchantu bhavantaḥ* 'May your honours be pleased to come where *āgacchantu* is the third person plural imperative; of the base *ā-gam* 'come' and *bhavantaḥ* is the masculine nominative plural of *bhavat* 'your honour.' *Bhavantaḥ* becomes *bhonto* in Pāli and is further corrupted into *honto* or *hunto* in the later Prākṛts (P.P.G.S. 476). An optional form was probably **bhanto* or **hanto* for the word *bhante* (=*bhavantaḥ*) 'sirs' is frequently used when addressing heads, as in Aśoka's letter to the Magadha Saṅgha where *bhante* punctuates the sentences. (I. A. Vol. V, page 257). The Apabhraṁśa forms for *bhavān* will be *hontu, huntu* and *hantu* respectively (P.P.G.S. 397) these and the imperative plural termination *-antu* have apparently become *-oṇḍu* and

-uṇḍu. The forms *ceppaṇḍu* and *cēyaṇḍu* are likely to be mistaken for the third person masculine negative, and the final vowels *a* probably differentiate the imperative; but we may have *ceppuṇḍu* and *ceppuḍu*. Thus *ēmaṇḍi*, *dayacēyaṇḍi* is really the hybrid formation *emi bhavantaḥ dayacēyantu*.

(ii) *E-du* is a suffix indicating measure or quantity which is used in composition, as mure-*du* 'cubit length' *jene-du* 'span-length,' *mane du* 'as much as a mana etc. This suffix appears to be derived from the Vedic suffix *yant* expressing the quantitative meaning of 'much' which occurs in *i-yant* 'so much' and *ki-yant* 'how much' (M.V. G. 402 (d)). In later Sanskrit *iyattā*, *iyattvam* meaning 'measure, quantity,' standard, limit, are from the pronoun *iyat*. In Apabhraṁśa the nominative singular of this pronoun will be *iyantu* or *entu*; the *-nt-* of these forms being cerebralized we get *eṇḍu* 'measure' of the Telugu inscriptions as in *māneṇḍu neyi pōyagala vāṇḍu* 'he must supply a *mana* of ghee' (E.I. Vol. VI, page 158). The nasal of this word has now dwindled into an ardhānusvāra (obscure nasal) the existence of which is recognised by grammarians (C. B. Sandhi, 11, Taddhita, 25).

There is a word *anta* in Telugu meaning 'measure, quantity' as in *ravanta*, *isumanta*, *konta* (=*okinta*) etc., which is also traceable to an Aryan origin and is probably imitated from the terminations of *etāvant* and *tāvant* 'so great,' *yāvant* 'as great,' *ivant* and *iyant* 'so great' (M.V.G.S. 402 [*e*]). This imitation must have been recent, long subsequent to the formation of *edu*.

(iii) *Vaṇṭi* as in *aṭuvaṇṭi* 'resembling that': *Tadvat* in Sanskrit means not only 'possessing it' but also 'like it'; in the former sense *-vat* is declinable and in the latter indeclinable. Though indeclinable its real form is *-vant* which will become *-vaṇḍ* in Telugu; with the oblique declensional suffix *-ti* the latter will become *-vaṇṭi* as in *atuvaṇṭi māvaṇṭi* 'resembling us,' *mīvaṇṭi* 'resembling you' etc. Compare the last two with the Vedic adjectival forms *māvant* 'like me,' *tvāvant* 'like thee' (M. V. G. 402 (e)). Adjectives signifying after the manner of, like etc., were probably made formerly with the suffix *-vant* (W.S.G.S. 517, 1233. f.) *māvant, tvāvant, yuṣmāvant, yuvāvant, ivant kivant, tāvant, etāvant yāvant.* Of these, however, only the last three are in use in the later language in the sense of *tantus* and *quantus.*

(iv) *anda* : One of the meanings of the Sanskrit word *anta* is 'neighbourhood' as in *antika, antevāsin* etc. The Aśoka inscriptions speak of *antaḥ* meaning 'neighbouring kings' and probably also 'protected princes.' This word appears to have become *anda* which in Telugu and Tamil means not only 'neighbourhood' but also 'protection.'

(v) *Pēraṇḍa* : The Sanskrit word *paryanta* becomes *peraṇṭa* in Prākṛt ; following the analogy of *anta* it should become *peraṇḍa* in Dravidian in the sense of 'the area surrounding a house, a backyard.' In classical Telugu the word appears to have lost the nasal and is written *peradu* as if it were a corruption of *pṛṣtha,* but the Telugus of the Tamil country preserve the nasal.

(vi) *edu* : Another example which may be mentioned here, but with some reserve, is that of the Prākṛt present participle in *ento*; for according to Vararuci's sūtras (VII-10 and 34) present participles may end in *ento* as well as in *anto* (*vide* Cowell's Vararuci Introduction, page xxxi, also Hemacandra 11-167 and 158). This *ento* might have given rise to the suffix-*edu* in the Telugu present participles *vaccedu, uṇḍedu* etc., but there appear to be no authenticated instances even in Telugu dialects where the nasal is preserved.

The above examples are enough to show that *-nt* in Sanskrit often becomes *-nd* in Telugu. The termination of *-vandu* and *-ondu* is thus derived from the Pāli and Apabhraṁśa terminations *-nto* and *-ntu* of the table in the previous paragraph.

The intermediate form between *-nt* and *-nd* is the conjuct consonant *-nr-* of Tamil. This intermediate *-nr-* appears to occur in a Telugu inscription of Satyāditya of Renandu which is supposed to be anterior to the 9th century A.D. (E. I. Vol. XI, page 337 *et ceq.*). The words of the inscription in which the above conjunct consonant occurs are:—

kāśyapagotrunṟu, *Satyādityunṟu*, *ēlucunṟi*, *vēvānṟu*, *vaccuvanṟu*, *uṇḍuvānṟu*;

but there are so many orthographical peculiarities in this inscription that it cannot be relied upon as furnishing indubitable evidence of the *-nṟ-* in Telugu. Further it has been suggested that *-nṟu* may probably stand for *-ndru* and may merely be the form; this explanation will not, however, apply to the word *ēlucunṟi*.

51. THE DRAVIDIAN MASCULINE SIGN *-n*.

It would appear from the discussion above that the termination of the nominative masculine singular of the Dravidian demonstrative pronoun varies from language to language, but in the oblique forms an *-n-* appears uniformly in all the languages under consideration. Thus we have in the accusative :—

Tamil *avaṉai*, Old Kanarese *avanam*,
Telugu *vānin*, Gōṇḍi *on (k) kai eāri*.

The Dravidian variations in the nominative singular have their counterparts in the corresponding singulars of Aryan present participles, thus :—

Vedic *bharan*, Māgadhī *bharam*,
Apabhraṁśa *bharantu*, Pāli *bharanto*,
Avestic *barəns*, *baras*, *baro drvae*.

The Vedic form is due to the elision of the final *-ts* in the masculine singular *bharants*; the Māgadhī *bharam* is probably due to a peculiar way of pronouncing the Vedic *bharan.* In all the Aryan forms there is an inherent conjunct *-nt* which is Indo-Germanic in origin and which owing to various causes undergoes the above modifications; in cases other than the nominative singular the Aryan *-nt* or *-t-* reappears.

The Indo-Aryan forms which contain this conjunct *-nt* are :—

(i) The present, aorist and future participles active formed with the suffixes *-ant, -syant,*

(ii) The past participle active formed with the suffix *-vant* and,

(iii) The possessive adjectives formed with suffixes *-vant, -mant.*

Grammarians recognise two forms of the stem in these classes of words—the strong and the weak—the former containing the conjunct *-nt* as in *bhavant,* the latter containing only the single consonant *-t* as in *bhavat.* All the masculine case-forms from and inclusive of the accusative plural are formed from the weak stem, the previous ones being formed from the strong stem. In the neuter gender only the nominative, vocative and the accusative plural are formed from the strong stem, the remaining case-forms being made with the weak. In classical Sanskrit and in the Vedic dialects the nominative singular always ends in *-n* in the masculine, as in *bhavan, bhagavan* and in *-t* in the neuter, as in *bhavat, bhagavat.* The feminine form is obtained by affixing *-ī* to the stem and is declined as a feminine noun in *ī* e.g. *bharantī, bhavatī, kṛtavatī, buddhimatī* etc.

In the Prākṛts, however, which are supposed to represent in some cases a condition of the spoken vernaculars even anterior to that of the Vedic dialects, there is very great laxity in the use of the strong and the weak stems, almost every case being formed in some of them either from the strong or from the weak stem indiscriminately (P.P.G. Ss. 396-397) ; (Duroiselle's Pali Grammar, Ss. 219-230).

In the Avestic language there are two weak stems *barad*, *baren* (Sanskrit *bharat*, *bharan*) and one strong stem *barand* (Sanskrit *bharant*). The masculine nominative singular is never of the form *baren* (Sanskrit *bharan*) but always of the form *baro*, *baras*, *drvae* (*vide* table in S. 49 above); the neuter nominative singular is always of the form *barad* (Sanskrit *bharat*). The stem *baren* occurs in the instrumental, dative and ablative plurals and may be used either for the masculine, or for the neuter in these case-forms as an alternative for the stem *barad*. Thus the Indo-Iranian *bharant-bhis*, *bharant-bhyas* which have become *bharad-bhis* and *bharad-bhyas* in Sanskrit appear as *baradbis*, *baradbyo*, *barenbis*, *barinbyo* in the Avestic language. For further particulars *See* K.A.G. Ss. 132-132.

The correspondence between the terminations of the masculine nominative singular of the demonstrative pronoun in Dravidian and those of the same case-forms in the Aryan participles and possessive adjectives etc., in *-ant*, *-vant*, *-mant*, is so exact even to details, that it leads irresistibly to the conclusion that the former are imitations of the latter, each Dravidian dialect imitating the contiguous Aryan dialect in this respect. The masculine nominative singulars ending in *-n* in Sanskrit are :—

bharan	present participle
vṛdhan	root aorist participle
bhariṣyan	future participle
kṛtavān	active past participle
dyutimān	possessive adjective
balayān	do

To these must be added :—

vidvān	perfect participle
balīyān	adjective (comparative degree).

Might it be that seeing this multiplicity of forms, all ending in *-n* in the masculine singular, many Dravidian languages adopted this letter as the sign of the masculine gender, and that subsequently the terminations of the nominative singular were changed in the various dialects in imitation of the contiguous Aryan dialects leaving the *-n* unchanged in the masculine oblique cases? The theory put forward in this book is that the Dravidian masculine sign *-n*, whether derived by imitation or by inheritance, is traceable to the Indo-Germanic ending *-nt*.

It is needless to point out here that the Sanskrit masculine forms mentioned above indicate only grammatical gender and may refer to irrational animals or inanimate things like *siṁha* 'a lion', *vyāghra* 'a tiger', *vṛkṣa* 'a tree,' *soma* 'the moon or the soma plant' which are all treated as of the neuter gender in Dravidian, as well as to males (and females, though rarely) of rational beings like *manuṣya* 'a man,' *amātya* 'a king's minister,' *dūta* 'a messenger,' *kṣattriya* 'a man of the *kṣattriya* caste,' *dārāḥ* 'wife.' In Tamil most nouns of the irrational (*aḵṟiṇai*) class, which now end in *-m*, may also optionally end in *-n* and some nouns of this class have only the latter form.

maram, maraṉ	'a tree'
aṟam, aṟaṉ	'virtue'
nilam, nilaṉ	'the ground'
iṭam, iṭaṉ	'a place'
pulam, pulaṉ	'one of the five senses'
vaḷam, vaḷaṉ	'fertility'
tiṟam, tiṟaṉ	'ability'
kaṭam, kaṭaṉ	'debt'.

The forms ending in *-ṉ* are usually considered archaic and poetical, but in the case of *kaṭaṉ* 'debt', and a few other words, it is the form ending in *-ṉ* that obtains in popular speech. In the case *kaṭukkaṉ* ' an earring,' *cōmaṉ* ' a cloth ', etc., there are no alternative forms ending in *-m*

It would seem that all nouns of the kind we are considering formerly ended in *-ṉ* and that such of them as belonged to the irrational class had their final subsequently changed to *-m* so as to make them correspond to the Sanskrit nominative neuter singular *jñānam* ' knowledge,' *bilam* ' an aperture,' *balam* ' strength ' etc., leaving the final *-n* unchanged in the case of high caste nouns of the masculine gender like *manitaṉ* ' a man,' *kaṇavaṉ* ' a husband,' *makaṉ* ' a son ' etc. Nouns of the feminine gender like *akkaṉ* ' an elder sister, *ammaṉ* ' mother,' have now become *akkā*, *akkāḷ*; *ammā*, *ammai*, *ammāḷ*; while *ammaṉ* ' a goddess ' still continue to be *ammaṉ*.

The oblique base of these high caste nouns (*uyartiṇai*) in the singular is the same as the nominative singular, but neuter nouns ending in *-m* form the oblique base by substituting *-t* for *-m*.

	Nominative singular.	Oblique singular.	Accusative singular.
Rational masculine	*makaṉ* ' a son '	*makaṉ*	*makaṉ-ai*
Neuter Old form	*aṟaṉ* ' virtue '	*aṟaṉ*	*aṟaṉ-ai*
Modern form	*aṟam*	*aṟat*	*aṟat-t-ai*
Old form	*iṭaṉ*	*iṭaṉ*	*iṭaṉ-ai*
Modern form	*iṭam*	*iṭat*	*iṭat-t-ai*

This reminds one of the Sanskrit *bharan* and *bharat*, and of the Avestic bases *baren* and *barad*.

52. THE DRAVIDIAN FEMININE SIGN -*ḷ*.

Professor Sten Konow says (L.S. Vol. IV, p. 220).

" Nouns denoting women and goddesses are, in almost all dialects treated as high-caste nouns in the plural. In the singular, on the other hand, there is a double tendency. Tamil, Malayāḷam and Kanarese use a separate female form of which there appear to be some few traces in other Dravidian languages, while all other dialects substitute the neuter. The analogy from the plural seems to indicate that this latter tendency is an innovation of the languages in question, and that the feminine singular or rational nouns did not originally agree with the neuter. I may mention as a possibility that the feminine singular suffix -*aḷ* in Tamil and Kanarese is only a modified form of the masculine -*aṉ*. It will be shown under the head of Gōṇḍi that there are distinct traces in that language of a system of inflection of nouns where rational masculine and feminine bases form an oblique base ending in -*n* while the oblique base of neuter nouns ends in -*t*. Though the latter form is now used in most nouns it is just probable that we have here to do with the last traces of an older state of affairs where the feminine singular like the feminine plural, agreed with the masculine."

The characteristic sign of the feminine gender in Tamil, Malayāḷam and Kanarese, is the letter -*ḷ* in the suffix -*aḷ*. The other Dravidian languages which contain traces of this termination are :—

Telugu which has the words *alu* 'a woman, wife', *kōḍalu* 'a daughter-in-law,' *celiyalu, cellelu* 'a younger sister,' *maradalu* 'younger female relation' *Kui kuali* 'a Kui woman', Kurukh *ali* 'a woman.' Telugu has also the adjective *āḍu* (literary *ā-ḍu*) 'female'.

The nominative plural of the above Telugu nouns in -*lu* are *āṇḍru, kōḍaṇḍru, celiyaṇḍru, celleṇḍru, maradaṇḍru* ;

and the combination -*ṇḍr*- appears in all the plural oblique forms of the nouns : *e.g.*

āṇḍranu, kōḍaṇḍra yokka etc.

The final -*ru* in the above forms is of course the plural sign, but what is the -*nd* ? There is no inflexional increment -*t*- in the oblique singular of these nouns and the -*ṇḍ* can not be due to any incremental -*t*. It is apparently the original from which the feminine sign -*ḷ* in *aḷu* etc., has been derived ; the original of *aḷu* must have been *andu* from which Telugu *ādu, ā* (*du* 'female' have also been obviously derived by the total or partial loss of the nasal -*n*-). We saw before, that the Indo-Germanic -*nt*- has been cerebralized in Telugu and has given rise to the masculine sign -*ṇḍu* as in *magaṇḍu* (husband), *alluṇḍu* 'son-in-law' etc. The -*n*- of these words became an *ardhānusvāra* (obscure nasal) as in *magu* (*du, allu*) *du* etc., and has now wholly disappeared in colloquial language as in *magadu, alludu* etc. By another process of corruption the same -*ṇḍ* (arising from -*nt*) has futher become -*l* as *naṇḍu, aḍu, aḍu* containing a cerebral should have become *alu*, but in this as in many other cases in Telugu *ḷ* replaces cerebral -*ḷ* found in Tamil, Malayāḷam and Kanarese as the sign of the feminine gender. Strange as it may seem both the masculine -*ṉ* and the feminine ending -*ḷ* appear to be derived from the same Indo-Germanic *d-nt*.

The feminine suffix -*aḷ* is, thus, not a modified form, as supposed by Professor Sten Konow, of the masculine suffix -*aṉ*, but both of them are modified forms of the Indo-Aryan -*ant* (Dravidian -*aṉṟ*, -*and*). There is, however, nothing improbable in the supposition made by him that in Gōṇḍi rational masculine and feminine bases had at one time oblique bases ending in -*ṉ* while the oblique bases of neuter nouns ended in -*t* ; for the Dravidian languages have obviously been imitating the endings of Aryan forms in this respect. We saw that there were two weak bases in the Avesta of the types *barad* and *bare̱n*. Some Indo-Aryan vernaculars might have had similar weak bases and it is possible that the finals *-d* and *-n* of these bases might have been adopted in some Dravidian dialects for irrational and rational oblique bases.

In Tamil, as we have seen, the development appears to have been different. All rational masculine and neuter bases originally ended in *-ṉ* (imitated from the nominative singular of the Sanskrit grammatical masculine) and the oblique bases also ended in *-ṉ*. Subsequently the final of the neuter bases was changed to *-m*, this *-m* being again changed to *-t* in the oblique forms. The evolution in Telugu differed from that both in Gōṇḍi and in Tamil. This lack of uniformity shows that Dravidian languages have been subject to powerful disturbing influences.

At pages 120-126 of his Grammar, Bishop Caldwell enters into a detailed disquisition as to the origin and inter-relations of the Dravidian signs of the masculine and the feminine singular, and arrives at the following conclusions :—

(1) Telugu *-nd*, Tamil, Malayāḷam and Kanarese *-ṉ* and Old Kanarese *-m* are identical; the masculine suffixes *-andu*, *-an*, and, *am*, of these languages are also identical;

(2) The Kūi word *āñju* 'a man' (which he writes *āñu*) is identical with the Tamil *āṇ* 'a male' and also probably with the Tamil *āḷ* 'a man, a person of either sex. The Kui *āñu*, he points out, is in some connections shortened into *anu*, and this fact, he thinks, renders it probable that the Dravidian masculine suffix *-an* is connected with the Kui *āñu* 'a man' and the Tamil *-an* 'a man'

(3) Similarly the Dravidian feminine suffixes *-aḷ* and *-aḷu* are, he says, derived from Telugu and Kui *āḷu* 'a woman,' which is probably connected with the Telugu adjective *ādu* 'female.'

As we have seen above the suffixes *āṇḍu*, *an*, *and*, *am*, can be said to be identical only in the sense that they are traceable ultimately to one and the same original; similarly Kui *āñu* and the Tamil *-an* and *-āḷ* are identical only in the sense that their suffixes are derived from a common original. It is probably incorrect to assume that the noun *āñu* has been shortened into the suffix *-āṉ* and the noun *āḷu* into the suffixes *-aḷu* and *-aḷ*; these words have required their meanings of 'a man' and 'a female' respectively in consequence of these suffixes.

There is a connection between the three words *āñu*, *āṇ*, and *āḷ*, on one side and the two words *āḍu* and *āḷu* on the other, which Bishop Caldwell has not noticed. In Telugu *āḍu* (adj.) means 'female' and *āḍudi* means 'a woman, but in Tamil *āṭuu* means 'a male' and *āṭavar* means 'males' in Telugu *āḍañgi* means 'a man of womanish character and ways'; the same word exists also in Tamil as *aṉṉakan*, (*aṉakaṉ*) 'a eunuch'. It would seem therefore that the terminations of the five words are derived from a common original, though the first three words denote 'a male' while the remaining two denote a female. This goes to confirm the inference stated above that the suffixes *-aḷ* and *-an* are modified forms of *-ant*.

These facts clearly demonstrate that there was no differentiation of sex in the originals from which these words and suffixes have been derived and that each Dravidian vernacular attached to them a masculine or a feminine signification according to its own convention.

53. THE DRAVIDIAN FEMININE SIGN *-di*.

We may next consider how the feminine suffixes *-aḷu* etc. Telugu and allied languages came to be superseded by the suffixes *-adi*, *ad* etc. Bishop Caldwell and Professor

Sten Konow consider *adi*, *ad* etc., as neuter singular demonstratives. The former says (C.D.G. page, 125) :—

" There is another mode of forming the feminine singular of appellative nouns, which is much used in all the Dravidian dialects and which may be regarded as specially characteristic of Telugu. It consists in suffixing the neuter singular demonstrative, its termination or modification of it to any abstract or neuter noun. The neuter singular demonstrative being used by Telugu instead of the feminine singular (' it ' for ' she ') this neuter suffix has naturally in Telugu supplied the place of a feminine suffix ; and though in the other dialects the feminine pronouns are formed by means of feminine suffixes, not by those of the neuter, yet the less respectful Telugu usage has crept into the department of their appellative nouns. In Tamil this neuter-feminine suffix is *-atti* or *-tti*. This will appear on comparing *veḷḷāḷ-atti* ' a woman of the cultivator caste ' with *veḷḷāḷ-* an ' a man of the same caste ' and *vaṇṇā-tti* ' a washer-woman ' with *vaṇṇā-ṉ* ' a washerman'."

Professor Sten Konow says (L.S. IV, page 290) :—

" Brāhūī does not distinguish the genders even in the case of rational beings. Most other languages of the family Kurukh, Malto, Kūi, Gōṇḍi, Kōlāmī and Telugu have no feminine singular but use the neuter instead. The same is the case in Kurumvārī a dialect of Kanarese, Kūi, and Gōṇḍi also use the neuter gender in the plural in order to denote feminine nouns..........there are also some traces of the use of a feminine suffix corresponding to the Telugu feminine and neuter suffix *-adi* in Tamil and Kanarese. Thus Tamil *vaṇṇāṉ* 'a washerman' *vaṇṇātti* 'a washer-woman' ; Kanarese *okkaḷati* ' a farmer's wife ' "

The neuter singular demonstrative pronoun is *-adi* in Telugu, and appellative nouns formed with this as suffix may no doubt give the feminine names *cinnadi* 'a young woman,' *golladi* 'a shepherd woman' etc. But the neuter demonstrative in Tamil and Kanarese is *-adu*, and it is *adu* even in the oldest specimens of these languages that have come down to us, the final *-i* of Telugu being due to the special phonetic laws of that language. Further the dental in *adu*, *adi*, *ad* is a media by etymology and by origin, and its medial sound is not merely due to the intervocal pronunciation of *a-t*; for it does not become a tenue when it becomes initial by metathesis as in Telugu *dāniki* 'to it.' It is not therefore easy to see how the "less respectful Telugu usage" would have given in Tamil and Kanarese, feminine nouns of the forms *veḷḷāḷatti*, *vaṇṇātti*, *okkaḷati*, and it is difficult to follow Bishop Caldwell's argument that these last are really neuter formations. The final *-ti* of these forms is probably a corruption of the Sans. *strī* 'a woman' which becomes *itthi*, *itthi*, *thi* in Pali ; compare, for example, Pali *caturittio* 'four women, *manussitthi*' 'a female of the genus homo (or a goddess or *apsaras*)', *natakitthio* 'actresses,' *taruṇithi* 'a young woman.' The *-ti* might also have arisen from imitation of the terminations of the Aryan participial and other forms ending in *-ti*, e.g.

kṛtavatī, *buddhimatī*, *balavatī*.

The former of these is the likely explanation, for the *-ti* of these last forms had very early become *-di* even in even Prākṛts, as Sanskrit, Prākṛt *bhodi*.

It is worthy of consideration whether the ending *-di* of Telugu feminine nouns should not be regarded as having been derived from the *-ti* of Aryan forms. If the masculine terminal sign of the Telugu *golla-du* has arisen from imitating the ending of *balavanta* we may well suppose the feminine sign *-di* of *golladi* to have arisen from imitating the termination of *balavatī*.'

54. THE ARYAN DEMONSTRATIVE ROOTS AND BASES.

In the last five paragraphs we have discussed the Aryan affinities of the signs which the Dravidian languages employ to distinguish gender in their demonstrative pronouns. It is proposed here to consider also the origin of the demonstrative roots and bases of the Dravidian languages and to ascertain to what extent they are related to the corresponding roots and bases in Aryan languages.

Demonstratives in Sanskrit : (M.V.G. Ss. 392-396 ; W.S.G. Ss. 503)

(*a*) *Ta* the pronoun of the third person serves also as a demonstrative pronoun in Sanskrit. *Tya* meaning 'that' is another far demonstrative obtained by a slight modification of *ta*. Besides these Sanskrit has pronouns formed from the demonstrative roots and elements *a*, *i*, *e*. The stems of these demonstrative pronouns are taken by Indian grammarians to be *tad*, *tyad*, *adas*, *idam* and *etad*, the forms which they assume in the nominative singular neuter. Of these *tad* and *tyad* are inflected like the pronoun of the third person.

(*b*) The near demonstrative *eta* obtained by prefixing *e* to *ta* means 'this here' and assumes the forms M. *eṣas*, F. *eṣā*, N. *etad* in the nominative singular. It is inflected like *ta* and *tya* and calls for no special remarks. The element *e-* is supposed by some to be the locative of the demonstrative root *a*.

(*c*) The near demonstrative which appears as M. *ayam*, F. *iyam*, N. *idam* in the nominative singular means 'this here' and employs the pronominal roots *a* and (in various modifications) *i* in its inflexions ; its paradigm is made up of forms derived from several stems. The following case forms are formed from the root *a*.

Instrumental. *enayā, ebhis, ābhis*
Dative. *asmai, asyai, ābhyam, ebhyas, ābhyas.*
Ablative. *asmai, asyās, ābhyām.*
Genitive. *asya, asyās, anayos, eṣām, āsām.*
Locative. *asmin, asyām, anayos, eṣu, āsu.*

The case terms *anena, anayā, anayos* appear to have been formed from a stem *ana-*; the *-n-* of this stem is supposed by some grammarians to have been inserted for preventing hiatus.

The forms *imau, ime, imās, imā, imāni*, seem to be formed from a stem *ima-*, this stem is supposed by some to be derived from the accusative *i-m* of *i*. The form *idam* is supposed to be made up of *i-d* (the nom. acc. neuter of *i*) and the suffix *-am*.

The forms *iyam* and *ayam* are both supposed to be formed from the root *i* to which the suffix *-am* is added.

The following roots and stems thus enter into the paradigm :—

a, i, id, ana, ima.

(*d*) The far demonstrative which appears as masculine *asau*, feminine *asau*, neuter *adas* in the nominative singular means 'that, there, you'. The fundamental stem used in every case, except the nominative singular, is *a-m* which is supposed to be the accusative masculine of the demonstrative root *a*. This *-am* gives rise to the extended stems *amū*, *amū* and *amī*.

The singular case forms *amum, amunā, amuyā, amuṣmin, amuṣyām* and dual forms *amū, amuyos* are formed from the stem *amu-*.

The dual form *amūbhyām*, and the plural forms *amūbhis, amūbhyas, amūṣām, amūsu* are formed from *amu*.

The plural forms *amī, amībhis, amībhyas, amīṣām, amīṣu* are formed from *ami*.

In *a-d* as the root *a* is extended by the pronominal *-d* and the suffix *-as*.

In the form *asau* the root *a* appears to be extended by -' ,-.

(*e*) The pronoun *ava* 'this' is found two or .ree times in the Ṛg-Veda and only in the genitive dual The pronoun *ama* 'this' occurs only once in the Atharv Veda, e.g., *amoham asmi* 'this am I'

(*f*) The pronoun *ena* is almost always use substantively, but its adjectival use like a demonstra..ive is aslo occasionally met with.

55. DEMONSTRATIVE IN THE AVESTIC LANGUAGE.

(*a*) Kanga's Avestic Grammar mentions the follow ing as the crude forms of the demonstrative pronouns in the Avestic language (Ss. 215-224).

i. m: *aēta ;* n : *aētad ;* f : *aētā.*

ii. m : *ima, a ;* n : *imad, id ;* f.: *imā, a.*

iii. m : *ava ;* n : *aom, avad ;* f : *avā.*

(*b*) The inflections of the first set corresponding to the Sanskrit *etad* do not call for any remarks.

In the inflections of the second set the following case forms appear :—

i. Nom. and Acc. Neut. Sing. *ad, imad, īd, id,* Plural *imā, ī :*

ii. Nom. masc. Sing. : *ayēm, aēm,* Plural *imē ;*

iii. Nom. fem. Sing. : *īm,* dual *ī,* Plural *imāe, imāese :*

iv. Acc. masc. Sing. : *imem,* Plural *i, imā ;*

v. Instr. masc. Sing. : *anā, ana,* Plural *aāais ;*
fem. Sing. : *āya, aha,* Plural *ābis ;*

Other forms are

vi. *aēibis, aēibyō, ahmāi, ahmād, aēṣām, ainghē, ainghāi.*

(*c*) The inflections of the third set are all formed from the base *av-*.

i. Nom. and Acc. Neut. Sing. : *aom. avad.* (Acc mas. sing. *aom.* Acc. fem. sing. *avām.*)

ii. Nom. Plural Masc. *avē.* Neut. *avē.*

iii. Acc. Plural Masc. *avē, avōi* Neut. *ava, avā, avata, avāe, ave,* Fem. *avāe, avanghāe.*

iv. Instr. Masc. and Neut. Sing. *avā, ava.* Plural *avāis.* Other forms are

v. *avahēta, avanghēta* etc.

Nominative singular forms for the Masculine and the Feminine are not given.

(*d*) All the demonstra ive roots and stems which occur in Sanskrit are also found here with the exception of those arising from the base *am-.*

(*e*) It appears from a comparison of the Avestic and Sanskrit demonstrative paradigms that the roots and elements *a, i, ē* (locative of *a*) and the bases *av-, an-, id-, ad-, im-* were already in existence in the Indo-Iranian period. Of these *a, i, av, an, id* are even older than this period and are of Indo-Germanic antiquity (Brugmann Vol. III, S. 409, pp. 329-331). The last of them is to obviously the same as the Latin *id* and the English *it.*

The stems *ima-* and *ad-* are not found outside Aryan and it is therefore inferred that the formation of new stems out of the accusative *i-m* and of *a-d* belongs to the Indo-Iranian period ; the formation of the stems *amū-, amū, amī* out of the accusative *a-m* which are not found in the Avestic language belongs perhaps to the pre-Sanskrit period.

56. DEMONSTRATIVE IN NEW PERSIAN.

(J. T. Platt's Persian Grammar, pp. 80 and 83.)

(*a*) The independent demonstrative pronouns are :—

īn 'this here , *ān* 'that there'

In is derived from the Paz : *īn*, which, it is stated, is probably from a primitive *ana*, cf. Sanskrit *ena*.

Ān is the same as the Paz : and Phl.: *ān*, Old Persian *anya* 'other' cf. Sanskrit : *anya*, Hindi : *ān*. Some scholars, however, refer *ān* to the zend *an- a* Sanskrit *an* or *an-a*.

(*b*) The genderless pronouns of the third person singular in the New Persian are :—

Singular *av*, but pronounced *ū* ; ⊔¯, *vai* ; ⊔¯, |, *ūe* (old), 'he, she, it's. These appear to be derived from the Avestic demonstrative *ava* : thus, *ū*=Paz : *ō*=Old Persian *ava* ; ⊔¯J | = Paz : *ōi*=Old Persian *ava*+*hya* ; ⊔¯ *vai* is probably a doublet of ⊔¯, |

Plural *Ī-ṣān* (archaic *ēṣān*) 'they'

(*c*) Besides these we also meet with the relic of another demonstrative *im* (=O.P. *ima*, S. *ima*) which invariably replaces the demonstrative *īn* before the words *roz* 'day', *shap* 'night' *sāl* 'year' and occasionally before the word *bār* 'time' (page 95).

(*d*) The affixed demonstrative pronoun ⊔¯—, *ī* (archaic *ē*) called the demonstrative⊔¯, or 'the *ya* that makes the noun determinate'. It is often termed 'the definite article' but it is really a demonstrative pronoun, and is generally interchangeable with the demonstrative *ān*. It is annexed to a noun in the singular or plural.

Remark. The demonstrative *ī* (*ē*) is derived from the Phl : *ē*=O. P. demonstrative pronoun *aita*. It is the same pronoun which forms the base of the personal pronoun *īṣān* (*ēṣan* third person plural of I) (page 99).

57. DEMONSTRATIVES IN MODERN INDO-ARYAN VERNACULARS (B. A. G. Vol. III, S. 68, pp. 316-320).

The far demonstrative 'that'.

	Nominative Singular.	Ablative Singular.	Ablative Plural.
Hindi	*u, ō, vah*	*us*	*un, unh*
Panjābī	*uh,*	*us, uh*	*unā, unhā*
Sindhi	*ū, hū, hō*	*un, hun*	*huni*
Guzarati	*ā*	*ā*	*ā, ō*
Bengali	*ō*	*uhā*	*uhā.*

The near demonstrative 'this'.

Hindi	*i, ih, ē, ēh, yah*	*is*	*in, inh*
Panjābī	*ih, ēh*	*is, ih*	*inā, inhā*
Sindhi	*ī, hī, hē*	*in, hin*	*hini*
Guzarati	*ē*	*ē*	*ēo*
Oriya	*ē, ēhi, ihi*	*ihā, ēha*	*ihā, ehā*
Bengali	*ē*	*ihā*	*ihā*

Although the Avestic form *ava* was practically unknown to the Indo-Aryan literary dialects, it appears to have existed in all the Aryan vernaculars of India, where it has been changed and shortened into *ō*, *ū* and *u* in the far demonstratives of these vernaculars. The same change took place, as we have seen, in New Persian.

Of the three demonstrative roots and elements in the Vedic dialects, *viz.*, *a*, *i* and *ē*, only *a* was used as an independent demonstrative pronoun in those dialects ; in the modern vernaculars all the three appear to be so used. Mr. John Beames remarks in his grammar (Vol. II, page 318) :—

" But it is perhaps useless to seek for the origin of these forms in any written works. They have their origin in all probability in a lower stratum of popular speech than ever found its way into writing before the time of Chand, whose forms, may, therefore, in this, as in so many other instances, be taken as the furthest point to which researches can at present be pushed back." If Mr. Beames had noticed the existence of the genderless pronouns -*ū* (archaic *ō*), *ī* (archaic *ē*) in modern Persian and had known that *ō* and *ū* are traceable to the Avestic *ava* while *ā* and *ī* are traceable to the Phl *ē* corresponding to the *ē* of the Sanskrit *eta-*, he would have seen that the Indo-Aryan popular speeches had preserved prehistoric forms which had disappeared from literary dialects.

58. THE DRAVIDIAN DEMONSTRATIVE ROOTS AND BASES.

We shall begin this section by reproducing the table of Tamil demonstrative and interrogative pronouns given by Bishop Caldwell at page 316 of his grammar and quoting his observations thereon. (C. D. G. pages, 315-316.)

1. The Tamil demonstrative and interrogative pronouns.

" The most common interrogative prefix is *e*. In all the Dravidian dialects this prefix is used in the formation o pronominals in precisely the same manner as the demonstrative bases *a* and *i*. It forms one of a set of vocalic prefixes (*a*, *i*, *u*, *e*) which occupy one and the same position, obey one and the same law and differ only in the particular signification which is expressed by each. The unity of principle pervading these prefixes will be clearly apparent from the subjoined comparative view. The forms which are here exhibited are those of the Tamil alone ; but in this particular all the dialects agree on the whole so perfectly with the Tamil, and with one another that it is unnecessary to multiply examples. I exhibit here an alternative (probably an older) interrogative base in *yā* which will be inquired into further on.

——	Proximate Demonstrative.	Remote Demonstrative.	Intermediate Demonstrative.	Interrogative *e* or
	i	*a*	*u*	*yā*.
Masc. Sing. ..	*ivaṉ hic* ..	*avaṉ ille* ..	*uvaṉ* ..	*evaṉ* or *yāvaṉ quisj.*
Fem. do. ..	*ivaḷ haec* ..	*avaḷ illa* ..	*uvaḷ* ..	*evaḷ* or *yāvaḷ quae.*
Neut. do. ..	*idu hoc* ..	*adu illud* ..	*udu* ..	*edu* or *yādu quid.*
Epic Plu. ..	*ivar-hi hae* ..	*avar ille illoe* ..	*uvar* ..	*ēvar* or *yāvar qui, quoe.*
Neut. do. ..	*ivei haec* ..	*avei illa* ..	*uvai* ..	*evei* or *yāvei quae ?*

"I need not call attention to the beautiful and philosophical regularity of this quadruple set of proximate, remote, and intermediate demonstratives and interrogatives. In no other language or family of languages in the world shall we find its equal or even its second. In addition to which, the circumstance that the demonstrative vowels are not only used in these languages with an invariable and exact discrimination of meaning which is not found in the Indo-European tongues (with the solitary and partial exception of the New Persian), but are also associated with a corresponding interrogative vowel of which the Indo-European tongues are totally ignorant, tends to confirm the supposition which I have already expressed, that the Dravidian family has retained some Prae-Sanskrit elements of immense antiquity; and in particular that its demonstratives, instead of being borrowed from Sanskrit, represent those old Japhetic bases from which the demonstratives of Sanskrit itself, as well as various other members of the Indo-European family were derived."

59. THE SO-CALLED INTERMEDIATE DEMONSTRATIVE *u*.

The intermediate demonstrative *u* is unknown to the popular dialects; Bishop Caldwell says (page 319) :—

"The medial *u* is occasionally used by Tamil poets, more frequently in classical Kanarese and in Tulu[1], to denote a person or object intermediate between the remote and the proximate". Again "In Tamil poetry we find an adverbial demonstrative of place, *umpar*, with the meaning of the intermediate demonstrative *u*, the correlatives of which are *ampar* 'that place' *impar* 'this place' and *empar* 'which place'; *umpar* means literally a place intermediate between two other places; but it is remarkable that it is also used in a secondary sense to signify 'on' 'upon' 'above' and even *uyar* 'height'

(1) In Tuḷu it is one of the two near demonstratives.

It is doubtful however whether any instance can be given from Cankam works or from any standard work in which *umpar* is used in the sense of intermediate place ; several instances can be given from old Tamil in which the word means ' there ', ' on the other side of '—not the intermediate place : e.g.,

(i) *paṉi paṭu cōlai vēṅkaṭattumpar*[1] " On the other side of the *Vēṅkaṭa* hills the groves of which attract the mist "

(ii) *pal vēr kaṭṭi naṉṉaṭṭumpar*[2] " On the other side of the beautiful land of (the chieftain) *Kaṭṭi* of many lances '

(iii) *neṭumoḻi-p-puḷḷi....nannaṭṭumpar*[3] " On the other side of the boastful Puḷḷis flourishing domain "

The signification ' on the other side of ' will naturally lead to the secondary and figurative sense ' upon ', ' above ' ' superior to ' ' height ' etc., some of which are noticed by Bishop Caldwell ; this latter sense will not arise from the meaning of ' intermediate place ' It may be noted in passing that one of the meanings of *umpar* is ' the sky the visible heaven '. The word *impar* ' on this side ' is the correlative of *umpar* and is used in Tolkāppiyam itself. It is doubtful whether *empar* is used by any old author. The word *ūṅku* derived from the same demonstrative *u* has the meaning ' better than ', ' superior to '.

(iv) *aṟattiṉ ūṅkākkam evaṉō uyirkku*[4] " What is more precious to human beings than (the practice of) virtue "

(v) *aṟattiṉ ūṅkākkamum illai.*[5] " There can be no greater good than (the practice of) virtue '

The word *u-p-pakkam* in the sense of 'the farther side' ' the side away from us ' ' the back ' as opposed to ' the front

1. Aham 211.
2. Kuruntokai, 11.
3. Aham, 211.
4. Kuṟaḷ, 31.
5. Kuṟaḷ, 32.

side' occurs in Kuṟaḷ 630. *Ūḻai-y-um uppakkam kāṇpar* 'they will make even fate turn back' that is, 'overcome it.'

The oldest Tamil work in existence which also happens to be a grammar mentions three demonstrative letters *a*, *i* and *u*. Of these, *a* admittedly refers to the distant thing or person and *i* to the proximate thing or person ; *u* is a convenient particle to refer to a third person or thing where there are three to be referred to, but commentators have apparently taken it to denote the intermediate person or thing so as to assign distinct functions to the three particles. The latter day interpretation of *u* as the intermediate demonstrative is thus not in consonance with its use in Old Tamil. It is not in consonance with its probable etymology. It has already been pointed out that *ava* has become *o* in Malayalam, Kūi and the Gondi dialects. It will be pointed out presently that it became *o* and later *u* (the pronoun of the third person) in Persian ; and that the far demonstratives *o* and *u* in the modern Aryan vernaculars of the North have the same origin. It is probable that Tamil *u* has the same origin ; its latter day use to denote the intermediate thing is wholly conventional and limited to literature.

In Tulu both *indu* and *undu* mean 'this'. In Kurukh *u* means 'that there'

We must therefore conclude that the demonstrative element *u* is of comparatively late origin. If we have to give a name to this *u* we must call it a *proximate demonstrative* from its usage in Tulu and a *remote demonstrative* from its usage in Kuru*kh* and in Old Tamil poetry.

60. THE SO-CALLED EUPHONIC-*v*-IN THE DEMONSTRATIVE PRONOUNS.

Dr. Kittel calls *u* the intermediate demonstrative ; it is not known to what extent such use obtained in Old Kanarese.

According to Bishop Caldwell the-*v*-in the pronominal forms *avan̲* etc. *ivan̲* etc., *uvan̲* etc., is wholly euphonic, inserted for the purpose of preventing hiatus between two vowels, as :

a-(v)-an̲, *i-(v)-an̲*, *u-(v)-an̲*, *e-(v)-an̲*. and *yā-(v)-an̲*.

In support of this view he draws attention to the circumstance that this-*v*-appears only when the termination indicating number and gender begins with a consonant, e.g.

a-(v)-an 'he' *a-(v)-al* 'she', *a-(v)-ar* 'they' (epicene) *a-(v)-ai* 'they' (neuter), *a-du* 'it'.

The exceptional forms assumed by the pronominals in Telugu, Goṇḍi, Tulu and Kanarese appear to militate against this view. Thus in Telugu the demonstratives are :—

	Singular.		Plural.
Masculine :	*vā-ḍu, vī-ḍu*	}	*vāru, vīru.*
Feminine ;	*adi, idi*	}	
Neuter :	*adi, idi*		*avi, ivi.*
(oblique	*dāni, dīni*	(oblique	*vāṭi, vīṭi. vani, vīni*).

In such of the forms in these paradigms as begin with a *-v-*, the demonstrative vowels *a* and *i* appear to have lost their initial position by metathesis but still the *-v-* persists. Bishop Caldwell says that in these forms the " *-v-* euphonic has advanced a step further and assumed the position of a demonstrative in the nominative as well as in the inflexion. That this *-v-*, however, is not a demonstrative and that the use to which it is put in Telugu is abnormal is shown by the fact that *da* and *di*, the inflexions of *adi* and *idi* the neuter singular demonstratives of the Telugu *d*, though certainly not a demonstrative nor even euphonic, but simply a sign or suffix of neuter singularity, has been advanced to a prominent position (by a similar euphonic displacement) as if it belonged to the root." (page 319.)

In Gōṇḍi the neuter plural demonstratives *av*, *iv* [1] show a *-v-* which is not wanted to fill any hiatus.

That this *-v-* is not euphonic but an integral part of the demonstrative itself is clear from Tolkāppiyam, the Grammar of Old Tamil, which besides mentioning the demonstrative roots ***a***, ***i***, ***u*** mentions also extended forms *av*, *iv*, *uv* of these roots. These extended forms, of the existence of which Bishop Caldwell seems to have been unaware, were used in Old Tamil as demonstrative adjectives as well as demonstrative pronouns in the neuter plural e.g.,

av-yāṉai 'that elephant' *av-yāṭu* 'that sheep'· similarly, *iv-yāṉai*, *iv-yāṭu* ; *uv-yāṉai*, *uv-yāṭu*.

Kaṇṇimai noṭi-y-eṉa avve māttirai (Tol : I. Sūtra-7).
'(Time taken in) twinkling the eye or snapping the fingers ; these are termed *māttirai* (in grammar)'.

These extended forms have become obsolete and are unknown to modern Tamil, but a grammatical rule provides that when words beginning with *y*-are compounded with ***a***, ***i*** and ***u***, ***av*** should be interposed between them (Naṉṉūl, 162) e.g. : ***a-yaṉai*** 'that elephant' becomes *avyāṉai*, etc.

61. THE TULU DEMONSTRATIVES.

The exceptional and abnormal forms of the Tuḷu demonstratives will appear from the following paradigms : —

	Singular.	Plural.	
Masculine:	***aye*** (rem) ***imbe*** (prox)	*ār* (rem)	***mēr*** (prox).
Feminine :	*āḷ* (rem) ***mōḷ*** (prox)		***mōkuḷu*** (prox).
Neuter :	***avu*** (rem) ***indu***, ***undu*** (prox).		***eikuḷu***.
Adv :	***avuḷu*** 'there' ***mūḷu*** 'here'		

1. The forms given by Professor Sten Konow (L.S. Vol. iv, page 486) are : ***aū***, ***iū***.

Bishop Caldwell's explanation of the forms containing-*m*-instead of-*v*-is that the latter letter which is merely euphonic has been hardened into -*m*-, and that this -*m*- has again been changed into -*mb*-. He explains *mēr* as having arisen from *imar* which, he says, was originally *ivar* as in the connected languages. Similarly he explains *mōḷ* as having arisen from *imaḷ*. This latter explanation is hardly acceptable, for the -*ō*-in *mōḷ* clearly shows that this word must have arisen from *umaḷ*, not from *imaḷ*. The circumstance that *u*- is earmarked by some as the intermediate demonstrative is no objection to this derivation, as in *untu* this same *u*- occurs in the Tuḷu near demonstrative.

Bishop Caldwell considers that in *indu* and *undu*, the neuter -*d*- has been nasalized ; but it would seem to be more correct to regard them has having arisen from the bases *im* and *um* which have given rise to **imaḷ*, **umaḷ* **umaḷu* or **umuḷu*.

The final -*e* in *āye*, *imbe* is perhaps due to Māgadhi influence. The long initial *a*- in *āye*, *āl*, *ār* probably arises from *av* or *ava*.

It is remarkable that all forms of the proximate demonstrative show a nasal, while those of the remote demonstrative (except the neuter plural) show a -*v*- or modifications of -*av*-. This reminds one of the Avestic *ima* and *ava*, in addition to which Tuḷu apparently had formerly stems formed from the base *um* corresponding to the base *uv* of poetic Tamil and poetic Kanarese.

These correspondences make it impossible for us to regard the Dravidian bases *av*, *iv*, *uv* as independent of Aryan bases, and to hold, as Bishop Caldwell does, that the final-*v* of these bases was euphonic in ultimate origin, or that the -*v* of *iv* has been hardened into *m* in Tuḷu. The contrary supposition that the -*v* in *iv* and *uv* has taken the place of an older *m* has more probability on its side.

62. THE SO-CALLED EUPHONIC *-n-* IN SOME VERBAL ENDINGS.

Bishop Caldwell says (page 319) : " In the higher dialect of Tamil *ṉ* is often used euphonically instead *-v-*, especially in the personal terminations of verbs. Thus instead of *iruntāṉ* (for *iruntavaṉ*) 'he was', the poets sometimes say *iruntaṉaṉ*, and for *iruntava* 'they (neuter) were', the form we should expect to find used *iruntaṉa* is universally used instead ".

It has already been pointed out that the Old Tamil form *iruntaṉṟu* 'it was', in which *-n-* occurs between *irunta*-and-*tu* militates against this explanation, and that the forms *iruntaṉaṉ*, *iruntaṉa*, *iruntaṉṟu*, etc., contain a separate suffix *-an-* inserted between the participle *iruntu-* and the personal endings *-aṉ*, *-aḷ*, *-ar*, *-tu*, etc. We may regard the combined suffix and personal endings, viz., *-aṉaṉ*, *-aṉal*, *-aṉar*, *-aṉṟu* etc., as being personal pronouns from the Aryan demonstrative base *aṉ-* similar to *avaṉ*, *avaḷ*, *avar*, *aḥtu* (*av-tu*) etc., formed from the base *av in* the verb forms *iruntavaṉ*, *iruntavaḷ*, *iruntavar*, etc.

63. THE RELATION OF DRAVIDIAN DEMONSTRATIVE TO ARYAN.

We are now in a position to discuss what relationship there is between the Aryan and the Dravidian demonstratives.

	Iranian.	*Indo-Aryan.*	*Dravidian.*
	Avestic.	Vedic.	Rem. Prose.
1.	*ad id* ..	*ad-as, id-am* ..	*ad id* (Gōṇḍī). *adi idi* (Telugu). *atu itu* (Tamil).
2.	*av im* ..	*av im* ..	*av iv* (Tamil, Gōṇḍī).
		am ..	*avai, ivai* (Tamil). *ava, iva* (Mal). *avu, ivu* (Kan). *avi, ivi* (Tel).
3.	*an*	*an* ..	*aṉ* (Tamil). occurring in the pronominal terminations of verbs.
4.	*a i* ..	*a i* ..	*a, u, i* (Tamil, Kanarese, Tuḷu).
5.	*ō ē* (Phl.) *ū, ī* (New Persian).	*ā, ū, ō, ī* .. (Modern Indo-Aryan).	(1) occurring in composition. *ō* 'that' (Gōṇḍī, Kui, Madras Gōṇḍī, Malayāḷam). *ū* (Tamil). (2) Independent indeclinable adjectives. *ā* 'that,' *ī* 'this.' (Kanarese, Tuḷu, Malayāḷam, Kurukh, Telugu). *ā, ē, ō* 'that' (Kūi). *ū* 'that' (Kurukh). *ē, ō* 'that' (Brāhūī).

(*a*) *ad*, *id*, *av*, *iv* :—

The Avestic *ad*, *id* and the Sanskrit *ad- as*, *id-am* are neuter singulars. In the neuter plural the bases *av*, *im* ; and *am*, *im ;* are used : the nominative forms being *avē*, *imā*, *ima*, *ī* ; and *amūni*, *imāni*, *imā*. In Old Persian the plurals are *avaiy*, *imaiy* (cf. Tamil *avai*, *ivai*).

In the Dravidian languages *ad*, *id* ; *adu*, *idu; adi*, *idi* ; are neuter singulars ; in the neuter plural the bases *av*, *iv* come into play, the nominative forms being *av*, *iv* ; *avai*, *ivai; avi*, *ivi* ; *avu*, *ivu*. The *d* of the Dravidian singulars is not due to any intervocal pronunciation of a hard *t*, but appears like the *d* of the Aryan *ad*, *id*, to be a media (which is foreign to Tamil) by origin ; for in Telugu it does not lose its medial sound even when it ceases to be intervocal, as *adi* 'that', *dāniki* 'to that', *idi* 'this', *dīniki* 'to this'[1]. The *v* of the Dravidian plurals is radical, not euphonic.

The Avestic *av* and *im* form the bases of masculine feminine and neuter pronouns with suitable gender signs —*ava* (m) *ava* (f), *avad*, *aōm* (n) ; *ima* (m) *ima* (f) *imad* (n). In the Indo-Aryan literary dialects, the base *av* plays little or no part having apparently been superseded by a new base *a-m* formed in the pro-Vedic period in imitation of *i-m ;* here *am*, *im* form the bases of pronouns with distinction of gender: Similarly the Tamil, etc., *av*, *iv* form the bases of pronouns: *avaṉ*, *ivaṉ*, *avaḷ*, *ivaḷ*, *aḥtu* (*av-du*), *iḥtu*, (*iv-tu*) etc.

The Dravidian demonstrative bases and their methods of inflexion thus appear to be idenctical with the Aryan demonstrative bases and methods of inflexion, but with this difference that in the Dravidian proximate base *iv*, *av* appears in the place of the *m of* the Aryan proximate base *im*. The *m*,

1. Contrast with this the Telugu imperatives *kammu agumu*, *kā* 'become ye' where the guttural becomes a tenuis when it ceases to be intervocal.

however, still persists in all the near demonstratives of Tuḷu, and perhaps in the forms *andu* 'that', *indu* 'this' of Telugu, and *anta* 'that', *inta* 'this' of Tamil.

It is therefore concluded that the Dravidian bases *ad*, *id*, *av*, *iv* are derived from the Iranian and Vedic bases *ad*, *id*, *av*, *am*, *im*. Of these *id* and *av* are of Indo-Germanic antiquity; *im* and *ad* were formed in the Indo-Iranian period, and *am* in the pro-Vedic period.

The change of *m* into *v* is very common in Indian vernaculars:

(*b*) *a*, *i*, *u*, *e*, *ā*, *ī*, *ū*, *ē*, *ō* :—

av also exists in the shortened forms of *ō*, *ū* in the Dravidian languages as in Persian and Modern Indo-Aryan, but with this difference that while, in the latter, these forms are by themselves demonstrative and personal pronouns, they occur only in composition in some of the Dravidian languages; *e.g.* Gōṇḍi *ōr*, 'he' Madras Gōṇḍi *ōṇḍu* 'he', Kūi *ōañju* '*he*', Tamil *ūnku* 'superior to, above'.

a, *ū*, *ē*, *ō* 'that' and *i* 'this' are used as indeclinable demonstrative adjectives in the Dravidian dialects marked (2) in item 5 of the table at the head of this para. Of these *a*, *ū*, *ō*, are shortened forms of *av* and *ī* of *iv*. It is remarkable that Kūi and Brāhūi should use *ē* as a remote demonstrative; compare the Tuḷu remote neuter plural *eikuḷu*. These three instances deviating from the Indo-Aryan practice remind one of the Phl. *ē* and Persian *ī*, the bases of *ēshan* and *īshan*, the plurals of the genderless pronoun of the third person; these bases are traceable through Old Persian *aita* to the Avestic demonstrative *aēta* corresponding to the Sanskrit *eta*.

In a specimen of the language of the Nilgiri Badagas published in the Linguistic Survey (Vol. IV, p. 403), the form *evam* occurs in the sense of 'this man'; if this is not a misprint, we have here an instance of the use of *e* in Dravidian as a near demonstrative.

The so-called intermediate demonstrative *u* appears to be only a shortened form of *ū* (*ō ; ava*). *uv* and *um* appear to be of comparatively late origin formed in imitation of *av*, *im*.

a and *i* as the remote and near demonstratives occur only in composition in the Dravidian languages, though the former figures as an independent demonstrative in the Avestic language and in Sanskrit. The separation of functions between *a* and *i* as the remote and near bases is more complete in Dravidian than in Aryan.

(*c*) *aṉ* :—The Aryan base *an* appears to have been imitated in the personal endings *aṉaṉ*, *aṉal*, *aṉṟu*, *aṉar*, *aṉa* of verb-forms occurring in literary Tamil. These endings are formed in the same manner as the endings of *iruntavan*, *iruntaval*, etc., are formed the demonstrative stem *av*. There is, however, one objection to the identification of Tamil *aṉ* with the Aryan demonstrative *aṉ*, for the former occurs not only in the verb forms of the third person but also in those of the first and second persons :—*iruntaṉaṉ* 'I was' *iruntaṉam* 'we were', *iruntaṉai* 'thou wert', *iruntaṉir* 'you were' All the above forms containing *aṉ* are wholly artificial and unknown to the spoken Tamil of the people ; and it is possible that the formations were originally confined to the third person in accordance with the demonstrative nature of *aṉ* but were subsequently extended by the poets to the first and second persons when the true nature of *aṉ* was lost sight of. Such a thing has happened in poetic Tamil even to the demonstrative base *av*, for we have the sporadic forms *cāṉṟavir* "*ye* (who) have become great," *kaṇṭavir*[1] "*ye* (who) saw." In Telugu also we have similar additions of first and second

1. Kali-t-tokai, 140.

person endings to third personal forms, *e.g.* *unnā(ḍu* 'he is,' *unnāru* 'they are,' *unnā(ḍanu* 'I am,' *unnāramu* 'we are' etc.

(*d*) *ta* : In the Telugu forms *āta(ḍu*, *ātanu*, *āta(ḍu*, *atanu*, *ita(ḍu*, *itanu*, etc., and the Kanarese forms *ātam*, *ītam*, *ūtam* the base *-ta* is subjoined to the vocalic demonstrative bases *a*, *ā*, *i*, *ī*, *u*, *ū*, in imitation of the Sanskrit *eta* and the Avestic *aēta*. The dentals of all these forms are tenues as also that of *atham* and *itham* the pronouns of third person in Tuḍa, common to all genders and numbers.

(*e*) The comparative table given at the head of this section is a practical and sufficient proof of the identity of the Dravidian demonstrative pronouns with some of those found in the Indo-Iranian group of languages and most of the lengthy discussion in Ss. 54-62 would have been unnecessary had not Bishop Caldwell obscured the subject by several incorrect propositions such as—(1) that the *-v-* of the forms *avaṉ* etc., and the *-n-* of the forms *anaṉ* etc., are euphonic ; (2) that *-u-* is an intermediate demonstrative; (3) that the *-m-* of the Tuḷu forms arises from the hardening of a euphonic *-v-* etc. He has also whittled down the affinities between the Dravidian and Aryan demonstratives to such an extent that there is nothing left of them but the identity of the initial vowels *a*, *i*, which again he assumes to be bases belonging to the old Japhetic stock. But we have seen that the demonstrative letters *a*, *i* originally existed in Tamil only as the initial of *av*, *iv*. Here is an illustration of how Bishop Caldwell's theories based on incomplete and incorrect information impede progress at every step.

64. INTERROGATIVE FORMS IN DRAVIDIAN.

Tamil : The personal, demonstrative and interrogative pronouns in use in Old Tamil are enumerated in two sūtras (rules) of Tolkāppiyam (Col. 164 and 169).

The former of these relating to high caste (rational) pronouns contains the following list :—

(1) *avaṉ*, *ivaṉ*, *uvaṉ* (Third person masc. sing.)
(2) *avaḷ*, *ivaḷ*, *uvaḷ* (do. do. femi. do.)
(3) *avar*, *ivar*, *uvar* (do. do. epicene plural.)
(4) *yāṉ*, *yām*, *nām* (First person).
(5) *yāvaṉ*, *yāvaḷ*, *yāvar* (Interrogative).

The latter rule referring to pronouns of the irrational and inanimate caste contains the following list :—

(1) *atu*, *itu*, *utu*
(2) *aḥtu*, *iḥtu*, *uḥtu* } (Third person neut. sing.)
(3) *avai*, *ivai*, *uvai*
(4) *av*, *iv*, *uv* } (do. do. do. plur.)
(5) *yātu*, *yā*, *yāvai* (Interrogatives.)

It is worthy of note that none of the modern interrogatives *evaṉ*, *evaḷ*, *evar*, *etu*, *evai*, beginning with a short *e* finds a place in either list. A word *evaṉ* is mentioned in Tolkāppiyam (Col. Kiḷavi. 31) and does occur in Old Tamil but it is genderless in the sense of 'why, what, for what purpose' For instance, it occurs *sixteen* times in Kuṟaḷ but always in the sense of 'why, what, for what purpose and never in the sense of 'who ?' (masc.); this *evaṉ* has given rise to *ēṉ*, *eṉṉa*, *eṉṉai* in modern Tamil. In mediæval Tamil poetry we find the forms *ētu*, *ēvaṉ*, *ēvar*, of which only *etu* has survived but with a meaning different from that of *ētu*. We also have in modern Tamil the words *yār*, *ār*, 'who ?'

Malayāḷam : These facts raise a presumption that the modern forms *evaṉ*, *evaḷ*, *evar*, *etu*, *evai* mentioned in Bishop Caldwell's tabular statement (S. 58 above) were unknown to the Tamil dialect dealt with in Tolkāppiyam. This presumption is strengthened, nay, is almost rendered a certainty by the circumstance that the Malayāḷam interrogatives all begin with long *ē* or *yā* and that the Kanarese set all begin with *yā*, *ā*, or *dā*. In Malayāḷam we have *ēvaṉ*, *ēvaḷ*, *ēvar*, *ēdu*, *ēva*; *yāvaṉ*, *yāvaḷ*, *yāvar* (*yār*, *ār*), *yādu*; *e* and *ē* are used as interrogative adjectives, the former occurring only as the initial of compounds like *ekkālam* 'what time,' *eppati* '*how*', *evvaṇṇam* 'in what manner, how' etc. None of the forms *yāvaṉ*, *yāvaḷ*, *yāvar*, *yātu*, *yāvai* is used by the common people either in Tamil or in Malayāḷam.

Kanarese : The Kanarese set all begin *yā*, *ā*, or *dā*. The interrogative adjectives of this language are *e*, *ē*, *ā*, *āva*, *yā*, *yāva*, *dāva*. Of these *e* forms the initial of compounds like *etta* 'what place or direction', *enitu* 'what quantity or number', *elli* 'where' *endu* 'when,' *ehage* 'in what manner'. The rest are not compounded but stand as separate words detached from the nouns qualified, *e.g.*: *ā-hottu* 'what time', *āva-mātu* 'which word' *dava ūru* 'what village', etc.

Tuḷu : The Tuḷu interrogatives are *dā* 'which' also *dāye* 'why ?' *dāne*, *jāne* 'what ?' *yēr* 'who ?'. This *yēr* appears as *dēr* 'who ?' in Brāhūī.

Telugu : The Telugu forms are masc. *eva*(*ḍu*, epicene plural *evaru*), fem. and neut. sing. : *edi*, *ēdi*, neut. plur. : *evi*, *ēvi*.

Kurukh and Malts have interrogatives beginning with *ne*.

65. THE ORIGIN OF THE DRAVIDIAN INTERROGATIVE FORMS WITH THE INITIAL *da*-.

It is well known that the initial *y*- of Sanskrit words always becomes *j*[1] in Prākṛts—:—e.g. *yaṣṭi* 'liquorice'

1. *Ader yo jah* (Var. II, 31) '*j* is substituted for an initial *y*.

yaśas 'glory' *yakṣa* 'a demi-god' etc., become *jaṭṭhi*, *jasī*, *jakkha* etc. Similarly the relative pronoun meaning 'who, which' which is indicated in Sanskrit by the type *ya* has become *ja* in Prākṛt and the modern Aryan vernaculars, and *yāvat* has become *jāva* through an intermediate *yāva*.

The Sanskrit palatal medial *j* is very often changed into *d* in Ardhamāgadhi and Singhalese languages; *e.g.*, *jugupsā* 'disgust', *jyotsnā* 'moonlight,' *rājan* 'a king', *tejas* 'lustre' *majjā* 'marrow, pith' have become *dugñchā*, *dosinā*, *rada*, *tedu*, *midul* (*vide* I. A. Vol. XI, pages 216-217). The word *jāmātā* 'son-in-law' appears as *dāmādā* in some North-Indian vernaculars. In Sanskrit itself the form *dampatī* 'husband and wife' is derived by some from *jampatī* (*jāyāpatī*). The Avestic *z* which in some cases is equivalent to Sanskrit *j*, becomes *d* in Persian.

In the Dravidian languages also *j* often changes place with *d* in words of North-Indian or foreign origin: *e.g.*, *jinisu*, *dinisu*, 'class, kind'; *javana*, *davana* 'the plant artemisia indica' etc.

The alternative forms *dāne*, *jāne* 'what' of Tuḷu indicate that the initial *d* of interrogative forms has probably arisen from a *j*; and the Tuḷu *yēr* 'who' corresponding to the Brāhūī *dēr* 'who', shows that the initial *-y-* has probably become *d-* through an intermediate *j*. It is therefore inferred that the Kanarese forms *yā*, *yāva*, *yāvanu*, etc., became *dā*, *dāva*, *dāvanu*, etc., through the intermediate forms *jā*, *jāva*, *jāvanu* etc. This is also the explanation which Dr. Kittel seems to suggest of the initial *d-* (K. K. G. S. 265, page 231).

66. THE INTER-RELATIONS OF INTERROGATIVE FORMS WITH INITIAL *yā*, *ē* AND *ā*.

Scholars hold wholly divergent views on this question.

(*a*) Bishop Caldwell says (C.D.G. pages, 316-317) :—

"Probably there was originally only one interrogative base, and if so, it must have been *yā* and *e* must have been corrupted from it. The process by which *yā* became *e* is tolerably clear. Ā evinces a tendency to become *ē* . . . In Tuḷu *yār* becomes *yēr.* This is a considerable step towards *e.* Then also *e* is commonly pronounced *ye*, and *ē* as *yē*; and in Telugu this *y* is frequently written as well as heard. This would facilitate the omission of the *y* in writing, when *yā* came generally to be weakened into *yē*. *Ē* alone would in time have the same force as *yā*, and would come to be regarded as its equivalent. The long form *ē* still survives in Malayāḷam *ēvan̠*, *ēvaḷ*, 'he, she', for, *ēvan̠*, *ēvaḷ*; and in the Tamil and Malayāḷəm *ēdu*, and the Telugu *ēdi.*"

Bishop Caldwell does not notice the Kanarese interrogatives beginning with *ā*.

(*b*) Dr. Kittle on the other hand regards *ē* as the original base and *yā* to have been corrupted from it. According to him "The interrogative pronouns *āvam* (*yāvanu*, *dāvanu*) *āvaḷ* (*yāvaḷu*, *dāvaḷu*) *āvudu* (*yāvudu*, *dāvudu*), *ār* (*yāru*, *dāru*), *āvuru* (*yēvuru*, *dāvuru*) rest on the interrogative *ē*; that becomes *yā* in the oblique cases of the mediaeval and modern dialects, which is another form of *ā*" (K.K.G.S. 265, page 231). In support of this view he also draws attention to the circumstance that "many Kannaḍa people pronounce and write the initial vowels *i*, *ī*, *e*, *ē* ungrammatically prefixing *y* to them . . . Regarding initial *e*, they use also *ya* instead of *ye*, e.g., *yanu*, *yammei* for *enu* 'an ox', *emmei* 'a buffalo'. Initial *ē* may also appear as *yā* e.g. *yālakki*, *yāke* for *ēlakki* 'cardamoms' *ēke* 'for what'; also when attached to an initial consonant : *e.g.* :—

dyāva, *myāle* for deva 'a god', *mele* 'above.'

As between *ē* and *ā*, he seems to think that it is immaterial which of these is taken as the original as "they are related and occasionally interchanged." (*Ibid.* S. 138, page 77.) He also considers the -*v*- in *āva*, *yāva*, *dāva* to be euphonic and that *āva* and *yāva* have been incorrectly assumed to be the bases of forms like *āvam* (*ē-v-am*), *yāvanu* (*ē-v-anu*), etc. (*Ibid.* S. 265, page 231). In his view *āvu* and *yāva* are mere substitutes for *ē*.

(*c*) Mr. C. P. Venkatarama Aiyar. The question, which of the three initials *ya*, *e*, *a* is primitive, is discussed in a paper entitled 'The Glides' written by Mr. C. P. Venkatarama Aiyar. In this paper, the author considers the etymology of a number of Old Tamil words[1] beginning with *yā* and of the alternative forms which these words assume with initial *e* or *a* either in Tamil itself or in the other Dravidian languages, and arrives at the conclusion that *ā* was the primitive initial and that the prothetic *y* was an on-glide necessitated by the difficulty of pronouncing an initial back-vowel. The opinions of Professor Juline Vinson and of Dr. L. D. Barnett of the British Museum, London are also quoted in the paper in support of these conclusions. Professor Vinson is quoted as saying that "the palatal semi-vowel is never initial in Tamil and primitive Dravidian. One might suppose that *ē* was primitive, that it changed into *yā*, then into *ā* ", "an *a* could never have been preceded by *ē* and perhaps the collection of the Dravidian forms points to the conclusion that the long *ā* was primitive". Dr. Barnett expresses himself thus :—

"In general I agree with your conclusion as to the initial *a*-being proto-Dravidian. The evidence suggests

1. (a) *yāṭu* 'a sheep, a goat', (b) *yāṇṭu* 'a year', (c) *yāmai* 'a tortoise', (d) *yāḷi* 'a lion', (e) *yāṟu* 'a river', (f) *yāṉai* 'an elephant'. (g) *yār* 'who', (h) *yāy* 'mother', which have also the alternative forms (a) *āṭu*, *eṭa*, (b) *āṇṭu*, *ē-ṭu*. (c) *āmai*, *ēve* (d) *āḷi*, (e) *āru*, *ēru* (f) *ānai*, *enu-gu* (g) *ar* (h) *ay*.

that the primitive Dravidian had no initial *y-* and that is sporadically developed later after the various languages had branched off."

67. THE INTER-RELATIONS OF INTERROGATIVE FORMS WITH INITIAL *ya*, *ē*, AND *a* (CONTD.)

(*a*) The above extracts show what wholly divergent views have been held by scholars on the question as to which of the three *yā*, *ē*, *ā* is the primitive interrogative base. The whole of the argument in 'The Glides' is based on the assumption that the Old Tamil words with the initial *yā* were all true Dravidian words, and that these or their originals existed in proto-Dravidian. This assumption can be disproved in the case of some at least of these words. For instance,

(1) *yāḷi* 'a lion.' The Sanskrit *vyāḷa*, *vyāḷika* mean 'a beast of prey.' An initial *vyā-* of Sanskrit words sometimes loses the *v-* in Tamil, cf. *vyāpāra* 'trade' which becomes *yāvāram* in Tamil and *vyāḷa* 'Thursday' is often pronounced *yāḷa*. *Vyāḷika* may thus become *yāḷi* and this may further change into *āḷi* by the loss of *y-*.

Vyāḷa also means 'a vicious elephant' in Sanskrit and has become *vēḻam* 'an elephant' in Tamil by another process of phonetic corruption. cf. *vyāghra* 'a tiger' which corresponds to *vēṅkai* in Tamil.

(ii) *yāy* 'mother.' This and several allied words occur in the Paiśāca languages of the North-west.[1] Thus English 'Mother' Wai-Ala *oie* ; Kalāsa *aya*; Gawar Bati *jai*; Pasai *ai*: *Garioi yai*; *śīnā* (dial) *āzē*.

Sir George A Grierson thinks that these words are connected with the Sansktit verb *jāyate* 'he is born'. The

1. Paiśāca Languages, page 75.

Sanskrit *jāyā* 'a wife' is also connected with this verb. Thus the initial of *yāy* arises from the Sanskrit *j*.

(*iii*) *yāṭu* 'a sheep, a goat' This appears to be an Indo-Aryan word of Indo-Germanic affinities. The English word goat appears with a palatal vowel or diphthong in Anglo-Saxon and most Teutonie languages, *e.g.* A. S. *gat*, Du. *geit*, Swed. *get*, Icel. *geit*, Ger. *geiss*, Gothic *gaitsa* (*vide* Skeat), Latin *haedus* shows an *h* (as is often the case in this language) instead of a palatal medial aspirate. The Sanskrit *eḍa* (*ka*) has the original *d* cerebralised and appears to have lost the initial aspirate which is however preserved in the Brāhūī *hēṭ*. The initial *yā* of the Old Tamil *yāṭu* has thus apparently arisen from an original *jhē* or *hē*.

The form *iṭaiyaṉ*, colloq. *etayaṉ* 'a shepherd' shows that the initial vowel was originally *ē* as in the Sanskrit *eḍa* (*ka*), Brāhūī *heṭ*.

(iv) *yāṇṭu* 'a year'. The cerebral -*ṇṭ*- was perhaps originally the alveolar conjunct -*ṉṟ*- ; if so, both *yāṇṭu* 'a year' and *ñāṉṟu*, *nāṉṟu* 'a day' must have been derived from an original **yāṉṟu*, and all these words are obviosuly connected with the Tamil *eṉṟu* 'the sun' and the Telugu *eṇḍa* 'sunshine.' There is nothing surprising in the names for 'day' and for 'year' being both connected with that of the Sun.

The Telugu *nāḍu* 'a day'. the Tamil *nāḷ* 'a day' are obviously derived from *nāṉṟu*, and the whole group appears to have Aryan affinities.

Some of the other words in the list can easily be shown to be foreign loans but they are not dealt with here as this will cause too great a digression from the subject on hand.

The illustrations given are, however, enough to show that the initial *yā*- of Old Tamil must have arisen in various ways from various sources.

It is stated in Tolkāppiyam[1] that Tamil words cannot begin with *y-* unless this consonant be combined with the long *ā*. Such words as did begin with *yā-* in Old Tamil have, most of them, now lost the initial *y-* in popular speech as this was apparently repugnant to the genuis of Tamil. Professor Vinson and Dr. Barnett are therefore perfectly correct in saying that there was no initial *y-* in primitive Dravidian. We can understand the creeping in of a prothetic *-y-* in the vulgar pronunciation of palatal vowels, but it is difficult to assent to Mr. C.P. Venkatarama Aiyar's assumption that in a certain stage of development an initial *y-* was found necessary in some of the most highly cultivated of the Dravidian languages, as an on-glide before the initial long vowel *ā*, and that this *y-* was subsequently dispensed with.[2]

(*b*) Words found in Old Tamil with the initial *ya-* should, *prima facie*, be regarded as foreign words which have since lost the *y-* in accordance with Tamil phonetic laws ; this is specially so with regard to the interrogative forms beginning with *ya-*. The Old Tamil initial *yā-* some-

---

1. *a-v-ōṭu allatu yakaramutalatu* (Tolkāppiyam, Eḻuttu. Moḻi Marapu, 32.)

2. The only example which Mr. Venkatarama Aiyar is able to cite in support of his view is that of the Pālis of Dinajāpur regarding whom Mr. G. H. Damant observed 'that they seem to be unable to pronounce initial *ṛ* and sometimes, initial *ā* ; and that thereforce they pronounce *āmi* 'I' as *hāmi* with a strong accent on the first syllable" (I. A. 1872). It is possible that *hāmi* is the correct form and pronunciation of the word in the language of the Pālis. In the lists of words given at page 1 of 'The Glides' *hāmi* is shown as the pronoun of the first person singular in the Chenchu language and we know that this word is cognate with the Hindi *ham* and is ultimately traceable to the Sanskrit *aham* : in the Naipali language *hāmī* is the first person plural nominative (B.A.G. Vol. II, page 302).

times appears as *ē*- in mediaeval Tamil and this *ē*- has been shortened into *e*- in modern Tamil ; and all the interrogative forms now current in the spoken Tamil of the people begin with *e* or *ē* :—

ē<u>n</u>, etu, e<u>n</u><u>n</u>a, enta, eva<u>n</u>, eva<u>l</u>, evar, ētu, evai.

None of the modern interrogative pronouns finds a place in either of the two (Old Tamil) lists of pronouns given already. In Tolkāppiyam[1] it is stated that there are only four Tamil words of one syllable ending in *-v* ; these words are stated in the commentaries to be the three demonstratives *av*, *iv*, *uv*, and a fourth word *tev*, 'an enemy' : the interrogative *ev* is not mentioned here. Neither does the short *e* referred to in the Na<u>n</u><u>n</u>ūl (sūtra 162) find a place among the interrogative letters which are stated to be only three *a*, *ē*, *ō*[2] though that this interrogative initially in composition as in *eppeyar*[3] 'what name' *evvayi<u>n</u>*.[4]

According to Modern Tamil pratice the pronouns *atu, itu, utu, etu, yātu* receive an inflexional increment *a<u>n</u>* before the case post-positions, *e.g.*

at-a<u>n</u>-ai, it-a<u>n</u>-āl, ut-a<u>n</u>-ōṭu,
et-a<u>n</u>-i<u>n</u>, yāt-a<u>n</u>-ai.

Tolkāppiyam prescribes this increment for *atu*, *itu*, and *yātu*, but does not speak of or mention *etu*. Similarly the neuter plurals *avai*, *ivai*, *uvai*, *evai yāvai*, now receive an inflexional increment *a<u>r</u><u>r</u>*- ; Tolkāppiyam, prescribes this increment for *avai*, *ivai*, *uvai*, *yāvai* but does not speak of or or mention *evai*.[5]

---

1. Vakara-k-ki<u>l</u>avi nā<u>n</u> mo<u>l</u>i-y-i<u>r</u><u>r</u>atu (E<u>l</u>uttu. Mo<u>l</u>i. 48).
2. Ā ē ō ammū<u>n</u><u>r</u>um vi<u>n</u>ā (E<u>l</u>uttu. Nū<u>n</u>ma<u>r</u>apu, 32).
3. E<u>l</u>uttu. Puṇariyal, 96.
4. E<u>l</u>uttu. Pu<u>l</u><u>l</u>ai 39.
5. Tol. E<u>l</u>uttu. Urupiyal—4, 5, 6, 28.

These facts leave little room for doubt that the interrogative pronouns with the short initial *e* came into use after the time of Tolkāppiyam, *i.e.*, after the beginning of the Christian era; they are even now unknown to Malayāḷam. The interrogative base *ya* and the pronouns formed therewith were apparently recent adoptions in Tamil at the time of Tolkāppiyam; recent because the *yā* had not yet been converted into *e* or *a*; e.g., *yāvaṉ* etc., into *evaṉ* etc. and *yār* into *ār*.

yā—THE EARLIEST INTERROGATIVE BASE.

If initial *e* is mispronounced as *ya* in popular speech, initial *yā* is also often mispronounced as *e*; Dr. Kittel's arguments for holding *e* to be the original interrogative base are therefore not conclusive.

The oldest specimens of Dravidian speech that have come down to us belong to Tamil and Kanarese. The Tamil interrogatives in these specimens mostly begin with *yā*, but there is also the form *evaṉ* 'why, what for' and the initial short *e* in interrogative compounds. The interrogatives in the oldest Kanarese specimens appear to begin with *e* or *a*; but as the Tamil specimens are earlier by some centuries than the Kanarese specimens it is allowable to assume with Bishop Caldwell that *yā* was the original interrogative and that *e* has arisen from the corruption of *yā*

The theory which assumes the *y*- in the initial *yā* of Old Tamil words to be an on-glide has little to recommend it.

68. AFFINITIES OF THE BASE *yā*-.

Assuming *yā*- to be the primitive base we shall proceed to enquire if it has any extra Dravidian affinities.

Bishop Caldwell says that the base *yā-* has no extra Dravidian relationship as the ordinary bases of the interrogatives in the Indo-European family and the Scythian group of languages begin with the gutteral *k* and he appears to think the Dravidian *yā-* to be isolated. He also observes (C.D.G. page, 332) :

" In the absence of a real relative pronoun, the interrogative is used as a relative in many of the Scythian languages. The base of the Sanskrit relative pronoun *ya* (*yas*, *yā*, *yat*) bears a close apparent resemblance to the Draivdian interrogative *yā*. The Sanskrit *ya*, however, like the derived North-Indian *jō*, and the Finnish *yo*, is used as a relative whereas the Dravidian *yā* is exclusively and distinctly interrogative.

" It has been conjectured that the Sanskrit *ya* though now a relative, was a demonstrative originally; and if (as we shall see that there is some reason for supposing) the Dravidian interrogatives *e* and *a* were originally demonstratives, it may be supposed that *yā* was also a demonstrative, though of this no direct evidence whatever now remains. If *yā* were originally a demonstrative, the connection which would then appear to exist between it and the Sanskrit relative would require to be removed a step further back ; for it is not in Sanskrit that the relative *ya* has the force of a demonstrative, but in other and more distant tongues, viz., in the Lithuanian *yis* ' he' ; and in the Slavonian *yam*, and the Zend *yim* ' him '."

(i) In saying that the Dravidian *yā* is " exclusively and distinctively an interrogative " Bishop Caldwell appears to overlook or ignore the circumstance that *yāvaṉ*, *yāvaḷ*, etc., and all the modern variations thereof are used both as relatives and interrogatives. In Cinnayya Sūri's Telugu Bālavyākaraṇamu the interrogative pronouns are called *yat-kim-arthakamu* 'Relative-interrogatives'. Illustrations of this double use will presently he given and reference will be made to Dr. Kittel's criticism, thereon, viz., that the 'so called' relative pronouns are interrogatives.

(ii) It is not in the Scythian languages alone that the interrogative is used as a relative pronoun. Indo-Germanic philologists tell us that the stem **i-o* which was originally anaphoric came to be used as a relative without losing its anaphoric value even in the pro-ethnic period of the Indo-Germanic languages, and that this relative **i-o* was displaced later by derivatives from the interrogative stem* *qo* and the demonstrative stem **to-* in several languages. (Brugmann Vol. III, pages 331-332). We can see this displacement of the relative stem in the use as relatives of the interrogatives *who, which what*, and of the demonstrative *that* in modern English in which no representative of the pro-ethnic relative stem **i-o* now survives. (in Teutonic *hu* and *th* correspond to the proethnic *h* and *t*).

69. THE RELATIVE PRONOUNS IN THE VEDAS AND THEIR IMITATION IN TAMIL (DRAVIDIAN).

In his Sanskrit Grammar (S. 512) Professor W. D. Whitney briefly notices two marked peculiarities in the Sanskrit use of the relative pronoun. One of these is "a very decided preference for putting the relative clause before that to which it relates ; thus,

Sanskrit, *yaḥ sunvataḥ sakhā tasmā Indrāya gāyata* (Ṛ. V. English, who (is) the friend of the somapresser, to that

Indra sing ye................

"The other arrangement where the correlative is put before the relative though frequent enough, is notably less usual". The second peculiarity noticed is "a frequent conversion of the subject or object of a verb by an added relative into a substantive clause ; thus,

Sanskrit : *pari no pāhi yad dhanam* (A.V.)
English : of us protect what wealth (there is)."

The examples given by Professor Whitney, only two of which are reproduced above, are taken from the whole range of Sanskrit literature, but those given below are from the Taittirīya Veda where the two peculiarities have been developed to an excessive degree and are most noticeable.

(i) Sans : *yē nas sapatnā apa te bhavantu* (T. S. IV-7-32).

Eng : *who* (are) our enemies let *them* be banished hence.

i.e., let *those who* are our enmies be banished hence.

Tamil : *yār eṅkaḷukku vairikaḷō avarkaḷ tolaintu pōvārkaḷāka.*

(ii) Sans. : *yam dviṣmo yaś ca no dvēṣṭi tam vō jambhē dadhāmi.*

Eng. : whom we hate and who us hates, him in your jaws I place.

i.e., I place in your jaws (for being crushed) him whom we hate and who hates us.

Tamil : *evaṉ ai nāṅkaḷ pakaikkiṟōmō evaṉ eṅkaḷai pakaikkiṟāṉō avaṉai uṅkaḷ kaṭaivāykkuḷ vaikkiṟēṉ.*

(iii) Sans : *Tā* (*vyāhṛtīḥ*) *yō vēda sa vēda Brahma* (T.A. 5-6).

Eng : Those (mystic words) *who* knows he knows Brahma.

i.e. he who knows those (mystic words) will realize Brahma.

Tamil : *Anta* (*vyākiruti-kaḷai*) *evaṉ-ō avaṉ Prahma t-tai aṟivāṉ.*

(iv) Sans : *ya ēnam viduḥ amṛtās tē bhavanti* (T. A-6-1).

Eng : *who* this (Being) know immortal they become.

i.e. Those who know this (Being) (will) become immortal.

Tamil: *Inta (-p-poruḷai) evarkaḷ aṟikiṟārkaḷ-ō avarkaḷ maraṇam illātavarkaḷ āvārkaḷ.*

(v) Sans: *yad aham veda tad aham dhārayāṇi* (T.A. 7-43).

Eng : What I know that let me remember.

i.e. May I not forget that which (what) I know (have learnt).

Tamil : *etai nāṉ terintu koṇṭirukkiṟēṉō- adai maṟa-vāmal iruppēṉāka.*

(vi) Sans : *yāni anavadyāni karmāṇi tāni sevita-vyāni nō itarāṇi* (T.A. 6-64).

Eng : *What* (are) blameless actions *those* should be performed, no others.

i.e., you should perform only such actions as are blameless.

Tamil : *evai nirtōṣamāṉa kāryam-kaḷ-ō avai-kaḷai māttiram tāṉ nīṅkaḷ śeyya-vēṇṭum.*

(vii) Sans : *yō vai tām Brahmaṇo veda amṛtenāvṛtām.*

Eng : who indeed that Brahman's knows light-encompassed.

Sans : *purīm tasmai Brahma ca Brahmā ca āyuḥ.*

Eng : citadel to him Brahman and Brahmā long life.

Sans : *kīrtim prajām daduḥ* (T.A. 1-27).

Eng : Fame progeny will give.

Brahman and Brahmā will bestow long life, frame, and progeny on *him who* knows that light—encompassed citadel of Brahman.

Tamil : *Anta pēr šoli ūlnta para prahmattiṉ kōṭṭaiyai evaṉ aṟikiṟāṉ ō avaṉukku paraprahmamum prahmāvum tīrkāyucaiyum, kīrttiyai-yum Cantali-yai-yum aḷi-p-pārkaḷ.*

The above are a few examples taken from the Taittirīya Veda of the relative pronouns derived from the base *yā-*; such constructions occur by many hundreds in the Āraṇyaka portions.

They are all practically interrogative constructions · in fact in the English and Tamil (Dravidian) renderings given above interrogative pronouns are used. In Sanskrit the relative construction is distinguished from the interrogative by the use of different sets of pronouns derived from the bases *yā* and *kā;* in English this distinction is indicated by a difference in syntax and in Tamil (Dravidian) by the use of the particle *ō*. Thus, in the English sentence 'He married the girl whom he loved from childhood' the collocation '*whom he loved from childhood*' has the force of an adjective qualifying the word 'girl'; if it was an interrogative the syntactical arrangement would be *whom did he love from childhood*. So in Tamil (Dravidian) *ārai pālyam mutal viḻaintār* 'whom did he love from childhood' is a question which requires an answer ; but *ārai pālyam mutal viḻaintār ō* 'whom he loved from childhood' assumes that he did love somebody from childhood and proceeds to predicate something about that person.

Sometimes the relative pronoun comes after its correlative as in the English idiom 'he, who etc.', 'that, which etc.' 'those which etc.'

(viii) Sans : *Dhūrva tam yō ' smān dhūrvati tam dhūrva yam vayam dhūrvāmaḥ* (T.S.I. 1-5).

Eng : Injure *him who* us injures, injure *him whom* we injure.

Tamil : *evaṉ eṅkaḷukkut tīṅku cey-kiṟāṉō avaṉai-k-keṭuttu-viṭuṅkaḷ.*

evaṉukku nāṅkaḻ tiṅku cey-kiṟōmō avaṉai-y-um keṭutlæ-vituṅkaḻ.

(ix) Sans : *sa ya etadannamanne pratiṣṭhitam veda prati-tiṣṭhati.*

Eng : he who this food in food fixed knows secures a firm position :

he who knows that this food is established on food secures a firm position.

Tamil : *Inta aṉṉattukku aṉṉamē ātāram eṉṟu evaṉ aṟiki-ṟāṉō avaṉ nilai peṟṟu vaḻvāṉ.*

More rarely the correlative is omitted as in the English idiom 'who steals my purse steals trash'.

(x) Sans: *Saiṣā bhārgavī vidyā. parame vyoman pratiṣṭhitā. ya evam veda pratitiṣṭhati.*

Eng : who thus knows secures a firm position.

Tamil : *eveṉ ippaṭi aṟikiṟāṉō avaṉ nilai peṟṟu vāḻvāṉ.*

The second peculiarity where the subject or object of a sentence is converted into a substantive clause by an added relative has naturally led to the insertion of the corresponding correlative also in most cases ; this amounts almost to a misuse of the relative construction. Such a construction is usually resorted to when a thing or person cannot be indicated by a single word or phrase ; but to convert a sufficiently expressive word or phrase into a clause by the addition of a relative except where such conversion is required for effect, is mere verbiage : thus :

(xi) Sans : *yaḥ pituranujāyāḥ putraḥ. sa purastānnayati.*

Eng : who (is) father's younger sister's son he leads in front.

Sans : *yo māturanujāyāḥ putraḥ. sa paścānnayati.* (T.B. 3-8-4).

Eng : who (is) mother's younger sister's son he drags from behind.

In these two sentences the relatives and their correlatives may both be omitted advantageously without any loss of perspicuity.

(xii) Sans : *ūrū tad asya yad vaiśyaḥ.*

Eng : His thighs (are) that which (is known as) the Vaiśya.

Here again the addition of a relative and its correlative seems to be wholly unnecessary. Such constructions are exceedingly numerous in the later portions of the Taittirīya Brāhmaṇa and Āraṇyakas. (*Vide* T. B. III—12-6 and 7; T.A. VI—64.)

The two perculiarities noticed by Professor Whitney and carried to excess in the manner illustrated above have made the relative construction look as if it was an interrogative one, and appear to take Sanskrit half way towards dispensing with one of the two pronominal sets as has actually been done in some Indo-Germanic languages.

70. DR. KITTEL ON THE RELATIVE CONSTRUCTION IN KANARESE.

Dr. Kittel thinks that the so-called relative sentences in Kanarese are really interrogative.

" It has been stated (already) that there are no relative pronouns in Kannaḍa and (that) their place is somehow supplied by the so-called relative participles. **** Occasionally, however, there occur sentences in the three dialects which might suggest the thought as if the interrogative pronouns were used as the relative ones, *e.g :*

(i) *Kan : Āvan adhika puṇyan avanē sēvyan ?*

Eng : who (is) a very righteous man he (indeed) is venerable.

But this translation is misleading ; the correct literal translation is 'who (is) a very righteous man? he (indeed) is venerable?

That the meaning of the above and similar sentences is thus to be explained by the interrogative pronoun followed by a demonstrative one becomes plainer by instances taken from the modern dialect in which the vowel *ō* of questioning is often used, *e.g.*

(ii) *Kan : Āneya mumbhāga yēvadō ? adu dāntabhāga.*
Eng : what (is) the forepart of an elephant's head, it is the *dantabhāga.*

(iii) *Kan : Yāvanu kelasa māḍuvanō ? avanu uṇṇuvanu.*
Eng : who work does ? he shall have a dinner. (K. K. G. S. 267).

He returns to the subject again in sections 329 and 330 of his grammar.

" When a relative participle with a demonstrative adverb of time, as *baruvāga* (*baruva*+*āga*) 'when I come ; when thou comest ; when he, she, it comes ; when we, you, they come is commonly used, the 'when' is occasionally expressed by an interrogative adverb of time followed by a demonstrative one, *e.g.*,

(iv) *Kan : nīvu yāvāga Puṇeyindu tirigi barnvirō āga avara bheṭṭi takolliri.*

Eng : you when from Puṇe back come then visit him, *i.e.*, when you come back from Poona visit him.

This is so to say an imitation of Sanskrit *yadā* 'when' and its correlative *tadā* 'then'. (*Ibid.* S. 329.)

" It might appear as if there existed relative pronouns and their correlatives in Kannaḍa (as in Sanskrit). That such an appearance is not based upon idiom has been indicated in S. 267, though in English the instances given there, would naturally suggest the existence of relatives and their correlatives, *e.g.*, 'who—he' 'who—she' However the pronouns resembling relative ones are interrogatives, and the correlatives are demonstratives, and therefore the instances quoted in section 267 and some additional ones in this paragraph are literally to be translated as follows :—

(v) *Kan : Dhanamullan āvan ? avanē indra ?*

Eng : who (is) a rich man ? he indeed is (a) prince *i.e.*, A rich man is a prince indeed.

(vi) *Kan : āval pativrate ? avale mānye.*

Eng : who (is) a faithful wife ? she indeed (is) venerable.

(vii) *Kan : yāvanu satkāryagalannu māḍuwanō ? avanu sukha paḍuttāne.*

Eng : who virtuous actions does perform ? he (is) happy.

Such instances appear to have originally been formed in imitation of Sanskrit ones with the relative *yad*, *yāvat*, *yathā* and their correlatives *tad*, *tāva*, *tathā*. (*Ibid.* S. 330.)

Dr. Kittel is incorrect in supposing that the particle *ō* in the modern examples *ii*, *iii*, *iv*, and *vii* is a letter of questioning. The real interrogative force lies in the pronouns *āvan*, *yāvadu*, *yāvanu*, *yāvaga*, *āval* and, as has already been pointed out in (*b*) above, the use of *ō* in the modern examples is to indicate that no question is asked.

Further, there is no point in saying that the Kanarese examples are all interrogative constructions, for the Vedic examples given above are practically interrogative constructions though the pronouns used are from the relative stem *yā-;* and it is in consequence of this practical identity that several Indo-European languages have discontinued the *yā*-stem and use interrogative pronouns instead, thereby effecting a simplification by getting rid of unnecessary forms. In many Scythian languages also the same pronoun serves as an interrogative and a relative. The remarks that "the pronouns resembling relative ones are interrogatives, and the correlatives are demonstratives "[1] applies equally well to modern English.

Dr. Kittel himself admits that the sentences[2] he has given to illustrate relative constructions in Kanarese "āppear to have originally been formed in imitation of the Sanskrit ones with the relatives *yad*, *yāvat*, *yathā* and the correlatives *tad*, *tāvat*, *tathā* ". The imitation goes back to the oldest specimens of the language which have come down to us, the change in the modern times merely consisting in the addition of the particle *ō* to distinguish a relative construction from the interrogative. Formerly the relative construction appears to have been indistinguishable from the interrogative in Kanarese.

Dr. Kittel does not see that the imitation referred to by him is not confined to mere *method* but involves also imitation and borrowal of materials (S. 41). The Sanskrit pronominal form *yāvant* which now means 'how much' (relative) originally meant 'which like' or 'whatlike' (W. S.G.S. 517); the masculine nominative singular of *yāvant*[3] is *yāvān* in Sanskrit and there is an indeclinable *yāvam* in Pāli. It is from the assumed base *yāva* of these forms, which also exists as an independent word in Pāli, and from its corruption *āva* that the Kanarese pronouns appear to be formed. *Āvam*,

---

1 In the Dravidian languages the demonstrative pronouns are the same as those of the third person.

2. He has given over twenty-five sentences of which only seven have been reproduced above.

3. Corruptions of *yāvant* in the forms *javan*, *jaun*, *jun*, *jiṇ*, *jin̲* etc. are now in use in some of the North Indian Aryan vernaculars as relative pronoun direct singular (H.G.G.S. 437-(4).)

āvan and *yāvanu yāvavanu* contain masculine suffixes imitated from Aryan (S. 51) ; the feminine forms *āvaḷ*, *yāvaḷu* contain a feminine suffix derived from Aryan (S. 52); the neuter forms *āvudu*, *āvuvu*, *yāvadu*, *yāvavu* are formed by affixing *udu*, *uvu*, *adu*, *avu*, all of Aryan affinities (S. 63) to the bases *āva* and *yāva*. Dr. Kittel calls the clauses containing these imitations interrogative forms. Quite so ; the forms are interrogative in the same sense in which 'who' and 'which' are interrogatives in English. They are both interrogative and relative

71-A. DRAVIDIAN INTERROGATIVE PRONOUNS ARE ALSO RELATIVE PRONOUNS.

The above discussion shows :

i. that the interrogative pronouns in the cultivated Dravidian languages (as in many Scythian and several Indo-European languages) are also relative pronouns, *i.e.*, that they are what the Telugu grammarians call *yat-kim-arthakamu* 'relative-interrogative'.

ii. that they are imitations of the Sanskrit relative pronouns, derived from the base *yā*-, which look so like interrogatives in their use in the latter Vedic literature.

iii. If the cultivated Dravidian languages had separate interrogatives formerly we must suppose that these have been completely superseded by the relative interrogative forms derived from Aryan.

71-B. DRAVIDIAN INTERROGATIVES BASES AND THEIR PROBABLE INDO-ARYAN ORIGINALS.

We shall now briefly enumerate the various developments and modifications which the original Indo-Aryan relative base underwent on Indian soil and indicate how the Dravidian relative-interrogative bases are traceable to them.

The root of the Indo-Aryan relative base is *ya* (m: *yas*, f: *yā*, n: *yad*), but in forming compounds the neuter stem *yad* is generally used. Professor Whitney says : "the use of *yat* as representative stem begins very early ; we have *yatkāma* in the Veda, and *yatkārin*, *yaddevatya* in the Brāhmaṇa ; later on grows more general. From the proper root come also a considerable series of derivatives : *yatas*, *yati*, *yatra*, *yathā*, *yadā*, *yadi*, *yarhi*, *yāvant*, *yatara*, *yatama;* and the compound *yādriś*" (W. S. S. 510). In *yāvant* 'which like' (original meaning) and *yādṛś* 'which like' the pronominal root *ya* is lengthened.

In Pāli[1] we have the adverbial forms *yāva* and *yāvam* with the modern meanings of 'until, while, as long as'.

71-C. A POSSIBLE ALTERNATIVE THEORY IN REGARD TO THE ORIGIN OF THE DRAVIDIAN INTERROGATIVE FORMS.

It is also possible to conceive of the Dravidian interrogative bases as having arisen from the Aryan interrogative root *k* combined with a palatal vowel or semi-vowel. The neuter interrogative form in Sanskrit is *kim* and the Sanskrit pronoun of quantity *kiyat* was *kivat* in the Vedas formed in the same manner as *tāvat* and *yāvat.* In modern Hindi the neuter interrogative is *kyā*. In all these cases the interrogative letter *k* is combined with a palatal vowel or semi-vowel. It is possible that the contiguity of these palatals palatalized the root letter itself which becoming weakened into *c* and *s* was ultimately lost. We saw already that the Skt. *kṛmi* 'ant' (Lith. *kirmi*) became **cīrma*, *cima* 'an ant' in Telugu and *irumpu*, *irumu*, *eṟumpu*, etc., in the other Dravidian languages of Southern India through the palatalization and ultimate loss of *k*.

In the Avesta there are in addition to the *k* forms special forms of the interrogative beginning with the palatal *c*:—*ci* 'who', *cid* 'which', *cati* 'how much' (l. A. V. S. 407, K. A. V. Ss. 228, 229).

---

1. Childer's Pāli Dictionary.

" Guzerati has " in addition to the *k* forms, " a unique interrogative (masculine) *so* (fem.) *si* and (neut.) *sum* the only approach to which is the Sindhi *ca* used only as a neuter " (B. A. G. Vol. II, page 324).

It is therefore possible that in the language of the Indo-Aryans who emigrated into South India in pre-historic times three were interrogative bases of which the initial was *ky*, *c* or *s* and that this consonant was weakened into *y*. Whether the initial of the earliest Dravidian interrogatives arose in this manner or was merely imitated from the Indo-Iranian relative base *ya* there seems to be no doubt, as will have been seem from section (*b*) above, that the Dravidian interrogative bases are derived from four different *yā-van*, *ya-d*, *yā-va*, *yā* which have the same suffixes as the Sanskrit *tā-van*, *ta-d* and the Prākṛt *tāva*, *tā*.

Sūtra IV-5 of Vararuci's Prākṛta Prakāśa says that the *va* of the words *yāvat*, *tāvat*, etc., is elided in Prākṛt and sūtra IV-6 says that the final non-conjunct consonant of words is also elided ; but as by that time (1st century B.C.) the initial *y*- had also become *j*- (II-31) the actual Prākṛt forms of *yāvat* (the relative pronoun of quantity) in Vararuci's time were *jā*, *jāva*[1]. An earlier form of *jāva* is the Pāli *yāva* ; it is reasonable to assume that *jā* tood had an earlier form **yā*.

The later forms of *jā*, *jāva* in Prākṛt were *jē*, *jēva*, *jēma*[2] (H.G.G.Ss. 438-1).

In several modern Aryan vernaculars of India the direct singulars of the relative pronoun have the forms *yē*, *jē*, *javan*, *jaun*, *jau*, *jō* (H.G.G. Ss. 437-4).

---

1. Vararuci II-31. *Ādēr yō jaḥ*. IV-5. *yāvadādṣu vasya* IV-6. *Antyahalaḥ*.

2. *M*, also appears in the other pronominal forms *ēma*, *tēma*, *kēma*.

Pronominal adjectival compounds with the suffix '*vant*,' conveying the meaning of 'after the manner of, like' were freely formed in the older language, *e.g.*, *māvant* 'like me,' *tvāvant* 'like thee,' *yuṣmāvant* 'like you,' *īvant* 'like this,' *kīvant* 'like what,' *tāvant* 'like that,' *etāvant* 'like this,' *yāvant* 'which like' (relative); and that of these only the last three were in use in the later languages in the sense of 'so much,' 'how much' (W.S.G. Ss. 517, 1233-*f*).

The forms *tāva*, *yāva*, *yāvam* of *Pāli*, *tā*, *tāva*, *jā*, *jāva* of the literary Prākṛts dealt with in Vararuci's Grammar (IV-5-6) have only the later senses of *tāntus* and *quāntus*. There is however reason to think that the older meanings of 'like that' and 'which like' must have persisted down to modern times in the popular dialects, for as noted above the forms *jēva*, *javan*, *jaun*, etc., are now used in some of the Aryan vernaculars of India as simple relative pronouns—which use is apparently derived from the sense 'which like'

We may compare also the Telugu forms *māvaṇṭi* 'like me,' *mīvaṇṭi* 'like you,' *aṭuvaṇṭi* 'like that' *iṭuvaṇṭi* 'like this,' *eṭuvaṇṭi* 'what like' where the suffix '*vant*' in the sense of 'like' is preserved.

(i) The Sanskrit masculine singular ending *n* when adopted in Tamil originally indicated only the singular number and was common to all the three natural genders. The Sanskrit masculine *yāvān* appears to have been one of the earliest relative-interrogative forms adopted in Tamil and other Dravidian languages and seems to be the original of the Kanarese interrogative pronouns *ēnu*, *ēn* common to all the three genders (K. K. G. Ss. 102-b, and 125) and of the genderless Old Tamil *evaṉ* which has become *eṉ* in modern times.

(ii) The interrogative *e* which appears initially in composition as in Tamil *eppeyar* 'what name,' *evvayiṉ* 'what place,' *emmaṉitaṉ* 'what man' and in Malayāḷam *ekkālam* 'what time,' *evvaṇṇam* 'what manner' has apparently arisen from the imitation of such compounds and combinations as *yatkāma* 'having which desire,' *yatkāraṇam* 'wherefore', *yatsukham* 'which pleasure,' *yadduḥkham* 'which grief,' etc., which would come to be pronounced *ekkāma*, *ekkāraṇam*, *eccukam*, *ettukkam* in Tamil and Malayāḷam. This *e* is another of the earliest relative interrogative forms adopted in the Dravidian languages.

(iii) The Tamil Malayāḷam forms *yāvaṉ*, *yāvaḷ*, *yāvar*, *yāvai*, and the Kanarese *yāva*, *yāvanu*, *yavavanu*, *yāvaḷu*, *yāvadu*, *yāvaru*, *yāvavu* are apparently derived from the old Indo-Aryan base *yāva*.

The Kanarese base *āva* and the derivatives *avaṉ* etc., are derivable from *yāva* by the elision of the initial *y*, as in *yānu* 'I' which has become *ānu*.

The Kanarese forms with the initial *d*- are derivable from the Prākṛt bases *jā*, *jāva*, the initial of which has become *d*-; these must have come in later than the forms with initial *y*-.

The Tamil Malayāḷam forms *ēvaṉ*, *ēvaḷ* etc., and the Telugu *ēvi* must have arisen from the weakening of the initial *yā* into *ē*.

In the forms *evaṉ*, *evaḷ*, etc., *evadu*, *evaru*, etc., the initial *ē* has been shortened.

The theory of Bishop Caldwell and Dr. Kittel that the *v* of the above forms is intervocal is untenable.

(iv) The assumed old Indo-Aryan *yā* corresponding to the Prākṛtic *jā* of Vararuci appears to be the original of the interrogative *yā* of Tamil and Kanarese, the interrogative *ē* of Malayāḷam, Kanarese and Telugu, the interrogative *ā* of Kanarese and the interrogative *dā* of Tuḷu.

It is also the base of the Tamil *yātu* ' which, what? ' which became *ētu*, *etu* later in Tamil, Telugu *ēdi*, *edi* are traceable to the same base ; as also *yār*, *ār* ' who ' of Tamil, Malayāḷam and Kanarese, *yēr* of Tuḷu, and *dēr* of Brāhūī. The Kuru*kh* and Malto interrogative *nē* can also be derived from the assumed Indo-Aryan *yā* as initial *y*- often changes into *n*- in Dravidian. Cf. Dravidian *yāṉ* ' I,' Sanskrit *yama* ' God of death,' *yuga* ' yoke ' which have become *naṉ*, (Telugu *nēnu*) *namaṉ* and *nukam* in Tamil.

72. MISCELLANEOUS DRAVIDIAN RELATIVE CONSTRUCTIONS.

(*a*) The particle *o*.

Several instances have been given already of relative constructions with the particle *o*.

Old Kanarese : *avan adhika puṇyan avanē sēvyam.*

Modern Kanarese : *yavanv adhika puṇyan -ō avanē sēvyanu.*

Telugu : *eva ḍu adhika puṇyamugalava do vā ḍē sēvpu ḍu.*

Tamil : *evaṉ atika puṇyam uḷḷvvaṉ-o avaṉē cēvikkattakkavaṉ.*

English : *who* (*is*) *a very righteous man he indeed* (*alone?*) (*is*) *venerable.*

The construction is the same in all the three languages and is an imitation of the Vedic relative construction, the particle *o* indicating that the construction is relative, not interrogative.

Sometimes the relative-interrogative pronoun is placed immediately before this *o*, *e.g.* :—

Kanarese : *adhika puṇyan yāvanō avanē sēvyanu.*

Telugu : *adhika puṇyamugalava du eva ḍō vā ḍē sēvyu ḍu.*

Tamil : *atika puṇyamuḷḷavaṉ evaṉō avaṉē cēvikkattakkavaṉ.*

English : *a very righteous man who* (*is*) *he indeed* (*is*) *venerable.*

These may be compared with the construction in the following Tamil verse—the very first in the Tiruvāymoḻi of the Vaiṣṇava saint Nammāḻvār.

1. Tamil : *uyarvaṟa uyarnalam uṭaiyavaṉ yavaṉ avaṉ.*

   English : unsurpassed goodness possessor who his (of him).

2. Tamil : *mayarvaṟu matinalam aruḷiṉaṉ yavaṉ avaṉ.*

   English : illusionless good intellect bestower who his (of him).

3. Tamil : *ayarvaṟum amararkaḷ atipati yavaṉ avaṉ.*

   English : sleepless immortal gods sovereign who his (of him).

4. Tamil : *tuyaraṟu cuṭarаraṭi toḻuteḻu eṉ maṉaṉē.*

   English : sorrow dispelling shining feet venerate my mind.

(Free Translation).

Oh my mind ! venerate the sorrow dispelling feet of Him who possesses unsurpassed goodness, who bestows illusionless intellects (on his worshippers), and who is the sovereign of the sleepless (unwinking) immortal gods.

The commentators explain that *yāvaṉ* in the above verse is not an interrogative but a relative.

We have seen that the far demonstrative base *ava* becomes *o* 'he' as in Madras Gondi *ondu* 'he,' Gondi or 'he,' Kui *o* anju 'he,' etc. In Malayāḷam or, *ol* are alternative forms of *avar, avaḷ.*

Might it be that the particle *o* in the relative constructions noted above was originally the genderless correlative *ava*, and that *evaṉō*, *evaḷo*, *evarō*, etc., are contracted forms of *evaṉava*, *evaḷava*, *evarava*, etc., corresponding to the English 'who so.' The fact that this *o* is re-inforced by a second correlative indicating gender and number is not an insuperable objection to this etymology as the *o* has latterly been mistaken for an interrogative particle.

(*b*) Another form of relative construction uses the particle *e*, *e.g.*

Tamil : *Nēṟṟu vantāṉē avaṉ iṉṟaikkum vantāṉ.*
Telugu : *Ninna vaccina de va ḍūde ḍukuda vaccinādu.*
English : yesterday came who he to-day also came.

It looks as if the *e* here was originally the relative-interrogative *ya*, common to all genders and numbers, and that *e-avan*, *e-aval*, etc., correspond to the English who he, who she, etc.

(*c*) The relative participles.

This is the name given by European grammarians to certain participles in the Dravidian languages which qualify nouns and are therefore called *peyar eccam* in Tamil. There is a participle corresponding to each tense form as follows :—

	Tamil.	Kanarese.	Telugu.
Past :	*ceyta* 'that did'	*geyda*	*cēsina*
	kāṭṭiṉa 'that showed'		
Present :	*ceykiṟa* 'that does'	*geyyuva*	*cēyutunna*
Future :	*ceyyum* 'doing' or 'that will do'	*geyyuva*	*cēyun.*

The majority of these are obtained by adding the particle *a* to the old non-pronominalized tense forms ; where the non-pronominalized forms still continue to be used as tenses, as in the Tamil *ceyyum* and the Telugu *ceyun*, no such addition is made.

Bishop Caldwell enters into a long disquisition as to the origin of the suffixed *a* and comes to the conclusion that it is the sign of the possessive case !! Dr. Gundert on the other hand appears to have been of opinion that the suffixed *a* was the same as the demonstrative base *a* (C.D.G., pages 411-414).

Dr. Gundert's view seems to be the correct one. As in Dravidian the subject of the action is tacked on to the verb-form and becomes enclitic thereto and as we have seen that in the Dravidian the same words are used to denote the correlative, the demonstrative and the third personal pronouns, it would seem correct to regard the suffixed *a* as the subject of the action expressed in the relative participles; in other words, the suffixed *a* of the relative participles should be regarded as corresponding to ' that ' in the relative clauses ' that did,' ' that showed,' ' that does ' in the paradigm above. If this view be correct the suffixed *a* will be the same *-av* the old demonstrative base which had lost its final *-v*; in Tolkāppiyam several verb-forms occur ending in *-av* which now end in *-a*.

It will be noted that the double use of *av-* in Dravidian as a demonstrative and as a relative corresponds to the double use of that in the same two senses in English. *Av* in Dravidian is also the base of the pronouns of the third person.

It may also be remarked in passing that without any addition for number or gender *av* is itself the pronoun of the third person in the neuter plural in Tamil. The original neuter plural forms must have been *iruntaṉar* ' they (neuter) were ' *pōkiṉṟaṉar* ' they (neuter) are going,' etc.; these have now lost the final *-v*[1] and exist *iruntaṉa*, *pōkiṉṟaṉa* etc., as if the neuter plural termination was merely *a*. This has led Bishop Caldwell into supposing that the Dravidian languages resemble Latin in having a neuter plural in short *a* (C. D. G. Introduction, page 76).

---

1. Tol. Col. 2: *uyartiṇaiyav v ē* for the modern *uyartiṇiaya vē* 'they belong the rational caste'.

Tol. Col. 3: *aḥriṇaiyav v ē* for the modern *aḥriṇaiya v ē* ' they belong to the irrational caste '.

73. SUMMARY AND CONCLUSION.

The supposed Dravidian Characteristics in Indo-Aryan are really Aryan Characteristics in the Dravidian.

We shall now proceed to summarise the results of the discussion of the various items in which the Dravidian languages are alleged to have affected Indo-Aryan speeches.

First in regard to vocabulary, it is well known that only about a fourth of the roots in Sanskrit can be traced in one or more of the other languages belonging to the Indo-Germanic group. Some scholars seem to hold that every root of the remaining three-fourths which Sanskrit has in common with Dravidian languages must have been borrowed by it from a Dravidian tongue, the contention being that though Dravidian languages are now spoken only in the South of the Peninsula there are reasons to believe that these languages were spoken at one time throughout the continent of India and that Indo-Aryan must have been in contact with Dravidian almost from the time of the arrival of the Aryans in India. On this supposition it is equally possible that the Dravidian languages might have borrowed the words from the Indo-Aryan and we saw in the last chapter that South Indian products such as rice, black pepper, ginger, etc., bear in South India names which have travelled southwards after the arrival of the Aryans in India and which are derived by curtailment from fuller forms found in Sanskrit.

The theory that the Dravidian languages were once spoken throughout India rests on premises which are more than doubtful and can be disproved in some cases. It is argued in support of this theory that there are certain peculiarities in Dravidian forms of speech which are not found generally in the Indo-Germanic group but which have been acquired by Sanskrit on Indian soil, and that this shows that there must have been formerly in use in the northern parts of India languages similar to the Dravidian languages spoken in South India at the present day. The chief peculiarities thus acquired are stated to be :—

1 The adoption of the cerebral series of letters by Sanskrit.

2. The use of participles for tense forms and a continued increase in the use of conjunctive participles in subordinate sentences.

3. The formation of the periphrastic future from present tense forms and of the active past participle from passive participles, and various other minor changes detailed by Professor Sten Konow in Vol. IV of the Linguistic Survey of India.

1. *Cerebral letters.*—The argument under this head appears to be due to a want of knowledge of the true phonology of the Dravidian languages. For, if cerebral sounds are a special feature of the Dravidian languages, alveolar or semi-dental sounds were an equally special feature which persisted in these languages long after Sanskrit had converted its alveolars into dentals and cerebrals and still persist in Tamil and Malayāḷam. This shows some foreign influence which has acted on Sanskrit and the Dravidian alike, not necessarily Dravidian influence on Sanskrit.

2. The use of participles for tense forms and of un-inflected participles in subordinate clauses is a necessary preliminary step in the process of evolution from the synthetic to the analytic stage and need not necessarily be in imitation of Dravidian.

3. The periphrastic future and the active past participle were inherited by Sanskrit from the Indo-Iranian period and were not evolved by it on Indian soil.

4. In regard to the change in the syntactical order of words it is obvious that when a synthetic inflected language drops its inflections and becomes analytical some convention is necessary as to the order of words for the purpose of avoiding ambiguity, and a change in the method of declension by prepositions into one declension by post-positions may lead to the complete reversal of the order of words in a sentence. In declining nouns by post-positions and in rendering pronouns enclitic to verbforms Indo-Aryan vernaculars and Dravidian both follow the Indo-Iranian system.

5. The loss of the subjunctive mood and of any infinitive forms in Sanskrit cannot possibly be due to Dravidian influence.

But these considerations become of minor importance in view of the deep-seated affinities, amounting in most cases to identities, between the demonstrative and the interrogative pronouns of Sanskrit and of the Dravidian languages.

(*a*) The adoption of *ṉ*, *ḷ* as the masculine and feminine signs, the replacement of the latter by *di* in the Āndhra group, the adoption of *ṇḍu*, *ñju*, *m*, *e* as the signs of the masculine nominative singulars in imitation of Prākṛtic terminations and the adoptions of *t* as the oblique declensional sign—all of which have arisen from the Indo-Germanic *nt*—are inconsistent with the assumption that Dravidian Grammar has not been affected by Indo-Aryan forms of speech.

(*b*) Even granting that the Dravidian interrogative base *ya* has no connection with the Aryan relative base *ya* it cannot be denied that the formations *yāvat*, *yāva*, *yā* and *yad* out of these bases are the same in both groups of languages and that the first three of these formations contain the Indo-Iranian *vant* and the Indo-Germanic *nt*. The formation *yāvān* in the sense of 'what like' which has given rise to the genderless *evaṉ*, *eṉ* of Tamil goes back to the oldest of the Vedic period while *yat* corresponding to the interrogative *e* of Dravidian is also old; while *yāva*, *jāva* and *jā* are found in some very old Prākṛts. These fact show that the imitation of Aryan forms began even in the oldest Vedic period.

(*c*) In regard to the demonstrative pronouns the Aryan bases *id* and *ava* are of Indo-Germanic antiquity while *ad* and *im* have been in existence since the Indo-Iranian period; the base *ava* is of exceedingly rare occurrence in the Vedas. Here some of the imitations by the Dravidian must have been from the pro-Vedic period.

Thus if we begin by supposing that the people of South India were originally speaking a group of non-Aryan languages we must,—to explain the borrowings noted in (*a*), (*b*), and (*c*) above —also assume that there emigrated into South India a large body of Aryans or of Aryanised people who must have separated from the main body of Aryans in the Vedic period when these Aryans were still in the Panjab and other portions of north-western India. This is also what, as we saw in the last chapter, was indicated by the general use in South India of names derived from the very old words *vrīhi*, *nīvāra*, *śuṣka* and *śṁgabēra*, the representatives of which are now but rarely met with in other parts of India.

That some of the oldest of these immigrants into Southern India must have come from North-West is specifically indicated by some north-western characteristics found in the Tamil vocabulary, as will be shown later on

74. Reasons for limiting the scope of the work to the cultivated Dravidian languages.

It occasionally happens that when we meet two persons, son and father, of strikingly similar features and apparently of the same age, we mistake the son for the father. This is exactly what has happened in the case of some Dravidian scholars who have thought that Sanskrit has imitated Dravidian. This is no doubt due in part to not noting that the Sanskrit forms must have been inherited from the Indo-Iranian period, but mainly to the assumption that the present Dravidian forms have been in use from time immemorial. The influences which to our knowledge have acted on the evolution of the Dravidian languages are such as to render this assumption highly improbable. These languages have been under the influence of Aryan dialects representing a higher culture and civilization for at least twenty or twenty-five centuries, and many Dravidian races have abandoned their mother tongues and adopted Aryan dialects; while many of the remaining indigenous languages are being rapidly aryanised. In this struggle for existence the dialects that will offer the greatest resistence to change will be those that have a literature and grammatical standard; but we have seen above in the case of the demonstrative and interrogative pronouns that even Tamil, Telugu and Kanarese are not above imitating Aryan models. Again the present tense suffixes in Tamil-Malayāḷam are not the same as those of Kanarese and Telugu. None of the three future tense suffixes in Telugu is found in Tamil or Kanarese, while not one of the four past tense suffixes in Telugu corresponds to the Kanarese past suffix. If these languages belong to the same family, was there not some uniformity originally in these essential forms? What were the external influences that destroyed the original uniformity, if there was one, and produced these extensive changes ? The Dravidian problem cannot be fully grasped unless we satisfactorily answer these questions.

The uncultivated Dravidian languages which have no known history will not be of much use in a historical treatment of the question. It is no doubt true that in many rude languages we often find idioms preserved, which throw light on the abraded forms of cultivated speeches. Thus the language of the Nilgiri Baḍagas who have remained isolated from the plains now for several centuries shows a literary condition corresponding in several respects with archaic Kanarese and the evidence furnished by it may be utilised in tracing the evolution of Kanarese forms. But this is a rare instance of a dialect isolated on a hill top and free from extraneous influences for centuries. Can the same be said of the majority of uncultivated speeches like Gōṇḍi, Gōlarī and Burgaṇḍī instanced already which are surrounded and interpenetrated by Aryan dialects and which are ful of flux and change and are fast dying out. There is no guarantee in the case of these languages that any peculiar form possessed by them *e.g.*, a *-k-* suffix for the past tense, or a *-t-* suffix for the present, is not a recent acquisition and to make use of such forms without a knowledge of their past history may lead to fallacious results.

It is therefore proposed in the following pages to confine attention to such Dravidian languages as have been cultivated and possess literatures, *viz.*, Tamil, Malayāḷam, Kanarese and Telugu, and to determine with the help of their literatures and inscriptions what grammatical forms were in use in them in the earliest period of their development. A comparison with the present grammatical forms will show what changes have taken place in them since that pro-Dravidian period and how these changes have been brought about. It is also necessary to know what Aryan languages were spoken in their neighbourhood prior to or during the time which corresponds to the pro-Dravidian period and what antiquity must be assigned to the literatures of these languages and the inscriptions written in them.

Before proceeding to enumerate the suffixes in use in the various Dravidian languages, it is proposed to describe briefly the earliest specimens of Indo-Aryan and Dravidian speeches that have come down to us either in the form of inscriptions or of literature and to determine what antiquity should be assigned to them. This description is not intended to be exhaustive as the object in referring to these specimens here is solely for the purpose of determining which are earlier, the Dravidian specimens or the Indo-Aryan specimens. When the Dravidian and the Indo-Aryan suffixes indicating the same tense or mood and having identical signification happen to have similar forms also, it may be sometimes doubtful whether Sanskrit borrowed from Dravidian or Dravidian borrowed from Sanskrit. If in such a contingency it can be established that Sanskrit has inherited the forms and has not evolved them on Indian soil, this will preclude the supposition that it has borrowed the forms from Dravidian. This point will be kept prominently in view and it will be noted in all such doubtful cases if the form existed in the Avestic language also.

CHAPTER IV.

Aryan literature and inscriptions.

75. The age of the Vedas.

When the Vedic Aryans first entered India they were no doubt divided into a number of clans speaking different but closely allied dialects. The Ṛg. Veda is the collection of the sacred hymns of these clans ; but as the hymns show few easily recognizable traces of dialectal differences it is supposed by some scholars that they have undergone a process of editing at the hands of those who complied them into their present arrangement, and that to this extent the language of Vedas must have deviated from the then spoken dialects. However this may be, the Vedas are the nearest approach that we have to the popular Aryan speech of their time.

There are irreconcilable differences of opinion among scholars in regard to the age of Vedas and in regard to the time of composition of many works in Sanskrit and Prākṛt. Whatever date one may choose as the date of any particular work, it is sure to be opposed to the views of some eminent scholar or another. In order to settle the relative priority of Aryan and Dravidian forms, it is very necessary that some rough estimate should be formed of the time when certain Aryan dialects which might have influenced Dravidian languages were actually in use as the spoken languages of the Aryan immigrants. The following summary of the divergent views held by scholars on this question, though far from exhaustive, will be useful in the fotmation of such an estimate in regard to the age of the Vedas and of some other literatures that have come down to us from antiquity. Classical, Sanskrit with its rigid grammatical rules is excluded from consideration here as it does not appear to have been the speech of the common people at any time.

LINGUISTIC ESTIMATES.

The Vedic period is divided by orientalists into several literary strata :—

(*a*) the age of the Chandas,

(*b*) the age of the Mantras when the hymns and prayers of the Saṁhitās were composed,

(*c*) the age of the Brāhmaṇas when the sacrificial ceremonial was elaborated; this age includes in its later phases the age of the Āraṇyakas and of the Upaniṣads ; and

(*d*) the period of the Sūtras.

The lower limit of even the latest phase of the Brāhmaṇa period cannot be fixed later than 500 B. C., for even the latest Upaniṣad doctrines are presupposed by Buddhism. Starting from this lower limit and allowing appropriate durations for the various minor layers of the Vedic literature estimates have been made of the time of composition of the earliest Vedic hymns. In this way Professor Max Muller arrived at 1200 B.C. as the date of composition of the Ṛg. Veda. Professor Weber's etsimate was 1500 B.C., while that of Dr. M. Haug was 2400—2000 B.C. In his History of Sanskrit Literature (1905) Prof. A. A. Macdonnell put the beginning of the Vedic age at 1500 B. C. and deprecated the tendency of some scholars to regard 2000 B.C. as its starting point, as he considered that such a huge period as 1500 years was not required " for a development of language and thought hardly greater than the difference between the Homeric, and the Attic age of Greece." More recently Professors A.A. Macdonnell and A. B. Keith have expressed the opinion that there is no cogent reason for fixing the date of the Ṛg Veda earlier than 1200 B. C. (Vedic Index. 1912—Introduction).

75-A. Boghas koi and tell-el-ommerṇa clay tablets.

In 1907 some excavations at Boghas Koi in Asia Minor brought to light a treaty of the 14th Century B. C. between the King of the Hittates and the king of Mitani in which the deities of both these nations are invoked and Hugo Winkler found among the Mitani gods the names of Mitra, Varuṇa Indra and Nāsatya. It appears frcm an article contributed by Dr. A. B. Keith to the Bhandarkar commemoration volume (1917 pp. 98-9) that H. Jacobi and Moulton consider the deities named above to be Indian deities brought to Northern Mesopotamia by an East Iranian tribe, but that Oldenberg takes the gods to be proto-Iranian while E. Meyer regards them as Aryan, *i.e.*, as pertaining to the period when the Indo-Iranians were living as one race. The view of Jacobi and Moulton of course implies that the Vedic pantheon was fully developed in that 14th century B. C. and that the beginnings of the Vedic culture must be placed earlier than this by several centuries. Dr. Keith inclines to the view that the names of the gods belong to some dialect of Western Aryan origin differing from both Iranian and Vedic.

Among subsequent contributions on the subject are the papers by Prof. Sten Konow on the Aryan Gods of the Mitani people (1921) summarised by K. P. Jayaswal in the Modern Review and an article by the late Prof. P. D. Gune in the Journal of the Iranian Association (1921, June). Prof. Sten Konow thinks that the Gods are Indian and Prof. Gune says that the names of the Gods have a decidedly Indian ring.

75-B. Astronomical estimates.

Various attempts have been made to detemine the time of the Vedas from references to astral positions which enable us to locate the equinoctial and the solstitial points of their epochs in particular asterisms. Vedāṅga Jyotiṣa says that the five-year *Yuga* of the Vedic calendar begins on the winter solstice day when the sun and the moon ascend the sky together with the Śiraviṣṭhās. It is admitted on all hands that this position of the solstice would have occurred about 1200 or 1100 B.C.

The Kauṣītaki Brāhmaṇa refers to the winter solstice as taking place on Māgha Amāvāsyā, and according to a calculation made by Dr. G. Thibaut in 1894 this position of the solstice would have occurred at about 1200 B.C.—the same as the time of composition of the Vedāṅga Jyotiṣa (I.A., Vol. XXIV ,pp. 85 to 100); but the calculation appears to be open to question as Dr. Thibaut following some commentary of Vināyaka takes the Amāvāsyā of Māgha to mean the new moon preceding the full moon of Māgha. But accepting the age of the Kauṣītaki Brāhmaṇa to be 1200 B.C., the age of the Vedic hymns must be put several centuries earlier. Dr. Thibaut himself put it at 1800 B.C. (Hindustan Review, January, 1904).

The late S. B. Dixit first drew attention to a passage in the Śatapatha Brāhmaṇa which describes the Kṛttikās as never swerving from the east. This position of the asterism at one of the equinoctial points appears to be in conformity with the scheme of the Taittirīya Brāhmaṇa which designates the *nakṣatras* as *devanakṣatras* and *yamanakṣatras* according as they lie north or south of the equator, the former headed by the Kṛttikās revolving south (in the northern hemisphere) *dakṣiṇena pariyanti* and the latter headed by *anūrādhās* revolving north (in the southern hemisphere) *uttareṇa pariyanti*. This position of the Kṛttikās will have occurred in the 3rd millenium B.C.; if this period is granted for the Brāhmaṇas the age of the Vedas will approximate to 3000 B.C.

Some European and American orientalists have persistently refused to accept such early dates for the Brāhmaṇas and the Vedas. Some of the arguments which, though repeatedly refuted, are adduced even now against those dates, are that the Brāhmaṇa passages relied upon are not capable of the interpretation put upon them, and that the Kṛttikā series of asterisms may have been borrowed late from Assyria. China, Arabia or some other country.

In 1915 Mr. B. V. Kameswara Aiyar, M. A. of Pudukkoṭṭa prepared for the Oxford Congress 1915 (which did not, however, come off owing to the world war) a paper reviewing in some detail the previous discussions on the subject of the age of the Brāhmaṇas. This paper, apparently considerably enlarged, was afterwards sent to the First Oriental Conference, Poona (1919) and has been published in Vol. XII (1922-221) of the Mythic Society's Journal, Bangalore. The main argument in the paper is that the position of the winter solstice as referred to in the Kauṣītaki was not, as argued, by Thibaut, the same as the position described in the Vedāṅga Jyotiṣa, but corresponded with the equinoctial position of the Kṛttikās implied in the Śatapatha and the Taittirīya Brāhmaṇas and that the age of the Brāhmaṇas must therefore be put back to 2000-2300 B.C.

It is unnecessary to refer to the speculations of Lokamānya B. G. Tilak (Orion) and of H. Jacobi (I.A. Vol. XXIII) in regard to Vedic passages alleged to contain reminiscences of still earlier positions of the equinoxes and the solstices, as it does not necessarily follow from such reminiscences that any portion of the Vedas had been composed in those very early times. These speculations though warmly welcomed by Buhler and Bloomfield met with strong adverse criticism from Whitney and Thibaut (I.A., Vol. XXIII, pp. 154-9, pp. 238-49, Vol. XXIV pp. 85-100, 361-69)

The unwillingness to admit a very great antiquity for the Vedic culture will become intelligible when we recollect the views of scholars engaged in connected departments of knowledge. The philologist draws attention to the practical identity of the Vedic idiom and the idiom of the Gāthās and to the circumstances that the Iranian tradition does not claim any very great antiquity for the Avestic literature. Some archaeologists are of opinion that it is not necessary to place the Indo-Germanic period earlier than 3000 B.C. or even 2000 B.C.

It will thus be clear that the lowest estimate given by any scholar for the age of the Vedic dialects is 1200 B.C. and the hgiest 3000 B.C. In view of this conflict of opinions it will be safe to assume 2000 to 1500 B.C. as the date when the Vedic dialects were actually spoken on Indian soil. This is slightly less than the 4000 years tacitly assumed by Sir G. A. Grierson for the evolution of modern Guzarātī from the Vedic dialects (L.S. ,Vol. IX, part II pp. 386-7).

76. The secondary prakrts.

(*a*) *Pāli.*—The inflectional Vedic dialects became corrupted in course of time into the Prākṛts and the Apabhraṃśas which are sometimes referred to collectively as the Middle Indian dialects ; these latter are called by some scholars Secondary Prākṛts—the Vedic dialects themselves being the Primary Prākṛts. The Secondary Prākṛts were still synthetic in character but the modern Aryan vernaculars evolved out of them that is, the Tertiary Prākṛts, are wholly analytical ; these last are supposed to have taken their present shape about 1000 A.D.

Of the Secondary Prākrts the first to come to notice was a dialect of Magadha in which the Buddha preached his gospel to the people; but none of the early Buddhistic literature composed in this dialect appears to have come down to us. Literary Pāli which became the sacred idiom of Southern Buddhism appears to be an artificail mixed form of speech having Māgadhī as its basis. Some scholars have held that it developed in the Āndhra country while others think that it was perfected in the North West and shows strong affinity to Paiśācī (Bhandarkar Commemoration Volume 1917, pp. 117, *et seq.*)

Of the Buddhistic works in, Pāli the Tripiṭaksa in their present form are supposed to have been composed in the 1st century B. C. while the Dhammapada and the jātakas did not take their present shape till the 5th century A.D. Though composed so late, those works show a literary condition earlier in many respects than that of the Aśoka inscriptions of the 3rd century B. C.; they were obviously composed in an artificial sacred language which had long ceased to be spoken by the people. The prose portions of the Jātakas, written in a free narrative style untrammelled by limitations of poetic composition show perhaps more traits of the original popular speech of the 5th century B.C. than the poetical portions of the above works, and give us an idea to what extent the Vedic dialects had become disintegrated by the time of the Buddha.

(*b*) *Aśoka Inscriptions.*—The earliest contemporaneous specimens that we have of a spoken Secondary Prākṛt are undoubtedly to be found in the inscriptions of Aśoka which belong to the middle of the 3rd century B.C. These inscriptions presented many difficulties of decipherment and interpretation, most of which have now been overcome by the labours chiefly of European Orientalists ; the results of these labours have been made available to Indian students in the pages of the Indian Antiquary and the Epigraphia Indica. The language of the inscriptions shows many local variations, but the ground-work is throughout Māgadhī, the Court language, which apparently was understood in all parts of Aśoka's empire from Afghanistan to Orissa and from the Himālayas to Mysore. The inscriptions are older by several centuries than the oldest Dravidian literature or inscriptions that have come down to us; and one of the suggestions in this book is that in cases where the grammatical terminations in the Aśokic forms are inherited from the Indo-Germanic or the Indo-Iranian period, these terminations may be regarded as the models or the originals of the identical Dravidian terminations. As there is no recognized grammar for Aśoka forms or readily available lists of them, the most noteworthy of them are noted down here for convenience of reference.

(*a*) In the Vedic and the Avestic dialects the use of the interposed *p* in the formation of casual bases is confined to *ā* stems ; but in the Aśoka inscriptions and the cave inscriptions of a later date the use of the interposed *p* occurs in other stems alsom as the following examples taken from the Rock Edicts I and II and the Hāthigumphā inscription will show (Corpus: Inscript, Vol. I, pp. 65, 67, etc.)

likhapitā, *pīḍāpayati*, *Kīḍāpayati*, *Kālāpitā*, *lopāpitā Khānāpitā*, *hārāpitāni*, *āharāpayaṭi*, from roots *likh* 'write, inscribe'; *pīd* 'affiict' ; *krīd* 'play' ; *kṛ* 'do' ; *rup* 'raise' ; *khan* 'dig'; *hṛ*, *āhṛ* 'bring, take.'

(*b*) There are about ten instances in the inscriptions of the use of what may be called indeclinable present participles which do not agree with the nouns they depend upon in number or gender. One instance is given here from Rock Edict No. XI. Shāhbaygarhī version :—

Ide| katavo| so| tatha| karatam| iha| loka| ca| āradheti.

Sanskrit. Idam| kartavyam| saḥ| tathā| kurvan| iha| loke| ca| ārādhayate.

(Corpus : Inscrip., Vol. I, p. 82).

The phrase *hevam ca kalantam* in the sense of 'by acting in this manner' occurs twice in the second separate Rock Edicts of Dhauli and Jaugada: the phrase *khane santam* in the sense of 'when opportunity arises' occurs in the latter (I.A., Vol. XIX, p. 102).

(*c*) In the Vedic the conjunctive participles are formed by means of the suffixes *tvā*, *tvī*, *yā* and *tyā*, the corrupt forms of these suffixes occurring in the inscriptions are *tu*, *ti*, *ta*, *cya*, *ye*, *i*.

Rock Edict. I., *ālabhitu*, *ālabhiti*, *ārabhit* 'having seized' from root *ālabh* (E.I. II, p. 448-9).

Rock Edict No. IV. *dasayitu*, *dasayita*, *draśayitu*, *darśeti* 'having shown' from the causal form of root *dṛś* 'see'

tistitu, *tistiti*, *ciṭhitu*, 'standing, having stood' from *sthā* 'stand' (I. A., Vol. XXI, pp. 13, 105; E.I. II, pp. 451-452).

Rock Edict No. X. *paritijutu*, *palitiditu*, *paricajitu paricaji* 'having abandoned' from *paritvaj* (I. A. XXI, p. 13; E. I. II, pp. 459 and 460).

Rock Edict No. XIII. *vijinitu*, *vijita* 'having conquered' from root *viji*; *śrutu*, *sutu* 'having heard' from *śru* 'hear' (I.A., Vol. XXI, p. 13; E.I. II, pp. 462-4).

Rock Edict No. XIV. *ālōcayitu*, *ālōcayitā*, *ālōceti* 'having considered' from root *āloc*;

Samchāya, *samkheye*, *samkhaye*, *sachāya* 'having abridged' from the causal form of '*samkṣi*.' (I.A., Vol. X, p. 272 XXI, pp. 8 and 13. E. I., II., pp. 465-6).

Separate Rock Edicts at Dhauli and Jaugaḍa.

jānitu 'having learnt or known' from *jñā* 'know'

kaṭu 'having done,' from *kṛ* 'do';

vēditu 'having learnt', from *vid* 'know';

anusāsitu 'having ordered or instructed' from *anuśās* instruct' (I.A., Vol. XIX, pp. 85, 87 ; XXI, p. 105).

Delhi Pillar Edict No. IV. *nisiyitu* 'having placed or entrusted' from the causal form of *niṣad* 'sit.'

Delhi Pillar Edict Nos. VII and VIII. *sutu* 'having heard' (I.A., Vol. XIII pp. 308-9 ; XVIII pp. 4 and 306. E.I. II, pp. 252 and 269).

Bairat second Rock. *adhigicya* 'concerning' from *adhikṛ* 'concern, relate to' (I.A., Vol. XX, p. 166).

Paḍeria and Nigilva inscriptions. *āgāca* 'having come' from *āgā* or *āgam* 'arrive' (E. I. V., pp. 4 and 6).

(*d*) In the Girnar inscriptions the conjunct consonants *tv* and *tm* are written *tp*, thus indicating a dialectal variety of pronouncing them; (I.A. Vol. IX, p. 285). *catpāro, ārabhitpā, hitatpāya, tadātpane, ātpapāsaṁḍa=catvaro, ārabhitvā, hitatvāya, tadātmane, ātmapāṣaṇḍa.*

(*e*) Attention may also be drawn to the equivalence of the vocables *am*= *ā* which Senart has established after an examination of a very large number of examples (I.A. Vol. IX, p. 283).

Dosaṁ, hidaṁ, naṁ, savataṃ, paṇaṁ—dosā, hidā, nā, savatā, panā.

(*c*) *The Prākṛts.*—It appears from the Aśoka inscriptions that the then Aryan vernaculars of Northern India contained at least two main dialects, an Eastern and a Western Prākṛt. The principal form of the Western Prākṛt was Śaurasenī, the language of the middle gangetic Dōāb and its neighbourhood, while that of the Eastern Prākṛt was Māgadhī or the language of Magadha, the present South Behar. Between the two was Ardhamāgadhī or half Māgadhī which is supposed to have been the language in which Mahāvīra, the Jain apostle, preached to the people; this is the language of the scriptures of the Śvetāmbara Jains. The dialect of the Berars or the country adjoining was Māhārāṣṭrī which later became the language of Prākṛt poetry. In the North-west there must have been a fourth dialect which later was known as Paiśācī. All that we know about these languages is founded on the literature in which they have survived and on the grammars written to illustrate that literature; but this literature cannot in many cases be considered as illustrating the actual vernaculars. (Grierson—L.S.)

(*d*) *Vararuci's Prākṛta Prakāśa*, traditionally referred to the 1st century B.C., deals with the grammars of Māhārāṣṭrī Māgadhī, Śaurasenī and Paiśācī. This grammar is of great importance to the philologist as showing the corruptions which the original Sanskrit forms had undergone by the beginning of the Christian era. Hāla's Saptaśatī, the earliest work that we have in the Māhārāṣṭrī Prākṛt is not probably earlier than the 3rd century A.D., while Rāvaṇavaho and Gauḍavaho must be a few centuries later. Māhārāṣṭrī is the language used by high class lady characters in plays, while Sanskrit is used by kings and other persons of high rank. Śaurasenī is usually found, it is said, in the prose passages of dramas, while Māgadhī, Paiśācī and other dialects are used by inferior characters.

(*e*) *Caṇḍa's Prākṛta Lakṣaṇam.*—This is also called the grammar of the Ārṣa Prākṛt, which many identify as Ardhamāgadhī, the language in which Mahāvīra conveyed his teachings. In the second century after Mahāvīra's death, there was a very severe famine in Magadha in consequence of which a portion of the Jain community is stated to have emigrated to the Karnāta country. During the absence of the emigrants, a council was held at Pātaliputra which collected the Jain canon consisting of the eleven Aṅgas and the fourteen Puvvas (—Sans. Pūrvas). There was subsequently a schism between the home-returned emigrants and the northern Jains, which was the foundation of the great division between the Digambaras (naked) and the Śvetāmbaras (white robed). The former refused to acknowledge the canon established by the council at Pāṭaliputra ; the Śvetāmbara canon as we now have them are in Ardhamāgadhī and were redacted at a second council held at Valabhī in Gujarat under the presidency of Devardhigaṇi in the year of 454 or 467 of the Christian era. (Hoernle's Uvāsagadasāo Introduction.)

The language of these canonical works shows a much later literary condition than the Buddhist literary works in Pāli, thus indicating that the language used by the redactors was of a later date than the standard Ardhamāgadhī of the pre-Christian centuries.

The term Ārṣam is explained by Hemacandra as meaning 'belonging to the Ṛṣis' and he adds that "in the Ārṣam Prākṛt every rule is deviated from and has its exceptions",[1] which is the characteristic of a spoken as opposed to a literary dialect. However this may be, the language of the Śvetāmbara canon is the only Prākṛt known to us besides that of the Aśoka inscriptions which uses the conjunctive participle in *-tu* ; these canonical works are also of interest to us as using the conjuntive participle suffixes *yānam* and *yāna* which have also found their way into the Dravidian languages.

(*f*) *Siddha Hemacandram.* Hemacandra (1088-1172 A. D.) a native of north Gujarat wrote this grammar called after himself and after Śrī Siddharāja his patron. The first seven Adhyāyas relate to Sanskrit while the eighth and the last Adhyāya treats of the following Prākṛts which must all have ceased to be spoken dialects in Hemacandra's time except perhaps the last :—Māhārāstrī, Sauraseni, Māgadhī, Paiśācī, Cūlikapaiśācī and Apabhraṁśa. Sir G.A. Grierson

1. Hemacandra I-3. commentary. "Ṛṣīṇām idam ārṣam" "ārṣe hi sarve vidhayo vikalpyante."

says that the Apabharaṁśa dealt with by the grammarian was the Nāgara form of the Śaurasena Apabhraṁśa (L.S. IX, part II, p. 326). This grammar clears up several points which are left doubtful or but imperfectly dealt with in Vararuci.

77. THE MODERN ARYAN VERNACULARS OF INDIA.

The Linguistic Survey of India undertaken in connexion with the census of 1901 and edited by Sir G.A. Grierson deals exhaustively with each of these vernaculars. Several comparative grammars have also been written of these languages. Two of these which will be frequently referred to in the course of the present book are John Beames's Comparative Grammar of the Modern Aryan of India, and A.F.R. Hoernle's Comparative Grammar of the Gauḍian Languages.

Beames's grammar recognises and deals with seven main vernaculars :—(1) Hindī (2) Pañjābī (3) Sindhī (4) Gujarātī (5) Marāthī (6) Oriyā (7) Bengālī.

Hoernle's grammar breaks up Hindī into West Hindī and East Hindī each of these comprising several dialects and adds a ninth Maipāti which with its dialects is called the North Gauḍ. The Marāthī language constitutes the South Gauḍ, Bengālī, Oriyā and East Hindī constitute the East Gauḍ ; while West Hindī, Pañjābī, Sindhī and Gujārātī comprise the West Gauḍ.

The Linguistic Survey divides the Old Secondary Prākṛts into two groups Inner and Outer, the Outer group comprising Māhārāṣṭrī, Ardhamāgadhī, and Māgadhī and the single Śauraseni forming the Inner group. The classification of the vernaculars derived from the Secondary Prākṛts is as follows :—

Eastern group : Bengālī, Assamese ; BihārīOriyā.
Mediate group ; Eastern Hindī.
Southern group : Marāṭhī.
North-Western group : Sindhī, Lahndā, Dradic or Paiśācī.
Central group : Western Hindī, Pañjābī, Rājatshānī, Gujarātī ; Bhīlī, Pahārī.

CHAPTER V.

THE OLDEST SPECIMENS OF DRAVIDIAN SPEECH.

78. TELUGU AND KANARESE SPECIMENS.

It is not proposed in this chapter to give any account of the literatures of the cultivated Dravidian languages or of the inscriptions in them, but merely to ascertain the oldest specimens of these languages that have come down to us either in the form of literature or of inscriptions and to determine the age of these specimens. This is necessary not only for the purpose of deciding the relative priority of large number of Dravidian and Aryan suffixes which are identical in form and in value, but also for the purpose of comparing the eldest Dravidian grammatical forms with the modern ones and of ascertaining what changes have taken place in them and how these changes have been brought about. In the case of Telugu and Kanarese there is little doubt or controversy as to the dates to be assigned to the oldest specimens and these languages will be dealt with first in the order stated.

Telugu. The extant Telugu literature begins in the 11th century A. D. and the earliest Telugu work is the renowned Nannayya Bhaṭṭarāka's translation of the Mahābhārata. A superior work of this kind could not have come into existence all at once and argues an antecedent literary cultivation of the language for several centuries.

Telugu inscriptions being earlier, the earliest of them being the Mālēpāḍu stone inscription of Cōḻamahārājā Ṣaktikomara of Siddhivēyu Rēnāṇḍu which is referred to the 8th century A. D. (E. I. XI, p. 337 *et seq*), and the Bezwada stone inscriptions of the two Yuddhamalla's, grandfather and grandson, which are referred to the latter part of the 9th and the early part of the 10th century. These are the only inscriptions discovered till now of a date anterior to the time of Rājarāja, the patron of Nannayya.

In addition to the conjunct consonant *-nṟ-* referred to in S. 50 supra as possibly an intermediate stage between the Sanskrit *-nt-* and the Telugu *-ṇḍ-*, the Mālēpāḍu inscription contains the following grammatical forms :—*cēśina*, *iccina*, *vaccuvānṟu*, *ēlucunṟi*. It will be pointed out hereafter that since the pro-Dravidian period, Telugu has undergone important grammatical changes ; some of these are the lengthening of the old verbal bases ending in vowels by a *cu* or a *su* (*yu*) suffix, the formation of a new past tense in *ina* and also probably a new present participle in *cun* or *tun*. It will be seen from the above forms occurring in the Mālēpāḍu inscription that these important changes had already taken place by the time of Śaktikomara, and it is to be presumed that other changes since the pro-Dravidian period, such as, the past tense in *ti* and the future forms in *ē* and *eḍa*, had also taken place by that time, Telugu had practically attained its present form by the 8th century and has undergone no important changes since. But several alternative forms which grammarians have preserved either as dialectic varieties or as archaic tenses given us a peep into much earlier stages of the languages.

The section relating to Telugu suffixes in Chapter VI is based on Campbell's Grammar of the Telugu Language and Chinnayasūri's Bālavyākaraṇamu.

Kanarese. According to the " Lives of Kannaḍa Poets " the earliest of the extant literary works in Kanarese are

(1) Kavirājamārga, a treatise on rhetoric ascribed to the Rāṣṭrakūṭa king Amōghavarṣa I (814-877) but surmised by some to have been the work of Śrī Vijaya the chief poet of his court, and

(2) Ādipurāṇa and Bhārata written by Ādipampa who belonged to the 10th century.

Kavirājamārga mentions the names of eleven noteworthy poets and the quotations made in the treatise from the works of previous poets place it beyond a doubt that the literary cultivation of Kanarese must have begun several centuries before the time of Amoghavarṣa. There is also a tradition that in the 7th century A. D. one Śrīvardhadeva, a Jaina priest, wrote a very extensive Kanarese commentary (not now extant) on Cūdāmaṇi consisting of 84,000 verses besides an abridgement thereof of 12,000 verses.

Kanarese inscriptions begin in the 6th century, the earliest of them being the short one at Bādāmi of the Western Cālukya king Maṅgaḷīsa recording a grant to the garland makers of a temple (I. A. Vol. X, page 60). Other early Cālukya records appear to be the Balagamve stone inscription of the time of Vinayāditya I (I.A. Vol. XVIII), about eight inscriptions of the time of Vijayāditya and of his son Vikramāditya II at Mahākūṭa, Paṭṭadakal and Aihole(I. A. Vol. X, Nos. 94, 99, 100, 101, 102, 105 ; I. A. Vol. VIII, Nos. 57 and 58) and the Āḍūr inscription of the time of Kīrti varman II (I. A. XI): there is also one inscription of Vikramāditya II in the Kailāsanātha temple at Conjeevaram at the time of his entry into that city after defeating Nandivarman Pallavamalla. Of the Rāṣṭrakūṭa grants the following two may be mentioned. The Paṭṭadakal inscription of the time of Nirupama I and the charter of Govinda III (I. A. Vol. XI). These and some others not mentioned here are earlier than the time of Amoghavarṣa.

The section relating to Kanarese suffixes in Chapter VI is based entirely on Dr. Kittel's Grammar of the Kannaḍa Language. Dr. Kittel thinks that there are three distinct stages in the history this language—Ancient, Medieval and Modern, and this division is followed in the discussion on Kanarese suffixes in the following pages (ancient 600 A. D. to 1250 A. D.; medieval 1250 A. D. to—1600 A. D.; modern 1600 A. D. to the present time (K. K. G. S. 109).

79. (*a*) TAMIL INSCRIPTIONS.

Tamil inscriptions in the Pallava country begin earlier than those in the Pāṇḍya or Coḷā kingdoms, and the earliest to which we are in a position to assign a date is the cave inscription of a vassal of the Pallava King Mahendravarman I at Vallam near Chingleput which is referred to the 1st half of the 7th century A. D. (S. I. I. I., Vol. II, part III, p. 340). There appears to be an earlier inscription, that at Tirunādar Kuṉṟu[1] in South Arcot, recording the Sallēkhana (religious suicide by fasting) of a Jaina mendicant, the date of which can be determined only on palaeographical grounds. The late Mr. T.A. Gopinatha Rao, Superintendent of Archaeology, Travancore, was of opinion that it belonged to the 5th or the 6th century. Both inscriptions are in what may be called modern Tamil. Other old Pallava inscriptions in Tamil are the Tamil portion of the Kūṟam plates of Parameśvaravarman which belongs to the 7th century; the Triplicane temple inscription of Dantivarman (E. I. Vol. VIII) and the Tamil portion of the Kaśākuḍi plates issued by Nandivarman Pallavamalla (S. I. I. Vol. II, part. III), both of which belong to the 8th century. The Tamil portions of the Vēlūrpāḷaiyam plates and of the Udayendiram plates appear to belong to the 9th century; to this century

1. Aimbattēḻ-aṉaśaṉam nūṟṟa Chandiranandi (trans.) Fifty-seven fasting that observed Chandirnandi āśirikar niśīdika. (trans.) religious teacher memorial (Sendamiḻ Vol. V, pp. 410-11). The memorial (stone) of the religious teacher Chandiranandi who (departed this life after) observing fifty-seven fasts.

also belong the two Kīḻ-Muṭṭugūr inscriptions of the time of Narasimhavarman and the two Āmbūr inscriptions of the time of Nṛpatuṅgavarman (E. I. IV). Several other inscriptions of the same period may be mentioned but they are all composed in modern Tamil, the characteristics of which can be ascertained from grammars.

It must be mentioned here in passing that we have numerous Prākṛit and Sanskrit records of Pallava kings which are centuries older than any of the Tamil inscriptions mentioned above and which enable us to construct a continuous genealogy of the kings of Kāñcī almost from the third century A.D. The earliest of these are the four Prākṛt copper plate grants known as those of Mayidavōlu (E. I. Vol. VI, page 84) Hīrahaḍagalli (E. I. Vol. I, p. 1) Dālura (E. I. Vol. VIII, p. 143) and Kondamudi (E. I Vol. VI, p. 315); the remaining one in Sanskrit.

Cōḷa Tamil inscriptions begin only in the 10th century and all of them are in modern Tamil. Some of the Pāṇḍya inscriptions belong to the 8th century. Jaṭilavarman Parāntaka was a famous Pāṇḍya king who ruled in the latter half of the 8th century and he is the donor in what are called the Smaller Śiṉṉamaṉur plates, the Madras Museum plates and the Vēḷvikkuḍi plates; all these three contain a Sanskrit portion and a Tamil portion; to this reign also belong two short rock inscriptions, one in Āṉamalai (E. I. Vol. VIII) and the other in Tirupparankuṉṟam (I. A.), and the Aramboli memorial stone now in the Travancore Museum (T. A. S. Vol. I, p. 153).

It is a remarkable circumstance that between the Brāhmī inscriptions of the pre-Christian centuries and the earliest Tamil inscriptions mentioned above, that is, for a period of one thousand years—there has been found no lithic or copper-plate record in the Pāṇḍya country in Sanskrit, Prākṛt or any other language.

(*b*) EARLY MALABAR INSCRIPTIONS.

Early Malabar inscriptions are in what may be called good Modern Tamil and begin in the 9th century ; and the earliest of them belong to the reigns of two kings-Ko-k-karunandaḍakkaṉ who ascended the throne of Malairājyam in 855 A. D. and his successor Vikarmāditya Varaguṇa who appears to have become king sometime in 866 A. D. There are seven inscriptions belonging to these two reigns of which five are in Tamil and the remaining two partly in Sanskrit and partly in Tamil (T. A. S. Part I., pp. 1 to 18; 187 to 200). A third king Rājaśekhara is also supposed to have reigned in the former part of the 9th century ; the Talamana *illom* copper-plate in Tamil belongs to this reign (T. A. S. Vol. II, part I, pp. 8 to 14).

Malayāḷam literature is admittedly quite recent. The Section relating to Malayāḷam suffixes in this book is based on Dr. Gundert's Grammar of the Malayāḷam Language and Mr. Seshagiriprabhu's Vyākaraṇāmṛtam.

(*c*) EARLY TAMIL LITERATURE.

The Tamil language has a body of literature supposed to be centuries older than the oldest of the above inscriptions and said to contain the productions of the poets composing the Third Caṅkam at Madura. A Caṅkam is a conference, or better, a school of poets representing a period of literary activity. It is stated that there were three such Caṅkams or periods, but only the works of the last stated to have come down to us. These are arranged in eight collections or anthologies :—(1) Kuṟuntokai, (2) Aiṅkuṟuṉūṟu, (3) Patiṟṟuppattu, (4) Naṟṟiṇai, (5) Puṟāṉāṉūṟu, (6) Akanāṉūṟu. (7) Kalittokai and (8) Paripāṭal. The poems comprised in the first six anthologies are short unconnected pieces, composed by various poets and dealing with various situations that may arise in the course of love, in married life, in war and in other affairs of life. The same remarks applies to No. 7 Kalittokai but the poems comprised in this anthology are comparatively longer and give us slight insight into the life of the people. No. 8 Paripāṭal originally consisted of seventy poems but only twenty-two of these are now available ; of these six relate to the god Viṣṇu, eight to Subrahmaṇya and the remaining eight to the river Vaikai. The anthologies appear to have taken their present shape long after the Caṅkam age and perhaps include many later pieces.

There are, besides, Tolkāppiyam the grammar of Old Tamil traditionally supposed to have been composed during the second Caṅkam and Iṟayaṉār Akapporuḷ, a work on erotics ; these two undoubtedly belong to the period to which the anthologies belong. Besides these ten works there is also a collection of ten long poems called Pattuppāṭṭu and two epics, Cilappatikāram and Maṇimēkalai which are stated to have been composed by the poets of the Third Caṅkam, but from linguistic considerations they must be placed between the last Caṅkam and the period of the Tamil inscriptions. These three works give a fair idea of the life of the people and of the culture attained by the early Tamils.

As the Caṅkam works contain the oldest specimens that have come down to us of the Dravidian languages, and as Tolkāppiyam, the grammar of Old Tamil, does not give any information as to the tense suffixes then in use, these works have been examined in detail from the point of view of tense suffixes and the results of the examination are given in the special section devoted to Old Tamil. Whenever reference is made to Old Tamil in this book, the language as contained in these works is meant.

80. THE OXYRHYNCHUS PAPYRUS.

We have to refer here to the language of the papyrus of the second century A. D. discovered at Oxyrhynchus about twenty years ago. The papyrus is discussed by Professor

E. Hultszch in an article in the J. R. A. S. 1904 and his conclusion is that the papyrus contains some specimens of Kanarese ; and many people believe that these are the oldest available specimens of that language. The following extracts from the above article will explain Professor Hultszch's position :

(*a*) " One of the papyri of the second century A.D. which Drs. Grenfell and Hunt lately discovered at Oxyrhynchus in Egypt, contains several passages in a barbarian language which is presumably an Indian dialect. This may be concluded from the facts that that text—a farce—is concerned with a Greek lady, named Charition, who has been stranded on the coast of a country bordering the Indian Ocean, and that the king of that country addresses his retinue by the words' Ἰνδῶν πρόμοι ' chiefs of the Indians'. In other places the same king and his countrymen use their own language. Twice one of the Greeks accompanying the heroine gives the Greek translation of a few Indian words.

1. 59. *βραθις* (or *βρκθεις*) =' let us draw lots for the shares,

1. 66. κυττως = ' give to drink ' ; ζοπιτ = ' quickly '

In line 64, *βραοις* occurs but no meaning is given.

A speech of the King is given which is repeated in the play in a slightly different manner but no meaning is given.

	1	2	3	4	5
lines 83, and 84,	βερη	κουζει	δαμυν	πετρεκίω	πακτει
Repetition.	βερη	. . .	. . .	πετρεκίω	δσμυτ
	κινζεη παξει				

6	7	8	9	10
πανουμ	βρηκτι	κατε	μαdοδυαμ	βρητουουενι

(*b*) Professor E. Hultszch is of opinion that the words are taken from the Kanarese language, and the following is his explanation :

ζοπιτ = *jhaṭiti* 'quickly ; κοττως=*kuḍisu* 'give to drink'
βραθις = *bēr āḍisu* ' let us play separately.'
β ραδις = *bēr āḍisi* (conjunctive participle of the above).

(1) βερη = *bērē* ' sepai ately ' ;
(2) κουζει = κινζη = *Koñca* ' a little ' ;
(3) δαμυν or δαμυτ = *madhuvam* accusative of *madhu* ' honey ' δ and μ being transposed ;
(4) πετρεκιω = *pātrakke*, fourth case of *pātra* ' a vessel ' ;
(5) πακτει or παξει—an incorrect rendering of *hāki* ' having put ' ;
(6) πανουμ = *pānam* ;
(7) βρητι = *bēr etti* ;
(8) κατε = *Kaṭṭi* ;
(9) μαδουαμ = *madhuvam* ;
(10) βρητουουενι=*bēr̲ ettuvenu.*

The meaning of the passage according to the Professor is " Having taken up the cup separately and having covered (it) I shall take wine separately."

(*c*) The following remarks are offered :—

(1) *Zopit* is now used in a Hindi dialect in the sense of ' quickly.'

(2) In the King's speech *pānam, madhu*. *pātram, kiñje* (=Prākṛt *kiñci*), and possibly also *bērē* are all words from Sanskrit.

(3) The apparent non-Sanskritic residuum thus consists of the conjunctive participle βαδις κατε, πακτει, παξει, and the finite verb βρητουουενι

Dr. Kittle's Dictionary does not give *pāku* as the old form of *hāku,* supposing that the old form was *pāku* the participial suffixes are τει and νει ; these might have arisen from the Sanskrit and the Prākṛit suffixes *-tya* and *-cya* which may become *-te* and *-ce* respectively.

Similarly βρητικατε may be the transformation of a single word *pṛthī -kṛtya.*

The passage is so full of words of Sanskritic origin that it belongs to an Aryan vernacular of the north. If Professor Hultszch's surmises are correct, then there was not much in pro-Kanarese which was not obviously derived from Sanskrit.

81. South indian scripts.

It is now generally admitted that the Indian Aryans became acquainted with a North Semitic alphabet about 1000 B.C. and that they elaborated it so as to suit their own highly developed phonetic system. This elaborated script was first publicly employed in the Aśoka inscriptions which were written in two characters, the Northern and the Southern. The Northern, that of the Kapurdigaṛhi near Peshawar is written from right to left, while the Southern employed in all other inscriptions is written from left to right. It is now also admitted that all the Indian alphabets of the present day are derived from the Southern variety of the Aśoka alphabet.

The scripts in use in Southern India are the Telugu-Kanarese, the Tamil-Grantha, and the Tuḷu-Malayāḷam besides the disused Vaṭṭeḻuttu or Round-hand formerly used exclusively in the Pāṉḍya-Cera country. The group Tamil-Grantha includes the modern Tamil script and the script used by Tamil Brāhmans in transcribing Sanskrit works; the affinities between these two groups shows that they must have been derived from a common original. Similarly the Kanarese and Telugu scripts included in the first group are traceable to a common original, as also the Tulu and Malayāḷam scripts included in the third group. It is now admitted on all hands that these three originals must have been derived from the South Aśoka alphabe

In regard to Vaṭṭeḻuttu Dr A. C. Burnell the earliest authority on the point was of opinion that "the South Aśoka and the Vaṭṭeḻuttu alphabets were independent adaptations from some foreign character, the first to a Sanskritic, the last to a Draviḍian language[1]." At page 38 of his South Indian Palaeography he said "This is the original Tamil alphabet which was once used in all that part of the peninsula south of Tanjore and also in South Malabar and Travancore where it still exists though in exceedingly limited use, and in a modern form. It may therefore be termed the Pāṇḍyan character, as its use extended over the whole of that kingdom at its best period; it appears also to have been in use in the small extent of country below the Ghats which belonged to the Cēra kingdom. As it was only gradually supplanted by the modern Tamil character beginning about the 11th century under the Cōḻas, it is certain that the Tolkāppiyam, Naṉṉūl, Kuṟal and all the other early Tamil works were written in it under the most flourishing period of the "Pāṇḍya" (or Madura) kingdom or before the tenth century when it finally fell under the Cōḻas. But though it is certain that the beginning of the Tamil literature may be safely put about the ninth century, there is nothing to show that there was in any way a literature before that time."

Again at page 49 he says "The ultimate origin of the Vaṭṭeḻuttu is again a difficult problem in Indian Palaeography. In the 8th century it existed side by side and together with the Grantha; it is therefore impossible to suppose that the Vaṭṭeḻuttu is derived from the South Aśoka character, even if the conclusive argument of the dissimilarity between the phonetic values of many of the corresponding letters be neglected."

1. Burnell's South Indian Palaeography, p. 40.

He was also of opinion that it was "impossible to put the introduction of writing into the Tamil country at so early a period as the third century B.C." (p. 83).

Every one of Dr. Burnell's speculations has been totally disproved by the recent discovery of a large number of Brāhmī inscriptions of the third or second century B.C., in the Pāṇḍya country.

Later authorities on the question of South Indian Palaeography are Dr. Buhler and Mr. T. A. Gopinatha Rao. Dr. Buhler enters into a detailed discussion of the development of the Tamil and Vaṭṭeḻuttu scripts in Sections 32 A and B of his Indian Palaeography. His conclusion is that the Tamil script is derived from the South Aśokan and that Vaṭṭeḻuttu was a cursive degenerate variety of Tamil. "Palaeographically Vaṭṭeḻuttu is the running hand of Tamil just as much as the modern northern scripts of office-clerks and tradesmen are to their originals, *e.g.*, the Moḍī of the Marāṭhās to Bālbodh, the Ṭākarī of Dogra in the Panjab to Śāradā."

In a paper on the evolution of Vaṭṭeḻuttu published as No. XVI of the Travancore Archaeological series (T.A. S. Vol. I, pp. 282 *et seq.*) Mr. T. A. Gopinath Rao says "To me it appears that Vaṭṭeḻuttu is most likely derived from the Brāhmī variety of the Aśoka alphabet like other alphabets of India, the Nāgarī, the Tamil-Grantha, and the Telugu-Kannaḍa groups. But it had a separate line of evolution. From the close analogy of the early specimens of the Tamil-Grantha characters we are sure that they must have been derived from the same mother alphabet, the Brāhmī of the Aśoka script." He then proceeds to consider each Vaṭṭeḻuttu letter and to show in what cases the independent evolution comes in.

Drs. Burnell and Buhler had only two inscriptions in Vaṭṭeḻulttu before them when they wrote their books ;

further they were unaware of the existence in Madura-Tinnevelly of cave inscriptions of the early Aśokan type with some orthographical affinities to the Ceylon cave characters and the Bhaṭṭiprolu casket script. The existence of these inscriptions was discovered only fifteen or twenty years ago and over forty of them are now known to exist.

Of the earliest Tamil inscriptions mentioned in S. 79-a above all the Pallava inscriptions are in the Tamil script and all the six Pāṇḍya inscriptions of the eighth century are in the Vaṭṭeḻuttu script, while, of the seven Malabar inscriptions of the ninth century, four are in the Tamil script and three in the Vaṭṭeḻuttu script. The Cōḷa inscriptions when they began to appear and the all later Pallava inscriptions were also in the Tamil script, and as the Cōḷas gained ascendency in the south, this script gradually displaced Vaṭṭeḻuttu in the Pāṇḍya country and in Malabar.

Brāhmī inscriptions have till now been found only in Madura-Tinnevelly where all the early Tamil inscriptions are in Vaṭṭeḻuttu exclusively. If any of these had been in the Tamil script there might be reason for supposing that the Pāṇḍya kings used two characters, one of which was a cursory variety of the other. Actual facts merely prove the gradual supersession by the Northern Tamil script of the southern Vaṭṭeḻuttu which, as pointed out by Mr. Gopinatha Rao, was probably an independent evolution from the Brāhmī script known in the south so early as the third century B.C. It is thus unnecessary to assume a separate foreign origin for the Vaṭṭeḻuttu.

82. THE AGE OF THE CAṄKAM WORKS.
Gajabāhu synchronism versus *Names of Solar signs etc.*

We are now in a position to discuss the period that should be assigned to Tolkāppiyam and other Tamil Caṅkam works. There are several conflicting theories on the subject and it is to be regretted that, notwithstanding several decades of critical discussion, there are still to be found, even among English-educated Indians, persons who still cling to theories based on mere legend about the existence of three Tamil Caṅkams each extending over several thousands of years which will take the beginnings of South Indian History and of Tamil culture to the last glacial period. The number belonging to this school is, however, rapidly diminishing.

Outside this school the only concession that is made to the antiquity of Tamil Literary culture is that prior to the time of the Tamil Vaṭṭeḻuttu inscriptions which begin in the Pāṇḍya and the Cēra country in the last quarter of the 8th century A.D. there was a period of great literary activity in Tamil which has in later times come to be traditionally known as the Caṅkam age.

The late Professor Seshagiri Sastri of the Presidency College, Madras, appears to have been the first scholar to furnish materials for a rational discussion of the question of the age of these works. He drew attention to a statement in the last chapter of *Cilappatikāram* that king Kayavāku of Ceylon was present in the court of the Cēra King Ceṅkuṭṭuvaṉ on a certain important occasion and identifying Kayavāku with the earlier Gajabāhu of Ceylon history, he was able to fix the age of Ceṅkuṭṭuvaṉ and of the incidents related in *Cilappatikāram* (not necessarily of the composition of the work in its present shape) as the 2nd century A.D.

This Gajabāhu-synchronism was adopted by the late Kanakasabhai Pillai as the basis of his work "The Tamils Eighteen Hundred years Ago." This author has constructed from the accounts given in the Caṅkam work genealogies of kings who are alleged to have ruled in the Tamil land from 50 to 150 A.D. of whom the most famous is stated to be Cōla king Karikāla. This account has been adopted in the Cambridge History of India.

The Gajabāhu synchronism also forms the sheet anchor of Dr. S. Krishnaswami Ayyangar's theories elaborated in 'The Beginnings of South Indian History' (1918). In a later work entitled 'Early History of Vaiṣṇavism in Southern India' (1920) the learned Doctor throws back the age of the first Āḻvars to the 2nd century A.D. on the ground that there is evidence that Poykaiyāḻvār was the author of *Iṉṉilai* included in the shorter Caṅkam works and therefore belongs to the Caṅkam age.

In regard to the Gajabāhu-synchronism it has been pointed out by adverse critics that the reference to Gajabāhu of Ceylon occurs not in *Cilappatikāram* itself but in two apparently later supplements subsequently added and that they should not be taken as contemporary references.

Various eminent scholars have pointed out from time to time that there is internal evidence in several works supposed to have been composed by prominent poets of Caṅkam age which shows clearly that these compositions belong to a much later age than the second century A.D.; and it is becoming more and more evident every day that the Caṅkam age should be put forward to the 5th or the 6th century A.D. It may be remarked in passing that the former of these is the estimate arrived at by Pandit M. Raghava Ayyangar of the Tamil Lexicon office, Madras and that the latter is the estimate arrived at by Mr. K. V. Subramania Ayyar, B.A. of the Madras Archaeological Department.

1. One of the foremost poets of the Caṅkam age was Cittalaiccāttanār who is believed to have composed the well-known epic *Maṇimekalai*. This work contains a reference to *Kuccara-k-kuṭikai*—'a small temple built in the 'Gurjara style'—and it has been pointed out by Mr. V. A. Smith

that if this is a reference to Gurjaras the work could not be much earlier than the 6th century A.D. as the Gurjaras are not heard of in Indian History before the middle of the 5th century A.D.

2. In another place the month of Vaiśākha is referred to in the work by the Rāśi name *iṭapa*-corrupt for Sanskrit *vṛṣabha*-. Various scholars have pointed out that the division of the year into solar months and the naming of these months by the corresponding Rāśis did not begin in Northern India till after the 5th century and that the adoption of this system in Southern India in the Tamil country must certainly have been later than its adoption in the north.

3. Tolkāppiyam itself (Poruḷ 135) contains the word *ōrai* in the sense of " a *lagna* auspicious or malevolent according to the position of the planets" and it has been pointed out that the Greek word *orā* or *horā* acquired this astrological significance only in the post-Ptolemaic astrology about the 3rd century A.D.

4. *Cilappatikāram* uses the word *Veḷḷivāram* 'Friday.' It has been pointed out that the Sanskrit word *vāram* acquired the technical sense of 'a week day' only about the 5th century A.D.

5. Stanza No. 229 of Puṟanāṉūṟu contains a clear reference to the ecliptic beginning with *Aśvini* while the reference in stanza 11 of *Paripāṭal* to the position of the sun in the beginning of the month of Āvaṇi (July-August) clearly indicates the same ecliptic beginning. These stanzas could not possibly be placed earlier than the 5th century.

The dates mentioned above are the lowest possible limits ; the poems and stanzas may be much later[1].

---

1. For a more detailed statement of this Question see article" Solar Signs in Indian Literature" by Mr. B. V. Kameswara Aiyar, M.A., in the Quarterly Journal of the Mythic-Society, Bangalore, October, 1921.

Professors G. Jouvean-Dubreuil of Pondicherry and P. T. Srinivasa Ayyangar of Trichinopoly appear to place the great Karikāla Cōḷa in the 5th century A.D., that is, four centuries later than the date given by Mr. Kanakasabhai Pillai.

83. THE AGE OF THE CANKAM WORKS (CONTINUED). *Possible want of a developed vernacular of uniform standard in the early post-Christian centuries.*

The following extract from appendix D to 'Studies in Jainism in South India' (1922) by Professor M. S. Ramaswami Aiyangar, M.A., of the Maharaja's College, Vizianagaram, deals with the question of the *Caṅkam* age from another point of view :—

"Writing many years before the discovery of the Caverns and the Brāhmī inscriptions of South India, Burnell thought that the Vaṭṭeḻuttu and the South Aśokan character were totally distinct importations and postulated a Semitic original in both the cases. The late Mr. T. A. Gopinath Rao in criticising the views of both Burnell and Buhler, has not only pointed out several points of similarity between Vaṭṭeluttu on the one hand and the other alphabets of South India but has successfully established the fact that Vaṭṭeḻuttu is derived from the Brāhmī variety of the Aśokan alphabet. We can therefore take it as proved that the most ancient Pāṇḍyan script Vaṭṭeḻuttu was derived from the Brāhmī inscriptions of the Madura, Ramnad, and Tinnevelly districts. Epigraphists are inclined to assign the end of the 3rd or the beginning of the 2nd century B.C. for the date of the Brāhmī inscriptions. This furnishes us with the lower limit for the period of any Tamil literary activity. The upper limit may be said to be furnished by the Vaṭṭeḻuttu inscription of the Pāṇḍyan king Jaṭilavarman Parāntakaṉ (last quarter of the 8th century A.D.), the earliest known record yet discovered written in Vaṭṭeluttu. In between these two limits must be sought the period of literary activity known as the Cankam Age. According to the orthodox school of Tamil scholars the sage Agastya was responsible for the evolution of the Tamil language and one of his twelve disciples, Tolkāppiyar, wrote the famous treatise on grammar, Tolkāppiyam. This grammarian is also believed to have been a member of the first and second Academies each of which existed for hundreds of years. Then was founded the last or the third Academy in which time more than 25,000 lines had been composed. Divested of legend and myth, we can reduce the traditional account to its proper limits thus. Long before Tolkāppiyar there was a period of literary activity, for there can be no grammar without literature. If it is true that Vaṭṭeḻuttu was the earliest Pāṇḍyan script and that, as has been remarked, it was derived from the Brāhmī inscriptions, we must allow at least three centuries for the development of a literature sufficiently wide to need a grammar. This would bring the date of Tolkāppiyar to the end of the 2nd century A.D. Allowing two more centuries for the first two Academies we may safely arrive at the conclusion that in all probability the third Academy was founded in the 5th or 6th century A.D., a period sufficiently near the epoch for which epigraphic records are available, when Vaṭṭeḻuttu was perfected and from which we have a continuous literary history.

It is well known that between the Brāhmī inscription of the south and the Vaṭṭeḻuttu inscription of the 8th century, A.D. referred to above there is absolutely no inscription written in any character or any coin-legend to enable us to fix with some certainty the chronology of the Pāṇḍyan kings. Scholars who, in season and out of season, sing the glories of the Cankam Age, its vast literature and spacious traditions, have not cared to inquire why, for a period of more than a thousand years, there has absolutely been no inscription. A few who thought about the subject argue that, notwithstanding the very early literary activity, the Tamils did not know or cultivate the habit of inscribing on stones and issuing copper-plate grants. This is too large an inference to be swallowed without critical examination. The early Tamils are said to be an intelligent and civilized race with a great deal of assimilating power. Not far off from their land the Pallavas were issuing copper-plate grants and in their own home they had the Brāhmī inscriptions. And they could have easily imitated the example of their contemporaries. The fact that they did not do so is due to want of a proper developed language of a uniform standard and not to their inability to understand the usefulness and value of inscription.

It might be argued that even supposing that the Caṅkam works were reduced to writing in the period not far remote from the time of Jaṭilavarmaṉ Parāntakaṉ, the Caṅkam scholars might still have handed down orally the innumerable verses. The Vedas, the Upaniṣads and the epics, one might say, were thus handed down from generation to generation by oral repetition. It is true that so far as religious poetry is concerned such a method might have been zealously adhered to. But most of the Caṅkam poems treat of love and war and are mostly panegyric in character and there is not much of religion in them. It is therefore hard to believe that the Caṅkam works intact would have been handed down to posterity in the manner of the Vedas. The conclusion of the whole matter is that such intense literary activity as the one that has been ascribed to the legendary Caṅkam is to be sought for in the time approximating the century for which we have the earliest known Vaṭṭeḻuttu records."

The remark in the above extract about the want of a proper developed language of uniform standard in the

Pāṇḍya country in the early post-Christian centuries will come as a shock to many Dravidian scholars who assume too readily that the Tamil language, as we now have it or as it was spoken in the period of the Caṅkam works, was always in use in the Pāṇḍya country.

We have to reckon now with the language of the Brāhmī inscriptions in the Pāṇḍya country. It is not any known Prākṛt nor is it Dravidian. It cannot be said that as in the case of the Aśoka inscriptions these Brāhmī records are royal ordinances written in the court-language ; for they are not intended to attract attention but are found inside caves which are generally difficult of access and appear to have served as abode to ascetics. Mr. H. Krishna Sastri says that the language of the records seems to be a mixture of Prākṛt and Dravidian and that it was probably the language of the people; but much of the supposed Dravidian element turns out on analysis to be Indo-Aryan. The aim of the present work is to show that whatever was the language of Southern India in times long past it has been radically changed by the Aryan speaking immigrants from the North.

None of the modern Aryan vernaculars of the north had assumed their present form before 1000 A.D. The Dravidian languages might have come into existence earlier, but we must accustom ourselves to the view that their beginnings are not far removed from the beginning of the Christian era.

CHAPTER VI.

84. THE TAMIL ALPHABET.

(*a*) *The order and classification of Tamil sounds.*

The Tamil alphabet contains thirty letters consisting of twelve vowels and eighteen consonants. The vowels are in order ***a, ā, i, ī, u, ū, e, ī, ai, o, ō, au;*** this is the same order as that followed in the enumeration of the Sanskrit vowels but with the omission of *ṛ, ṟ and ḷ.* The consonants are *k, ṅ, c, ñ, ṭ, ṇ, t, n, p, m, y, r, l, v, ḻ, ḷ, ṟ, ṉ.* The last four of these are unknown to the Sanskrit alphabet. Of the remaining fourteen, the first ten constitute the gutturals, palatals, cerebrals, dentals and labials arranged in the Sanskrit order of consonants but containing only two under each class, a tenuis and a nasal. The remaining four sounds *y, r, l, v* are what are called *antas-sthās* 'intermediate' in Sanskrit and also follow the Sanskrit order. It is stated in the perface[1] to Tolkāppiyam that this order of letters has never changed, *i.e.*, that it has been in existence from the very beginning.

Besides these thirty sounds there are three others called *kuṟṟiyalikaram* or 'the *short i̊*' *kuṟṟiyalukaram* or 'the *short u̇*' and *āytam* having a symbol consisting of three dots (.˙.). There were three *i's* in the Tamil alphabet *ī, i̊, i* of which the last had only one-half the quantity of the second and one-fourth the quantity of the first; similarly there were three ***u's ū, u, u̇*** of which the third had only one-half the quantity of

1. A short metrical preface supposed to be written by a so-disciple of the author of Tolkāppiyam :—

mayaṅkā marap ṉ eḻuttu muṟai kāṭṭi

"he explained the never changing order of letters".

the second and one-fourth that of the first. The *āytam* corresponds to the *visarga* of Sanskrit. These three letters are called dependent letters and it is stated that their sounds partake of the sounds of the letters to which they are attached.

The eighteen consonants are divided into three classes (1) *vallinam* 'hard class' consisting of the tenues *k, c, ṭ, t, p, ṟ*; (2) *mellinam*, literally 'soft class', consisting of the nasal *ṅ, ñ, ṇ, n, m, ṉ* corresponding to the tenues in the previous class, and (3) *iṭaiyinam* or the intermediate class *y, r, l, v, ḻ, ḷ*. The term *mellinam* (soft class) which would ordinarily connote mediae is obviously a misnomer, for the letters included in the class have only nasal sounds and they can be said to be soft only in the sense that they indicate that the tenues following them should be pronounced like mediae, *i.e.*, that *ṅk, ñe, ṇṭ, nt,* and *mp* should be pronoucd as *ṅg, ñj, ṇḍ, nd* and *mb*. An pointed out already *ṟ* and *ṉ* are alveolar sounds which are placed at the end of the alphabet, though their place of articulation is between the dentals and cerebrals; and *ḻ* and *l* though placed after *y, r, l, v* have places of articulation which lie between those of *y* and *r*.

Of the three dependent letters the *short i* and *short u* were originally apparently intended to indicate glide sounds. The short *i*, however, plays no part in modern Tamil and played but little part in old Tamil; it need not be considered here. The short *u* has now become an overgrown off-glide and is dealt with below.

(*b*) *The Āytam.*

The third sound called *āytam* has also practically disappeared from Tamil but its name furnishes an important clue in the development of the Tamil idioms and should be considered here. The *visarga* in Sanskrit when followed by tenues had sounds corresponding to the class to which these tenues belonged. Thus, when followed by a guttural tenuis the *visarga* had the sound of a spirant something like that of *c* in *loc* and was called *jihvāmūlīya* (produced at the root of the tongue) as in *Rāmaḥkaroti* ' Rama does '. When followed by *c* it was converted into *ś*, when followed by a cerebral tenuis it became *ṣ*, and when followed by a dental it had the sound of *s*. When followed by a labial tenuis it was sounded like the English *f* and was called *upadhmānīya* (produced at the lips) as in *Rāmaḥ paśyati* ' Rama sees '. The Sanskrit language had coined separate symbols for *ś*, *ṣ*, and *s* the sounds which the *visarga* acquired when followed by palatal, cerebral and dental tenues but it had no separate symbols for the sounds described as *jihvāmūlīya* and *upadhmānīya*. The *visarga* itself, slightly modified, was written in these two cases and the grammar contained a general rule that the sound of the *visarga* in such cases was dependent upon the consonant following, *i.e.*, the *upadhmānīya* and the *jihvāmūlīya* were described as *parāśritau* ' dependent on the following (sounds)'; and they with some other letters were described as *āśritasthānabhāginaḥ* ' having the same place of articulation as the letters on which they depended '.

In Tolkāppiyam the *āytam*, the *short ī* and the *short ù* are described as *cārpu eḻuttu* ' dependent letters ' and one of its rules[1] specifically says that they do not occur independently and that their sounds are determined by those of the letters on which they depend. A special rule in regard to *āytam* says that it always precedes a tenuis *valliṉam* and its sound is determined by this consonant. This characteristic resembles that of the *visarga* when it is *jihvāmūlīya* and *upadhmānīya*. Several instances will be found below to show that Tamil, when adopting Sanskrit words containing the conjunct consonant *śr* omits this conjunct. The word *āśritam*, when dealt with in this manner will become *āitam*, i.e., *āyatm*

1. Tolkāppiyam I, Piṟappiyal—19.

which is the name in Tamil of the dependent letter we are now considering. Humanly speaking there is no doubt that the word *āytam* is the same as the Sanskrit word *āśritam* in a Tamil garb.

85. THE TAMIL MALAYALAM SCRIPTS.

Absence of symbols for *e* and *o* in the old scripts.—

All the thirty-three sounds enumerated above had special symbols in writing except the *short i*, the *short u*, *e* and *o*. We gather from Tolkāppiyam that the symbols for *e*, *o* were also then used for *ē*, *ō* respectively but with a dot over them like that placed over consonants not moved by vowels. The *short i* appears to have been left without any mark to distinguish it from the ordinary *i;* whether there was any symbol for the *short u* will be considered later. The sounds *e* and *o* whether appearing initially as in *evaṉ oṭi* or in combination with consonants as in *katu*, *col*, continued to be marked with dots till after the close of the 12th century, for the grammar Naṉṉūl written about that time contains a rule that *e* and *o* should be marked with a dot to distinguish them from *e* and *o*. The celebrated missionary *Beschi* says in his grammar of *Koḍuntamiḻ* that the upper loops which now distinguish *ē* and *ō* in combination with consonants from *e* and *o* in similar combination *kē* (கே), *ke* (கெ); *kō* (கோ), *ko* (கொ) were first introduced by himself. Initial *ē* (ஏ) and *ō* (ஓ) had apparently come to be distinguished from initial *e* (எ) and *o* (ஒ) even before the time of Beschi.

As pointed out by Bishop Caldwell long ago the fact that the original Tamil script made no distinction between the long and the short *e* or between the long and the short *o* but had only one character for the long and short vowels tends to show that the script was in imitation of an alphabet framed originally for the expression of Sanskrit sounds containing only *ē* and *ō*, not for those of the Dravidian languages which had both *e*, *o* and *ē*, *ō*. This point is now placed beyond a doubt by the investigations of Dr. Buhler and Mr. T. A. Gopinatha Row.

(*b*) THE TAMIL AND VATTELUTTU SCRIPTS.

Early inscriptions show that there were two scripts formerly in use in the Tamil country. One of them originally used in the Pallava inscriptions, has gradually spread to the Cōla and the Pāṇḍya territories and has developed into the modern Tamil script and entirely displaced the Vaṭṭeḻuttu which was formerly used exclusively in the Pāṇḍya-Cēra country and in which the oldest Tamil works must have been written. It is admitted on all hands that the modern Tamil script is ultimately traceable to the South Aśokan script, but Dr. Burnell was of opinion that Vaṭṭeḻuttu was an independent adaptation from a foreign character. Dr. Buhler in discusses this question Ss. 32-A and 32-B of his Indian Palaeography and comes to the conclusion that Vaṭṭeḻuttu is a cursive degenerate variety of the Tamil script derived from the South Aśokan. Dr. Buhler and Dr. Burnell had only two Vaṭṭeḻuttu inscriptions to base their conclusions upon ; but the late Mr. Gopinatha Row, Archaeological Superintendent, Travancore, whose work lay in the land of Vaṭṭeḻuttu inscriptions, has re-examined this question in detail (T. A. S., Vol. I.,pp. 283 *et seq*) and comes to the conclusion that Vaṭṭeḻuttu is an independent evolution from the Brāhmī script. This is *prima facie* very probable as numerous inscriptions in the Brāhmī script of the early Aśokan type have recently been discovered in the Pāṇḍya country ; Mr. Gopinatha Row shows in fact how each Vaṭṭeḻuttu letter is evolved from the South Aśokan. Drs. Burnell and Buhler were unaware of the existence in the Pāṇḍya country of these Brāhmī inscriptions belonging to the 3rd and 2nd centuries B. C.

(c) MALAYALAM ALPHABET AND SCRIPT.

Though Malayāḷam is a late off-shoot from Tamil, it has in modern times admitted all the sounds of Sanskrit in its literature. The Malayāḷam and Tuḷu scripts are traceable to a common original which again is admittedly derived from the South Aśokan.

86. INDO-ARYAN WORDS IN TAMIL.

(*a*) *Classification of Tamil words.*—According to Tolkāppiyam and Naṉṉūl Tamil words are divisible into four classes : (i) *iyaṟcol,* (ii) *tiricol,* (iii) *ticai-c-col,* (iv) *vaṭacol. Iyaṟvcol,* literally ' natural words ', includes all words in common use ; *tiricol,* literally ' altered words ', includes all unusual words confined to poetry, literature and the sciences. These are the two main divisions of Tamil proper which, again, may be either ' pure ' *cen-tamiḻ* or ' corrupt ' *kaṭuntamiḻ.* The word *ticai* in the third class *ticai-c-col* is related to the Sanskrit word *deśya* and appears to imitate the name of the third class in the threefold classification of Prākṛt words as (*a*) *tatsama,* (*b*) *tadbhava,* (*c*) *dēśya. Centamiḻ* and *koṭuntamiḻ* are literally ' straight Tamil ' and ' crooked Tamil ', and the adjectives *cem* and *koṭum* are derived as well be shown later, from the Sanskrit words *sama* ' straight ' and *kut* (*ila*) ' *curved* '.

(*b*) *Vaṭacol. Rules for the transcription of Indo-Aryan words in the Tamil script.* Although the Tamil alphabet was wholly inadequate to represent Indo-Aryan words containing mediae, aspirates, sibilants and the vowels *ṛ*, *ṝ* and *ḷ* Tolkāppiyam is very particular that in transcribing such words only Tamil letters should be used and that letters special to the Sanskrit alphabet should be avoided ; the grammar adds that it does not matter if the words thereby lose their original shape and sound provided the new forms are suitable. The result has been that Indo-Aryan words admitted into Tamil literature have been greatly altered, sometimes beyond all recognition ; this has also been their fate in popular speech. Naṉṉūl, a grammar written perhaps more than ten centuries after Tolkāppiyam, contains a rule which says that in transcribing Indo-Aryan words we might use letters which are common to Tamil and Sanskrit or letters special to the Sanskrit alphabet or both classes of letters. But this deviation from the Tolkāppiyam rule is only apparent, for another rule of Naṉṉūl lays down that the special letters of the Sanskrit alphabet should be transliterated in the Tamil script in accordance with a table of equivalents prescribed. These special letters are stated to be ·—the four vowels *ṛ*, *ṝ*, *ḷ*, *ḹ*, the anusvāra or nasal *o*, the visarga, the aspirate tenuis, the media, and the aspirate media of each of five classes of mutes and the consonants *ś*, *ṣ*, *s*, *h*, *kṣ*, *ṣp* and it is laid down that these should be transliterated as follows in the Tamil script ·—

(i) all mediae, aspirate tenues, and aspirate mediae should become tenues of their respective classes ;

(ii) *ṛ* > *i* or *iru ;* as *dṛṣṭi* 'sight', *vṛddhi* 'increase' *tiṭṭi*, *virutti.*

(iii) *j* > *y ;* as *aja* ' a goat ', *paṅkaja* ' a lotus ' > *ayam*, *paṅkayam.*

(iv) *ś* > *c* or *y ;* as *śālā* ' a hall ' *śmaśāna* ' cemetry ' > *cālai*, *mayāṉam.*

(v) *ṣ* > *c* or *ṭ ;* as *ṣaḍguṇa* ' six qualities ', *puṣṭi* ' nourishment ' > *caṭkuṇa*, *puṭṭi.*

(vi) *s* > *c* or *t ;* as *sūtra* ' thread ', *vatsarāja* ' proper name', > *cūttiram*, *vattarāya.*

(vii) *h* > *a* or *k ;* as *hāra* ' a garland ', *gṛah* ' a house ' > *āram*, *kirakam.*

(viii) *kṣ* > *kk ;* as *pakṣa* ' a side ' > *pakkam.*

(ix) final *ā*> *ai*; as *mālā* 'a garland, a wreath'> *mālai*.

(x) final *ī*> *i*; as *purī* 'a town', *kumārī* 'daughter'> *puri*, *kumāri*.

(xi) Other rules given in Naṉṉūl in regard to the changes to be made in Indo-Aryan words are that words beginning with *r*, *l*, *y* should have the on-glides (1) a, *i*, or *u*, (2) *i* or *u* and (3) *i* respectively.

(xii) In regard to conjunct consonants, Naṉṉūal lays down that when *y*, *r*, *l* are the second members of the nexus the conjuncts must be broken up by interposing the vowel *i*; that if *m*, *v* are the second members, the vowel *u* should be interposed; that *a* should be interposed when the second member is *n*; and that if *r* is the first member *u* should be interposed, as :—*vākya* 'a sentence', *vakra* 'crooked', *śukla* 'white', *padma* 'a lotus', *pakva* 'cooked, mature', *ratna* 'a gem', *sarpa* 'a snake';> *vākkiyam*, *vākkiyam*, *cukkilam*, *padumam*, *pakkuvam*, *aratanam*, *caruppam*.

Nothing is stated in regard to the vowels *ṛ*, *ḷ*, or the *anusvāra* and *visarga*. The above are the rules which Tamil writers have adopted for their guidance when transcribing Indo-Aryan words in the Tamil script and words so transliterated are placed by them in the fourth class *vaṭacol* of Tamil words.

(*c*) *Corruptions in popular speech*. Drāviḍa is not the only part of India in which a progressive civilization has necessitated the admission of a large number of Indo-Aryan words into the vernacular vocabularies. The same has happened in the Malayāḷam, Kanarese and Telugu speaking countries but the cultivators of these languages have expanded their alphabets as so to preserve the Indo-Aryan words with as little change as possible. It is only the old cultivators of Tamil, with the grammarians at their head, that were very particular that the borrowed words should be transcribed in the defective Tamil script in accordance with certain rules laid down by them. If their object was that people should in course of time forget the northern origin of these words and come to regard them as independent words of the South they have succeeded most wonderfully in their object as is evidenced by the current Dravidian theory and by the contention of many Dravidian scholars that Sanskrit has borrowed largely from Dravidian, especially from Tamil.

The whole of this paper is devoted to the discovery of a portion at least of the Indo-Aryan words to which the disguised Dravidian words owe their origin. There is not much difficulty in discovering the originals consciously altered in accordance with the rules laid down by Tamil grammarians, though even here one often meets with puzzles ; *e.g.*,

Indo-Aryan.		Dravidian
Jamadagniḥ	'the father of Paraśurāma'	*Iyamaṅki*
Prahlādaḥ	'the son of Hiraṇya'	*Piruṅkalādaṉ*
Bahvṛca	'having many verses', a term applied to the Ṛg-Veda.)	*Paviḻiyam* *Pauṭikam*
Muhūrtaḥ	'a measure of time' (48 minutes)	*Muluttam*

But long before the time of Tolkāppiyam, before perhaps writing began, Indo-Aryan words had, owing to the limited range of sounds of which South-Indian mouths and vocal organs were capable, become altered to an extent undreamt of by the authors of Naṉṉūl and Tolkāppiyam. This may be illustrated by taking the case of the Sanskrit vowel *ṛ* which should change into *i* or *iru* according to the rule of Naṉṉūl, but has actually changed into *a*, *i*, *u*, *e*, *ē*, *ar*, *ir*, *ur* etc., in popular speech as will be seen in the following examples.

ṛ becomes	Sanskrit	Intermediate forms	Tamil
a	*mṛgaḥ* 'a deer, a beast'	*maga* (Pāli form)	*mā* (1) 'a deer' (2) 'a beast' *māṉ* 'a deer'
i	*tṛṇ* 'to eat, to graze'		*tiṉ* 'to eat'; also *tuṇ* (coll.)
u	*vṛṇ* 'to eat, to consume'	*vuṇ*	*uṇ* 'to eat
e	*ṛkṣaḥ* 'a bear'	*ekkhu*	*eṇau* 'a bear'
	pṛ-ṇu 'to be delighted'		*peṇ* 'to be detighted, pleased'
	pṛṇ 'to delight'		
e	*pṛ-ṇā* 'to cherish, to nourish'		*pēṇ* 'to cherish, to support'

ṛ becomes	Sanskrit	Intermediate forms	Tamil
ar	*ṛtam* 'a sacred custom' (Vedic) a pious action'	*artam* (Iranian)	*aṟam* 'virtuous action, charity'
	mṛd 'clay, mud'	*maḍ*<*mard*	*maṇ* 'earth, mud'
ir	*vṛddha* 'grown, large'	*viḍḍh*	*viḻ-u* 'large'
ur	*kṛtta* 'cut off, mutilated'	*kurta*	*kuṟṟam, kuṟai* 'a defect, a fault'
	pṛ 'to protect'		*pura* 'to protect, to rule as a king'

(Note.—Similar transformations of *ṛ* occur also in the Aryan venaculars of the North.)

The words shown in the last column are now regarded as pure Tamil words but they are all obvious Sanskrit *tadbhavas;* such *tadbhavas* are to be found by hundreds in the class of words cherished by Dravidian scholars as *centamiḻ* and in the classes named as *koṭuntamiḻ* and *ticai-c-col.* The rest of this section will be devoted to the discovery of the laws of letter-change which have transformed Indo-Aryan words in this extraordinary manner and of a portion at least of the missing links lost and forgotten, perhaps for over two thousand years.

87. THE TELUGU ALPHABET.

(*a*). *The Telugu sounds* :—The standard Telugu grammar by Cinnayya Sūri enumerates 36 letters as belonging to pure (*acca*) Telugu. There are twelve vowels as in Tamil *a*, *ā*, *i*, *ī*, *u*, *ū*, *e*, *ē*, *ai*, *o*, *ō*, and *au*. After the vowels come a nasal *a* called *anusvāra* or *bindu* and an obscure nasal called *ardhānusvāra* (half-nasal.). The consonants are twenty two in number : *k*, *g*, *c*, *j*, *ṭ*, *ḍ*, *ṇ*, *t*, *d*, *n*, *p*, *b*, *m*, *y*, *r*, *l*, *v*, *s*, *h*, *l*. The first fifteen of these are arranged in the order guttural, palatal, cerebral, dental and labial, each class having a tenuis and a media ; between the palatals and the cerebrals come *c* and *j* having the value of *ts* and *dz* which are the sounds assumed by *c* and *j* when moved by non-palatal vowels. The class-nasals capable of appearing independently, otherwise than in conjunction with the corresponding tenues and mediae, and having separate symbols are *n*, *n*, *m*. The *bindu* and the *ardhānusvāra* may take the place of class-nasals before the corresponding tenues and mediae.

The grammar does not mention the harsh *r* of Telugu, called *śakaṭa rēphamu*, as a separate letter of the alphabet as it considers that the harsh *r* is only a variety of the ordinary *r*; but as the *cakaṭa rēphamu* of many Telugu words corresponds to the alveolor *ṟ* of the corresponding Tamil-Malayālam words there is no doubt that it was originally an alveolar but that its original value has now been forgotten. We saw already that the literary Tamil *cuṟṟu* 'coil, envelope' passed into *cuṭṭu* having the same meaning in Telugu. In the following instances taken from Cinnayya Sūri's grammar, what ought to be *ṟṟ* in Telugu becomes *ṭṭ* similarly :—*kuṟu* small, short'+*usuru* 'life, breath'=*Kuṭṭusuru* (kuṟṟusuru), *ciṟu* 'small'+*eluka* 'rat'—*ciṭṭeluka* (ciṟṟeluka). Where *ṟṟ* does occur, it is pronounced like *rr*, as in *erra* 'red', *kurra-vārḍu* 'a lad, young man'

Recent epigraphical researches seem to show that the Tamil sound *ḻ* was also formerly used in some Telugu words. Throughout the historic period all the letters and sounds of Sanskrit have been freely admitted into the Telugu language and literature.

(*b*) *The original Telugu alphabet possibly had only tenues and no mediae.*

(1) Though the Telugu alphabet possesses characters to represent unaspirate mediae, some Sanskrit words containing aspirate and unaspirate mediae are written with tenues in the *tadbhava* forms. Examples :—

Sanskrit.	Telugu.
garbhaḥ 'pregnancy, embryo'	*kaḍupu*
	karuvu
dṛtiḥ 'a leather bag'	*titti*
dṛś in dṛśyate 'is seen, appears'	*teliyu*
dhiṣṇyam 'a prepared seat'	*tinni*
	tini
rājan 'a king'	*rāzu*
	rācu
mṛgaḥ 'a deer'	*megamu*
	mekamu
nibham 'pretence, pretext, fraud'	*nepamu*
	nevāmu

brāhmaṇaḥ 'a Brahman' Korava *penāmbra*[1] 'a Brahman' Telugu *penimiṭi* 'husband'

1. L.S. of India, Volume IV, pp. 324-395.

NOTE.—In the Tamil country Brahmans refer to their wives as *pomman-āṭṭi*, where *pomman*<*bomman* 'a Brahman' (Hindi)<S. Brāhmaṇa, and *āṭṭi*, is a feminine termination; and Brāhman women refer to their husbands as Brāhmaṇa. *Penimiṭi* 'husband' is apparently the oblique base of a lost word of the form *penamar*; for in the specimen of the Korava dialect referred to in the footnote, a Brāhman woman refers to her husband as '*penāmbra*,' which word is explained to be a corrupt form of Brāhmaṇa. This shows that Brāhman women of the Telugu country also refer to their husbands as Brāhmaṇ. Compare *okaṭi* in which the original uninflected form appears to have been lost.

These examples seem to show that there must have been a period, perhaps the oldest, when as in Tamil, there were only unaspirate tenues in Telugu. Of the Prākṛt languages mentioned by old grammarians the only one which did not possess any medial sounds was the *Cūlika Paiśācikā*[1] of Hemacandra which substituted the first and second sounds of each *varga* for the third and fourth sounds.

This rule obtains in certain Cūlika Paiśacī words given by Pischel in para. 191 of his Prākṛt grammar; here *p* is substituted not only for *b* but also for *v* in some instances. Thus Govinda and Keśava appear also as Gopinta and Keśapa.

Certain varieties of Ārṣa Prākṛt dealt with in Caṇḍa's Prākṛt grammar appear to have followed a rule similar to the one quoted above; for the MSS. marked C and D[2] by

1. Hem. (IV-325). *Cūlika-Paiśācikē tṛtīyaturīyayōr ādyadvitīyau*; "In Cūlika Paiśācikā the first and the second letter of the *varga* are substituted for the third and the fourth respectively."

2. Sūtra III-11 (a). *tṛtīyacaturthayōḥ*, *prathamadvitīyau*; "The first and second letters take the place of the third and fourth letters respectively." (Hoernle's Caṇḍa, p. 48 Appendix C-D.)

Dr. Hoernle and obtained from Western India contain a similar rule.

(ii) On the other hand in another class of *tadbhavas* in Telugu the first and second letters of a *varga* are often replaced by the third and fourth letters, the fourth again being replaced often by *h*. Examples :—

Sanskrit.		Telugu.
arthaḥ	'meaning'	*ardhamu*
aśvatthaḥ	'a kind of tree'	*aśvaddhamu*
vīthī	'a road, street'	*vīdhi*
kuḍyam	'a wall'	*gōḍa*
mukham	'face'	*muhamu*
sukham	'pleasure'	*suhamu*
putrikā	'a damsel'	*boṭṭiya, boṭṭe*
paṅktiḥ	'a row'	*banti*
putraḥ	'a son'	*biḍḍa* (*piḷḷai* in
Śauraseni *puḍḍ*		Tamil).

Note.—The substitution of *dha* for *tha* occurs only in the colloquial speech in some localities.

The above examples remind us of the usual Ārṣa rules[1] 'The third letter takes the place of the first,' 'The second and fourth letters take the places of the first and second.'

In '*kudaramu, gur̲r̲amu*,' we have both tenuis and media.

(iii) These inconsistent and puzzling substitutions obviously relate to words borrowed at different periods in the history of the language, and one is often left in considerable doubt as to which of two or more likely Sanskrit words is the original of any particular *tadbhava* in Telugu.

88. The Kanarese Alphabet.

(*a*) *Kanarese sounds.*—In his Kanarese grammar Dr. Kittel, following the works of previous Indian gram-

1. Caṇḍa III-12 *Prathamasya tṛtīyaḥ.*
Caṇḍa III-11. *Prathamadvitīyayōr dvitīyacaturthau.*

marians, says that there are 47 indigenous letters in true (*acca*) Kannaḍa, *viz.*, twelve vowels as in Tamil and Telugu *a*, *ā*, *i*, *ī*, *u*, *ū*, *e*, *ē*, *ai*, *o*, *ō*, *au*; an *anusvāra* or general nasal and thirty-four consonants:—*k*, *kh*, *g*, *gh*, *ṅ*; *c*, *ch*, *j*, *jh*, *ñ*; *ṭ*, *ṭh*, *ḍ*, *ḍh*, *ṇ*; *t*, *th*, *d*, *dh*, *n*; *p*, *ph*, *b*, *bh*, *m*; *y*, *r*, *ṟ*, *l*, *v*, *s*, *h*, *ḻ*, *ḷ*. The first twenty-five consonants are arranged in the order of guttural, palatal, cerebral, dental, labial, each class consisting of five including a nasal as in Sanskrit.

The letter *ḻ* was in extensive use formerly but both *ṟ* and *ḻ* have fallen into complete disuse in modern times. Dr. Kittel has, however, introduced them in his Kannaḍa-English Dictionary as he thought "that without them, Kannaḍa and its language cannot be understood.' Dr. Kittel also says in the Preface to his Dictionary "True Kannaḍa has no aspirated consonants except in a few imitative sounds although in later years through Brahmanical influence they have crept into writings and certain circles of society; unaspirated consonants have therefore been substituted wherever the aspirated were not sanctioned by grammar." Similarly the dental *s* has been substituted for the palatal spirant ś in all true Kannaḍa words and in *tadbhavas*. Acting on these principles he has divided the Kannaḍa vocabulary into two main divisions—true Kannaḍa and Sanskrit derivatives—exhibiting the former in bolder type than the latter in his Dictionary.

(*b*) *Uncertain orthography*.—Notwithstanding these emendations the Dictionary exhibits uncertainty in regard to the initial mute of a considerable number of words—as to whether the initial is to be a tenuis or a media. The following are a few instances of such uncertainty out of those that have been noted:—

gey, *key* 'to perform, do.'
geḷeya, *keḷeya* 'a companion, friend.'

goṅke, kuṅke 'the throat.'
gaṭṭu, kaṭṭu 'a bank, shore.'
gīru, kīru 'to scrape.'
guḍi, kuḍi (1) 'a flag,' (2) 'a circle.'
gūnu, kūnu 'a hump.'
gūḍe, kūḷe 'a basket.'
dombi, tombe 'a crowd, a mass.'
dumbi, tumbi, dumbe, tumbe, 'a large black bee.'
dāṭu, tāṇṭu 'jump, pass over.'
diḍḍu, tiṭṭu 'an eminence, elevation.'
daṇi, taṇi 'to grow fatigued.'

It is not clear whether all or any of the alternative forms are mere provincialisms, or whether they have been admitted into the language at different periods of its history. It is probable that, as in Telugu, there was a period when there were only tenues, no mediae, in Kanarese. The following Kanarese words may be mentioned as unmistakable instances in which tenues have been substituted for the mediae of Sanskrit words :

1. K. *taddu, daddu*<*S. dadru* 'a cutaneous disease.'
2. K. *teṅkaṇa*<*dakṣiṇa* 'southern'
3. K. *titti, tidi*<S. *dṛti* 'a pair of bellows.'
4. K. *pubbu, purbu, hubbu* < S. *bhrū, bhruva*<' the eye brow.'

Another peculiarity of Kanarese is that a number of words beginning with *ca* have alternative forms beginning with *ce*: a few examples may be mentioned here :

cakke, cekke 'a fragment.'
caṇḍu, ceṇḍu 'a ball to play with.'
cadaru, cedaru, kedaru 'to scatter.'
cambu, cembu 'the red metal.'
caṭṭi, ceṭṭi 'an earthen pot.'
canda, cenda 'beautiful.'

This reminds one of the rule of Tolkāppiyam that no Tamil words should begin with *ca* the result of which was that several Sanskrit *tadbhava* words in Tamil which would otherwise have begun with *ca* were written with the initial *ce*.

(*c*) Telugu and Kanarese scripts are traceable to a common original which is derived from South Aśokan.

89. SPIRANTAL PRONUNCIATION OF SINGLE TENUIS IN TAMIL IN CERTAIN POSITIONS.

(*a*) Bishop Caldwell notices the absence of symbols for mediae in Tamil and thinks that according to the phonetic laws of the language surds and sonants are mutually convertible into one another and that one character serves for both these sounds.

"This rule" he says, "does not apply merely to the written characters of the language, but is the expression of a law of sound which is inherent in the language itself.

"There are distinct traces of the existence of this law in all the Dravidian dialects ; but it is found most systematically and most fully developed in Tamil and Malayāḷam. The law, as apparent in the Tamil-Malayāḷam system of sounds, is as follows : *k*, *t*, *t*, *p*, the first unaspirated consonants of the first, third, fourth and fifth *vargas*, are always pronounced as tenues or surds (*i.e.*, as *k*, *ṭ*, *t*, *p*) at the beginning of words, and whenever they are doubled. The same consonants are always pronounced as medials or sonants (*i.e.*, as *g*, *ḍ*, *d*, *b*) when single in the middle of words. A sonant cannot commence a word, neither is a surd admissible in the middle, except when doubled ; and so imperative is this law, and so strictly is it adhered to, that when words are borrowed from languages in which a different principle prevails, as

Sanskrit or English, the consonants of those words change from sonants to surds, or *vice versa*, according to their position, *e.g.*, *danta*, Sans. 'a tooth', becomes in Tamil *tantam*; Sans. *bhāgya*, 'happiness,' becomes *pākkiyam*.

"A similar rule applies to the pronounciation of *c* or *ś* (the Tamil *c*), the first consonant of the second varga."

Bishop Caldwell states that the sonants of the surds *k*, *c*, *ṭ*, *t*, *p* are *g*, *j*, *ḍ*, *d*, *b* respectively and does indeed recognise that the values of intervocal *k* and single *c* are not those of the English *g* and *j* but of the Irish *gh* and the Sanskrit *ś* which are guttural and palatal spirants. The pronounciation of *k*, *c*, as *g*, *j* in Tamil occurs only after nasals and Bishop Caldwell's law of 'The convertibility of surds and sonants' fails even according to his own showing in the case of these two consonants. It will be shown presently that it also fails in the case of *p*.

(*b*) *Sounds now actually heard in speech.* Single non-initial *k*, *c* and *p* are never pronounced now like *g*, *j*, *b*, in common speech and though single non-initial *ṭ* and *t* generally have the sounds of *ḍ* and *d* there are indications to show that their pronunciation was different formerly. The name *mellinam* given to nasals would seem to indicate that non-initial *k*, *c*, *ṭ*, *t*, *p* were perhaps once sounded as mediae only when combined with nasals and that in other cases they were pronounced spirantally. The actual sounds heard now are as follows:

The letters *k*, *t*, *p* at the beginning of words and these same doubled as *kk*, *tt*, *pp* in the middle of words are pronounced hard like tenues; *k* and *p* are also sounded hard in the conjunct consonants *ṭk*, *ṟk* *ṭp*, *ṟp*. A single *t* in the middle of words whether intervocal or preceded by *y*, *r*, *n* or *l* is generally pronounced like a media. The letter *k* is sounded like *g* after *ṇ*, *ṅ* and *ṉ* and the letter *p* is sounded like *b* after *ṇ*, *m*, and *ṉ*; In other cases however *k* whether intervocal or preceded by *y*, *r*, *l*, *ḷ* or *ḻ* is pronounced like a deep guttural spirant—something like *ch* in *loch ;* and *p* whether intervocal or preceded by *y*, *r*, *l*, *ḷ* or *ḻ* is pronounced somewhat like the English *f*. It has been considered unnecessary, however, to have separate characters for these sounds and they are represented by *k* and *p*. The letter *c* is never sounded like a palatal tenuis except when doubled or preceded by the consonants *ṟ* or *ṭ*; When preceded by the *ñ* it is pronounced ike *j* ; in all other cases whether at the beginning of words or in their middle it is pronounced like the palatal spirant *ś*. The character for *ṭ* is never sounded hard except when doubled as *ṭṭ*; in all other cases it is sounded like *ḍ*.

On a careful consideration of the available facts it would seem that the original tendency was to sound non-initial tenues like mediae, only when in combination with nasals and to pronounce non-initial single *k*, *c*, *ṭ*, *t*, *p* as spirants. The spirants corresponding to guttural, palatal and labial tenues are sounded without difficulty and these sounds still hold the ground, *c* coming to have the spirantal sound even initially. The following are some of the examples. *pakal* ' a day '; *tōkai* ' a tail'; *akil* ' aquilaria agollocha '; *cey-kiṟatu* ' it does '; *ciṟu* ' small'; *kacappu* ' bitterness '; *varupavaṉ* ' he who comes '; *mārpu* ' the chest'; *iyalpu* ' nature ' which are pronounced as *pahal*, *tōhai*, *ahil*, *śeyhiradu*, *śiru*, *kaśappu*, *varufavaṉ*, *mārfu*, *iyalfu*. The form *ahil* is imbedded in the Hebrew *ahilom*, *ahiloth*, occurring in the proverbs in the Old Testament and must be as old as the 5th or the 4th century B. C. Intervocal single *p* has, in consequence of this spirantal pronunciation, been replaced by *v* except in a very few instances ; there are special reasons for its retention in the few forms in which it is retained and here it is sounded like *f* :—as *irupatu* ' twenty '; *aṟupatu* ' sixty ' *eḻupatu* ' seventy ' etc.; the forms *iruvatu*, *aṟuvatu*, *eḻuvatu* are more common. The spirant of *t* appears to be more difficult to pronounce and it has in consequence come to be sounded like the class media *d* although one occasionally hears the spirantal sound as in '*seyθal*', 'doing', *poθal* 'going' *varuθal* 'coming'

The spirant of *ṭ* appears to be the most difficult to sound and this is probably the reason why *ṭ* is pronounced as *ḍ* except when doubled ; but the attempt to pronounce it spirantally has converted it in very many cases into *ḻ* which next to *ṣ*, appears to be the nearest approach to a cerebral spirant. Example :—

(i) S. *kaṭakam* 'a house, abode'	*kaḻakam* 'a house of assembly'.
(ii) S. *peṭakaḥ* 'a box'	*pēḻai*.
(iii) S. *pīḍā* 'pain, annoyance, agony'	*pīḻai*.
(iv) S. *pīḍ* 'to pain, torment'	*pīḻ-i*.
(v) S. *nāḍī*, *nāḍi-kā* 'a measure of time equal to twenty-four minutes'	*nāḻi*, *nāḻi-kai*.
(vi) S. *nāḍi* 'a tube, a tubular vessel'	*nāḻi* 'a measure of capacity originally made of the hollow joint of bamboo'.
Pāli has *nāḻika* in the sense of a measure of capacity	
(vii) S. *aṣṭakam* (1) 'any group of eight'	*āḻakku*.
(2) 'the eighth part'	*āḻākku*—'the 8th part of one measure'
>Pkt. *āṣṭak*, 'compare' S. *aṣṭa* 'eight'> *āth* in Hindi.	

(viii) S. *prati* (instead); 'in compensation for, as equivalent to'	*paṭi*>*paḻi* 'requital, amends, revenge'
(ix) S. *ēḍakaḥ* 'a ram, a wild goat'	*ēḷakam*.
(x) S. *jaṭiḥ* 'clotted hair'	*ceḻi-yaṉ* 'having clotted hair' (c.f. *caṭaiyaṉ*) 'a name frequently occurring in the list of Pāṇḍya kings'
(xi) S. *meṭhıḥ*, 'the post to which cattle are tied when threshing corn'.	*mēḻi* 'the plough'
K. *mēṭi* 'plough-tail'.	
(xii) S. *garuḍaḥ* 'the Brahminy kite'	*kaluḻaṉ*.
(xiii) S. *bhaṭṭārakaḥ* 'a common name for a temple deity'.	*paṭārar*, *paḻārar*, (Malayāḷam)
(xiv) S. *cūḍikaḥ* 'having a lock of hair on the crown of the head'	*cōḻiyar* 'a class of people having a crown-tuft'
(xv) S. *kaparḍikā* 'a small shell or cowry'.	*coḻi* 'a small cowry'.
Hindī. *kauḍī*, Marāṭhī &c.	*kavuḍī*.
(xvi) S. *taḍitvāṉ* 'possessing *taḍit* or lightning, a cloud'	*eḻili* 'a cloud' literally 'possessing *eḻil*'. Tuḷu *teḍil*, *seḍil*, H. *sidil* 'lightning, thunder'

The above are all instances of intervocal *ṭ* or *ḍ* having been transformed into *ḻ*; a large number of examples will be found elsewhere in this book in which the final consonants *ṭ* or *ḍ* undergo the same transformation.

It may be remarked in passing that *ṣ*, *ḷ*, *y* of Indo-Aryan words are often converted into *ḻ* in Tamil and that it is questionable whether there are many Tamil words in which the sound *ḻ* is original.

90. THE OFF-GLIDE OR FINAL ENUNCIATIVE VOWEL IN DRAVIDIAN WORDS.

(*a*) *Practice in different dialects.* In most Dravidian languages there is a tendency to pronounce a short vowel after every final consonant.

Telugu. This rule is absolute in Telugu where no word can end in a consonant except rarely in poetry. For this reason all Telugu verbal bases end in -*u* which is put in solely for purposes of enunciation; for it disappears before the initial vowels of suffixes, and when a suffix begins in a consonant which is capable of combining with the last consonant of the base, the final -*u* disappears, sometimes optionally, so as to allow this combination to take place. Examples :—

Conjunctive participles.	*koṭṭu*+*i*=*koṭṭi* 'having beaten'.
do	*naḍacu*+*i*=*naḍaci* 'having walked'
Imperative.	*cēyu*+*i*+*cu*=*cēyiñcu* 'cause to be done'.
Present participle.	*koṭṭu*+*tun*=*koṭṭutun* 'beating'
do.	*naḍucu*+*tun*= *naḍucutun* / *naḍustun* 'walking'.
do.	*cēyu*+*tun* *cēyutun*, *cēstun* 'doing'.

Kanarese. In Kanarese there is now no verbal theme which ends in a consonant, all roots which in Old Kanarese ended in consonants having had affixed to them an enunciative *u* which disappears before suffixes, beginning with vowels. All nominal bases which in Old Kanarese ended in a consonant now generally appear with a euphonic final *-u* or *-i*.

Tamil. Tamil is not so particular in regard to the final short vowel of consonantal endings and its grammar says that Tamil words can end in the consonants *ñ*, *ṇ*, *n*, *m*, *ṉ*, *y*, *r*, *l*, *v*, *ḻ*, *ḷ*; but a short *-ŭ* is heard after every final *k*, *c*, *ṭ*, *t*, *p*, *ṟ* whether these consonants are pronounced as tenues or like mediae as they usually are after nasals. This *-ŭ* is what the grammarians call *kuṟṟukaram* 'short *ŭ*' which has only one-fourth the quantity of a long vowel, the rule being that the final *-u* is short in every word ending in *kŭ*, *cŭ*, *ṭŭ*, *tŭ*, *pŭ* *ṟŭ*, if the word consists of more than two syllables or has in it a long vowel or a conjunct consonant. This stands to reason, for where, as in the Dravidian languages, the normal accent falls on the first syllable of a word then the final *-ŭ* is necessarily short in all words consisting of more than two syllables or having a long syllable. This short *-ŭ* disappears before suffixes and words beginning with vowels.[1]

Including this short *-ŭ* among vowels we may say that verbal bases in Tamil may end in any vowel except *e* and in any consonant except *k*, *c*, *ṭ*, *t*, *p*, *ṟ*, *n*. It follows from this that all short *ŭ* verbal bases in Tamil are practically consonantal bases, as this short *ŭ* disappears before suffixes beginning with vowels. For a similar reason all Telugu verbal bases with a few exceptions may be regarded as consonantal bases.

---

1. The grammatical rule as to short *ŭ* has in modern times to be extended so as to include such words as *eṇṇu* 'think', *eḷḷu* 'disregard', *avāvu* 'desire.'

Malayāḷam. Bishop Caldwell says :—" In Malayāḷam, a short *a* sometimes replaces the short *ŭ* of Tamil. Dr. Gundert considers this a peculiarity of the Malayāḷam of Cochin and Syrian Christians. Foreigners who are led more by the written sign than by the spoken sound, have often, he says, been led to regard this letter as *a*. The short *ŭ* of Tamil is still further shortened in Northern Malayāḷam, so that in the Northern districts it is not written at all, but a small circle or a dot merely over the letter is used to express this sound. The same usage prevails still more extensively in Tuḷu in which the pronunciation of this *ŭ* is still more like the Hebrew *shvā*." (C. D. G. p. 18).

Mr. Seshagiri Prabhu in his Malayāḷam Grammar (Vyākaraṇāmṛtam S. 46) says that the final short *u* is usually pronounced as short *a*. He adds that the final *-u* of Sanskrit words and of finite verbs in the present and the past tense is a full *u* while the final *-u* of present and past participles is short.

The remark of Dr. Caldwell that the off-glide *ŭ* is represented in some places not by the symbol for *u*, but by a small circle or a dot over the final consonant is worthy of note.

(*b*) *The genesis of the Tamil* kuṟṟiyalukaram *or short ŭ.* It is well known that in most of the Aryan venaculars of Northern India the final short vowel, specially short *a*, of words of two or more syllables is generally quiescent. This will be obvious from well-known names of great persons familiar to everybody such as Kēśava Candra Sēna, Rāma Mōhana Rāya which are pronounced Kēṣab Candar Sēn and Rām Mōhan Rōy.

Words like *kaṭuka(ḥ)* 'pungency', *lōka(ḥ)* 'the world etc., as shown in the statement below will be pronounced in the north as *kaṭuk*, *lōk*, etc., and will become *kaṭuku*, *(u)laku* etc., in Tamil.

Sanskrit.	*Intermediate.*	*Tamil.*
kaṭukam 'a compound of ginger, black and longer pepper'	*kaṭuk*	*kaṭuku* 'mustard'
kaṭukaḥ 'pungency'		
lōkaḥ 'the world'	*lōk*	*ulaku.*
rājan 'a king'	*rāj*	*aracu.*
rājaḥ		
akṣaḥ 'an axle'	*acch*	*accu.*
amātyaḥ.		
Pāḷi Prāk, *amaccō* 'a minister, a king's counsellor'	*amacc*	*amaccu.*
śakaṭam 'a cart'	*cakaṭ*	*cakaṭu.*
kapaṭam 'fraud, trick'	*kapaṭ*	*kavaṭu.*
dūtaḥ 'a messenger'	*dūt*	*tūtu.*
dyūtam 'gambling'	*jūt*	*cūtu.*
vādaḥ 'dispute, controversy'	*vād*	*vātu.*
vikalpaḥ 'option, alternative'	*vikalp*	*vikaṟpu.*
rūpam 'form, figure'	*rūp*	*urupu, uruvu, uru.*
valayaḥ 'a bracelet'	*valay*	*vaḷai.*
kuvalayam 'a blue lotus'	*kuvalay*	*kuvaḷai*
nīram 'water'	*nīr*	*nīr.*
samaraḥ 'battle'	*samar*	*amar.*
tuvaraḥ 'astringency'	*tuvar*	*tuvar.*
kēraḷaḥ 'name of a dynasty'	*kēraḷ*	*cēral.*
analaḥ 'fire'	*anal*	*aṉal* 'the heat of fire.'
bālaḥ (1) 'a tail'	*bāl*	(1) Tam. *vāl.*
vālaḥ (2)'hair'	*vāl*	(2) *Mal. vāl.*
mālaḥ 'Viṣṇu'	*māl*	*māl.*

Sanskrit.	*Intermediate.*	*Tamil.*
sthūṇā 'a post, a pillar'	*thūṇ*	*tūṇ.*
araṇam 'a refuge'	*araṇ*	*araṇ* 'a stronghold'.
araṇa 'not fighting'		*araṇmaṉai* 'a fortified house'.
mīnaḥ 'a fish'	*mīn*	*mīṉ.*
idhmaḥ 'fuel, especially that used for sacred purposes, as on funeral occasions, etc.		*īma-p-puṟaṅkāṭu* 'a burning ground.' *īm*[1] 'the burning ground.'
karma(n) 'action, labour, work'		*kam.*[2]

The tabular statement above brings out in a marked manner the difference already pointed out between Telugu and Tamil. In Telugu all final consonants require a short vowel while in Tamil it is only final mutes that require it :— thus, the Tamil *nīr* 'water', and *tuvar* 'astringency' exist as *nīru* and *togara* in Telugu. All the Tamil words shown in the last column as requiring a final *ŭ* end or should end in mutes in the Indo-Aryan vernacular and the speakers of these languages experience no difficulty in pronouncing these mutes as finals. Thus even an illiterate Marāṭha when he means 'all the world' Sans. *sarvaḥ lōkaḥ* says *sab lōk* and the off-glide, if any, in the two words *sab* and *lōk* is almost imperceptible. But *sab* is impossible according to the rules of Tamil grammar and *lōk* becomes *olaku* in popularTamil, equivalent to *(u)laku* of literary Tamil.

Having regard to the present practice in Indo-Aryan vernaculars, it would seem that in Tamil mute endings had at first only a slightly perceptible off-glide and that since this glide began to be marked in writing it has gradually

1,2. These two words are found in Tolkāppiyam (I. Puḷḷi, i. 33).

increased in quantity to half that of a short *ū*. The remarks quoted above, that the short *ŭ* of Tamil is still further shortened in Nothern Malayāḷam and is not written at all in some parts of the West coast, lend support to this supposition.

It is also possible that this off-glide was not marked at all originally and that there was nothing to distinguish it from a consonantal ending. The Tolkāppiyam rules in regard to this matter are as follows :—

'All final consonants should be marked with dots' (I. Puṇar. 2).

'They say that the short *ŭ* is of the same nature' (*Ibid.* 3).

The second rule may be taken to mean that the off-glide was not to be distinguished from a consonant but commentators have understood the rule differently[1].

We have to remember that the off-glide *ŭ* is not now written in the northern districts of Malabar and in Tuḷu and was not marked in some mute endings quoted by Kumārila Bhaṭṭa.

The very existence of *kuṟṟiyalukaram* in Tamil appears to indicate that a very large number of Indo-Aryan forms with mute endings were adopted in Tamil which the Dravidians found it difficult to pronounce without a perceptible off-glide.

Of course even a normal final *-u* in a long word will become shortened when the accent is shifted to the first syllable. But why should the grammatical rule associate this final *ŭ* with the tenues *k, c, ṭ, t, p, ṟ*, to the exclusion of other finals? This fact shows that the genesis of the *kuṟṟiyalukaram* is not to be sought for in a shifting of the accent but in an off-glide necessary in pronouncing final mutes.

---

1. *Meyyīṟu ellām puḷḷi-y-oṭu nilaiyal* (I. Puṇar. 2). *Kuṟṟiya lukaramu maṟṟeṉa moḻipa* (*Ibid.* 3).

91. CHANGE OF THE FINAL MUTES *t*, *d*, *ṟ*, *ṭ*, *ḍ* INTO *ḷ*, *ṉ*, *ḻ*, *ṇ*, *ḷ* IN TAMIL WORDS.

(*a*) *Alternative to the off-glide.* Sometimes the final mute of Tamil words undergoes a change if it happens to be a dental, a cerebral or alveolar and no enunciative *ŭ* is added. Then *ṭ* and *ḍ* become one of *ḷ*, *ṇ* or *ḷ* which have very nearly the same place of articulation as themselves; while *t*, *d* and *ṟ* will be changed into *ḻ* or *ṉ* which have nearly the same place of articulation as themselves. Thus *māṭu* 'cattle' *pāṭu* 'ruin' 'loss', *iruṭṭu* 'darkness', *poruṭṭu* 'a thing of importance' may appear as *maḷ* (a dialectic form) *pāḻ iruḷ* and *poruḷ* while *eṭṭu* 'eight' may appear as *eṇ* without any enunciative *ŭ* or off-glide.

(*b*) *A living rule in Malayāḷam.* Some Sanskrit words and compounds used in Malayāḷam end in -*t*, or have -*t*- or -*d*- as the final letter of the first member of the compound and these letters are sounded like *l* in that language. Thus the Sanskrit *ad*-, *ud*- (a prefix), *tad*, *mad* etc., in *adbhutam* 'wonderful', *utsāham* 'energy', *tātparyam* 'design, object'. *camatkāram* 'surprise', *gadgadam* 'stammering, faltering' etc., are pronounced *al*, *ul*, *tal*, *mal*, *gal*, *albhutam*, *ulsāham*, *tālparyam*, *camalkāram*, *galgadam*, etc., in Malayāḷam. Some of these compounds exist also in Tamil, but here *t* and *d* are replaced by *ṟ* when they happen to be the final letters of the first members of compounds as in *aṟputam*, (*adbhutam*) 'wonderful', *Paṟpaṉāpaṉ* (*Padmanābhan*) 'a proper name', *taṟkālam* (*tatkālam*) 'that time', *muṟkam* (*mudgam*) 'a kind of pulse'. So also *Marut* 'a storm God'; *jagat* 'the world, *tasmāt* 'therefore', *gurumukhāt* 'from the mouth of the teacher' are pronounced *Marul*, *jagal*, *tasmāl*, *gurumukhāl*. Similarly final -*ḍ* has the sound of -*ḷ*; thus *ṣaḍ* 'six', *madhuliḍ* 'a bee', *parivrāḍ* 'an ascetic', are pronounced *ṣaḷ*, *madhuliḷ*, *parivrāḷ* in Malayāḷam. Sanskrit words ending in *ṭ*, *ḍ*, *t* or *d* are not now in use in Tamil.

This change of *t* and *d* into *l* and *ṟ* is an indication that their sounds were not originally dental but alveolar.

We know that even among the Vedic Aryans there was a tendency to pronounce *ḍ* as *ḷ* and *l*. Thus the word *iḍā* 'the earth, speech' appeared also in the form *iḷā*; and in the first line of the first verse of the Ṛg-Veda '*agnimīḷe purohitam*' 'I praise Agni the priest', the followers of the Ṛg-Veda pronounced *īḍe* as *īḷe*. A similar tendency now rendered very general is in full operation in Malayāḷam, a late off-shoot from Tamil, and gives us a most important clue as to the original form of a large number of Dravidian words which now end in *l*, *ḷ*, *ḻ*, *ṇ*, *ṉ*. We are in the habit of regarding these finals as original and of supposing that *kāl* 'wind', *poruḷ* 'a thing of importance' *iruḷ* 'darkness, night', *pāḻ*, 'waste', *maṇ* 'mud, earth', *paṇ* 'a song', are the original forms of words and that *kāṟṟu*, *poruṭṭu*, *iruṭṭu*, *pāṭu*, *maṭṭi*, *pāṭṭu*, etc., having the same significations are derived from them by the addition of the suffix -*ṭu* or -*ṭi*. But the above living tendency in Malayāḷam raises the presumption that the finals *l*, *ḷ*, *ḻ*, *ṇ*, *ṉ* may in a large number of cases have been derived from *t*, *d*, *ṟ*, *ṭ*, *ḍ*; and this presumption is greatly strengthened when the Dravidian words having the above finals are compared with the corresponding Indo-Aryan words having the same meaning. The theory submitted by the present writer for the consideration of scholars is that in the vast majority of cases these finals are secondary, and have taken the place of the original dental, alveolar and cerebral mutes.

(*c*) The following examples will illustrate this alternative change of finals when the enunciative *u* is not added.

(i) Tamil and Malayāḷam. *mel*, *meṉ* 'soft'; *mella* 'slow'; *mirutu*, *metu* 'soft, quiet, slow'. Kanarese *medu*, *mel*, *mella*, *mellane*.

The Sanskrit adjective *mṛdu* 'soft, quiet, slow' may become *mirudu* by the insertion of a glide vowel (*svarabhakti*) or *medu* by the conversion of *ṛ* into *e*; both these words are in use in Tamil. But *metu*, may lose the final *u*, and be converted into *mel*, *meṉ*, by change of the final *t* into *l* or *ṉ*. Example :— *melliṉam*, *meṉkaṇam* 'soft kind'—grammatical names for *mediae*; *meṉpāl* 'soft kind' a literary word for 'soft cultivable ground' which is also called *marutam* in Old Tamil; *mella mella-p-pōṉaṉ* 'he went slowly'. The Kanarese lexicographer Dr. F. Kittel and the Malayāḷam lexicographer Dr. Gundert recognise that *mel* is a *tadbhava* of the Sanskrit *mṛdu*.

The oscillation of the final between *l* and *ṉ* should be noted; *l* appears before vowels and *ṉ* before tenues—as in *melliṉam* 'soft kind,' *melleḻuttu* 'soft letter'; *meṉpāl*, *meṉkaṇam* 'soft kind.' The same oscillation is seen in the Tamil and Malayāḷam *val*, *vaṉ* 'hard, strong,' derived from the Sanskrit *balam* 'strength, force'; *valliṉam*, *vaṉkaṇam* 'strong class (of consonants)' *i.e.*, tenues :—*valleḻuttu* 'a strong letter or sound, a tenue'; *vaṉpāl* 'hard kind (of ground)'

Similar oscillations are observable between *ḷ* and *ṇ* in the following couplets (a) *veḷ*, *veṉ* 'white,' (b) *vaḷ*, *vaṇ* 'generous', (c) *oḷ*, *oṇ* 'shining,' (d) *teḷ*, *teṇ*, 'clear, pure,' (e) *eḷ*, *eṇ* (1) 'sesamum' (2) 'light, of little value,' (*f*) *naṭu naḷ*, *naṉ* 'middle.'

(ii) Tamil, Malayāḷam and Kanarese : *mel* 'to masticate, chew'; *medi*, *midi* 'tread, grind.'

The Sanskrit root *mṛd* (v. tr.) 'tread or grind' has become *mal* and *maḷ* in Prākṛt. In Tamil, Malayāḷam and Kanarese, it has produced the root *mid-ī* 'tread' and *mel* 'masticate, grind' (with the teeth); the latter form has been produced by a process of corruption similar to what we have noticed in the adjective *mel* 'soft' from Sanskrit *mṛdu* 'soft.' Dr. Gundert recognises that these forms are *tadbhavas* of the Sanskrit root *mṛd*.

(iii) Tamil, Malayāḷam and Kanarese *maṇ*; Telugu and Kanarese *maṭṭi*; Telugu *maṉ*, *maṉṉu*; all meaning 'mud.

The Sanskrit *mṛd* 'mud, clay' takes the termination *ti* and *kā* and becomes *mṛttikā* 'mud.' This becomes *maṭṭiyā* and also *maṭṭi* (losing the suffix) in Telugu having the same meaning; the word *maṭṭi* 'mud' exists also in Tamil and Kanarese. The original Sanskrit word *mṛd* must by an analogy become *maḍ* or *maṭ* which change into *maṇ* in Tamil, Kanarese and Malayāḷam and into *maṉ* *maṉṉu* in Telugu, all meaning 'mud.' Dr. Kittel recognise, that Kanarese *maṭṭi* is derived from Sanskrit *mṛd* 'mud.'

(iv) Tamil, Malayāḷam *tiṉ*, *tiṉṉiya* 'strong, stout, firm,' *tiḍam*, *tiṭpam* 'firmness'· Kanarese *diḍa*, *duḍa*, 'strong stout, firm.'

The Sanskrit *dṛḍha* 'strong, firm,' gives rise to the Tamil-Malayāḷam *tiḍam*, *diḍa*, *duḍa* by the mere change of *ṛ*, into *i* or *u*. Deprived of the final *a* it should become *tiṭ* in Tamil, but as Tamil words cannot end in tenues, it is converted into *tiṇ*. The word *tiṇṇa* exists also in Kanarese where it also means 'largeness, greatness, excessiveness' which senses are also inherent in the Sanskrit '*dṛḍha*.'

(v) Tamil and Malayāḷam: *cimiḻ* 'a casket' 'a little round box.' The Sanskrit *sampuṭa* having the same meaning exists as *cempuṭam* in Tamil but when it loses its final *a* it becomes *cimiḻ* which passes for a pure Tamil word. No Tamil word can begin with *ca*.

(vi) So has the Sanskrit '*dramiḍa*' or '*drāviḍa* (Prākṛt *damiḍa*) become *tamiḻ*.

92. SANSKRIT WORDS SHORTENED OR OTHERWISE ALTERED IN TAMIL IN CONSEQUENCE OF A SHIFT OF ACCENT TO THE FIRST SYLLABLE.

(*a*) Tamil words generally accented on the first syllable.

It is generally stated that the Dravidian languages are destitute of accent; but as pointed out by Bishop Caldwell these languages do possess an accent which is upon the first syllable of every word. This is specially so in the case of Tamil. Of course when a speaker has to emphasise a particular idea or to lay stress upon a particular mode of action he has to modulate the voice so as to emphasise syllables other than the first; there is also a class of verbs in Tamil-Malayāḷam in which the final vowel has to be stressed for the purpose of indicating that the verb is used transitively or causatively. Omitting these exceptional cases we may say generally that in ordinary Tamil speech the pitch of the voice is highest on the first syllable of every word and gradually falls till the last syllable has the lowest pitch ; the result of this is that the final syllables of all words are slurred over. It has therefore happened that many words of three or more syllables borrowed from Sanskrit appear in an exceedingly curtailed form in Tamil. In several of the illustrative examples given below it is only the Prākṛtic corruptions of Sanskrit words that have thus been further shortened in Tamil; but it is thought unnecessary to distinguish such cases here.

Sanskrit.	Tamil.
1. *pārāvataḥ* ' a dove '	*puṛavu*, *puṟā*, *prā* (vulgar).
2. *vraiheya* ' relating to paddy.'	*vai* ' paddy stalks.'
3. *nīvāraḥ* ' wild paddy '	*nel* ' the paddy plant, paddy grain.'
4. *taiṣī* ' name of a month '	*tai*.
5. *mārgaśīrṣī* do.	*mārkaḷi*.
6. *ānuṣī* do.	*āṉi*.
7. *vaṁśaḥ* 'the bamboo'	*vēy*.
8. *apavarakaḥ* ' a room partitioned off '	Mal : *pura* ' a room.'

	Sanskrit.	Tamil.
9.	*pariśīl* 'practise'	*payil* 'practise, do again and again.'
10.	*martya(m)* 'the body'	*mey* 'the body.'
	Pkt. *macca(m)*	*mai* 'birth, incarnation.'
11.	*kārya(m)* 'action'	*kai* 'action.'
	Pkt. *kacca(m)*.	
12.	*pākya(m)* 'to be cooked or matured'	*pai* 'green.'
	pacya(m) 'uncooked, immature, therefore green.'	
13.	*vandhyā* 'a barren woman'	*mai* 'barren.' Mal. *macc* .
14.	*bhastrā* 'a leathern bag'	
	pātrikaḥ 'a vessel, cup'	*pai* 'a bag.'
	pracitiḥ, praciḥ 'a hoard.'	
	Pāli : *pacci* 'a collection, a bag.'	

These examples are all dealt with elsewhere.

(*b*) Initial *i* or *ai* often replaced by *e* and initial *u* and *au* by *o*.

In Sanskrit, the vowel gradations are :—(i) *i. u.* (2) *e, o*; (3) *ai, au*. Indo-Germanic philologists have demonstrated that of these *e* and *o* constitute the natural stage and that they are transformed to *i, u* in less accented syllables, while *ai, au* represent the highest grade. The semi-vowe s *y* and *v* occupy the same position as *e* and *o* and become *i* and *u* in less accented syllables ; this change of the semi-vowels into the lowest grade vowels is called *Saṁprasāraṇa*.

As the highest pitch in a word is generally on the first syllable in Tamil, it has happened that all words in which the vowel of the first syllable was *i* or *u* in Sanskrit or in Old Tamil now exhibit *e* or *o* in the speech of the people· thus *ikal̲* (v. tr.) 'despise,' *icaivu* 'agreement,' *iṭam* 'a place,' *ṇ akkam* ' endship,' *itam* 'agreeableness,' *in̲ām* 'a reward, *imai* (v. intr.) 'wink the eye,' *iyal* 'nature,' *ilai* 'a leaf' *kukai* 'a cave,' *kucavan̲* 'a potter,' *kuṭam* 'a pot,' *kuṇam* 'quality,' *cumai* 'a load,' *curai* 'a kind of gourd,' *pulampu* (v. intr.) 'weep,' *kuvaḷai* 'a lily' are pronounced in the ordinary speech of the people a : *ekal̲, eśaivu, eḍam, eṇakkam, e am, en̲ām, emai, ēr̲kan̲avē, elai, kokai, kośavan, koṭam, koṇam, śomai, śoṛai, polambu, kovaḷai*. Similarly the first vowels of Indo-Aryan words if they happen to be *ai* or *au* are changed into *e* or *o* in their *t atsama* forms in Tamil.

(*c*) Initia l *vya* s very often replaced by *ve* and *vicc versa*.

	Sanskrit.	Tamil.
1.	*vyāghraḥ* 'a tiger'	*vēṅkai* 'a tiger.'
2.	*vyālaḥ* 'a vicious animal.'	*vēl̲a(m)* 'an elephant'
3.	*vyāpāraḥ* 'trade'	*vēpāram* 'trade.' *pēram* 'bargaining,' *vēlai* 'work, business.'
4.	Tel. *bēḍa* 'a two anna piece.'	Kanarese Dialect: *byāla* 'a silver coin' (*vide* specimen of Gōlarī L. S. Vol. IV).
5.	*vyaṅgaḥ* 'deformed, deficient, a cripple.'	*veṅk(an̲)* 'a pauper.'
6.	*vyarthikaḥ* 'useless, vain'.	*veṭṭ(i)* 'useless.'
7.	*vyayaḥ* 'loss, expenditure'	Tel: *vecc(amu)* 'expenditure.'

	Sanskrit.		Tamil.
8.	*vyañjanam*	'seasoning'	*veñcaṉ(am)*
9.	*vyavasāyaḥ*	'agriculture'	*vevacāy(am)*
10.	*vyasana*	'misfortune, grief.'	*vecaṉ(am)* 'grief.'

Sometimes the presence o a *y* in a word converts the first vowel *a* into *e*.

11.	*anya*	'other, different'	*ēṉai* 'other.'
12.	*kalya(m)*	'morning'	*keḻa-k-ku* 'the east.'
13.	*paryasta*	'turned upside down.'	*peṟaṭṭu* (v. tr.) 'turn upside.' *peṟaḷ* (v. intr.) 'down.'
14.	*saṁyak*	'fully, accurately, well' Pāli *sammā*	*cemmai, cevvai* 'good condition, welfare,'
15.	*samaya*	'opportunity, fit time.'	*cevvi* 'opportunity, fit time.'

The words *vyāpāra* and *pēram* now express the business of traders involving only sale or change of goods; but the first of them *vyāpāra* originally connoted the general idea of business including offices under Government. Thus in the Old Pallava Prākṛt inscriptions the word *vāpata* (<vyāpṛta) referred to officers employed by the king in his service.[1]

The word *vēlai* which is only another form of *bēra* and which now means 'an office, work, business,' thus appears to be derived from *vyāpāra*.

---

1. Sivakhandavammo dhannakaḍe vāpatam ānapayat i (E. I., Vol. VI., p. 86). Śans: *Śivaskandavarmā dhānyakaṭake vyāpṛtam ājñāpayati*. Eng.: Śivaskandavarama commands the officer in Dhānyakaṭaka."

The Telugu *bēḍa* and the Kanarese *byāla*, which are merely other forms of the Tamil *vyāḻam*, both mean 'silver coin' or in Tamil *veḷḷi-k-kācu*. It would thus seem that the Tamil word for Thursday has the same meaning as the Tamil name for Friday, viz., *veḷḷi*, (suitable names for the brightest heavenly bodies next to the moon) words are traceable to the Sanskrit *śvitra(m)* and *śvaitra(m)* 'whiteness.'

The word *veṅkaṉ* is used to indicate a pauper, humorously, in popular speech.

Paryasta had become *palaṭh*, *palaṭ* in some Prākṛts (H.G. G.S. 143).

(*d*) *Va* in an initial conjunct often changes to *o*.

Sanskrit.	Tamil.
kvath 'boil'	*ko-ti* (v. intr.) 'boil'
śvānaka 'a dog'	*cōṇaṅki* 'a kind of dog.'
dhvani 'sound'	'*toṉi*'
jvara 'fever'	*coram*
jval (v. intr.) 'shine, burn'	*coli*.

(*e*) Samprasāraṇa. On the other hand *ya* and *va* at the end of words where the pitch of the voice is lowest are converted into *i* and *u*. Thus *tva* and *yā* the conjunctive participle suffixes of classical Sanskrit which became *tu* and *i* in Prākṛt are also in use in Dravidian. In the following words final *-ya* has been changed to *-i* in Tamil :—(i) *Pāṇḍya* 'name of a dynasty,' (2) *kanyā* 'an unmarried girl' (3) *sandhyā* 'time of twilight,' (4) *veśyā* 'a harlot,' (5) *hatyā* 'slaughter,' (6) *Ahalyā*, 'a proper name,' (7) *vandhyā* 'a barren woman' have become (1) *Pāṇṭi*, (2) *kaṉṉi* (3) *canti*, *anti* (4) *vēci*, (5) *atti*, (6) *Akali*, (7) *vanti*.

This change called Samprasāraṇa has produced various forms in Sanskrit which appear to have their counter-parts in Tamil words of Sanskritic origin; but it is difficult to say whether the changes took place in Sanskrit itself, before the words were borrowed in Tamil or after the adoption of the words in Tamil. For instance the roots *yaj* (v. tr.) 'sacrifice and *vac* (v. tr.) 'speak,' *vap* (v.tr.) 'sow,' *vas* (v. intr.) 'shine,' *vas* (v. intr.) 'dwell,' have the past participles passives *iṣṭa, ukta, upta, uṣṭa* or *uṣita* and verbal nouns *iṣṭi, ukti, upti, uṣṭi*. In these cases the accents in Sanskrit being on the suffixes *-ta* and *-ti*, the initial *ya-* and *va-* of the roots have undergone Samprasāraṇa. Similarly and for similar reasons in the perfect the original re-duplicated bases *yayaj, vavac* etc., assume the forms *iyaj, uvac, īj (iij), ūc (u uc)*.

Certain Tamil words like *uruḻ* (v. intr.) "roll' and ūḻ (v. intr.) 'come round' appear to be derived from the re-duplicated bases *varvart, vavart*, which, when *rt* is changed to *ṭṭ*, would assume the forms *varvaṭṭ, vavaṭṭ*. These last by the Samprasāraṇa of the *v*'s appear to have become *urūṭṭ uūṭṭ* (*ūṭṭ*) and ultimately *uruḻ, ūḻ*. It is best to regard the Samprasāraṇa to have taken place in Sanskrit itself where the accent was on the terminations.

93. NORTH-WESTERN CHARACTERISTIC IN DRAVIDIAN WORDS, ESPECIALLY TAMIL WORDS DERIVED FROM IN O-ARYAN.

Sir G. A. Grierson divides[1] the modern Aryan vernaculars of India into two classes with reference to their mode of treatment of the double consonants in the Apabhraṁśa words which they have inherited.

"It is a commonplace of the history of all Indo-Aryan languages, that the various Prākṛts from which they are derived are full of words containing double consonants. As an example we can take the Sanskrit *bhaktaḥ* 'cooked

1. L. S., Vol. VIII, Part I, pp. 237-8.

rice' which becomes *bhattu* with a double *tt* in Apabhraṁśa Prākṛt. In most of the modern Indo-Aryan vernaculars (especially in West Hindī and Gujarātī) these double letters are simplified by the rejection of one of them and the preceding vowel is lengthened in compensation. Thus almost universally *bhattu* is represented in modern languages by *bhāt*. But in the Lahndā and Pañjābī this is not the case. The double letter is retained and the preceding vowel remains short. In Sindhī and the Dardic languages and sometimes in Lahndā the compound is, it is true, simplified, but the preceding vowel almost always remains short. There is no compensatory lengthening. Thus Sindhī has *bhatu,* not *bhātu* and the Dardic Kashmiri *bata* not *bāta.* This absence of compensatory lengthening is a most important distinction between the Aryan languages of the North-West, and those of the rest of India. It separates them at once as two definitely distinct groups. In the North-West a double letter is either preserved or is simplified without affecting the preceding vowel. In the rest of India it is nearly always simplified and the preceding vowel is then always lengthened".

Of the twenty-one words given by Sir G. A. Grierson in illustration, the following eleven occur in Tamil also.

Sanskrit.	Pañjābī	Sindhī.	West-Hindī.	Tamil.
(i) *bhaktam*[1] 'cooked rice'	*bhatt*	*bhatu*	*bhat*	*pattu* 'boiled rice' *patam* 'the state of being boiled'

1. In the Tamil country vessels to which boiled rice or other cooked foodstuffs are adhering are regarded as ceremonially impure and are called *pattu* vessels; the name

	Sanskrit.	Pañjābī.	Sindhī.	West-Hindī.	Tamil.
(ii)	*uccakaḥ* 'high'	*uccā*	*uco*	*ūcā*	*ucci* 'the zenith, the crown of the head'
(iii)	*śabdaḥ* 'a sound'	*sadd*		*sād*	*cattam* 'a sound'
(iv)	*cakram*[1] 'a wheel'	*cakk*	*cāku*	*cak*	*cekku* 'oilman's wheels'
(v)	*śuṣkakaḥ* 'dry'	*sukkhā*	*sukō*	*sūkhā*	*cukku* 'dried ginger'
(vi)	*carma*[2] 'skin'	*camm*	*camu*	*cām*	*cemmāṉ* 'leather worker' T. *ceruppu* 'sandals' also in Mal. Kan. and Telugu.

---

pattu being usually explained as being due to the circumstance that cooked things 'adhere' (*paṟṟu*) to the vessel.

The word *patam* is usually taken to be the same as the Sanskrit *padam* meaning 'station, place, position' and is usually understood to mean 'proper condition' in the phrase *cōṟṟu-p-patam* 'the extent to which food has been softened by boiling.'

The explanation of *pattu* and *patam* given in the last column above is new.

1, 2. According to Tolkāppiyam no Tamil word can begin with *ca*.

	Sanskrit.	Pañjābī.	Sindhī.	West-Hindī.	Tamil.
(vii)	*karṇaḥ*[1] 'an ear'	*kann*	*kanu*	*kān*	*kaṇ* 'the 7th case post-position.
(viii)	*karma* 'an action'	*kamm*	*kamu*	*kām*	*kām* 'work, employment' *kammiyar* 'workmen'
(ix)	*raktakaḥ* 'red'	*rattā*	*ratō*	*rātā*	(*i*) *rattam* 'blood'
(x)	*pṛṣṭham*[2] 'the back'	*piṭṭh*	*puṭhi*	*pīṭh*	*puṭṭam* 'the back', *piṭari* 'the nape of the neck.'
(xi)	*darbhaḥ* 'a kind of grass'	*dabbh*	*ḍābhu*	*ḍābh*	*turumbu* 'a straw'

All the eleven words show the characteristic of the North-Western group.

The following list of additional words may be given.

	Sanskrit.	Actual or probable Prākṛt. form.	Dravidian.
1.	*cūrṇakaḥ* 'power'	*cunno*	T. *cuṇṇāmpu* 'slaked lime.' Tel. *sunnamu* 'lime used with betel'

1. *Api karṇe* in Sanskrit means 'near', 'close to'; so the Tamil *kaṇ* has been taken to be related to the *S. karṇaḥ*. It may also be taken as related to the Tel. *kaḍa* 'side proximity.'

2. *Piṭari* in literary Tamil is *ciṟu puṟam* 'small back' and is obviously a diminutive form like the Indo-Aryan *pagri* 'a turban' (from the Hindi *pag*) and *tukaḍi* 'small bit' (from the S. *Sṭoka*).

Sanskrit.	Actual or probable Prākṛt form.	Dravidian.
2. *vyākhyānakaḥ* 'commentary'	*vakkhano*	T. *vakkaṇai.* 'preliminary or superfluous words, explanation.' K. *vakkaṇai, vakkaṇe, vakkaṇa.*
3. *kāṣṭhakaḥ* 'wood, forest'	*kaṭṭo*	T. *kaṭṭai* 'wood firewood'; *kāṭu* 'a forest' also in Kan. and Tel.
4. *kāṣṭhakaḥ* 'limit'	*kaṭṭho*	T. *kaṭai,* Kan. *kaṭṭa, kuṭa, kaḍe* Tel. *kaḍa* 'end, limit.'
5. *arghakaḥ* 'price, value, cheapness'	*aggho*	Tel. *agguva* 'cheapness Kan. *agga, hagga.* (1) worth, value, (2) 'cheapness'
arghyakaḥ 'saleable objects'	*aggho*	Tam. *akkam* 'grain'
6. *vargakaḥ* 'class, kind'	*vaggo*	T. *vakai*; K. *bage* 'a class, kind.'
7. *vijñap* 'cause to hear, inform'	*vinnav*	T. *viṇṇap(pam),* K *binna, binnappa* Tel.: *vinnappa,* 'a petition.' T. *vinavu, vinā* (v. tr.) 'enquire, question.'

Sanskrit.	Actual or probable Prākṛt form.	Dravidian.
8. *viṣṭiḥ* 'labour rendered to Government without hire'	....	*veṭṭi(vēlai)* 'unpaid labour'.
9 *uṣṇakaḥ* 'heat'	*unho*	*uṇa(ṅku)* 'be dried' *uṇa(kku)* 'to dry' *uṇar, ular* 'to dry.'
10. *śuktiḥ* 'oyster shell'	*sippi*	*cippi, ippi,* 'pearl oyster.'
11. *vyuptakam* 'sown'	*vrittam*	T. *vittu, vitai* 'seeds' K. *bittu,* Tel. *vittu*
12. *vyuṣṭiḥ* 'the dawn, the day-break'	..	T. *viṭi(yal)* 'day-break.' (Coll.) *veṭi(yal.).*
13. *vyṛddhi* 'non-prosperity, ill-luck'	*viddhi*	T. *miṭi* 'poverty.'
14. *vandhyā* 'a barren'	..	T. *mai mac mac* 'barren'. K. *banji* Tulu. *bajjai.* Ma. *macci.*
15. *martya (m)* 'the body'	*maccu.*	T. 1. *mai mac* as in *immai* 'this body that is, 'this birth.' 2. *mey* 'the body.'
16. *kārya(m)* 'to be done, an action,	Pr. *kajja* T. Prac: *kacca* (Var: III-17 and X-11).	*kai kac kac* 'action, work' *kai arutal* 'to be incapable of action' as through excessive grief.

	Sanskrit.	Actual or probable Prākṛt form.	Dravidian
17.	*pāky(m)* 'uncooked, therefore green'	*paccu*	T. *paccai, pacumai* 'green oolour.' *pacum, paim* 'green' *paiṅ(kiḷi)* 'a green (parrot).'
	pācya(m) 'to be cooked'		*payir* 'green crops.
18.	*bhastrā* 'a leathern bag'		
	pātrakam 'a vessel'	*pacci*	*pai pac pac*
	pracitiḥ, praciḥ 'a collection, hoard'	*pacci* 'a bag'	'a bag.'
19.	*parva(n)* 'the day of the full or new moon'	*pavvu*	Kan. *habbu* 'a festival.' T. and Mal.: *vāvu* 'holiday, change of the moon.' T. and Tel: *uvā, uvavu* 'full moon.'
20.	*piṣṭakaḥ* 'a ground substance, flour, meal'	*piṭṭo*	*piṭṭu, puṭṭu,* 'meal cake' Kan. and Tuḷu *puḍi*, Tam. Mal. and Tel: *poḍi* 'powder.' T. *puḻuti, pūḻi, pūti* 'dust.'
21.	*vyarthaḥ* 'useless, vain fruitless'		T. Mal. and Tel. *veṭṭi* 'useless, spoiled.'

Sanskrit.	Actual or probable Prākṛt form	Dravidian.
'wasted'		T.: *vī*, *vīṇ*, Mal: *vīṇ* 'spoiled, useless. wasted'. Kan: *bidu*, 'waste, uncultivated land.'
22. *śvitraḥ* 'related to white'		Mal: *veṭṭam* 'light'.
śvetaḥ 'the white colour, the planet Venus' from the root *śvit* 'to be white, to be bright.'		T. and Mal: *veḷḷi* 'silver, the planet Venus' *veḻiccam* 'light,' *viḷaṅku* 'to shine,' *viḷakku* 'a lamp Kan: *beḷḷi* 'silver, the planet Venus,' *beḷagu* 'to shine' Tel: *veṇḍi* 'silver' *beḍa* 'a silver coin worth two annas'
23. *varta-te* 'he is; lives, conducts himself'	*vaṭṭai*	T. *vaḻa(ṅku)* 'be accustomed *vāḻ* 'live, be'
24. *vardha-te* 'he grows, continues, flourishes, cuts, distributes.'	*vāḍḍh-ai*	T. *vaḷ-ar* 'grow' *vāḻ* 'flourish' *veṭṭu* 'cut' *vāḷ* 'a knife, a sword' *vāl* 'shining' *vaḻa(ṅku)* 'distribute'

(1) Instead of slaked lime South Indians were formerly using powdered camphor with betel leaves. *Karpūra-cūrṇasamyuktam tāmbūlam pratigṛhyatām* 'Please accept (this)

tāmbūlam with the powder of *karpūra*' is the formula now used when offering pansupari to a deity.

(2) The word *kādu* in No. 2 ; and the words *vāvu* (No. 19) ; *pūli* (No. 20) ; *vīl, vīn, bīdu* (No. 21) ; *bēda* (No. 22) *vāḷ, vaḻ* (Nos. 23 and 24) ; show lengthening of the vowels which is a west-Hindi characteristic. This may be due to later immigrants from *madhyadeśa*.

(9) May also be derived from the Sanskrit *vana* 'dry.

(13) In Nos. 14, 15, 16, 17 and 18, the loss of one *c* weakens the remaining *c* and it is converted into the semi-vowel *y* and ultimately vocalised.

(18) The *pacci* means 'a bag' in Pāli and appears to be derived from or related to the Sanskrit *pracitiḥ* meaning 'a hoard, a collection' just as *sañci* related to the Sanskrit *sañcitiḥ* also meaning 'a hoard, a collection,' literally, has come in the Dravidian idioms to mean 'a bag' *i.e.*, a receptacle for hoard or collection. But from Pischel's Prākṛt Grammar it appears that some scholars connect a form *pacci* with the Sanskrit *patrin*.

(22) *Śvitram* has latterly come to signify a kind of leprosy but its original meaning was 'whiteness' or 'brightness.'

94. Changes undergone by the palatal *c* original and substituted.

The Tamil alphabet possesses the single symbol *c* to represent the following sounds of the Sanskrit alphabet, viz., *c, ch, j, jh, ś* and *s*. Tamil *c* has the sound of the unaspirated palatal tenuis only when doubled and in the combinations *ṟc, ṭc*; it is pronounced like the English *j* in the combinations *ñc* and has the sound of the palatal spirant *ś* in all other cases. This spirantal sound is liable to be weakened into *y*, especially when intervocal, and is often lost. There are a number of *tadbhavas* in Tamil in which the Indo-

Aryan conjunct *śr* becomes *c* and in several of them even this *c* is dropped later. Sanskrit words beginning with the conjuncts *śm*, *śn*, etc., often lose the initial *ś* and *s* when adopted in Tamil, these conjuncts also undergo various other changes as will be seen from the following examples. It may be said generally that the changes which the Tamil *c* has undergone disguise a larger number of *tadbhavas* than the change of any other single letter. The instances given below are by no means exhaustive.

In the following instances the Sanskrit *śra* and *śṛ* have been dropped after being changed into *ś* in some cases, probably in all.

Sanskrit.	Meaning.	Tamil form.
śramaṇa	a Buddhist mendicant	*camaṇa, amaṇa*
śrāvaṇa	name of a month,	*āvaṇi*
śroṇā	name of a constellation.	*ōṇam*
śraviṣṭhā	do.	*aviṭṭam*
śreṣṭhi	foreman of a guild, a wealthy merchant.	*ceṭṭi*
Pāli : *sēṭṭhi*	'a title given by kings'	
śreṇi	a line, a row	
Pāli : *nisseni*		*ēṇi* ' ladder '
Telugu : *nicceṇa*	a ladder	
śrotra	Revealed scriptures;	*ōttu* ' conversancy with the Vedas '
āśrita	' dependent ' (adj.)	*āytam* (a dependent letter)
śrāṇam	' boiled meat etc.'	Mal.: *kōḻi āṇam* ' ' chicken broth '
śṛṅgabēra	' green ginger '	*iñci*, 'green ginger'
Pāli : *singibera*	Pāli : *hingur, ingur.*	

In the following instances the initial *ś* and *s* of conjuncts have been dropped.

śmaśru	'hair'	*mayir*
śmaśāna	'a cemetery'	*mayāṉam*
snāna	'bathing, washing'	*naṉai* (v.t.) wet
sneha	'oil'	*ney* 'ghee'
	'friendship'	*nēyam.*
		necam 'friendship'
snuṣā	'a daughter-in-law'	*nuḻai*
śrōṇa, *ślōṇa*	'a cripple'	**lōni, noṇai.*

In the following examples initial *śṛ*, *śṛ(a)*, *śl(a)* have been reduced to *c*.

śṛṅkhalā	'a chain, a fetter'	*caṅkili* 'a chain'
śṛṅga	'the tusk of an elephant.	*ciṅkam* 'the tusk, etc.'
śṛṅgāra	'handsome, property'	*ciṅkāram* 'beauty' 'adornment'
śṛṅgī	'a very poisonous plant'	*ciṅki*
śraddhā	'trust, confidence'	*caṭṭai* 'regard, respect'
śravas	'the ear'	*cevi* 'the ear'
śrāvaka	'a disciple of the Hinayana school'	*cāvakaṉ*
śrapaya-ti	'he cooks, boils'	*camai* (v.t.) 'cook'
śleṣman	'phlegm'	*cempa* 'cough among animals' T. *irumal,* K *kemmu* 'cough'

In the following list, *ś* and *s* wherever occurring have been dropped.

śālmali	'the silk cotton tree'	*elova, ilavu.*
mārgaśiras	'Name of a month'	*mārkaḻi*
sīsa	'lead'	*īyam*
Siṁhaḷa / Pāli : *Sihaḻa*	'Ceylon (a transliteration of *cīyaḷam*)'	*Īḷam*
sahasra	'one thousand'	*āyiram*
sūcī	'a needle'	T : *ūci* Tel. *sūdi* Mal: *tūśi.*

(T. *ūci* may perhaps have come from the S. *vēśī* 'a needle')

sabhā	'an assembly'	*avai*
saṁśaya	'doubt'	*aiyam.*
sarṣapa / Pāli : *sasapa*	'mustard'	Tam : *aiyavi,* Tel: *ava(lu)*
ācārya	'a priest, a preceptor'	*āciriya, ācā(ṉ) aiya(r)*
suparṇa	'having beautiful feathers'	*uvaṇaṉ*
samaya	'fit time, opportunity'	*amayam*
śulka	'a toll'	*cuṅkam, ulku*
sarpa (*sarapa*)	'a snake'	*aravu*
śandhyā	'evening'	*anti*
śarkarā	'sugar'	*akkāram*
śāṭaka	'a cloth'	*āṭai*
ālāpa-sallāpa	'intimate and familiar conversation'	*aḷāvaḷāvu.*

In the following list *ś*, original and substituted, has been weakened into *y* or lost.

(*ā*) *kāśaḥ* 'the sky,' *kayam*	*kās* (v.i.) shine	*kāy* (v.i.) 'shine'
		kāy (v.i.) 'be hot'
vac 'speech'	(Vedic) mouth	*vāy*
deśaḥ	'a country,'	*tēyam,*
yacch(*yam*) (v. t.)	give	*ic ic*
	tēm	*ī* (give)
kruś (v. i.)	'cry out, bawl'	*kūy, kū,*
vāśī	'a sharp knife'	*vay* 'sharpness'
		vāci 'an axe, adze.'

95. Other changes in initial sibilants and palatals.

In Tolkāppiyam it is stated that no words can begin with *ca, cai, cau*; this rule does not find a place in Naṉṉūl. It is clear that in the interval between the periods of the two grammars a number of words had been admitted into the Tamil language beginning with *ca, cai, cau.* Even now there are not many words beginning with *cai* or *cau* and these are all obviously Indo-Aryan words. There are, however, a number of words in Tamil beginning with *ca* which are supposed to be pure Tamil ; but in view of the presumption raised by the rule of Tolkāppiyam these words must be regarded as foreign.

In the following list of *tadbhavas* initial *ca, śa śṛa, ja, jha* and *sa* of Indo-Aryan words are converted into *ce* or *ci.* There appears once to have been a sense of incongruity in combining palatal consonants with a non-palatal vowel. Palatals so combined are now pronounced dentally in Telugu and in Kanarese. Many words beginning with *ca* have alternative forms beginning with *ce.*

Sanskrit.		Tamil.
(i) *cakram*	'an oil mill'	*cekku* 'an oil mill'
(ii) *carman*	'leather'	*ceruppu* 'sandals' *cem-(m-āṉ)* 'a leather worker'
(iii) *car, caḻ*	'go, move'	*cel* 'go, pass'
(iv) *śravas*	'the ear'	*cevi* 'the ear'
(v) *śāḻmali*	'the silk-cotton tree'	Kan. Tam : *elava*: *ilava* 'silk-cotton tree apparently through *celama*'
(vi) *samabhāgaḥ*	'equal share, one-half'	*cemppākam* 'exact half.'

In the following words also the Sanskrit *sama* meaning 'equal, straight' has become *cem*.

(viii) *ceṅkōl* 'straight sceptre (*i.e.*) righteous government'

(ix) *centamiḻ* 'straight or correct Tamil'

(x) *centūkku* 'straight metre'

Nos. (viii), (ix), (x) are the opposites respectively of *koṭuṅkōl* 'tyrannical governmet,' *koṭuntamiḻ* 'corrupt Tamil' and *vañci-t-tūkku*. Here *koṭum* and *vañci* mean 'crooked', the former being cognate with the Sanskrit *kuṭila* 'crooked' and the latter with Sanskrit *vak-ra* (*vañc*) 'crooked.'

(xi) *sampuṭaḥ* 'a round casket'	*cimiḻ*
(xii) *savarṇaḥ* 'like, similar'	*civaṇ* 'to be similar' a *sautra* root from Tolkāppiyam.
(xiii) *jaṭin* 'having clotted hair'	*ceḻi-y-aṉ*
(xiv) *ja(ya)vaḥ* 'barley' Pkt: *javō*	*cev-(v-arici)* 'barley grain husked'
(xv) *jhaṭi* a small tree, a shrub, a bush'	*ceṭi* 'a plant :a young tree'

(xvi)	*yamaḷa* 'one of a couple' Pkt : *jamaḷa*	*cevili* 'a female companion' as in *cevili-t-tāy* 'mother's companion'
(xvii)	*samyak* 'correctly truly, entirely,' Pāli : *sammā*	*cevvai* 'well, completely'. *cemmai*
(xviii)	*samayaḥ* 'season, opportunity'	*cevv-i* 'fit or proper time, opportunity'
(xix)	*cayaḥ* 'the hand'	*cey*(v.t.) 'do', Tel: *cēyu* (v.t.) 'do' *cēy* 'the hand'

The following words and a large number of others beginning with *ca* must be presumed to have been admitted into the language after the time of Tolkāppiyam.

Tamil.	Sanskrit.	Tamil.	Sanskrit.
Caṅkam 'a multitude, and assembly'	*saṅghaḥ*	*cakaṭu* 'a cart'	*śakaṭam.*
Caṅku 'a conch shell'	*śaṅkham*	*caṇal* 'hemp'	*śaṇam*
Cavam 'a corpse'	*avam*	*cakkarai* 'sugar'	*śarkarā*
Cavai 'an assembly'	*sabhā*	*cantaṉam* 'sandalwood'	*candanam*
Camai (v.t.) 'cook'	*śrapaya-ti*	*caṭai* 'matted hair'	*jaṭā.*

In the following list, the initial sibilant or palatal of Sanskrit words appears as *t* in Tamil. &c.

(i)	*śrī* (subs.) 'wealth, beauty, lustre, high position, dignity'	*tiru* (subs.) 'wealth, beauty' (adj.) 'divine'

	ciṟa (v.i.) '*be* elegant, graceful, eminent'
	cir (subs.) 'beauty, prosperity, greatness'
(ii) *śrītvam* (subs.)	*celvam* (subs.) 'riches, affluence'?
(iii) *śrīmān* (subs.) 'an epithet of *Viṣṇu*'	*tirumāl* (subs.) 'a name of Viṣṇu'
(iv) *sēnā* (subs.) 'an army'	*tāṉai* (subs.) 'an army, a weapon'
	cēṉai (subs.) 'a host, an army'
(v) *svarga* (subs.) 'the heavens'	*tuṟakkam* (subs.) 'the world of the Gods.'
(vi) *sūcī* 'a needle'	*tūci* (Mal.) 'a needle'
	ūci (Tam.)

The interchange of initial *s* and *t* is exceedingly common also in Malayāḷam and Tuḷu. The following are a few of the instances noticed in Gundert's Malayāḷam-English and Manner's Tuḷu-English Dictionaries.

saṅgam	*taṅgam*	'love, affection'
sañci	*tañci*	'a bag'
samaram	*tamaram*	'a fight, a battle'
sabhā	*tavā*	'an assembly'
sasyam	*tasya, tai*	'a shoot, any young tree'
sēvi	*tēvi*	'serve, worship'
śona	*tōna*	'incessant rain'
sōlu	*tōlu*	'be defeated'
seḍil	*teḍil*	'thunder'
sare	*tare*	'the head'
sale	*tale*	'a rope for climbing palm trees'
seli	*teli*	'pure, clear'

The change of intervocal *s* to *d* is also very common in Tamil and Malayāḷam. Thus, the Sanskrit *manas* ' the mind', *māsaḥ* ' a month ', *mās* ' the moon ', *āsanam* ' a seat ', *śāsanam* ' an order ', *vāsaḥ* ' residence ' etc., become *manatu, mātam, mati, ātaṉam, cātaṉam, vātam* ? etc., in Tamil.

(vii) *oṣṭhau* 'the lips, Paic : *osaṭ*	*otaṭu* ' a lip '
In Prāk. *ṣṭ* is changed into *saṭ* (Var : x-6).	*utaṭu* ' is the standard form '
(viii) *śiras* (subs.) 'the head' Avestic *sarah* Paiśācī *sōr* (Grierson Paic : Lang p. 73)	Tuḷu : *sare, tare,* Dravidian : *talai* ' the head ' is probably derived from a form *saraka*.

96. CHANGES OF THE ORIGINAL *p* SOUND IN TAMIL.

1. It was pointed above that (*a*) initial *p*, (b) doubled *pp* wherever it may occur, and (c) *p* in the nexuses *ṭp, ṟp*, are pronounced hard like tenuis, (d) that *p* in the conjuncts *mp, ṉp, ṇp* are pronounced like *b*, and (e) that in every other position single *p* occurring in Tamil words is sounded like the English *f*. This *f* sound which must once have been common in Tamil speech has in course of time been further weakened into the labio-dental *v* and in consequence we find that the original intervocal *p* has been converted into *v* in almost all cases and that the final *vu* has generally been lost except when preceded by *i*. Thus the only cases in which the letter *p* is retained in Tamil words are those included in (a), (b), (c), (d) and the excepted cases in (e).

(a) *paḻam* ' a fruit, *pāmpu* ' a snake ' *piṟa* (v.i.) ' to be born ', etc.

(b) *karuppu* ' blackness,' *appam* ' a cake,' etc.

(c) *puṭpam* ' a flower,' *uṟpavam* ' origin,' *viṟpatti* learning,' etc.

(d) *vēmpu* 'the margosa,' *paṉpu* 'quality,' *aṉpu* 'affection,' etc.

(e) verbal participles ending in *pu* in Old Tamil and still retained in poetic Tamil :

(i) *ōṭupu* 'running,' *oṭipu* 'breaking,' *ceypu* 'doing' *varupu* 'coming', etc.,

(ii) *ceypavaṉ* 'doer', *varupavaṉ* 'comer' etc.

(iii) *mārpu* 'the breast,' *cārpu* 'support, reliance' *cālpu* 'greatness, superiority,' *iyalpu* 'nature, inborn quality.'

(iv) *irupatu* 'twenty,' *aṟupatu* 'sixty,' *eḻupatu* 'seventy.'

The words in (c) are obvious Sanskrit derivatives and are few in number.

The participles in e. (i.) occur only in poetry ; the words in e. (ii.) are agent-nouns from these obsolete participles which are still in use and the *p* is probably retained in them for the sake of euphony, to avoid the repetition of *va* as in *ceyvavaṉ varuvavaṉ*. The words in e. (iii.) found in Old standard works have acquired a status of their own.

2. The following are a few examples of Sanskrit words in which intervocal *p* has been replaced by *v*.

Sanskrit.	Tamil.	Sanskrit.	Tamil.
vāpī 'a well'	*vāvi*	*dīpaḥ* 'a lamp'	*tīvam*, also *tī*
pāpam 'sin'	*pāvam*	*ātapaḥ* 'sun's heat'	*ātavam*
kopaḥ 'anger'	*kōvam*	*śāpaḥ* 'a curse'	*cāvam*
tapas 'penance'	*tavacu* *tavam*	*upamā* 'likeness'	*uvamam*
nāpitaḥ 'a barber'	*nāvitaṉ*	*kapaṭam* 'fraud, deceit'	*kavaṭu*

These examples can be multiplied indefinitely. People acquainted with Sanskrit recognise the Tamil words as *tadbhavas* at once.

3. In the following examples the final *p* and *v* of words of Sanskrit origin have been lost.

Sanskrit.	Intermediate.	Tamil.
(i) *gopaḥ* (subs.) 'one who guards or protects'. The word exists in Mal. & Kan. in the sense of 'a shepherd' chief of a district, a king'	*gōp	(1) *kōvu, ko* 'a king' (2) *kōṉ* 'a king' *kōpaṉ*
(ii) *garbhaḥ* (subs.) 'a foetus, an embryo'	*garubh	*karuvu, karu* 'an embryo'
(iii) *puṣpam* (subs.) (1) a flower, a blossom; (2) the menstrual discharge'	*pupph	(1) *pūvu, pū* 'a flower' (2) *pūppu* 'menstrual flow'
(iv) *rūpam* (subs.) (1) 'form, shape (2) the inflected form of a noun or verb, the sign of that inflection'	*rūp	(1) *uruvu, uru* 'form, shape' (2) *urupu* 'a case-sign of nouns'
(v) *rogaḥ* (subs.) 'disease, sickness'	*rōv	(1) *nōvu, nō* 'sickness' (2) *nōvu, nō* 'pain'
(vi) *śephaḥ, śepaḥ, śevaḥ* (subs.)	*cēp	(1) *cēvu, cē* 'a bull' (2) *cēval* 'a cock'.
(vii) *gumphaḥ* (subs.) from *guph, gump* (v.t.) 'string together, as	*goph	(1) *kōvu, kō* (v.t.) 'string as beads' etc.

pearls, flowers etc.'		(2) *kōvai* 'a string as of beads'
(viii) *eva* 'a particle added to emphasise or streng then the idea expressed'	**ēv*	*ē* 'a particle expressing *tēṟṟam* certainty'
(ix) *dēvaḥ* (subs.) 'a god a deity'	**dēv*	*tēvu, tē* 'a god',
(x) *dvīpaḥ* (subs.) 'an island'	**dīp*	*tīvu* 'an island', also *tī* as in *tīyar* 'islanders'
(xi) *dīpaḥ* 'a lamp, lantern' from *dīp* (v.i.) 'flame, burn'		*tī* 'fire' as in Sans. *dīpa-varti* 'lamp-wick' *tī-vaṭṭi* 'a torch'
(xii) *kūpaḥ* '(1) a well (2) a mast'		T (1) *kūval* 'a well' (2) *kūmbu*, K. '*kūva*, *kū* 'a mast'

These changes and losses should not be regarded as modern or recent; the laws exemplified by the words given have been in operation from the time of the earliest extant Tamil literature. The words *pū* 'flower' and *cē* 'a bull' occur in Tolkappiyam (I. Uyir. 66, 67, 72) referrable to the early centuries of the Christian era. The words (a) *urupu*, (b) *aḷapu*, (c) *tiripu*, among others, are assigned special technical meanings in that work as distinguished from their further corruptions (a) *uru*, (b) *aḷavu*, (c) *tirivu*. Thus (a) *urupu* is 'a case form' while *uru* is 'form of shape' generally. (b) *aḷapu* is 'metrical measure' of sounds while *aḷavu* is 'measure' generally. (c) *tiripu* is 'change of one sound into another' while *tirivu* is 'change' generally. These technical terms have come down from earlier grammarians and retain their original spelling.

4. We may lay down as a general rule that final *vu* is always dropped if preceded by *u* and may be dropped if preceded by *o* or *e*. If preceded by *a* the final *avu* may optionally be replaced by ā as in the following cases :—

viṉavu (v.i.) enquire	*viṉā*	*pukavu* 'food,eating'	*pukā*
aravu 'a snake'	*arā*	*iravu* 'night'	*irā*
uṇavu 'food'	*uṇā*	*kaṉavu* 'a dream'	*kaṉā*
nilavu 'moon-light'	*nilā*	*uvavu* 'the full moon'	*uvā*
cuṟavu 'a shark'	*cuṟā*	*puṟavu* 'a dove'	*puṟā*

These instances might be multiplied. The majority of them are instanced as *tadbhavas* elsewhere in this book.

5. In the following Sanskrit derivatives the initial vowel of the prefix *upa* is lost and *p* is found converted into *v*.

(i) *upādhyāyaḥ* 'a teacher, a religious preceptor'	T. and M. *vādhyār;* also T. *ōccar*. Tel : *ayya*, Kan. *uvajja*.
(ii) *upāyaṉam* 'a present, gift'	T.M.K. and Tel: *vayaṉam* 'present of sweet-meats etc., at feasts etc.'
(iii) *upe-upōyaḥ* 'to fall, falling to one's lot, to befall, as luck'	T. *vāy* 'to be obtained luckily without expectation'
(iv) *upāvr* (v.i.) 'go near to, hasten near', a Ṛg-vedic root made up of the prefix *upa* and *vṛ* 'go towards'	T.M. *vā*, *var*, *vār;* Tel. *bā*, *bar*, *bār ;* Tel. *vaccu*. (v.i.) 'come, approach'
(v) *Upendraḥ* 'Literally almost Indra'; usually applied to 'Viṣṇu' as brother of Indra; also used in Kan. in the senses of 'Indra, a king'	T. M. *vēntaṉ* 'Indra, a king'

6. In the following Sanskrit derivatives the initial vowel of the prefix *upa* or *apa* is lost or transposed but the labial remains tenuis.

(i) *upadhā, apidhā, pidhā* 'cover, conceal'	*pidhī-ya-tē* 'it is concealed'	T. *poti ;* T. and M. *patuṅku* ; Tel. *podugu.* Kan. *pudi, pode, poduṅgu,* 'cover, conceal'
(ii) *upavasthaḥ* 'a fast day'		Tel. *pastu* 'a fast' also *pastilli.*
upavastam[1] 'a fast'		T. and M. *paṭṭiṇi* 'a fast' Mal. *paṣṇi* 'a fast'
		T. and M. *pāḍu* 'fasting and waiting' probably derived from a disused *paṭṭu.*

In Telugu *pastilli* 'a fast'—*pastu*+*illi* both of which also mean 'fast'. In Tamil *pāṭu-kiṭa* is 'to remain fasting within the precincts of a temple for propitiating the deity'; in Malayāḷam *pāḍu-iri* is 'to remain fasting in or before a debtor's house till he pays the debts, to dun by fasting'. The word *pāḍu* here is apparently derived from a Tamil *paṭṭu* corresponding to Telugu *bastu. Paṭṭiṇi* and *paṣṇi* corresponding to Telugu *pastilli* may derived from *upavāsatithi* 'a fasting *tithi*'.

(iii) *upāśakam* 'asylum', resting place'	T. *pācarai* 'a fortified retiring place in or near battle-field where wounded are lodged and the king retires for the night'.

1. The conjuncts *st* and *sth* often become *ṭṭ*, *ṭṭh* as in *ṭhāṇā*, *sthāna:* 'a police station', *ṭhēvaṇi : sthāpani*(?) 'a deposit'. *puraṭṭu, paryasta* 'turn upside down'.

(iv) *apāra* 'boundless, unlimited'	Tel. *pār-mādu* 'mother -earth'
apārā 'the earth'	T. *pār* 'the earth'
(v) *apasarpaḥ* 'g l i d i n g away'	**pasap; pap* of Kumārila Bhaṭṭa.
prasarpaḥ 'creeping along'	T. *pāmpu,* Kan. *hāvu,* Tel. *pāmu* 'a snake'

In Hindī, the Sanskrit *sarpaḥ* 'a snake' exists as *Sāmp* a nasal.

7. The *v* of Sanskrit words is sometimes found converted into *p* in Tamil. The probable explanation of this is that Tamil adopted the words from some Aryan dialects which had changed the *v* and *b*.

Sanskrit	Tamil
kāvyam 'a poem'	*kāppiyam.*
divyam 'divine'	*tippiyam*
gandharvaḥ 'a celestial musician'	*kantarppa(n)*
vardhaya 'serve food, make offerings to the deity'	*paṭai* (c.f.) K. *badisu*
Pārvatī' 'the goddess Durgā'	*pārppati*
vasaḥ 'a boy child'	*payya(n)*

8. In the following instances the initial *p* of Sanskrit words appears to have been changed into *v;* the reason is not apparent.

pratimā 'an image, an idol'	T. *paṭimam* 'shape', T. *vaṭivam* 'form',
parvan(ṇī) 'a festival'	T. *vāvu* 'holiday for a festival'.

97. Dravidian roots and words derived from the Sanskrit roots

vṛt and *vṛdh*

Some of the commonest of Tamil and Telugu roots now regarded as 'pure Tamil' (Cen Tamiḻ) and 'pure Telugu' (Acca Telugu) can be easily shown to be of Indo-Āryan origin. We shall begin by writing down all the Dravidian roots and words traceable to the Sanskrit roots *vṛt* and *vṛdh* both of which are clearly of Indo-Germanic origin corresponding to *vart* 'turn, turn oneself, become, be' and *vardh* 'grow, increase' of the list of Āryan roots.[1]

The conjunct consonants *rt*, *rth*, *rd*, *rdh* often become *ṭṭ*, *ṭṭh*, *ḍḍ*, *ḍḍh* in Prākṛt. In many cases they do not undergo any cerebralization but are found as *tt*, *tth*, *dd*, *ddh*. As pointed out in the following pages, some of these conjuncts occasionally become alveolars in Dravidian. The vowel *ṛ* undergoes various modifications of which *ar*, *ir*, *ur*, *a*, *i*, *u*, *e*, *ē* may be mentioned.

The Sanskrit root *vṛt* has the form *vartate* 'it exists'; this appears as *vaṭṭati*, and later as *vaṭṭai* in the Prākṛts, of which the root-form may be taken to be *vaṭṭ*.

Similarly the root *vṛdh* has the form *vardhate* 'it increases'; and this appears as *vaḍḍhati*, and later as *vaḍḍai*; of which the root-form may be taken to be *vaḍḍ*.

In the languages of the West Hindī group (these two root-forms will usually become *vāṭ* and *vāḍ* but in the North-Western group they may remain as *vaṭṭ* and *vaḍḍ*, or lose a a consonant and become *vaṭ* and *vaḍ*.

---

1. Appendix to Skeat's Etymological English Dictionary.

For reasons already explained these roots cannot end in *ṭ* or *ḍ* in Tamil. They must take an enunciative final *u* or change their final consonants into *ḷ*, *ḻ* or *ṇ* and become *vaḷ*, *vaḻ*, *vāḷ*, *vāḻ*, *vaṇ* etc.

Some of the meanings of the roots *vṛt* and *vṛdh* given in Apte's Sanskrit-English Dictionary are :—

vṛt	1. Choose, like. 2. distribute, divide.	*vṛtyate.*
	3. be, exist, abide, subsist. 4. turn, roll on, revolve. 5. act, behave, conduct or demean oneself.	*vartate.*
	6. speak, relate, describe. 7. shine. 8. do, practise. 9. brandish, flourish, whirl round.	*vartayati.* (causal)
vavṛt	choose, select, love.	*vāvṛtyate.*
vṛdh	1. grow, increase, thrive, prosper.	*vardhate.*
	2. continue, last.	
	3. felicitate, congratulate.	*vardhayati*
	4. speak.	*vardhyate.*
	5. shine.	
vardh	cut, divide, share.	*vardhayati.*
varh, valh	speak, give.	*varhate.* *valhate.*
valh	shine, be pre-eminent or excellent.	*valhayati.* *valhayate.* *valhate.*

vaṇṭ	divide, apportion.	*vaṇṭati.* *vaṇṭayati.* *vaṇṭayate.*
vaṇḍ	share, apportion.	*vaṇḍati.* *vaṇḍayati.* *vaṇḍayate.*

The last four roots appear to be Prākṛtic forms of *vart* and *vardh* taken back into Sanskrit.

The following Dravidian roots may be derived from the Prākṛtic forms of the above roots.

Tamil (1) *vāḻ* (v.i.) 'exist, live', e.g.,

kiṇaru vāḻ tavaḷai 'frogs living in wells'

kōṭu vāḻ paravai 'birds living on the branches of trees'; *vāḻ-nāḷ* ' life-time'

(2) *vāḻ* (v.i.) 'behave or conduct oneself'

vaiyattu vāḻvāṅku vāḻpavaṉ vāṉuṟaiyum
teyvattuḷ vaikka-p-paṭum (Kuṟaḷ)

'He who conducts himself after the manner of the world (the wise) will secure a place in heaven.'

(3) *vāḻ* (v.i.) 'flourish, thrive', 'last, continue', 'rule,reign'

vēntaṉ vāḻka, vēntaṉ vāḻiya 'Long live the king'; *vāḻttu, vaḻuttu* 'bless' are causal forms.

M: *vāḻi* 'a ruler', Tam. *vaḻuti* 'a title of Pāṇḍya kings'

(4) *vaḻa-ṅku* (v.t.) 'distribute'

cakkarai vaḻaṅkiṉāṉ 'he distributed sugar (to the assembled people)'

(5) *vaḻa-nku* (v.i.) 'be practised ; *vaḻakkam* 'practice, habit', 'behaviour' (a derived noun) also belong here.

(6) *vāṭu* (v.i.) 'use, make use of, employ'

vāḍuka 'practice, habit, custom' is a derived noun; as also Tam : *vāṭikkai* 'habit, custom'

(7) *vaḍḍiñcu* (v.t.) 'distribute cooked food to the people seated'

Tam : *vaṭṭi*, Kan : *baḍisu* (v.t.) 'distribute or serve out food or victuals'.

Tam : *paṭai*, Aryan *badai* (v.t.) 'serve food'

All are apparently derived from the Skt. *vardhay* having the same meaning[1].

(8) *vaṇḍu* (v.t.) 'cook food'. It originally probably meant 'distribute cooked food' but now applies to the chief duty of the cook, *viz.*, 'cooking'.

vaṇṭakamu is 'the portion distributed'.

The distribution of cooked food being the chief way in which rich men helped the poor in very early times ; the root *valh* derived apparently from *vaḍḍh* has come to mean 'give'.

Tamil :—

(9) *vaḷḷal* means 'a great giver', also *vaḷḷiyar* 'generous givers'.

(10) *vāḷ* (v.i.) 'speak' exists in Tamil, only in the negative forms *vāḷā*, *vāḷātu*, 'silently', *vāḷāmai* 'silence, taciturnity'.

(11) *vāḷ* (adj.) 'shining' e.g. *vāḷ-nutal* 'bright forehead'. The noun *oḷi* 'light' belongs, apparently to this.

---

1. It will be seen that the Dravidian words are derived from a causal form c.f. '*yāgum vaḍḍhēmi sāma* snall serve rice-gruel sir' (V.F.J.) Vol. VI, p. 366 9d.

NOTE.—There is no verb *vāḷ* 'shine' now in use in Tamil.

(12) *veṭṭu* (v.t.) 'cut, hack' apparently comes from *vaḍḍ* 'cut'.

The noun *uḷi* 'a carpenter's chisel' perhaps belongs to this.

(13) *vaṭi* (v.t.) 'sharpen'; (adj.) 'sharp'

(i) *vaṭivēl* 'a sharp lance', (ii) *vaṭittal* sharpening a crow bar etc., (iii) *vāḷ* (subs.) 'a sword', (iv) *vāḷi* (subs.) 'an arrow', Telugu (vi) *vāḍimi* 'sharpness', (vii) *vaḍraṅki* (Sanskrit *vardhaki*) 'a carpenter' also come under this head.

(14) *vaḷa-r* (v.i.) 'grow, increase'.

(i) *vaḷarum payir* 'growing crops', *vaḷarum piṟai* 'the waxing moon', (iii) *vaḷarum pirāyam* 'the adolescent period'.

We have till now considered only the roots arising from the bases *vart* and *vardh*. But *ṛ* may also change into *ir* giving rise to forms like *virt, virdh,* and undergo other modification. The roots may be reduplicated or may take prefixes; and the initial *va* may undergo *Samprasāraṇa.*

(15) *uruḷ* (v.i.) 'roll, revolve'.

The reduplicated form *varvart* 'turn round and round' will become '*varvat*' which by the *Samprasāraṇa* of *va* will become *vuruṭṭi, uruḷ.*

(16) *ūḻ* (v.i.) 'come round and round'. Not in use as a verb, but *ūḻam* in the sense of 'a turn of duty' is in use in Malayāḷam. The reduplicated *vavart* 'turn round and round' will become *vavaṭ* and by the *Samprasāraṇa* of *va* will become (*ūṭ*) *ūḻ.*

(17) *ūḻ* (v.i.) 'grow very old, decay'; *ūḻal* (subs.) 'things spoiled or decayed'.

The reduplicated form *varvardh* will become *ūḻ* as above.

(18) *ūṭu* (v.i.) 'feign dislike or anger as a woman to her lover'.

The Sanskrit *apāvṛt* (v.t., v.i.) 'turn away from, repulse' which in conjugation will take the form *apāvart* (*-a-tē*) will become *ūvaṭ* in some Prākṛts and may have given rise to the Tamil root. The prefix *apā-* becomes *ō*, *u*, and sometimes *ū* in Pāli (c.f. Ep. Ind., Vol. V, p. 5).

(19) Tam : *uḷ* (v.i.) 'be' (a defective verb). Telugu *uṇḍu* (v.i.) 'be'.

By the *Samprasāraṇa* of *va* and may further be nasalized into the form *uṇḍu*. The form *vāṭ* is the verb-substantive in Oriya.

(20) *viḻu*, *viḻ* 'large'.

These appear to be traceable to *virddha* for *vṛddha* 'grown old, large' which will become *viḍḍu*, and finally; *viḻu* and *viḻ*.

(21) Tam: *vāṭṭi* (subs.) 'a turn, repetition' (vulgar). Telugu *māṟu* (subs.) 'a turn, repetition'; *māṭiki* 'frequently' (literally, 'every time'). These words appear to be connected with the Sanskrit *āvṛtti* repetition, turn' and *āvṛt* (subs.) 'coming round and round'. The Sanskrit forms have become corrupted into *āvaṭṭi* and *āvart* and by a transposition of the initial vowel have given rise to *vāṭṭi*, *māṟṟu* or *māṟu*.[1]

Some instances have been given of the changes of *rt* into *ṟṟ* and of the change of initial *v* to *m*.

(22) Tamil : *vil* (v.t.) 'sell'. Tam : and Tel : *māṟu* (v.t.) 'exchange, barter'. Kan : *bil* 'sell', *bāḷu* 'sell for, exchange for'.

---

1. In the Telugu *vāṇḍu* 'he' and *vīṇḍu* 'this man', the initial *a* and *i* (of the Tamil *avaṉ* and *ivaṉ*) have been transposed.

The word *vartakam* in Dravidian now means 'trade, exchange or barter' and if we can infer from this that *vṛt* has the meaning of 'exchange or barter' as undoubtedly *parivart* has, then we may suppose that *vṛt* took the form *virt* and was ultimately corrupted into (*viṟṟ*) *vil* and *bil*.

Āvart will also then have 'exchange or barter' as one of its meanings and may be transformed finally into *māṟṟu* or *māṟu* (*vide* item 21) and *bāḻu*.

In the two forms *āvṛtti* and *āvṛt* considered above the prefix *ā* displaced by metathesis produces the form *vāṭṭi*, *māṭi* 'repetition, turn', and *māṟṟu*, *māṟu*, *bāḻu*, 'exchange, barter'. But there are a few Tamil verbal bases containing alveolars which appear to be derived from the Sanskrit *vṛt* of Indo-Germanic origin corresponding to the Latin *vert* but there is nothing in the Tamil bases corresponding to the prefixes which give the special meanings to *vṛt* in the Aryan languages.

(23) The Tamil : *maṟu* (v.t.) 'deny, refuse' apparently derived from *vṛt* (*vart*) with no prefix conveys the idea of the English 'controvert'.

(24) The Tamil *veṟu* (v.t.) 'loathe, feel disgusted' probably derived from the same base *vṛt* (*vart*) with no prefix conveys the meaning of the English '*aversion*' (from 'avert').

(25) We may also mention here the words *maṟṟu*, *maṟu*, involving the sense of 'the other'; *maṟṟavaṉ* 'the other man' *maṟu-nāḷ* 'the next day', *maṟupaṭi* 'again, a second time'.

(26) The following derivatives from *vṛt* and *vṛdh* in use in Tamil may also be noted down here.

vaṭṭam (*vṛttam*) 'a circle'; *vaṭṭu* 'a circular piece in gambling'; *vaṭṭil* (*vartula*) 'a circular plate'; *vaṭṭai*, *vaṭṭi*; *vaḻi* 'a way' (*vartis* 'a way'); *vaṭai* (*vaṭaka*) 'a round cake', *vaṭṭi* (*vṛddhi*) 'increase or interest (on loans)'.

CHAPTER VII
DRAVIDIAN SUFFIXES
TAMIL I.

98. CLASSIFICATION OF ROOTS

Tamil roots and verbal bases may be grouped under three classes with reference to the principles laid down already: (A) accented, (B) unaccented, (C) accented when transitive or causal, but unaccented in other senses.

A. To the accented group belong :—

1. The verb substantive *iru* 'be' and above fifty roots of obscure formation ending in *-a* and consisting of two short syllables. Examples :—

naṭa 'walk'	*maṟa* 'forget'
tiṟa 'open'	*paṟa* 'fly'
tuṟa 'abandon'	*iḻa* 'lose'
ira 'beg'	*uḻa* 'labour'
pura 'protect'	*kaṭa* 'cross'
iṟa 'die'	*kiṭa* 'be, lie uncared for'

2. All bases of obvious Āryan origin formed by affixing *i* to *a* Sanskrit or Indo-Āryan root or base. Examples :—

Base	Sans:root	Base	Sans:root
paṭi 'read'	*paṭh*	*kōpi* 'be angry'	*kup*
mari 'die'	*mṛ*	*pali* 'be fruitful'	*phala*
vaci 'dwell'	*vas*	*puci* 'eat, enjoy'	*bhūj*
vāci 'read'	*vāc*	*naṭi* 'dance, pretend'	*naṭ*

3. All causal bases containing one or both of the causative suffixes *vi* and *pi*. Examples :—

ceyvi 'cause to be done' *naṭappi* 'cause to be performed'
koṭuppi 'cause to be given' *aṟivi* 'cause to be known'
uṭuppi 'cause to be put on' *terivi* 'cause to be known'
ceyvippi 'cause to be done' *naṭappivi* 'cause to be performed'

4. A number of miscellaneous bases including adjectives and nouns used as verbs. Examples :—

pār 'see' *veṟu* 'dislike, be disgusted with'
kā 'protect, wait' *uru* 'take shape'
koṭu 'give' *peru* 'become large'
eṭu 'take' *ciṟu* 'become small'
paṭu 'lie down' *veḷu* 'become white'
uṭu 'put on, dress oneself with' *karu* 'become black'
paḻu 'become fruit'
kal 'learn'
vil 'buy' *kāy* 'yield, produce as fruit etc.'
nil 'stand, cease moving'

B. (1) Of the unaccented group the most numerous are those ending in the short enunciative *ŭ*. Examples :—

āṭŭ 'play' *ōṭŭ* 'run'
ēṟŭ 'ascend' *kāṭṭŭ* 'show'
maṅkŭ 'become dim' *taḷḷŭ* 'push aside'
eṇṇŭ 'count, think' *eḷḷŭ* 'disregard'

(2) The following are some of the bases of this class not ending in short *ŭ* :—

vai 'abuse' *pāy* 'flow (as water)'
ey 'shoot' *ōy* 'cease'
koy 'cut' *puku* 'enter'
cey 'do' *naku* 'laugh'
pey 'pour, rain' *uku* 'be scattered'
aḻu 'weep' *toṭu* 'touch'
uḻu 'plough' *iṭu* 'give alms'
toḻu 'venerate' *paṭu* 'suffer'
kāy 'be heated'

C. The following are some of the roots which are accented or unaccented according to sense :—

iṭi 'powder, become powdered'

aḻi 'destroy, be destroyed'

oḷi 'conceal, hide oneself'

oṭi 'break, be broken'

uri 'peal off (as the skin), be pealed'

eri 'burn, be burnt'

viṭu 'disentangle or cause to leave, leave'

keṭu 'ruin, be ruined'

maṟai 'hide, be lost to view'

uṭai 'break, be broken'

arai 'grind, be ground'

aṭai 'put into, go into'

karai 'dissolve, be dissolved'

NOTE :—This complex classification may be contrasted with the uniformity that has been attained in Telugu.

99. THE PRESENT TENSE SUFFIXES *-kiṟu*, *-kiṉṟu*.

Paradigms Suffix *-kiṟu* reduced to *-ku* in some cases.

Corrupt forms. Explanation of dialectical forms.

(*a*) The present tense suffixes are *-kiṟu* and *-kiṉṟu*. The suffix *-kiṟu* is universal in the popular dialect ; it is also now used in literary works though unknown to Old and Mediaeval Tamil. The suffix *-kiṉṟu* is confined to a literature and is not heard in the common speech of the people.

Present tense paradigms

Accented base *paṭi* 'read'

		Singular		Plural
1.		*paṭi-k-kiṟ-ēn*		*paṭi-k-kiṟ-ōm*
	(Coll.)	*paṭi-k-kṟēn*	(Coll.)	*paṭi-k-kṟōm*
2.		*paṭi-k-kiṟ-āy*		*paṭi-k-kiṟ-īr*
	(Coll.)	*paṭi-k-kṟāy*	(Coll.)	*paṭi-k-kṟīr*
3.	M.	*paṭi-k-kiṟ-āṉ*		*paṭi-k-kiṟ-ar*
	F.	*paṭi-k-kiṟ-āḷ*		
	(Coll.) M.	*paṭi-k-kṟāṉ*	(Coll.)	*paṭi-k-kṟ-ār*
	F.	*paṭi-k-kṟāḷ*		
	N.	*paṭi-k-kiṟ-atu*		*paṭi-k-kiṟ-atu*
	(Coll.)	*paṭi-k-kṟ-atu*	(Coll.)	*paṭi-k-kṟ-atu*

Unaccented base *ōṭu* 'run'

		Singular		Plural
1.		*ōṭu-kiṟ-ēṉ*		*ōṭu-kiṟ-ōm*
	(Coll.)	*ōṭu-ṟ-ēṉ*	(Coll.)	*ōṭu-ṟ-ōm*
2.		*ōṭu-kiṟ-āy*		*ōṭu-kiṟ-īr*
	(Coll.)	*ōṭu-ṟāy*	(Coll.)	*ōṭu-ṟ-ār*
3.	M.	*ōṭu-kiṟ-āṉ*		*ōṭu-kiṟ-ār*
	F.	*ōṭu-kiṟ-āḷ*		
	(Coll.) M.	*ōṭu-ṟ-āṉ*	(Coll.)	*ōṭu-ṟ-ār*
	F.	*ōṭu-ṟ-āḷ*		
	N.	*ōṭu-kiṟ-atu*		*ōṭu-kiṟ-atu*
	(Coll.)	*ōṭu-ṟatu*	(Coll.)	*ōṭu-kiṟ-atu*

In colloquial speech the *i* of *kiṟu* is elided after accented bases, the whole syllable *ki* being lost after unaccented bases. The third person neuter is often *naṭakkutu*, *ōṭutu*, *pōkutu*, *ēṟutu* etc., both in the singular and in the plural in vulgar speech. In the grammatical dialect no elision takes place, and *-kiṉṟu* may be substituted for *-kiṟu*; the third person neuter plurals in this dialect are *paṭikkiṉṟaṉa, ōṭukiṉṟaṉa, pōkiṉṟaṉa* etc.

(*b*) In the case of the verb substantive *iru* 'be' and of *kiṭa* 'be, lie uncared for' which are both accented the present tense suffix *-kiṟu* which in the colloquial language becomes *-kṟu* by the loss of the vowel *i*, finally becomes *-ku* by the assimilation of *ṟ* to *k*. Examples:—

		Singular	Plural.	Singular	Plural
1.		*irukkēṉ*	*irukkōm*	*kiṭakkēṉ*	*kiṭakkōm*
2.		*irukkāy*	*irukkīr*	*kiṭakkāy*	*kiṭakkīr*
3.	M.	*irukkāṉ*	*irukkār*	*kiṭakkāṉ*	*kiṭakkār*
	F.	*irukkāḷ*		*kiṭakkāḷ*	
	N.	*irukkutu*	*irukkutu*	*kiṭakkutu*	*kiṭakkutu*
		irukku	*irukku*	*kiṭakku*	*kiṭakku*

This use of *kiṭakku* and *irukku* originally *kiṭakkṟu* and *irukkṟu* in the neuter without personal endings is probably a remnant of their former use in all person and numbers without personal terminations. The Labbai hawkers even now use *irikkiri*, in the third person neuter without any personal ending. *Muttu irikkiri, pavaḻam irikkiri* etc. 'Pearls there are, coral beads there are (with me)'.

(*c*) *Corrupt forms:*—The forms of the verb substantive undergo corruptions of other kinds among the lower working classes and in Tamil dialects.

Thus in the town of Madras *irukkiṟāṉ* 'he is' becomes *īkiṟāṉ* with loss of *ru* and compensative lengthening of the initial *i*; and also *kīṟāṉ* by a shifting of the accent and the consequent loss of the intial *i*.

(*d*) The Linguistic Survey gives specimens of Tamil dialects spoken by Tamil tribes who have wandered from the Tamil country and are settled in the Bombay Presidency,

Berar and the Central Provinces. In these dialects the suffix *kir* enters into the formation of the present tense :—

Korava or Yerukala. *igarū* "he is", *igadu* "it is" *sāgārē* "I die". (L.S.N., Vol. IV, p. 320.)

Kaikāḍī. *igarī* "I am", *igada* "It is", *igadgā* "they are". In Berar *kiri* " I am " etc. are used instead. (L.S.N., Vol. IV, p. 335.)

Burgaṇḍī.	Singular	(1) *sīrē* (2) *sirā* (2) sir
	Plural	(1) *sirū* (2) *sirū* (3) *sirū*

S in the above is interchangeable with *c*. Thus *cir* "he is", *ciṟu* "they are" are also found. Such forms correspond to *kiri* 'I am' of the Kaikāḍī dialect. (L.S.N., Vol. IV, pp. 343 and 344.)

The correct explanation of these corrupt forms appears to be that the substantive base *iru* which becomes *i* in Kaikāḍī and Korava is elided altogether as in some forms of vulgar Tamil in Madras, *k* being palatalized at the same time. Professor Sten Konow appears, however, to take the *kir* of these forms to be a verb substantive and to identify the present tense suffix -*kiṟu* with this verb substantive. (L.S.N., Vol. IV, p. 296.)

100. THE PAST TENSE SUFFIXES

t-iṉa. Various forms of the conjunctive participle.

(*a*) The characteristic signs and letters of the past tense are mentioned in grammars as *t*, *ṭ*, *ṟ* and *iṉ* ; here *t* and *ṭ* include also the corresponding medial sounds *d* and *ḍ* which they have after unaccented roots. Of these six signs *ṭ*, *ḍ* and *ṟ* are merely modifications which *t* undergoes when combining with the final consonants of verbal bases. Thus *l*+*t* becomes *ṟṟ* or *ṉṟ*, *ṉ*+*t* becomes *ṉṟ*; *ṇ*+*t* becomes *ṇṭ*; and *ḷ*+*t* becomes *ṭṭ* or *ṇṭ*.

Examples: 1st person singular:—

kal+t+ēṉ=kaṟṟēṉ 'I learnt'
vil+t+ēṉ=viṟṟēṉ 'I sold'
cel+t+ēṉ=ceṉṟēṉ 'I went'
vel+t+ēṉ=veṉṟēṉ 'I conquered'
tiṉ+t+ēṉ=tiṉṟēṉ 'I ate'
uṇ+t+ēṉ=uṇṭēṉ 'I ate'
kēḷ+t+ēṉ=kēṭṭēṉ 'I heard'
koḷ+t+ēṉ=koṇṭēṉ 'I bought'

The original signs of the past-tense-forms will hence be only two, *viz.*, *t* and *iṉ*; there is reason to believe that *iṉ* was not in use in the oldest stage of the language and that the short *ŭ* bases which now use *iṉ* in the formation of their past relative participles and tense forms then used the suffix *i*, which they use even now in forming their conjunctive participles.

(*b*) The past is the only tense in Modern Tamil which has a verbal participle from which tense-forms can be derived by adding personal terminations. These participles (conjunctive) are derived by suffixing *tu* or *i* to the base and the forms which they assume for the various classes of roots described above are as follows:—

(i) Accented. A (1) *iruntu, kiṭantu, naṭantu, maṟantu* from *iru, kiṭa, naṭa, maṟa.*

(ii) All other accented roots. A (2), A (3), A (4), and C. *paṭittu, naṭittu*; *ceyvittu, naṭappittu*; *kāyttu, kaṟṟu*; *pārttu, paṭuttu*; *iṭittu, oḻittu*; from A (2) *paṭi, naṭi*; A (3) *ceyvi, naṭappi*; A (4) *pār, kāy, kal, paṭu*; *and* (C) *iṭi, oḻi.*

(iii) Unaccented roots ending in short ŭ. B (1) *ōṭi, kāṭṭi, ēṟi, eṇṇi, eḷḷi* from *ōṭŭ, kāṭṭŭ, ēṟŭ, eṇṇŭ, eḷḷŭ.*

(iv) All other unaccented roots, B (2) and C *vaitu, eytu, koytu, ceytu, peytu, aḻutu, uḻutu, toḻutu; toṭṭu, iṭṭu, viṭṭu; ceṉṟu, veṉṟu, koṉṟu, koṇṭu, iṭintu, oḷintu.*

From B (2) *vai, ey, koy, cey, pey, aḻu, uḻu, toḻu; toṭu, iṭu, viṭu; cel, vel, kol, koḷ;* (C) *iṭi, oḷi.*

(*c*) In colloquial speech *-ttu* and *-ntu* become *-ccu* and *-ñcu* after *y* and palatal vowels, and *-ṉṟu* becomes *-ṉṉu* always. Thus *paṭittu, iṭittu, iṭintu, oḷintu, uṭaittu, maṟaintu, ceṉṟu, koṉṟu,* etc. become *paṭiccu, iṭiccu, iṭiñcu, oḷiñcu, uṭaiccu, maraiñcu, ceṉṉu, koṉṉu* etc. The past relative participles are formed by adding *a* to these conjunctive participles:—*naṭanta, ceṉṟa, koṇṭa, kēṭṭa* etc.

(*d*) It will be seen that bases ending in short *ŭ* form their conjunctive participles with the suffix *i*; relative participles and finite verbs (agent nouns) derived from these conjunctive participles will be *ōṭiya* 'that ran', *kāṭṭiya* 'that showed', *ēṟiya* 'that ascended' etc., *ōṭiyāṉ* 'he ran,' *kāṭṭiyōm* 'we showed', *ēṟiyār* 'they ascended' etc. These forms were current in Old Tamil but have now been displaced by forms containing the tense sign *iṉ*—*ōṭiṉa, kāṭṭiṉa, ēriṉa, ōṭiṉāṉ, kāṭṭiṉōm, ēṟiṉār* etc.; there is, however, no conjunctive participle containing the suffix *-iṉ* either in Old or Modern Tamil.

(*e*) Bases not ending in short *ŭ* form their conjunctive participles with the suffix *tu*, the initial *t* of which is doubled after accented bases not included in class A (1); the number of unaccented bases after which *tu* is sounded as *du* can be counted on one's fingers. After all other unaccented bases and after accented bases included in class A (1) *tu* becomes *uṭu*.

(*f*) Conjunctive participles are sometimes used in the sense of present participles. Examples :—

Ōṭi vantāṉ 'he came running'. *naṭantu vantāṉ* 'he came walking'. *āṟṟai nīnti-k-kaṭantāṉ* 'he crossed the river swimming'.

To avoid ambiguity the auxiliary participle *viṭṭu* is often added to indicate a past signification; and the auxiliary participle *-koṇṭu* is added to indicate a continuing action. Examples :—

cāppiṭṭu viṭṭu 'after having eaten'
muṭittuv ṭṭu 'after finishing', 'having finished'
tūṅki-k-koṇṭu irukkiṟāṉ 'he is sleeping'

Viṭṭu is the past verbal participle of *viṭu* 'leave'; *koṇṭu* is supposed to be the past verbal participle of the reflexive auxiliary *koḷ*.

101. THE FUTURE TENSE-SUFFIXES *-p, v.*

Examples from old inscriptions showing the original gerundive sense of the suffixes :—

(*a*) The characteristic letters of the future are *p, v.*

Base		Singular	Plural
iru 'be'	1.	*iruppēṉ*	*iruppōm*
vā 'come'	2.	*varuvāy*	*varuvīr*
tiṉ 'eat'	3. M.	*tiṉpāṉ*	*tiṉpār*
		tiṉpāḷ	
	n.	*irukkum*	*irukkum*
		varum	*varum*
		tiṉṉum	*tiṉṉum*

The letter *v* arises from the weakening of *p* after unaccented roots; *p* after nasals is pronounced *b*. The neuter termination *-um* arises from the elision of *k* in *-kum* after unaccented roots.

(*b*) The neuter forms in *-kum* and *-um* are the remnants of an old conjugation which appears to have been used formerly in other persons also, as it is even now in Malayāḷam; in vulgar speech they are in some places even now used in the Tamil country in the 3rd person masculine and feminine singular.

The forms in *-kum* and *-um* express simple futurity or the habitual present. The forms in *p* and *v* rarely express mere futurity; in most cases they imply contingency, will, obligation, or promise. In colloquial speech simple futurity is often expressed by the present forms in *kiṟu*. *nāḷaikku varukiṟēṉ* 'I will come to-morrow'.

(*c*) There is a 3rd person neuter singular form in *p* or *v* which was formerly much used in laying down rules and regulations; the following examples are taken from a Tamil inscription of the 9th century containing regulations for the management of a temple and of the attached seminary in Travancore (T.A.S., Vol. I, pp. 1 to 18).

(1) *paṇi kuttu-k-kāl paṭāmal ceyvippatu* 'The business should be done without obstruction'.

(2) *muppattāṟu kuṭam nīr koṭuppatu* 'Thirtysix pots of water should be given'.

(3) *kuṟaivaṟa koṭuppatu* 'should be given without any deficiency'.

(4) *poruvār aṟṟai-k-kalam iḻappatu* 'Those who gamble (quarrel) shall lose the day's meals'.

(5) *poṉ taṇṭamum paṭṭu kaṭamaiyum koṭuppatu* 'The tax should be paid in addition to the fine of gold'.

(*d*) A form ending in *-vum* implying order or command occurs frequently in letters addressed to inferiors. Examples:—

Cīkkiram aṉuppavum 'let (it) be sent soon'

Patil uṭaṉē eḻutavum 'reply immediately'

(*e*) Another class of words expressing obligation are derived from *kaṭava*—which is joined to an infinitive.

Ceyya-k-kaṭavēṉ 'I shall be bound to do'

Koṭukka-k-kaṭavāy 'You shall be bound to give'

Celutta-k-kaṭaviyar 'They shall be bound to pay'

102. OTHER FINITE VERB FORMS

Imperatives, *Benedictives*. and *Injunctives*

(*a*) *Imperatives.* The imperative second person singular is the verbal base itself; the plural is formed by adding *-um*, *-miṉ* or *-miṉir* to the base; *-um* and *-kaḷ* together form a double plural. Examples :—

Singular	*Naṭa* 'walk';	*cey* 'do'.
Plural	*Naṭavum*,	*ceyyum*;
	Naṭamiṉ,	*ceymmiṉ*;
	Naṭavuṅkaḷ,	*ceyyuṅkaḷ*.

El and *al* are also imperative suffixes; the former is always used in prohibiting; the latter may be used in enjoining or prohibiting. *Ka* may be added to the negative *al* in the singular and may be added in the plural.

(1) *Naṭavēl*, *naṭavaṟka*, *naṭavaṉmiṉ*, (pl.) 'do not walk'.

(2) *Makaṉ eṉal makkat pataṭi eṉal* 'do not call him a man (but) call him the chaff of mankind'.

(3) *Olluvatu ellām ceyal* 'do everything possible'.

There is also a permissive imperative with the suffix *-kaṭṭum* or *-kaṭṭu* of which the initial *k* is elided after unaccented roots. Examples :—

Avaṉ paṭikkaṭṭum 'let him read'

Nāṉ varaṭṭā 'may I come ?'

Avaḷ pokaṭṭum 'let her go'

The forms are the same for all persons, numbers and genders.

(*b*) *Benedictives* and *injunctives* are obtained by adding *ka* to the verbal bases; they are the same for all persons, numbers and genders. The initial *k* is elided after unaccented roots.

Aracaṉ vāḻa 'long live the king'
Avarkaḷ ellārum keṭa 'may they all perish'
Naṭakka 'walk'; *uṭkārka* or *uṭkāra* 'sit'

These forms have a precative sense in the 2nd person and are much used by Śrī Vaiṣṇavas.

There is a very rare variant *aṟpir* or *āppir* of *al-miṉ* the suffix of the negative imperative plural which is sometimes used in cursing and is a strong injunctive. Examples:—

tuṟakkam pukāppir 'you shall not enter heaven'.

103. Eccam or incomplete Forms

Relative participles—Adverbial participles

Tamil grammars arrange incomplete forms under two heads—*peyar-eccam* and *viṉai-y-eccam*. The former is what European grammarians call 'relative participles', while the latter head includes infinitives, subjunctives, conjunctive participles, etc.

(*a*) Relative participles are of the forms:—

	Present	*Past*	*Future*
Paṭi 'read'	*Paṭikkiṟa* 'that reads' *paṭikkiṉṟa*	*Paṭitta*	*Paṭikkum*
cey 'do'	*ceykiṟa* 'that does' *ceykiṉṟa*	*ceyta*	*ceyyum*
kāṭṭu 'show'	*kāṭṭukiṟa* 'that shows' *kāṭṭukiṉṟa*	*kāṭṭiṉa*	*kāṭṭum*

(*b*) The second class—*viṉai-y-eccam*—of incomplete forms are stated in Naṉṉūl to be of the following types:—

ceytu, ceypu, ceyyā, ceyyū, ceyteṉa, ceya, ceyin, ceyyiya, ceyyiyar, ceyvāṉ, naṭappāṉ, ceypākku.

Of these the first five are stated to show the past tense, the sixth to show the present tense, and the remaining six, the future.

The type *ceytu* which includes the type *kāṭṭi* is what has been called the conjunctive participle ; it is by suffixing *a* to this that the past relative participle is obtained. Participles from which present relative participles have been similarly derived by suffixing *a* are not now in use.

The types, *ceypu*, *ceyyā*, *ceyyū*, *ceyteṉa* are now wholly confined to the literary dialect; the first three of these are really present participles in sense.

The type *ceyiṉ* is a subjunctive form.

The types *ceya, ceyyiya, ceyyiyar, ceyvāṉ, naṭappāṉ, ceypākku*, are all infinitives of purpose. Of these, only the first is in use in the colloquial dialect. The other five are found only in the literary dialect. The last three *ceyvāṉ, naṭāppāṉ, ceypākku* are practically unknown to Old Tamil and are not mentioned in Tolkāppiyam.

104. MISCELLANEOUS FORMS

Verbal nouns—Infinitives—Subjunctives

(*a*) *Verbal nouns:*—These are usually formed by adding *-al, -tal, -pu,* etc., to the base. There is reason to believe that the *t* in *tal* is only a formative letter interposed between the suffix and the base. The origin of this *t* and the other formative letters will be adverted to in a later chapter. Examples:—

(1) *ceyal, ōṭal, ēṟal* 'doing, running, ascending'.

(2) *naṭattal, ceytal, ōṭutal* 'walking, doing, running'.

(3) *necavu* 'weaving', *uḻavu* 'ploughing', *aṟuppu* 'reaping'.

(*b*) *Infinitives*:—

(i) The infinitive of purpose is the 4th case of the verbal noun in *al* or *tal*.

ceyaṟku (*ceyal*), *ceytaṟku* (*ceytal*), *ōṭaṟku* (*ōṭal*), *naṭattaṟku* (*naṭattal*).

(ii) Infinitives of purpose are also formed by adding *a* or *ka* to the verbal base, *k* being elided as usual after unaccented roots. Examples:—

paṭikka, ceyka, ceyya, āṭuka (*āṭa*).

These forms are also used in the senses of: (1) so as to, so that; (2) at the time that, when, while. Examples:—

(1) *avaṉai viḻa utaittār* he kicked him so as to cause him to fall down'.

(2) *poḻutu viṭiya vantārkaḷ* 'they came when the day was breaking'.

In Old Tamil and often in poetry *-ppa* is used instead of *-kka* after accented roots. Examples:—

naṭappa, iruppa.

(iii) Forms like *ceyyiya, ceyyiyar,* 'for doing', *ōṭuvāṉ* 'for running', *naṭappāṉ*, *naṭappākku* 'for walking', are also used as infinitives of purpose in poetry.

(*c*) *Subjunctives.* The suffixes in use are : *ēl, āl, iṉ, il.*

The first of these is used with finite verbs (future chiefly), the second chiefly with past verbal participles, and the third and the fourth with the uninflected. Examples:—

naṭappāṉēl 'if he will walk'.

maḻai peytāl, 'if it rains'.

avaḷ variṉ 'if she comes'.

avar uṇṇil 'if they eat'.

105. Causal Bases

These bases are formed in literary Tamil by adding *vi* or *pi* to the root according as this is unaccented or accented; the original suffix was throughout *-pi*, but this has been softened to *-vi* after unaccented roots. Examples:—

ceyvi, varuvi, naṭappi, niṟpi.

These casuals appear to have been adopted late and have not yet displaced the old causal bases corresponding to the conjugations of pro-Dravidian period; these old bases maintain their ground and are preferred in popular speech to the later literary forms.

Non-causal root or base	Causal base	Non-causal root or base	Causal base
naṭa 'walk'	*naṭattu*	*eḻumpu* 'rise'	*eḻuppu*
nil 'stand'	*niṟuttu*	*tirumpu* 'turn'	*tiruppu*
vā (*varu*) 'come'	*varuttu*	*kiḷampu* 'get up'	*kiḷappu*
iru 'be, sit'	*iruttu*	*peruku* 'increase'	*perukku*
aḻuntu 'sink'	*aḻuttu*	*uruku* 'melt'	*urukku*
poruntu 'fit'	*poruttu*	*iṟuku* 'become tight'	*iṟukku*

The genesis and the formation of these old bases will be fully dealt with when dealing with pro-Dravidian aorists and past tense forms.

NOTE.—Many causals formed with the suffixes *vi* and *pi* have, in course of time, acquired shades of meaning slightly different from the old causals formed with the suffixes *-tu*, *-pu*, *-ku*.

2. TAMIL DIALECTS

106. KORAVA OR YERUKALA

The Koravas or Yerukalas are a wandering tribe of basket and mat-makers, pig-breeders, etc. They are found all over the Madras Presidency and in several districts of the Bombay Presidency. (L.S., Vol. IV, p. 318.)

(*a*) The present tense is formed in this dialect as in Tamil:—*aḍikēri* 'I strike', *hōgārē* 'I go', *aḍikir*, 'I shall strike', *sāgārē* 'I die', *igarū* 'he is'. The suffixes *kēr*, *kēr*, *gār* are clearly identical with the Tamil *kkiṟa kiṟa*. (L.S.Vol. IV, 320.)

(*b*) The past tense is formed by adding the suffixes *sa*, and *na*, or, in most cases, in the same way as in Tamil:—*aḍasā* 'thou struckest', *hōnū* 'he went', *kuḍatū* 'he gave', *kuḍatā* 'she gave', *vañcu* 'it came'.

107. KAIKADI

Kaikāḍīs are a wandering tribe of mat-makers found in the Bombay Presidency, Berar and Central provinces (L.S., Vol. IV, 333.)

(*a*) The present tense of the verb substantive is as follows:—*igarī* 'I am' *garā* 'thou art' *igarū* 'he is' *igada* 'it is', *igar* 'we are' *igrāng* 'you are' *igrāng* 'they are' *igadga* 'they (neuter) are'. In Berar we find *kiri* etc. used instead. (L.S., Vol. IV, 335, 666, 668.)

(*b*) The present tense of finite verbs is formed by adding a suffix *ak* (*gak*) or *ar*. Thus *iḍḍukī* 'I strike', *varāk*

'It comes' *kōgākī* 'I go', *nikyakā* 'thou art'. In Kolaba *pogārē* 'I go', *sonārē* 'I say', *śeyārō* 'he is doing'. In Ramdrug *sagārī* 'I die'. (L.S., Vol. IV, 335.)

(*c*) The past tense is formed by means of the same suffixes as in Tamil.

Forms such as *śeidutu* 'he has done', *yakpisutu* 'he spent' are compounds. Compare Tamil *uṟṟēṉ* pronounced *uttēṉ* 'I was'. Forms such as *bhēṭitsnō* 'he met', *vantsa* 'it came', *tiṅgantsga* 'the pigs ate', should be compared with the vulgar Tamil forms such as *paṭiccān* 'he learned', *paṭiccatu*' it learnt'; *āccu*, *āccutu* instead of *āyiṟṟu* 'it became', 'it was'; *Āsa* 'it was' in a specimen received from Akola, directly corresponds to the vulgar Tamil *āccu*.

In Ellichpur we find forms such as *pesus* 'he said', *guḍtusu*, 'he gave'; *hōsu* 'he went'. They appear to contain the suffix *-tsa* or *-tsu* of the 3rd person neuter. Similar forms occur in Burgaṇḍī also.

(*d*) The future apparently corresponds to the Tamil present. Thus *ikarī* 'I shall be', *eḍkirī* 'I shall arise', *iḍrī* 'shall strike', *hōgrī* 'I shall go'. (L.S., Vol. IV, 335.)

(*e*) *Kaikāḍī* thus agrees with vulgar Tamil in most respects. Like other Tamil dialects, in several points, it agrees with Kanarese, and it must therefore be derived from an older form when Tamil and Kanarese had not as yet been differentiated so much as is the case at the present day. (L. S., Vol. IV, 333.)

108. BURGANDI

Burgaṇḍī is the dialect of another vagrant tribe in Nimar and the Central India Agency. It is closely connected with *Kaikāḍī*, but is apparently dying out. (L.S., Vol. IV, 343.)

(*a*) The following are the forms of the present tense of the verb substantive. (L.S., Vol. IV, 343.)

Singular	Plural
1. *sirē*	1. *sirū*
2. *sirā*	2. *sirū*
3. *sir*	3. *sirū*

S is in this verb interchangeable with *c*. Thus we also find *cir* 'he is', *cirū* 'they are'. Such forms correspond to *kirē* 'I am', and so forth in some forms of *Kaikāḍī*. (L.S., Vol. IV, 344.)

(*b*) The past tense of the verb substantive is given as *nīḍis* in all persons and numbers. The first specimen, however, contains the plural form *nīḍisu* 'they were'.

(*c*) The present tense of finite verbs is formed much as in *Kaikāḍī*. Thus *nikakē*, 'I live', *sāgākē* 'I die', *pōgākē* 'I go', *tiṅgākō* 'let us eat', *siyākō* 'let us do', *tiṅgakū* 'they eat'.

(*d*) The past tense is formed by one of the suffixes *s* (or *c*) and *n*. Thus *aḍsē* 'I struck'; *aḍsa* 'thou struckest'; *aḍic* 'he struck'; *aḍcū* 'we, you, or they struck'; *pōinē* 'I went'; *pōina* 'thou wentest'; *pōs* 'he went'; *pōinō* 'we went'; *pōinang* 'you or they went'; *señjē* 'I did'; *sēja* 'thou didst'; *señjō* 'we did'; *akna* 'thou madest'; *tiṅgasū* 'they ate'; *nikasū* 'they lived'.

The 3rd person singular always ends in *s* or *c*. Thus *thōrac* 'he sent', *patas* 'he saw', *pōras* 'he ran', *ēnpiskus* 'he wasted', *vañc* 'he came'. *Is* or *as* is sometimes added. Thus *mandisōs* and *mandisis* 'he began'; *pēsis* or *pesus* 'he said'; *sējus* 'he did'.

(*e*) There are several other forms which apparently contain a suffix *-yō*. Thus *vaṅgyōt* 'I drove'; *vaṅgus* and *vaṅgyōtus* 'he drove'; *ēleyōs* 'he went'; *vagyōs* 'it happened'.

Forms such as *elyō nīḍis* 'he had gone', *lit.* 'gone he was' seem to point to the conclusion that this *-yō* is the suffix of a past participle passive. It is therefore probably borrowed from *Rājasthānī*.

A perfect is *vañcir* 'he has come'. It is formed from the conjunctive participle *vañc* by adding *ir*, another form of *sir* ' he is.'

(*f*) The future is apparently formed as in *Kaikāḍī*. Thus *aḍikra* 'thou wilt strike'; *agarē* 'I shall be'; *agar* and *agyōgar* 'he will be', *Mētarisuṅga* 'I shall fill', is in its termination apparently a *Rājasthānī* form. Other forms are *khālakē* 'I shall go', *sarlē* 'I shall say', *Koḍturē* 'I shall give', *pōrakē* 'I shall throw'.

Note.—Everything stated above in regard to Tamil dialects is taken almost *verbatim* from the Linguistic Survey of India.

OLD TAMIL

Note.—*Tol-kāppiyam* is our main authority for the grammatical forms of Old Tamil but the work does not refer to tense-suffixes as such though of course it gives verb-forms containing such suffixes; in fact the term *iṭainilai* does not occur in the work at all. One is therefore left in considerable doubt as to which of the suffixes of modern Tamil were in use in that early period. The commentaries supply the omission, but having been written several centuries after the date of Tolkāppiyam, they will naturally include later developments and formations, and are not reliable authorities in all cases for the grammatical forms of the archaic period. It has therefore been thought necessary to examine all the verb-forms occurring in Tolkāppiyam itself and the Caṅkam and other early Tamil works mentioned already. The results of this examination may be summarised thus—It is surmised that the omission in Tolkāppiyam to enumerate or classify the tense-suffixes may partly be due to the difficulty of saying except with reference to the context what tense any particular participle indicated. It is also possible that the grammarians then regarded a pronominalised verb as made up of a participle and a pronominal ending and had not yet risen to the conception of a tense suffix or sign.

109. THE PAST TENSE.

This was the only tense in Old Tamil which denoted a definite time; all other tenses were practically aorists.

The signs of the past tense were as in modern Tamil *t*, *d* (intervocal *t*), *nt* and *i* or *iṉ*, but poets occasionally formed the conjunctive participles with *i* even in the case of bases which did not end in short *ŭ*. Example :—

micaii 'having eaten' from *micai* 'eat'; *malaii* 'having warred' from *malai* 'war', *kuṟii* 'having intended' from *kuṟi* intend.

Such forms occur in Tolkāppiyam itself.[1] It is not possible to say now whether this was merely a poetical license or was a characteristic of the living language of the time.

Finite verbs formed conjunctive participles ending in *i* were as numerous in Old Tamil as the finite verbs containing the tense suffix *-iṉ*, but past relative participles always ended in *-iya*, and not one ending in *-ina* could be found in the earliest works. Both the relative participles in *-iya* and the finite verbs formed from conjunctive participles ending in *-i* have now fallen into disuse except in a few stereotyped cases like *vēṇṭiya* ' required', *nāṭiya* 'desired', etc., but the

1. *Vide* Tolkāppiyam I, 83; 121; 141; 226; II, 40; 57; 115; 163.

existence of the former in colloquial Malāyaḷam and of the latter in colloquial Telugu would show that they were once in common use in the speech of the people in the Tamil land also.

110. THE T-AORIST

This suffix was different in origin from the *-t* suffix of the past tense and was confined to the 1st and 2nd persons only. The suffix combined with the personal endings took the forms: 1st person (sing.) *-tu*, (plur.) *-tum*; 2nd person (sing.) *-ti* or *-tai*, (plur.) *-tir*. The use of *t* in many of the following examples merely shows the intervocal pronunciation like that of the *t* of the past tense. The aorist *t* also changed to *ṭ* and *ṟ* in combination with the final of the base. Examples :—

(1) *niṉaiti* 'you think'.

(2) *kāṇṭi* 'please see'.

(3) *cēṟi, ceṉṟī, ēkuti* ' please go'.

(4) *eṉṟi* (1) 'you will say'. (2) 'you say'. (3) 'you are in the habit of saying'.

(5) *irattir* (1) 'you will beg'. (2) ' you beg'

(6) *viṉavutir* 'you will ask'.

(7) *kaṭattir* 'you cross'.

(8) *varutum* 'we will come'.

(9) *puṉiṟu nāṟutum* 'we smell of confinement (childbirth)'.

(10) *varuntutum* 'we will suffer'.

(11) *oṉṟutum* ' we will be with you'.

The above examples show that these *t* forms constituted an aorist tense. These aorist forms were in extensive use in Old Tamil, but they are now unknown to the spoken

Tamil of the people and are but rarely used in literary Tamil having been superseded in both these dialects by tense-forms containing the suffixes-*kiṟu* and -*kiṉṟu*. The Old Tamil *t* forms correspond to the aorist tense in Telugu and must have been in popular use in old times. Their total disappearance from colloquial speech is doubtless due to the confusion between them and the dental past forms.

111. THE K-AORIST

This suffix used sometimes with, sometimes without personal endings, took the following forms:—1st person singular -*ku*, 1st person plural -*kum*, 3rd person singular and neuter plural -*kum* which usually became -*um* after unaccented roots; but -*k* was never elided in the 1st person. -*Ku* and -*kum* in the 1st person often had an infinitival force. The ordinary personal endings were sometimes added to -*ku* in the 1st person. Examples :—

(1) *teḻikku* 'I assure (you)' (Kali: 88, 91).

(2) *mey toṭuku* 'I touch (your) body' (=I swear) (*Ibid.* 95).

(3) *niṉ aṇi nalaṉ nukarku* 'I will enjoy your graces'. (Pattu: VIII-181.)

(4) *nāṭaṟi naṉ maṇam ayarkam* 'we shall have a proper wedding in public'. (Pattu: VIII-232.)

(5) *uṉṟan arum tuyar kaḷaikēṉ* 'I will remove your unbearable suffering'. (Cilap : XV-6, 68.)

(6) *yāṅku aṟikōm ayya* 'How can we know, sir'. (*Ibid* VII-6.)

(7) *irakku vārēn* 'I will not come to beg'. (Patiṟṟu: 61.)

(8) *naṭukku nōy kaimmikum* 'The trembling increases. (Cilap: XVIII.)

(9) *mayaṅkum eṉ neñcu* 'my mind reels'. (*Ibid.*)

(10) *villavaṅkōtai vēntaṟku uraikkum* 'Villavaṅkōtai replies to the king'. (Cilap: XXV, 151.)

(11) *kāṇku vanticiṉ* 'I have come to see'. (Patiṟṟu: 16.)

(12) *uraikkēṉ, paṭarkēṉ* 'I shall say, I shall go'. (Maṇi: Chap. XI, XII.)

It is obvious from the above examples that *-ku* in the 1st person signified the present or the future. With the personal endings *-eṉ*, *-am*, *-ōm* it signified the future; such *k* forms with personal endings are now confined to the negative voice. The use of *-kum* in the 1st person plural was rare; here *-m* is the sign of the plural number. *-Kum* and *-um* in the 3rd person singular and neuter plural often signified the present in addition to their usual sense of the future and the habitual present; here *-m* has taken the place of a previous *-p*.

112. THE P-AORIST

(*a*) Tense forms with the *-p* suffix expressed not only futurity, obligation, promise etc. as in modern Tamil, but were often used with a present signification. One well-known instance of the use of *p* (*v*) to signify the present, which has survived into modern Tamil is in the attestation of documents where each witness writes *aṟivēṉ* after his signature, which means 'I know'. The suffix was also extensively used for forming the *nomen actionis* and the *nomen agentis*.

(1) *yāṉ aṟikuveṉ atu paṭṭateṉṟu uraippōṉ* "He replies saying 'I know how it happened'." (Cilap: Patikam-*l*. 11.)

(2) *makiḻ viḻā-k-kāṇpōṉ* 'he who *witnesses* the joyous festival'—that is—'while witnessing the joyous festival'. (Cilap : VI-*l*. 34.)

(3) *poṉṉurai kāṇpōr* 'gold assayers'. (Maṇi: XXVIII.)

(4) *varuvārum pōvārum* 'comers and goers'.

(5) *koḷvārum koṭuppārum* 'buyers and sellers', literally 'receivers and givers'.

(6) *naṭavu, uṭaippu, tiṟappu, ōyvu;* 'transplanting, breach, opening, cessation'.

These action and agent nouns are also very freely formed in modern Tamil.

(*b*) The 3rd person epicene plural suffix *-mār* which formed a future adverbial participle (an infinitive of purpose, in sense) may be mentioned here. (Tolkāppiyam II-209; Naṉṉūl 326.)

Ā koṇmār vantār 'They came to lift cattle'; *eḷḷumār vantārē iṅku* 'They came here intending to deride'.

In these instances and in the other examples given in grammars, *mār* appears to form agent nouns in the future tense. *Eḷḷumār* may well be regarded as made up of *eḷḷum* and *aṟ*, and *koṇmār* of *koḷḷum* and *ār*, *ār* being the ordinary epicene 3rd person plural suffix and *eḷḷum* and *koḷḷum* being future relative participles. The forms will then be the same as those of agent nouns referred to below, and it is also seen that they can be replaced in the above examples by *eḷḷuvār* and *koḷvār*.

(*c*) A plural termination *mār* also occurs in poetry in combination with the negative *al*, the combined *aṉmār* being the suffix of the negative imperative second person epicene plural: *pāṭiṉ maṉṉarai-p-pāṭaṉmār emarē* 'May not bards like myself sing (the praises of) ignoble kings.' (Puṟam. 375.) *Kāma* * * * *nōymali varuttam kāṇaṉmār emarē* 'May our class not suffer (witness) the pangs of unrequited love.' (Naṟṟiṇai 64.)

Cēṉāvaraiyar, the commentator on Tolkāppiyam explains *kāṇaṉmār* and *pāṭaṉmār* as the negatives of the finite verbs *kāṇpār* and *pāṭuvār* (that is as made up of *kāṇ+al+p+ār* and *pāṭu+al+v+ār*) and that *-p* and *-v* have been replaced by *-m* in the new compound.

113. BENEDICTIVES, INJUNCTIVES, AND PRECATIVES

One of the suffixes *-i*, *-iya*, *-iyar* was added to the root or base and the combination thus formed was used as a benedictive in all persons, numbers, and genders, without any further inflection.

vāḻi tōḻi 'may you flourish! friend' equivalent to the English 'God bless you! friend'.

vāḻiya nalaṉē 'may good (virtue) flourish'.

vāḻiyar vēntaṉ 'long live the king'.

poy-y-ākiyarō 'may (it) turn out false'. (Puṟam. 233.)

Benedictives and injunctives were also formed by adding *-ka* to the base. These were originally used only in the 3rd person as in Old Kanarese, but appear to have been gradually extended to other persons also. These forms had a precative sense in the 2nd person.

keṭuka niṉ avalam 'may your grief disappear'. (Pattu. VI-209.)

peṟuka til yāṉē 'may I get (it)'. (Puṟam. 306.)

vāraṟka tilla 'please do not come' (Kuṟuntokai 360.)

(*Note.*—*til* and *tilla* express wish.)

114. PEYARECCAM OR RELATIVE PARTICIPLES

(*a*) These are of the following types in Modern Tamil:—*ceyta* 'that did', *ceykiṉṟa* or *ceykiṟa* 'that does', and *ceyyum* 'that will do'.

In Old Tamil the types were *ceyta*, *ceyyum*, and *ceymmaṉa* (Tolkāppiyam II-224); thus showing perhaps that *kiṉṟu* and *kiṟu* had not come into use as signs of the present tense in those old days. Further *ceyyum* which now indicates future time was then the present and the aorist relative participle.

(*b*) There appears to be no instance of the use of *ceymmaṉa* as a future participle in Caṅkam works; but several instances occur in Tolkāppiyam itself of verbs with the suffix *maṉa*.

(1) *eṉmaṉār pulavar* 'learned men say'.

(2) *tiriyumaṉ payiṉṟē* (I-172) '(it) will change often'.

(3) *moḻimaṉār* (II-165) '(they) say'.

(4) *icaikkumaṉ collē* (II-1) 'words will connote'.

(5) *muṭiyumaṉ poruḷē* (II-233) 'the sense will become complete'.

In some of these cases the sense conveyed is not future but indefinite present.

(*c*) *Agent nouns*.—In Modern Tamil agent nouns like *ceytavaṉ*, *ceytavaḷ*, *ceykiṉṟavaṉ*, *ceykiṉṟavaḷ*, are formed from the relative participles *ceyta*, and *ceykiṉṟa*, but none from the future participle *ceyyum*. In Old Tamil such nouns were formed from *ceyyum* also.

(1) *uṇarumōr*, *teḷiyumōr* 'those that know'.

(2) *viyakkappaṭumōr* 'those that are admired'.

(3) *koyyumōṉ*, *vāḻumōr* 'reaper, residents'.

(4) *tam kuṭi niṟumār* 'those that establish (settle) their subjects'.

In Modern Tamil the above words assume the forms *uṇarvōr*, *teḷivōr*, *viyakkappaṭuvōr*, *koyvōṉ*, *vāḻvōr*, *niṟuppōr*, or *uṇarpavar*, *teḷipavar*, *viyakkappaṭupavar*, *koypavaṉ*, *vāḻpavar*, *niṟuppavar*.

Note.—The agent noun *naṭappavaṉ* 'walker, he who walks' from the accented root *naṭa* exists also as *naṭappōṉ*, the syllables *ava* being shortened into *ō*. Agent nouns from the unaccented roots *koy* 'cut', *vāḻ* 'reside', *teḷi* 'know' etc. should be *koyvavaṉ*, *vāḻvavaṉ*, *teḷivavaṉ* etc. and their shortened forms *koyvōṉ*, *vāḻvōṉ*, *teḷivōṉ*, etc.; but the longer forms exist only as *koypavaṉ*, *vaḻpavaṉ*, *teḷipavaṉ*, etc. through the operation of the law of dissimilation.

(*d*) In Puṟanāṉūṟu there are about twenty-five instances in which relative participles of the type *ceyyum* have *-tu* added to them. These may be regarded as neuter singular verbs or as agent nouns formed in the above manner.

(1) *nīrkkōḻi kūyppeyar-k-kuntu* 'the water-fowl scratching (scratches) the sail'. (395.)
(2) *micai-p-pāyuntu* 'jumping above'. (24.)
(3) *ariyal āruntu* 'drinking toddy'. (395.)
(4) *muttākuntu* 'becoming pearls'. (380.)
(5) *karai cērkkuntu* 'bringing to the shore'. (343.)

115. VINAIYECCAM OR ADVERBIAL PARTICIPLES

(*a*) In Old Tamil these were of the types, *ceytu*, *ceyyū*, *ceypu*, *ceyteṉa*, *ceyyiya*, *ceyyiyar*, *ceyiṉ*, *ceya*, *ceyaṟku*. (Tol. II.)

(*b*) Of these, *ceya* and *ceyaṟku* were infinitives, *ceyaṟku* being the fourth case of the verbal noun *ceya*, 'doing'; *ceyyiya* and *ceyyiyar* had mostly an infinitive sense though occasionally used as conjunctive participles also. *Ceyiṉ* was a subjunctive form, *Ceyyū* and *ceypu* were present participles though sometimes used with a past signification; *ceytu* which included the type *kāṭṭi* 'having shown' was the conjunctive participle proper. *Ceyteṉa* always indicated past time.

(*c*) The types *ceyvāṉ*, *naṭappāṉ*, *ceypākku* of Naṉṉūl are not mentioned in Tolkāppiyam. But there are a few instances (three have been counted)[1] of the types *ceyvāṉ*, *naṭappāṉ* in Caṅkam works. They appear to be imported Malayāḷam forms which occur largely in later literature but have failed to secure a place in the popular speech. Kuṟaḷ appears to be the earliest work, in which the suffix *pākku* occurs.

(*d*) There is reason to believe that infinitives of the type *ceya* like *paṭikka*, *pōka*, *tiṉṉa*, *vara* etc., originally ended in *l*, for there are forms like *āṭal toṭaṅku* in old poetry where we now say *āṭattoṭaṅku* 'begin to dance'. This surmise becomes a certainty when it is seen that *geyya* and *geyyal* 'doing' are both regarded as infinitives in Kanarese and that Kanarese grammarians regard the former as arising from the latter by the elision of the final *l*. (K.K.G.,S. 187 (2.). The following instances of the full form may be quoted from Naṟṟiṇai.

(1) *aḻal toṭaṅkiṉaḷ* 'she began to weep'. (371.)
(2) *koyal toṭaṅkiṉar* 'they began to cut'. (306.)
(3) *peyal toṭankiṉa* 'they began to pour'. (371.)

(*e*) Infinitives and subjunctives of accented roots are always of the form *naṭakka*, *naṭakkiṉ*, and *naṭakkil*, in modern colloquial Tamil. In Old Tamil they were always of the forms *naṭappa* and *naṭappiṉ*, and formations with double *-kk-* are very rare in really old works. The frequent occurrence of *-kk-* in infinitives and subjunctives is a sure sign of lateness. Other subjunctive terminations were *ēl* and *āl* as in modern Tamil.

(*f*) There were no instances of any adverbial present participles, but late in the Caṅkam period or after the close of it an abortive attempt appears to have been made to form present adverbial participles with the suffix *kiṉṟu*. Only three or four instances of such participles have been counted.

---

1. Pari : VII. 1. 57; X. 1. 9; Kali: 97.

Nīṭu-kiṉṟu ōṅkiya oru peruṅkōyil 'a large temple that grew up lengthening'. (Maṇi.)

kuḻavi aḻukiṉṟu eṉakku pāl tammiṉ nīr āṭṭumin eṉṟaḻātu "when an infant weeps it does not weep saying 'give me milk, wash me'.[1]"

This use of *kiṉṟu* may be compared to that of the auxiliary *koṇṭu* in colloquial Tamil as in *tūṅki-k-koṇṭu* 'sleeping'.

116. Other special features in Old Tamil

(*a*) *Inflected verbs used as new bases.* The rule that the second person singular imperative is the verbal base itself was often made use of by poets to start a new series of verbal formations from the special forms which this imperative singular occasionally assumed. Thus, in the examples given already, *kaṇṭai, ceṉṟī*, are special forms of the second imperative singular; from these as bases new finite verbs were formed like *kaṇṭaippai* 'please see' *ceṉṟīka* 'please go'. Such forms appear to have perplexed commentators who pass them by with the remark that the forms are corrupt.

(1) *kaṇṭaippai* 'please see' (Kali. 89.)

(2) *vantīyaṉ* 'he will not come' (Kali. 71.)

(3) *maṟantiṭṭōy* 'you have forgotten' (Kali. 28.)

(4) *iruntaikka* 'please remain (here)' (Cilap. XIX, 67.)

(5) *kēṭṭaikka* 'please hear' (Cilap. XVIII, 49.)

(6) *veṉṟīka vēntaṉ* 'may the king be victorious' (Kuṟaḷ 1268.)

In the above examples the inflected forms *kaṇṭai, vantī, maranti, iruntai, kēṭṭai, veṉṟī* are taken as identical with the uninflected bases *kāṇ* 'see', *vā* 'come', *maṟa* 'forget', *iru*

1. Iṟaiyaṉār Akapporuḷ with Nakkīrar's commentary (p. 126). Other instances will be found at page 53, *Ibid.*

'be', *kēḷ* 'hear' *vel* 'conquer' and are inflected a second time.

(*b*) *Kiṟu.* This suffix is conspicuous by its absence not only in Old Tamil but also in inscriptions and literature for a long time afterwards. It does not occur at all in Cintāmaṇi or Kamparāmāyaṇam. As it is not found in Malayāḷam, Kanarese, or Telugu, we may conclude that it was a late immigrant into the Tamil land.

Note.—*Kiṟu* occurs once in Maṇimēkalai (XXIX, *l.* 299, 300), but such an isolated instance may really owe its existence to the ignorance of copyists who might not have known that *kiṟu* is a late suffix.

(*c*) *Kiṉṟu.* This suffix occurs but rarely in Caṅkam works—the number of occurrences being only about 43 in something like 20,000 lines; it is always found in these works in combination with the verb *ā* 'become' and without personal endings (except in one or two instances) just as *kunnu* is now used in Malayāḷam.

(1) *nakai ākiṉṟē tōḻi* 'it is (has become) matter for laughter, friend'. (Naṟṟiṇai 245.)

(2) *kavai ākiṉṟatu ayya* 'it is common talk, Sir' (Naṟṟiṇai 354.)

(3) *nōy ākiṉṟē* 'it has become painful, distressing'. (Kuṟuntokai 224.)

(4) *peṇṇuru oru tiṟaṉ ākiṉṟu* 'one side is a female form'. (Puṟam. Intro.)

(5) *iṉi niṉaintu irakkam ākiṉṟu* 'it is grief to think of it now'. (Puram. 243.)

In many of these instances, it is difficult to say whether *ākiṉṟu* should be split up as *ā*+*kiṉṟu* and construed 'it becomes', or as *āku*+*iṉ*+*tu* and construed 'it has become', in one or two instances the latter appears to be the correct interpretation. The use of *kiṉṟu* in finite verbs without personal terminations is exceedingly rare outside Caṅkam works. There is only one instance in these works of *kiṉṟu* entering into a relative participle like *ceykiṉṟa*. Such relative participles and finite verbs with personal terminations begin to appear in Cilappatikāram and Maṇimēkalai, and are more frequent in Cintāmaṇi; they are quite common in Kamparāmāyaṇam and in the religious poetry of the Nāyaṉmārs and the later Āḻvārs. The earliest inscriptions in Malabar being in Tamil, *kiṉṟu* has found its way into Malayāḷam literature.

NOTE.—A relative participle with *kiṉṟu*—*cērkiṉṟa*-occurs once in Paripāṭal (XXII-*l*-25) ; *ākiṉṟatu* occurs twice in Naṟṟiṇai (227, 354) and *ākiṉṟēṉ* occurs once in Kalittokai (108). But for reasons already stated such isolated instances should not be relied upon as evidencing the use of such relative participles and verb-forms in the Caṅkam period. Even if such occasional use is admitted its infrequency will show that the suffix was then new and just coming into vogue. *Kiṉṟu* occurs a few times without personal terminations in the poetry of the Āḻvars[1]; in two or three of these the forms may be construed as verbal nouns.

(*d*) *kuṉ*. This suffix spelt indifferently as *kuṉ* or *kiṉ* was used extensively to form the *nomen agentis* in cases where modern Tamil uses *kiṟu* or *kiṉṟu*. Such formations were decidedly on the decrease at the time of the twin epics and are scarce now.

(1) *neykuṉar*=*neykiṟavar*='weavers'.

(2) *mīṉ piṭikkuṉar*=*mīṉ piṭikkiṟavar* 'fishermen'.

1. Tiruvāymoḻi I-4-9 ; I-10-5 ; V-1-1, 7.

(3) *āṭuṉar, pāṭuṉar, ceruṉar*='dancers, songsters, warriors'

(*e*) *Special expletive.* Tolkāppiyam enumerates a large number of expletives, many of which are used with the imperative second person; these appear to be terms of address or remnants of old conjugations which had fallen into disuse even in the time of that ancient grammar. Some of the more important of these expletives are *miyā, ika, mō, maṭi, ikum, ciṉ* (II-274). Of these *ciṉ* is referred to as *iciṉ* by later writers; this and *ikum* may also be used with persons other than the second. *Iciṉ* is always used with the past verbal participles and there are about a hundred instances of its use in the works of the Caṅkam period.

(1) *Kaṇṭu vanticiṉē* 'I came seeing *i.e.*, I saw as I was coming'. (Patiṟṟu. 15.)

(2) *uraitticiṉ* 'please say' (Aiṅkuṟu. 59.)

(3) *kēṭṭiciṉ* 'please hear' (Kuṟuntokai 30.)

(4) *uyarnticiṉōr* 'great men'· literally 'elevated men' (Puṟam. 214.)

(5) *kaṇṭikum allāmō* 'Have we not seen?' (Aiṅkuṟu. 121.)

(6) *kaṇṭika, kaṇṭai, kaṇṭaikka, kāṇika* 'see!' (Kali. 105.)

(7) *kaṇṭiku* 'see'.

(8) *ceṉṟika* 'go', 'may (he, she, it or they) go'.

These expletives have no counter-parts in the other Dravidian languages and will not be examined in detail in this book.

4. MALAYĀḶAM

117. (a) Personal endings

This question whether personal endings were ever in use in popular speech in Malabar is referred to briefly by Gundert in his Grammar; he seems to think that, as these endings are found used in poetry and old prose works, it may be inferred that they were once current in popular speech also but have since been discontinued. (G.M.G., S. 198.) Mr. Seshagiri Prabhu discusses this question in para. 155 of his *Vyākaraṇāmṛtam*; he says that tense forms are used with and without personal terminations in poetry but that such terminations are wholly wanting in prose works. He suggests the possibility that the partial use of personal endings in poetry in imitation of Tamil might have been necessitated by the exigencies of metre, but leaves the question unsettled as he thinks that it is difficult of decision. As already indicated it is assumed in this work that the Dravidians were at one time using as finite verbs what have since come to be regarded as participles. There is nothing improbable in the supposition that Malayāḷam, which in other respects has changed the least since ancient times, still preserves the old habit of using participles as tense forms and it is unnecessary to assume that the people adopted the use of personal endings at one time and have again discontinued their use. Malabar literature and inscriptions have been greatly influenced by Tamil.

(*b*) Strong and weak verbs

The classification of roots is the same as in Tamil, but Malayāḷam grammarians give the names 'strong' and 'weak' to the two classes which have been designated above as 'accented' and 'unaccented'; this is a mere question of names and is of no importance. It is, however, different when these grammarians take the stem of the verb to be the form which it assumes in the infinitive, not the simpler form which it has in the 2nd imperative singular. Thus *naḍakka* 'to walk', *koḍukka* 'to give', *kēḻkka* 'to hear', *pōka* 'to go', are taken as stems instead of *naḍa, koḍu, kēḻ, pō*. This has the effect of obscuring the real nature and form of all suffixes beginning with *k*. Thus the suffix of the present tense which really is *kuṉṉu* becomes *uṉṉu* in Malayāḷam grammars as the initial *k* is removed from the suffix in the analysis of *naḍakkuṉṉu* as *naḍakka*+*uṉṉu* instead of *naḍa*+*kuṉṉu*. In this book the 2nd person singular is taken as the base or stem of Malayāḷam verbs. Bishop Caldwell thought that the Malayāḷam present tense suffix was *kuṉṉu*, a modified form of the Tamil suffix *kiṉṟu*. (C.D.G. pp. 384-4.)

118. THE PRESENT TENSE

The suffix, which is also the termination, is *kuṉṉu*, the initial of which is generally elided after unaccented bases. Example :—*naḍakkuṉṉu*, *kēḻkkuṉṉu*, *keḍuṉṉu*, *varuṉṉu*. Dr. Gundert thinks that the present tense suffix was formerly—*iṉṟu* (corrupt form *iṉṉu*) and that this was subsequently changed to *uṉṉu* (G. M. G., S. 303); that is to say, he derives the Malayāḷam suffix *kuṉṉu* from the Tamil suffix *kiṉṟu* of the inscriptions and literature. It seems more reasonable, however, to assume that the forms *kiṉṉu* and *kuṉṉu* must have developed independently of each other, though both are perhaps derived, as will be indicated later, from the same Aryan source. The form *kiṉṉu*, originally *kiṉṟu*, must have come from the Tamil country and the latter occurs in the Travancore Tamil inscriptions of the 10th and 11th Centuries A.D. The forms *vāḻkiṉṟa* and *vāḻiṉṟa* 'ruling' occur in the inscriptions of the time of Sthāṇu Ravi, and *ceykiṉṟa* 'doing' occurs in an inscription of the time of Bhāskara Ravi Varman. (T.A.S., 1916, pp. 67, 80, 40.) The latest occurrences of *kinṟu* traceable in published inscriptions are found in an inscription of 1603 belonging to the time of Vīra Ravi Varman where the forms *aruḷinṟa* 'gracing' and *koḷḷinṟa* 'taking' occur. (T. A. S., Vol. I, pp. 176-77.) The suffix *kunṟa* appears in the Parūr Romo-Syrian inscription of 1624 (T.A. S., Vol. I, p. 300) where we have the relative participle *cellunṟa* 'passing' and in the Pālayam plates of 1662 embodying the agreement between the Dutch East India Company and the Royal family of Cochin, the Malayāḷam forms in *kunnu* are freely used. (T.A.S., Vol. I, pp. 30 *et seq.*) The suffix *kunṟu* corrupted later into *kunnu* and derived probably from an original Tamil-Malayāḷam stock must have been in use among the lower classes, while *kinṟu* and *kinnu*, which it ultimately supplanted, were confined to literature and inscriptions.

119. THE PAST TENSE

The suffixes of the past verbal participle which is also used as the tense form are the same as in Tamil —*viz.*, *tu*, *du* (intervocal *t*) and *i*, but the conjunct consonants in the participles have become palatalized or otherwise modified; thus *-nṟu* has become *-nnu*, *-ttu* has become *-ccu* after *y* and palatal vowels, *-ndu* has become *-ñju* and *-ññu* after *y* and palatal vowels, and *-nnu* in other cases. Example :—

(1) *irunnu, naḍannu, paṟannu.*
(2) *paḍiccu, ceyiccu, mēyccu, pārttu.*
(3) *ōḍi, kāṭṭi, eṇṇi.*
(4) *iḍiñju, aḷiñju, mēyñju* ; *iḍiññu, aḷiññu, mēyññu, cennu, vennu, konnu.*

120. (*a*) THE FIRST FUTURE TENSE

(*a*) The suffix-termination is *kum*, the initial *k* of which is doubled after accented roots and generally elided after the unaccented. Example:—

keḍukkum, kēḷkkum, ākum, pōkum, śuḍum, uḷum.

(*b*) *The second future tense.* In poetry and old literary works the final *-m* of the first future forms are often found omitted and the preceding *u* sometimes lengthened also. Sometimes the future takes the terminations *pu* which becomes *vu*, *vū* after unaccented roots; *vu* becomes *mu* after nasal stems.

These forms are collected by grammarians under the head 'second future tense' and it is to these forms that personal endings are found added in literature. Example:—*koḍuppu*, *vayppu*, *śelvu*, *pōvu*, *koḍukkuvāṉ*, *rakṣikkuvaṉ*, *vīḻvan*, *mudivar*, *tīrppaṉ*, *uṇmu*, *tiṉmu*, *kaṇmu*.

121. OTHER FINITE AND MISCELLANEOUS VERB FORMS

(*a*) *Relative participles.* The present and past relative participles are formed by adding *a* to the corresponding tense forms. The future relative participle is the first future form. Example :—

(1) *naḍakkuṉṉa*, *ōḍuṉṉa*, *varuṉṉa*.

(2) *ōdiya*, *ēṟiya*, *koṉṉa*, *paḍicca*, *aḻiñja*.

(3) *keḍukkum*, *pōkum*, *cuḍum*.

Agent nouns are formed from all these relative participles and from the second future forms.

(1) *naḍakkuṉṉavaṉ*.

(2) *ēriyavaṉ*.

(3) *vāḻumavaṉ*, *iḍumavaṉ*, *vāḻvavaṉ*, *iripyaṉ*, *colluvar*.

(*a*) *Imperative.* The imperative second person singular is the root or base itself. The plural appears to be a future form and is obtained by adding *-in* to the second future. Example :—

(Singular) *pō*, *iru*, *koḍu*.

(Plural) *varuviṉ*, *kaṇmiṉ*, *uṇkiṉ*, *nilpiṉ*, *kēḷpiṉ*.

(*b*) *Optative.* The optative is obtained by adding *-ka* to the root or base and is the same for all numbers, persons and genders. The initial *-k* of this suffix is doubled after accented roots and never elided after unaccented roots. Example :—

koḍukka, taruka, karuka, ceyka, āḍuka.

(*c*) *Permissive imperative.* There is another optative called also permissive imperative, which is obtained by adding *-ṭṭe* to the ancient form of the infinitive to be mentioned presently. This is used only in the first and third persons. Example :—

irikkaṭṭe, pōkaṭṭe, varaṭṭe.

(*d*) These forms correspond to the permissive imperatives in *kaṭṭu* and *kaṭṭum* of Tamil; they must therefore be regarded as obtained by adding *kaṭṭe* to the root, *k* being elided after unaccented roots.

(*e*) *Infinitives.* The following ancient forms occur in literary works:—*naṭakka, ceyya, āṭa, tara, tiṉṉa, aṟiya*—in which *k* has disappeared after unaccented roots as in Tamil. In colloquial language, however, the *k* appears in every infinitive:—

tinnuka 'to eat', *ceyka* 'to do', *āḍuka* 'to play', *taruka* 'to give', *aṟika* 'to know'.

Forms of the types *ōṭuvāṉ, kāṇmāṉ, naṭappāṉ* are infinitives of purpose in common use. These are supposed to be formed by adding *-āṉ* to the second future.

(*f*) *Subjunctives.* These are formed by adding *-al* to the past verbal participle or *-il* to the base; in the latter case a *-k-* always intervenes between the base and the suffix as in colloquial infinitives. Example :—

(1) *kuṭuttāl, pukkāl, kaṭṭiyāl, paṭiccāl.*

(2) *ākil, uṇkil, ceykil, colkil, varikil.*

(*g*) *Causals*. These are formed as in Tamil by adding *-pi* (*ppi*) to accented roots and *-vi* to some unaccented roots; but most unaccented roots add only *-i*. Examples:—

(1) *appi*, *pūppi* (*pukuppi*), *kappi* (*kalpi*).

(2) *a̱rivi*, *ceyvi*, *peruvi*, *taruvi*.

(3) *ka̱ṉi*, *colli*, *vaḻi*.

As in Tamil, the old causal bases corresponding to the conjugations of the pro-Dravidian period exist side by side with the above forms. Example :—

kāṇi	*kāṭṭu* ;	*naḍappi*	*naḍattu* ;
varuvi	*varuttu* ;	*aḍakkippi*	*aḍakku*.

NOTE.—Dr. Gundert thinks that forms like *naḍappi* and *arivi* arise by adding *i* to the verbal nouns in *-pu* and *-vu*. The explanation given in this book is different.

5. KANARESE

122. THE FINAL *u* OF KANARESE BASES

(*a*) There are apparently no roots or verbal bases in modern Kanarese which end in consonants, bases formerly ending in consonants having been lengthened by a final *u*. It cannot be said that this *u* was put in as a help to enunciation, for it is found added even to roots which formerly ended in vowels—*ī* 'bring forth', *mī* 'bathe', *bē* 'be burnt up', *nōy* 'pain', *sāy* 'die'—which have now become *īyu*, *mīu*, *bēyu*, *nōyu*, *sāyu*. In Old Kanarese, on the other hand, it was only roots ending in explosives and sibilants that required a final enunciative *u*. Examples:—

aḷku 'fear'	*oggu* 'meet together, join'
naccu 'trust'	*māju* 'hide'
kuṭṭu 'beat'	*āḍu* 'play'
muṭṭu 'surround'	*pordu* 'join'

tappu 'commit an error' *tabbu* 'embrace'
nagisu 'cause to laugh' *tīrchu* 'finish'

In the formation of the present-future relative participles and the future tense almost every root is now assumed to end in *u* or may be so assumed.

(*b*) It will be pointed out hereafter that in Tamil-Malayāḷam a pleonastic suffix *-ku* was always interposed between the base and the future tense signs *pu-vu* or *m*, and that in the case of unaccented roots the combined suffix *-kum* has now mostly become *-um* in these two languages. As the Tamil-Malayāḷam future *m* appears as *v* in Kanarese, and as all bases in the latter languages are unaccented, the *u* in the present-future participles *mīyuva*, *nōyuva* etc., probably corresponds to the *u* of the *um* of Tamil-Malayāḷam.

(*c*) If we were certain that the initial *u* of the Kanarese present participle suffixes *-utā*, *uttā* is radical and not taken over from the base, we can give an additional explanation of the almost universal use of the final *u* which obtains at present in Kanarese bases. These suffixes are unknown to Tamil-Malayāḷam and probably did not exist in pro-Dravidian. In their original forms *-uttum*, *utte*, *-uttam*, they were probably just coming into use when Kanarese first comes within our ken in the 6th, 7th, and 8th centuries of the Christian era in the inscriptions of the Western Chālukya and Rāṣṭrakūṭa kings. Forms like *bēyuttā*, *nōyuttā*, *naḍeyuttā*, and *īyutum*, side by side with *kāḍuttum* 'fighting', *isute* 'throwing', *kettute* 'quivering', where the explosives and sibilant bases undoubtedly required an enunciative *-u*, would naturally lead to the assumption that in the former cases also the uninflected forms were *bēyu*, *nōyu*, *naḍeyu*, and *īyu*.

123. THE PRESENT TENSE SUFFIXES *-utā*, *uttā*.

This is a tense formed by adding the personal endings to present verbal participles which are as follows :—*irutā*, *iruttā, naḍeyuttā, baruttā, nōyuttā, aḻūtā* etc. The following is the paradigm of the verb substantive *iru* 'be':—

	Singular	Plural
1.	*irutēne*	*irutēve*
2.	*irutī, iruti*	*irutīri*
3.	*irutāne* } *irutāḷe* }	*irutāre*
	irutade	*irutāve, irutave*

This tense form is entirely a creation of modern times; in the ancient and mediaevel dialects the present verbal participles were always used in subordinate constructions as follows :—

rājyam geyutt-ire 'while reigning'.
āḷutt-ire 'while ruling'.
nōḍutta bandam 'he came seeing'.

The forms of the suffixes as given by Dr. Kittel appear also to have differed slightly in various periods. They were *-uttu* and *utte* in the oldest period, *-utum, ute,* and *uttam* in the ancient and mediaeval dialects, *-uttam,* somewhat later in the mediaeval, *-utā* and *uttā* in the mediaeval and the modern, and *-uta* and *-utta* in the modern (196, 172).

These suffixes are apparently related to the present tense suffixes *-tun* and *tā* of Telugu, and it is doubtful whether their initial *u* is radical. This *u* does not appear in the present tense forms of any of the Kanarese dialects dealt with in the next section.

The theory elaborated in K.K.G. 173 that *utu* the primitive form of these suffixes is a variant of the pronominal *udu* has little to recommend it.

The final *e* in the first and third persons of the paradigm above is stated by Dr. Kittel to have been added for the sake of emphasis (K.K.G. 196). This is not a satisfactory explanation. Why should the present alone, of all the tenses, require an emphasis? And why should this *e* be unnecessary in the tense forms of the second person? According to a list given by Bishop Caldwell (C.D.G. p. 512) the pronouns in the Kōta language, a dialect of Kanarese, have an *e* attached to them except in the second person singular:— (1) *āne*, *nāme*; (2) *nī*, *nīve*; (3) *avane*, *avare*. If the Kanarese present tense which is entirely a creation of modern times was developed in a dialect which had pronouns like the Kota pronouns, there will be an *e* at the end of all the forms of the tense except those of the second person singular; this is probably the correct explanation of the final *e*.

124. The old present tense suffixes *tappa* or *dappa*.

In old Kanarese the present tense was formed with a suffix having the above form and supposed to be made up of the past verbal participle suffix *-tu* or *du* and the present future participle of the base *agu*, 'be, become'.

Kuḍidappem	'I drink'	*Kaltappam*	'he learns'
Endappem	'I say'	*Naḍedappanu*	'he walks'

Here *kuḍidappem* according to the above explanation is a compound form made up of *kuḍidu* 'having drunk' and *appem* 'I shall be', 'I am'.

In the mediaeval period when the *p's* were generally converted into *h*'s the verbs formed as above took forms like *kuḍidahem*, *kaltahanu*, *endahem*, *naḍedahanu*. In modern Kanarese this *h* has disappeared in most cases and the vowels of the personal endings have been lengthened, thus giving rise to forms like the following :—

bandēnu (*baru* 'come'), *nuḍidaru* (*nuḍi* 'speak'), *ādēvu* (*agu* 'be'). Further in the case of *u* bases a practice has grown up of using the participles *māḍi*, *nōḍi*, *kuṭṭi*, etc. in the formation of this tense instead of *māḍidu, nōḍidu, kuṭṭidu* etc. as in the old times. Thus the tense forms now are:—

māḍyēnu, māḍēnu, māḍyēvu, māḍēvu, instead of *māḍidēnu, māḍidēvu.*

Dr. Kittel notes also a change in the meanings of these tense forms and remarks that the ancient and mediaeval present tense which has been corrupted in the above manner "is now-a-days used to convey the idea of uncertainty or possibility, and may be called the contingent present-future tense". (K.K.G. 195.) It would seem, however, that a future sense was always inherent in the tense, for *appem, appam* etc. are future by formation; and Dr. Kittel himself gives at page 429 of his grammar an instance of this present used in a future tense:—

Akka ninage tandappem 'I shall bring for thee, sister'

125. The past tense

This is obtained by adding the personal endings to the past verbal participles of verbs. The following examples will illustrate the ways in which these participles are formed.

tiḷidu (*tiḷi* 'perceive')	*iḻidu* (*iḻi* 'descend')
karedu (*kare* 'call')	*paḍedu* (*paḍe* 'acquire')
sattu (*sāyu* 'die')	*ittu* (*īyu* 'give')
uttu (*uḻu* 'plough')	*niltu* (*nilu* 'stand')
tindu (*tinu* 'eat')	*kondu* (*kollu* 'kill')
āsattu (*āsaṟu* 'become weary')	*tattu* (*taṟu* 'happen')
mutti (*muttu* 'surround')	*kuṭṭi* (*kuṭṭu* 'beat')

Most *u* bases now form their verbal participles with the suffix *i*, but in forming the past tense of such bases a *d* is interposed between the suffix and the personal endings; that is to say, the personal endings are added to a hypothetical participle in *-idu*. In the case of bases not ending in *u* of which the participles end in *-du* or *-tu* or the modifications which these undergo in combination with the final consonants of the bases the personal endings are added directly to the participles. Thus Kanarese adheres, and has always adhered, to a dental suffix in the formation of its past tense. This dental is predominatingly *d*, but it appears also exceptionally as *t*, chiefly in some *i*, *e*, *n*, and *r* stems, and undergoes other modifications in some other cases.

Example :—*antu*, *niltu*, *uttu* (*uḷtu*), *artu*, *māḍidenu*, *nuḍiday*, *kēḷdiri*, *āsattaru*.

NOTE 1.—From the universal appearance of a dental in the past tense forms, in the past relative participles, and in the old present tense in *tappa* (*dappa*), we may infer that the past verbal participles formerly ended always in *du*, *idu*, *tu*, and that the participles in *i* were a later innovation which have not succeeded in finding their way into tense forms.

NOTE 2.—The initial hypothesis in this book is that the Dravidians originally used *verbal* participles in the place of finite verbs and that personal endings were subsequently added to these participles; and in accordance with this hypothesis all tense forms are derived from verbal participles. This method differs from that of Dr. Kittel who derives the past and future tenses of Kanarese from the corresponding *relative* participles.

126. THE FUTURE TENSE

The sign of this tense and of the corresponding relative participles called the present-future participle by Dr. Kittel is *v*. Examples :—

Root	Relative participle	Tense form (1st person singular)
baru 'come'	*baruva*	*baruvenu*
pūjisu 'worship'	*pūjisuva*	*pūjisuvenu*
belagu 'shine'	*beḷaguva*	*beḷaguvenu*
uṇ 'eat'	*uṇṇuva*	*uṇṇuvenu*
tin 'eat'	*tinnuva*	*tinnuvenu*
nuḍi 'speak'	*nuḍiyuva*	*nuḍiyuvenu*
naḍe 'walk'	*naḍeyuva*	*naḍeyuvenu*

Modern Kanarese effects this uniformty of formation by the device of inserting a *u* between the tense-sign and the base. In old and mediaeval Kanarese there were many future forms with *p*, *b*, and *h*, instead of with *v*. (K.K.G. 183.) Thus :—

1. *baru* 'come' and *iru* 'be' which were formerly written *bar* and *ir*, as also *tar* 'give', *kūr* 'love' and *gōr* 'fish' had relative participles with *p* :—

> *barpa*, *irpa*, *tarpa*, *kūrpa*, and *gōrpa*; the *p* of these forms could be doubled.

In the mediaeval dialect the first four of these appear as *bappa*, *ippa*, *tappa* and *kūpa* (for *kūppa*).

2. Similarly many bases ending in *ṟ*, *ḻ*, and *n* used *p* in the future; -*māṟpa* (*māṟ* 'do'), *āṟpa* (*āṟ* 'be strong'), *agaḻpa* (*agaḻ* 'dig'), *ānpa* (*ān* 'touch, meet').

3. Some bases ending in *ṇ* and *n* used *b* :—*uṇba*, *umba* (*uṇ* 'eat'), *enba*, *emba* (*en* 'say'), *tinba*, *timba*, (*tin* 'eat'), *nānba* (*nan* 'get wet'). Most of these could also use *b* alternatively in the modern dialect.

4. In causal and other stems formed by suffixing *isu* or *su* to the roots and in bases ending in *gu* there were two

ways of forming the future in the ancient dialect. Either the *v* was added as now, or the last syllable *su* or *gu* was elided and *pa* was added. The *p* of this *pa* could be doubled in causal verbs and not in others, unless the penultimate vowel of the base was short. Examples:—

pūjipa, pūjippa 'worshipping'; *alapa, alappa* 'shaking'; *beḷapa, beḷappa,* 'shining'; *āguva, appa, apa* becoming; *pōguva, pōpa, hopa* 'going'.

5. In the mediaeval dialect the forms *appa, ippa, tappa, bappa* etc. became *aha, iha, taha, baha* etc.

The above examples seem to show that the original future suffix was *p,* and that *v* has arisen from the soft pronunciation of *p* after unaccented roots. This *p* was doubled after the causal *i* and some other short vowels, thereby showing the existence of accent at a remote period on the final short vowels of bases. But the *p* had become weakened into *v* even in the ancient dialect thereby showing that there has been no stress on the final vowel in the known history of the language.

A special conjugation confined only to the third person and with suffixes *kum, gum, ku, gu,* was formerly in vogue and was used in all tenses without variation for number or gender. The most common of these suffixes was *gum* which was added to most verbal bases ending in consonants and vowels. *Kum* appears to have been used chiefly after some *ḷ*, *l*, *r*, and *n* bases; *ku* appears late in the ancient dialect and *gu* occurs only in the mediaeval. Causal and other bases formed by means of the suffix *isu* may drop the particle *su* and take *kum*; *kkum* was an alternative for *kuṃ* in verbs of Sanskrit derivation. Examples:—*māḍugum, paḍegum, naḍegum*; *irkum, tarkum, nilkum, tōrku, esegu, enisugu, enikum*; *vartisugu, vartikku.* (K.K.G. 203.)

This conjugation has now gone out of use and its only remnants in Modern Kanarese are *bēku* and *sāku*. *Bēku* of which *bēḻku* is the fuller form is derived from *bēḍu* (Tamil *vēṇḍu*, Telugu *Vēḍu*) and has the same meaning as the Tamil *vēṇḍum* 'it is wanted'. *Sāku* or *Sālku* is derived from *sāl* and has the same meaning as Tamil *śālum*, Telugu *chālunu* 'enough'.

Note.—The doubling of *k* in verbs of Sanskrit derivation with the elision of *su* shows that the suffix in such verbs was originally only *i* and that there was an accent on it before it became extended by *su*. It is also obvious that *kum* and *ku* were the original suffixes and that *gum* and *gu* arise from the soft pronunciation of *k*.

127. IMPERATIVES

The forms brought together by Dr. Kittel (K.K.G. 205) under the head Imperatives include not only Imperatives proper but also Optatives and Benedictives. It is not however, necessary for the purpose of this book to separate these forms.

(*a*) *Future forms used as Imperatives etc.*—

(1) Imperative first person singular is the same as the first person singular of the future tense. Example—*māḍuvem*, *māḍuve*, *māḍuvenu* 'I shall do' *i.e.*, 'let me do.'

(2) *Imperative first person plural*—Suffixes *am*, *a*, *ā*, *anu*, *anaa*, and *ṇa* are added to the present future participles. *Am* a contracted form of *ām* 'we' was used in the ancient dialect; this *ām* became merely *a* inthe mediaeval dialect; in the modern dialect *a*, *ā*, *anu*, *ana*, and *aṇa* all originating from the old *am* are used.

Example—(1) *māḍuvam* (2) *māḍuva* (3) *maḍuva, māḍuva, māḍvana, māḍōṇa, māḍūṇa,* 'let us do'.

(3) *Imperative second and third persons*—The third person neuter singular of the future tense is used for both singular and plural.

Example—*māḍuvadu* in the modern, *māḍuvudu* in the ancient and mediaeval dialects.

(*b*) Suffix *ali*. *First and Third persons*

This suffix is not found in the ancient dialect. It is used in the mediaeval dialect in the third person and in the modern dialect in the first and third persons.

Example—*māḍali* 'let (me, us, him, her, it, or them) do'.

(*c*) Suffixes *go, ke, kke*. *Third person*

These suffixes were used in the singular and plural of the third person in the ancient and mediaeval dialects.

Example—*īge* 'let him etc. give' *maḻke* 'let him etc. do'.

(*d*) Suffixes *a, im, i, iri*. *Second person*

(1) *Singular*—The verbal base itself or the base with the suffix *a* in all the three dialects. Example: *māḍu, māḍa,* 'do (thou)'.

(2) *Plural*—The suffix *im,* a contracted form of *nīm, īm* 'you' was used in the ancient dialect; this *im* became *i* in the mediaeval and modern dialects which also use the suffix *iri* pronounced *ari* by the vulgar. Example: *māḍim, māḍi, māḍiri,* 'do you'.

(*e*) It is evident from (*a*) above that from very ancient times the tense which had *p, v,* or *b* for its sign represented not merely futurity but also implied obligation or promise; compare the following quotations from ancient inscriptions.

(1) *ōr-m-mattarge ir-k-kuḷa jōlam kuḍuvudu* 'Two *kuḷas* of *jōlam* (zonna) should be given for each *mattar* of land'. (I.A. Vol. X, p. 167—about 700 A.D.)

(2) *I sthānaman -aḷva goravar akhaṇḍita brahmachāri-y-apudu.* 'The Śaiva mendicants holding this office should practise celibacy.' (E.I. Vol. VII, p. 201—about 865 A-D.)

(3) *Brahmacharyya - hīnaran - ī samayada goravarkkaḷ kaḷevōr.* 'The Goravars of this community shall remove those who break the vow of celibacy.' (*ibid.*)

128. Miscellaneous verb forms

Infinitives—These end in *al*, *alu* or *a*, the last of these arising from the loss of the final *l* in *al*. As in Tamil the following senses :—

(1) for the purpose of, (2) so as to, so that, (3) at the time that, when, while.

In the first of these senses the fourth case of the verbal noun in *al* or *alu* is also used. The suffix *e*—sometimes *ge*—is also used in the third of the above senses. (K.K.G. 187, 188, 365.)

uṇal bandam 'he came to eat.'

nuḍiyalke bandam 'he came to speak.'

arthi, bēḍal, dāniyittam 'when the beggar, begged the liberal man gave.'

gāyakam pāḍe devam mechchidam 'when the singer sang the king was pleased'.

The above examples illustrate the use of the infinitive in old and mediaeval Kanarese. In the modern dialect the use of *al* is confined to the so-called passive construction as in *iral patta, kēḻalpatta* etc. and the use of the suffix *e* appears to be confined to poetry.

Subjunctives—The conditional was formed in the ancient and mediaeval dialects by adding certain suffixes to the present-future and past relative participles; in the modern dialect the suffix is added to the past relative participle.

The suffixes were *oḍe* in the ancient and mediaeval dialects, *aḍe* in the mediaeval, and *are* in the mediaeval and in the modern: *oḍe* being the original form of which the other two are corruptions apparently. (K.K.G. 314.)

Example :—

baruttiddare	'if (you) are coming.'
kēḷiddare	'if (I) had listened to.'
illadiddare	'if (the sun) were not in existence.'

129. CAUSAL BASES

The most usual causative suffix is *isu* which appears as *su* in bases ending in *y, l, e, i* and occasionally *asu*. In the ancient and mediaeval dialects the common suffix was *chu* in the case of bases ending in *r, l, ḷ, ḻ* and occasionally *ichu* was affixed in the mediaeval dialect. (K.K.G. 151.)

Original verb	Causal base
iru 'be'	*irisu*
en, enu 'say'	*enisu, enasu*
hāku 'put'	*hākisu, hākasu*
kā, kāy, 'guard'	*kāyisu*
kāy, kāyu, 'grow hot'	*kāyisu, kāsu*
niṭṭu, 'length'	*niṭṭisu*
taḷir 'shoot, sprout'	*taḷirchu*
aḻal 'grieve'	*aḻalchu*

Original verb		Causal base
uruḷ	'roll'	*uruḷisu*
		uruḷchu
		uruḷichu
maguḷ	'turn round, return'	*maguḷchu*
		maguḷisu
keral	'cry, shout'	*keraḷchu*
		keralichu
tīru, tīr	'be finished'	*tīrisu*
		tīrchu
sōr	'drop, drip'	*sōrchu*
sōru	'drop, drip'	*sōrisu*

The suffix added to Sanskrit words to form verbs is also *isu*. In the ancient and mediaeval dialects a euphonic *v* was interposed between Sanskrit words ending in vowels and the suffix; in the mediaeval dialect this euphonic *v* is occasionally changed into *v*. (K.K.G. 151.)

Examples :—

(sans)	*bhram*	'roam, wander'	*bramisu*
(sans)	*suddha*	'clean'	*śuddhavisu*
(sans)	*bhinna*	'different'	*bhinnavisu*
(sans)	*tāra,*	'high, shrill'	*tāravisu*

130. EARLY LOSS OF ACCENT IN KANARESE

(*a*) Reference has already been made to the alternative forms assumed by causal stems and roots of Sanskrit derivation in the present-future inflection and in the special conjugation in *kum, gum* :

enisuva enipa; *pūjisuva, pūjippa*;
enisugu, enikum; *vartisugu, vartikkum.*

Bases with the suffix *gu* had also alternative forms in the present-future inflection:—*beḷaguva, beḷapa, beḷappa*: *tolaguva, tolappa*, *tolapa*. The forms in which *su* is rejected take us to a stage of the language in which causal stems and stems of Sanskrit derivation ended only *i* and show that the real causative suffix is *i* and not *su* as supposed by Dr. Kittel. (K.K.G. 151.) The forms in which *gu* is elided take us to a stage in which *beḷagu*, *tolagu* etc., were merely *beḷa*, *tola* etc.

(*b*) The above alternative forms also show that there was once a stress on the final short vowel of verbs; but this must have been long antecedent to the date of even the earliest inscriptions. For even in the records of the Chālukya kings we have forms like the following :

aḻivōn	for Tamil	*aḻippōn*	'destroyer'
aḻidōn	for Tamil	*aḻittōn*	'he who destroyed'
paḍedōr	for Tamil	*paḍaittōr*	'he who obtained'
pudidudu	for Tamil	*putaittatu*	'fixed in the ground'

These are all transitive verbs strongly accented in Tamil.

As already noted in 122-3 there are a considerable number of exceptional cases in which the tenues *t*, *p*, *k* are still retained though the roots have lost their accent.

131. BIJAPURI

The Kanarese spoken in Bijapur is locally known as Bijāpurī, but it does not differ so much from the standard form of the language as to deserve to be called a separate dialect. (L.S. Vol. IV, p. 381.)

The dialect sometimes uses contracted forms instead of the fuller forms of the standard. The conjugation of verbs is mainly regular. The pronominal suffixes are very commonly dropped in the first and third persons singular :

andā for *andanu* 'he said', *hōdā* 'he went'
hōde 'I went', *koṭṭa* 'he gave', *bandā* 'he came'

The following forms deviating from the standard may be noted.

sāyatāne 'I die', *yeḷatēni* 'I will arise.'
hōgatēni 'I will go', *antēnu* 'I will say.'
sattavā 'who was dead', *hōdavā* 'who had gone.'

132. GOLARI OR HOLIYA

This is the dialect spoken by the Gōlars or Gōlkars and Hōliyas of the Central Provinces. The former are a nomadic tribe of herdsmen and the latter are a low caste of leather workers and musicians. (p. 385.)

(*a*) The short final vowel of verbal forms is usually dropped. Gōlarī in this respect agrees with old Kanarese. We also find a final *m* in the 3rd person singular as in old Kanarase. The past tense of bases ending in *u* is formed by adding *d* directly to the consonant preceding *u* without inserting an *i*; the same principle also prevails in old Kanarese. (387.)

(1) *sikdun* for *sikdanu* 'has been found.'
kyāḷdum for *kēḷdanu* 'he heard'; *nōṛdun* for *nōḍdanu* 'he saw.'
māṛdun for *māḍdanu* 'he did.'

Another peculiarity is that these shortened tense forms ending in *dun* are employed in places where it will be sufficient to use conjunctive participles.

(2) *sāythīn* (p. 390), *sāitin* (392) for *sāyuttene* 'I die' *tintān* (392) for *tinuttāne* 'he eats'; *antān* (394) for *anuttēne* 'I will say'; *māṛtan* (393) for *māḍuttāne* 'he makes.'

In these instances the verbs undergo contractions by the dropping of the final vowels and the elision of the intermediate *u*. These shortened tense forms are also used as participles :—

dūrum (far from)	*nōdrum* (saw)
appu (the father)	*magun* (the son)
bartan (coming) (392)	

(3) *hōgāin* 'I will go'; *anāin* 'I will say'; *tināi* for *Tināin* 'I will eat' (392), *māḍēva* 'we will make' (391).

These may be regarded as corrupt or contracted forms of what the authors of the Linguistic Survey call the second future and what Dr. Kittel calls the contingent present-future. (K.K.G. 195.)

(4) *āhām, āhān* 'he is'; *nittun, nuttum* 'he stayed.' In these two instances a final *m* is used alternatively in the third person masculine. (pp. 388-9, 390, 392.)

(*b*) Conjunctive participles such as *māḍ-ke* 'having done', *huk-ke* 'having gone' are due to the influence of the surrounding Aryan dialects. The same is probably also the case with forms such as *yad-kō* 'arising', *andākō* 'saying' etc. (p. 387.)

Though the dialect forms its past tense with the dental sighs *t* and *d* it seems to have forgotten the conjunctive participles from which such past tense forms have arisen and hardly uses them except in compound tenses such as *sōt-hōgidun* 'dead gone was', *kaḍḍ-hōgidun* 'lost gone was', *tindbūṭun* 'had eaten' where the suffixes *tu, du* appear to be used (391). Instead of these old conjunctive participles the dialect has formed new ones by adding suffixes ke, kō, etc. to the bases in imitation of Aryan dialects. The subjoined lists give the participles occurring in the four specimens received from four different localities for purposes of the Linguistic Survey; it will be seen that the suffixes have not the same form in all the specimens.

(1) *ming-kyā*, *ming-kyō* 'sleeping', *tera-kō* 'having opened', *kalt-kō* 'having stolen', *itakō* 'having been kept', *hiḍ-kō* 'having stolen', *hōgyā* 'having gone'. (pp. 388-9.)

(2) *māḍ-ke* 'having made' *kuk-ke* 'having gone', *vad-kō* 'having arisen', *nōḍ-ke* 'having seen', *ōḍ-ke* 'running'. (pp. 390-1.)

(3) *sōch-kō* 'thinking' (p. 392).

(4) *Tā-kō* 'talking', *hōk-ki* 'having gone', *veda-kū* 'having arisen', *ōḍ-ki* 'having run', *tind-ku* 'eating' and *an-ku* ' saying ' (pp. 394-5).

It will be seen from below under the section 'Present Tense Suffixes' that there are similar variations in the forms of the suffixes in the Aryan dialects which Gōlarī has imitated.

133. KURUMVARI

This dialect is spoken by Kurumvars, a wild pastoral tribe in Chanda. These seem to be identical with the Kurbas or Kurumbars of the Nilgiri Hills and neighbouring districts.

Words undergo contractions by the omission of intermediate and short final vowels. The *d* of the past tense is usually dropped; when the base ends in *n*, however, the past tense sign is retained. Though a dialect of Kanarese, Kurumvārī agrees in many respects with Telugu and differs from the other language (396-7).

(1) *antdu* for *anuttade* 'she says'; *antunalla* for *anuttānealla* 'he says'; *tarturn* for *tarutāne* 'he brings'; *kānistaru* for *kānisuttare* 'they appear'; *koḍtadu*

for *koḍuttade* 'it gives'; *keṭdu* for *keṭṭadu* 'bad thing' (399).

(2) *māḍenu* for *māḍidenu* 'I did'; *ōgine* for *ōgidanu* 'he went'; *jami-āḍini* for *jami-āḍidenu* 'he collected'; *andade* (*anditu*) 'she said.'

(3) verbal participle—*Āḍ-kuṇṭa iddaru* 'were playing'

134. Badaga

Badaga is spoken by the Badagas of Nilgris. It is a very ancient form of Kanarese. Thus the sounds *ḻ* and *ṟ* are still found in it *e.g.* *makkḻu* 'children', *hoṟsivi* 'put on'. The 3rd person masculine termination ends in *ṁ*; the pronoun of the first person is *nām* 'I', dative, *yenaga* 'to me.' The past tense of the verbs agrees with old Kanarese. As in Tamil *ch* is substituted for *s* (401).

(1) *avaṁ* 'he'; *appaṁ* 'father'; *evaṁ* 'this man'; *kunnavaṁ* 'the younger'; *takkavaṁ* 'fit man'; *keṭṭavaṁ* 'bad man'; *sattavaṁ* 'dead man'; *hōdavam* 'who had gone'.

(2) *nām* 'I'; *ninnadutām* 'thine alone'

(3) *Kḻēgidam* 'he sent'; *māḍidem* 'I did'
ikkidaṁ 'he gave'; *māḍidam* 'he made'
korachidam 'he called'; *gīdem* 'I served'
ennaṁ 'he said'; *bannaṁ* 'he came'
paṭṭaṁ 'he felt'; *iddaṁ* 'he was'

(4) *manicha* 'man'; *dēcha* 'country'
chīle 'robe'; *baricha* 'year'

(*b*) Other points worthy of note are :—

(1) Though *ch* is substituted for *s*, the causal verbs invariably retain the sibilant :—
māḍiside '(thou) hast caused to be made';
hōṟisivi 'put on'; *korachisiyumbadu* 'to be called

(2) The conjunctive participles are invariably made with the suffixes *tu* and *i*.

(3) The infinitives are the datives of verbal nouns ending in *du* mostly.

āpaduga 'to become'; *mēsōduga* (*mēsuvaduga*) 'to feed or graze': *tumbisōduga* (*tumbisuvaduga*) 'to fill'; *korachisiyumbaduga* 'to cause to be called'; *barak-oḷḷāndu* 'refusing to come'.

(4) The following tense forms may be noted :—
sattane 'I die'; *iddane* 'he is'; *haḍade* 'is obtained'; *idde* 'thou art'.

7. TELUGU

135. One advantage which Telugu has over the other Dravidian languages is that with a single exception its pronouns end in different syllables :—(1) *nu*, *mu*; (2) *vu*, *ru*; (3) *ṇḍu*; or *ḍu*; *ru*; *di*, *vi*. This fact enables it to contruct its tense forms by affixing these single syllables to its participles without interfering with the forms of the tense suffixes. Another feature in Telugu is that all its verbal bases end in an enunciative *u* which disappears before tense suffixes beginning with a vowel; this appears to have been the case even from before the time of Śaktikomara of Rēnāndu seven thousand, that is to say, from the 8th century probably. How this has been brought about and what changes Telugu has introduced in the roots which it inherited from the pre-Dravidian language will be apparent from the following comparison of some Telugu bases with the corresponding Tamil roots.

Tamil	Telugu	Tamil	Telugu
iḍu 'give'	*iḍu*	*naḍā* 'walk'	*naḍuchu*
tiṭṭu 'abuse'	*tiṭṭu*	*maṟa* (Kan) 'forget'	*maṟachu*
śāl 'be sufficient'	*chalu*	*tiṟa* 'open'	*teṟachu*

Tamil	Telegu	Tamil	Telegu
tiṉ 'eat'	*tinu*	*śey* 'do'	*chēyu*
kāṇ 'see'	*kanu*	*koy* 'cut'	*kōyu*
naḍa 'walk'	*naḍachu*	*kala* 'mix'	*kalayu*
uri 'peel'	*oluchu*	*neyvi* 'cause to be woven'	*nēyinchu*
nali 'crush'	*naluchu*		
kuḍi 'drink'	*kuḍuchu*	*kaṭṭuvi* 'cause to be built'	*kaṭṭinchu*
koyvi 'cause to be cut'	*kōyinchu*		
		path (Sans) 'read'	*paṭhinchu*

Roots ending in *u* in Tamil like *iḍu* and *tiṭṭu* are adopted without change, while roots ending in consonants like *śāl*, *kāṇ*, and *tiṇ*, have an enunciative *u* affixed to them. Some roots generally corresponding, but not always, to accented roots in Tamil have a *chu* affixed to them, while *kala* has *yu* affixed to it; others like *śey* and *koy* have an apparent *u* added to them, but the addition is really *yu*. The final vowel *i* in *kuḍi*, *uri*, and *nali* is changed to *u* for securing harmonic sequence with the *u* of the final syllable *chu*. In causal verbs and verbs of Sanskrit derivation as *nēyinchu*, *paṭhinchu* etc., the causative suffix *i* is an indispensable sign and cannot be altered; therefore a conjunct consonant *nch* has to be interposed between it and the final *u* so as to suspend the operation of the law of harmonic sequence. It would seem that in former times this conjunct could be formed either by doubling of the *ch* or by nasalising it; for both *ettichchu* and *ettinchu* occur in Yuddhamalla's inscription of the 9th century. The forms *tinipichināḍu* and *tappichakoni* occur in a specimen of the Dāsarī dialect. (L.S. Vol. IV, page 601.)

This uniformity has enabled Telugu to reject all conjunctive participles except those ending in *i*. It has four differently formed past tenses, two present tenses, three tenses which may be utilised to express the future and finally an aorist tense. Notwithstanding this richness of forms the language is easier to learn than Tamil or Kanarese and its grammar is shorter as exceptions to general grammatical rules are fewer in Telugu than in the other languages.

136. THE PRESENT TENSE (*a*) SUFFIX—*chun* or *tun*.

The tense formed with these suffixes is a compound tense obtained by combining the verb substantive with the present participle; it is the recognised grammatical present tense. The present participles take the forms :—*koṭṭuchun, kuṭṭutun; naḍachuchun, naḍachutun, naḍastun; viṇutun, viṉṭun; konutun, koṇṭun; chēyuchun, chēstun.*

In colloquial speech the *drutam* or the final *n* of the present participle is dropped, and the preceding vowel sometimes also lengthened.

koṭṭutu, naḍuchutu, chēstu, koṇṭū,
viṇṭū, konuchū, konchū, vinuchu.

The tense forms with pronominal endings are:—

koṭṭuchunnānu, naḍuchutunnānu, naḍastunnāru,

chēyuchunnavi, koṇṭunnānu, vinuchunnāmu.

(*b*) Suffix *tā* or *chā*-. The participle formed with this suffix has no independent existence in the grammatical language; the forms *koṭṭutā, naḍustā, koṭṭuchā* etc., occur only as colloquialisms and provincialisms. From these a simple tense is formed by adding personal endings :—

koṭṭutānu, naḍuchutānu, chēstānu, vastāḍu,
koṭṭuchānu, konchānu.

These forms have a future signification and are in colloquial use ; the forms in *chā* are said to be used mainly by the religious Brāhmans of the northern districts.

137. The past tense

(*a*) *Suffix i.*—The past verbal participles of all bases are formed only with this suffix :—

koṭṭi, naḍichi, chēśi, chēsi, vini, iḍi.

The only tense form now extant derived from this participle is the third person epicene plural :—

Koṭṭiri, naḍichiri, chēśiri, viniri, iḍiri.

These forms supply the defects in the other past tense forms mentioned below.

NOTE—It will be seen from 147 that in Bēraḍī, one of the Telugu dialects, the third person masculine form of the past tense is also based on this verbal participle, Example :

Cheppiḍi 'he said', *pōkayḍi* 'he did not go'

The change of *ru* to *ri* and of *ḍu* to *ḍi* is due to harmonic sequence.

(*b*) *Suffix yā*—The tense formed with this suffix occurs only in colloquial usage, and does not possess forms for the third person feminine and neuter. It is usually supposed to be a corrupt form of the tense formed with the suffix *ina* below. Thus *koṭṭinānu, āḍinānu, chēśināvu, kōśināru, naḍichināḍu, pilichināru* are supposed* to have become corrupted in popular speech into *koṭṭiyānu, āḍiyāmu, chēśiyāvu, kōśiyāru, naḍichiyaru, pilichyāru.* The *y* is however not pronounced or written after *ch* and *s* and the past forms of the bases ending in *chu* and *yu* are written *naḍichānu, chēśānu, kōśānu, pilichānu,* the *ā* being pronounced like the *ā* in the English word '*bade*'. The same pronunciation of *ā* is heard in the past forms *paḍḍānu, cheḍḍāmu, iḍḍāḍu* of *paḍu, cheḍu, iḍu.*

---

*Seshagiri Sastri's Telugu Philology, Verbs, pages 35-37.

It must also be noted here that the usual explanation given of the third person plural forms *koṭṭiri*, *chēśiri*, *kōśiri* etc. is that they are further corruptions of the corrupt forms *koṭyāru*, *chēśaru*, *kōśaru* etc.

The view taken in this book is that the past tense forms with the tense suffix *yā* are much older in Tamil and Telugu than the past tense forms in *ina*. There are now no participles formed with the suffix *yā* either in Tamil or Telugu, but they appear to exist in some Telugu dialects as will be seen from the forms given in Section 8 below. As in the neo-Aryan vernaculars of the north the *yā* suffix has become corrupted into *i* which is now the regular conjunctive participle suffix in Telugu.

(*c*) Suffix *enu*=(*yāna*)—The participle formed with this suffix is used as a finite verb without personal endings in the third person singular and neuter plural:—*koṭṭenu*, *naḍichenu*, *chēśenu*, *kōnenu*, *paḍenu*. The final *nu* of these forms is often omitted in colloquial speech, and the forms are pronounced *koṭṭe*, *koṭṭya*, *vachche*, *vachchya*, *koneya** is very common in the Telugu dialects where sometimes they are also used as conjunctive participles.

In the case of the 13 roots mentioned below the suffix *enu* may optionally be changed into *iyenu*. Thus instead of *konenu*, *paḍenu*, *nagenu* etc. we may also say *koniyenu*, *paḍiyenu*, *nagiyenu* etc. *Koniye*, *padiye*, *nagive* etc.

anu	'say'	*nagu*	'laugh, smile'
konu	'buy, take'	*tegu*	'break'
tinu	'eat'	*tagu*	'suit, fit'
chanu	'go'	*digu*	'descend'
kanu	'see, bring forth'	*paḍu*	'fall'

* The alternative pronunciation *koṭṭya*, *vachchya*, *konya*.

vinu	'hear'	*cheḍu*	'be corrupted'
iḍu	'place, put'		

NOTE—The alternative forms assumed by the conjunctive participles and the suffix *enu* give rise to a surmise that the suffixes *i* and *enu* are probably corrupt contracted forms and that they perhaps contained an *y* formerly.

(*d*) *Suffix ina*—The tense forms are :—*koṭṭinānu, paḍinānu, chēśināvu, kōśināru, naḍachināḍu, naḍachinadi, chēśinavi.*

This is the only tense form of the past which is not defective; there is no corresponding verbal participle now in use. The past relative participles of all Telugu roots are formed with the suffix *ina*:

koṭṭina, paḍina, chēśina, kōśina, naḍachina.

The thirteen roots mentioned in (*c*) above have alternative forms for their relative participles :—

konna, tinna, paḍḍa, cheḍḍa, tagga etc. with the exception of *chanu* and the four ending in *gu* they have also alternative past tense forms corresponding to these participles: *konnānu, paḍḍaḍu.*

NOTE—The view taken in this book is that the suffixes *enu* and *ina* are derived from the Ardhamāgadhī suffix *yāna* which found its way into Telugu rather late.

(*e*) Suffix *ti* or *iti*. The tense formed with this suffix is the recognised grammatical tense of the past, but it is wanting in the forms for the third person. There is no corresponding verbal participle now in use.

Example—*koṭṭitini, naḍichitimi, naḍistivi, chēstiri.*

The *ni* of the first person singular is often omitted; the change of the personal endings *nu, mu, vu, ru* into *ni, mi, vi, ri* is for the purpose of securing harmonic sequence of vowels.

138. THE FUTURE TENSE

(*a*) Suffix *ē*—This suffix is in widely extended use among the common people in the Telugu districts and in the Telugu dialects; it expresses the contingent future :—

paḍēvu 'you might fall', *paḍēru* 'they might fall', *koṭṭēnu, āḍēvu* etc. The third person singular and neuter plural forms are exceptional.

koṭṭēni, koṭṭīni, chēśēni, chēśīni.

(*b*) Suffix *eda*—This is the suffix of the grammatical future.

Koṭṭedanu, chēśedamu, naḍachedavu, kōśedaru.

The *nu* of the first person is often omitted.

The third person singular and neuter plural forms are exceptional :—

koṭṭeḍini, naḍacheḍini, chēśeḍunu, kōśeḍunu.

(*c*) Suffix *kala*—Another grammatical feature is formed by combining *kalanu, kalamu, kalavu, kalaru, kaladu, kalaäi, kalavi* with the infinitive; it implies ability or obligation :—

Cheyagalanu, poyaεgaladu, chaduvagalavā? With this may be compared the forms *kalavāṇḍu, kalāṇḍu* of the inscriptions:—

manēṇḍu neyyi pōyangalavāṇḍu '(he) is bound to supply a mana of ghee'?

139. THE AORIST TENSE SUFFIX *du*

This suffix is used only in the first and the second person; the form for the second person plural is also used for the epicene plural of the third person. For the third person singular and neuter plural the bare stem with the suffix *nu* is used.

	Singular	Plural
1st	*naḍachudunu, naḍatunu*	*naḍachudumu, naḍatumu*
2nd	*chēyuduvu, chētuvu*	*chēyuduru, chēturu*
3rd M.	*chēyunu, chēśunu*	*chēyuduru, chēturu* (M. and F.)
3rd F.	*cheyunu, chēśunu*	
3rd N.	*chēyunu, chēśunu*	*chēyunu, chēśunu*

140. Imperatives and Benedictives

The Imperative First person—This occurs only in the plural and includes the speaker and the person addressed.

(1) *koṭṭudamu* *koṭṭudāmu*

(2) *chēyudamu* *chēyudāmu*

chētamu *chetāmu*

(3) *naḍuchudamu* *naḍuchudāmu*

naḍutama *naḍutāmu*

Note—In the case of roots ending in *chu* and *yu* the *chudu* and *yudu* of the aorist, and *chudu, yuda* and the *chuda* and *yudā* of the imperative are optionally replaced by *tu, ta* and *tā* respectively. In causal verbs we have three alternative forms :—

koṭṭinchudunu	*koṭṭintunu*	*koṭṭimpudunu*
divinchudamu	*divintamu*	*divimpudamu*
dīvinchudāmu	*dīvintāmu*	*dīvimpudāmu*

The Imperative Second person :

(*a*) singular (1) the bare root, (2) suffix *mu*.

Example—*koṭṭu, koṭṭumu, chēyu, chēyumu.*

(*b*) Plural suffixes *aṇḍu, uṇḍu, uḍu.*

Example—*koṭṭaṇḍī, chēyaṇḍī, chēyuṇḍā, kōyuḍī, venudu.*

Note—The forms *Koṭṭandu, chēyaṇḍu,* are likely to be mistaken for the third person masculine singular of the negative verb; the affixes *i, ī, ā* usually added to the imperative plural distinguish these from the negative, but we may have *koṭṭuṇḍu, chēyuḍu.*

(*c*) In the case of roots ending in *chu* the following peculiarities must be noticed. (Campbell's Telugu Grammar rules 359, 361, 362.)

(1) one class of roots including *niluchu* 'stand', *lēchu* 'rise', *piluchu* 'call', *naḍuchu* 'walk', replace *chu* by *vu* before the imperative terminations.

Example—*niluvumu, niluvaṇḍī, piluvuḍu, lēvaṇḍī.*

(2) A second class including *ūḍuchu* 'sweep', *tuḍuchu* 'cleanse by rubbing', *mōchu* 'bear a burden', *valachu* 'love' optionally replace *chu* by *vu:*—

Example—*ūḍchumu, ūḍvumu, mōchaṇḍī, tuḍuvuṇḍu.*

(3) A third class including *rāchu* 'rub', *kāchu* 'attend', *tūchu* 'weigh', *enchu* 'think' retain the *chu* always and have no optional forms.

Example—*rāchamu, kāchaṇḍī, tūchuṇḍu.*

(4) The fourth and the last class including causals optionally replace—*chu* by *pu.*

Example—*dīvinchumu, dīvimpumu, dīvinchaṇḍi.*

The Imperative Third person.—Suffixes *eḍun, tan.* This is really a benedictive form and is used in blessing, cursing etc.

nīku mēlu kaligeḍunu *mūku mēlu kalugutanu*	'May you have prosperity'.

When followed by a word with an initial vowel the final *n* of *eḍun* and *tan* is changed into *m.* (C.B. verbs 26 and 28.)

Example—*mīku mēlu kaligeḍumaniye.*
mīku melu kalugutamaniye.

141. Some miscellaneous forms

(*a*) *Bālavyākaraṇamu* (C.B. verbs 27) mentions an imperative form obtained by adding the demonstrative pronoun *adi* to the third person singular of the aorist:—*chēyunadi*. 'you should do, he should do, it should be done', *uṇḍunadi*, *prōchunadi* etc.

This form corresponds to the third person neuter singular of the tense formed with the sign *p* or *v* in Tamil and Kanarese. Tamil *koḍupadu*, Kanarese *kuḍuvadu* 'should be given'. (98 C 124 a.)

(*b*) The forms *pōnī* 'let it go', *rānī* 'let it come', *uṇḍani* 'let it be, let it alone' may be mentioned here. These imply permission or assent on the part of the speaker though supposed to be formed by the addition of the verb *ī* 'give, allow' to the infinitive as thus :—

rānī=*ran*+*ī* 'allow to come', *ī* being here supposed to be another form of the imperative *immu*. But a comparison with the corresponding forms in Tamil and Kanarese does not support this derivation.

(*c*) The form *kāka* used as an auxiliary in benedictives is the only remnant of the old benedictives in *ka*; it is the optative form of *agu* 'be', 'become' and is equivalent to the Tamil *ākuka* 'may it become'.

Example—*uṇḍeḍugāka*, *avugāka*, 'may it become'.

142. Miscellaneous verbal forms

(*a*) Verbal nouns : Suffixes (1) *aḍamu* (2) *ṭa*

Example—*koṭṭaḍamu*, *chēyaḍamu*, *koṭṭuṭa*, *chēyuṭa*, *chēsuṭa*, *pōyaḍamu*, *pōyuṭa*, *pōsuṭā*.

Note—Bases ending in *vu* change the *vu* into *su* when taking the suffix *ṭa*.

(*b*) *Infinitives.*—Suffixes are (1) the fourth case of verbal nouns (2) *an* or *a*.

Example—*chēyaḍāniki, pōsuṭaku, chēyan, chēya, pōya.*

The forms in *an* and *a* are used in the senses of (1) for the purpose of (2) so as to, so that, (3) when, while. The fourth case of the verbal noun is used only in the first of these senses. In the last of the senses the forms in *-an* and *a* are often strengthened by *kan* as *undagan, chēyagan.*

(*c*) Before the infinitive suffixes *an* and *a* and the verbal noun suffix *-aḍamu* the final syllable of roots ending in *chu* is replaced by *vu* or *pu* in the same manner and to the same extent as before the endings of the imperative second person.

(1) *niluva, nadavaḍamu, piluvan, lēvaḍamu.*

(2) *ūḍchan, ūḍvan, tuḍuchanḍamu, tuḍuvaḍamu.*

(3) *rāchan, rāchaḍamu, kāchan, kāchaḍamu.*

(4) *dīvinchan, dīvimpan, dīvinchaḍamu, dīvimpaḍamu.*

(*d*) Subjunctives suffixes (1) *ēni*, (2) *an* or *ā* and (3) *ē* (*tē*). The first of these is used with finite verbs, the others with verbal participles.

(1) *koṭṭinānēni* 'If I beat' *Chēśinānēni, chēstineni*

(2) *koṭṭina* 'If I, we, you, he, she etc., beat' *koṭṭinā, chēśina, chēsina.*

(3) *koṭṭite* 'If I, we, you, he, she, etc. beat' *chēśite, chēstē.*

The last of these appears to be a *drutaprakṛitika* as it appears with the final *n* in some of the dialects. Also compare the combination *chēstē*+*emi*=*chēstenēmi* 'what if it is done?'

(*e*) Relative participles:

(1) Present—*chēyuchunna, chēstunna, dīvinchuchunna, dīvimpuchunna, dīvinchutunna, dīvistunna.*

(2) Past—*Chēśina, koṭṭina, naḍichina.*

(3) Indefinite—*koṭṭu, chēyu, chēseḍu, chēsē, chēśeḍi, chēsēṭi.*

The indefinite forms *koṭṭu, chēyu* are *drutaprakṛitika* and should be regarded as the third person singular aorist used like the Tamil tense form *śeyyum* in the sense of a relative participle. They give rise to agent nouns, the *druta* making its appearance when the following pronoun has an initial vowel.

Example—*Koṭṭuvāru, chēyuvāru, chēyunataḍu.*

(*f*) Verbal participles:

(1) Present—*chēyuchun, chēstun, chestū.*

(2) Past—*koṭṭi, chēśi, naḍichi.*

143. Causal bases

(*a*) With a few exceptions roots ending in *chu* form their causal bases by changing *chu* into *pinchu*:—*piluchu* 'call' *pilipinchu. maṟachu* 'forget', *maṟapinchu. teṟachu* 'open' *teṟapinchu. naḍachu* 'walk' *naḍapinchu.*

Exceptions—*lēchu* 'rise' *lēpu. vachchu* 'come', *rappinchu. niluchu* 'stand', *nilupu. echchu* 'increase', *echchinchu. mōchu* 'bear', *mōpu. chachchu* 'die' *champu. chūchu* 'see', *chūpu* or *chūpinchu.*

(*b*) Roots not ending in *chu* generally form their causal bases by changing the final *u* into *inchu.*

koṭṭu 'strike', *koṭṭinchu. chēyu* 'do' *chēyinchu. aṇṭu* 'touch', *antinchu. panḍu* 'ripen' *panḍinchu. kōyu* 'cut' *kōyinchu.*

There are about sixty exceptions to this rule of which some are mentioned below:—

(1) *Kāgu* 'boil' *kāchu.* (2) *dāgu* 'conceal oneself' *dāchu.* (3) *tūgu* 'weigh' *tūchu.* (4) *ūgu* 'be rocked' *ūchu.* (5) *kungu* 'sink' *kunchu.* (6) *vangu* 'bend' *vanchu.*

(7) *maragu* 'be habituated', *marapu.* (8) *medugu* 'be injured', *medupu.* (9) *malugu* 'be extinguished', *malupu.* (10) *tunugu* 'be broken', *tumpu, tunchu.* (11) *kālu* 'burn' *kāluchu.* (12) *kūlu* 'fall down', *kūluchu.*

144. Miscellaneous observations

The *y* of the roots ending in *yu* like *chēyu, kōyu* etc. becomes sibilant when moved by the initial vowels of the suffixes of the past and the future tenses: *i, enu, ina, iti, ē, eda, eḍunu, eḍini, ēni, īni*; but not when moved by the initial vowels of the infinitive suffixes *an, a* or of the verbal noun suffix *aḍamu* or of the causative suffix *inchu*; this *y* also optionally becomes sibilant before the verbal noun suffix *ṭa*, *y* and *ch* become sibilant when by the loss of the final *u* of roots they come in intimate contact with the *t* of the suffixes *tun, tā, ti.* The intimate contact of this *t* with the *n* of the roots *anu* 'say', *konu* 'buy', *tinu* 'eat', *vinu* 'hear' etc. renders both of them cerebral.

The alternative forms in the imperative first person and the aorist first and second persons in which the final *chu* and *yu* of the roots are rejected and the *d* of the suffixes is replaced by *t* indicate a stage when there was no *chu* or *yu* added to the roots and the tense sign was *t* as in the old Tamil *t* aorist; the *d* of Telugu in the forms under consideration is thus merely due to the intervocal pronunciation of an original *t.* It is remarkable that the third person aorist forms in *t* should be wanting both in Tamil and in Telugu.

The alternative causal aorist forms *koṭṭintunu, koṭṭimpudunu* and *kottinchudunu* appear to indicate that the causal base was originally only *koṭṭi* (as now in Malayāḷam) then *koṭṭimpu* and lastly *koṭṭinchu.*

The hard and medial pronunciation of *t* in *naḍutunu, naḍutamu* and *koṭṭudunu* respectively appears to indicate that *naḍa* or *naḍu* was originally an accented root in Telugu as it is now in Tamil; this surmise will hold good with reference to all roots now ending in *chu* or *yu*.

The infinitive forms *niluvan* (intransitive) and *nilupan* (causal) would seem to indicate that the present Tamil practice of accenting some verbs when transitive and pronouncing them without any stress when intransitive was probably in vogue in Telugu also formerly.

These alternative forms and other relics which are preserved in Telugu are of great help to the philologist in tracing the development of Telugu roots and of Dravidian forms generally.

CHAPTER VIII

TELUGU DIALECTS

145. KOMTAU

This is the speech of the shop-keepers of Chanda and does not differ much from the standard Telugu as spoken by the people in this Presidency. (L.S. Vol. IV, pp. 594-5.)

Indefinite tense: *aṇṭādu* 'he says', *chastā* 'I die'. Conjunctive participles end in *i*.

Kāmāṭhī—This is a dialect of Telugu spoken by the *Kāmāṭhīs* or bricklayers of Bombay and its neighbourhood. The language has been much influenced by the neighbouring Aryan forms of speech but is still a pure Dravidian dialect. (p. 596.)

Indefinite tense: *aṇṭāḍu* 'he says', *sastā* 'I am dying', *pōtā* 'I will go', *chēstāmu* 'we will make'.

Future : anēnu 'shall say'.

Conjunctive participles end in *i*.

The past third person singular ending in *enu* in the standard Telugu always ends in *yā* in this dialect: *Āyā* 'it became', *pōyā* 'he went', *uṇḍya* 'he stayed', *chapyā* 'he said', *sūśy* 'he saw'.

146. DASARI

Dāsaris are wandering beggars in Belgaum. Some of them speak Kanarese, others Telugu. (pp. 599-601).

Indefinite tense : tastā 'I die'.

Conjunctive participles end in *i*.

The past third person singular ending in *enu* in the standard Telugu always ends in *e* in this dialect :—*ane* 'he said', *āye* 'it became', *cheppe* 'he said'.

The oblique forms of the indefinite relative participles are peculiar: *tinēṭa* 'eating', *uṇḍeṭa* 'being'.

Verbal nouns are formed from the participles in *eḍu:*— *pāḍa-eḍḍi* 'singing', *chāli-baṭṭaḍḍi* 'dancing', *eyaḍḍi* 'obtaining or becoming'. Note also *mēpaḍānki* 'to feed', *anipicha-konaḍaḍānki* 'to be called'.

The suffix of causal verbs has the form *ichu* or *ichchu,* not *inchu :—tinipichināḍu* 'he has made feast', *anipichakona-ḍam* 'causing to be called', *tappichkoni* 'having been lost'.

147. Beradi

The Bèraḍs are an aboriginal tribe of Belgaum scattered all over the district who speak a dialect of Telugu in which Kanarese forms are occasionally used. (pages 602-6.)

Indefinite tense : pōtānu 'I am going', *ostān* 'I will come', *ostāyi* 'it will come', *sastān* 'am dying'. Conjunctive participles are formed with *i.*

The past third person Masculine often ends in *iḍi :*— *śeppiḍi* 'he said', *śikkiḍi* 'he was found', *uḍḍi* (*uḍiḍi*) 'he was', *pōkayiḍi* 'he did not go'.

The following past forms containing the suffix *ti* occur without personal endings : *aḍigiti* 'he asked', *mīrk agati* (agiti) 'I did not disobey', *isak-agati* (agiti ?) 'you did not give', *osti* 'I came'.

Verbal nouns : Ōsand 'coming', *kēsand* 'doing'.

The subjunctives often end in *tēn: agitēn* 'but', *Iyākudten* 'if (it) was not', *pōten* 'if (we) go'.

148. Vadari

This is the speech of a wandering tribe of quarrymen in the Bombay Presidency, the Berars and other districts. (pages 607-18.)

Indefinite tense : sastānu 'I am dying', *pōtānu* 'I will go', *cheputānu* 'I will say'. The following forms are puzzling: *kuḍisāmu* (615) 'we are enjoying', *kuḍiśyavu* 'thou enjoyest' (615), *sachchyāna* (611) 'I am dying'; they may be regarded as corruptions of forms containing the *cha* suffix, that is of the forms *kuḍuchuchāmu, kuḍuchuchāvu, chachchuchanu.*

Future *pōyāru* (pōyēru) 'They will go' (613), *paḍēru* 'they might fall' (614), *pōyēnu* 'I will go', *cheppēnu* 'I will say'. (618.)

Conjunctive participles end in *i* except in two cases where they are shown as ending in *ya* ; but in these two instances the forms may also be construed as final verbs in the third person singular. Conjunctive participles and past tense forms are often strengthened by an auxiliary of the form *kin, kēn, kōn* even if the verb is not used reflexively.

Conjunctive participles : *phaliśi-kinya* (*pilchikoni*), (615) 'having called', *nābisi-kinya* (615) 'having taken off', *niṅchikōni* (609), 'having filled', *tiskōni* (611) *tiskēni* (617) 'taking', *ankōni* (611) 'having said', *naḍas-kōni* 'having behaved', *kuḍakēni* 'joining' (617), *yegarkoṭṭi-koni* (618) 'spent having made', *poikyāsi* 'having gone' (617).

The past tense forms in the third person singular may be noted. *Sarpu-kinya* 'he spent', *kuḍyas-kinya* 'he collected', *karchis-kinya* (609) 'he spent', *anyā* 'she said' (615), *pāḍlēpyā* 'he wasted' (611) *uṇḍya* 'she was', *uṇḍe* 'there were' (613), *dōśe* 'it appeared' (613), *ane* 'he said' (613), *sikke* 'he was found'.

Verbal nouns *aḍēdi* 'dancing', *udēdi* 'music' (610)

CHAPTER IX

PRO-DRAVIDIAN AORISTS

149. The pro-dravidian aorist

In Chapter VII are brought together all the Dravidian suffixes which it is proposed to deal with in this book. Some of them are special to individual languages and must have been adopted by these during their individual development after separation from the common parent tongue, while other suffixes common to two or more languages must have been in use from the pro-Dravidian and pro-ethnic periods. It is necessary to classify the suffixes according to the periods in which they first came into use. The verbal bases themselves have undergone great changes, most of them being now longer by one syllable *ku*, *tu*, *pu*, *chu*, or *su*, than in the pro-ethnic period. As an examination of the changes which the bases have undergone throws considerable light on the nature and age of the suffixes we shall deal with these changes first. In groups of languages other than the Dravidian such formative additions which result in the mere lengthening of the roots arise from tense or modal suffixes—the special significations of which had become lost in course of time. It is assumed that the five formative syllables mentioned above owe their origin to similar causes and have arisen from tense and modal suffixes of the pro-ethnic and pro-Dravidian period, and we proceed to consider to what extent it can be explained on the basis of philology.

There was undoubtedly a *k*- conjugation in the pro-Dravidian period which was one of the earliest grammatical forms of that period and of which the following remnants have come down to us.

Language	*Grammatical suffixes*	*Person and number in which used*	*Tenses indicated by suffixes*
Old Tamil (108)	*kum* (*um*)	3rd person singular and neuter plural	present future and habitual present
do.	*ku* (singular) *kum* (plural)	1st person	Future and present
Modern Tamil (98-b)	*kum* (*um*)	3rd person singular and neuter plural	Future and habitual present
Modern Malayalam (117-a)	*kum* (*um*)	All persons and numbers	Future
Literary Malayalam (117-b)	*ku* (*u*)	All persons and numbers	Future
Old Kanarese (123)	*kum* (*gum*) *ku*, *gu*	3rd person all numbers	All tenses

Telugu (136). *Koṭṭunu*, *chēyunu*, etc. of the aorist third person is of the same form as the Tamil *śeyyum* and if it is open to us to say that a *ku* has been elided in the Telugu forms as has probably been the case with the Tamil *śeyyum* (98 a) then Telugu will be brought into line with the other languages.

We have to reconstruct the pro-Dravidian *k*- conjugation from the above remnants. The theory put forth in this book is that this *k* conjugation merely consisted in adding *ku*, that is, *k* with the enunciative *u*, to all roots and using the combination in all persons, numbers and genders without any personal endings and probably in all tenses except perhaps the definite past. The *m* of *kum* is the sign of another conjugation (which came to be superadded to *ku*, except in the case of the first person forms in Old Tamil where *m* is the sign of the plural number.

The initial *k* of the suffix was doubled after accented roots and pronounced intervocally as *h* or *g* after unaccented words. In Kanarese *k* was retained only in certain harsh combinations (123 b) like *rk*, *lk*, *ḷk*, etc., and after the causative and the Sanskritic *i*, and became *g* in all other cases. As stated in 98 b. the *um* of Tamil arises from the elision of *k* in *kum* after unaccented roots ; a similar explanation probably holds good for the *u* of literary Malayalam. The *kū* and *ū* of literary Malayalam may be supposed to arise from the elision of the final *m* and the compensatory lengthening of the preceding *u* in *kum* and *um*.

150. Root-extension in Tamil and Malayalam

Examples have been given in 95 *c* of verbal bases in modern Tamil which are transitive or intransitive according as they are accented or unaccented. The number of such bases appears to have been much more numerous in the pro-Dravidian period and the *k* conjugation must have given rise to two tense forms—transitive (or causal) and intransitive—corresponding to each base. Thus corresponding to the base *kuṟu* which now means 'short (adj.)', there were two forms *kuṟukku* and *kuṟuku* which were probably first used as aorist tenses without personal terminations ; when such terminations subsequently came to be added and other conjugational signs came to be super-added and the original forms ending in *ku* ceased to be looked upon as finite verbs. They are now treated merely as extended uninflected verbal bases, and in the case of many of them the original roots have now no separate existence in the language.

Intransitive	*Transitive or causal*	*Original root*
kuṟuku 'become short'	*kuṟukku* 'shorten'	*kuru* 'short' (adj.)
peruku 'swell as a flood'	*perukku* 'cause to swell'	*peru* (a) large (adj.) (b) become large
paḻaku 'become familiar'	*paḻakku* 'train, accustom'	*paḻa* 'old' (adj.)
karuku 'become black by heat'	*karukku* 'blacken by heat'	*karu* (1) black (adj.) (2) become black
uruku 'become liquid'	*urukku* 'liquefy'	
iṟuku 'become tight'	*iṟukku* 'tighten'	
vilaku 'step aside'	*vilakku* 'put aside'	

In the vast majority of cases, however, the *k* of *ku* has become softened to *g* and also nasalised in the intransitive form.

vaṇaṅgu 'be bent, bow'	*vaṇakku* 'cause to bend'	*vaṇai*, *vaḷai* 'bend' (v.t., v.i.)
iṇaṅgu 'agree, suit'	*iṇakku* 'cause to agree or to suit'	*iṇai* (v.t., v.i.) 'suit'
uṇaṅgu 'be dried'	*uṇakku* 'cause to dry'	*ushna* 'heat' (subs)
aḍaṅgu 'be enclosed or subdued'	*aḍakku* 'enclose, subdue'	*aḍai* (v.i.) go in (v.t.) put in
oduṅgu 'step aside'	*odukku* 'put aside'	*ottu* 'go aside'
puḻuṅgu 'be boiled or heated'	*puḻukku* 'boil or heat'	*prush* (Sanskrit) 'burn, consume'
tuḷaṅgu } *viḷaṅgu* } 'become bright'	*tuḷakku* } *viḷakku* } 'burnish'	
amuṅgu 'be immersed' (in a fluid)	*amukku* 'immerse'	
iṟaṅgu 'come down'	*irakku* 'let down'	

kuluṅgu 'shake'	*kulukku* 'cause to shake'
śuruṅgu 'shrink'	*śurukku* 'shorten'

There are many instance. in which only one member of the couplet, either the transitive or the intransitive, exists in Tamil :—

tiruku (v.t.) 'twist'	*pudukku* (v.t.) 'renovate'
oḻuku (v.i.) 1. 'leak' 2. 'behave'	*meḻuku* (v.t.) 'daub a place with dung, mud, chunam etc.'
viḻuṅgu (v.t.) 'swallow'	

It is hardly necessary to add that in the case of every verb, transitive or intransitive, ending in *-gu,* or *-ku* a causal base can be formed by the addition of the suffix *-vi.*

It is unnecessary to give separate examples for Malayāḷam as almost all the couplets given above exist also in that language though with occasional shades of difference in meaning.

151. ROOT-EXTENSION IN KANARESE

In Kanarese also we find a large number of roots lengthened by a *ku* or *gu* suffix, but the system of accenting roots have been early discontinued in that language we find fewer couplets than in Tamil and even in those few the distinction noticed in Tamil that the suffix *ku* (*k* hard) generally occurs in causal or transitive bases and the suffix *gu* in the non-causal or intransitive bases is but rarely observable.

Aḍagu, *adaṅgu* (v.i.) 'be compressed' and

aḍaku (v.t.) 'press into a narrow compass'

furnish a rare instance of a couplet in which the Tamil distinction is preserved. In the following instances both members are used indifferently either as transitives or intransitives or both :—

muḻugu *muḻuku*	(v.i.) 'sink under water'
tāgu *tāku*	(v.i.) 'joint' (v.t.) 'come in contact with' 'attack'
toḍagu *toḍaku*	(v.t.) 'commence, undertake'; *todagu* is also used intransitively.
minugu *minuku*	(v.i.) 'shine, glitter'

In the vast majority of cases the bases do not occur in couplets, and we find only one member either with a *gu* or a *ku* suffix:

beḷagu (v.i.) 'shine'; (v.t.) 'cause to shine'
tūgu (v.i.) 'be suspended' 'rock, swing'
kargu, kaḻgu (v.i.) 'turn back'
karagu, kargu, karangu (v.i.) 'melt, dissolve' (v.t.) 'melt'

tolagu (v.i.) 'go away', 'fail', 'disappear'
toḷagu (v.i.) 'shine', 'be full of splendour'
naḍugu (v.i.) 'tremble'

nalagu *nalugu*	(v.i.) 'be crumpled', 'grown weak', 'droop
maḍagu *maḍangu*	(v.t.) 'lay down', 'put', 'hide'
maṇagu *malagu*	(v.i.) 'bend', 'be submissive'
malagu *malangu*	(v.i.) 'lie down', 'recline'
mingu *miṟugu* *misugu*	(v.i.) 'shine', 'glitter'

kalaku } (v.t.) 'stir', 'perturb'. *kalaku* is also used
kalanku } intransitively.

kedaku (v.t.) 'stir', 'dig up'
keṇaku (v.t.) 'stir', 'provoke'
kuluku (v.t.) 'shake', 'agitate'

niluku
niliku
nilku
nilaku } (v.i.) 'stretch one's self', 'stand on tip-toe'

There was a rule in Old Kanarese (K.K.G. 183-7) that bases ending in *gu* could form their present future relative participle either in the usual way by adding *va* to the base, or by eliding the final *gu* and then adding *pa*; as remarked in 127 a. above this optional form must have arisen in a stage of the language when the bases in question had not been extended by the suffix *gu*. The grammar does not mention similar optional forms in the case of bases ending in *ku*; but it cannot be inferred from this omission that these bases were later formations. For *kalaku* and *kuluku*, for instance, in the above list occur also in Tamil and probably go back to the pro-Dravidian period.

152. ROOT-EXTENSION IN TELUGU

(*a*) Telugu also contains a good number of verbal bases ending in *gu* and *ku*, but these bases do not generally occur in couplets and in the few that so occur both members appear to be intransitives.

Examples—

vakku } (v.i.) 'become lean or emaciated'. The forms probably have arisen from *valuku* and *valugu*,
vaggu } e.g. *valiyu* (v.i.) having the same signification.

chituku } (v.i.) 'be crushed or broken, break, burst'.
chidugu }

visuku
visugu } (v.i.) 'be tired or disgusted, be sick of'

In several cases the bases that look like couplets are really unconnected with each other and are etymologically different.

Examples—

aḍugu } (v.t.) 'ask, question, beg, demand'
aḍuku } (v.t.) 'pile up, arrange in a set or series'

ēgu } (v.i.) 'go, repair, proceed, resort'
ēku } (v.t.) 'pick or clean cotton; defame, expose'

chinugu } (v.i.) 'be torn or rent'
chinuku } (v.i.) 'fall into drops'

uḍugu } (v.t.) 'give up, leave, desist from'
uḍuku } (v.i.) 'boil, simmer; be annoyed, or vexed'

dōku } (v.t.) 'dig slightly so as to loosen the soil'
dōgu } (v.i.) 'go on all fours as an infant'

tolagu } (v.i.) 'move, step aside, disappear'
toḍagu } (v.i.) 'begin, be commenced'

tolaku, toḍaku (v.i.) 'be slightly shaken, be spilled'

sāgu (v.i.) 'go on, proceed; take effect, be effective'

sāgu (v.i.) 'extend, lengthen, prostrate one's self'

sāku, sāku (v.t.) 'rear, bring up, foster, train up.'

(*b*) There is not perhaps a single couplet in Telugu resembling the Tamil ones instanced in 147 above where the bases ending in *ku* (*k* hard) are the transitive or the causal forms of the corresponding intransitive and non-causal forms ending in *gu*, or *hu* (*k* inter-vocal). Of the Telugu roots ending in *gu* a few form their causals by changing *gu* into *pu*, but the vast majority of them change *gu* into *chu* or add the suffix *inchu*.

Bases			Causal and some other derived forms	
adagu / *aṇagu*	(v.i.)	'be suppresed, submit.	(caus.)	*aḍchu*, *aḍaginchu*, *aṇachu*
			(der.)	*adakuva*, *aṇakuva* 'humility'
kalagu	(v.i.)	'be confused or disturbed'	(caus.)	*kalachu*
			(der.)	*kalakuva*, *kalaka* 'confusion'
maḍagu / *maḍugu*	(v.i.)	'be folded, bend'	(caus.)	*maḍchu*, *maḍuchu*
			(der.)	*maḍaka* 'a fold'
penagu	(v.i.)	'be twisted'	(caus.)	*penachu*
			(der.)	*penakuva* 'a quarrel'
kāgu	(v.i.)	'be heated, grown hot'	(caus.)	*kāchu*
			(der.)	*kāka* 'heat, anger'
ūgu	(v.i.)	'be rocked, swing'	(caus.)	*ūchu*, *uginchu*, *ūpu*
			(der.)	*uka* 'swinging'
tolagu	(v.i.)	'vanish', step aside, disappear'	(caus.)	*tolachu*, *tolaginchu*
malagu	(v.i.)	'turn back, be twisted	(caus.)	*malachu*, *malapu*
			(der.)	*malaka* 'a bend
vēgu	(v.i.)	'be fired, sorrow'	(caus.)	*vchu*, *vēyinchu*
			(der.)	*vēki* 'fever'
tunugu	(v.i.)	'be cut to pieces, be broken'	(caus.)	*tunchu*, *tunuchu*, *tumpu*
			(der.)	*tunuka* 'a fragment'
eṟugu	(v.t.)	'know, under-stand'	(der.)	*eṟukava*, *eṟuka* 'know-ledge'
kaḍagu	(v.i.)	'endeavour, strive, attempt'	(der.)	*kaḍanka*, *kaḍaka* 'endeavour'

Bishop Caldwell's explanation of the suffixes *chu* and *inchu* (C.D.G. pp. 96 to 98, 347 to 354) is that they arise from the palatalization of *ku* and *ikku*. This explanation is entirely untenable; for there are many Telugu forms as in the table above in which the *k* of the original *ku* suffix has not been palatalised and it will be shown later that the predecessors of *chu* and *inchu* are not *ku* and *ikku* but *pu* and *impu*.

153. THE PLEONASTIC KU SUFFIX

It is well to note here that we have no evidence that *ku* or *gu* was ever used as a tense sign in Telugu whether with or without personal endings. There is evidence that they were so used in the third person in Old Kanarese without personal endings; we also know from specimens that have come down to us that *ku* was so used in the first person in Old Tamil and in all persons in literary Malayāḷam.

Kum and *gum* were used in Old Kanarese in the third person as tense signs without personal endings; and *kum* and *um* are now so used as tense signs in third person in Tamil and in all persons in Malayāḷam. Assuming the identity of the Telugu *nu* in the aorist forms *chēyunu*, *koṭṭunu* etc., with the *m* of the Tamil aorists *śeyyum*, *varum*, etc., it has been surmised that a *ku* or a *gu* has been elided in these Telugu forms. There is however, no necessity for making the surmise; for if *nu* arises from *m* the sign of a separate conjugation, it may itself express the tense of the Telugu forms without being tacked on to *ku* or *gu*. In this alternative view the Telugu forms *chēyunu*, *koṭṭunu* etc. will not come under the *k* aorist, but under the *p*- conjugation to which *m* belongs.

There are several unaccented verbal bases in Tamil to which a *ku* is often pleonastically added. Thus we have *seykuvēṉ* 'I shall do', *pōkuvōm* 'we shall go', *varukuvīr* 'you will come' etc. in addition to the usual forms *śeyvēṉ*, *pōvōm*, *varuvīr* etc. In Malayāḷam we have the forms *koḍukkuvān* 'he will give' *naḍakkuvāṉ* 'he will walk' etc., side by side with *koḍuppāṉ*, *naḍappāṉ* etc. In old Kanarese also in the special conjugation with *kum, gum, ku, gu* (K.K.G. 203) they used to add *gu* pleonastically to the base.

māḍikugum 'he will cause to make'
āgugugum 'it becomes'
nilgugum 'she will stand'

etc., side by side with *māḍikum, āgugum, nilgum* etc.

In negative verbs, a *ku* suffix is often pleonastically added to the verbal base in Tamil and Malayāḷam: *Koḍukkāṉ* 'he will not give', *naḍakkāṉ* 'he will not walk' etc., side by side with *koḍāṉ*, *naḍavāṉ* etc. In modern Malayāḷam the use of the suffix is obligatory in the case of accented roots.

The above are relics of an old practice of adding *ku* to every root before proceeding to conjugate it.

The infinitives and subjunctives of all roots in Modern Malayāḷam contain a *ku* suffix :

naḍakka, naḍakkil, tarika, tarikil, śeyka, śeykil.

In non-literary Tamil a doubled *K* invariably appears in the infinitives and subjunctives of accented roots; in the case of unaccented roots the use of *k* is unnecessary though often optionally allowed:

variṉ, śeyyiṉ, uṇka, uṇṇa, uṇkiṉ, uṇṇil, śeykiṉ.

The fuller forms of Malayāḷam may be taken as proof that a *ku* suffix which had lost its original signification continued to be added to every root in some inflections; the initial *k* of this suffix when it was not doubled was often elided in Tamil and in literary Malayāḷam.

It has been stated in 112 C. above that the infinitive suffix *a* has arisen from the loss of *i* in *al*, and the question arises whether infinitives and verbal nouns in Tamil and

Malayāḷam were formed by the addition of *kal* in the pro-Dravidian period. This question must be answered in the affirmative. The verbal nouns in *kal* appear to have been replaced by formations in *tal* and are now exceedingly rare in Tamil in the case of roots which have not been permanently lengthened by a *ku* suffix. Two of such rare instances are,

koḍukkal 'giving' and *mōkkal* 'smelling'

koḍukkal vāṅgal 'lending and borrowing, money transactions'

mōkkalum mōndaṉaṉ (Kali. 54).

Per *contra* may be quoted cases in *al* where we should expect *tal* or *kal*:—

Kuḍiyal eṇṇai 'oil fit for (human) consumption'.

154. THE PRO-DRAVIDIAN '*t*' AORIST

There is no trace of a *t* aorist even in the oldest specimens of Kanarese that have come down to us; but it existed in Old Tamil and exists now in Telugu:

Language	*Suffixes* *Singular*	*Plural*	*Persons in which used*	*Mood or tense indicated*
Old Tamil (107)	*tu*	*tum*	1st person	aorist
	ti, tai	*tir*	2nd person	aorist
	tunu	*tumu*	1st person	aorist
	tuvu	*turu*	2nd person	aorist
		turu	3rd person epicene	aorist
		tamu	1st person	Imperative
		tamu	(includes the person addressed).	

The *t* of the suffixes will be pronounced like *d* after unaccented roots in Tamil and after all roots in Telugu except where *chu* and *yu* of the roots are optionally omitted. The *m* of *tum* in Old Tamil is a plural sign; *i*, *ai*, and *ir* in Old Tamil and *nu*, *mu*, *vu*, *ru*, *amu*, and *āmu* in Telugu are personal endings or their final syllables. It is remarkable that this aorist should be defective in the third person in both these languages.

The theory put forward in this book is that this conjugation must have originally consisted in merely adding *tu*—that is *t* with the enunciative *u*—to all roots and using the combination in all numbers and genders. The initial *t* of the suffix was doubled or pronounced hard after accented roots and sounded inter-vocally after other roots ending in *pu* to unaccented bases *tūṅgupu* 'hanging', *vāṅgupu* 'taking', *paḍupu* 'falling', *iḍupu* 'placing'; the *p* of the suffixes having the value of the English *f*. Such participles are exceedingly common in Paripāḍal.

The meanings of the p *forms*—The illustration given in 98 (c), 124 (a, e) under Tamil and Kanarese suffixes make it abundantly clear that the original significance of the *p* sign was necessity or obligation which, as usual, has in most cases degenerated into mere futurity. In Old Tamil the *p* forms were also used with a present signifaction; in Kanarese relative participles with the *p* (v.b.) sign are called by Dr. Kittel present-future participles and have an aorist sense.

155. PU BASES IN TAMIL, MALAYALAM AND TELUGU

In this and the two succeeding articles are brought together a number of Dravidian forms containing suffixes of which *p*, *b* or *v* forms the essential part, but it must not be supposed that they all contain the future suffix which originally connoted (98 b above) necessity, obligation, promise etc.; most of them do not.

There are in Tamil-Malayāḷam a number of *pu* causal bases, the non-causal forms of these end in *mbu*.

Non-causal	*Causal*
eḻumbu 'rise'	*eḻuppu*
tirumbu 'turn'	*tiruppu*
kiḻambu 'rise'	*kiḻappu*
kūmbu 'shut, close (as a flower)	*kūppu*
nirambu 'to be filled'	*nirappu*
kuḻambu 'become turbid'	*kuḻappu*

Kanarese has some of these forms, but as in the case of the *ku* and *tu* suffixes as the tenues and mediae have not separate functions assigned to them. Thus *tiruppu*, *tirumbu* and *tiruvu* are all transitive verbs; *eḻbu* is intransitive while *erbu* is transitive and *ebbu* is both.

Telugu makes a first show under the head of *pu* causals but the non-causal forms of these bases have suffixes belonging to other conjugations.

Non-causal	*Causal*
tirugu ' turn '	*trippu, tippu*
nalugu 'be crushed'	*nalupu*
maragu 'be habituated'	*marapu*
malugu 'be extinguished'	*malupu*
medugu 'be beaten in mortar'	*meduupu*
mēyu 'graze'	*mēpu*
māyu 'be tarnished'	*māpu*
lēchu 'rise'	*lēpu*
chachchu 'die'	*champu*
mōchu 'bear to burden'	*mōpu*

There are besides bases like, *chiduku* 'burst '; *sāgu* 'be stretched'; '*dangu*' 'be beaten in mortar'; *chinugu* 'be torn'; *tunugu* 'be broken'; *tegu* 'be cut'; *digu* 'descend'; *trāgu*, 'drink'; *uḍugu*, 'leave'; *zarugu* 'slide, pass', which have alternative causal bases besides *chidupu*, *sāpu*, *dampu*, *chimpu*, *tumpu*, *tempu*, *dimpu*, *trāpu*, *udupu*, *zarupu*.

where *chu* and *yu* of the roots are optionally omitted. The *m* of *tum* in Old Tamil is a plural sign; *i*, *ai*, and *ir*, in Old Tamil and *nu*, *mu*, *vu*, *ru*, *amu*, and *āmu*, in Telugu are personal endings, or their final syllables. It is remarkable that this aorist should be defective in the third person in both these languages.

The theory put forward in this book is that this conjugation must have originally consisted in merely adding *tu*—that is *t* with the enunciative *u*—to all roots and using the combination in all numbers and genders. The initial *t* of the suffix was doubled or pronounced hard after accented roots and sounded inter-vocally after other roots ending in vowels; where the roots ended in consonants the *t* of the suffix underwent suitable modifications in combination with these consonants. The *t* aorist forms in Old Tamil were often indistinguishable from the past tense forms in *t* or *d*; and the confusion arising in consequence was no doubt the main reason why those forms have been discontinued in Tamil. If this aorist had ever existed in Kanarese it must have been discontinued in that language for this same reason. There is no such confusion in Telugu where the aorist forms are clearly distinguished from the past tense forms in *ti*; further, these past forms do not appear to have existed in the pro-Dravidian period and are probably of late origin.

§ 154 (*a*). THE PRO-DRAVIDIAN *p* CONJUGATION

From the analogy of the *k* and *t* aorists we should expect that in the pro-ethnic period the *p* conjugation merely consisted in affixing *pu*—that is, *p* with the enunciative *u*—to the root or base and using the form so obtained in all persons numbers and genders without personal endings. But even the oldest specimens that we have in Tamil and Kanarese combine personal endings with the *p* sign and we have no evidence that *p* tense forms were ever in use without such endings except in literary Malayalam. In the tense forms of these three languages *p* is doubled or pronounced hard after accented bases, becomes *b*, sometimes *m*, after nasal bases, and is softened into *v* after other unaccented bases.

Tense forms with the *p* or the *v* sign do not occur at all in Telugu. They are supplemented in Tamil in the 3rd person by forms obtained by adding *kum* (*um*) to the base; these latter are the only forms in use in colloquial Malayalam. Old and mediaeval Kanarese possessed a special conjugation for the 3rd person in *kum* (*gum*) besides the *p*, *v*, *b*, forms applicable to all persons.

(*b*) Alternative forms with the pleonastic *ku* Suffix.

Putting together the Tamil and Malayalam forms with the tense sign *p* given in §98, §109, and §117, it follows that formerly there was an alternative method of forming this tense in which a pleonastic *ku* was interposed between the suffix *pu* and the root. In all these alternative forms *pu* was necessarily weakened into *vu* as the final short *u* of the extended bases was unaccented. Thus there must have been forms like *kodukkuvu* 'giving, will give', *rakshikkuvu* 'protecting, will protect', *vaykkuvu* 'placing, will place'; *pōkuvu* 'going, will go', side by side with *koduppu, rakshippu, vayppu, pōvu*; when personal endings were subsequently added, these alternative forms would have become *koduk-kuvaṉ*, *rakshikkuvaṉ* and *vaykkuvaṉ*, *pōkuvaṉ* of literary Malayalam.

The final *vu* of these alternative forms appears to have been a very unstable sound and it is apparently in consequence of this that *m* has been substituted for it in the popular dialect giving rise to the forms *kodukkum*, *rakshikkum*, *vaykkum*, *pōkum* (vide § 155, §156-a, below). This appears to be the origin of the suffix *kum* of Tamil, Malayalam and archaic Kanarese.

In Old Tamil there were in use verbal participles of the form *seypu* 'doing', formed by adding *pu* to unaccented bases—*tūṅgupu* 'hanging', *vāṅgupu* 'taking', *paḍupu* 'falling', *iḍupu* 'placing'; the *p* of the suffixes having the value of the English *f*. Such participles are exceedingly common in *Paripadal*.

(*c*) THE MEANINGS OF THE *p* FORMS.

The illustrations given in § 101 (c), § 127 (a, e,) under Tamil and Kanarese suffixes make it abundantly clear that the original significance of the *p* sign was necessity or obligation which, as usual, has in most cases degenerated into mere futurity. In Old Tamil the *p* forms were also used with a present signification; in Kanarese relative participles with the *p* (*v*, *b*) sign are called by Dr. Kittel present-future participles and have an aorist sense.

§ 155. *pu* BASES IN TAMIL, MALAYALAM, AND TELUGU.

In this and the two succeeding articles are brought together a number of Dravidian forms containing suffixes of which *p*, *b*, or *v*, forms the essential part, but it must not be supposed that they all contain the future suffix which originally connoted (§ 101-b above), necessity, obligation, promise etc.; most of them do not.

There are in Tamil, Malayalam a number of *pu* causal bases, the non-causal forms of these end in *mbu*.

Non-causal	*Causal*
eḻumbu 'rise'	*eḻuppu*
tirvmbu 'turn'	*tiruppu*

kiḷambu 'rise'	*kiḷappu*
kūmbu 'shut, close (as a flower)'	*kūppu*
nirambu 'be filled'	*nirappu*
kuḻambu 'become turbid'	*kuḻappu*

Kanarese has some of these forms, but as in the case of the *ku* and *tu* suffixes, the tenues, and mediae have not separate functions assigned to them. Thus *tiruppu*, *tirumbu* and *tiruvu*, are all transitive verbs; *elbu* is in transitive while *erbu* is transitive, and *ebbu* is both.

Telugu makes a fair show under the head of *pu* causals, but the non-causal forms of these bases have suffixes belonging to other conjugations.

Non-causal	*Causal*
tirugu 'turn'	*trippu*, *tippu*
nalugu 'be crushed'	*nalupu*
maragu 'be habituated'	*marapu*
malugu 'be extinguished'	*malupu*
medugu 'be beaten in a mortar'	*medupu*
mēyu 'graze'	*mēpu*
māyu 'be tarnished'	*māpu*
tēchu 'rise'	*tēpu*
chachchu 'die'	*champu*
mōchu 'bear a burden'	*mōpu*

There are besides bases like, *chiduku* 'burst'; *sāgu* 'be stretched'; '*dangu*' 'be beaten in a mortar'; *chinugu* 'be torn'; *tunugu* 'be broken'; *tegu* 'be cut'; *digu* 'descend'; *tragu* 'drink'; *udugu*, 'leave'; *zarugu* 'slide, pass', which have alternative causal bases besides *chidupu*, *sāpu*, *dampu*, *chimpu*, *tumpu*, *tempu*, *dimpu*, *trapu*, *udupu*, *zarupu*.

156. THE 'P' INFLECTIONS IN TELUGU

A large number of Telugu bases end in *chu* and this syllable enters into the conjugation of these bases in almost every mood and tense; as pointed out in 143 this was not so formerly, and in the earliest stages of the language these bases were without any *chu* suffix. This will also be evident from the circumstance that the corresponding roots in other Dravidian languages have no such suffix and are still one syllable shorter than the Telugu bases. Thus, *maṟachu*, 'forget', *naḍachu* 'walk', *kuḍuchu* 'drink' are only *maṟa*, *naḍa*, *kuḍi* in Tamil. An examination of the special and optional forms which the Telugu *chu* bases assume in the infinitive and imperative moods and in the negative voice clearly shows that the suffix *pu* formerly played a much larger part than now in the inflection of Telugu verbs. For the purpose of this examination reference should be made to the four-fold division of *chu* bases adopted from Campbell's grammar and given in 140 *supra*.

(*a*) The verbs included in the first of these four classes replace *chu* by *vu* when inflected for the imperative second person, the infinitive, and the verbal noun, and in the negative forms. Campbell's grammar (rule 359) enumerates 15 verbs as belonging to this class and the number includes some of the commonest of Telugu roots in daily use such as *lēchu* 'rise', *niluchu* 'stand', *naḍachu* 'walk', *maṟachu* 'forget', *piluchu* 'call,' *kuḍuchu* 'suck, eat', *karachu* 'bite', *ēḍuchu* 'weep', *viḍuchu* 'quit' etc. Some of the inflections of the base *lēchu* are compared below with those of its causal form *lēpu*.

Imperative	*Inf. and verbal noun*	*Negative*
lēvumu, *lēvaṇḍi*	*lēvan*, *lēvaḍamu*	*lēvaka*, *lēvani*
lēpumu, *lēpaṇḍi*	*lēpan*, *lēpaḍamu*,	*lēpaka*, *lēpani*

The comparison shows that there must have been a couplet *lēvu* and *lēpu* identical in meaning with the Tamil couplet *eḻumbu* and *eḻuppu* and identical also in form; for the Telugu *lē* is the same as Tamil *el* but with metathesis of the initial vowel and while *p* is softened into *v* in the non-causal form in Telugu, it becomes *b* nasalized in Tamil. Similarly we have the couplets *niluvu, nilupu*; *naḍuvu, naḍupu*; and in all the three cases the hard pronunciation of *p* occurs in the causal form thereby showing that the radicals *lē, nilu, naḍu,* must have been accented when used in a causal sense. The hard pronunciation of *p* can be secured in Tamil only by doubling it.

In regard to the other roots belonging to this class the causal forms do not end in *pu* but in *pinchu* as *maṟapinchu, kuḍipinchu, pilipinchu,* and although the inflections of the non-causal bases follow those of *lēchu,* as *maṟavan, kuḍuvan, piluvan* etc., the inflections of the causal bases are longer and also have optional forms: *maṟapimpan, maṟapinchan* etc. But if it is assumed that this *pinchu* arises by adding *inchu* to a previous *pu* or that it has replaced a previous *pu* suffix then the conclusion is irresistible that all the bases belonging to the first class existed formerly in couplets having *vu* and *pu* as their final syllables. The recollection of non-causal bases ending in *vu* is still so strong that the final *chu* is rejected absolutely in the inflections now under consideration.

(*b*) Campbell's grammar enumerates 18 roots (rule 363) as belonging to the second class which optionally replace *chu* by *vu* in the above inflections: most of these are common roots in daily use such as:

mōchu 'bear a burden'; *naluchu* 'squeeze or crush';
tuḍuchu 'cleanse by rubbing'; *ūḍuchu* 'sweep';
īḍuchu 'drag or pull'; *vaichu* 'place or put';

piluchu 'draw up anything with the breath';
prōchu 'protect.'

Taking the base *mōchu* the inflections of the couplet may be exhibited as follows :—

mōchumu, mōchaṇḍi; mōchan, mōchaḍamu; mōchaka, mōchani.

mōvumu, mōvaṇḍi; mōvan, mōvaḍamu; mōvaka, mōvani.

mōpumu, mōpaṇḍi, mōpan, mōpaḍamu mōpaka, mōpani.

Here also we can reasonably infer that there were formerly couplets of the form *mōvu* and *mōpu* but that the tradition of the *vu* suffix had been lost in some parts of the Telugu country when the *chu* suffix became permanently incorporated with the root and that the grammarian has thus had to recognise a double usage. The only root of this class which forms its causal with the *pu* suffix is *mōchu*; in all other cases the causal is formed by replacing *chu* by *pinchu.*

(*c*) The third class of roots which retain the final syllable *chu* in the inflections now under consideration are in less common and daily use than the two previous classes; Campbell's grammar (Rule 361) enumerates 26 roots as belonging to this class of which the following are more common perhaps than the rest;—

kāchu 'attend'; *rāchu* 'rub'
gruchchu 'string (pearls etc.); *puchchu* 'rot, send'
tūchu 'weigh'; *āchchu* 'owe'
nōchu 'perform a ceremony'; *ēchu* 'harass, torment'

It cannot be said that these are new bases which did not exist in the pro-Dravidian period, for most of them have corresponding roots in Tamil and all of them form their causals by adding *pinchu.* If these bases had formerly non-causal forms with the suffix *vu* all tradition of such forms has been entirely lost.

(*d*) The fourth class which optionally replace the final syllable by *pu* comprise all the remaining *chu* bases; they are mostly causals formed by adding *inchu* or *chu* to the root, as;

koṭṭinchu, kōvinchu, aḍaginchu, kāluchu, kūluchu.

These bases must have originally assumed the suffix *pu* when taking the inflections now under consideration but a double usage has grown up as in the second class of verbs considered in (*b*) above. The above optional replacement occurs also before the *du* of the aorist and *chunu* of the present tense.

The net result of the examination is that in a certain stage in the development of Telugu all bases now ending in *chu* assumed the suffix *vu* or *pu* before undergoing certain inflections and that such of them as assumed the suffix *vu* must have had causal forms ending in *pu*.

157. Miscellaneous 'p' forms

(*a*) Infinitives and subjunctives of accented roots in Tamil which were formed by adding *ppa*, and *ppin* to roots (112 e) come under the *p* conjugation. Thus *naḍappiṉ*, *naḍappa, niṟpin, maṟappa* etc., must have arisen by affixing *a* and *iṉ* to the obsolete bases *naḍappu, niṟpu, maṟappu* etc., which apparently went out of use as being needlessly long; for we have still the roots *naḍa* 'walk' *nil* 'stand' and *maṟa* 'forget' conveying the same meaning. It is worthy of note that while Telugu has had and still has inflections arising from the couplets *niluvu, nilupu*; *naḍavu, naḍapu* etc., corresponding to the unaccented and accented forms of the primitive roots in the non-causal and causal sense respectively, Tamil should have retained only the inflections of accented roots in a large number of cases and that in some of these cases the sense conveyed should be intransitive and causal, as for instance, *naḍa, paṟa, nil, iru.*

(*b*) A very large number of nouns are formed in Tamil and Malayāḷam by means of the suffixes *pu* and *vu* ; some of these are action nouns while others have acquired special significations. Examples :

kaḍippu 'beating, a drum stick' ; *tīrppu* 'a settlement'
ōṟpu 'patience' ; *uḻavu* 'ploughing'
tōṟpu 'defeat' ; *viḻippu* 'waking'
iḻuppu 'dragging spasms' ; *veṟuppu* 'disgust'

Malayāḷam sometimes uses also *ma* where Tamil uses only *pu* or *vu*; thus *tīrppu, tīrmma* 'a settlement'; *uḻavu, uḻama* 'tillage'; *ōrmma* 'recollection, thought'; *tōlma* 'defeat'. Nouns formed from verbs by the addition of *pu* or *vu* are also numerous in Telugu.

māpu 'dirt'; *mōpu* 'burden'; *vāpu* 'swelling'; *penupu* 'nourishing'; *koluvu* 'service'; *taḍavu* 'delay'; *niluvu* 'what is left'.

(*c*) These nouns must be carefully distinguished from abstract nouns or nouns of quality formed mostly from nouns and adjectives by means of the suffixes *pu, vu, mi, mai* etc., which have a different origin unconnected with the *p* conjugation :

Tamil : *karuppu*; *karumai* 'blackness'; *śivappu* 'redness'; *veṇmai* 'whiteness'; *arumai* 'rarity'; *pudumai* 'newness'.

Telugu : *telupu*, 'whiteness'; *nalupu* 'blackness'; *pērimai* 'greatness'; *magatimi* 'manliness'.

(*d*) There is a peculiarity in the formation of verbal nouns in Tamil, Malayāḷam and Kanarese by means of the suffix *vu*, which must be specially noted ; it is that the vowel preceding *vu* should *not* be *u*. In Tamil we may form nouns from accented roots ending in *u*, *iruppu* 'abode'; *uḍuppu* 'dress'; *aṟuppu* 'harvest' etc. without changing the final *u* of the roots, but when *pu* becomes *vu* the suffix added is practically *avu* when the roots end in *u* or a consonant. Thus the nouns from *uḻu* 'plough', *uṟu* 'be related', *naḍu* 'transplant', *puku* 'enter'; *miku* 'exceed', *varu* 'come', *śel* 'go', *kaḷ* 'steal', *uṇ* 'eat' are *uḻavu*, *uṟavu*, *naḍavu*, *pukavu*, *mikavu*, *varavu*, *śelavu*, *kaḷavu*, *uṇavu*; but we may have *kaḻivu* 'passing', *iḻivu* 'descending', *kuḻivu* 'depression', *iḻavu* 'loss', *iravu* 'begging' without any change in the final vowels *a* or *i* of the roots. These remarks apply also to Malayāḷam. A similar state of things appears to prevail in Kanarese. Chapter X of Dr. Kittel's Grammar contains examples of verbal nouns ending in *vu*, but the penultimate vowel is never *u*. Where the root ends in *u* the suffix is either *va*, *vi*, or *avu* :—

> *iravu* 'being'; *olavu* 'pleasure'; *baravu* 'coming'; *ikkuva* 'placing, putting'; *hannuva* 'making ready', 'equipping' (K.K.G. 243-(20-24).)

Several nouns ending in *uvu* have lost their final syllable in Modern Tamil. Thus the Telugu *biguvu* 'tightness', *koluvu* 'service' are now commonly known as only *bigu* and *kolu* in popular Tamil; while *uruvu* 'shape', *karuvu* 'embryo' etc., tadbhavas from the Sanskrit *rupa*, *garbha* etc., have become *uru*, *karu* etc.

On the other hand Telugu grammar has verbal nouns ending in *uvu* :

> *biguvu* 'tightness', *eguvu* 'flight', *koluvu*, 'service', 'assembly', *niluvu*, 'what is left'.

158. THE TENSE SIGNS *m* AND *nu*

(*a*) The tense sign *m* is a substitute for *v*.

There are various considerations which show that the *m* of the suffixes *kum* (*um*), *gum* has arisen from a previous *v*.

(i) In Tamil the future sign appears as *p*, *v* or *b* according to connection, that is as the roots are accented or unaccented, or end in nasals :—

naḍappēṉ, *varuvēṉ*, *kāṇbēṉ*.

In Malayāḷam the second future sign appears as *p*, *v* or *m* in the same circumstances :—

koḍuppu, *śelvu*, *kāṇmu*, *koḍuppāṉ*, *varuvāṉ*, *kāṇmāṉ* (117b.)

(ii) The same plan is followed in the imperative second person plural in Malayāḷam, and Bishop Caldwell was the first to point out that the various forms assumed by this imperative plural were based on the plan of the future. (C.D.G. pp. 421-2):—

koḍuppiṉ, *varuviṉ*, *kāṇmiṉ* where *iṉ* is the second person plural termination.

Tamil uses are invariable—*miṉ* or *miṉir* as the plural imperative suffix for all classes of verbs :—

Koḍumiṉ, *varumiṉ*, or *vammiṉ*, *kāṇmiṉ*, in the negative form, however either *p* or *m* may be used *kāṇaṉmiṉ*, *pukaṉmiṉ*, *kāṇaṟpir*, *pukāppir* for *pukaṟpir*. (99 a, b.)

There are other negative imperatives in Old Tamil where *m* takes the place of *p*. Thus in the verbs *kāṇaṉmīr* 'may they not witness' and *pāḍaṉmār* 'may they not sing'. *m* according to a commentator or Tolkappiyam arises from the future sign *p* (109 c.)

(iii) The agent nouns formed in Malayāḷam and Old Tamil from the aorist relative participle ending in *kum* or *um* have identically the same sense as the agent nouns formed with the suffixes, *p*, *v* or *b*; thus *uṇarumōr*, *teḷiyumōr*, *kāṇumōr*, *kāṇmor*, *vāḻumōr*, *koyyumōṉ* have the same sense as *uṇarvōr*, *teḷivōr*, *kāṇbōr*, *vāḻvōr*, *koyvōṉ*. (111 c.)

(iv) We may also note here the ordinals formed with the suffix *ām* in Tamil and Malayāḷam and with *ava* in Telugu. Thus *āṟām* in Tamil and Malayāḷam and *āṟava* in Telugu mean 'the sixth'; their lengthened forms meaning 'sixth thing' are *āṟāmadu* in Malayāḷam, *āṟāvadu* in Tamil and *āṟāvadi* in Telugu. The suffix *ām* is a shortened form of the future relative participle *ākum* 'becoming'.

In all these cases, *p*, *v*, and *b* give place to *m*. In the alternative archaic *p* aorist obtained by interposing the pleonastic *ku* between the suffix *pu* and the root or base (vide 155 b above) the *vu* of the final *uvu* of *naḍakkuvu*, *pōkuvu* etc. was likely to be lost; it looks as if the stable *m* took the place of this *vu*.

(*b*) The final *nu* of the Telugu aorist third person is a substitute for *m*.

The Telugu aorist *cheyunu* is identical in meaning and in application with the old Tamil *śeykum* and *śeyyum*, and all the three are also used as aorist relative participles without regard to the number or gender of the nouns qualified; and agent nouns are formed from all :—

Tamil : *śeyyumavaṉ*, *śeyyumavar*.
Telugu : *chēyunavāḍu*, *chēyuvāḍu*, *chēyuvāru*.

There are several instances in which Telugu is known to have changed the final *m* of grammatical particles into *n*. The copulative conjunction *um* of Tamil, Malayāḷam and Old Kanarese appears as *unu* in Telugu, the benedictive suffixes *tan* and *eḍun* appear to have originally ended in *m* for when followed by a vowel these particles become *tam* and *eḍum*. Vide also 141 a, above where it has been pointed out that Telugu *chēyunaḍi*, 'should be done' etc., have an impressive signification like the Tamil *koḍuppadu*, 'Kanarese *kuḍuvadu*' 'should be given'.

Having regard to the identity of use and meaning it may be reasonably inferred that there was an identity in form also originally and that the Telugu *n* in the aorist third person has arisen from a previous *m* which arose out of the pro-Dravidian gerundive and future sign *p* (*v*).

It may be mentioned here that Bishop Caldwell also thought that the Tamil *um* was identical with the Telugu aoristic *nu* (C.D.G. pp. 406-9); but his explanation of *um* was entirely different from that given in this book *viz.* that *u* has arisen from pleonastic suffix *ku* and that *m* is a substitute for *v* which again was a softened *p*.

CHAPTER X

PRO-DRAVIDIAN PAST TENSE FORMS

159. Dravidian conjunctive participles have no passive force.

Attention was drawn in 48 above to Prof. Sten Konow's remark that 'In the Dravidian a participle is active as well as passive'. This statement requires qualification. There are certain elliptical phrases such as :—

Tamil : *śeyda vēlai*
Kanarese : *māḍida kelasa*
Telugu : *chēśina pani*

which are usually translated as 'the work done'. This rendering may give rise to the supposition that the Dravidian past relative participles correspond to the Sanskrit past participle passive *kṛita* 'done', *bhinna* 'broken'; but if the elliptical subject is supplied it will be at once be apparent that the above participles are wholly active in sense.

Tamil : *avaṉ śeyda vēlai*
Kanarese : *avanu māḍida kelasa* } 'The work he has done'
Telugu : *vāḍu chēśina pani*

This will also be evident from the verb forms with personal endings. Thus Tamil : *aḍittāṉ*, Kanarese : *hōḍedanu*; Telugu : *Koṭṭinādu,* will mean only 'he struck', never 'he was struck'.

Bishop Caldwell fully recognises the active character of these participles (C.D.G. p. 400) and Dr. Kittel is careful enough to translate such phrases as *kalta pāṭha*, *bareda pustaka* etc., by ' the lesson which (somebody) has learnt, the book which (somebody) has written'. (K.K.G. pp. 328, 421.)

The same observations are applicable to present, future, and aorist relative participles such as Tamil: *seykiṟa*, *seyyum*; Kanarese : *maduva*, Telugu : *chese* etc., and to the elliptical phrases *seykiṟa velai*, *seyyum velai*, *maduva kelasa*, *chēse pani* which are often rendered 'the work that is being done'. In these and in the other examples given above a misconception may arise from the circumstance that the neuter nouns which the participles qualify are the objects of the action; no misconception can possibly arise in the examples *paḍitta piḷḷai* 'the boy that read', *paḍikkiṟa piḷḷai* 'the boy that is reading'.

It is necessary to emphasize here that the Dravidian conjunctive participles are wholly active in meaning; these participles were once used as finite verbs in the past tense in the active voice as they are even now in Malayalam and in some uncultivated Dravidian dialects (42). There are no instances in which these participles or the tense forms derived from them were ever used in the passive or impersonal construction with the subject of the verb in the agent or the oblique case.

160. Tamil-Malayalam Conjunctive participle

(*a*) Tamil: The suffixes denoting past tense in Tamil and Old Tamil are *tu*, *i*, in and have been briefly dealt with in 97, 106. In all periods of the Tamil language known to us conjunctive participles have been formed with the suffix *i* in the case of short *u* bases and with the suffix *tu* in the case of the other bases. In Old Tamil several bases not ending in short *u* used the suffix *i*; it is impossible to say whether this represented the popular usage of the time or was merely a poetical license. If the former the suffix *i* must have had a wider range of application then. Though there is little doubt that these participles must once have been used as finite verbs we do not find instances of such use even in the oldest specimens of Tamil known to us.

In Old Tamil bases ending in short *u* had tense forms containing the suffix in side by side with forms containing the suffix *i* (*iy*) ;

ēṟinan, *ōḍinan*, *kattinan*. etc. side by side with
ēṟiyan, *ōḍiyan*, *kattiyan* etc.

But relative participles were always forms with the latter suffix; the forms of these participles were *ēṟiya*, *ōḍiya*, *kāṭṭiya*, etc. not *ēṟina*, *ōḍina*, *kāṭṭina* etc. In modern Tamil relative participles and tense forms of short *u* bases are formed only with the suffix *in*.

(*b*) Malayalam : Conjunctive participles are forms as in Tamil with the suffixes *tu* and *i*; these participles are used also as tense forms. The suffix *in* is not in use in spoken Malayalam as a sign of the past tense, but instances occur in literary works of past tense forms containing this suffix. Relative participles have the same form as in Old Tamil *ēṟiya*, *ōḍiya*.

(*c*) Is *y* merely a *ya* sruti? The *y* in the forms *ēṟiya*, *kāṭṭiya*, *ēṟiyan*, *kāṭṭiyan* etc., is usually considered to be a *ya* sruti an inorganic consonant put in to fill the hiatus between the final *i* of the conjunctive participles and the initial vowel of the suffixes, as thus *ēṟi* (*y*) *a*. But several considerations may be urged which render it more likely that the final *i* of these participles is not original but has arisen from a previous *ya*. The Sanskrit words *kanyā* 'an unmarried girl or woman' *pāṇḍya* 'the name of a people', *vandhyā* 'a barren woman' *sandhyā* 'evening, dusk' etc., have become *kanni*, *pāṇḍi*, *vandi*, *andi* in Tamil. *Tolkappiyam* (I-2-25)[1] says that *i* can replace *y* and *vice versa* at the end of words. The bases *pō* 'go' and *ā* 'become' have conjunctive participles *pōy* and *āy*. Tamil does not tolerate *y* as the second member of a conjunct consonant but inserts a glide vowel *i* between ; thus *pāṇḍya* must have been adopted as *pāṇḍiya* in Tamil and must have become successively *pāndiy* and *pāndi*. Similarly, if *ya* was the original suffix of the conjunctive participles it would have become successively *iya*, *iy*, *i* in consonantal bases *ēṟiya*, *ēṟiy*, *ēṟi* and the *y* of the form now under consideration will not be merely euphonic and adventitious, as the personal endings might have come to be added to the participles at a time when these still retained *y*.

161. KANARESE CONJUNCTIVE PARTICIPLES

The suffixes used in Kanarese are *tu* and *i*. Since the 6th or the 7th century A.D., when this language first comes within our ken there has been a progressive extension of the use of *i* in the formation of its conjunctive participles. In old Kanarese the use of *i* was limited to sibilant bases and to such explosive basis as required a final *u* for proper enunciation; but a continued increase in the number of *a* bases has led to an extension, though not to an equal extent, of the use of the suffix *i*. Notwithstanding this change the relative participles and tense forms derived from every verb contain, and have always contained the dental sign *t* or *d*. This gives rise to the presumption that in the older stages of the languages when conjunctive participles were used as tense forms without personal endings these participles must have been formed in the case of all bases with the suffixes *tu*, *du*, or *idu*, and that the suffix *i* is a later innovation adopted perhaps partly in

1. *Ikara yakaram iṟudi viravum* (Tol.1. *moḷimarapu*. 25.)

imitation of contiguous languages, but mainly because the shorter form in *i* was more convenient. For, if forms in *i* were in use in those older stages we should have had, as in Old Tamil and in Malayalam, relative participles and tense forms without any dental sign in the case of the bases which then used the suffix *i*.

It might be argued per contra that the tense forms were as supposed by Dr. Kittel (K.K.G. 189-192) derived from the past relative participles. Then the question arises how were the relative participles themselves derived? These participles have acquired their present meanings only as derived from verbal forms used in former times as tense forms without personal endings. Thus Tamil, Malayalam *śeydu* and Kanarese *geydu*, both meaning 'having done' without regard to number or gender, have given rise to *śeyda* and *geyda* which mean 'that has done' applicable to all numbers and genders. Similarly, Malayalam *śeykunnu* and Tamil *śeykinṟu*, both of which mean 'doing', have given rise to *śeykunna* and *śeykinṟa* meaning 'that does', and applicable to all numbers and genders; so also the Kanarese hypothetical *geyyuv* 'does or will do', must have given rise to *geyyuva* 'that does or that will do'. It has been pointed out in 72 (*c*) above, following the view of Dr. Gundert, that the suffixed *a* of these relative participles is the subject of the action expressed by the participles. It has also been surmised that this suffixed *a* is short *av* which, like the English 'that' is both a demonstrative and a relative. The supposition that past relative participles in Kanarese are derived from the conjunctive participles ending in *du* is fully in accordance with the mode in which such relative participles are derived in Tamil-Malayalam, and with the way in which present future relative participles are derived in Kanarese. The presumption that all conjunctive participles in Kanarese must formerly have been formed with a dental suffix is almost irresistible.

162. TELUGU CONJUNCTIVE PARTICIPLES AND PAST TENSE FORMS

(*a*) Suffixes *i*, *chi*, *si*. In Telugu all verbal bases from their conjunctive participles with the suffix *i*, but as all old vowel bases have been lengthened by one syllable *chu* or *yu* (*su*), the real addition in the case of these stems in *chi* or *si*. Thus *ād* 'play', *aḍagu* 'be submissive', adopted without change in Telugu form their participles with the suffix *i*; *āḍi*, *aḍagi*; but *naḍa* 'walk', *maṟa* 'forget', *tuṇi* 'be out to pieces', *pukai* 'smoke', which have become lengthened by a syllable in Telugu form their participles by the addition of *chi* or *si*; *naḍachi*, *marachi*, *tunisi*, *pogasi*.

The only tense forms corresponding to these participles is the third person epicene plural:—

āḍiri, *chēsiri*, *naḍachiri*, *aḍgiri*;

to this may be added the third person masculine singular forms *cheppidi* 'he said', *uddu* (*udidi*) 'he was', *sikkidi* 'he was found', *ayidi* 'he became' given in 144 above as current in the Beradi dialect.

(*b*) Suffixes *ya*, *chya*, *eya*. Telugu grammarians do not, however, derive the above third person epicene plurals from the conjunctive participles *āḍi*, *naḍachi*, *aḍagi*, *chēs*, but consider them as contactions of the colloquial and vulgar forms *āḍayāru*, *naḍichyārau*, *aḍagyāru*, *chēsyāru*. These tense forms in *ya* correspond to the old Tamil forms referred to in 161 c., and here also the question arises whether the suffixes *i*, *chi*, *si* of the conjunctive participles are original or have arisen from *ya*, *chya*, *sya*.

(*c*) Suffixes *e*, *enu*. The suffix *enu* gives rise to forms like *kōnēnu*, *pāḍēnu*, *chēsēnu*, *naḍichēnu* etc., used in the third person singular and neuter plural. These forms often drop their final *nu* and assume also the forms *kōnyēnu*, *kōniyē*, *kōnya*, *chēsya*, *pāḍya*, *pāḍiyēnu*, *pāḍiye* etc., in colloquial speech and in the Telugu dialects. Here also the question arises whether *e* is original or *ya*, and if the latter, what is the origin of the final *nu* in *enu*.

There are many instances in Telugu in which *e* has arisen from an original *ya*. Thus Sanskrit *kanyā* 'an unmarried girl or woman' has become *kanniya* and *kanne* in Telugu; Sanskrit *dhishnya* 'a seat' has become *tinniya* and *tinne* 'a pyal'; *sandhyā* 'morning and evening twilight' has become *sande*, and *anyamu* 'other' has become *annēmu*. Again consider the following Telugu couplets.

1.	*paggiya*, *pagge*	'skill, cleverness'
2.	*mulliya*, *mulle*	'a bag or bundle of jewels or money, wealth'
3.	*diviya*, *dive*	'a light, a lamp'
4.	*bumiya*, *bume*	'a disguise, deceit, trick'
5.	*bottiya*, *botte*	'a small girl, a lass'
6.	*middiya*, *midde*	'a terrace, terraced house'
7.	*pindiya*, *pinde*	'a small berry'
8.	*mattiya*, *matte*	'a small ring worn on the toe'
9.	*pudiya*, *pude*	'a small ball or bend'
10.	*paliyamu*, *palemu*	'a camp, an army'

It is well known that the Sanskrit conjunct consonant *jn* becomes *gy* in Prakrit and that the Sanskrit *jñāna* 'wisdom', *ājñā* 'order' etc., exist as *gyān*, *āgyā*, in Hindi (H.G.G. 18-24). Similarly we can see that *prajñā* 'wisdom', 'intelligence' must become *pagyā*, which latter has apparently given rise to the first couplet *paggiya*, *pagge*. The second couplet is obviously traceable to the Sanskrit *mūlyam* 'capital', 'principal pride'. The words *bumiya*, *diviya*, *bottiya* are obviously *tadbhavas* from *bhūmikā* 'an actor's costume', *dīpikā* 'a light', *putrikā* 'a daughter', and are clearly the original forms of *bume*, *dive*, *botte*. In regard to the other five couplets and many others that may be cited we cannot say offhand whether the form in *e* or that in *iya* is the original one, but must wait till we know their etymology. But the instances given above are enough to place us on our guard against the tacit assumption usually made (L.S.IV. p. 608) that the standard forms *pade*, *kone*, *chepe* etc., are the original ones and that *padya*, *konya*, *chepya* etc. arise from mispronunciation. The contrary supposition is the more probable one ; as a matter of fact it will be seen later that *e* has arisen from *ya*.

(*d*) Suffixes *ina* and *ti*. There remain two other suffixes *ina* and *ti* which enter into past tense forms in Telugu; but there are no conjunctive participles formed with these suffixes in use at present. Of these *ina* is unknown to Kanarese and Malayalam and is but partially employed in old Tamil and literary Malayalam ; *ti* is altogether unknown to all these three languages. It is therefore surmised that these two suffixes were not in use in the pro-Dravidian period and are late accretions. This surmise is greatly strengthened by the character of the bases in which these suffixes are found used in Telugu.

163. Pro-Dravidian past-tense suffixes.

(*a*) The past tense suffixes of the pro-Dravidian period are then (1) the dental suffix *tu* which in most cases changed into *du*, *ndu*, and *ttu*, the last two of which further changed into *nju* and *chchu* after palatal sounds in Malayalam and vulgar Tamil ; and (2) the palatal suffixes *i*, *si*, and *chi*, which were perhaps original in some cases, but must have arisen from previous *ya* and *chya* in the vast majority of cases.

Telugu must have formed its conjunctive participles and past tense forms entirely with palatal suffixes ; there is no relic in this language of any pro-Dravidian dental suffix; if any dental suffix was in use, it must have been wholly superseded and replaced by the above palatals.

Reasons have already been given in 159 above for holding that all non-causal bases in Kanarese must have formed their conjunctive participles with a dental suffix. Thus non-causal *u* bases like *alku* 'fear', *ettu* 'take', *muttu* 'surround', *kuttu* 'strike', which in Old Kanarese formed their conjunctive participles with the suffix *i* must in a still earlier stage have had participles of the form *alkidu*, *ettidu*, *muttidu*, *kuttidu* etc. These participles would have had the same form as the conjunctive participles of the causal forms of the above bases. For as the causal suffix was then only *i*, not *isu* (127), the causal stems of the above bases will be *alki*, *etti*, *mutti*, *kutti*, etc., and the participles of these stems also will be *alkidu*, *ettidu*, *muttidu*, *kuttidu* etc. It is apparently to make distinction between the two sets of participles that Kanarese appears to have adopted *chi* for forming the conjunctive participles of its causal and Sanskritic stems ending in *i*. When the accent on this *i* was lost, the palatal tenue *ch* would have had a tendency to be pronounced like the palatal aspirant *s*:, but as this sound is not tolerated in Kanarese the tenue *ch* has ultimately become *s* and the original *chi* has been softened into *si*. As is generally admitted this *si* has the same etymology as the Telugu *chi* and *si*.

In Tamil both *tu* and *i* were in use; the latter was not confined then as now to short *u* bases.

(*b*) What is the cause of this diversity of usage? Was there not a period in which all Dravidian languages had common past tense suffixes? It is impossible to answer the question satisfactorily with the materials at our disposal, but it may be pointed out that this diversity has its counterpart in the usage that obtained in the Prakrits which arose out of the disruption of the Vedic dialects. The Vedic dialects themselves had dental and palatal suffixes for forming conjunctive participles. Of the four languages dealt with in Vararuchi's *Prākrita Prakāsa* the first three, *viz.*, Maharashtri Paisachi and Magadhi formed their conjunctive participles with *una* (iv-23) *tunam* (x-13) and *dani* (xi-16) respectively, which arose from *tvana* and *tvanam* by forms of the Vedic dental suffix *tva* while the fourth Sauraseni formed its participles with is pronounced *iya* or *iy* which arose from the Vedic palatal suffix *ya*. This same diversity of usage is observable in the modern Aryan vernaculars of India of which Marathi and Eastern Rajasthani use suffixes derived from the Vedic *tvanam*, while Hindi, Bengali, Oriya, Sindhi, Gujarati Punjabi, Naipali use suffixes arising from the Vedic palatal suffix *ya* (H.G.G. 491) through the Sauraseni *ia*.

(*c*) It was seen in 10 above, that Gondi and Golari while possessing past tense forms containing dental tense signs have practically forgotten their old conjunctive participles from which these tense forms must have been derived, and are forming new ones in imitation of the adjoining or surrounding Aryan dialects by means of the suffixes *kun*, *ke*, *ku* etc. It would seem that this imitation has been going on from the time that the Dravidian Languages first came in contact with the Aryan dialects ; for the pro-Dravidian suffixes mentioned in (*a*) above, *viz.*, *tu*, *i*, *si*, *ya*, *chya* seem to be identical in form and in value with the suffixes used in pre-Christian centuries, especially about the time of Asoka and for one or two centuries previously. It is proposed to discuss here the relationship of these Aryan suffixes to the corresponding Dravidian ones. The discussion properly belongs to later chapters devoted to the etymology of Dravidian suffixes, but some of these pro-Dravidian forms appear to have given rise to new formative additions to Telugu and Kanarese roots, *viz.*, *chu*, *su*, and *nchu* and it is necessary to consider the origin of these formative additions here even at the expense of having to repeat the arguments over again later.

The Aryan forms that are proposed to consider here are (1) the conjunctive participles and (2) the sigmatic aorists; and it will be necessary to exhibit the changes undergone by these forms at different stages of their evolution. Four stages have been chosen, *viz.*, (*a*) the Vedic stage, (*b*) the Pāli stage, (*c*) The Asokic stage and (*d*) the stage at the time of Vararuchi. The least artificial portion of the extant Pali literature and that nearest to the popular speech of the time is probably the prose portions of the Jataka stories, and one of these stories taken at random, *viz.*, the *Mugapakkha Jātaka*, has been analysed for the purpose of exhibiting the Pali stage of the above forms.

164. Aryan conjunctive participles.

The practice of using the gerund of verbal noun as an indeclinable participle seems to date from the Iranian period. In the Avesta the gerunds were formed by adding the suffixes *tva*, *ta*, or *ya* directly to the root, but it is not clear whether these gerunds were always indeclinable (KA.V. 564; J.A.V. 718). The value of these gerunds was the same as that of the English participles—'making', 'doing' etc.

(*a*) *Vedic dialects.*

In the Vedas the suffixes added were *tva* and *ya*, the former being added generally to simple roots and the latter being used with roots compounded with a prefix (*upasarga*). If the compounded root ended in a short vowel *tya* was used instead of *ya*. It is stated that in the Rig Veda the suffix *ya* is long in fully two-thirds of the occurrences (W.S.G. 989, 983 (*a*)).

The Vedic gerunds have the force of indeclinable participles past or present, qualifying the actor whose action they describe: Examples:—

sru 'hear'	*srutvā*	: *driś* 'see'	*darśayitvā* (caus)
jna 'know'	*jnatvā*	: *vid* 'know'	*viditvā*
sthā 'stand'	*sthitvā*	: *kri* 'do'	*kritvā*
viji 'conquer'	*vijitya*	: *āgam* 'come'	*āgatya*
āloch 'consider'	*ālochya*	: *ālabh* 'seize'	*ālabhya*
adhi-kri 'concern'	*adhikritya*	: *anu-śās* 'rule'	*anuśāsya*

The by-forms of *tva* were *tvi* and *tvaya*; two other by-forms *tvanam* and *tvinam* are mentioned by grammarians, but they do not occur in the existing Vedas though they have left representatives in Prakrits. The suffix most used in the Rig Veda is *tvi*.

(*b*) *Pāli.*

An analysis of the forms in the *Mugapakkha Jātaka* shows that out of over (260) conjunctive participles used therein only 11 are formed with the suffixes *ya* and *tya*. These are:—

1.	*āhachcha* (*āhatya*)	'having struck'
2.	*adhitthāya* (*adhishṭhāya*)	'standing on'
3.	*patthāya* (*prasthāya*)	'having started, starting from'
4.	*utthāya* (*utthāya*)	'having risen'
5.	*ōruyha* (*avaruhya*)	'having descended'
6.	*āruyha* (*āruhya*)	'having ascended'
7.	*paggahya* (*pragrihya*)	
8.	*Pahāya* (*prahāya*)	'leaving, abandoning'
9.	*patichcha* (*pratitya*)	
10.	*nissaya* (*nissritya?*)	
11.	*ōdāya* (*avadāya*)	

All the remaining forms numbering over 250 and arising from 107 simple and compounded roots are formed with the suffix *tva* with a connecting *i* where necessary. Nearly one-half of the roots are compounded with prepositional prefixes. The following may be cited as examples:—

*āharitvā, abhishinchitvā, vivaritvā, ukkhipitvā, *(utkshipitvā), abhiruhitvā, ālabhitvā.*

It is clear that the rule of classical Sanskrit that *tva* should be used with simple roots and *ya* with compounded roots was known to Pali. The rule of Pali grammarians in regard to the use of *ya* and *tya* may be noted here. *Tya* which regularly becomes *chcha* is merely a form of *ya*, initial *t* being inserted between the gerundial suffix *ya* and a root ending in a vowel. Example :—*pā i* 'depart' *ya* = *pā i t ya*=*pētya* = *pēchcha* 'having departed' (D.P.G. 470 (*c*)). It will be noted that in this rule *tya* is not restricted, as in Sanskrit, to roots ending in short vowels, but may be used with roots ending in long vowels also.

(c) *Asoka inscriptions:*

The conjunctive participles occurring in the various Asoka inscriptions have already been detailed in (§145) above. These end mostly in *tu* or *itu*, a few in *ti* or *ta*, two in *chya* or *cha*, and one with a doubtful reading in *i*. The forms *sutu, dasayitu, darsēti, dasayita, janitu, vēditu, tistiti, tistitu, chithitu, katu, vijinitu, vijita, agacha, ālocheti, ālocayita, ālochayitu, adhigichya, anuśāsitu*; *ālabhitu, ālabhiti, ārābhit*, may be compared with the Sanskrit and the Vedic forms given sub-para. (*a*) above.

The forms *adhigichya* occurs in Asoka's letter to the Magadha Sangham and is important as showing what we might have anticipated, that *cya* is one of the forms into which *tya* is corrupted (I.A.Vol. XX. p. 166).

The form *agacha* occurs in the Paderia and Nigilva Edicts and is important as showing that *tya* may be added to roots ending in long vowels (E.I.Vol. V. pp. 4 and 6).

Conjunctive participles formed with *ttu, ittu, chcha*, occur also extensively in the canonical works of the Svetambara Jains written in the Ārsha Prakrit otherwise called Ardhamāgadhi. These forms will be found collected in Pischel's *Prakrit Grammar* 577, 587, Cf. also Chanda's sutra II. 19, which mentions *ttu* and *chcha* among others, as signs of the past tense.

The above forms clearly represent a stage later than that of the Pali forms.

(*d*) *Vararuchi's Prakrits:*

The suffixes given by Vararuchi have already been mentioned in 161 b supra., *viz.*, *una*, *tunam*, *dani*, and *ia*. The last of these which was in use in Śauraseni will have been pronounced *iya* with a *ya* sruti, and as the final of words of more than one syllable is usually elided in popular speech the suffix must have had a tendency to become shortened into *iy*; in fact it became *i* in Apabhramśa (P.P.G. 594) and is *yi* or *i* in most of the Aryan vernaculars of Northern India (H.G.G. 491).

It is obvious from the above (1) that in a widely understood Aryan speech in use about the time of Asoka, conjunctive participles were formed mostly with the suffixes *tu* or *itu*, occasionally with the suffixes *i*, *chya*, *chcha*, or *cha*, the last three of which were added to roots ending with vowels; and (2) that in Śauraseni which has been followed by most of the Aryan vernaculars of the North the suffix used was *iya* (or *iy*) arising out of the Vedic *ya*.

165. Aryan sigmatic aorists

Aorist formations including what are called the sigmatic or the sibilant aorists are common to Greek and Sanskrit, and this fact may be taken as proof that these formations must have originated in the Indo-Germanic period. In the Avestic language where the Indo-Germanic *s* becomes *h* these aorists are formed with *h*.

(*a*) Sanskrit grammarians recognize four varieties of the sigmatic aorist in the Vedic literatures but we are concerned here only with two of them, *viz.*, those called the *s* aorist and the *ish* aorist, of which the paradigms in the active voice are as follows:—

	s aorist of kri 'do'		*ish aorist of pu 'cleanse'*	
	SINGULAR	PLURAL	SINGULAR	PLURAL
1.	*akārsham*	*akārshma*	*apāvisham*	*apāvishma*
2.	*akārshīh*	*akārshṭa*	*apāvih*	*apāvishṭa*
3.	*akārshīt*	*akārshuh*	*apāvīt*	*apāvishuh*

The value of the aorist forms in the Vedic language was that of a completed past or 'perfect' translatable by 'have done', but in the later or classical language they are simply preterites exchangeable with imperfects and perfects (W.S.G. 825).

The forms given in the paradigms above became greatly corrupted and shortened in the Prakrits. The initial augument totally disappeared in course of time as also the final consonants (sometimes syllables), and all persons and numbers appear to have been reduced to one and the same form—kārshi, or kāsi, and pāvi—though literary Pali distinguished persons and numbers by new formations based on *kāsi* and *pāvi* which last were appropriated to the third person singular. In some of the northern dialects the final *si* of the shortened forms appears to have been pronounced *hi*.

(*b*) Pali : Pali grammarians say that the aorist is the only true past tense in Pali, and this statement is fully borne out by an analysis of the past tense forms in the *Mugapakkha Jātaka.* In this Jātaka past tenses are occasionally expressed by past participles, but where tense forms are used these are almost invariably aoristic formations and no forms corresponding to the Sanskrit perfect (*liṭ*) or imperfect (*laṅ*) are found.

Singular third person is formed by adding *i* to consonantal stems and *si* to vowel stems.

Examples.—

ārabhi 'he began';	*chintēsi* 'he thought'
paridēvi 'she cried aloud'	*ārochēsi* 'he informed'
ōtari (*avatari*) 'he descended'	*akāsi* 'he did'
yāchi 'she begged';	*anasi* 'he knew'
niṣīdi 'he sat down'	*adasi* 'he gave'.

the augument being retained in the case of *ekach* roots like *ka*, *jna*, *da*.

The second person singular has the same form as the third person singular. To this latter are added *m*, *mha*, and *ttha* in the first person singular, first person plural, and the second person plural, respectively. In the third person plural *msu* is added to the third person singular or *um* replaces the final *i* of this singular.

Duroiselle says that the sigmatic aorist is used with roots ending in vowels and the *s* is inserted to join the endings to the root or to the base (D.P.G. 420).

(*c*) *Asoka inscriptions.*

A few aorist formations of the kind we are now considering occur also in the Asoka inscriptions.

(1) *ārabhisu*, *ārabiyisu*, *ālabhiyisu* 'they were slaughtered' (E.I. ii. p. 449) Rock edict. 1).

(2) *mā anulochayisu*, *mā locheshu*, *mā alochayisu* 'let them not permit' (E.I. ii. pp. 452-453) Rock Edict IV.

(3) *nikrami* 'he went forth'; *nikramishu* 'they went forth' (E.I. ii. p. 457) Rock Edict VIII.

(4) *mā manishu* 'let them not consider' (E.I. ii. pp. 463-465) Rock Edict XIII.

(*d*) *Vararuchi's Prakrits.*

But the greatest simplification in the formation of the past tenses is recorded in Vararuchi's sutras VII. 23 and 24.

VII-23. *ia bhūte.* VII-24. *ēkachi hia.*

"*Ia* is substituted for the affix after a root in a past tense; if the root is a mono-syllable then *hia* is substituted". The substitutions are the same for all numbers and persons without distinction; that is to say, *hasia* from the root *has* 'laugh', may be used in the sense of "I, we, thou, you, he, she, it, they, laughed", and *kāhia* from the root *ka* 'do', may be used in the sense of "I, we, thou, you, he, she, it, they, did." Cowell the editor of Vararuchi says that the reference to *ekach* is not clear and suspects corruption in the text. He therefore quotes Hemachandra's corresponding sutras III-162, 163, which make the point clear.

III-162. *si, chi, hia, bhūtārthasaya*

III-163. *vyanjanād ia.*

"*si, hi,* and *hia*, are substituted for the affixes of past tenses; if the root ends in a consonant then *ia* is substituted" that is to say in all persons and numbers. *si* and *hi* here have apparently arisen from the aorist forms; it is not obvious how *ia* and *hia* arose.

It is obvious from the above that the aorist forms gradually displaced the imperfect and the perfect—the *laṇ* and the *liṭ* of the grammarians—in popular speech, and had themselves become greatly shortened, assuming the same invariable forms in all numbers and persons:—

kāsi, kāhi, kāhia from *ka* (*kri*) 'do' and *hāsia* from *has* 'laugh'.

166. The derivation of the Telugu past tense in *ya*, and *e*: *cha*, *che*; *se*; and of the Telugu conjunctive participles in *i*, *chi*, *si*, from Aryan conjunctive participles.

It is clear from the account given above of the changes undergone by the Vedic forms that some of the Secondary Prakrits formed their conjunctive participles with the palatal suffixes *ya*, *chya*, and their corruptions, and that according to the rule of Pali grammarians *ya* was added to bases ending in consonants, and *chya* to bases ending in vowels. Let us suppose a Prakrit forming its participles in this manner to be contiguous to the Dravidian dialect which has now become Telugu and that the speakers of this dialect employ Prakritic suffixes in the formation of verbal participles from Dravidian roots. Taking the following Dravidian roots,

(1) *koṭṭu* 'strike', *anagu* 'be suppressed', ending in consonants, and (2) *naḍa* 'walk', *kuḍi* 'drink', *nali* 'be bruised or bruise', ending in vowels the participles will be *koṭya*, *koṭṭiya*, *anagya*, *anagiya*, *naḍachya naḍachiya*, *kuḍichya*, *kuḍichiya*, *nalichya*, *nalichiya*; and these will have been used at first in all persons and numbers as finite verbs in the past tense in the active voice (42-b). If we suppose the final vowels in these forms to be long as in the majority of instances in the oldest Vedic dialect (W.S.G. 993 (*a*)) the tense forms with personal endings are at once obtained from them by adding *nu*, *mu*, *vu*, *ru*, etc., the third person singular and neuter plural alone being left without personal endings (42-c). The forms thus pronominalized *koṭyana*, *naḍachyana* etc., will be used as final verbs in the sentence, while the original forms *koṭya*, *naḍachya* etc., will thenceforth be regarded and used as conjunctive participles. The non-pronominalized forms *koṭya*, *naḍachya* etc., used in the third person singular and neuter plural will

in course of time assume the forms *koṭṭiye*, *koṭṭe*, *naḍachiya*, *naḍache* etc. (160-c). These will also be the forms assumed by the conjunctive participles *koṭya*, *naḍachya*, etc., but this function is in modern times, restricted to *koṭṭi*, *naḍachi*, arising in the manner shown below. It is possible that the suffixes were not imitated so early as the Vedic period, but only at the Vararuchi period or even later during Apabhraṁśa times when they had become *iya*, *iy*, *i*.

The forms used as conjunctive participles and in the third person singular and neuter plural will have been *koṭṭiya*, *naḍachiya*, *koṭṭiy*, *naḍachiy*, *koṭṭi*, *naḍachi*; the first two will, by and by, have become the modern finite verbs *koṭṭe*, *koṭṭiye*, *naḍachē*, *naḍachiyē*, respectively (160-c), while the others will have become *koṭṭi* and *naḍachi*, the modern conjuctive participles.

In the case of unaccented roots the *ch* of the *chya* will be weakened into the palatal spirant *s* and may even become the dental *ṣ*; while in the case of accented roots it will have a tendency to become doubled which will effectively preserve its sound as a tenue. In the case of the root *nali* which is both accented and unaccented the verbal forms arrived at in the manner indicated above will be *nalichyānu* etc., *nalisyānu*, etc., *nalisyānu* etc., *nalichē*, *nalisē*, *nalisē* etc., *nalich nalish*, *nalisi* etc.

167. The Telugu past tense in *i* possibly derived from the Aryan sigmatic aorist.

It is also possible that Telugu speakers imitated the Aryan sigmatic aorists the successive deterioration of which has been described in 163. In this case the Dravidian roots combined with the Aryan suffixes will be:—

koṭṭi, *ana gi*, *naḍassi*, *kuḍissi*, *nalissi*, *nalisi* each of which was a complete paradigm representing all persons and numbers. The doubled *ss* shows the result of accent. If Vararuchi forms had been imitated, the finals of these forms will have been long at first, and in consonantal bases the suffix will have been *iya* (163-d), in Sanskrit a double *ss* is often written and pronounced *ts*, as in the aorist *avatsam* 'I dwelt' from the root *vas* 'dwell' and in the locative plural *vidvatsu* 'among learned men' from *vidvas* 'a learned man'. The conjunct *ts* represents the dental pronounciation of the palatal *ch*; the doubled *ss* in some of the above forms might thus have been replaced by *ch*.

When personal endings come to be added, the combined finite verbs will most of them ultimately assume the forms: *ana giri*, *nalichidi*, *kuḍichini*, *naḍachini*, *nalisivi* etc. It is possible that the forms like *ana giri*, *pillichiri* etc., arose in this way and not as supposed by grammarians from contractions of forms like *ana gyāru*, *pilichiyāru* etc. It is imposible to say at present whether the imitation of the Aryan aorists ever produced a full paradigam; only the forms for the third person are met with now.

168. THE GENESIS OF THE FORMATIVE SYLLABLES *chu* AND *yu*.

(*a*) It is hardly necessary to note here that the Telugu past tense, the genesis of which is described in the last two articles, is the colloquial tense in popular use which is not even noticed in grammars. It is the oldest of the Telugu past tenses.

What is stated above as to the formation of this tense is only a theory framed so as to accord best with the known facts of the case. The oldest specimens of Telugu known to us belong probably to the 8th century A.D., while the past tense suffixes which the language has imitated were certainly in use in the Aryan vernaculars of India in the 3rd Century B.C., if not earlier. We do not know when these suffixes were adopted or what changes Telugu underwent during these 1000 years. All that may be said with some certainty is that the palatal past tense of Telugu appears to be made on the model of Aryan palatal conjunctive participles and possibly in a few cases, of the sigmatic aorists. But it is not known which Telugu dialects followed the aorist model and which the participial model and whether any followed both. It is also not known whether there were any dental past forms in Telugu and, if so, how these came to be superseded. It is however, certain that as in the case of the Aryan languages there must have been great differences from place to place in the spoken dialects and several attempts must have been made to introduce uniformity. We have evidence of one such attempt about the close of the pro-Dravidian period.

Comparing the verbal forms *koṭyānu, koṭṭē, koṭṭi* of the consonantal base *kottu* with the forms *naḍachyānu, kuḍichyānu, nalisyānu, naḍachē, naḍachi, kuḍichē, kuḍichi, nalichē, nalichi, nalisā, nalisi,* of vowel bases, it must have been thought that the effective past suffixes in all forms were really *ya, e,* and *i,* and that the bases of *naḍachyānu* etc., should be *naḍach, kuḍich, nalich, nalis,* with the enunciative *u* the forms of the bases would be *naḍachu, kuḍichu, nalichu, nalisu,* and having regard to the law of harmonic sequence of vowels the last three should further change into *kuḍuchu, naluchu,* and *nalusu.* It is not clear why the last which assumes the alternative form *nalusunu* in the aorist should further change into *naliyu;* perhaps the change of *s* to *y* suspends the law of harmonic sequence. The vowel bases *naḍa, kuḍi, nali,* have thus become lengthened into *naḍachu, kuḍuchu, naluchu, naliyu* through a mistaken etymology.

(*b*) The following may be given as instances of the very large number of couplets of extended bases which the palatal past tense has produced out of primitive vowel bases.

	Non-causal	Causal
pogayu	'smoke'	*pogachu*
merayu	'shine'	*merachu*
egayu	'fly up, soar'	*egachu*
payu	'become separated'	*pachu*
nuliyu	'be twisted'	*nuluchu*
vaḍiyu	'fall in drops'	*vaḍuchu*
tuniyu / *tunugu*	'be cut to pieces'	*tunuchu*

But there are many stray bases which do not thus occur in couples: for Example:

taniyu	'become satisfied'	*taḍiyu*	'become wet'
taḍayu	'delay'	*uliyu*	'sound'

are intransitive without corresponding transitive bases ending in *chu*; *guniyu*, *gunuchu*, 'dance, dangle' are both intransitive; *dorayu* 'be fitted, resemble'; *tiriyu*, *tiruchu*, 'beg, live by alms', *enayu* 'resemble, mingle'; are both transitive and intransitive.

Aḍiyu, 'break' occurs as a transitive verb in Yudhamalla's inscription *lingambu aḍisi* 'having broken the idol'; but the form current now is *aduchu*.

169. THE GENESIS OF THE SUFFIXES *inchu*, *chu*.

It has been pointed out more than once already that the causal bases and bases derived from Sanskrit words originally ended in *i*, not in *inchu*, as *koṭṭi*, *anagi*, *naḍapi*, *kuḍipi*, *nalipi*, *puji* 'adore', and *bhuji* 'eat' from Sanskrit *puj* and *bhuj*. There appears to have been a specially marked accent on the final *i* of such bases, for when *cya*, *che*, *chi* of the past tense come to be added to these bases the initial *ch* is actually written double or has an anusvara put before it, while in the case of the ordinary accented roots like, *naḍa*, *kuḍi*, *nali* mere pronunciation of *ch* as a tenue *is* considered sufficient; as in *naḍachi, kuḍichi, nalichi.* In the earlier of the two Yuddhamalla inscriptions the form *ettichche* 'caused to be raised' occurs side by side with *vēlvarinchinan* 'if (they) drive (them) out', *upēkshinchinan* 'if (they) neglect'. *Vide* also causal forms without anusvara in §143 above under Telugu dialects.

The causative and the Sanskritic *i* is apparently considered to be a distinctive sign and it is deemed very necessary to retain it. It is apparently for this purpose that this *i* is given a special accent and the following consonant doubled or nasalized so as to suspend the law of harmonic sequence.—

Koṭṭinchu, anaginchu, naḍapinchu, bhujinchu etc.

Another class of causals consists of bases like *tola chu, pena chu, aḍa chu, ana chu,* which have non-causal forms ending in *gu*:—

Tola gu, pena gu, aḍa gu, ana gu.

Here the question is whether these causals should be regarded as contracted forms of *tola ginchu, pena ginchu* etc., or as arising from the primitive accented roots *tola, pena, aḍa, ana* an ardhānusvāra being inserted before *chu* in imitation of the ardhānusvāra before *gu*. The formations probably belong to a period when the unextended roots *tola, pena, aḍa, ana,* were in use in the language side by side with the extended bases *tola gu, pena gu, aḍa gu, ana gu,* and also perhaps *tola ku, pena ku, aḍa ku, ana ku,* and may be derived from the unextended roots by the addition of the suffix *chu*.

170. Classification of verbal forms.

(*a*) *Pro-Dravidian and pro-Telugu forms.*—It is necessary to emphasize here that the extended roots ending in *chu*, and *yu* the latter standing for *su* or *su* were originally employed only in the formation of the past tense. On referring to the section Telugu suffixes and to 154, it will be observed that the tenses and moods in which *chu* and *yu* are optionally or necessarily rejected are :

(1) the aorist tense including first person imperative,
(2) the imperative mood second person,
(3) the infinitives, also the verbal nouns in *adamu*,
(4) the negative forms.

These with the past tense are sufficient for all ordinary purposes of a spoken language and they all existed probably in the Pro-Dravidian, certainly in the pro-Telugu period.

(*b*) *Modern verbal forms.*—The tenses and forms in which the suffixes *chu* and *yu* are not even optionally removed are:—

(1) the present participles formed with the suffixes *tun*, *chun*, *ta*, *cha*;

(2) the past tenses formed with the suffixes *ti*, *in*, *enu*, and

(3) the future tenses formed with the suffixes *e* and *eda*; *edunu* and *edini*.

As has been indicated more than once in the foregoing pages these formations appear to have come into existence after the old vowel bases had been extended by the suffixes *chu* and *yu*.

(*c*) *Difference in the behaviour of old and new tense and mood suffixes.*—The following table exhibits the forms assumed, from time to time, by some typical bases in the four tenses and moods which have existed in Telugu from the pro-Dravidian period. As the negative forms follow the infinitives closely they are not shown separately.

Base	Aorist	Imperative	Infinitive	Causal	Conj-part
1. *koṭṭu*	*koṭṭudunu*	*koṭṭumu*	*koṭṭan*	*koṭṭi* *koṭṭimpu* *koṭṭinchu*	*koṭ ya* *koṭṭi*
2. *nalugu*	*nalugudunu*	*nalugumu*	*nalugan*	*naligi* *naligimpu* *naliginchu*	*naligya* *naligi*
3. *naliyu*	*nalutunu* *naliyudunu*	*naliyumu*	*naliyan*	*veyi* *veyimpu* *veyinchu*	*nalisya* *nalisi*
4. *piluchu*	*pilutunu* *piluchudunu*	*piluvumu*	*piluvan*	*pilipi* *pilipimpu* *pilipinchu*	*pilichya* *pilichi*
5. *koṭṭinchu*	*koṭṭintunu* *koṭṭimpudunu* *kottinchudunu*	*koṭṭimpunu* *koṭṭinchumu*	*koṭṭimpan* *koṭṭinchan*	*koṭṭimpi* *koṭṭimpimpu* *koṭṭimpinchu*	*koṭṭinchya* *koṭṭinchi*

The first line opposite to each base shows the oldest forms; these have *ch* only in the past tense. The behaviour of *y* in the bases *naliyu*, *pogayu* etc., shows that in the basic period the bases were merely *nali* or *nalu*, *poga etc.* ending in vowels, as they are even now in Tamil. When extended by *chu* they assumed the shapes *naliyu*, *pogayu* etc., in the intransitive forms instead of *nalusu*, *pogasu* etc. When the suffixes *mu*, *undu*, *an*, *adamu* and the causal *i* which belong to the pro-Dravidian period came after them no change takes place in *y*. But if the present participial suffixes *tun*, *ta*, or the past and future suffixes, *in*, *ti*, *enu*, *e*, *eda* come after them *y* at once begins to hiss, thereby showing that it is not now a *ya* sruti but a substitute for *s*.

This contrast brings out clearly what verbal forms were in existence in the oldest period of the language and what forms were added to the languages after the extension of vowel bases by the suffixes *chu*, *su*. This classification is, however, open to the criticism that alternative forms without *chu* or *su* might once have existed in the case of some at least of what are classified as late editions. This is possible but we have to base our classifications on the evidence actually available; the classification may have to be altered if additional alternative forms are found to exist.

(*d*) *Gradual encroachment of the syllables chu and pu on old moods and tenses.*—The table given in the previous sub-para also shows that vowel bases not already extended by the suffix *gu* assumed three different forms in the pro-Dravidian period according to tense and mood. This will be clear from the forms:—

pilutunu piluvan pilichi:

and *koṭṭintunu koṭṭimpan koṭṭinchi*, which show that the non-causal *koṭṭi* had each three different model forms.

pilu piluvu piluchu
and *koṭṭi, kottimpu, koṭṭinchu,* used
respectively in (1) the aorist and the imperative first person, (2) the imperative second person, the infinitive and the verbal noun, and (3) the past tense.

Since then *pu* and *chu* bases have been encroaching upon moods and tenses which did not originally belong to them. The alternative forms

koṭṭintunu, koṭṭimpudunu, koṭṭinchudunu,

show that they have both encroached upon (1) while *koṭṭinchan* and *mochan* show that the suffix *chu* has encroached upon (2). The suffix *chu* has now established its right to enter into the formation of all moods and tenses, and has come to be regarded as an inseparable addition to a very large number of the old vowel bases. But there must have been a long period in which *koṭṭimpu, koṭṭinchu,* were regarded as alternative verbal bases before the latter gained the final victory. It is probably to this period that the alternative present participles *koṭṭimpuchu* and *koṭṭinchuchu* should be referred.

The causal form *pilipinchu* with a hard *p* shows that the *v* in *piluvu* is a softened form of *p*.

171. Special forms of conjunctive participles

In Tamil, Malayalam and Kanarese there are a number of *u* bases of which the conjunctive participles and past tense forms are formed by doubling the last consonant of the bases. The doubled consonant has always the tenual sound even in cases where the original consonant was a media.

	Base	*Conjunctive participles*
	Tamil	
1.	*uku* 'be spilt or scattered'	*ukku*
2.	*toku* 'be collected or gathered'	*tokku*
3.	*naku* 'laugh, smile'	*nakku*

	Base	*Conjunctive participles*
	Tamil	
4.	*miku* 'remain, be left over'	*mikku*
5.	*puku* 'enter'	*pukku*
6.	*aḍu* 'cook'	*aṭṭu*
7.	*iḍu* 'put, place, give alms'	*iṭṭu*
8.	*paḍu* 'suffer'	*paṭṭu*
9.	*toḍu* 'touch'	*toṭṭu*
10.	*viḍu* 'leave'	*viṭṭu*
11.	*keḍu* 'be spoilt'	*keṭṭu*
12.	*naḍu* 'plant'	*naṭṭu*
13.	*aṛu* 'cease, become extinct'	*aṛṛu*
14.	*peṛu* 'beget, bring forth'	*peṛṛu*
15.	*seṛu* 'hate, kill'	*seṛṛu*
16.	*iṛu* 'break, be severed'	*iṛṛu*

No separate examples are given for Malayalam as most of the Tamil words above are also found in that language.

Kanarese

All the Tamil words shown above as ending in *ḍu* are also found in Kanarese and form their conjunctive participles in the same manner; the following may also be mentioned:

	Base	*Conjunctive participles*
1.	*isu* 'discharge, shoot'	*ichchu*
2.	*pasu* 'divide, apportion'	*pachchu*
3.	*bisu* 'unite firmly, solder'	*bichchu*
4.	*egu* 'be spilt'	*ekku*
5.	*pogu* 'enter'	*pokku*
6.	*nagu* 'laugh'	*nakku*
7.	*migu* 'remain'	*mikku*
8.	*sigu* 'fall into the hands of'	*sikku*

Dr. Kittel's explanation is that in all these cases the *t* of the conjunctive participle suffix *ti* changes into *t*, *ch* or *k* as the case may be. This explanation is hardly satisfactory. One can understand *dt* becoming *tt* in sandhi but it is hard to believe that *st* and *kt* became *chch*, *kka* respectively.

In Telugu the thirteen roots enumerated in 134 *c*, above form their conjunctive participles by adding the suffix *i* but they have alternative past relative participles obtained by doubling their last consonants and eight of the thirteen have also alternative past tense forms obtained by doubling these consonants.

The past participles and finite verbs in which the last consonants of the roots are doubled can be satisfactorily derived from past forms containing the Vedic gerundial palatal suffix *ya*. Ordinarily when a Sanskrit conjunct consonant containing *y* as its second member passes into Prakrit, the second member is often absorbed by the first consonant which is then doubled. In fact, according to Vararuchi's rules (III-2, 50, 51)[1] absorption and doubling seem to be the rule and the resolution of the conjunct by the interposition of a glide vowel between seems to be the exception. Prakrit instances of such resolution will be found collected in P.P.G. 134. The following instances of the doubling of the first consonant without changing it are taken from P.P.G. 279, 572.

(*i*) *kya*, *kka*, *chāṇakka*, *chāṇakya* (a proper name);
paraka, *parakya* 'alien, hostile';
vāka, *vākya*(*m*) 'a sentence'
sakka, *sakya* 'practicable'

(*ii*) *kkhyā*, *kkhā*, *ākkhāi*, *ākhyāti*, 'narrates'
sokkha, *saukhya*(*m*), 'pleasure'

1. *Vide* next page at foot.

(*iii*) *gya*, *gga*, *jogga*, *yogya*, 'fit'
veraga, *vairāgya*(*m*), 'indifference to the world'
sohagga, *saubhāgya*(*m*), 'good fortune, blessedness'

(*iv*) *chya*, *chcha*, *muchchai*, *muchyatē*, 'is liberated'
vuchchadi, *uchyatē*, 'it is stated'
vācha, *vāchya*, 'blameable'

(*v*) *jya*, *jja*, *jujjai*, *yujyatē*, 'it is fit and proper'
rājja, *rājya*(*m*) 'kingdom'

(*vi*) *ṭya*, *ṭṭa*, *tuṭṭai*, *truṭyati*, 'it breaks, falls asunder'
loṭṭai, *luṭyati*, 'it wallows on the ground'.

(*vii*) *ḍya*, *ḍḍa*, *kuḍḍa*, *kuḍya*(*m*), 'a wall';
piḍḍai, *pīḍyatē*, 'it is molested'

(*viii*) *ḍhya*, *ḍḍha*, *aḍḍha*, *āḍhya*, 'rich, wealthy'

(*ix*) *pya*, *ppa*, *kuppai*, *kupyati*, 'he becomes angry'; *suppau*, *supya ām* 'let it sleep'; *ānappa*, *ājnapyā* 'to be enjoined'; *viṇṇapa*, *vijñāpyā* 'fit to be communicated or reported'.

(*x*) *bya*, *bb*, *bhya*, *bbha*, *pibba*, *pibya*, 'to be drunk'; *abbhantara*, *ābhyantara*, 'interior, intimate'

III-2 *Adho mānayam.*—The consonants *m*, *n*, *y* are elided when last in a conjunct.

III-50 *Sēshadēsayōr dvitvam aṇādau.* Wherever after performing an elision or substitution enjoined by a rule, a single consonant comes to represent a conjunct this letter is always doubled except in the beginning of a word.

III-51. *Vargēshu yujah pūrvah.* When the doubling enjoined by the previous sūtra takes place wherever the single representative is an aspirate it is to be doubled by prefixing its own non-aspirate.

abbhuvavanna, *abhyupapanna* 'consoled', 'protected'
ibbha, *ibhya*, 'wealthy, opulent'.

The above examples make it clear that if we formed the past tenses of the original roots *nak*, 'laugh', *puk* 'enter', *naṭ*, 'plant', *aṭ* 'cook', with the Vedic suffix *ya* the tense forms will be *nakyan*, *pukyan*, *naṭyan*, *aṭyan*, and these may change into *nakkān*, *pukkān*, *naṭṭān*, *aṭṭān* by the absorption of *y* and the doubling of the previous consonant. The doubled consonant may have arisen in many cases in this manner and the conjunctive participles may have subsequently coined from the tense forms. This is put forward as an alternative theory to Dr. Kittel's view who supposes that the sign *t* of the past tense has in every case mentioned above been changed into the last consonant of the root.

In Telugu forms *padda du*, *chedda du* etc., in which *a* has the sound of the *a* in the English *bade* would seem to indicate the previous existence of *ay* which has been absorbed (§134-b).

172. Suffix *tya* or *chya* in Kanarese

The syllable *su* in the Kanarese causative suffix *isu* appears to have the same origin as the Telugu *chu*. If we suppose Kanarese causative bases to have ended in the suffix *i* as they undoubtedly did in Telugu, the past participles with the *tya* suffix will take the forms:—*madichya* 'having done', *hakichya* 'having put', *kayichya* 'having heated' etc., and as Kanarese had early lost the habit of accenting the vowel endings of verbal bases, these forms would ultimately have become *madisi*, *hakisi*, *kayisi*, as Kanarese does not tolerate the palatal aspirant *s*. As in Telugu new lengthened bases formed with these suffixes will be *madisu*, *hakisu*, *kayisu* etc. That the Kanarese causal stems originally ended with *i* that there was then an accent on this *i*, and that the syllable *su* was a latter addition are proved by the alternative forms like *maḍipa*, *maḍikum*, *maḍik-*

kum etc., side by side with the forms *madisuva*, *maḍisugum*, which have survived to modern times. (§ 127).

173. Suffix *tya* in Tamil

It has been supposed in 161 above that, in the pro-Dravidian period, Tamil formed its conjunctive participles for vowel bases solely with the suffix *tu* (*ttu* and *ndu*). There are however, certain causal and other forms which are best explained on the supposition that an attempt had been made in the pro-Dravidian or pro-Tamil period to form conjunctive participles with the suffix *tya*. Many vowel and consonantal bases now form their causals by means of the syllable *tu*;

Root		*Causal form*	*Root*		*Causal form*
naḍa	'walk'	*naḍattu*	*sel*	'go'	*seluttu*
puku	'enter'	*pukuttu*	*varu*(*vā*)	'come'	*varuttu*
iru	'be'	*iruttu*	*tiṅ*	'eat'	*tiṅṛu*
nil	'stand'	*niṛuttu*	*uṇ*	'eat'	*ūṭṭu*
			kāṇ	'see'	*kāṭṭu*

If we suppose that an attempt had been made to form conjunctive participles in *tya*, the participles of the accented, that is causal forms of the above named roots would have been:

naḍatti	*selutti*
pukutti	*varutti*
irutti	*tiṇṛi*
niṛutti	*ūṭṭi*
	kāṭṭi

which might, by mistaken analogy, have been supposed to arise by the addition of the conjunctive participle. Suffiix *i* to the Causal bases shown above.

In Old Tamil there are sporadic instances of the suffix *tu* being suffixed to non-causal bases, thus roots *puku* 'enter' and *pō* 'go' are sometimes inflected with a pleonastic *du*[1], as if there were then in use the non-causal bases *pukudu* and *pōdu* but these have not survived in Modern Tamil.

Two causal bases *kāychchu, pāychchu,* derived from the roots *kāy* ' be heated, dry' and *pāy* 'to flow (as water)', require special mention here. Bishop Caldwell argued (C.D.G. pages 49, 99 and 350) from the supposed analogy of Telugu and on the basis of vulgar pronunciation in the extreme south of the Tamil country that *kāychchu* had arisen from the palatialisation of *kk* in an assumed *kāykku* and that *pāychchu* arises from *pāykku.* The form *kāyttu* appears as the causal bases of *kāy* in *Silappadikaram* (XXI-55) where *kāyttiya* is used in the sense of 'for the purpose of burning'. The form *pāyttu* is stated to have been found in an old Tamil inscription[2] in the sense of 'irrigate'. It is thus clear that the *chchu* of the two bases arises from *ttu,* not from *kku.*

We must refer here to a small number of couplets in Tamil in which the suffix *tu* pronounced *du* and nasalized produces a non-causal base while the same suffix pronounced hard and doubled produces the corresponding causal base. Examples:—

---

1. (*a*) '*pukudinum*' 'even if it enters' (Silap. XVI. I-179) *nin manai p pukudāḷ* ' she will not enter your house (Maṇi: XXIV-81).

(*b*) *pōdu* 'go'; *pōduvār* 'they will go'; *pōduval* 'I will go', *pōduvāḷ* 'she will go'; *pōdēn* 'I will not go' (*Silap.* and *Mani.*)

2. The late Professor M. Seshagiri Sastri quotes (foot-note page 16 *Tamil Philology*—verbs) the phrase *pāytta-p-pervaraka* 'They will be entitled to irrigate' from a copper plate grant obtained from Kumbakonam.

tirundu	'be rectified'	:	*tiruttu*	'rectify'
porundu	'be joined, fit'	:	*poruttu*	'join, cause to fit'
varundu	'suffer, be afflicted	:	*varuttu*	'cause suffering afflict'
alundu	'be indented or depressed'	:	*aḻuttu*	'depress, press'

There appear to be no corresponding couplets in Telugu or Kanarese though some of the above bases are found in these languages also:—

Kanarese: *aldu*, *addu*, 'dip' (trans.); 'sink in a fluid' (intrans.)
pordu, *poddu*, *pondu*, 'join' (trans.) 'obtain' (trans.)
tirdu, *tiddu*, 'make straight' (trans.)

Telugu: *diddu* 'correct, rectify' (trans.)

174. ACTION NOUN SUFFIXES IN TAMIL

The forms mentioned in the previous para raise the presumption that formerly in certain Tamil dialects conjunctive participles might have been formed in all cases with the suffix *tya*. This surmise is rendered a certainty by the fact that the suffix *tal* may be added to all bases to form action nouns.

The usual action noun suffixes are *al* and *tal*, the former of these is added to unaccented bases, the latter may be added to any base accented or unaccented. Examples:—

Base	*Action noun*	*Base*	*Action Noun*
sey 'do'	*seyal* *seytal*	*iruttu* 'cause to sit'	*iruttal* *iruttutal*
viḻu 'fall'	*viḻal* *viḻudal*	*kiḍa* 'be', 'remain'	*kiḍattal*
ōḍu 'run'	*ōḍal* *ōḍutal*	*nil* 'stand' *paḍu* 'lie down'	*niṟṟal* *paḍuttal*

šel 'go'	*šellal*	*naḍa* 'walk'	*naḍattal*
	šellutal	*iru* 'sit'	*iruttal*
naḍattu 'cause to walk'	*naḍattal* *nadattutal*		

The real action noun suffix is *al* and *tal* is merely *tal* where *t* arises from the old habit of adding a pleonastic *tu* to every root. Even apart from this when the final vowel of a root is accented and the suffix begins with a vowel the expiratory accent requires a consonant to spend itself on, as it were. There is no such necessity for a consonant in the case of unaccented roots where the interposition of *t* when it occurs is merely due to an old habit and is therefore optional.

There are, in use in colloquial Tamil, a large number of words originally action nouns which in many cases have now acquired special significations.

Roots		*Derived nouns*
kāy	'heat, be heated'	*kāychchal* 'fever'
kūy	'make a loud noise'	*kūchchal* 'loud outcry'
mēy	'graze'	*mēychchal* 'grazing pasture'
irai	'make a noise'	*iraichal* 'noise'
kaḻi	'discharge'	*kaḻichchal* 'looseness of bowels'
eri	'burn'	*erichchal* 'burning sensation'
alai	'go to and from, wander'	*alaichchal* 'wandering'
ōy	'cease'	*ōychchal* 'feeling of tiredness' cessation.
tuṇi	'be bold'	*tuṇichchal* 'temerity'
pāy	'flow (as to water to crops) spring':	*pāychchal* 'irrigation', to spring as of a tiger, cat, etc.
viḷai	'grow'	*viḷaichal* 'growth', 'yield'
oḍi, oḍai	'break'	*oḍisal, oḍaisal* 'broken things'
tēy	'be worn out'	*tēysal* 'worn out things'
maḍi	'become earth-eaten'	*maḍisal* 'earth-eaten things'

In all these cases the initial *t* of the action noun suffix coming after the sounds *i, ai, y* has become palatalized.

CHAPTER XI

CAUSAL FORMATIONS

175. The Modern Dravidian Method of forming causals.

The manner of forming causal bases in the cultivated Dravidian languages has been explained in §§102, 118 (*g*), 126 and 140. As a general rule and subject to exceptions every vowel base could, in the pro-Dravidian period, be converted into its causal form by merely accenting its final vowel. (§91). This method has now become obsolete in Kanarese and obtains only to a limited extent in Tamil and Malayalam, while in Telugu there are now practically no bases ending in vowels. The modern method of forming causals is as follows :—

(1) *Tamil:* The invariable causative suffix is *pi* which becomes *ppi* after accented vowel bases and is softened to *vi* after unaccented bases. The suffix is added to all roots whether ending in vowels or consonants.

(2) *Malayalam :* Causal stems are formed as in Tamil, by the addition of *pi* (*ppi*) to accented roots and *vi* to unaccented roots. But most unaccented roots add only *i.*

(3) *Kanarese:* The most usual causative suffix is *isu* which appears as *su* in themes ending in *y*, *l*, *e*, and *i* and occasionally as *asu*. In the ancient and medieval dialects the causative suffix was *chu* in the case of themes ending in *r*, *l*, *ll*, and occasionally *ichu*, was affixed in the medieval dialect.

(4) *Telugu:* With a few exceptions bases ending in *chu* form their causatives by changing into *pinchu*. Roots

not ending in *chu* generally form their causals by adding *inchu* ; in some cases the final syllable is changed into *chu*. In the case of the following verbs and some others the final *chu* is changed into *pu*:—

naluchu, tēchu, mōchu, chūchu.
nalugu, malugu, medugu, tunugu.

(5) All the above languages form a large number of bases from Sanskrit words by the addition of *inchu* (Telugu), *isu* (Kanarese), and *i* (Tamil and Malayalam) to suitable bases. Examples :—

Sanskrit word	*Telugu*	*Kanarese*	*Tamil and Malayalam*
bhuj 'eat'	*bhujinchu*	*bhujisu*	*bhuji*
jaya 'victory'	*jayinchu*	*jayisu*	*jayi*
śayana 'lying down'	*śayaninchu*	*śayanisu*	*śayani*

Some bases are also formed in Telugu by suffixing *ilu* or *illu* to Sanskrit bases.

Sometimes in the ancient and medieval dialects of Kanarese a euphonic *y* is used before the *isu*; in the medieval dialect this euphonic *y* sometimes changes also into *v*.

176. Bishop Caldwell's explanation of the causative *i, vi, pi*.

What is the origin of this causative particle *i* and of the *p* which is prefixed to this *i* in the case of all causals in Tamil, and in the case of many causals in Telugu and Malayalam? Bishop Caldwell says in his book at page 354:

'*Origin of the Dravidian Causal particle* i.' The oldest form of the Indo-European causative particle is supposed to be the Sanskrit *aya* (with *p* prefixed after a root in *a*). *aya* becomes *i* in old Slavonic, and the apparent identity between this *i* and the Dravidian *i* is noteworthy. Notwithstanding this, it does not seem to me either necessary or desirable to seek for the origin of Dravidian particles out of the range of the Dravidian languages, if those languages themselves provide us with the tolerably satisfactory explanation. The Dravidian causative particle *i* may be supposed to have been derived from *i* 'give'.

In regard to the *p* which precedes the *i*, Bishop Caldwell says in his book at page 353:

"The Tamil future tense signs seem to throw light on themselves to which the causal particle *i* is affixed. It is remarkable, at all events, that these three (future) signs, *v*, *b*, *pp* are identical with the formatives of the causal verb, in what-way-soever this identity may be accounted for, so that if we know which of these three signs is used by any verb in the formation of its future tense, we know at once how the causal of the same verb is formed. Compare:

varu v ēn 'I will come' with *varu v i* 'cause to come';

eḍu pp ēn 'I will take up' with *eḍu pp i* 'cause to take up, erect';

paḍi pp ēn 'I will learn' with *paḍi pp i* 'cause to learn, teach'.

"The explanation of this curious coincidence seems to be that the Tamil future was originally a sort of abstract verbal noun, which came to be used as a future by the addition of pronominal signs, whilst the same abstract neuter noun was converted into a causal (as we have seen probably the case also with Telugu causals in *pinchu*) by the addition to it of the causal particle. The addition of the causal particle in all cases in Kanarese to the verbal root would seem to indicate an older period of Dravidian speech." (Page 354.)

Bishop Caldwell notes the apparent identity between the Aryan (Slavonic) suffix *i* and the Dravidian *i* but does not consider it necessary or desirable to seek for the origin of Dravidian particles out of the range of Dravidian languages. This is only one of a large number of identities which he has ignored or rejected as being merely apparent. A philologist should be guided in these matters not by what one may consider necessary or desirable but what the history of the forms shows to be the actual root in fact.

What Bishop Caldwell regards as three identities between *v*, *b*, *pp* of the future and of the causals is only one identity for every *p*, whatever its origin, will become *v*, *b* and *pp* after unaccented, nasal, and accented bases; *e.g.* *varu v ēn* 'I will come.'; *kān b ēn* 'I will see'; *naḍa pp ēn*, 'I will walk'.

Further what Bishop Caldwell calls abstract neuter nouns are in many cases used as causals in Tamil, Malayalam and Telugu without the causative suffix *i*. Thus Tamil *eḻuppu* 'raise', *nirappu* 'fill', *tiruppu* 'cause to turn'; Telugu *nalupu* 'crush'; *champu* 'kill'; *medupu* 'beat in mortar' and a number of other *pu* bases enumerated in § 153 above are even now used as causal bases. It will also be seen from § 154 above that the causal forms of a large number of lengthened *chu* bases formerly ended in *pu* and that *pinchu* or *inchu* was a later innovation.

Lastly it may be remarked, in anticipation, that the causative *p* and the future *p* appear to have different origins.

177. The Aryan method of forming causals

The causal formations in Sanskrit are what are called *ṇich-antas* by Hindu Grammarians; the *ṇich* being nothing more than a suffix *i* (ommitting *ṇ* and *ch*) which is invested with certain characteristics, in consequence of which it causes *vriddhi* and *guṇa* changes in the vowel of the root to which it is attached. It is well known that the substitution of high grade and long grade vowels for simple vowels, generally results from a shift of accent (M.V.G. Vowel Gradation).

As a thematic vowel *a* invariably follows the causative particle *i* in tense forms it is itself converted into *e* and becomes *aya* in combination with the thematic vowel in all tense forms. The accent on the *a* of *aya* is called the causal accent by foreign grammarians. A few examples will illustrate this:—

Root	*Original suppositious forms*	*Strengthened form*	*Final form*
chi 'collect'	*chi i a*	*chai e a*	*chāyaya*
śru 'hear'	*śru i a*	*śrau e a*	*srāvaya*
kri 'do'	*kri i a*	*kar e a*	*kāraya*
char 'move'	*char i a*	*char e a*	*chāraya*

In the above illustrations the modified roots end in consonants, and the *a* of *aya* has merely to attach itself to these consonants. But when the root ends in *a* there is a necessity for the insertion of a consonant to fill the hiatus between this *a* and the initial *a* of *aya*; and this consonant has always been *p*, from the Indo-Iranian period. Examples:

Root	*Original form*	*Strengthened form*	*Final form*
sthā 'stand'	*sthā i a*	*sthā ay a*	*sthāpaya*
dā 'give'	*dā i a*	*dā ay a*	*dāpaya*

(*b*) In course of time the use of this interposed *p* in the causal formations began to be extended also to bases not ending in *a*. Even in the Vedas it had come to be used with some bases ending in *i* and *ri*. For instance:

ji 'conquer' *jāpaya*; *kshi* 'possess' *kshēpaya*;
śri 'resort' *(ud)śrāpaya*; *ri* 'go' *arpaya*.

In *snāpaya*, *jñāpaya*, *srāpaya*, from the roots *snā* 'bathe', *jñā* 'know', *srā* 'boil', the root vowel is shortened. (M.V.G. 558.)

We have seen that in the Asoka inscriptions the interposed *p* had come to be used almost with any kind of base and even with bases ending in consonants as in *krīḍāpayati*, *pīḍapayati*. In the literary Prakrits the causal stem was made from all roots by the addition of the equivalent of *apaya*, i.e., by *aye* or *ave*. (W.S.G. 1042-n.)

(*c*) Although the causal sign *aya* appears in almost all tense forms it was not expressed in several important verbal formations even in standard Sanskrit, the only indication that these formations are causal, being the strengthening of the roots by a *guna* or a *vriddhi* change of their vowels or the presence of the interposed *p*. In the past participle passive the causative particle *i* though expressed does not undergo *guna* change.

Verbal noun	*Conjunctive participle in ya*	*Gerundives in ya and aniya*	*Past participle passive in ta*
māraṇam 'killing'	*pratiṣṭhāpya* 'having established'	*sthāpaya*; *sthāpanīya* 'that ought to be established'	*sthāpitam*
srāpanam 'cooking'	*anusārya* 'having followed'	....	*sāritam*
ājñāpanam 'commanding'	....	....	

All causal past passive participles are formed with *i*, *ta*, with strong grade of root syllable. (Brug. Vol. IV, 795). Brugmann considers that the *i* of this suffix is etymologically connected with the causative particle *aya* and that it is an organic part of the base, is in fact a root determinative from which the *aya* of the causative and of the Sanskrit denominative forms may have arisen (§§ 789 and 798). These suffixes appear to be traceable to the Indo-Germanic period. Brugmann's view is that the causal past participles passive Sanskrit roots and denominative bases for instance of *vrit* 'turn round', *dhri* 'carry support', *vri* 'hinder', *mantra*, 'counsel', *tarka* 'guess' are formed from the extended bases *vart i*, *dhar i*, *var i*, *mantr i*, *tark i*.

On the other hand, foreign Sanskrit grammarians for instance, Professors Whitney and Macdonell, consider the *i* of the causal past participle passive suffix *i tą* to be an inorganic union vowel. (M.V.G. 575 c; W.S.G. 1051 b.) In their view the causative suffix in Sanskrit is *aya* and they appear to regard the causative *i* (*nich*) of the Indian grammarians to be an artificial device.

That it is not an artificial device is clear from allied forms in other Indo-Germanic languages—especially Germanic and Balto-Slavonic (Brug. IV 804-807). Brugmann also considers the *p* of the Indo-Iranian suffix *paya* to be a root-determinative (797 *ibid*). Allied forms in other Indo-Germanic languages leave little room for doubt that the Indian grammarians must be following some hoary tradition when they take *aya* to be made up of *i* (*ṇich*) *a*.

(*d*) Another class of denominative inflexions, also of Indo-Germanic origin, which may be mentioned here are those of stems in which the final *a* is lengthened.

Professor Whitney notes that such inflexions may in Sanskrit be in the middle of the active voice and that middle forms have an intransitive or reflexive meaning; *e.g.*, *kaluṣāyatē* 'is or becomes turbid', *taruṇāyatē* 'is rejuvenated', *śithilāyatē* 'grows loose'.

There are certain verbal bases in Tamil which are formed by lengthening the final *a* of nouns. These appear to be in imitation of the above denominative stems.

(1) *śōka* (i) be afflicted with grief, (ii) faint, fall in a swoon.

from *śōkam* (i) grief, (ii) fainting, loss of consciousness.

(2) *annā* 'open the mouth looking upward' from the Dravidian *anna m* high, upwards.

(3) *angā* 'yawn, open the mouth'. *c.f.* Telugu *angil i* Kanarese *angal i* 'the palate'.

(4) *ēma* { 'be overjoyed, self-conceited, be exhila-
(5) *śemma* { rated'. These words appear to be derived from *ēmam* and *śēmam* meaning 'security, happiness, joy', which are corruptions of the Sanskrit *kshēma* 'security'.

(6) *iṟumā*. A third base having the same meaning is *iṛumā* the original form of which is not clear.

(*e*) It would seem from the examples given in §553 of Pischel's *Prakritic Grammar* that in popular and vulgar dialects such Apabhramaśa *Ardhamāgadhi*, and Jaina Mahārāṣṭrī, the causative suffix may be suppressed in tense forms also, the lengthening of the roots or the presence of *p* being the only indication that the forms are causal. Following are some of the examples given Pischel—

Prakritic form	*Corresponding Sanskrit form*
padai	*patati* for *pātayati* 'fell'
marai	*mārati* for *mārayati* 'kill'
nasai, *nasavai*	{ *nāśati for nāśayati* { *nāśapati* for *nāsāpayati* 'destroys'
vēdanti	*vēdanti* for *vēdayanti* '(they) inform'
thavai	*sthāpati* for *sthāpayati* 'frees'
hasavai	*hasapati* for *hāsāpayati* 'causes to laugh'
bhamavai	*bhramapati* for *bhrāmāpayati* 'causes to whirl'

karavai — *kārapati* for *Kārāpayati* 'causes to be done'
vinnavai — *vijñāpati* for *vijñāpayati* 'informs, requests'
palavai — *pralāpati* for *pralāpayati* 'laments'
nimmavai — *nirmāpati* for *nirmāpayati* 'creates'
adhavai — *ādhāpati* for *ādhāpoyati* 'causes to be placed'

Other forms which may be quoted here from Pischel are:—

Ŝamthavanti, *vidhavai*, *patthavai*, *haravai*.

This practice seems to have begun even in the Indo-Iranian period; for in Kanga's Avestic Grammar it is stated: 'In some rare instances the causal is formed by changing or lengthening the radical vowel without subjoining the characteristic *aya*. (K.A.G. 523.)"

Examples :

Root	*Iranian form*	*Sanskrit form*
sad 'fall'	*sāzdum* 'hew ye' for	*sādayadhvam*
naś 'perish'	*nāśmi* 'I destroy' for	*nāśayāmi*
śru 'hear'	*śrūta* 'well proclaimed'	*śrāvita*
mru 'die'	*mrūra* 'killing'	*māraṇa*.

(*f*) The above is a very brief account of causal formations in the Aryan languages. It is impossible in this book to go into greater details—in fact, it is unnecessary to do so. The main points to be noted in the above analysis are:—

(1) the causative suffix *i* which bears an accent and which the Indo-Germanic philologists call a root-determinative. It is changed to *e* when the thematic *a* follows and becomes *aya* in combination with this *a*.

(2) the accent on the vowel of the root which in consequence undergoes *guṇa* or *vriddhi* change:

(3) when the root thus strengthened does not end in a consonant the interposition of the consonant *p* between the final vowel of the root and the causative suffix;

(4) the absence of the causative *aya* or *i* in several verbal formations, the strengthening of the roots and the presence of the interposed *p* being the only indications that the formations are causal;

(5) the continual extension of the use of the interposed *p* to other vowel bases and even to consonantal bases, the optional use of *apaya* for *āpaya* in the Asoka inscriptions and of *av* (*ap*) in popular idioms without the causative sign *aya* (*e*) or *i*.

(6) the absence of the causative sign even in tense formations in popular idioms such as Apabhramśa, Ardhamāgadhi' and Jaina Mahārāstrī; and

(7) the existence of such tense formations, though in rare instances, without the causative sign *aya* or *i* even in the Avestic literature.

178. Comparison of Aryan and Dravidian Methods

(*a*) *Telugu:*—Let us take the following examples given by Pischel: *thavai*, *patthavai*, *samthavai*, *vinnavai*, *nimmavai*, *adhavai*, *nasavai* of which the bases should have originally had the forms :

sthap for *sthāp* 'fix, place'; *prasthap* for *prasthāp* 'despatch, dismiss';

samasthap for *samsthāp* 'place, fix'; *vijñap* for *vijñāp* 'inform, beg';

nirmap for *nirmāp* 'cause to be built';

adhap for *adhāp* 'cause to be deposited';

nāsap for *nāśāp* 'destroy'

the vowels preceding the final *p* are shortened in these examples and there is no indication that the forms are causal except the presence of *p*.

The Telugu causal stems of the bases mentioned in 140, 153 above, deprived of the enunciative *u* will be *nalup*, *tep*, *mop*, *chup*, *nalup*, *malup*, *medup*, *tunup*; these correspond exactly in formation to the Aryan stems and appear to be in imitation of them.

Again let us consider the pro-Dravidian or pro-Telugu forms (§168 a.) of a base now ending in *chu*, say, *naḍachu* 'walk':—

> *causal: naḍa p adamu, naḍa p an, naḍa p ani;*
> *non-causal: naḍa v adanu, naḍa v an, naḍa v ani*
> *causal: naḍa p undu*
> *non-causal: naḍa v undu, naḍa chya, naḍa tu nu.*

We see that Telugu uses this interposed *p* only for the purpose of filling the hiatus between vowels; the tenual pronunciation of *p* shows that the Dravidian accent in the case of causal forms has not been forgotten. This observation may be objected to on the ground that the forms *naḍa tu nu* and *naḍa chya*, containing the tenual pronunciation of *t* and *ch* occur in the non-causal paradigm. True: this is one of the whims that are often noticed in the languages spoken by millions of people in which the selection of forms cannot be expected to be conducted always on a logical basis. Telugu retains the non-causal forms *agasi*, *pogasi*, side by side with the causal forms *agachi*, *pogachi*. Similarly it might have retained the non-causal form *naḍasi*, corresponding to the causal for *naḍachi*; but it has not done so, and we have to accept the fact. Having selected the causal forms *naḍa pu du nu* and *naḍa p i* it has rejected *naḍadunu* and *naḍasi*, if these forms ever existed in the language, and has relegated *naḍa tu nu* and *naḍa chya* to the non-causal paradigm.

The same remarks apply to many other roots ending in *chu*. In Tamil also we have the anamoly that the non-causal bases *naḍa* 'walk', *paṛa* 'fly', etc., are unaccented only in the past tense.

(*b*) *Tamil:*—As has been pointed out in 95 b, there are a number of verbal bases in Tamil which the rule that the final vowel should be accented when the base is used causatively is strictly observed. The number of such vowel bases was much larger in the older stages of the language and it will have been seen from the examples given in §95 (4) that even the vowels of consonantal bases were accented in some cases.

The accent in the Indo-Aryan languages was musical or pitch accent and affected the gradation of the vowels accented; while in the Dravidian languages the accent was merely a stress on the vowel the result of which was to double the initial consonants of the suffixes attached to the bases. In the examples quoted above from Pischel mere accentuation of the root-vowels *i.e.*, a change in their gradation was enough in popular speech to convert a verbal base to its causal stem, and similar examples quoted above from the Avesta would seem to show that this method is as old as the Indo-Iranian period, not an innovation on Indian soil.

The suggestion of the present writer is that the Pro-Dravidian and Tamil method of accenting the final vowel of a root to convert it into its causal stem is an imitation of the methods adopted in the popular Indo-Aryan idioms. This method has, as has been pointed out in §147-149, 153, 171 produced a large number of lengthened bases.

As in Telugu the *p* of the *pu* causals *eḻuppu*, *tiruppu*, *kiḷappu*, *kuppu*, *nirappu*, *kuḻappu*, etc. (§ 153) merely arises from an imitation of the Aryan interposed *p* ; this *p* is used also in the literary dialect in the infinitives and subjunctives of accented roots to fill the hiatus between two vowels. In the popular peech the hiatus in filled by *kk* (§ 112 e).

179. CAUSATIVE SUFFIXES *ilu* or *illu*, *i*, *pi* (vi)

(*a*) There is a root *il* or *ilu* of the 10th conjugation which is thus referred to in the Dhātupāṭha lists of roots:—

'*ila prēranē*' *ila* is used in the sense of 'urging or driving'. But *prēraṇā* in grammar also denotes the 'causal form' and the Aryan cultivators of the Telugu language are in the habit of adding this *il* (or *ilu*) to Sanskrit roots and using the compounds as Telugu verbal bases in the same manner as the *prēraṇā* (causative) suffix *i* is added to Sanskrit bases for the purpose of converting them into Dravidian bases.

khid	*khēdillu*	'be afflicted';
śubh	*śōbhillu*	'shine';
chit	*chintillu*	'think or reflect';

(Campbell's Grammar §371)

These forms differ from the Tamil-Malayalam denominatives given in §173 (5) only in containing *illu* instead of the suffix *i*.

(*b*) The suffix *i* is apparently an imitation of the Indo-Iranian *i* which was originally a root-determinative and has given rise to the *aya* of the Sanskrit causals and determinatives. The only verb-forms in which it is now seen unchanged are the causal past participles passive.

(*c*) The suffix *pi* (*vi*) which may be added to all Tamil bases without exception and to all vowel bases and to some consonantal bases in Malayalam is also an adaptation from the Indo-Iranian forms. It stands in the same relation to the Indo-Iranian *paya* that the suffix *i* stands to *aya* and is made up of *p* and *i*; Brugmann considers this *p* also to have been a root determinative in its inception.

(*d*) The Dravidian and the Indo-Iranian thus agree in the following respects :—

(1) Accenting the vowel of a root to convert it into its causal stem. The accent changed the gradation of the vowel in Indo-Iranian, it merely led to the doubling of the initial tenues of suffixes coming after vowel bases in Dravidian. Where the suffix began with a vowel a tenue had to be interposed between the root and the suffix.

(2) Formation of causal and denominative stems by the addition of *aya* in Indo-Aryan and of *i* including *isu*, *inchu*, in Dravidian. There is reason to believe that *i* was the original of *aya*; in any case the two suffixes are etymologically related.

(3) Formation of causal stems by *paya* in Indo-Aryan and of *pi* (including pinchu) in Dravidian, the two suffixes being related in the same way as *aya* and *i*.

(4) Formation of denominative bases by lengthening the final *a* of nouns.

180. The Lengthening of the pro-Dravidian roots.

(*a*) So far as we can form a conception from a comparison of the materials available in the cultivated Dravidian languages, the verbal bases of the pro-Dravidian language consisted of:—

(1) consonantal bases like,
koṭṭu, 'beat'; *tiṭṭu* 'abuse'; *tannu*, *taḷḷu* 'push'; *kaṭṭu* 'bind' etc.

(Note :—The final *u* of these bases is enunciative.)

(2) *aḍa*, *ana*, *kala*, *maḍa*, *maḍu*, *pena*, *tola*, *tuna*, *eru*, *kaḍa*, etc. (§149 *b*)

(3) *naḍa*, *mara*, *kara*, *le*, *nilu*, *mo* etc. (§154 (*a*))

(4) *nāli*, *pōga*, *ēga*, *nuli*, *vaḍi*, *me*, etc. (§166)

It is difficult to say now whether all these radicals were used as verbal bases, and in the case of any of them whether the Tamil final vowel was *a* or *ai*, *i* or *u*. Some of these radicals are still in use in Tamil as verbal bases but the final vowels in that language are not the same as shown above in some cases.

These radicals were converted into their causal stems by laying a stress or accent on their final vowels.

(*b*) one of the suffixes used in the pro-ethnic period began with a *k* and now exists in the form *ku*.

It has lost its original signification, whatever that was, and is now become permanently attached to the root, forming what is called a root extension or a formative syllable (§150). In Tamil this *ku* has given rise, in many cases, to causal and non-causal couplets. (§147.)

aḍaṅgu *aḍakku* *maḍaṅgu* *madakku*
piṇaṅgu *piṇakku* *oḍuṅgu* *oḍukku*

Telugu possesses lengthened non-causal bases ending in *gu* corresponding to the radicals shown in (*a*) (2) above, but not accented bases ending in *ku* or *ku* (§149 *b*).

It is difficult to say for certain now whether causal forms with a *ku* suffix were ever in actual use in Telugu though it is probable that they were.

(*c*) Another particle which became permanently attached to the root even in the pro-Dravidian period was the letter *p* which in its inception was a junction consonant and was adopted to fill the hiatus between two vowels—the final vowel of the base and the initial vowel of the suffix—in imitation of the interposed causative *p* in low colloquial Aryan idioms. The causative meaning itself was expressed by the stress on the radical vowel. This gave rise to two forms—one with a tenual *p* and the other with a *v* or *mb*. Of these a limited number of bases ending in *pu* are now in use as causal stems in Telugu ; in Tamil-Malayalam there is a small number of couplets ending in *mbu* and *ppu*.

(*d*) The formative syllable *tu* which plays such an important part in the case of Tamil and Malayalam bases is hardly noticeable in Telugu or Kanarese. It arose out of the Vedic conjunctive participle suffix *tya* and has given rise, in Tamil and Malayalam, to a number of causal bases in *ttu* and a limited number of couplets in *ndu* and *ttu* (§171).

(*e*) A fourth suffix beginning with a tenue which was in use in the pro-Dravidian period as a past tense suffix was *chya* which became *sya* after unaccented roots, and has given rise to the Telugu formative syllables *chu* and *su* and a couplet of roots corresponding to each radical of the kind shown in (*a*) (4) above.

(*f*) in addition to these there were the causative suffixes *i*, *pi* which have since become lengthened into *isu*, *inchu*, *pinchu* but which have not yet permeated down to all colloquial strata. They appear to have been superimposed on the previous pro-Dravidian causals which they are displacing (§177).

(*g*) One of the old radicals which have been lengthened by each of the formatives *ku*, *pu*, *chu*, is the Telugu *nali:*

	Non-causal	*Causal*
(1)	*nalugu*	*naluku* } *naluchu* }
(2)	*naluvu* } *naliyu* }	*nalupu*
(3)	*nalusu* } *naliyu* }	*naluchu*

Successive lengthening of the stem in order of time are, for instance,

kottu, *kotti*, *kottimpu*, *kottinchu*

kottu, *kotti*, *kottimpu*, *kottimpi*, *kottimpimpu*, *kottimpinchu*

naḍa, *nadapu*, *naḍapi*, *naḍapimpu*, *naḍapinchu*

CHAPTER XI-A

ARYAN GERUNDIAL SUFFIXES

181. Aryan gerunds at various stages

(A) *Iranian.*—The practice of using the gerund or verbal noun as a verbal participle dates at least from the Iranian period. In the Avesta the gerund was formed by the addition of *-thva* (changeable to *-tva* after *s* and *ṣ*), *-ta*, or *-ya* -directly to the root. This form had generally the same signification as the Latin gerund in *-ndum*, e.g., *vāta* 'blowing' *stōta* 'praising', *phramainya* 'thinking', *phrajathva* 'smiling'. (K.A.C. para. 564.)

(B) *Old Indo-Aryan.*—The so-called gerund in Sanskrit is a stereotyped case (doubtless instrumental) of a verbal noun, having the force of an indeclinable participle which qualifies the actor and denoting an action which accompanied or (more often) preceded that signified by the principal verb of the clause. (W.S.G. § 989.)

(1) *Vedic dialects.*—The following suffixes occur in the Vedas *-tvi*, *tva*, *tvya*, *tya*, and *ya*. Some Grammarians also mention *-tvanam*, and *tvinam*; but these have nowhere been found in the Vedas available to us. In the *Rig Veda* in the greatest majority of cases (full two-thirds) the final of *ya* is long. (W.S.G. § 993.) In the Vedic dialects these gerunds expressed an action which accompanied or more often preceded that of the finite verb. (M.V.G. § 589.)

(2) *Classical Sanskrit.*—The suffixes of the conjunctive participle in classical Sanskrit were *tva* and

ya the latter being used for compounded roots and the former for simple roots; *ya* became *tya* after roots ending in short vowels.

NOTE.—It will be noted that gerunds had not always a part signification.

(C) *Prakritic Corruptions.*—The above suffixes underwent various modifications, changes and corruptions in the Prakrits.

(*a*) the forms found in the Asoka Inscriptions have been dealt with in great detail in § 76-B above. They are in order of frequency *tu*, *-ti*, *-ta*, *cha*, *-chya*, *-ya*, *ye*. Of these *-tu* arises from *-tva* by the Samprasāraṇa of *-va*.

-ta also arises from *-tva* but the absorption of *-va* in *-t* *-ti* is taken by Dr. Buhler to arise from the Vedic *-tvi* by the absorption of *-v*, but M. Emile Senart would derive it from *tya* by the Samprasāraṇa of *-ya*. (*Vide* Indian Antiquary, Vol. XXI, page 13.)

-cha and *-chya* arise from *-tya* palatalisation. *-ye* arises from the Vedic *ya*.

These corrupt forms are attached to the roots by a connecting *-i* where necessary.

(*b*) *The Prākṛita Prakāśa* of Vararuchi gives for

1. *Mahārāṣṭrī* : *una* (IV-23). This comes from *-tvanam* or *-tvana* through the following intermediate forms: *tuna*, *dna* and *una*.

2. *Paiśāchī*: *-tunam* (X-13) Examples:—*dātunam* 'having given', *kātunam* 'having done', *ghettunam* 'having taken'; this suffix arises from *tvanam* by the Sampraśāraṇa of *va*.

3. *Māgadhī*: *-dani* (XI-16) Examples:—*sahidani* 'having borne', *karidani* 'having done'.

4. *Saurașenī:* *-ia* generally; and in addition *jadua* and *kadua* for the two roots *gam* and *kri* (XII-9-10) *-ia* arises from the Vedie *-ya* and *dua* from the Vedic *-tva*.

(*c*) The *Prākṛita Lakshaṇam* of Chanda gives : *-ttu*, *-tta*, *chcha*, *-ttum*, *-tuna*, *-ttu*, *-o*, *-ppi* (II-19).

Chcha in the list appears to arise from *-tya* perhaps also from *-tta* preceded by *-i* or other palatal vowel; *-ppi* arises from Vedic *-tvi*; *-tuna* arises from *-tvana*; and *itum* is merely *-ttu* with a final anusvāra.

Vandittu (*van* 'alone'); *Chaittu* (*tyaj* 'abandon')
Janitta (*jñā* 'know'); *Thichcha* (*sthā* 'stand')
hochcha (*bhū* 'be'); *Sunittu* (*śru* 'hear')
kinita (*kri* 'do'); *Karisitta* (*krish* 'drag or plough')
pechcha (*pre* 'go or die')

These forms are very common in the canonical works of the Śvetāmbara Jains.

(*d*) *Pallava Prakrita Inscriptions.*—The forms in *-tuna*, *-tuna* and *-tunam*, occur in the Pallava grants discovered in the Telugu country.—

atichhituna -atichchidya (?), *atikshipya* (?)
Katuna, *katunam*, *Kritvā*
natuna, *natunam*, *jnātva*.

Similar forms also occur in the Amraoti, Jaggayapet and Bhattiprolu inscriptions.

(*e*) *Siddhahēmachandram* of Hēmachandra gives:—

(1) *Śaurasēni*; *-ia*, *-duna*; and *gadua* and *kadua* for the two special verbs and *gam* and *kri*—(IV -271-272)

(2) *Paiśāchi* *-tuna* Examples:—*Gamutana*, *ramtuna*, *hasituna* (IV -312)

(3) *Apabhramsa.*—*-i*, *-iu*, *-ivi*, *-avi*, *-eppi*, *-eppinu*, *-evi*, and *-evinu* (IV-439-40). Here *-i* is what is left of *-ya*; it was originally *-ia* but the *-a* has been lost in course of time. (P.P.G. para. 594.)

The Apabhramsa referred to here is supposed to be the Nāgara Apabhramsa, and the rules given have reference apparently to this dialect as it appears in literature. The Śauraśenī referred to is apparently the traditional one of the old grammarians put into the mouths of inferior characters in dramas.

(*f*) *Pischel.*—The above lists contain the chief modifications of the *-ktva* suffix as given by the old Prakrit grammarians. A few of the more important of the other forms collected by Pischel from works in Prakrit and given in his *Prakrit Grammar* are subjoined:—

(1) *-ttanam* arises from the *-tvanam* of the Vedas. It is common in the Jaina works in Ardhamāgadhi. (P.P.G. para 583.)

(2) *-chchana*, *-chchanam*; These forms appear to have arisen from an extension of the Vedic *-tya*, just as *-ttana* and *ttanam* have arisen from a lengthening of the form of *-tva*; *-chchana*, and *-chchanam* are common in the Jaina canonical works. (P.P.G. para 587.)

(3) Similarly *-yanam* and *-yana* have arisen by an extension of *-ya*. These also are common in the Angas of the Śvetāmbara Jains and are probably confined to these works. (P.P.G. 592.)

A curious misapprehension appears to have arisen with reference to these forms. The *-nam* has apparently been regarded by grammarians as a separable participle, inserted for the purpose of imparting grace to words and phrases, *i.e.*, for 'Vākyālaṅkāra'; and that is apparently why the suffixes *-ttaam*, *-ttana*, *-chchanam*, *-chchana*, *-yanam*, and *yana*, have not been noted separately in Chanda's or Hemachandra's Grammar. As will be seen below the people have always regarded *nam* and *na* as integral parts of the suffixes.

NOTE:—It will be seen that the rule of classical Sanskrit regarding the use of *-tva* and *-ya* is ignored in Prakrits: Mahārāshṭrī, for instance, uses *-una* for all roots, and Paiśāchī *-tunam*.

(*D*) *Modern Aryan Vernaculars.*—The suffixes used in the Modern Aryan vernaculars are.—H.G.G. 491; B.A.G. Vol. III. pp. 229-33:

(1) *Marathi*:— *-una* from *-una* of Mahārāshṭrī which again is traceable to *-tvana*.

(2) *Eastern Rajasthani*:— *-u*, *-ne*, arising from *tvanam* the final *-am* of which becomes *e*.

(3) *Gujarati*:—*i* or *-i-ne*, the latter of which may be derived from *-ya-nam* (§ 182).

(4) *Eastern Hindi*	*e* or *i* or quiescent.
(5) *Western Hindi*	*-i* or quiescent.
(6) *Punjabi*	*-i* or quiescent.
(7) *Sindhi*	*-i* or *-e*
(8) *Naipali*	*-i*
(9) *Oriya*	*-i*
(10) *Bengali*	*-iya*

The forms in (4) to (10) are derived from the Vedic *-ya* through the Śaurasenī *-ia*.

As has been stated in § 10 above through the habitual neglect of the final short vowels the conjunctive participles often assume the form of the bare stem and it has become necessary to strengthen them by derivatives from *kri* which take the forms *Kari, kei, ko, ke, ku, ki.* Other strengthening suffixes met with are *-kun*, *-kana*, *-kane*, etc. which are variously explained by scholars; the present writer thinks that these may be derived from *kriṇu* which becomes *-kun* in Prakrit and *-kun* in Paiśachī and Persian. (§ 193 a.)

182. THE COLLOQUIAL PAST TENSES IN TELUGU IN *-ya*, *-i* and *-e*

(*a*) The Aryan suffixes entering into the formation of these tenses are *-ya* and *tya* and their corruptions *-i*, *-chya*, *-sya*, *-chi*, *-si*. The formation of these tenses is the backbone of the theories put forward in this book, and has been dealt with in detail in Chapter IX. It will be sufficient here to merely mention the main conclusions arrived at there.

(1) the verbal participles used as finite verbs in the beginning must have been formed in the Telugu area by suffixing *-ya* to consonantal and *-chya* to vowel bases (164). It is probable that *tya* was suffixed in the Tamil area to Tamil bases in a certain stage of the development of that language (§171); it is just possible that the Vedic *-tya*, not the Prakriti *-chya*, was originally used in the Telugu area also and that it subsequently became palatalized;

(2) *-chya* became *sya* after unaccented bases.

(3) The pronominalization of the participles produced the finite verbs *-koṭvānu*, *naḍachyānau*, *chēsyānu* etc.

(4) The non-pronominalized tense forms of the third person *-koṭ ya*, *naḍachya*, *chēsya*, become the finite verbs *-koṭṭe*, *naḍache*, *chēse*. (§ 164.)

(5) The forms not used as finite verbs became the conjunctive participles *kotti*, *naḍachi*, *chēsi*. (§ 164.)

(6) Possibly the terminations *-i*, *si*, of the Aryan sigmatic aorists were used in parts of the Telugu area, giving rise to the pronominalised forms like *koṭṭiri*, *naḍachiri*, *chēsiri*; also *koṭṭidi*, *naḍachidi*, *chēsidi* as in the Beradi dialect. (§ 165.)

(7) The accented and unaccented vowel bases were at the beginning of the Telugu period lengthened by the syllables *-chu* and *-su* (*yu*) respectively, through a mistaken notion that the tense signs of these bases were *-ya*, *-e*, and *-i*, as in the case of consonantal bases. (§ 166-a.)

(8) There was a special accent on the causative suffix *-i* which led to the doubling or nasalization of tenses coming after it, as in the suffixes and forms *-inchchu*, *-inchu*, *-impu*, *-intu*; a similar special accent being also the cause of the causative suffix *chu*. (§ 167.)

(9) The necessary or optional rejection of the additional syllables *-chu* and *-yu* in some of the tenses and moods is a sufficient reason for presuming that these tenses and moods are Pre-Dravidian or pre-Telugu and for holding that the other tenses and moods have come into existence some time after the beginning of the Telugu period. The conversion of *-yu* into *-su* in the latter tenses and moods appears to confirm this view, (§ 168-c.)

(10) Since the beginning of the Telugu period the additional syllables *-chu* and *-pu* have been encroaching upon tenses and moods which did not originally belong to them; *pu* itself being in later times displaced by *-chu* except in a few causal stems. (§ 168-d.)

(11) The syllables *-chu* and *-su* in the causative suffixes *-ichu*, *-isu* of Kanarese have the same origin as the final syllable *chu* of the lengthened Telugu verbs.

(12) It is possible that the suffix *-tya* was used in the Tamil area; it did not, however, produce any tense form but merely gave rise to a very large number of causal leases in *-ttu* and to the verbal noun suffix *-tal* which latter can now be employed to form the *nomina actionis* from any Tamil verbal base. (§ 171-2.)

(*b*) In a paper entitled "The tense signs in Dravidian" sent to the Poona Oriental Conference of 1919, the present writer gave an alternative explanation that the Telugu formative syllable *-chu* and *-su* were probably modifications of the imperative second person singular endings *-ssu* and *-su* of Prakritic verbs. A fatal objection to this supposition is that the syllable *-chu* is rejected from the imperative second person singulars of certain classes of verbs ending in *-chu* and is replaced by *-pu* or *-vu*. The same objection is also fatal to Bishop Caldwell's supposition that *chu* is a corruption of *-ku*; for the predecessor of *chu* in old verbal forms is *-pu*. not *-ku*.

183. The Tamil, Malayalam, and Kanarese Suffix *-tu* (§95, 115, 122).

The similarity of this suffix to the Asokic conjunctive participle suffix *-tu* (*-itu*) of which it appears to be an imitation is too striking to be ignored. It is unnecessary to consider here the changes which the *-t* of this suffix undergoes in colloquial and vulgar speech and in combination with final consonants of bases.

In standard Kanarese the suffix appears as *-du* predominatingly with a connecting *-i* where necessary. In standard

Tamil and Malayalam it becomes *-ittu* after accented bases generally and *-du* or *-ndu* after other bases. It also becomes *-ndu* after *iru* 'be', *kida* 'lie' and a number of other accented roots enumerated in §95-A above.

As remarked in §97 (*e*) the number of unaccented bases in which *-tu* appears as *du* in Tamil can be counted on one's fingers; in the vast majority of unaccented bases the suffix is found as *-ndu* which apparently corresponds to the *-du* of Kanarese as can be seen from the following words common to Tamil and Kanarese.

Tamil	*Kanarese*
marundu 'medicine'	*marudu*
virundu 'feast'	*birdu, biddu*
uḷundu 'black gram'	*urdu, uddu*
parundu 'a kite'	*paddu, haddu*
porundu 'fit, unite'	*produ, poddu*

In the past tense forms *konṟān, venṟān, śenṟān, koṅḍān, māṅḍān* etc. of *kol* 'kill', *vel* 'conquer', *sel* 'gȯ', *koḷ* 'buy', *māḷ* 'die' etc. It is *nd*, not *d*, that nasalises the final of the bases.

It is noteworthy that the accented roots *iru, kiḍa, naḍa,* etc. should have conjunctive participles of the form *irundu, kiḍandu, naḍandu* etc., instead of *iruttu, kiḍattu* and *naḍattu* etc. These last are likely to be mistaken for the causal forms of the roots which also contain *it* and the nasalised *-ndu* is preferred probably to distinguish the conjunctive participles from the causals.

184. Telugu-Tamil Suffix *ina* (95 and 134-*d*)

To trace the Telugu-Tamil past tense in *-ina* we shall begin with the consideration of the much younger Gujarati conjunctive participle suffix *-i, -ne,* of which various explanations have been given at different times. The suffixes used in Gujarati are *-l -ne* of which the former *is*, as we have seen (§179 D) derived from the Vedic *ya* through Śaurasenī *-ia*.

Some appear to have attempted to derive the latter from the Mahārāshṭrī *-u-na*, but unsuccessfully (B.A.G. Vol. III, page 233). Sir G.A. Grierson appears to have thought that it was contracted form of *-i -tane* another Prakrit conjunctive participle suffix (L. S. IX, Part II, page 389) of which the latter part-*tane* he takes to be connected with the *tana* of *Keratanau.* In the old Western Rajasthani from which Gujarati is derived the conjunctive participle suffix is *i-nai*, and Dr. L. P. Tessitori, Udine, in his notes on the grammar of that Language (I.A. Vol. XLIV, pp. 105 and 119) is of opinion that Gujarati *-i-ne* is derived from *i-nai* of Western Rajasthan and that *nai* is a declensional post position, short for *kanai* (*kanhai karnasmin*). He also rejects the usual explanation which derives the long *i* from the Apabhramśa *i* of the Prakrit.

(1) '*Sambandhinah Karatanau*' (Hem. IV, 422 20) '*Kara* and *tan* are used to express connection.'

He thinks that both *-i* and *-kanai* are locative cases and that *-i-nai* (*i-kanai*) is a locative absolute.

The explanation given in this book differs from the explanations both of Sir G. A. Grierson and Dr. Tessitori.

The conjunctive participle suffixes *yanam* and *yan* which occur in the religious works of the Jains furnish a solution of the difficulty; if we admit *nam* to be an integral part of the suffix *yanam* as it has always been admitted to be of *-tvanam* and *tunam*, the whole difficulty disappears. If Eastern Rajasthani could produce *-u-ne* from *-tvanam* by Samprasāraṇa of *va* and the elision of *t* we should not be surprised at modern Gujarati having arrived at *-i-ne* from *yanam* by the Samprasāraṇa *ya*. Final *am e* is a common change. It is but natural that *-i-ne* and other modified forms of *yanam* should be found now in use in Gujarat and the parts adjoining, for it was at the council of Vallabhi in 454 or 467 A.D. that the Śvetāmbara Canon, as we now have it was fixed. (§76 e.)

We can conceive how these scriptures though in the main dating from the council of Pataliputra might have had to be recomposed in parts from time to time in the Aryan vernacular current in Gujarat which appears to have been the scene of Jaina activities for a considerable period. The originally separable particle *nam if ti* was separable had come to be incorporated with the suffix in popular speech. The following are a few instances of the use of *yanam* and *yana* in the Acaranga Sutta:—

(1) *Ausanto samana tumam chevedam panagajatam padiggahena va-ussinchiyanam*[1] *vattiyanam ginhahi*[2] (1; 7; 8).

(2) *Bikhupadiyae chhappena va dussena va valgana va aviliyana*[3] *paripiliyana*[4] *parisaiyana*[5] *shattu dalaejja* (2; 1; 8; 1).

(3) *Aggam cha mulam cha vigimcha dhire palickkindi yanam*[6] *nikkammadamsi* (1; 2; 1).

Some of the degenerated forms of *-yanam* and *-yana* now in use in Gujarati and the adjoining countries taken from the L.S. Vol. IX, Parts II and III are noted below:—

(*a*) The language of the semi-civilized tribes of Eastern Broach: The suffix *-n* is usually added to the past tense (II p. 389). *Rahyan* 'we lived'; *gayan* 'we went' conjunctive participles *ka-in* 'having done', *chod-in* 'having left'. It is obvious that *yan* in the above examples is *yana* without the final a.

(*b*) Ghisadi spoken by a tribe of blacksmiths who wander over Southern India: *Jay-ina*, *hoy-ina*, *pad-ina*, *kay-ina*. Some-

1. *Utsichya*, 2. *apavartya*, 3. *apīdya*, 4. *paripādya*, 5. *parissāviyana*, *parisrāvya*, 6. *parichchidya*.

times the final *a* is dropped *kar-in* 'having done'. (II 453 at sec).

(*c*) Nahikantha Bhili (II p. 13) Conjunctive participles *pad-i*, *pad-in-ne*, *pād-i-ne*,

(*d*) The Dhar state Bhili (III p. 52) Conjunctive participle suffixes -1, *-i-ne* (*i*-na).

(*e*) Raj-i-a Bhili (0.85) Conjunctive participle suffixes *-i*, *-i-ne*.

(*f*) Panchali (III 138) *qat-i* 'having divided; *ach-in* 'having seen'; *kar-in* 'having done'.

(*g*) Khandesh Bhili (III p. 154) *pad-i*, *uda-i*,

(*h*) Nimar Bhili (III p. 174-5) *kai -ina*, Jaina

(*i*) Baori (III p. 183-4) *kar-in*, *uth-in*, *chekkh-in*

The above examples are enough to show in what directions *-yanam* and *-yana*, become modified in the language of the uncultured, and how the Tamil-Telugu tense in *-ina* could have been derived from these suffixes.

If in addition to *-yanam* and *-yana* we can assume *a* by form in *-yan* as in *rahyam* and *gayam* of Eastern Broach we get a form like the Telugu *koṭyan* which can be used for all persons and numbers without personal endings. In the illustrations given in 160 c above *-anyam* and *pilyam* have become *annemu* and *palemu* in Telugu. Similarly, the suffix *-yan* in the forms *koṭyan*, *naḍachyan* etc., will become *enu* in Telugu and produce the forms *koṭtenu*, *naḍachenu* etc. How faithfully has Telugu preserved the drutam here?

The non-pronominalised forms of the third person *viz.* *koṭṭe* (§164) and *koṭṭenu* thus arise from two different suffixes *-ya* and *-yan*, and are independent of each other. It is therefore unnecessary to explain as do the Telugu grammarians the origin of *koṭṭē* by assuming that *koṭṭēnu* loses its final in popular speech. Of course, the form *koṭṭēnu* might in popular speech lose its final and also become *kotte.*

The relative participles can be formed only with *-ina* in Telugu. In old Tamil they could be formed only with *-iya* but both the participle and the past tense are now formed only with *-ina* in spoken Tamil. The new Forms have penetrated into the literature of Malabar but they are unknown to the people's Malayalam which still forms its relative participles in *-iya.* It is assumed in this book that the past tense in *-ina* is a late form as the suffixes *chu* and *su* are not rejected in *ina* forms of *naḍachu*, *chēyu*, etc. It may be argued on the other side that the tense may be regarded as formed with the suffixes *-yana* and *-chyana* the latter being suffixed to unextended roots like *naḍa*, *chē*, etc. The use of *-ina* with the lengthened roots is not the only evidence of its modernness. We have also to take into consideration the late appearance of the suffixes *yanam* and *yana* in Prakrit literature, the absence of *ina* in Kanarese and Malayalam, and its partial and limited use on Old Tamil.

185. THE TELUGU SUFFIX *ti*

As noted in §179 (*a*) above, there is a difference of opinion in regard to the original of the Asokic *ti*, Dr. Buhler suggesting *-tvi* while M. Emile Senart inclines to *-tya.* However this may be, there seems to be little doubt that the Telugu past tense forms *koṭṭitini*, *koṭṭitimi*, etc. contain this suffix. The forms of this tense as contained in the first specimen of the Beradi dialect of Telugu published in the *Linguistic Survey of India* (IV, 604) contain no prenominal endings. The original Telugu form must also have been of the type *koṭṭiti* without personal endings, the final *u* of the *une* being changed into *i* to secure harmonic sequence of vowels.

CHAPTER XI-B

ARYAN PRESENT PARTICIPLE SUFFIXES

186. Aryan indeclinable present participles

The present participle *i.e.* the *Śatranta* of the Sanskrit grammarians was always declined in Aryan literature so as to agree with the noun it qualifies in number, gender and case, and even when it forms the first member of a compound tense in modern Aryan vernaculars of the present participle is generally declined and agrees in gender and number with the subject of the verb. But this is not always so and whenever a new Aryan vernacular uses an indeclinable that is an adverbial present participle in the formation of its present tense the authors of the *Linguistic Survey* remark that this is due to the influence of the adjoining Dravidian languages which never inflect their participles.

As pointed out in §46 however the use of the adverbial present participle was not unknown to the Old Aryan vernaculars and the Asoka inscriptions, the earliest specimens that we have of spoken Prakrit, furnish instances of the adverbial present participle.

Three Neo-Aryan vernaculars, Gujarati, Marwari and Marathi also use adverbial present participles and Dr. L.P. Tessitori explains these forms as absolute plural genitives of present participles. (I.A. Vol. XLIV, p. 97.)

"The so called adverbial present participle", he says, "is formed by the inflecting into *a* the present participle. Thus from *Karatau* we have *karata*, from *hutau huta*. In the same way as present participles, adverbial participles too may optionally retain the dental nasal when used in poetry.

I explain it as an absolute plural genitive contracted from Apabhramsa *antaha* or *antaha*"

The forms *santam*, *anupatipajantam*, *kalantam*, *karatam*, *katam*, occurring in the Asoka Inscriptions have all to be understood under this explanation as genitive plurals used absolutely; *karatam* is of course the genitive plural of *karat* in Prakrit corresponding to *Karatam* of classical Sanskrit and the first three of the above Asokic forms can also be described as genitive plurals if we overlook the superfluous nasal, as apparently Dr. Tessitori would. In any case, here are obvious case forms of present participles used adverbially which do not agree with the subject in number or gender and we have to accept the fact. Other forms that occur in Asoka's edicts are *kalanta* and *karu*.

One illustration of the use of such participles has already been given in § 76 B; two more are given below :—

Delhi Pillar Edict VIII (I.A. Vol. XVIII, page 301)

Hevam hi anupatipajantam hidatapalate
thus indeed following here below and in the next world
aladhi hoti
gain is.

"For by acting thus they gain (happiness) here below and in the next world."

Separate Rock Edict II Dhauli (I.A. XIX, p. 96)

Hevam kalantam tuphe svagam aladhayisatha
thus doing you heaven will obtain.

Those who wish to have more details about the use of these participles in the Asoka Inscriptions and how scholars have vainly and variously endeavoured by suitable commendations to make the participles agree with the qualified nouns may consult:—I.A. Vol. V. pp. 260, 277, Vol. X, p. 210, Vol. XVIII, pp. 301, 306, 307, Vol. XIX, pp. 7, 46, 102. E.I. Vol. II pp. 252, 460. M. Emile Senart is inclined to regard them as accusative absolutes equivalent to nominative absolutes.

In Dr. Hoernles *Grammar of the Gaudian Languages* it is stated that in the evolution of the Aryan vernaculars of India "in the main a gradual alternations of the nasal has taken place. The nasal consonant of the Sanskrit becomes *anusvara* in Prakrit, and *anunāsika* in Gaud, and finally drops off altogether". (H.G.G. 23.) In the examples given in illustration of this statement it often happens that when the *anusvāra* becomes *anunāsika* the preceding vowel is often lengthened. Thus, Sanskrit *simha* 'a lion', *hamsa* 'a swan', *chandra* 'the moon', becomes *sih*, *has*, *chad*, in East Hindi.

Thus the Asokic participle *karatum* may have become *karata* which is the form of Dr. Tessitori's adverbial present participle and also *karata* by the ultimate dropping off the nasal sound. The form *karata* is also what we obtain by the equivalence of the final *am* -*a* which E. Senart has established. (76 B.e.)

It may be remarked in passing that the Sanskrit periphrastic future which has its roots in the Indo-Iranian period shows that fifteen or twenty centuries before even the date of Asoka inscriptions the Asiatic Aryans were forming compound tenses, by affixing the first and the second persons of the verb substantive *as* or *ah* '*be*' to an indeclinable form derived from the root to be conjugated (§47 above). In all countries the spoken vernaculars evince a tendency to drop unnecessary inflections to the influence of adjacent foreign idioms.

187. (*a*) The Telugu Suffix-*ta*

This might have arisen by imitating the ending *tam* of Prakrit genitive plurals used adverbially in the Asoka inscriptions. In Emile Senart's analysis we saw that final *am* becomes *-a*. (76 B.e.) This lengthening of a vowel as compensation for the loss of a nasal is also deducible from colloquial Telugu where the suffix *ta* is mostly in use ; for

koṭṭinum, *chēstun*, *gurramulu*, became in colloquial speech, *koṭṭinā*, *chēstū*, *gurrālu*.

The old Kanarese suffix *-uttam* has become *uttā* in modern times. With the equivalence *am -a* the Telugu colloquial present participle in *-ta* and the colloquial tense formed with this particle are brought into agreement with the Asokic adverbial present participles ending in *tam*. Examples—

Koṭṭutam—Koṭṭuta, *chēyutam—chēyutā*, *chēstā*.

These colloquial forms *koṭṭuta* 'beating', *chēstā* 'doing', etc., it will be noted are strikingly similar in formation to the Hindustani forms used by the Madras Mussalmans *e.g.* *Khata hai* 'he is eating', *sota hai* 'he is sleeping ' etc.

The Telugu suffix *-cha* used by certain religious Brahmans of the Northen Circars is supposed to be a corruption of *-ta*.

As the suffix *-ta* occurs only in colloquial speech and is unknown to literature it is not possible to say whether it was borrowed as *tam* or *ta*.

(*b*) The Kanarese suffixes *uta*, *utta*.

The original of these suffixes was apparently *-uttam* the compensatory lengthening of *-a* being due to the loss of the final nasal. Are the initial *-u* and the doubled *-t* radical? Neither of these occur in the forms in use in the Kanarese dialects which however preserve the tenual pronunciation of *-t*.

The pre-Dravidian *-t* of the past tense suffix generally became *-d* after Kanarese roots which had lost their accent. Is the doubled *-t* in the present case a device of the Jain cultivators of Kanarese to preserve the tenual pronunciation of the *-t* of the present participle suffix, and was the initial *-u* put in to prevent this *-t* from combining with finals of the roots? If so, the Kanarese suffixes are identical with the Telugu suffixes *-tam* and *-ta* already considered.

If, however, the initial *-u* and the doubled *-t* are taken to be essential elements of the suffix then we must seek for the original of *-uttam* in the languages which were contiguous to Kanarese in the pro-Kanarese period when it appears to have been first adopted. The form *huttam* may be regarded as a Mahārāshṭrī *tadbhava* of the genitive plural—*bhavatām* of the participle *bhavat*; for *apahutta* is used in *Saptaśate* (5-36) as a *tabdhava* of the present participle *aprabhavan* 'unable, incompetent'. If so, *uttam* (*huttam*) may be taken as an indeclinable Aryan present participle used as an auxiliary to Kanarese bases just as the Aryan conjunctive participles *ki*, *ke*, *ke*, are used by Golari to form Dravidian conjunctive participles like *maḍ-ke* 'having made', *oḍ-ki* 'having run' *tin-ku* 'having eaten' (10-*a*). According to Dr. L.P. Tessitori in the old Western Rajasthani the indeclinable present participle *hutaii* (*bhavantakam*) of the auxiliary *bhū* 'be' is often added pleonastically after present participles used adjectively or absolutely; sometimes *Karataii* (*karantakam*) is so used. The participles *hutaii* is also used after participles used as adjectives. (I.A. XLIV, pp. 96-104.) Here *hutaii* which like *huttam* is an indeclinable present participle from *bhu* 'be' is used as an auxiliary in Aryan vernacular; the two uses are similar tnough *uttam* (*huttam*) is added to the bare root in Kanarese not to a participle.

188. The Telugu and Old Tamil *-t-aorist*

Dr. Tessitori's examples of adverbial present participles are apparently taken from standard literature but in colloquial and rustic dialects we can find several other examples of the indeclinable present participles besides the genitive plural.

Hindi has two sets of forms ; one indeclinable, originally ended in *-ant* and still exists in several rustic dialects with the termination *-at*. Chand inserts or omits the nasal at pleasure to suit his metre as

bhajjan 'possessing' *sunat* 'hearing'
rajant 'shining' *sajant* 'arraying'
subhant 'being beautiful' *kathant* 'being out'
chadhat 'mounting'

Tulsi Das chiefly uses the latter form as *jat* 'going ; *gunjat* 'humming'; *dhyāvat* 'meditating'; *pavat* 'finding'; *bhavat* 'being pleased' ; *gavat* 'singing'.

The form is also common in most mediaeval poets ; *dharat* 'placing'; *padat* 'falling'; *sōhat* 'being beautiful'; *lasat* 'appearing' ; *chahiyat* 'looking'; *jiyat* 'living'; *bandhat* 'being bound'. It survives in all the dialects of the Eastern Hindi area in Oudh, Riwa and Bhojpuri and even in the Gangetic Doab" (B.A.G. Vol. III, pp.123-4). Two forms are observable in Marathi or rather two sets of forms. The indeclinable ends in *-t*, *-tam*, and *-tamna* as *sutat*, *sutatam*, *sutatamna*, The first of these agrees with Hindi. B.A.G. Vol. III, p. 125.

In the Bhojapuri dialect of East Hindi the present definite and the imperfect tenses are formed by affixing to the present participle *-at* in various persons of the verb substantive. Here the present participle does not change for number or gender. (L.S. Vol. V, Part II.)

There are also present participles in the Hindi area of the forms (H.G.G. 299):—

khat 'eating'; *det* 'giving'; *hot* 'being'; *rovat* 'weeping'; *piat* 'drinking'.

The participles in the Telugu aorist of vowel bases corresponding to *marachu* 'forget'; *chēyu* 'do'; *koyu* 'cut'; *kuduchu* 'drink', before these roots were lengthened by the suffixes *-chu*, and *yu*, must have been of the form *marat*, *chat*, *kot*, *kudut*; or with the enunciative final *-u maratu*, *chetu*, *kotu*, *kudutu*. These last have apparently produced the forms:—
marachudu, *chēyudumu*, *koyuduvu*, *kuduchudru*. So also in Old Tamil the forms:—

Kadattir 'you are crossing'; *nadattum* 'we shall walk'; *pōtum* 'we are going'; are derived from the participles *kadat*, *nadat*, *pōt*.

The Hindi and the neo-Aryan participles are formed with the Vedic-Avestic present participle suffix *-at* transmitted through the Prakrits. The Dravidian has apparently drawn from the same source which has been in existence at least since 2,500 B.C.

§189. The Aryan Declinable Present Participles

(*a*) We saw in Chapter III that the Dravidian languages have also imitated some of the terminations of the Indo-Iranian declinable participles. The termination of the crude form of Indo-Iranian Active *Parasmaipada* present participle is usually taken to be *-at*, but the real termination is *-ant* of which the *-nt* is Indo-Germanic and appears, for instance, in the English words 'solvent', 'adherent', 'dependent' etc. In declension, however, either *n* or *t* is rejected in most of the Indo-Iranian forms, *-nt* appearing only in the remaining few: in the Iranian language and the Prakrits both *n* and *t* are rejected in a few forms, and the declension is on the whole very irregular.

The correspondence between the terminations of the Tamil *avan*, Badaga and Old Kanarese *avam*, Tulu *aye*, Kui *eanju*, Telugu and Gondi *vandu*, *vadu*, *ondu*, on the one hand, and those of the Vedic *bharan*, Māgadhi and Ardhamāgadhi *baram*, Avestic *dravas*, *baras*, Apabhramśa *hasantu*, and the inference to be drawn therefrom, have been exhaustively dealt with in Chapter III above (§§49-53). It will be sufficient here to recapitulate the main results arrived at there.

The Dravidian singular termination *-n* was traceable to the Indo-Germanic *-nt* being an imitation of the final letter in the Sanskrit participle and possessive forms *bharan* 'bearing', *bharishyan* 'about to bear'.

Guṇavan, 'possessing good qualities', *buddhiman* 'possessing intellect'; *an* originally indicated the Sanskrit grammatical masculine, neuter, and feminine as in the Tamil *manidan* 'a man', *araśan* 'a king', *idan* 'a place', *marai* 'a tree', *akkan* 'elder sister', *avvan* 'mother'. Subsequently, the final *-n* became generally restricted to the male sex and was replaced by other terminations in the remaining two sexes e.g. *manidan*, *araśan*, *idam*, *maram*, *akka*, *avva*, or *avvai*.

The Telugu and Madras-Gondi *-ndu*, the Kuinju Badaga *m* which are masculine terminations, the feminine terminations *-l* of Tamil and Kanarese, *-lu* of Telugu, and *kui* and *di* of Telugu, and the oblique suffix *-t* of neuter nouns in Tamil, are also traceable to the same Indo-Germanic *-nt*.

(*b*) It might be objected that the Telugu masculine termination generally appears as *-undu* not as *-andu* which is the form corresponding to the Prakritic present participle termination *-anto* or *-antu*. True: but the Sanskrit masculine names ending in *-a* end mostly in *-u* in Apabhramśa (P.P.G. 363) from which they were adopted as *-U* stems in Telugu, and were being declined as such when the new masculine termination *-ndu* was added in the nominative case. c.f. *Bālavyākaraṇamu*, *Tatsama-parichchēdamu*, (Sutra 21) according to which the Sanskrit *Pratipadikas Didda*, *Rāma*, *Bhārghava*, and *Rājapurusha*, should appear as *Diddu*, *Rāmu*, *Bhārgavu*, and *Rājapurushu* in Telugu declension.

In Tamil also *Dūta* 'messenger', *Amātya* 'minister', *Gōpa* a proper name, *Rāma* 'a proper name' etc., sometimes appear *Dūtu*, *Amachchu*, *Gōpu*, *Rāmu* etc.

(*c*) It has also been suggested in § 152 above, but with some reserve, that the alternative form *-ento* or *-entu* of the Prakritic participial termination may have given rise to the Telugu participial termination *-edu* in such words as *chēśēdu* 'which or who is doing'; *kottēdu* 'which or who is beating'.

These have alternative forms *chēsē*, *kottē*, in which the final *du* is dropped and the preceding vowel is lengthened in compensation. With the oblique declensional suffixes *-i*, *-ti*, these participles take the forms *chēsedi*, *kottedi*, *chēsti*, *kotteti* (§142).

In the Dāsari and Vadari dialects (§146-8) verbal nouns are formed by suffixing *-du* to the indefinite participles ending *edu*, e.g. *udedi* 'singing', *ādedi* 'dancing', *pāda eddi* 'singing' etc. In the former dialect the oblique form of the participle shows the suffix *-ta* e.g. *tineta* 'eating', *undeta* 'remaining'.

(*d*) In old Tamil the future relative participle was of the type *seymana* 'that will do', and there are several instances of forms containing this suffix, Ex. *enmanār pulavar* 'learned men say', *moḻimanār* 'they say' etc. and indicating the indefinite present (114 a-b). These arise probably from the imitation of the Aryan present participle suffix *-mana*. The suffix appears also as *vana* in some cases in Tamil literature.

CHAPTER XI-C

ARYAN ABSTRACT NOUN SUFFIXES

190. (*a*) The Aryan Suffixes *-tva* and *-tvana*

These two suffixes, the latter of which is an extension of the former, are used in the Vedas and in later Sanskrit to form neuter abstract nouns and adjectives (M.V.G. 17, 218). *Examples* :

bhrātṛtva 'brotherhood', *amṛitatvā* 'immortality', *sakhitvana* 'friendship', *rakshastva* 'sorcery', *kavitvana* 'wisdom'.

Of these *-tvana* becomes *-ttana* in Prakrit[1].

Examples

pīnattanam 'fatness', *mūdhattanam* 'folly'. This *-ttana* has been adopted practically without change in cultivated Dravidian in the form *-tanamu* or *-tanam*.

Examples :

Telugu : *chinnatanamu* 'smallness'; *peddatanamu* 'greatness'
Tamil : *kettatanam* 'badness'; *nallatanam* 'goodness'
Kanarese : *kelyatana* 'friendship'; *vīratana* 'valour'

(*b*) The Dravidian suffixes *-pam* and *-pu* (155-C). It has already been pointed out that in the Girnar inscriptions of Asoka the Sanskrit absolutive suffix *-tva* was written *-tpa* (§176); this peculiarity of pronunciation extended also to other words in the inscription in which the conjunct consonant *-tv* occurred. e.g. *Chatvāro* became *chatpāro*.

This process carried a step further has converted all conjuncts *-tv* into *-pp* in some dialects. Thus the suffix *-tvana*

---

(1) *taltvayōr dattanau* (Var. IV-22)—
-da and *-ttana* are respectively substituted for the suffixes *-tal* and *-tva*.

forming abstract nouns and nouns of condition became *-ppana* in Śaurasēni, and this form has been transmitted to all the neo-Aryan vernaculars where *-ppa* and *-ppan* are the suffixes of abstract nouns.

Examples :

motappa 'fatness', *bālakappan* 'childhood', *guruppan* 'heaviness' (H.G.G. 228-231); while the Vedic absolutive suffixes *-tvi* and *-tvinam* have become *-ppi* and *-ppin* in the Apabhramśa (P.P.G. 300, 588). From Mr. Beame's Grammar we also learn that in Hindi and Sindhi, in addition to the terminations *-pana*, *-panu*, *-pani*, containing *n* and *ni* and arising from *-tvana*, there are also abstract noun terminations *-pa*, *-po*, *-pp*, *-p*, etc. which must have arisen from *-tva* and *-tvaka*, and which show that *-tva* itself had become *-ppa* and *-pa* (B.A.G. Vol. II, p. 75).

There are certain nouns of quality ending in *-pu* or *-pam* in Dravidian.

Telugu : *telupu* 'whiteness', *erupu* 'redness', *pasupu* 'yellowness', *nalupu* 'blackness'

Tamil : *oṭpam* 'clearness' *nuṭpam* 'minuteness'; *tiṭpam* 'firmness', *veḷuppu* 'whiteness'; *śivappu* 'redness'

These terminations appear to be derived from the Vedic *-tva* and *-tvana*.

Kanarese having converted its *-p's* into *-h's* these suffixes do not occur in that language.

(*c*) The Dravidian suffixes *-mi*, *-mai* (§155-C). These occur as suffixes of abstract nouns and appear to be only different forms of the suffixes mentioned in (*b*) above, and to have also arisen from the Aryan suffix *-tva*.

Tamil : *perumai* 'greatness'; *veṇmai* 'whiteness'; *kūrmai* 'sharpness'

Telugu : *perimi* 'greatness'; *magatimi* 'manliness'

It is noteworthy that the change of *-p* to *-m* in the abstract noun suffixes occurs in Bengali and Oriya where *mi* or *ami* occur side by side with, and more frequently than, *pan*, *pam* etc.

luchami 'profligacy', *chadami* 'roguery', *dhilami* 'largeness' (H.G.G. 230).

The Tamil *mai* may also be compared with the ending *mā* of the Sanskrit words.

aṇimā 'minuteness'; *mahimā* 'largeness';

garimā 'heaviness'; *laghimā* 'lightness' as the final of Sanskrit words is usually pronounced *ai* in Tamil, e.g. *makimai* 'greatness', '*mālai*' etc. for the Sanskrit *mahimā*, *mālā* etc.

CHAPTER XI-D

THE ARYAN VERB-FORMS

kri, krinu. and *grihna*

§191. *Kri* IN THE ARYAN LANGUAGES

(*a*) *The Vedas*: The practice of using *kri* as an auxiliary to other verbs is as old as the Vedas in Sanskrit.

The earliest use of *kri* in this manner occurs in the periphrastic perfect, as in *vidam chakāra* 'he learnt', *vidam chakruh* 'they learnt' etc., where the various persons of the perfect of *kri* were made to govern the accusative of a noun form derived from the root conjugated. But forms other than the perfect of *kri* have also been in use as auxiliaries even from very early times (W.G.G. 1091-4).

svadaha karōti	*vashat kuryāt*
śritam kritya	*naganam kritya*
syēti akuruta	*krūrī kurvanti*

(*b*) *Modern Aryan Vernaculars*: As pointed out in §-c above, in the Aryan vernaculars of the north, *kri* is very largely used as an auxiliary in forming conjunctive participles. The forms it takes in Hindi are *kari*, *kar*, *karka*, and *karkar*; *ke* which arises from *kari* is used in the Hindi rustic dialects (B.A.G. Vol. III p. 231). Other derivatives from *kri* used for the purpose in the modern Aryan vernaculars of India are *ki*, *ku*, *kō*.

In Eastern Rajasthani which uses *kar* in verbal participles the initial *k* of the suffix is elided as in unaccented Tamil roots (H.G.G. 491) Thus in the broken dialects of the Dangs the following contracted forms occur:—

lair, *uthir*, *dēkhar*, *ār*, *jār*, *karar*, *hōr*, for the following forms *laikar* 'having taken', *uthikar* 'having risen', *dēkhkar* 'having seen', *ākar* 'having come', *jākar* 'having gone', *karikar* 'having done', *hōkar* 'having been' (L.S. Vol. IX, Part I, pp. 346 and 309). Alternative forms like *bōlar*, *bōlarkai*, *bōlarkan*, *bōlarkain*, occur in some of these dialects (p. 343 *ibid*). This shows that the strengthening additions are some times duplicated *kar*, *karkai*, *karkan*, *karkain*.

The auxiliary also enters largely in the formation of verbal participles in Marwari, Punjabi, and Braja. (I-A Vol. XLIV 105); and in most other Hindi dialects.

In Oriya which has the conjunctive participle with *kari* as in *dēkhikari* 'having seen', *kari* is often pronounced *kiri* in common speech (B.A.G. Vol. III, p. 232).

§192. *kri* IN THE DRAVIDIAN LANGUAGES

(*a*) One of the suggestions in this book is that *kiru* the suffix of the present tense in Tamil is nothing but the Sanskrit root *kri* 'do'. When one has to deal with an unfamiliar verb, one generally combines it with a familiar verb meaning '*do*', and this is what we should expect Northerners to have done with Dravidian Verbs.

ōdu- kir- ēn	*nada- k- kir -ēn*
run do I,	walk do I,

are 'I do run', 'I do walk', in English, but in the inverse order 'Run do I' and 'Walk do I' are the exact renderings of the Tamil forms. English knowing Indians, especially school boys, often indulge in such hybrid formations when speaking in their vernaculars:—

Tamil :	*enda*	*varusham*	*pāss*	*seydāy*?
English :	what	year(in)	pass	you did?
Tamil :	*avanai*	*dismiss*	*seyduvittārkal*	
English :	him	dismiss	they have done.	

(*b*) The suggestion that the Tamil *kiru* is the same as the Sanskrit *kri* 'do' is not a new one, but was made moer than fifty years ago by the late Rev. D. G. U. Pope in certain grammatical notes of the Toda language appended to Colonel Marshall's book entitled 'A *Phrenologist among the Todas*'. But Bishop Caldwell and those belonging to his school who believed that the Dravidian languages had attained their development long before the arrival of the Aryans in India simply ignored the suggestion. Bishop Caldwell's view is that *kiru* is merely another form of *kinru*, and in regard to the latter he appears to accept the derivation given by Drs. Kittel and Graul, *viz.* that the suffix is made up of *ku* a future sign, and *inru* meaning 'today', or 'now' (C.D.G. p-385).

Some varieties of Kaikadi and Burgandi, two of the dialects dealt with in §§ 104, 105, have forms of the verb substantive like *kire, kiri*, 'I am'; *chir* 'he is'; *chiru* 'they are'; *sire* 'I am', and *sir* 'he is'; etc. Dr. Sten Konow appears to take the bases of these forms *viz. kir, sir*, to be the verb substantive *kir* being the oldest, and considers that the Tamil present tense *nadakkirēn* contains this verb substantive (L.S. Vol. IV. p. 296).

As stated in §99 a, above, the true explanation of the Burgandi and Kaikadi forms is that, as in the Madras vulgar Tamil, they arise through successive contractions *ikirān, kirān*, of the standard form *irukkirān*; this explanation receives support from the existence of the intermediate forms *igari, igara, igaru*, etc. in Kaikadi (§107).

(*c*) The suffix *kiṟu* as a present tense sign is not of old standing in any of the Dravidian languages. The only members of that group in which it is used are Tamil, and the dialects thereof spoken by Tamil tribes now settled in Dakhan, in which the suffix appears as, *gar, kar*, or *kir* (L.S. Vol. IV-pp. 318-47). The Kurmis of Dravidian stock settled in Manbhum and Kharsawan also use *kri* as an auxiliary:—*shabekeris* 'existing thou doest'; that is, 'you are' (L.S. Vol. V. part ii-p. 147). When it is remembered that the auxiliary is unknown to Telugu, Kanarese, and Malayalam, and also to Old Tamil, the conclusion seems to be irresistible that it is a late immigrant from the north.

(*d*) The various derivatives from the Sanskrit *kri* or *kinṟu* which are used in the Dravidian languages and which are noted in succeeding articles are:—

The formative syllable *ku* (§193) the non-reflexive auxiliaries *kun*, *konu*, *kal* (§195 c §196 c), the present tense suffixes *kinṟu*, *kunṟu*, *kunnu*, (§196 d) perhaps the Telugu present suffix *chun* (§197 c), the suffixes *kadava*, *kala*, the permissive imperative suffixes *kattu*, *kattum*, *katta* (§203 a), and the benedictive suffixes *ka*, *ge*, *ke*, *kke* (§203 b).

193. The Dravidian Formative Syllable (§147-9) *ku*—Hindi Analogies

(*a*) In colloquial speech the *i* of *kiṟu* is pronounced most indistinctly *i.e.* as if the words *ōdukiṟēn*, *nadakkiṟēn*, were *ōdukaṟēn nadakkaṟēn*. Two of the roots one most frequently hears in Tamil colloquial speech are the auxiliaries *iru* 'be', *kida* 'be', 'lie uncared for'. In the present tense suffix was only *ku*; the third person neuter is *irukku*, *kidakku* (§99 b above). Such contractions of *kiṟu* to *ku* occur also after other accented roots; whether accented or unaccented, the third person neuter has only *ku* in the speech of the uneducated classes; e.g., *ākudu*, *pōkudu*, *varukudu*, *nadakkudu*, as if the non-pronominalised forms were *āku*, *pōku*, *varuku*, *nadakku*. This change of *kiṟu* (Sanskrit *kri*) to *ku* in modern times raises the presumption that the formative suffix *ku* of the pro-ethnic period which now forms the final syllable of many roots in the cultivated Dravidian languages has also arisen from *kri*.

(*b*) Dr. Hoernle mentions several cases of compound roots in Hindi where an auxiliary *kri* has dwindled into an affix -*k* (H.G.G. -p. 353). Hoernle's examples are:—

	Hindi		*Sanskrit*
1.	*phuk* 'blow'	from	*sphut* 'blow, blossom'
2.	*bukk* 'bark'	,,	*brū* 'say, call'
3.	(alternatively)	,,	*vad* 'speak'
4.	*dhakka* 'destroy'	,,	*dhvamś* 'destroy'
5.	*phakk* 'swell'	,,	*sphat* 'expand'
6.	*chikk* 'pain'	,,	*chrit* 'hurt'
7.	*tank* 'bind'	,,	*tanch* 'contract'
8.	*bahak* 'stray'	,,	*bahis* 'outside'
9.	*uchak* 'be raised'	,,	*uchcha* 'high'
10.	*kasak* 'pain'	,,	*kash* 'injure'
11.	*rok* 'hinder'	,,	*rudh* 'surround, obstruct'
12.	*chuk* 'cease'	,,	*chyut* 'ceasing', *chyn* 'cease'
13.	*chamak* 'glitter'	,,	*chamatkri* 'be clever, show off'.

What has happened in modern times may have taken place in the past. The Dravidian -*ku*, it will be noted, is merely an affixed *k* as in Hindi, but with an enunciative *u* added.

The modern Tamil suffix -*kiru* is a recent borrowing of the same *kri* which had become *ku* in the pro-ethnic period.

§194. THE DRAVIDIAN REFLEXIVE AUXILIARIES *koḷ* AND *konu* TRACEABLE TO THE SANSKRIT *ghun*.

(*a*) There are several circumstances which led to the presumption that the auxiliaries, Tamil *koḷ*, and Telugu *konu*, are traceable to the Sanskrit stem *grihṇa*. The vowel *ri* of Sanskrit is more or less artificial, and takes various forms in popular speech. Even in classical Sanskrit it became *ar, ir,* and *ur*[1] as in the forms *karōti* 'he does', *chikīrshati* 'he wishes to do', *kuruta* 'do', which the root *kri* 'do' takes in various tenses, and we saw that in the Dravidian languages the Sanskrit *kri* took the forms *kir, ger, gar.*

These changes of *kri* are also exemplified by the modification which the root *grih* 'take, accept' undergoes. This root becomes *ghe* and its conjugational stem *grihna* becomes *ghen* in Prakrit[2]. Other modifications which this stem underwent in popular speech were apparently *ghin, ghun* and *ghrin,* which have been re-adopted in classical Sanskrit[3]. These forms illustrate another phonetic law in Sanskrit, *viz.* that when the aspirate *h* is lost in one part of a verb it sometimes appears in another part as compensation[4].

The root *ghun* 'revolve', 'whirl round', seems to be the Prakrit form of *ghuru* having the same meaning and has been re-adopted in Sanskrit.

The two roots *ghun* derived from *grihn* and *ghurn* belong to the *bhu* class of Sanskrit roots, and take the forms *ghon* in conjugational tenses, and the second of them meaning 'revolve' 'whirl round' is changed into *ghol* in Prakrit (6), *l* replacing the final *n* of *ghun.*

(*b*) The reflexive use of *koḷ* and *konu* may be illustrated as follows :—

---

1. '*ur an raparah*' 'The forms *ar, ir, ur,* often take the place of *ri* Pāṇini).

2. Vararuchi VIII 15-16.

3. *ghini, ghuni, ghrini, grahaṇe* (D.P.) "the roots *ghin, ghun, ghrin,* have the meaning 'taking' or 'accepting"

4. Thus in the im-....

Tamil (1) *eḍu* 'take', *eḍuttu-k-koḷ* 'take for yourself'

(2) *talayilaḍi* 'strike on the head'—

talayilaḍittu-k-koḷ 'strike yourself on your head'.

Telugu—*kottu* 'strike', *kottuko* (*kottu-konu*) 'strike yourself'

(*c*) Dravidian reflexive auxiliaries *koḷ* and *konu*.

But there is another class of idioms containing participles from *koḷ* and *konu* which have no reflexive force. We saw in §100 f above, that in Tamil conjunctive participles are often used in the sense of present participles and that to avoid ambiguity the participle *koṇḍu* is added to impart a continuative force.

Similarly in Telugu, it is generally supposed that in all such phrases as *chēsi-koni* 'doing', *chūchukoṇṭu* 'seeing' etc., it is the reflexive auxiliary that is in use. The grammarian has, however, seen that *konu* imparts no reflexive force to the verb in some cases, and takes *konu* to be a mere *śvārtha* auxiliary in such cases as *pandu-koni* 'lying down' (C.B. verse 108). It is also noticeable that in colloquial speech *konu* is often pronounced *kun*.

In these and similar cases, the auxiliary used does not seem to be related to the Sanskrit *ghun* (*grihna*) but appears to be derived from the Vedic *krinu*.

§195. The Vedic krinu and the Dravidian kun, konu, kol, kinru, kunru, kunnu.

(*a*) Prākkrit *kun* and Paiśāchi *kun*. The root *kri* is used in the Vedas generally as *kriṇu* with the class sign *nu* added, and *kriṇu* becomes *kuṇa* which is extensively used in literary Prakrit poetry[1], *kar* being used in colloquial speeches like Saureseni

1. *Kriṇah kuṇo vā* (Vararuchi VIII-13) *kuṇo* is optionally used for the root *kri* . e.g. *kuṇai* or *karai* 'he does'

In the Paiśāchi dialect which substitutes *n* for *ṇ*, *kuṇ* becomes *kun* (2).

The Avestic *kriṇu* has also become *kun* in Modern Persian.

These roots *kuṇ*, *kun*, are inflected in the languages concerned as roots of the *a* conjugation :

(*b*) Tamil and Telugu auxiliaries *kun* (§113 d). The Paiśāchi form *kun* appears to have found its way as an auxiliary verb into Tamil, Malayalam, and Telugu. In old Tamil it was extensively used in the formation of the nominal agent where modern Tamil uses *kiṟu*:—

mīnpidikkunar	'fishermen'	*mīnpidikkiṟavar*
viṟkunar	'sellers'	*viṟkiṟavar*
varunar	'comers'	*varukiṟavar*
ikaḻunar	'despisers'	*ikaḻkiṟavar*
uḍalunar	'fighters' (enemies)	*uḍalkiṟavar*[2]

It has been pointed out in §192 (*c*) that the non-reflexive auxiliaries —Tamil *koḷ*, and Telugu *kon*—should be derived from the Vedic *kriṇu*.

It will have been seen from §10-b that Gōṇḍī strengthens its conjunctive participles by the addition of *kun* which, the editors of the *Linguistic Survey* think, is borrowed from Aryan; and it has been pointed out in § 148 that in the Telugu dialect *Vadari* conjunctive participles and finite verbs are often strengthened by participles, *kinya*, *kosi*, *koni*, derived from an auxiliary of the forms *kīn*, *kon*, *ken*, though the verb thus strengthened in not used reflexively. These facts are best explained on the supposition that just as the Aryan vernaculars of the North

1. *ṇo nah* (Vararuchi X-5) "in the Paiśāchi language *ṇ* becomes *n*"

2. In the last three examples *ku* is elided after unaccented roots.

strengthen their participles by other participles derived from Śaurasēni *kar*, the Dravidian languages use participles derived from the Paiśāchī *kun* for a similar purpose.

(*c*) *Indo-Aryan particles kan, kne, kane.*

It has been stated (Kellog) that certain rustic dialects in the Hindi area use the suffix *kne* to form present participles. Eastern Rajasthani uses *kane* to form conjunctive participles. Newari *kne* and Naipali *kan* e.g. *gari-kan* 'having done', *khai-kan* 'having eaten', *basi-kan* 'having sat' (H.G.G. 491). These suffixes are very similar to the Dravidian suffixes above, and are possibly derived from the Vedic *kriṇu* which as shown above, might take the forms *kan*, *kin*, and *kun*. Compare the Hindi continuative particle *-kne* with the particle of almost 'identical form in vulgar Tamil': *nān pārttu-knē vandēn*—'I looking came' *i.e.*, 'I was looking as I came. Here *kne* is usually supposed to be corrupt for *konde*, *-kondu e*.

This is not, however, the explanation given by some scholars who have drawn attention to the existence of those forms *vide* § 198 below.

196. (2) TAMIL MALAYALAM SUFFIXES *kinṟu*, *kunru*, *kunnu* (§ 196 a AND 195).

The Malayalam present tense suffix *kunnu* was *kinṟu* formerly (14). The suffix *kinṟu* is the present tense sign of literary Tamil. We have seen that this suffix was rare in Sangam works, and that there were only a few instances in Old Tamil of its being used in the formation of adverbial present participles (III.f) Two of the instances are *nīdukinṟu ōngiya* 'that grew up lengthening ', *kuḻavi aḻukinru*,' a child crying'—'a child when crying'.

In colloquial and vulgar Tamil *nṟ* is pronounced *nd* and the literary *kinṟu* pronounced *kinḍu* and confounded with *koṇḍu* the past verbal participle of the reflexive auxiliary *koḷ* is in use in such phrases as *tūṅgi-k-koṇḍu-irukkinṟān* 'he is sleeping ; *āḍi-k-koṇḍu-irukiṟārkaḷ* 'they are playing'.

Kunṟu and *kinṟu* are apparently identical. Their first syllables *kun* and *kin* being Prakritic adaptations of the Vedic *kriṇu* 'do' ; but what is the second syllable *ṟu*? This evidently arises from a suffix *tu* the initial *t* of which is changed to *ṟ* when combining with *n* ; and the affinities of *kinṟu* and *koṇḍu* will be evident when the following sentences are compared:—

Tamil	: *āḍi-k-koṇḍu irundārkaḷ*	They were playing.
Telugu	: *āḍu-kuntu unḍiri*	
Kanarese	: *āḍ-kunṭa iddaru*	

The Kanarese form is taken from a specimen of the Kurumvāri dialect given at page 399 of Volume IV of L.S.I. but *āḍ-kunṭa* is really a Telugu form. In all the three cases the participles have a continuous sense and have no reflexive force; the bases of these suffixes must be derived from *kriṇu* not from *ghun* or *ghol*. The final *tu* of the suffixes *kinṟu* and *kunṟu* is probably the aorist sign of the pro-Dravidian period, this sign is not now added directly to the root as in *naḍattum* 'we walk', *naḍattir* 'you walk', of Old Tamil, but to the auxiliary *kin* 'do', which is suffixed to the root as in the *naḍakkinṟīr* 'you walk'.

197. TELUGU PRESENT TENSE SUFFIXES *-chun* AND *-tun* (§136*a*)

(*a*) These suffixes are *drutaprakritakas*, and there is no doubt that-*chun* and-*tun* are the real forms, though they are written sometimes as *chu* and *tu* without the *drutam*, or as *chunnu* and *tunnu* as if the conjunction *nu* were added. One of the explanations given of *chun* is that it is a corruption of the Malayalam *kunnu*; but *kunnu* is only a modern form, the original of which was *kunru* (§117) and this would correspond to *chunḍu* in Telugu, not *chun*.

It is highly problematical whether *-ku* would palatalise into *-chu* after Telugu *u* bases ; if this be possible, we can compare *-chun* with the *svārtha* auxiliary *kun* which was also employed largely in the formation of the *nomina agent* in Old Tamil.

It is also doubtful whether the suffix *-tun* can be derived from the grammatical *-chun*. The tendency to change is just the other way and we assumed in §187 a that the suffix *ta* of the Telugu colloquial present tense becomes changed to *cha* in the speech of certain religious Brahmans.

Can *-tun* be derived from the Paiśāchi conjunctive participle suffix *-tuna* employed in the Prakritic inscriptions in the Telugu area? (§181). The Aryan gerundial suffixes had not always a past signification and often expressed an action which accompanied that of the principal or finite verb (§§ 164, 181). They might impart a present signification to participles as sometimes in Tamil:

naḍandu varukiṟān 'he comes walking'

āṟṟai nīndi -k-kaḍa-k-kiṟān 'he crosses the river swimming'

(*b*) Bishop Caldwell thought that *tunnu* and *chunnu* were made up of *chu* plus *unnu* and *tu* plus *unnu*, *-unnu* being understood by him to be a participle of the verb substantive *unḍu* 'be'; he was also of opinion that the first part *-tu* of *-tunnu*, the *t* of the Telugu aorist and *-tu* the present participle suffix of Kanarese were orignally identical (C.D.G. p. 382). The suffix *-tun* is as was pointed out in Chapter X (170 *b c*) a late adoption while the *-t* of the Telugu aorist belongs to the pro-Dravidian period. Similarly, the Kanarese present participle suffixes were probably adopted for the first time by Jain cultivators of Kanarese in the post-Christian centuries. Their initial *u* and double *tt* supposing these to be radical, show them to be connected with some such Aryan form as *huttam* (*bhavatām*) (§187 b). These considerations seem to be fatal to Bishop Caldwell's theory.

(*c*) The suffix *tun* is not likely to have arisen from a previous *-chun*. Further in the forms *tu* and *tu*, it is so widely spread in the Telugu Districts and so deeply rooted in the speech of the common people, that it must be regarded as an independent suffix perhaps derived from the Paiśāchi *-tun* of the Prakritic inscriptions. The suffix *-chun* is perhaps a palatalised form of the Paiśāchi *-kun*.

CHAPTER XI-E

§198. Aryan Gerundive, Imperative, Infinitive Verbal-Noun Suffixes.

Final *n* in Telugu often corresponds to *l* in Tamil (including Malayalam and Kanarese).

As one goes through the volumes of the *Linguistic Survey of India* one is struck with the frequently recurring remark that the infinitive has the same form as the future passive participle. This is so in Naipali, Kumauni, Rambani, Poguli, to quote only a few of the very many instances that have been noticed. Even where the forms are not absolutely identical they are nearly so, having been derived from the same verbal formations. Another point that may be noted here is the absolute identity of the infinitive and the verbal noun in many languages ; for the infinitive is only a case form of the verbal noun. The gerundive is also often the base of the future tense and may be used as an imperative.

These observations apply almost verbatim to the cultivated Dravidian languages, but before developing these points we shall draw attention to certain correspondences in these languages:

	Telugu	Kanarese	Tamil
verbal base	*cheyu*	*geyyu*	*sey*
imperative	*cheyani*	*geyyali*	*seyal*
infinitive	{ *cheyan*	*geyyal*	*seyal* (O. Tamil)
	{ *cheya*	*geyya*	*seya*
verbal noun	*cheyan*	*geyyal*	*seyal*
	{ *chestin(i)-ani*		*seydēn-ēl*
subjunctives	{ *chesin-an* }		*seyd-āl* }
	{ *chesin-a* }		*sey-in* }
			sey-il }

Compare also Telugu-Tamil couplets —

Chanu	'go'	*sel*
konu	'buy'	*koḷ*
	'accept'	
tannu	'push aside',	*taḷḷu.*

In Telugu verbal noun from *konu* is *kolu.*

The above examples bring out that a final *n* of particles and words in Telugu often corresponds to *l* in Tamil and Kanarese, and that in all these languages the infinitive loses its final consonant and has an alternative form ending in *a.*

In Tamil itself there are several instances in which the final of participles may be *n* or *l* —

(*i*) the old instrumental locative suffix *an* is now *al.*

(*ii*) one of the old locative suffixes *in* is now *in* or *il.*

(*iii*) one of the subjunctive suffixes is *in* or *il.*

(*iv*) The word *mēl* 'above' appears as *mēn* in Tolkāppiyam.

(*v*) *val* 'hard', and *mel* 'soft', have also the forms *van* and *men.*

(*vi*) One of the verb endings in the first person singular is either *an* or *al.*

cf. also table showing correspondence of finals in §91.

Outside the Dravidian area the inter-change of *l* and *n* is common in many of the Bhilli dialects dealt with in Vol. IX Part III of the *L.S. of India* (pp. 3-4) as in the Bhilli of Kapipla (p.84), the Naikadi, of Panchmahals and Surat (pp. 91 and 93), Gamati (p. 119), Ranawat (pp. 142-4).

§199. ARYAN GERUNDIVE SUFFIXES *-tva*, *-ya*, *aniya*, *tavya*.

Aryan gerundives: Gerundives were generally formed in the Avesta by suffixing *-thwa*, *thwya* (changeable to *tva* and *tvya* after *ṣ* and *s*), *tya*, *ata*, or sometimes *ta* or *ya*. These suffixes imply that the action which the verb expresses 'must be done', 'is allowed', or 'deserves to be done' (K.A.G. 565) : Examples:—

Kārshya 'fit for cultivation'; *gāthwya* 'what ought to be sung', *yāzata* 'fit for adoration'

In Sanskrit gerundives are ordinarily and regularly formed with the suffixes *-ya*, *tavya*, *aniya*. Derivatives in *-ya* having a gerundival sense were being made in all periods of the language from the earliest down; the other two are of more modern origin. Some of the other formations of a kindred kind found in the Vedas are *ya*, or *tva*, and *enia* or *enya* (W.S.G. 962, 968).

Examples:—

nāvya	'to be praised'	*yudhēnya*	'to be combated'
yōdhya	'to be fought'	*saparyēnya*	'to be adored'
kartvā	'to be done'	*kartavya*	'to be done'
hantvā	'to be slain'	*śrōtavya*	'to be heard'
		varjanīya	'to be avoided'
		mananīya	'to be contemplated'

(The examples for *ya*, *enya*, and *-tva* are taken from A.A. Macdonell's *Vedic Grammar* 578-581).

§200. THE SANSKRIT *-aniya* GIVING RISE TO THE DRAVIDIAN *-ani*, *-an*, *-admu*, *-du*, *-udu*, *-edun*.

The Sanskrit aniya. This suffix has given rise to a large number of suffixes used in the Aryan vernaculars of the north to form future participles both active and passive, verbal nouns, and infinitives. *Aniya* became *ania*, *anaa* in Prakrit. The last of these has become *ana* (feminine *ani*) in East Hindi and some other languages, and is used to form declinable future passive participles and verbal nouns both of action and of agency over a large area. There are also terminations *-an* *-an* similarly used. (H.G.G. 315-21; B.A.G. Vol. III pp. 236-8) Mr. Beames mentions a suffix *an* derived from the Sanskrit verbal noun suffix *-ana* which was formerly used to form infinitives over a large area. *An* still survives in Kanuji (*ibid* p. 236). Specimens given in the *Linguistic Survey* Vol. IX, Part I, show that this suffix also survives in Musalmani (p.61), Antarbedi (p. 81), Bundeli (p. 93) and elsewhere.

(i) Gerundives and verbal nouns in East Hindi (H.G.G. 317-19)

de 'give' *-den, dena,* or *deni* 'what is to be given', 'a debt'

le 'take', *-len, lena, leni* 'what is to be taken, a receipt'

len den 'intercourse, traffic'

baj 'be played' *bajan, bajana* 'what is to be played, a musical instrument.

odh 'put on, wear' *-odhana, obdhani* 'what is to be put on, a cloak or sheet'

kud 'leap' *-kudan* 'leaping'

dol 'move' *-dolan, dolani* 'movement'

kah 'speak' *-kahan- kahani* 'speaking'

kar 'do' *karan, karani* 'action'

rah 'remain, live' *-rahan, rahani* 'existence, living'

sun 'hear', *sunan, sunani* 'hearing'

(ii) Obsolete forms of the infinitive from Old Western Hindi literature (B.A.G. Vol. III p. 236)

bandhan 'to stop'; *chalan* 'to go'; *juran* 'to join';
ian 'to go'; *dekhan* 'to see'

These indeclinable infinitives still survive in Kanuaji, Musalmani etc. *Vide* also *Linguistic Survey* references noted above.

The above examples indicate in what directions the original gerundival suffix *-aniya* and the verbal noun suffix *an* of Sanskrit have become corrupted. Even apart from the forms current in the Modern Aryan vernaculars we could have inferred that *-aniya* and *-ana* would have become *-ani*(y) and *an* in popular speech which generally elides the final short vowels. (§ 90).

(*a*) Telugu *-ani* (§ 140 *b*). The Aryan suffix *-aniya* must have become *ani* as in *pani* 'that ought to be drunk'. It is suggested here that the suffix in the Telugu forms *poni* 'let (it) go", *rani* 'let (it) come', *vādu chēyani* 'let him do it' is an imitation of the Aryan gerundive suffix which in some areas is used to form politer imperatives (*Cf.* L.S. Vol. IX Part IV, pp. 34, 470). These Telugu forms are usually construed as if compounded of the infinitive or verbal nouns *ran*, *pon*, *cheyan*, and the root *i* or *ichchu* 'give' and another form *ranivva du* ' he will not allow (it) to come' is formed from it on this supposition.

The corresponding Kanarese imperatives *geyyali* in the singular and *geyyalim* in the plural are not thus construed (§ 127 *b*). The Tamil imperative *seyal* has the same form as the verbal noun *seyal* (§ 196) and appears to have been formed in a manner similar to the shorter Hindi forms which are both gerundives and verbal nouns but with this difference that the Aryan final *n* becomes *l* in Tamil. Thus the Kanarese and Tamil forms do not support the construction usually put on the final *i* of *cheyani*, *kottani* etc. The suffix *ani* in these imperatives appears to be merely an imitation of the Aryan *aniya* or *ani*.

* * * *

CHAPTER XII

§216. The Current Dravidian Theory has the Support of a Continuous Tradition of over Eighteen Centuries

What is then the explanation of the theory now almost universally accepted that the Dravidian languages have no radical and deep seated affinities with Sanskrit, a theory which has behind it the support of a continuous tradition of over eighteen centuries? The original stock of Indo-Aryan words which the pre-historic immigrants from the North-West must have brought with them appears to have undergone a process of gradual deterioration in South Indian mouths. The causes that tended to this deterioration have already been exemplified above. The foremost of them was the extremely limited number of consonantal sounds to be found in South Indian speeches which were even fewer than the sounds to be found in the rudest of Aryan dialects like the *Chūlika Paiśāchika* mentioned by Prākṟit grammarians. The second was the change from the Indo-Aryan system of varied accents to the South Indian monotony under which the highest stress was on the first syllable of each word and the pitch gradually decreased in the succeeding syllables ; this naturally led to the loss or deterioration of all syllables in a word except the first or the first two, and also to a change the first vowel of each word. A third was the entire absence of sibilants in South Indian speeches, and the consequent deterioration and final omission of all sibilants from Indo-Aryan words. A fourth was the South Indian habit of pronouncing non-initial single *k* and *p*, and initial and non-initial single *ch*, as spirants. This has led to the complete loss of non-initial *k* and *ch* in a very large number of words and to the conversion of non-initial *p* into *v* in almost all words. Another cause was the inability of South Indians to pronounce an initial *r, l, y* which has led to the insertion of an initial on-glide or the substitution of other letters in the place of the first two and the entire omission or nasalisation of the last. A similar inability to pronounce a final *t, r* and *t*, has led to the conversion of these sounds into *l, ṉ, ḷ, ṇ, ḻ*. Owing to the steady operation of these causes, it must in course of time have become impossible to see any connection between these altered words and the speech of the northern Aryans. More important than all these was the difference in grammatical structure and syntax; while the Aryan speeches were highly synthetic, the Southern idioms arising out of their *debris* were mainly analytical, with a tendency to become agglutinative again.

All but the memory of the pre-historic Aryan immigration under the leadership of Agastya had been lost by the beginning of the Christian era, and the original stock of Indo-Aryan words brought by the immigrants having been altered beyond all recognition in the speech of the South Indians it came to be tacitly assumed—when attention was first directed to the materials and structure of South Indian idioms—that this altered vocabulary was part of the indigenous speech of the land except in regard to recent obvious borrowings from Sanskrit, and that the immigrants had forgotten their mother tongue and had adopted the language of the land in its stead. Kumārila Bhatta (7th Century A.D.) refers, in his *Tantravārtika*, to the South Indian languages as *Drāviḍādi Bhāshā* evidently under the impression that these languages were foreign to Sanskrit, and he had no idea that the basic portion of the vocabularies of these languages and the suffixial elements entering into the composition of their verb-forms had been borrowed from the Vedic idioms, or from Sanskrit. In fact he mentions with disapproval the attempts of certain contemporary writers to adopt words from these non-Aryan languages into Sanskrit after giving them an Aryan shape by means of suitable affixes.

Earlier than this (during the Sangam period which was a time of great literary activity in the Tamil land) nobody appears to have thought that the Tamil language was in any way indebted to Sanskrit except of course in regard to obvious loan words and easily recognisable Sanskrit derivatives. These words and derivatives were placed in a special class as of Sanskrit origin. And as time passed, the theory that Tamil was a distinct language gained further strength, and was incorporated in the Purāṇas and other sacred writings.

From the very beginning, owing to the increasing needs of a progressive civilization and to the requirements of a rapidly developing philosophy and religious system, the *tatsama* and the semi-*tatsama* Sanskrit element in the South Indian vocabularies has been steadily increasing, and it now occupies considerably more than half their volume. During the middle of the last century, certain orientalists, perceiving the very large number of obvious Sanskrit derivatives in these vocabularies, started a theory that the Dravidian languages were descended from Sanskrit like the Aryan vernaculars of northern India, but the theory was very short-lived, and was abandoned after the publication of Bishop Caldwell's *Dravidian Grammar.*

§ 217. THE CURRENT DRAVIDIAN THEORY REQUIRES RECONSIDERATION.

The aim of the present book is to secure a reconsideration of the current theory of Dravidian Languages on the ground that the theory is based on a mis-apprehension of the real facts of the situation, and is supported by assumptions some of which can be easily disproved. A complete treatment of the question requires an investigation of the subject under the three heads, vocabulary, nominal declension, and verbal inflexions. The vocabulary of the Tamil language alone consists of about fifty or sixty thousand words. Omitting obvious Sanskrit derivatives, the ultimate roots to which the remainder can be reduced must be at least a thousand, and having regard to the fact that a very large number of roots will require detailed individual investigation, it will be impossible to investigate the affinities of all the Dravidian roots within the limits of a single volume, or even of two. It was in consequence of this that the scope of the present work was limited to the consideration of tense and mood signs which are limited in number and belong to the fundamental structure of the languages. If these signs could be proved to be of Aryan origin, it would necessarily follow that the original languages of South India must have been under the influence of Aryan languages from very early times. The present state of the Dravidian question is such that we are unable to discuss the origin of these tense and mood signs without previously disposing of a large number of misconceptions and untenable theories about Dravidian languages and Dravidian culture, which have come into existence since the publication of Bishop Caldwell's *Dravidian Grammar* in 1856. It has thus come about that discussion of these and similar subsidiary matters occupies more than half the present work. The tense and mood signs are dealt with in Chapters VII-XI of the book, and the results of these chapters are summarised in § 208-9 of Chapter XI.* The space devoted to the consideration of these signs is less than one half of the book, the remainder of the book being devoted to a discussion of the subsidiary questions mentioned in the last article as the outworks and entrenchments of the Dravidian theory.

(*a*) The supposition that there was a pre-Aryan Dravidian culture is wholly based on the assumption that the words for '*rice*', '*peacock*', *ginger*' etc. in European languages are derived from their Tamil names. This question is dealt

* These sections are missing [Ed.].

with in Chapter II of the book, and the conclusion arrived at there is, that to the extent to which the names of the commercial products of South India are evidences of any civilization they demonstrate the civilization of an Aryan speaking population. (§ 34).

(*b*) The alleged influence of the Dravidian Languages on Sanskrit vocabulary and grammar is discussed in Chapter III and the conclusion arrived at there (§ 73) is —

(1) that the cerebral letters of the Sanskrit alphabet are not due to the influence of the Dravidian Languages— some of which retained their alveolars down to historic times and two of which still retain them;

(2) that the grammatical forms which Sanskrit is supposed to have derived from the Dravidian languages were not evolved by it on Indian soil but were inherited by it from the parent Aryan tongue ;

(3) that the other changes which Sanskrit has undergone on Indian soil are changes incidental to a transition from a synthetic stage to the analytical stage, as in the parallel cases of English, and Modern Persian ; and

(4) that there is therefore no reason to suppose that the Dravidian languages were once spoken throughout India.

In the course af this discussion, we came upon the startling discovery that the final *ṉ*, *ḷ*, *ḍi*, representing respectively the masculine, the feminine, and the neuter, singulars in Dravidian are derived from the Indo-Germanic *nt* as also the terminations *ṉ*, *ṇḍu*, *ndu*, *m*, *aa*, indicating the masculine nominative singulars in various Dravidian dialects ; and that the Demonstrative and the interrogative bases *av*, *iv*, *ad*, *id*, *yāva*, *yat*, *yā* have been derived from the Indo-Aryan languages.

(*c*) In Chapters IV, V, and VI, it is pointed out that the earliest available specimens of Indo-Aryan speech are at least one thousand years older than the earliest specimens of

Dravidian speech, that the *vaṭṭeḻuttu* is derived from the Brāhmī script (§82) and the Agastya tradition is based on solid fact (§ 92).

The fact that the Dravidian tense and mood signs are derived from Aryan particles and words, though it raises a strong presumption that the two groups of languages must have radical affinities will not appeal so much to the general reader as identity of names for the commonest objects and things. Opportunity has therefore been taken as in §§ 6, 7, 8, 31, 40 and in Chapter VI generally, to illustrate by copious examples, the change through which the old Indo-Aryan words have acquired their present South Indian forms and in §§ 210-13* more than one hundred Dravidian verbal bases mostly of ordinary occurrence have been shown to be derived from Indo-Aryan roots. It will be seen from these that such common words as :—

Substantives:—

talai 'head'; *mayir* 'hair'; *śevi* 'ear'; *neṟṟi* 'the forehead'; *mūkku* 'nose'; *udaḍu* 'the lip'; *vāy* 'the mouth'; '*piḍari*' 'the nape of the neck'; *kai* 'the hand'; *aḍi* 'the foot'; *āḍu* 'sheep'; *māḍu* 'cattle'; *māṉ* 'a deer'; *erumai* 'a buffalo'; *kudirai* 'a horse'; *vēngai* 'a tiger'; *pāmbu*, *aravam* 'a snake';

nāḍu "country'; *ūr* 'village';

puṟā, *prā* 'a dove'; *vai* 'paddy stalks'; *śēy*, *kuḻandai* 'a child'; *pēy* 'a demon'

Common verbs:—

naḍa 'walk'; *nil* 'stand'; *uṭkār* 'sit';
tūngu 'sleep'; *tiṉ* 'eat'; *vāḻ* 'be, live, flourish'
aḍi 'beat'; *kaḍi* 'bite'; *aḻi* 'destroy';
veṭṭu 'cut'; *tongu* 'hang'; *uri* 'peel off the skin';
piṟa 'be born'; *paṟa* 'fly'; *uḷ* 'be'.

* These sections are also missing.

The known history and civilization of South India appears thus to be a history and civilization of Aryan-speaking immigrants from the North and so far no facts have been adduced ta make us doubt the statements in the Rāmāyaṇa that Agastya found South India inhabited by cannibals. Archaeology says that when the Aryans penetrated into Southern India, they found the country inhabited by men in the neolithic stage of culture. The South Indian words for 'paddy', 'rice', 'ragi'; for 'plough', 'cattle', buffaloes', and 'sheep'; and for 'boats' and 'rafts' appear to be derived from North Indian names brought by Aryan speaking immigrants.

§218. Linguistic Evidence Showing a Pre-Historic Aryan Immigration into South India.

(i) It has been shown in Section 93 above that Sir George Grierson divides the Prakritic languages of India into two groups which may conveniently be referred to as the North-Western and the West-Hindi groups and that Tamil contains a very large number of words which show the North-Western characteristics These are, no doubt, a few cases in which the vowels of Prakritic forms are lengthened as in the West-Hindi group but these may be due to importations from the Hindi area in post-Christian centuries.

(ii) The language of the Brahmi inscriptions of the second and the third century B. C. recently discovered within the limits of what was of old known as the Pandya kingdom is neither Tamil nor any known Indo-Aryan idiom. It is supposed to be a mixture of Tamil and Prakrit, but much of what is thought to be Tamil in them namely, *nādu*, *ūr*, *kuṭupilā*, are derived from Indo-Aryan. This shows Indo-Aryan activity in the Pandya country from before the 3rd century B.C. (§ 24).

Attention has already been invited (§ 83) to the presumption which these inscriptions raise, *viz.* that Tamil as known to us, even the oldest dialect of it had not perhaps come into existence at the time of these inscriptions.

§ 219. Aryan Immigration into South India and the Dakhan—In the Historic Period.

Having summarised the results arrived at in this book in regard to the composition and structure of the cultivated Dravidian languages we shall proceed to consider what evidence there is to show that there have emigrated into the Dravidian area large bodies of Aryans and Aryanised immigrants from the North.

We know that throughout the Historic Period of South India—that is, from the beginning of the Christian era and for a few centuries earlier—there has been a steady movement of people into the land of the Dravidians from North India.

The Maurya Period :

The earliest recorded movement is perhaps that of a portion of the Jain community which left Magadha during the reign of Chandragupta Maurya, in consequence of a prolonged famine, and emigrated to the Karnata country[1]. There appears to be a tradition[2] that the Tulu country and the adjoining parts were colonised by another migration under the leadership of Tulu, a son of Chandragupta, while the existence of Asoka inscriptions at Siddhapura, Brahmagiri, etc., shows that the Maurya empire had been extended,

1. Introduction to Hoernle's Uvasagadesa.

2. *Narrinai* by Pandit Narayanasami Aiyar—p. 73 of *Aganandooru.*

down to Mysore even before the time of Asoka. These and the conquest of Kalinga by Asoka in the 3rd century B.C. must have been accompanied by numerous and large settlement of Aryan speaking northerners in Dravidian India. Some of these Mauryan settlements continued to exercise sway in the Konkan till the 6th century A.D. when they were subjugated by the Chalukya King Kirti Varman. It has been conjectured by Dr. S. Krishnaswami Ayyangar, M.A., not perhaps on reliable evidence, that the Mauryan power extended at one time as far as the Podiyil Hill in Tinnevelly.

The Andhra Period :

The Andhra Dyansty of the Dakhan which came into prominence simultaneously with the decline of Maurya power in the North exercised sway for four and a half centuries over the Telugu, Kanarese, Tulu and Maratha areas. The capital of the Andhra which was originally Srikakulam on the Kistna in the District of Kistna appears to have been transferred to the Bombay Karnatic when the Dynasty extended its sway across the Peninsula and later to Paithan on the upper waters of the Godavari. Almost all the kings of the dynasty assumed the titles of Satavahana and Satakarni, and some of them were great patrons and lovers of learning. But as none of the vernaculars now spoken in the Dakhan areas ruled by the dynasty—Marathi, Konkani, Telugu, Kanarese, Tulu, Kui, etc.—appear to have come into existence then, the inscriptions belonging to the period of the Satakarnis are in Prakrit or Sanskrit, and the languages of the Court and of literature in their dominion appear to have been Paisachi and Maharashtri.

The Pallava Period and after :

The Pallavas of Kanchi succeeded to the power of the Andhras on the east coast and their dominions which at first lay in the Telugu area had been extended as far as the

Palar by the middle of the 3rd century A.D. The Pallavas appear to have come from the North-West, their name being supposed to be a variant of Pahlava, which again is a corruption of Parthiva, a Parthian, and it is supposed that the founder of the dynasty secured the nucleus of the later Pallava empire by marrying a daughter of the Andhra king Sivaskandasatakarni. From about the middle of the 3rd to the 8th century A.D. the Pallava dynasty played a great part in the history of Southern India, and exercised a dominating influence, varying in degree from time to time, over the other Tamil kingdoms of the Cholas, the Cheras, and the Pandyas. The kings of this dynasty had great partiality for nothern learning and culture, and it is probable that the southward migration of Aryans and Aryanised peoples from the Arakhan into Southern India continued during the Pallava period. Such of the Pallava copper-plate inscriptions as have survived to modern times bear indubitable evidence that many of the earliest of the small Brahmin settlements with which Southern India is now dotted have come into their present places at the invitation of Pallava kings. This policy was continued by the Cholas and the Pandyas when they threw off the Pallava yoke. This migration southward has continued, though on an exceedingly limited scale, down to modern times as is evidenced by several isolated settlements of Telugu, Kanarese, and Maratha peoples, who have come into the land of the Tamils in the wake of later conquerors.

Two places situated in South India and supposed to have been peopled by Brahmans are mentioned in Ptolemy's Geography Book IV—Chapter I S. 8 and 74. The first of these Bramagaras is situated in Limyrika (Damarike) in Ptolemy's map, and has been taken to be equivalent to the Sanskrit Brahmagara 'the abode of the Brahmans'. In regard to the second Ptolemy says "in like manner the parts under Mount Bettigo are occupied Brakhmanoi Magoi as for as the Batai with this city Brahkme." In regard to this city Bishop Caldwell asks "can this Brahkme be Brahmadesam, an ancient town on the Tamraparni, not far from the Podogai mountain (Mount Bettigo) which I have found referred to in several ancient inscriptions". Others are of opinion that the city and tract should be sought for in the Kanarese country about the upper Kaveri. Even the oldest Tamil works available make reference to Brahman settlements in various parts of the Tamil country, and also to various Jain and Buddhistic settlements. But it is doubtful whether these Brahman settlements and those referred to Ptolemy belong to Aryan immigrations during the historic period or to people who settled in the Tamil country in pre-historic times.

APPENDIX I

I am forwarding to your address to-day copies of a paper entitled 'The Aryan Affinities of Dravidian pronouns' which I read at '*The Third All-India Oriental Conference*' held at Madras last December.

2. I have now been before the public for some years proclaiming that the languages spoken in Southern India in the pre-Aryan period of Indian History could not have been of the Dravidian family comprising Tamil, Malayalam, Kanarese, Tulu, Telugu etc.; that these Dravidian languages are in all their essential characteristics mainly a creation of Aryan and Aryan-speaking immigrants from the North; that whatever were the original languages of Southern India they must have been replaced by the new Dravidian idioms by the beginning of the Christian era except in the case of the names of a few numerals and perhaps, of a varying number of special South Indian products; that from such extensive changes, amounting to practical displacement, we may safely argue that the immigrants, typified by Agastya, must have settled here in large colonies; and that what is known as the Dravidian civilization of the South is merely the civilization of these Indo-Aryan immigrants from the North.

3. The following particulars will show why the Dravidian idioms should be regarded as a creation of Indo-Aryan immigrants from the North:—

(i) There are about one hundred suffixes used in the cultivated Dravidian languages for indicating the tenses and modes of verb-forms. Most of these tense and mode signs are of Indo-Aryan origin.

(ii) The personal terminations of Dravidian finite verbs indicating the number, gender, and person, of the agent are also of Aryan origin; as also the pronouns of which these terminations are early forms.

The Dravidian Demonstrative and the Relative-Interrogative pronouns have the same bases as in Indo-Iranian; the number and gender signs of the Dravidian pronouns are corruptions of Aryan terminations. The Dravidian Reflexive pronouns are derived from Sanskrit words used for this purpose in the Vedic dialects. Dravidian pronouns of the First and Second persons have remote Aryan affinities.

(iii) The basic portion of the Dravidian vocabularies consists largely of words of Indo-Aryan origin though, owing to the extremely limited character of Tamil and other early Dravidian alphabets, these words have been grossly corrupted and are very difficult of recognition.

Item (i) above formed the subject of a paper entitled "Tense Signs in Dravidian" which I sent to the *Poona Oriental Conference* (1919), and a summary thereof was printed in the *Conference Proceedings*, *Volume I*, but the paper itself has not, I am sorry to say, yet been published. This delay has enabled me to perfect my theory in many of its details, and I am taking steps to bring out my work soon. Item (iii) and several other important matters have been dealt with in my *Readership Lectures* delivered last year in the Calcutta University; these lectures will come out soon, I hope. Item (ii) is dealt with in the present paper of which I am sending you copies herewith.

4. My views differ from those of all previous scholars because they contented themselves with comparing the Dravidian languages with Classical Sanskrit, and naturally saw no deep seated affinities. When one language is extensively affected by another we should seek for the source of influence not in the artificial language of high literature but in the spoken idioms of the common people. It is

necessary to compare Dravidian idioms with the Vedic dialects and the Prakrits of pre-Christian centuries, before we can decide the question of Aryo-Dravidian affinities. Such a comparison will irresistibly lead to the conclusions I have stated above.

APPENDIX II-A
THE ARYAN AFFINITIES OF DRAVIDIAN PRONOUNS.

By

MR. R. SWAMINATHA AIYER, B.A., MADRAS

The Current Dravidian Theory.

The class of words known as Pronouns belong to the most fundamental elements of a language. I propose to bring together in this paper a body of facts which seem to show unmistakeably that the Demonstrative, the Relative-Interrogative, and the Reflexive, pronouns of the Dravidian languages are of Āryan origin ,that their Personal pronouns have some Āryan affinities and that most of the gender and number signs in these pronouns are also of Āryan origin. These facts are totally opposed to the assumption made by Western scholars that the Dravidian languages had attained their development long before the arrival of the Āryans in India and to the current Dravidian theory of which that assumption is, as it were, the sheet anchor. This theory is undergoing a process of evolution and it is not the same now that it was forty or fifty years ago. Bishop Caldwell, who is regarded as the father of Dravidian philology, maintained that the Dravidians were not an autochthonous Indian race but were Turanian immigrants who entered India by the North-West, that the Dravidian languages had become fully developed long before the arrival of the Āryans in India, that these languages had no structural relationship with Sanskrit, that their affinities were mainly Turanian, occasionally Semitic, and that where the affinities were Aryan, these did not come into existence on Indian soil, but belonged to the pre-Āryan period of the pre-historic past when the Indo-Europeans and Turanians were living as one undivided race.

This theory elaborated in great detail in Bishop Caldwell's *Comparative Grammar of the Dravidian Languages* (1st Edition 1857, 2nd Edition 1875) found general acceptance at one time, but is dissented from in several important particulars at the present day. As pointed out by Professor Sten Konow in his introduction to the Dravidian languages in Volume IV of the *Linguistic Survey of India* (1906), it is now generally recognised that these languages constitute an isolated family in India and that the attempt to connect them with other linguistic families outside India has been a failure. Professor Sten Konow is also of opinion that all attempts to show a closer connection with the Indo-Germanic family have proved just as futile, and that there is no philological reason to connect the Muṇḍā group with the Dravidian.

While it is assumed that the Dravidian languages have remained unaffected in structure by the contiguous Indo-Āryan idioms, most Dravidian scholars hold that these idioms have, by contact with Dravidian languages, undergone important changes not only in their vocabulary but also in phonology, grammar, and syntax; and Professor Sten Konow (Vol. IV of the *Linguistic Survey of India*) gives a pretty long list of items in which Sanskrit and other Indo-Āryan tongues are stated to have undergone changes by imitating Dravidian idioms. The most important item under phonology is the adoption of the cerebral series of letters in Sanskrit, and as these letters are found even in the oldest Vedas composed while the Āryan immigrants were still confined to the Panjab it is inferred that these immigrants must have been in contact with the Dravidians from the very beginning and that the Dravidians though confined now to the Dakhan and Southern India, must once have occupied also the West and the North-West of India.

§ 2.—*The Present Writer's Conclusions*

The conclusions which I have arrived at after a detailed examination of the question extending over several years are entirely at variance with the current theory:—

(i) There are about one hundred suffixes employed in the cultivated Dravidian languages for the purpose of indicating the tenses and modes of verb-forms. I find that most of these suffixes are of Indo-Āryan origin.

(ii) The personal terminations of Dravidian finite verbs and the pronouns of which these terminations are in many cases early forms are also most of them of Āryan origin.

(iii) The basic portion of the Dravidian vocabularies consists largely of words of Indo-Āryan origin though, owing to the extremely limited character of Tamil and other early Dravidian alphabets, these words have been greatly corrupted and are very difficult of recognition. These conclusions clearly indicate that what are known as Dravidian languages are in all their present essential features a creation of Āryan and Āryanised immigrants from the North. Further, the existence in the Tamil language of words and forms which are met with in the Vedas and in the Avestic language but have disappeared from the post-Vedic Indo-Āryan tongues, would seem to show that these immigrants must have separated from the main body of Indo-Āryans in the North-West in pre-historic times—in the pro-Vedic or even pre-Vedic period. It also follows from the above that the tradition about Agastya's immigration to the south is not a mere myth, and that what is known as the Dravidian civilization of the South is merely the civilization of these Āryan and Āryanised immigrants.

The above conclusions are tantamount to a total negation of the current Dravidian theory in all its details and will have no chance of being listened to by the literary world unless they are presented with all the arguments which I have to urge in their support ; a piecemeal treatment of the question in a number of small papers is therefore out of the question. Some of my conclusions formed the subject of a paper entitled "Tense Signs in Dravidian" which I sent to the Poona Oriental Conference, 1919, and a summary thereof was printed in the Conference Proceedings, Volume I, but the paper itself has not yet been published. In my Readership lectures delivered at the Calcutta University in August last, I have dealt with the influences alleged to have been exercised by the Dravidian languages on the Indo-Āryan phonology, grammar and syntax; the conclusion arrived at there is that what are called Dravidian characteristics in Indo-Āryan phonology and inflexional system are really Indo-Aryan characteristics in Dravidian, and that in this matter many Dravidian scholars have mistaken the reflection for the original and the original for the reflection. In the course of those lectures I have had to deal exhaustively with the gender-distinguishing pronouns of the Dravidian languages. For the sake of completeness I am dealing with all Dravidian pronouns in the pressent paper but my treatment of the gender-distinguishing class will be as brief as possible consistently with perspicuity.

APPENDIX II-B.

§ 3 (1)—*Summary*.

We shall now summarise the conclusions arrived at in this paper.

(*a*) *Demonstrative*. The Dravidian demonstrative bases may be arranged in the following order of importance as determined by wideness of use.— *av, iv, ad, id, aṉ, im, am, um, ud, uv*. The circumstance that *n* appears in the Tamil forms *av-yāṉai*, and *ivaṉ*, and that *v* and *m* appear as initials in such forms as Telugu *vāṇḍu, vindu*, etc. and Tuḷu *mēr, mōḷu*, and *mōkuḷu*, clearly shows that these consonants should not be considered as euphonic. Of the above bases *av, im, ad, id*, and *āṉ* are common to Indo-Iranian and Dravidian, *am* is common to Indo-Āryan and Dravidian. The bases, *um, ud, uv* are Dravidian formations, the initial *u* arising out of *av* common to Indo-Iranian and Dravidian.

The Dravidian adjectives *ā, ū, ō, ē, ī* are also found in the later Iranian and Indo-Āryan dialects, but used as pronouns.

(*b*) *Relative-Interrogatives*. The same sets of pronouns are used both as relatives and as interrogatives in Dravidian as in many other languages of the world. The chief Dravidian interrogative bases are:— (1) *e*; (2) *evaṉ, ēnu, ēmī*; (3) *yāva*; (4) *āy*. These are derived respectively from the Indo-Āryan relative bases (1) *yad*; (2) *yāvān, yāvam*; (3) *yāva*; (4) *yā*. The last two exist as *ēva, āva, ē, ā* in later Dravidian. The Prakrit relative bases *jāva, jā*, have given rise to the Dravidian bases *dāva, dā*. The base *ya* has also been changed into *nē*.

(*c*) *Gender and number signs in demonstrative and interrogative pronouns*.

(i) The signs of the masculine singular are *ṉ, ṇḍu*, (*ḍu, du, ñju, r, m*). All these have arisen from imitation of the terminations of the Indo-Āryan present participle in *ant* in the masculine singular nominative; the signs *ṇḍu*, (*ḍu*, *ḍur*) arising from the cerebralisation of the *nt* of these participles which is Indo-Germanic in origin. The termination *e* in Tuḷu is imitated from Ardhamāgadhī.

(ii) The sign of the feminine singular *ḷ* or *lu* is derived from *ṇḍ*, the cerebralised form of the same Indo-Germanic *nt*; this *ṇḍ* lost the nasal and the remaining *ḍ* was converted into *ḷ*.

(iii) Two other signs of the feminine singular are *di* and *tti*. The former of these is taken from the neuter singular *adi* 'it'; the later is derived from the Sanskrit *stri* 'a woman.'

(iv) The neuter inflexional increment *t* appears to have been taken over from *bharat*, the nominative neuter singular of the Indo-Āryan present participle in *at*.

[Note. The *v*-forms of the Dravidian demonstrative and interrogative pronouns have throughout this paper been exhibited as derived from the bases *av*, *iv*, *yāv* by attaching to these number and gender signs arising from the termination *ant*. Most of these forms can also be derived from the Vedic *īvant*, *yāvant* and the possible **āvant*.]

(*d*) *Reflexives*. The so called reflexive base *ta* appears to be identical with the Indo-Āryan demonstrative base *ta*. The pronouns *tāṉ*, *tām*, formed from this base were originally, really demonstrative or third personal pronouns. But their oblique forms *taṉ*, *tam* were indistinguishable from two nouns *taṉ*, and *tam* derived later from the Sanskirt *tanu* 'body', *tman* 'soul or body', used as reflexives in Sanskrit. The result is that the pronoun *tāṉ* has come to be called 'the reflexive pronoun', although it has not yet lost all its demonstrative uses, and although when it is used in reflexive constructions the reflexive force is in most case furnished not by itself, but by the added particle *ē* or the reflexive verb *kol*.

It is a moot point whether the forms *tām*, *tāṅgaḷ*, *tamaru*, *tāvu*, used as honorific pronouns of the second person in various Dravidian dialects, should be derived from the pronoun *tam* or the noun *tam* (from *tman*).

(*e*) *The number signs in personal and reflexive pronouns.*

(i) The plural sign *m*. There is no doubt that this sign is related to, though not actually derived from, the Dravidian copulative conjunction *um* which appears mostly in what are literally *dvandva* compounds. It is probable that this *um* is the same as the Indo-Germanic dual particle *u* with an inorganic nasal attached. The inclusive plural of the first person, *viz.*, *nām* appears to be the same as the Indo-Aryan dual *nau*.

(ii) The plural sign *kaḷ* must have arisen from the plurals, formed with *ḷ* or *lu*, of noun stems containing the pleonastic suffix *ka*.

(*iii*) The plural sign *ḷ* or *lu*. It is possible that this has arisen from the Indo-Germanic *nt* in the same manner as the feminine suffix *ḷ* or *lu*.

(*f*) *The bases of personal pronouns.* It is clear that the final *n* and *m* of these pronouns are the singular and the plural suffixes. It has been pointed out in § 24 (*b*) above, that the initial *n* and *m* also might not be radical in some cases but might have arisen adventitiously in various ways. If this view is accepted, the primitive bases will be reduced to *ā*, *ē*, *ī*, or *yā*, *ye*, *yī*. There is nothing corresponding to these in Indo-Iranian, and if the affinities of these bases are Āryan, we have to go back in search of the originals to a period when the Vedic *aham* and the Iranian *azem* had not acquired their affixes.

It will have been clear from what has gone above that pre-historic forms of great antiquity, lost to literature, are often preserved in the submerged popular patois despised by men of culture, and that they crop up again most unexpectedly in modern times. Thus the Indo-Iranian demonstrative *ava*, obsolescent in the Veda and unknown to later Sanskrit and to the Prakrits, comes to the surface in the modern Indo-Āryan vernaculars in the form *ō*, *ū*; the original form has throughout been preserved in Dravidian. If it is admitted that there was a large immigration of Indo-Āryans into South-India in pre-historic times, we should not be surprised at their speeches preserving Āryan forms not found in the available Iranian and Indo-Āryan literature. But the materials available are not sufficient to justify anything more in regard to the bases of the personal pronouns than the general observations contained in § 24 above.

§ 3 (2)—*Conclusion.*

The identity of the demonstrative, the relative-interrogative, and the so-called reflexive bases of the Dravidian languages with those to be found in the Indo-Āryan and Iranian languages; the adoption of the Indo-Āryan relative stems in the Dravidian relative-interrogative system; the derivation of the Dravidian masculine, feminine, and neuter, pronominal signs from the endings of the Indo-Āryan present participles in *nt*; the adoption of the Sanskrit words *nau*, *tanu*, and *tman*, in the Dravidian pronominal system; to say nothing of the other influences referred to in the course of this paper, such as those of the pleonastic suffix *ka* and of the dual sign *au*; all these clearly indicate that the present Dravidian theory should be totally abandoned.

One thing comes out most clearly from the discussion in this paper; *viz.*, that some knowledge of Vedic Sanskrit and of the Indo-Āryan vernaculars of pre-Christian centuries is necessary to deal adequately with the questions involved in Dravidian philology.

APPENDIX III

NOTE.—*To the foot-note at page* 15

The author first propounded his views in a series of lectures delivered in Tamil under the auspices of the TAMILIAN EDUCATION SOCIETY, MADRAS, and they were published in 1922-23 in the Society's magazine *The Tamilian's Friend*, Vol. VI, as an appendix.

At page 4 of his written out matter, we find a list of words picked out from Caldwell. They are :—

(*a*) *Eṇṇuppeyarkaḷ* : oṉṟu, iraṇṭu, mūṉṟu.

(*b*) *Sarvanāmaṅkaḷ* : nāṉ, nī, nām, nīr, avaṉ, avaḷ, avar.

(*c*) *Uṟuppuppeyarkaḷ* : talai, mayir, śevi, kaṇ, mūkku, vāy, kai, kāl, aṭi.

(*d*) *Vastuppeyarkaḷ* : nilam, nīr, tī, vaḷi, pūṉai, nāy, āḍu, maram, kōḷi.

(*e*) *Vinaippeyarkaḷ* : naḍa, nil, iru, vā, pō, uṇ, paḍu.

(*f*) *Muṟaippeyarkaḷ* : tantai, tāy, āy, aṇṇaṉ, tampi, taṅkai, piḷḷai, makaṉ, koḻuṉaṉ.

See also pages 18 and 19 of this book where some of these words are considered.

BIBLIOGRAPHY

A

ĀDIPURĀNA—263
AGE OF THE MANTRĀS, 159
AINKUṞUNŪṞU—266, 378
AKANĀNŪṞU—201, 266
AKAPPORUL (IṞAYANĀR)—26, 375
ANCIENT AND HINDU INDIA (1920)—*By* V. A. Smith, (A.H.I.) 78
ĀRAṆYAKAS—249
ĀRYAN AFFINITIES OF DRAVIDIAN PRONOUNS—40, 42
ASOKA INSCRIPTION—(A.1), 254
ATHARVA VEDA—80
AVESTA—114, 452, 494, 234,
AVESTIC GRAMMAR—*By* Kanga, 173, 174, 175, 183, 194, 233, 485

B

BAIRAT SECOND ROCK INSCRIPTION—(B.S.R.I.) 257
BĀLAVYĀKARAṆAMU (TELUGU)—*By* Chinnayasuri, (B.K.) 222, 262, 411
BEGINNINGS OF SOUTH INDIAN HISTORY—*By* Dr. S. Krishnaswami Ayyangar, 275
BHAGAVAD-GĪTA—168
BHANDARKAR COMMEMORATION VOLUME—250, 254
BHĀRATA—*by* Adipampa, 263

C

CORPUS INSCRIPTION (COR. 1) 63, 66, 112, 121, 126, 129, 130, 165, 190, 198, 214, 222, 223, 240, 304, 280, 387, 420, 439, 444, 442, 474, 521, 539

CŪDĀMAṆI—263

CŪLIKA BAISACI KE—(HEMACANDRA)—293

D

DANISH PHILOLOGY, (Rask)

DELHI PILLAR EDICT—(D. .E.)

DEMONSTRATIVE IN SANSKRIT (DE. S) (M.V.G.) 392, 396

DHAMMAPĀDA, 254

DHATUPĀṬHA, 154

DICTIONARY (MALAYĀḺAM AND ENGLISH)—*By* Dr. H. Gundert (Dic.)—7, 11

DICTIONARY—*By* Dr Kittel, (*See* Kittel) 268

DICTIONARY OF ECONOMIC PRODUCTS OF INDIA—*By* Watts, 129

E

EARLY COMMERCE OF BABYLON WITH INDIA—(Published in J. R. A. S.—1898), 91

EARLY HISTORY OF INDIA—*By* V. A. Smith (E.G.I.) 71, 132

EARLY HISTORY OF VAISHNAVAISM IN SOUTH INDIA—*By* S. Krishnaswamy Iyengar, 275, 509, 512, 517, 519, 520, 534

ĒKĀGNIKĀNDA (II-1—Veda)—113

ENCYCLOPAEDIA BRITANNICA—61

EPIGRAPHIA INDICA—(E.I.) 22, 28, 179, 181, 254, 256, 257, 261, 215, 391, 394, 454 457, 458, 499, 503, 509

EPICS—168

ETYMOLOGICAL DICTIONARY OF THE ENGLISH LANGUAGE—*By* Skeat,, 105, 117, 340

G

H

I

INDIAN ANTIQUARY—88, 135, 178, 214, 251, 254, 256, 394, 454, 504, 507, 508, 511, 590

INDIAN CENSUS, (1921) (I.C.) 3

INDIAN ANTIQUARY (I.A.) 11, 34, 49, 50, 57, 88, 108, 111, 112, 135, 140, 178, 214, 219, 231, 1252, 254, 259, 263, 394, 454, 503, 507, 509, 511, 520

INNILAI, 275

IṞAIYAṈĀR AKAPPORUḶ, (With Nakkirar's Commentary)—375,

J

JAIN CANONS (11 Angas, and 14 Puwas), 258

JĀTAKAS—STORIES—254, 452

JOURNAL OF THE ROYAL ASIATIC SOCIETY (J.R.A.S)—81, 82, 100

JOURNAL OF THE ORIENTAL CONFERENCE

JOURNAL OF THE IRANIAN ASSOCIATION (J.I.A.) 250

JOURNAL OF THE MYTHIC SOCIETY (QUARTERLY), 252, 276

K

KALI-T-TOKAI (KT), 28, 210, 266, 267, 368, 374, 375, 377, 378, 430

KANNADA (KANARESE) ENGLISH DICTIONARY—*By* Dr. Kittel 10,110, 135

KAMPA ṞAMĀYAṈAM—376, 377

KAVIRĀJAMĀRGA (AMŌGHAVARṢA)—262, 263

KURNOOL DISTRICT MANUAL—*By* Gopalakrishna Chetty

KAUSĪTAKĪ BRĀHMAṆA—139, 251, 252,

KOSMOS INDIKOPLEUSTES,—121, 122

KURAL, 201, 202, 375

KUṞUNTOKAI—201, 266, 360, 371, 376, 378

L

M

N

NATURAL HISTORY—*By* Pliny (N.His) 54
NARRIṆAI, 266, 370, 376, 377, 543
NIGHANTUS, 109

O

OLD TESTAMENT—299
ORIENTAL CONFERENCE POONA, (JOURNAL—PROCEEDINGS OF THE—252, 501
ORIENTAL CONFERENCE TRANSACTIONS OF THE (Poona)—95, 146, 552
OXYRHYNCHUS (EGYPT) PAPYRUS—2nd CENT. A.D. (Discovered *By* E. Hultszch—Grenfell and Hunt), 267, 268

P

PADERIA AND NIGILVA INSCRIPTION; (See Inscription)
PAIŚĀCA LANGUAGES—*By* Grienson 21
PĀLI DICTIONARY—*By* Childer 233
PĀLI GRAMMAR, DUROISELLES—454
PARIPĀṬAL—77, 266, 267, 276, 374, 377
PATTU-P-PĀṬṬU—37, 170, 328, 371
PATIṚṚU-P-PATTU—266, 269, 278, 368, 378
PERIPLUS (McCRINDLE'S TRANSLATION)—*By* Schoff, W. H. 48, 49, 50, 51, 52, 54, 56, 57, 60, 61, 71, 73, 82, 101, 106, 111, 115, 130, 121
PERIPLUS, 116, 122, 125, 126, 127
PERSIAN GRAMMAR—Platt, 195
PEUTINGERIAN TABLES, 71
PRĀKṚTA PRAKĀSA—*By* Vararuchi—234, 257, 258, 451, 495
PRĀKṚTA LAKṢAṆAM (P.L.) Canda)—258, 293, 496
PROCEEDINGS AND TRANSACTIONS OF THE POONA ORIENTAL CONFERENCE, 95, 501

'STUDIES IN SOUTH INDIA' (1922)—*By* M. S. Ramaswami Iyengar
'STUDIES IN JAINISM IN SOUTH INDIA,' (1922)—*By* M. S. Ramaswami Iyengar
SŪTRAS—249
SVĒTAMBARA WORKS
SVĒTAMBARA CANONICAL WORKS, (S.C.W.) 47

T

TAITTIRIYĀ BRAHMAṆA (T.B.) AND ARAṆYAKAS (T.A.) 227, 228, 251, 252
TAITTIRĪYA SAMHITA (T.S.) 87, 138, 140, 226
TAITTIRĪYA UPANIṢAD, 20, 223, 226,
TANTRAVĀRTIKA—*By* Kumarlla Bhatta, 2, 537
TELUGU PHILOLOGY—*By* Seshagiri Sastri, 405
THE TAMILS, EIGHTEEN HUNDRED YEARS AGO (1904)—*By* M. Kanakasabhai Pillai, 48, 66, 72, 274
TIRU-K-KUṞAḶ, 201, 202, 342
TIRUVĀYMOLI—*By* Nammalvar (Ti.) 236, 238, 277, 377, 381
TOLKĀPPIYAM 28, 144, 170, 201, 204, 211, 212, 219, 221, 240, 267, 273, 276, 278, 281, 283, 284, 286, 287, 289, 297, 306, 307, 319, 329, 331, 334, 336, 365, 366, 370, 372, 378, 439
TRAVANCORE ARCHAEOLOGICAL SERIES, 27, 28, 260, 272, 285, 356, 380, 381
TRIPIṬAKAS, 254
TULU—ENGLISH DICTIONARY —*By* Manners—332

U

UPANIṢADS—249
UVASAGADASAO — INTRODUCTION—*By* Hoernle, 259 269 543

V

W

ERRATA

NOTE.—All those concerned in seeing this scholarly book through the Press regret the errors which are likely to irritate the scholarly readers. Most of them are of the mechanical kind — transposed or missed letters, missing or mis-placed diacritical marks, mis-directed or wrong references. The scholarly reader will spot most of them. The less obvious errors, and some sample errors of the kinds indicated, alone are noted here. We request the readers' forbearance, and hope to be forgiven.

Page	*Line*	*Error*	*Correction*
36	7	Telugu battigo completely, entirely	(should go as the third line)
86	23	as	(omit)
103	2–3	Eastern . . . . and	(omit)
113	19	*-n-*	-ṟ-
115	21	fear	bear
123	2	woop	wood
123.	22	order	border
124	1	erailing	trailing
126	1	might taws	(transpose)
126	last	stores	stones
134	16	come caṭṭan	become caṭṭān
157	3	vēṟṟu	veṟṟu
157	4	uṟṟu	ūṟṟu
157	16	avaṟṟitiruntu	avaṟṟiliruntu
157	17	then	them
181	11	The three words should go correctly below the three words in line 10	

183	last	balayān	balavān
199	last column 1st line	after or add ya	
218	25	day the	day and the
224	last but one line	even-o	evan-aṛivānō
226	1	soli ūl̲lnṭa	ol̲i śūl̲nta
226	2	arikirān ̣o	ar̲ikirānō
226	4	cantali	c̲āntati
290	12	eṇau	enku
290	13	pẹn	pēn
292	24	tinniy	tinniyu
292	25	tinn	tinnu
292	26	raz	razu
293	19	sounds	sounds respectively
300	13	peṭakaḥ	pēṭakaḥ
314	4	ṇ akkam	iṇakkam
314	10	e am	etam
315	11	katyam	kalyam
315	25	power	powder
328	13	ava(lu)	āva(lu)
332	3	tir	cir
366	21	forms	formed by
397	20	above (3) Bijapuri	insert **kanarese Dialects**
419	25	from	from disused
419	25	proceed	proceed on this assumption
496	11	alure	adore
501	5	(12)	This section had been numbered as (13) in the TS and there was a gap above it of about 5 lines. There may have been a (12) which is now missing.

ERRATTA

Page	*Section*	*Errata*	*Correction*
420	149	(98-b)	(S.101)
,,	,,	Old Tamil (108)	Old Tamil (S.108)
,,	,,	(117-a)	(S.120)
,,	,,	(117-b)	(S.120)
,,	,,	(123)	(S.126)
,,	,,	(136)	(S.139)
,,	,,	(98-a)	(S.101)
421	,,	(123-b)	(S.126-5)
,,	,,	(98-b)	(S.101)
433	156	(143)	(S.143)
433	,,	140 Suapr	(S.140 Supra)
436	157	(112-e)	(S.115-e)
439	158	(99.a,b)	(S.102-a)
439	158	(109.c)	(S.112.c)
440	,,	(111.c)	(S.114.c)
440	,,	(141.a)	(S.144)
443	160	(97-)	(S.100)
,,	160	(106-)	(S.109)
447	162	144	(S.147)
,,	,,	144	(S.147)
,,	,,	161.c.	(S.160.C)
450	163	159	(S.161)
,,	,,	127	(S.129)
454	164	(S.145)	(not known)
455	164	(161-b)	(S.160-c)
459	166	(42-b)	(S.42-b)
460	167	163	(S.165)
461	167	(163-d)	(S.165)
464	169	143	(S.143)
,,	170	Suffixes and	Suffixes (S.168) and
,,	,,	to 154	to S. 154
470	171	134-,,	S.137-c

Page	*Section*	*Erratum*	*Correction*
472	171	134-b	(S.137-b)
473	172	(127)	(S.130)
477	175	(102)	(S.105)
,,	,,	(118 (g))	(S..121 (g))
,,	,,	126	(S.129)
,,	,,	140	(S.143)
,,	,,	91	(S.92)
480	176	153	(S.155)
,,	,,	154	(S.156)
487	178	140	(S.143)
,,	,,	153	(S.156)
488	,,	95-b	S.98.b.
,,	,,	—	S.98 A-4
,,	,,	(147-49)	(S.150-151)
,,	,,	153	(S.155)
,,	,,	153	(S.155)
489	178	(112-e)	(S.155-e)
,,	179	173 (5)	S.175 (5)
490	180	149-b)	(S.152 b)
,,	,,	154 (a)	S.157 (*a*)
,,	,,	166	S.168 (*b*)
491	,,	147	S.150
,,	,,	149(*b*)	S.152 (*b*)
492	,,	(c) A fourth	(e) A fourth
495	181	76-B	S.76-(*b*)
498	,,	182	S.184
499	182	(164)	(S.166)
,,	,,	(171)	(S.173)
,,	,,	(164)	(S.166)
,,	,,	(164)	(S.166)
500	,,	(165)	(S.167)
,,	,,	(166-a)	(S.168-a)

ERRATTA

Page	*Section*	*Erratum*	*Correction*
,,	,,	(167)	(S.169)
,,	,,	(168-c)	(S.170-c)
,,	,,	(168-d)	(170-d)
501	,,	(171-2)	(S.174)
,,	183	tu (5,115)	tu (S.98, 117)
502	183	95-A	S.98-A
,,	,,	97 (e)	S.100 (e)
,,	184	Ina (95 and 134-d)	(S.100 and 137d)
503	,,	(179.D)	(S.181.D)
505	,,	160-c)	(S.162-c)
,,	,,	(164)	(S.166)
506	185	179 (a)	S.181.c. (a)
508	186	76 B	S.76 B (*b*)
,,	509	76 B.e.	S.76 B (e)
510	187	76 B.E.	S.76. B (e)
74	17	*Para*.3. Vedic pantheon (11 169-173)	
Similarly		*Errata.*	*Correction*
in page 75		(1146-48)	(11.46-48)
,,		(1148-49)	(11.48-49)
,,		(1149-51)	(11.49-51)
,,		(1152-53)	(11.52-53)
,,		(1154-55)	(11.54-55)
,,		(1156-57)	(11.56-57)
,,		(1160-61)	(11.60-61)
,,		(1162-64)	(11.62-64)
,,		XIV (11111-12)	(11.111-12)
421	150	(95-c)	(98-c)
425	151	(127-a)	(S.130)
426	152	147	(S.150)
429	153	112 c	(S.115.e)

Page	*Section*	*Erratum*	*Correction*
430	154	(107)	(S.110)
431	,,	98 (c)	(S.101)
,,	,,	(124 a,e)	(S.127)
,,	,,	(98.b)	(S.101)